T0350008

THREADS
OF
EMPIRE

THREADS

OF
EMPIRE

*Loyalty and Tsarist Authority
in Bashkiria, 1552-1917*

CHARLES STEINWEDEL

INDIANA UNIVERSITY PRESS

Bloomington & Indianapolis

Publication of this book was made possible, in part, by a grant
from the First Book Subvention Program of the Association
for Slavic, East European, and Eurasian Studies.

This book is a publication of

Indiana University Press
Office of Scholarly Publishing
Herman B. Wells Library 350
1320 East 10th Street
Bloomington, Indiana 47405 USA

iupress.indiana.edu

© 2016 by Charles Steinwedel

Studies of the Harriman Institute
Columbia University

The Harriman Institute, Columbia University, sponsors the Studies of the
Harriman Institute in the belief that their publication contributes to scholarly
research and public understanding. In this way the Institute, while not necessarily
endorsing their conclusions, is pleased to make available the results of some of
the research conducted under its auspices.

Manufactured in the United States of America

Library of Congress Cataloging-in-Publication Data

Names: Steinwedel, Charles.
Title: Threads of empire : loyalty and tsarist authority in Bashkiria,
    1552-1917 / Charles Steinwedel.
Description: Bloomington : Indiana University Press, 2016. | Includes
    bibliographical references and index.
Identifiers: LCCN 2015028816| ISBN 9780253019264 (cloth : alkaline paper) |
    ISBN 9780253019332 (ebook)
Subjects: LCSH: Bashkortostan (Russia)—Politics and government. |
    Bashkortostan (Russia)—Intellectual life. |
    Russia—Relations—Russia—Bashkortostan. | Bashkortostan
    (Russia)—Relations—Russia. | Russia—Officials and employees—Russia
    (Federation)—Bashkortostan—History. | Intellectuals—Russia
    (Federation)—Bashkortostan—History. | Allegiance—Russia
    (Federation)—Bashkortostan—History. | Authority—Political
    aspects—Russia (Federation)—Bashkortostan—History. |
    Imperialism—Social aspects—Russia (Federation)—Bashkortostan—History.
    | Social change—Russia (Federation)—Bashkortostan—History.
Classification: LCC DK511.B33 S74 2016 | DDC 947/.43—dc23
LC record available at http://lccn.loc.gov/2015028816

1 2 3 4 5 21 20 19 18 17 16

To Franny

CONTENTS

ACKNOWLEDGMENTS

THE GENEROUS SUPPORT of many people over many years made this book possible. I thank Mark von Hagen for introducing me to the study of empire and for his patient guidance. I am grateful to Richard Wortman for generously sharing his broad and deep knowledge of imperial Russia. Steve Kotkin's seminar at Columbia first helped me see the potential of a local study to understand a much larger system. Fred Corney, Peter Holquist, and Yanni Kotsonis have read and discussed drafts of this project since its very inception. I have benefitted immensely from their acute, critical minds and their generosity. Jane Burbank helped steer me toward writing a more expansive book and has been a source of inspiration, insight, and advice.

A work covering such a long period of time has only been possible with the help of many who were willing to give me essential feedback on the manuscript. Willard Sunderland, Adeeb Khalid, and Rob Nemes deserve special thanks for reading the entire work and improving it greatly. Ilya Gerasimov, Alexandra Haugh, Francine Hirsch, Marina Mogilner, David Ransel, Matt Romaniello, William Rosenberg, Sasha Semyonov, Roshanna Sylvester, Paul Werth, and Ben Zajicek helped me to refine and sharpen key parts of the manuscript.

I thank Janet Rabinowitch of Indiana University Press for her support of the project, and for pushing me to write a better, broader book. Upon Janet's retirement, Bob Sloan helped me make the best finished product possible. I thank him, Michelle Sybert, Kira Bennett Hamilton, and Janice Frisch for their efforts. I thank Erick Howenstine for making the maps. I am grateful to Matt Romaniello for locating and scanning an image from the University of Hawaii's collection, and to Aleksandr Iskovskii and Wang Xiyue for their help with obtaining images for the book.

Organizers and participants in a variety of workshops and seminars have improved the manuscript with their thoughtful readings of my work. I thank Yanni Kotsonis and the Jordan Center at New York University; members of the Midwest Russian History Workshop who attended sessions hosted by Ben Eklof and David Ransel at Indiana University and Alexander Martin at Notre Dame University; Norihiro Naganawa and his colleagues from Japan's National Institute for Humanities and Kazan University; Eugene Avrutin, Diane Koenker, John Randolph, and Mark Steinberg and the University of Illinois; Mark von Hagen, Jane Burbank, Anatolyi Remnev, and Pavel Savel'ev, the Ford Foundation, Omsk State University, and the Samara Municipal Administration Institute; Nick Breyfogle and the Mershon Center at Ohio State University; and Uli Schamiloglu and the University of Wisconsin.

For their generous financial support of my research, I thank the American Council of Teachers of Russian, the Harriman Institute, the International Research and Exchanges Board (IREX), the Social Science Research Council, the COR Grant Committee at Northeastern Illinois University, and the Slavic Research Laboratory at the University of Illinois.

I thank the library staff at Columbia University, the University of Illinois, the Slavic Reference Service at the University of Illinois, Northeastern Illinois University, the Russian National Library, the Russian State Library, and the State Public-Historical Library of Russia for their assistance in locating often-obscure materials. I thank the staff of the Bakhmeteff Archive at Columbia University, the Central State Historical Archive of the Republic of Bashkortostan (TsGIA RB), the Central Archive of Social Organizations of the Republic of Bashkortostan (TsAOO RB), the Scholarly Archive of the Ufa Scholarly Center of the Russian Academy of Sciences (NA UNTs RAN), the Natsional'nyi Archive of the Republic of Tatarstan (NA RT), and the Russian State Historical Archive (RGIA). Their professionalism in often-difficult circumstances made my project possible.

This book could not have been written without the support of historians in Ufa who generously shared in print and in person their great knowledge of their local history with an outsider. Although they might not fully agree with my interpretation of their past, I hope my work demonstrates my conviction that their history is of great importance. In Ufa, I thank especially, Bulat Davletbaev, Andrei Egorov, Zufar Enikeev, Marsel' Farkhshatov, Il'dar Gabdrafikov, Larisa Iamaeva, the late Rail G. Kuzeev, and Father Valerii. Valentina Latypova and Danil Azamatov were particularly helpful and challenging interlocutors. My experience in Ufa and knowledge of the highways and byways of Bashkortostan would have been much poorer without Yuri Afanasev, Fanis Gubaidullin, and Ildus Ilishev. I thank Fanis for his help with Bashkir translations.

In Kazan, I thank Alter Litvin for providing an academic home for me and for introducing me to Ilya Gerasimov and Marina Mogilner, who became generous friends and insightful commentators on my work. I thank Natasha Fedorova, Rustem Tsiunchuk, and Diliara Usmanova for sharing their wide knowledge with me. I thank Elena Campbell, Irina Novikova, Katya Pravilova, and Sasha Semyonov for their help and support in St. Petersburg. In Moscow, Igor and Sveta Baksheev were the most generous hosts and friends a person could hope for.

Chapter 6 contains in revised form material from my article "The 1905 Revolution in Ufa: Mass Politics, Elections, and Nationality," which originally appeared in *The Russian Review* 59, no. 4 (October 2000): 555–576. I thank the editors for their permission to reprint this material.

My greatest disappointment in the long gestation of this project is the fact that some who powerfully influenced me are not here to share the results. Richard Hellie helped me see the importance of early Russian history and believed in me. I still return to insights Leopold Haimson provided during the initial writing. His passion, wisdom, and intellect are sorely missed. Ina Vladimirovna Zhiznevskaia was like a mother to me in Kazan. I miss our talks about history on her balcony. Anatolyi Remnev was among the kindest and most knowledgeable historians of Russia I have had the pleasure of knowing. Susan Rosa was an ideal critic, colleague, and friend. They left us far too soon.

I thank Diane Nemec-Ignashev, Diethelm Prowe, and William Woehrlin for an excellent start in Russian and in history at Carleton College. I had the pleasure of working with Jeffrey Brooks at the University of Chicago and benefited from his insights and support. At Northeastern Illinois University, I thank my colleagues in the History Department, as well as Sophia Mihic and Russell Zanca, for their support and determination to maintain high standards.

My last thank-yous are ones for which words can never suffice. I thank Henry and Mary McCarl for welcoming me into their family and supporting me in so many ways. I thank my sisters Sandy and Steph for their encouragement. I thank my parents, Robert and Donna Steinwedel, for their love and unceasing support of me and my education, through thick and thin. My son Daniel and daughter Susannah have only known me when I have had this project on my desk in some way. I consider it a most important achievement that they have not seemed to notice this much and do not wonder where I was in their younger years. Watching them grow strong and curious has helped me to keep in mind what really matters in life. My greatest thanks are for Francesca, who met me not long before I started work on this project. The fact she has remained with me and been a steadfast supporter of my project for over two decades testifies to her extraordinary devotion. She always has been the first one to hear my ideas for the book and the reader of the last draft. I simply could not have done it without her, nor can I imagine life without her.

ABBREVIATIONS

Biulleten' otdela narodnogo obrazovaniia	BONO
Cahiers du Monde Russe	CMR
Cahiers du Monde Russe et Soviétique	CMRS
Chast'	ch.
Comparative Studies in Society and History	CSSH
Delo	d.
Desiatina	des.
Edinitsa khranenii	ed. khr.
Fond	f.
Gosudarstvennyi Arkhiv Rossiiskoi Federatsii	GARF
List	l.
Kniga	kn.
Materialy po istorii bashkirskoi ASSR	MPIBA
Ministerstvo Narodnogo Prosveshcheniia/Ministry of Education	MNP
Ministerstvo Vnutrennykh Del/Ministry of Internal Affairs	MVD
Natsional'nyi Arkhiv Respubliki Tatarstan	NA RT
Nauchnyi Arkhiv Ufimskogo Nauchnogo Tsentra Rossiiskaia Akademiia Nauk	NA UNTS RAN
Opis'	op.
Orenburg Muhammadan Ecclesiastical Assembly	OMEA
Pol'noe Sobranie Zakonov Rossiiskoi Imperii	PSZRI
Rossiiskaia Akademiia Nauk	RAN
Rossiiskaia Gosudarstvennaia Biblioteka	RGB
Rossiiskii Gosudarstvennyi Istoricheskii Arkhiv	RGIA
Rossiiskii Gosudarstvennyi Arkhiv Drevnikh Aktov	RGADA
Russkii arkhiv	RA
Sbornik Russkogo Istoricheskogo Obshchestvo	SRIO
Tom	t.
Trudy Orenburgskoi Uchenoi Arkhivnoi Komissii	TOUAK
Tsentral'nyi Arkhiv Obshchestvennykh Ob"edinenii Respubliki Bashkortostan	TsAOO RB
Tsentral'nyi Gosudarstvennyi Istoricheskii Arkhiv Respubliki Bashkortostan	TsGIA RB

Ufimskie eparkhial'nye vedomosti (Ufa Eparchial Gazette)	UEV
Ufimskie gubernskie vedomosti (Ufa Provincial Gazette)	UGV
Vestnik orenburgskogo uchebnogo okruga	VOUO
Vestnik rossiiskogo geograficheskogo obshchestva	VRGO
Vypusk	vyp.

THREADS
OF
EMPIRE

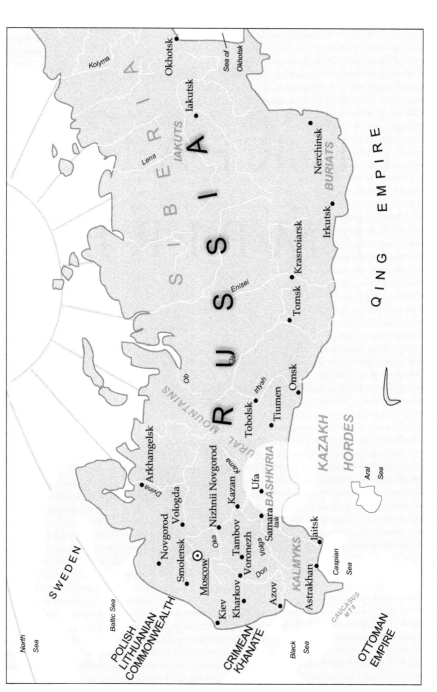

MAP 1.1. The Muscovite tsardom in the late seventeenth century.

Introduction

> To live as our fathers and grandfathers lived will not do. The village resident more and more feels that his life is connected by thousands of invisible threads not only with his fellow villagers, with the nearest *volost*, but this connection goes much further. He dimly perceives that he is a subject of a vast state, and that events taking place far from his place of birth can have a much greater influence on his life than some event in his village.
>
> —PETR KOROPACHINSKII, Ufa Provincial Zemstvo Chairman, 1906

WHEN PETR KOROPACHINSKII addressed the mostly rural population of Ufa that he hoped would read a new *zemstvo* newspaper, he captured the province's political environment after the revolution of 1905.[1] That revolution had catalyzed the development of a new political consciousness among the empire's residents. Many people who earlier had passively accepted the political order now had to decide whether to join thousands of people taking to the streets or to heed calls to action found in a flood of political pamphlets. Koropachinskii sought to use print and public discussion to shape the consciousness of the diverse population of the province, located about 750 miles east of Moscow. Koropachinskii's project was a distinctly twentieth-century one. He aimed to connect newly politically literate people of all faiths, nationalities, and social statuses to a new kind of state he believed was in the making after the near-collapse of tsarist authority in 1905.

Viewed from a long-term perspective, however, Koropachinskii's project was the latest in a series of efforts that had begun centuries before when leaders of the overwhelmingly Turkic and Islamic local population of what would come to be called Bashkiria had begun to swear oaths of loyalty to Tsar Ivan IV (the Terrible) in the 1550s. Over more than 350 years, the tsar and his officials had sought to tie this population to the imperial center, to find ways to make local populations accept tsarist rule, and to provide resources—mostly taxes and soldiers—to support the empire's goals and activities. Who would be connected to the center, what would connect them to the center, and how the tsar and central officials would constitute and present their authority varied greatly over the centuries.

Throughout the period 1552 to 1917, imperial officials' fundamental challenge remained: to cultivate loyal servitors of the tsar who could represent and stabilize imperial authority. This search for stability was far from straightforward. In 1906, Koropachinskii wrote of "invisible threads"—the creation of shared cultural understandings that would link residents of a great state. Before the 1730s, these threads lacked strength or connected only a narrow stratum of men, primarily Russian-speaking and Russian Orthodox servitors and some native elites. Such an elite sufficed to achieve the limited imperial goals at the time. In the mid-eighteenth century, little but quite visible force kept Bashkiria in the empire. The tsar's army suppressed major rebellions about once per generation. During the reign of Catherine II in the 1770s, imperial officials sought to expand the loyal elite in Bashkiria by drawing Russian Orthodox nobles to the region, restoring noble status to Muslims who had lost it in the preceding century, and officially recognizing local Muslim clerics while acculturating all elites into the culture and practices of the empire. Members of the diverse elite would serve as intermediaries between imperial authority and the people below them in the social hierarchy. As one Muslim religious leader put it, Catherine did "not consider various faiths, just loyalty of the heart."[2] The effort to create a loyal, diverse elite largely succeeded. Unrest in Bashkiria was infrequent and of low intensity from the 1770s until the wider, all-imperial revolution of 1905. Only after 1905 did the simultaneous emergence of mass politics and visions of a culturally homogenous nation-state call into question the ability of non-Russian, non-Orthodox Christian elites both to be loyal to the emperor and to maintain the respect of the broader mass of people.

Loyalty typically has not been a central category with which to examine the Russian Empire, or for that matter other empires. The word "loyalty" appears in many works, but it is rarely analyzed or reflected upon.[3] Since, in common speech, loyalty is defined as a powerful devotion to a ruler or to a state, loyalty can fit awkwardly with the study of empires, which are associated with a distance between ruler and ruled, coercion, and a lack of democracy. For this reason, in the imperial context, an oath of loyalty often appears to be a "manifestation of subservience" that a ruler forces upon his or her subjects rather than a sign of true devotion.[4] As Max Weber reminds us, however, loyalty may be "hypocritically simulated" on "purely opportunistic grounds," "carried out in practice for reasons of material self-interest," or out of "weakness . . . because there is no acceptable alternative." What is most "important is that a particular claim to legitimacy is to a significant degree . . . treated as 'valid.'"[5]

As R. J. W. Evans put it in his study of the early modern Habsburg monarchy and its German lands, "loyalty became a calculation, not a sort of disembodied idealism."[6] Such a calculation of loyalty remained an important element of cohesion in the empire, one that changed over time. If we see loyalty as rooted in changing practical concerns, ones that can form the basis of a more lasting identification with a state or ruler, the concept opens new possibilities for exploring the relationship between ruler and ruled.[7]

In a similar way, imperial officials did not extend status and privileges to local elites out of kindness or generosity but out of perceived necessity. As William Rosenberg has argued, an imperial formation is a solution to a particular set of challenges or goals.[8] For most of the Russian Empire's history, the challenge of empire was to maintain order and economic production necessary to support tsarist rule over a vast space with a diverse population. Mobilizing sufficient people to secure the steppe, which stretched hundreds of miles to the south, east, and west of Bashkiria, was an exceptionally costly undertaking. It was easier to make local elites part of an imperial elite that could then be used to mobilize members of the local population with fewer direct links to imperial authority. In building an imperial elite in Bashkiria and throughout their realm, imperial officials faced a "dilemma of empire" common to imperial regimes around the world. Imperial officials had to manage space and population in such a way as to incorporate them into the empire, yet without undermining the empire's "differentiated governance of differentiated populations" that allowed the center to arbitrate among diverse elites.[9] Officials sought to give people, or at least their elites, sufficient stake in the empire to ensure loyalty while maintaining the hierarchy necessary to preserve privileges and to provide the sense of "imperial destiny" and grandeur that connected the emperor and his elite servitors.[10]

To reveal the threads of empire, one must capture these dynamic relationships among historical actors and with political authority. The very identity of historical actors, relationships among them and with central authority, and the geography of these relationships changed over time. Although Bashkirs became associated with the region and informally it became known as Bashkiria, the population was always diverse and changing. Those known by the ethnonym "Bashkir," or *Bashqort*, made up a confederation of tribes who had paid tribute to the Kypchak Khanate, or "Golden Horde" according to later Russian sources, and who spoke different dialects, had different ways of life, and paid tribute to different suzerains after the khanate's collapse. Bashkirs established distinctive relations with the Muscovite state and became a legal estate group in the Russian Empire. In the late nineteenth and early twentieth centuries, intellectuals and imperial administrators alike perceived them as a nation. The relationships of Bashkirs with political authority changed, too. As the Bashkir estate was incorporated into the empire, it incorporated culturally varied migrants from nearby areas. By 1917, some began to identify as members of other estates or national groups. The territory associated with Bashkirs changed from a loosely defined area mostly utilized by semi-nomadic pastoralists to land collectively owned by members of the Bashkir estate. In the eighteenth and nineteenth centuries, most of Bashkiria was part of Kazan Province, the Ufa governor-generalship, or Orenburg Province. Finally, after 1881, its core was known as Ufa Province. In the twentieth century, some promoted the idea that this land should be a national territory for Bashkirs, and its core became the basis of the Bashkir Autonomous Republic in 1919. Thus, the history of Bashkirs and what would become the Bashkir Republic is the history of constant, multipolar negotiation about the names and identity of people, their status, and their territory. Bashkirs' history is one of conflict and integration into first the empire and then the empire's European core. As such, the case of Bashkirs and Bashkiria tells much about the imperial state, legal status within it, and its changing practices of governance. Study of Bashkirs and Bashkiria illuminates the threads that sustained the Russian Empire for more than two centuries as well as the causes of the empire's demise, when the tsar's diverse subjects and even some who governed the empire discovered new, seemingly more attractive principles of political authority and cultural solidarity in 1917.

These concepts of difference, intermediaries, and hierarchy are crucial to understanding empire.[11] However, I am less interested in either endorsing an abstract definition of empire or advancing a new one than in capturing the uncertainties, variability, and processes of change in a particular "imperial formation."[12] Limiting the territorial focus of the study makes it possible to address changing conceptions and representations of the empire in the center that powerfully informed local strategies of rule.[13] A limited territorial focus also makes it possible to avoid the understandable desire to reduce the empire's formation to one dimension or to one fairly brief moment in time.[14] Since the breakup of the Soviet Union focused attention on empire in the late 1980s, historians have produced in-depth analyses of key elements of imperial rule such as diplomacy, violence, religious confession, ethnographic knowledge, or nationality.[15] Each of these is important in understanding Bashkirs and Bashkiria.

This book will address multiple categories and practices over a long period of time, with particular attention to the nexus of legal status or estate status (*soslovie* in Russian), religious confession, and nationality that was particularly important to imperial rule in Bashkiria. Whether and how estate status can be used to describe imperial society as a whole has been a subject of continuing controversy in the profession.[16] This book will not answer that question. The concern here is with the imperial dimension of estate status and its interaction with other categories of imperial rule. The best-developed literature on estate status and empire addresses the Jews, a legally distinct cultural/religious group that, like Bashkirs, became a nationality in the Soviet Union.[17] Estate status was a politically important category of imperial rule over the entire lifespan of the empire. The identification and analysis of ethnic, national, or religious differences is key to empire, but building an empire requires also the creation of differences that cut across existing divides in the body politic. Imperial officials worked to make a loyal elite that would identify with the tsar by elevating some of the tsar's subjects over others, by formally recognizing and confirming their elite status, and by granting land and other privileges.

This book will focus on two types of estate status in particular: nobility and Bashkir status. The emperor granted noble status in Bashkiria that was characteristic of the empire as a whole. Noble status brought important members of Bashkiria's elite into a status group with mutual loyalties and allegiance to the sovereign. Nobles could become part of the cultural world of the ruling dynasty and, after Peter the Great, part of its westernized elite. The granting of noble status became an instrument of particular significance in Bashkiria, which had a large Muslim population. Muslim nobles were much more common in Bashkiria than in the Russian Empire as a whole. According to Ramil' Khairutdinov's analysis of 1897 census data, nearly 70 percent of all Muslim hereditary nobles in European Russia resided in Ufa province alone.[18] Bashkir was itself an estate status, indicating a particular set of privileges and obligations that distinguished Bashkirs from those in other estates, such as peasants and merchants. Bashkir estate status originated in the sixteenth century, when Bashkir elites swore allegiance to Ivan IV (the Terrible, reigned 1533–1584). In exchange, they received privileged status, and their tribes received rights to the land they occupied. Due to imperial officials' concern to secure the vast steppe frontier, Bashkir land and status distinguished them from elites in Kazan to Bashkiria's west, where Tatars did not make up a distinct status group, and in Siberia to Bashkiria's east, which were legally *inorodtsy* or aliens.

An important challenge to the estate-based hierarchy came in the late nineteenth century, when competition with European states and economic changes caused imperial officials to seek more direct connections with more of the population in order better to school the tsar's subjects in the goals of the state and to create more skilled, knowledgeable, and hence more productive people. The tsar and his officials, in and after the Great Reform era of the 1860s, attempted, as Eric Hobsbawm has written, "not merely to command the obedience of their peoples as subjects, but to rally their loyalty as potential citizens."[19] Yanni Kotsonis characterizes the Great Reform era as one in which nearly all parts of the population were expected to exhibit "a participatory, civic ethos and a sense of commitment (*grazhdanstvennost'*)," while formal citizenship was left aside.[20] The reforms and their motivations transformed the nature of estate and provided a space for national ideas to gain power.

Bashkirs' experience of empire complicates the most common ways scholars frame the imperial Russian state's relationship with non-Russian, non–Orthodox Christian groups. Historians have often presented incorporation into the empire as a process that proceeds in stages toward a goal of full assimilation. As Marc Raeff writes, for instance, "conquest or acquisition was the first step, incorporation the second, and assimilation the final goal."[21] Other historians have elaborated on this step-by-step process and officials' desire to create a homogenous population.[22] Such a goal certainly existed in the minds of some officials, especially toward the end of the empire.[23] Similarly, the process of building an imperial state could look the same from the perspective of a Russian-speaking peasant or a Bashkir-speaking semi-nomadic pastoralist.[24] In the Bashkir case, step-by-step movement toward assimilation is difficult to discern, however. Strategies and goals of incorporation varied considerably over time.[25] Periods of rapid expansion when empire could mobilize resources, such as the 1550s and the mid-eighteenth century, alternated with periods of little change when imperial officials could not or chose not to. Periods of extreme violence, such as the 1730s, alternated with periods when such violence was largely absent, as in the nineteenth century. Major elements of the empire's fabric, such as serfdom and Peter I's poll tax, were extended to Bashkiria but not to Bashkirs themselves. Most imperial officials did not intend to eliminate differences but rather to organize them. Imperial officials assumed that differences among the emperor's subjects existed and recognized them in law until the end of the Old Regime.[26] Rather than assimilation, Bashkirs experienced what Benjamin Nathans has described as acculturation, "a form of adaptation to the surrounding society that alters rather than erases the criteria of difference."[27]

BASHKIRS IN IMPERIAL AND INTERNATIONAL CONTEXT

Empires by definition are large polities encompassing vast spaces. For this reason, some of the most influential recent writing on empire addresses the subject on a grand scale. Such works address the Russian Empire as a whole, compare the Russian Empire with its rivals, or situate it among empires in history.[28] The gains from thinking big about big things are obvious, and I have learned much from these works. This book takes a different approach, one that emphasizes the local.[29] Works on the Russian Empire that trace the history of a region from the mid-sixteenth until the twentieth century are few and often have different emphases.[30] People and resources varied greatly within the empire. As Ronald Suny has argued, the "different forms of rule" and "uneven socioeconomic transformations" in the empire placed the empire's peoples in "distinct historical contexts."[31] Finding one place representative of the empire is therefore impossible. Nonetheless, Bashkiria's diversity of peoples, ways of life, and terrain, together with its geographic position at the eastern edge of European Russia, help us understand the processes by which the tsar and his servitors conquered territory and incorporated it and its population into the empire.

Just as contemporaries compared the empire's regions, so they compared the Russian Empire with its rivals. For this reason, it behooves historians to beware of connections and similarities among empires. Doing so is a challenge. My scrutiny of Bashkiria extends over more than three centuries, which complicates comparisons with other, shorter-lived or differently timed analyses of empire. Subjects of comparison that work for some periods—for instance, the Russian empire's land policies in Bashkiria and those of the French in Algeria in the nineteenth century—do not work for other time periods, such as the seventeenth century, well before the French arrived. I address this challenge by comparing the Russian Empire with its international rivals on a chapter-by-chapter basis. That is, I will address in each chapter the comparison most relevant to that particular time period. The Ottoman Empire and Habsburg monarchy will receive particular focus not only because they were also continental, contiguous empires but also because over the Russian Empire's last two centuries it was particularly entangled with them.[32] The Ottoman Empire was Russia's most consistent military rival, and Muslim people and ideas moved easily across the border. The Russians fought for and against the Habsburgs at different times. All three empires were at least partly European in population and self-conception but often found themselves reacting to European political, economic, and social developments.

THE SETTING

Bashkiria's location on the borderland between European and Asian Russia made empire-building a particular challenge to imperial officials. Russia's capitals, first Moscow and then St. Petersburg, lay far away. Yet Bashkiria's limits were not international boundaries, which by the 1850s lay hundreds of miles to the south. In the 1850s, writer Mikhail Avdeev characterized his native region, straddling the Ural Mountains and stretching from the forests of the north across the steppe toward Central Asia, as the place where "Europe meets with Asia, the steamship meets the camel, [where] the dance hall of the noble assembly . . . is thirteen miles from the nomadic tent."[33] A much more prominent local writer, Slavophile Sergei T. Aksakov, also noted the mix of cultural forces but was more skeptical than excited by European influences. Aksakov wrote in his 1856 classic *The Family Chronicle* that when he had first come to love his native land, it was called the Ufa governor-generalship (*ufimskoe namestnichestvo*). This expression mixed the local Turkic word for "small" or "hilly" that had been given to the provincial capital, Ufa, at its founding in the late sixteenth century with the Slavic word for regional administration before the 1770s.[34] When, in the nineteenth century, Ufa became part of Orenburg Province, the latter name with a foreign suffix sounded strange to Aksakov's ears. He thought the diverse population that had flocked to the region diminished its charm.[35] Writing in 1904, Bashkir official and man of letters Mukhametsalim Umetbaev shared Aksakov's view. He blamed "overseas companies and merchants" for stripping his native land of its "bountiful cattle, bees, and forests."[36] Bashkiria was a place where Petersburg-trained engineer Avdeev drank the Bashkirs' fermented milk beverage *kumys* daily, Aksakov wrote of a Russian eloping with the daughter of a prominent Muslim, and Umetbaev published his thoughts on Pushkin for the poet's centennial in 1899.[37] In Bashkiria, Russian Orthodox met Muslim, Slavic met Turkic, modernity met antiquity, and Asia met Europe.

Just as the Bashkir people who gave the region its name moved and changed, so did the limits of the space called Bashkiria. Defined most broadly, Bashkir settlement extended west to the Volga River, which was an insurmountable barrier to moving livestock herds; northwest to the Kama River; and east to the Tobol River. For most of the period addressed here, however, Bashkiria was a smaller territory, that of Ufa and Orenburg Provinces in the nineteenth century along with small parts of adjacent Viatka and Perm Provinces and western Siberia. In the late imperial period, Ufa and Orenburg Provinces occupied about 185,000 square miles, a bit more than California or Sweden, and had a population in 1897 of just over four million people. With the different application of the Great Reforms to Orenburg and Ufa, our focus will turn to Ufa Province, the more populous of the two provinces and the one with the most turbulent history in the early twentieth century.

The Ural Mountains shaped Bashkiria in fundamental ways. The highest point in the Southern Urals, Mount Iamantau, reaches 1,640 meters, or 5,380 feet, about 985–1,315 feet below the highest peaks in the eastern United States and only about one-third the height of Alpine peaks. Peter the Great's geographers used the Urals to mark the boundary between Europe and Asia.[38] Peter's officials themselves were most interested in Ural minerals: gold, iron, coal, nickel, and silver. The mountains also provided a refuge for those fighting the tsar's forces. Major rivers such as the Iaik River (renamed the Ural River in 1775), in Bashkiria's south, and the Ufa River, which flowed west from the

Urals, provided water and fishing grounds, but only one river, the Belaia, linked Bashkiria, via the Kama River and the Volga River, to the Moscow region and the empire's center. Until regular riverboat service commenced in 1870 and the railroad came through in the 1880s, connections to European Russia were slow and difficult.[39]

The mountains meet the steppe to the east, west, and south. To the west, the Urals' foothills flatten out roughly by the time one reaches the city of Ufa. The sparsely populated and flat steppe to the south of the Urals critically shaped the region's history. People could move from Central Asia in the southeast toward European Russia in the northwest or vice versa with few natural impediments. The diversity of the region's topography and climate supported demographic diversity. Coniferous forests dominated much of the land north of the city of Ufa. Deciduous forest and farmland struggled for supremacy from about Ufa until trees gave way to the steppe in the south. The forests provided timber and supported hunting and the gathering of berries and honey—Bashkir honey is a local specialty. Land to the south and west of the forests supported settled agriculture and the production of rye, wheat, barley, and millet. As the soil became drier and poorer to the south and east, agriculture became difficult, and animal husbandry took over. People in Bashkiria were famous into the twentieth century for raising livestock, mostly horses and sheep but also goats, cattle, and the camels used to form caravans for trade with Central Asia.

THE PEOPLE

Providing ethnonyms for groups in Bashkiria's population risks suggesting that they were primordial and static, which was not the case, as we will see in the chapters ahead. Nonetheless, it helps to become familiar with the range of names and terms encountered in the text. Bashkirs who swore loyalty to Ivan IV in the sixteenth century led tribes formed from Ugric, Kypchak, and Finno-Ugric elements, the relative weight of which is in dispute.[40] From early on, the tribes displayed characteristics that influenced how they would encounter the expanding Muscovite state. Most Bashkirs were primarily semi-nomadic cattle breeders, which distinguished them from their sedentary neighbors to the north and west and from the fully nomadic Kazakhs to the south and east. By the sixteenth century, Bashkirs typically spent the winter months in settlements, which allowed some protection from the region's brutal cold. In the heat of summer, they drove their herds north into cooler and moister pastures and into the foothills of the Urals. Exposure to settled peoples in the north and west influenced some Bashkirs to practice agriculture. Arab traveler Ibn-Fadlan noted the presence of Islam in Bulgar, a city located on the Volga River south of Kazan and the center of the region's first Islamic state, when he traveled there in 922 CE. The local population, in turn, received Islam from Bulgar.[41] After Islam became the official religion of the Kypchak Khanate under Uzbeg Khan (1312–1342), the spread of Sunni Islam throughout Bashkiria intensified.[42] From at least the sixteenth century on, some local Muslims traveled to Central Asia to study and brought back connections to Sufi brotherhoods, especially the Naqshbandi order. Bashkirs speak a Turkic dialect very similar to that of Kazan Tatars, which facilitated connections with Central Asia.[43] The Mongol conquest, along with Tamerlane's spread of Chagatay, or what Russian sources often refer to as Turki—the high literary language of the Turkic lands in the fifteenth century—made the local population part of the Turkic, Muslim world that stretched from China to southern Europe.[44]

Unlike some peoples in the former Soviet space, contemporary Bashkirs claim little tradition of independent statehood. They paid tribute to someone. Some Bashkir clans may have united under the leadership of a khan before the Mongol conquest in 1207–1208, while others were subordinate to the Bulgar Khanate.[45] After the Mongol conquest, however, Bashkirs remained subordinate to them and to their successors. Both Russian imperial sources and Bashkir sources use the concepts of tribe, or *plemia,* and clan, or *rod,* seeing clan as Bashkirs' fundamental political unit.[46] With the advent of the Kypchak Khanate in 1243, the area's rulers applied to the region a quasimilitary organization. Chinggisid rulers received control of land based on the number of soldiers it sustained. This helped to shape Bashkir tribal organization as well. According to Bashkir legend, khans assigned each Bashkir clan a *tamga,* or mark; a battle cry; a tree; and a bird. The organization of Bashkirs in such a manner facilitated the extraction of resources, including *desiatinnyi obrok*—the tax of one of every ten head of livestock—as well as *iasak,* the tax or tribute that all from the poorest to the wealthiest had to pay, and conscription for the khan's military.[47] With the breakup of the Kypchak Khanate in the late fourteenth century, the population became subordinate to at least one of three entities: the khan of Kazan, who ruled the west of Bashkiria; the Siberian khan, who ruled the eastern slope of the Ural Mountains; and the Nogai Horde, which governed the southern steppe regions of Bashkiria.

The fall of Kazan in 1552 and Bashkirs' swearing of allegiance to the tsar have crucially influenced relations among Bashkiria's population. Muscovite law distinguished a Bashkir hereditary landowner (*votchinnik* in Russian, *asaba* in Bashkir)—those with recognized rights of property ownership—from a *pripushchennik,* or a person "let in" to Bashkir lands regardless of their ethnicity, although some non-Bashkirs still assimilated into Bashkir communities through marriage or adoption.[48] *Teptiars* were closely associated with Bashkirs throughout the period under study. Their origins are not entirely clear—their name may derive from the Persian word *defter*, or "register," indicating that they were listed as somehow separate from Bashkir communities among whom they lived. For much of the period of this study, they represented a distinct legal status or estate group, but as Teptiars and Bashkirs became closer in status, they became more similar culturally, too. The Soviet government officially merged them for census purposes in 1926.[49]

Other groups with a significant presence in Bashkiria include Kazan Tatars, the Turkic-language-speaking, Muslim people who generally practiced settled agriculture or trade and who provided much of the area's religious elite and merchants. They were most heavily concentrated in the northwest of Bashkiria and in what was the Kazan Khanate before 1552 and Kazan Province in the Russian Empire. The Bashkir and Tatar languages are mutually intelligible. Tatar was the written Turkic language in the region before 1917. As we shall see, there have been considerable shifts in identification between the two groups.[50] Large numbers of Tatars moved east in order to avoid missionary campaigns that followed the Russian conquest of Kazan in 1552 and to avoid taxation in the eighteenth century. Some consider the Turkic *Meshcheriaks* or *Mishars* a Tatar subgroup, while others see them as an ethnic group that originated in the Oka River basin. In either case, many moved to Bashkiria in service of the Russian state and there became a distinct legal status category.[51] The group known as the *Chuvash* bears a strong influence of Bulgar Turkic but lacked Islamic influence until more recently.[52] They, too, migrated from Bashkiria's northwest. They practiced agriculture and raised livestock in southern portions of Bashkiria. Most converted to Orthodoxy, although some remained animist or became Muslims.

Finnic peoples have been present in Bashkiria and especially in the forests of the north for as long as Bashkirs, but those who were animist also moved to the region after 1552 in order to avoid Christianization. The largest such group is the *Mari* (*Cheremis* before 1917). Although the largest Mari population lived north and west of Bashkiria, the so-called Eastern Mari had a significant presence throughout the period under study. They practiced settled agriculture, hunted, and kept bees. More than one Bashkir *shäzhärä*, a genealogical chronicle common to Turkic people, indicates Mari elements in the clan's ancestry.[53] The *Udmurt* (*Votiak* before 1917), another Finnic people who left the Kama River basin in the sixteenth century to avoid forced conversion, also settled primarily in Bashkiria's northwest and remained largely an animist people. The last group of migrants to the region, the Russians, came mostly from the north and west of Bashkiria. They brought the Russian language and Russian Orthodox faith with them.

If we look south of Bashkiria, the picture becomes still more complicated. Security requirements on the southeastern border catalyzed the formation of the Ufa Cossacks in the 1620s. Like Cossacks elsewhere in the empire, Ufa Cossacks were a distinct legal status group distinguished by their military form of organization. Instead of paying taxes, Cossacks served on the Orenburg defensive line that was intended to protect the tsar's subjects from incursions from the steppe. In exchange for service, they received plots of land and sometimes salaries and privileges, such as fishing rights. The small number of Ufa Cossacks, only four hundred by 1700, were folded into the larger Orenburg Cossack Host in 1755. Muslims and animists served in substantial numbers in the Orenburg Cossack Host. Three Kazakh hordes lay across the defensive line until their decisive incorporation into the empire in the 1820s. Commonly referred to as "Kirghiz" before 1917, Kazakhs were distinguished by political considerations and way of life. Like Bashkirs, Kazakhs were Islamic and spoke a Turkic language. Unlike Bashkirs, however, Kazakhs were organized into hordes under the rule of a khan who claimed descent from Chinggis Khan. They also were fully nomadic—they lacked winter quarters and practiced less agriculture. Since the city of Orenburg was founded in 1735 in order to command the steppe trade, much of the empire's diplomacy with Central Asia flowed through Orenburg. Kazakhs and other Central Asian peoples frequently made their way through Bashkiria.

Beginning in the second half of the nineteenth century, peoples from all over the empire migrated to Bashkiria in search of land and employment. Improved transportation made the region easily accessible to much more of the empire's population than previously. Peoples more commonly encountered in the empire's western borderlands, such as Poles and Jews, had long been present in Bashkiria, but after 1905 they became more prominent numerically and culturally. Germans, Ukrainians, and Latvians, among others, were drawn to Bashkiria because it was easier to obtain land there than in the empire's west, or because violence and war in 1905 and 1914–1917 pushed them from their homes and sent them east as refugees. Bashkiria's major cities, Ufa and Orenburg, grew rapidly in population. Managing class relations in the cities and in Urals mining towns became more urgent for tsarist officials than sorting the region's Muslim and animist populations into estate status groups. In this respect, Bashkiria became much more like the rest of the empire.

The constitution of groups is certainly a focus of empires and of this book. Empires also make individual lives by structuring careers and possibilities for identity and belonging. Members of important Turkic and Muslim families will figure prominently in the book. Most notable is the Tevkelev family, which demonstrated how the tsarist state could provide a locus of loyalty in changing ways. The Tevkelevs, a Tatar princely line from the Kasimov region, entered the tsar's service in the seventeenth century. Kutlu-Mukhammad Tevkelev, born 1674 or 1675, served as a translator for Peter the Great. In 1734, he changed his name to Aleksei Ivanovich Tevkelev and became the second in command of the Orenburg Expedition. His son and grandson made careers in the military and, like Kutlu-Mukhammad, were known by both Turkic and Russian names. Beginning with Kutlu-Mukhammad's great-grandson Salim-Girei, Tevkelevs seldom used Russian names in public life.[54] In 1865, Salim-Girei became the mufti of the Orenburg Muhammadan Ecclesiastical Assembly (OMEA), the leading Muslim official in the empire's east. Kutlu-Mukhammad Batyr-Gireevich, the nephew of the mufti, became a political activist in Ufa Province. He served as a member of the provincial zemstvo and was elected to all four State Dumas, leading the Muslim Fraction in the Duma's last three convocations (1907–1917). In later chapters, other Muslim and Bashkir families such as the Umetbaevs and Syrtlanovs figure prominently. Their experience of empire illustrates the possibilities for Muslims and Bashkirs to be loyal subjects of the emperor and how expectations of loyal subjects changed over three centuries of imperial rule.

SOURCES

Working in the archives, one realizes that an empire is, among other things, a vast machine for the collection, analysis, and presentation of information. Since this book centers on the empire, its institutions, and those who worked within them, at the core of the book lie sources imperial officials produced, collected, and organized into archives. Archival documents provide much essential information, especially as to how state officials perceived the population, categorized it, and sought to influence its behavior. The writings of those outside the imperial administration who sought to influence the behavior of imperial officials also appear in the archives. Russian was the lingua franca of the empire, and for this reason sources for the book are overwhelmingly in Russian. Even in an empire with a diverse governing elite and a diverse population, those who sought to influence the empire wrote in Russian. Of course, this does not mean that all who are quoted in the book would identify as Russian.

Many of the book's sources came from provincial archives in Kazan and Ufa. In an administration as centralized as the Russian Empire aspired to be, the flow of memoranda, reports, and other materials between the metropole and the provincial leadership shaped how the area was understood and represented in the center. Much of the information sent from the provinces to the center was collected at the request of the center, and materials in central archives are generally better organized than those in the provinces. Yet not everything that appeared in the provinces found its way to the center. Moreover, even in cases where reports were prepared in the provinces in response to central directives, provincial archives at times contain drafts with marginalia and crossed-out material that says much about the attitude of those in the provinces compiling the reports.

Archival documents have their limitations. Much of the personal detail that renders the human dimensions of imperial governance does not make it into bureaucratic documents. I have therefore made extensive use of diaries and memoirs of those who served in the region. Some of these can be found in archives, but others appear in hard-to-find published sources. They provide glimpses of the personalities and characters of those who otherwise presented themselves only in flat, bureaucratic prose. How else would we learn that in the 1840s Governor-General Perovskii spent much of the summer in what he called his *kochevka,* or nomadic summer encampment,[55] that Governor Kliucharev, appointed in 1906, was a raving anti-Semite,[56] or that "Red Prince" Kugushev wore Tatar clothing as he moved about his estate, even though his family had converted from Islam and Russified over a century before? The periodical press first appeared in the region in the mid-nineteenth century. Central newspapers and journals often featured local informants or even printed material omitted from local newspapers. I have used both the central and local press extensively in chapters that address the period after 1860.

1

STEPPE EMPIRE

1552–1730

THE CONQUEST OF Bashkiria marked Moscow's emergence as a steppe empire, one that governed steppe nomads as previous empires and its Eurasian rivals did, by developing different systems of administration for sedentary and nomadic peoples. The contrast in systems became clear after 1552, when Ivan IV's army conquered the Kazan Khanate. The 1550s were a difficult time in Bashkiria according to many Bashkir chronicles.[1] Harsh winters and floods cut the size of herds and harvests, leaving many people hungry.[2] Even before Moscow conquered Kazan, conflict strained Bashkir relations with the Nogai Horde, a larger tribal confederation that had dominated Bashkiria's south since the mid-fifteenth century. Disagreements with the khan of Kazan provoked violence and caused some Bashkir clans to support Moscow instead of Kazan.[3] With Ivan IV's triumph, the Nogai Horde splintered. Many Nogais who had supported Kazan fled to the southwest and left their lands empty.[4] Parts of the Bashkir elite, seeking to take Nogai land and prevent the Nogais' return, turned to Ivan IV as a new "khan" who had assumed the title "Tsar of Kazan."[5] In return, the tsar's men promised Bashkir clans that they would interfere little in Bashkir life if the clans submitted to Muscovy. According to the Karagai-Kypchak chronicle, Ivan declared: "Let no one run away as the Nogai ran away, having abandoned their iurts (tents) and having left their land behind. Let everyone preserve his faith [and] observe his customs."[6] Russian sources generally echo Bashkir chronicles. In 1553, according to the Nikon chronicle, Ivan IV sent to every district (*ulus*) surrounding Kazan documents stating that there was nothing to fear. The new sovereign wanted all to pay iasak, a tax or tribute, just as they had paid it to the "former tsar of Kazan."[7]

Although many scholars have emphasized Bashkirs' "voluntary joining" with the Muscovite state, most Bashkirs did not feel that they had much of a choice.[8] According to the Iurmat chronicle, Tatigach, the clan's *bei*, went to Kazan to swear allegiance because he was "unable to think of anything else" when faced with pressure from Moscow and the Nogais.[9] Bashkir leaders apparently believed that neither custom nor their own military forces would allow them to take over the land of the departed Nogais.[10] So, beginning in the mid-1550s, first Bashkir clan elders in Bashkiria's northwest and then those in Bashkiria's south and east journeyed to Kazan, where they "bowed their heads" to the tsar, now called the *Ak Bii,* the "White Bei," and became his "slaves."[11] Ivan IV became *padishakh,* the Persian word for "king" or "shah." Bashkirs agreed to pay iasak.[12] Some Bashkir chronicles specifically mention that their clans received charters registering their land with Muscovite authorities. The Nikon chronicle states simply that Bashkirs, "having bowed," paid iasak.[13] Muscovite rule moved beyond defensive lines and Kazan's settled population onto the open steppe.

By contrast, Moscow's conquest of Kazan, which preceded events in Bashkiria, was much more dramatic and bloody. Moscow and Kazan had long been rivals who often negotiated and sometimes fought. In the fall of 1552, Ivan IV led a massive army that attacked and lay siege to the city of Kazan. After a standoff lasting several weeks, Muscovite forces undermined and destroyed Kazan's main tower on September 4; they demolished its other fortifications a month later.[14] After the siege, much of Kazan's male population was put to death, and the khanate's elite was forced to convert to Russian Orthodoxy and exiled to the empire's interior. Mosques were destroyed and replaced by churches. Muslim Tatars were pushed out of the city's core to a low-lying space outside the city walls or exiled to the countryside. Moscow Metropolitan Makarii led the Russian Orthodox Church's effort to present the conquest as a victory for church and dynasty, overseen by God.[15] Ivan IV commissioned the Cathedral of the Intercession on the Moat, also known as St. Basil's Cathedral, on Red Square in 1555 to commemorate his victory.[16] The conquest also produced one of the most revered icons in the Russian Orthodox tradition, the Kazan Mother of God, which appeared in 1579.[17] The Church created a new archbishopric in Kazan, which became one of the most influential in Muscovy.

The harshest treatment of the city was relatively short-lived. Forced conversions largely ceased by about 1555. As Matthew Romaniello has shown, the dramatic defeat of the khan did not restructure life for most of his former subjects, and Muscovite control of the territory took over a century to realize.[18] Many Muslims converted and entered the tsar's service. Many others, however, served but did not convert while still holding high positions at court and in the military and receiving land and Christian serfs.[19] Nonetheless, the elimination of the khan, the destruction of much of the city and its elite, and the construction of churches instead of mosques at the city center marked a major change in the political landscape. Kazan's conquest has come to be seen as the beginning of the Russian Empire.

Conquest of Bashkiria's primarily nomadic populations had different meanings for Moscow than did the conquest of Kazan's sedentary population. No cathedrals commemorated Bashkirs' oaths of allegiance to Moscow. When Bashkir elders transferred their loyalty to the "White Bei," Ivan IV inserted himself into a set of relationships in a manner quite consistent with previous practices. Muscovite rule of Bashkiria greatly resembled that of its predecessors in nomenclature of administration, in taxation, and in military service.[20] From a Bashkir perspective, Muscovite rule may well have been preferred to that of the Nogais, who were not Chinggisid, did not have legitimacy as such, and had shown little respect for the governing practices of the Kypchak Khanate that preceded the Nogais. Muscovite forces even occupied many of the same spaces as Kazan and Nogai administrations. With the passage of time, however, Muscovite administrative practices gradually and often unintentionally changed the region and Bashkirs' status within the empire. Muscovite promises of land for payment of iasak became codified as *votchina* rights, what I will refer to as "hereditary landholding," and prevented Bashkirs from being enserfed—a process much of Russia's peasant population experienced in the seventeenth century.[21] Bashkiria continued to be organized in *dorogas* (Turkic *daruġa*); native elites were appointed *tarkhans* and served the Muscovite military in lieu of tax payments. The practice of Islam was not hindered. A combination of land rights and reduced taxation gave Bashkirs privileged status within the empire, drew people to Bashkiria, and created an increasingly diverse population there. The extension of the tsar's sovereignty to Bashkiria represents a variant of "bargained incorporation" that Karen Barkey analyzes in the Ottoman case.[22] Rather than using force first as in Kazan, Moscow negotiated Bashkir subordination. Bashkirs sought to work with Moscow in order to gain land from and protection against the Nogais, and Moscow was happy to gain authority in Bashkiria with little commitment of men and material. The swearing of allegiance reflected the interests of Bashkirs and of Moscow's rulers, even if some Bashkir elites felt they had little choice. Certainly, the two sides were not equal. Playing a relatively weaker hand, Bashkirs took to arms when they thought the empire was reneging on its side of the bargain. The case of Bashkiria did not become paradigmatic; instead, it indicates the flexible and varied nature of Muscovite expansion, which was persistent but lacked system and consistency.

BOWING TO THE WHITE BEI

The residents of Bashkiria had long been subjects of one power on the steppe or another and often several at once. Taking an oath to the tsar meant that Bashkirs were shifting allegiances as they had done before. Even before 1552, as

Edward Keenan and others have pointed out, Muscovy was "an integral part" of the world of the steppe, both economically and politically.[23] A complex diplomacy characterized Muscovy's relations with three political entities to its east and south: the Khanates of Kazan and Crimea, the leaders of which claimed descent from Chinggis Khan, and the Nogai Horde, centered in what is now northern Kazakhstan. All three emerged from the ruins of the Kypchak Khanate in the late fourteenth century. The struggle for position among these steppe powers motivated Ivan IV to lead his armies against Kazan in 1552. Bashkir clans of the Volga-Urals region played only a supporting role in the conflicts among the larger political entities. Regardless of whether Bashkirs lived closer to Kazan and paid tribute to that khan, lived in the south and paid tribute to the Nogai Horde, or lived in or east of the Ural Mountains and paid tribute to the Siberian khan, they had to pay someone. The collection of iasak was the key to asserting sovereignty.[24] In exchange for iasak and supporting their suzerain militarily, Bashkirs received the right to use land, which was considered under the control of the respective khan or ruler, and, in principle, protection from others who might threaten their land, lives, or possessions.[25] Clans living in the west and northwest of Bashkiria had paid tribute to the khan of Kazan, so their swearing of allegiance to Ivan IV followed fairly quickly after Ivan's triumph. Clans located farther from Kazan in the central, southern, or southeastern parts of Bashkiria had paid tribute to the Nogai Horde. Their oaths to Ivan IV followed in the years 1555–1557. Bashkir clans farther east and further from Moscow's influence turned to Muscovite authority after Moscow decisively defeated the Siberian khan in 1598. Notably, Bashkir leaders swore allegiance to the tsar as individual representatives of a clan, not collectively. The clan leader typically received tarkhan status, and sometimes another clan leader became an elder (*starosta*).[26]

The new relationship between Bashkirs and Ivan IV demonstrated substantial continuity in terminology and practices. The vocabulary of administration remained mostly the same. The Kypchak Khanate had appointed officials, called *daruga*s, who seem to have been heads of administrative units and whose primary responsibility was tax collection. Under the Kazan Khanate, the word seems to have shifted in meaning from a person to the territory he administered.[27] In the second half of the sixteenth century, tsarist officials divided Bashkiria into four dorogas: the central and southern portions of Bashkiria lay in Nogai Doroga, the east and northeast lay in Siberian Doroga; the north-central portion lay in Osinsk Doroga, and the west and northwest lay in Kazan Doroga.[28] This nomenclature remained until the late eighteenth century. Russians took the word "volost" that identified the administrative unit below the doroga from the Turkic word *ulus,* which meant the same thing. As we might

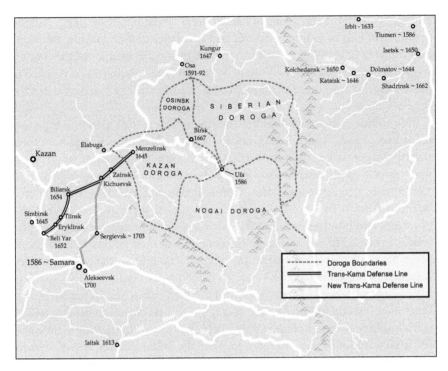

MAP 1.1. Bashkiria in the seventeenth century.

expect from a semi-nomadic population often on the move, the primary attachment of Bashkirs was to a particular leader of the volost, rather than to a territory.[29]

Similarities in language reflected similarities in practice. As Bulat Aznabaev indicates, Bashkirs accepted Ivan IV's sovereignty in the same manner that they swore loyalty to the Kypchak Khanate or its successor khans. Bashkirs travelled to the capital of their sovereign, and their emissaries brought gifts for the new ruler. The ruler's representatives conferred privileged status, here tarkhan status, on the heads of Bashkir clans just as the Kypchak Khans had; and the tsar's men conferred particular lands on Bashkirs, as the Kypchak Khanate's rulers had. The payment of tribute and the provision of military servitors protected Bashkirs' use of the land. Those who paid and served became hereditary landowners.[30] Land was not the private property of individual Bashkirs, and the state could limit the alienation of the land. Collectively, however, Bashkirs could use their land as they desired. Religious differences played very little role in Russian-Bashkir relations. This, too, had precedents on the steppe.

The Mongols, in the words of one scholar, were "situationally tolerant." As long as local religious institutions did not lead resistance to Mongol rule, the Mongols accepted these religious institutions and in some cases granted them privileges.[31] For the most part, the Muscovite government continued this practice in Bashkiria. Not even those attacks on Islam characteristic of Kazan reached the region.[32]

Continuities between Bashkir sovereigns before and after the 1550s extended to physical space, too. Until the early eighteenth century, tsarist authority remained largely within the spatial bounds established by previous sovereigns. Bashkir interests and landholding conditioned the introduction of a Muscovite military-administrative presence. In 1573, Bashkirs petitioned the tsar for a fortress in Bashkiria itself. They argued that paying iasak in the city of Kazan, two hundred miles to Bashkiria's west, was burdensome. They also sought to bring Muscovite military forces closer to their lands so that Moscow could better protect them against the Nogais, who refused to accept Bashkirs' defection to Moscow. Shortly thereafter, in 1586, work began on a new garrison town named Ufa well beyond Moscow's fortified line at the Kama River. The tsar's men literally followed in the footsteps of their Nogai predecessors—the tsar's military governor (*voevoda*) in Ufa took the place of the Nogai governor. Ufa itself was located near the intersection of the Belaia and Dema Rivers, where a Nogai fortress had stood as a tax collection point.[33] The Russian administration remained reluctant to infringe on Bashkir land ownership well after Ufa's founding. The tsar largely limited the distribution of service lands (*pomest'e*) in Bashkiria to lands Bashkirs had taken when the Nogais fled. When the tsar's men did infringe on Bashkir land rights in the sixteenth and early seventeenth centuries, Bashkirs usually defended their rights successfully.[34]

Muscovite military fortifications mostly remained on the fringes of Bashkir land throughout the seventeenth century. All but three of the thirty-one fortresses built in the seventeenth century were located in northwestern Bashkiria along the Kama River or in northeastern Bashkiria along the Iset River on the Siberian side of the Urals, just east of what is now Ekaterinburg.[35] Other than Ufa, the two exceptions were Menzelinsk and Birsk. Located on the Menzelinsk River not far from where it flows into the Ik River, Menzelinsk was constructed in 1645 and staffed by mounted troops and members of the Polish elite, the *shliakhta*, who had been exiled east after Russia's war with Poland. The Birsk fortress, located on the Belaia River about forty miles north of Ufa, had started as an agricultural settlement with court peasants on the site of a former Nogai stronghold. After Bashkirs attacked the settlement in a 1662–1664 uprising, imperial forces fortified it.[36] This was the extent of the Muscovite presence in Bashkiria until the 1730s. Muscovite authority inserted itself into political positions the khans and Nogais had held and largely occupied the same space as well.

Ufa remained an island of tsarist influence in a sea of non-Orthodox, non–Russian speakers. Tsarist servitors remained few well into the eighteenth century. The majority of them in Ufa were nobles sent from Kazan in order to establish a military presence in Bashkiria. Some, such as twenty-seven members of the Polish nobility, ended up in Ufa as exiles.[37] In the 1620s, forty-four men from twenty-one families comprised the Ufa nobility. By the end of the century, the number had risen to 197 men from sixty-two families, but a core of fifteen families present since the 1620s remained most influential and numerous. These two hundred or so men were charged with maintaining order, collecting iasak, and mobilizing military recruits in a territory the size of Italy. In the seventeenth century, the Slavic peasant presence remained small, too. In 1637, only 619 peasant households were found in Ufa Province, and over half of those were on the northwestern border with Kazan.[38]

The nature of service in Ufa certainly did nothing to attract more men. As Bulat Aznabaev puts it, "transfer in service to Ufa, even if not because one was disgraced, represented an extremely unpleasant event in the life of a serviceman." The tsar's servitors fought his battles frequently: against the Kalmyks from 1638 to 1648; against Bashkirs, Siberian Tatars, and Kalmyks in the 1660s; and against Bashkirs and Cossacks in the 1680s. From 1647 to 1718, Ufa was besieged five times. Nobles suffered in such attacks. Fully one-third of the Ufa service elite had to be replaced after armed conflict in the 1660s, and many fled.[39] By Muscovite standards, the Ufa nobility was not wealthy either. Ufa servicemen fighting for the tsar received land as a reward. The Law Code of 1649 forbade Muscovite servicemen from acquiring Bashkir land, and these prohibitions were repeated in 1663, 1695, and 1696.[40] The tsar's servitors' landholdings increased by as many as fifteen times during the sixteenth century. Since very few servicemen owned more than a modest number of serfs, however, they had a limited ability to make their land productive.[41] Trends in serf ownership in Bashkiria differed from those in the empire as a whole. As the number of serfs expanded in the empire, the number of serf owners and serfs held in Bashkiria actually declined from 566 households with 786 serfs in 1647 to 386 households with 667 serfs in 1718.[42] Without the labor necessary to work their lands, Ufa servicemen remained poor compared to those in central regions.

How did a small and not particularly distinguished service elite govern such a large territory? Local officials did so primarily by relying upon the same native elites who had delivered taxes and recruits to the Nogais and khans before the tsar's men arrived. After 1552, as the Slavic nomenclature *volost* replaced the Turkic *ulus,* Russian records began to refer to Bashkir beis as "elders," or *starostas*. In most cases, though, Muscovite authorities used the same terms to identify and categorize the native elite as their predecessors had. The Muscovite government borrowed the practice of awarding tarkhan status from its predecessor, the Khanate of Kazan.[43] The khan had granted the status of tarkhan primarily to the beis who headed Bashkir clans in the Ik River basin on the khanate's southeastern frontier. For example, Sakhib-Girei, khan of Kazan, granted nine men tarkhan status in 1523.[44] Under tsarist rule in the seventeenth and early eighteenth centuries, tarkhans were an elite that resembled the Russian nobility but with fewer privileges. Bashkir tarkhans were exempt from most obligations levied by the tsar's men. Most, though not all, tarkhans neither paid iasak nor had to discharge the transit tax or maintain roads and river crossings. Tarkhans also collected taxes and administered land use among Bashkirs, which had advantages. Since the Russian state did not keep tax rolls in Bashkiria, tarkhans presumably had some discretion in assigning tax burdens and could probably skim a bit off the top, too.[45] Finally, the tsarist administration typically supported tarkhans against efforts by nonprivileged members of Bashkir communities to limit their powers. Tarkhans lacked, however, the two most important privileges granted to Orthodox noblemen: they could not legally own land (other than as part of a clan) or serfs. So, tarkhans were expected to collect taxes and defend the realm, but they lacked the primary privileges that supported such service elsewhere in the empire.[46] The fragmentary evidence on the number of tarkhans that survives indicates a range of 90 to 187 in the second half of the seventeenth century. The majority of tarkhans were located in Nogai Doroga, probably due to the military importance of southern Bashkiria.[47]

For the most part, existing relationships between tsarist authority and local elites sufficed to mobilize local forces to support the tsar. Tarkhans' primary obligation was to protect the Bashkir steppe from incursions by Nogais and Kazakhs to the south and east and to join the empire's struggles against enemies in the west. Tarkhans would appear with their entourages for military service in support of the Ufa garrison. In the 1630s and 1640s, for instance, tarkhans fought alongside servitors from Ufa against Kalmyk raiders. Tarkhans also fought with Prince Pozharskii against the Poles during the Time of Troubles in 1612; fought for Peter the Great against the Ottomans in Azov in 1695–1696; and fought against the Swedes in the Northern War that raged for most of Peter's reign.[48] Tarkhans also conducted diplomacy for the tsar on the Kazakh steppe and in Central Asia. They were not considered part of the imperial administration, however, and could not be ordered to serve at the tsar's pleasure.[49]

Other elites in Bashkiria had some subset of the privileges accorded tarkhans, thus connecting their interests to those of the Muscovite state to different degrees. Bashkirs identified as elders (*starostas* or, in the seventeenth century, *starshinas*), along with Muslim religious leaders, the *akhunds* and imams, did not have to pay iasak. Nor did service Tatars, sometimes bearing the title of *murza* (in Tatar, *mirza*, which is usually also translated as a prince) and sometimes identified as Meshcheriaks, who were sent from west of the Volga to Bashkiria beginning in the early seventeenth century in order to reinforce the local elite.[50] By 1699, 748 Meshcheriaks or service Tatars had moved to Bashkiria.[51] Two other types of servitors did not receive privileges but became sources of tarkhans. Bashkir clan leaders in a number of areas held the title of *duvan* (*divan*), a term used by Kazakhs, and many such leaders became tarkhans after they swore allegiance to the tsar. Finally, distinguished Bashkir warriors called *batyrs* sometimes received tarkhan status for their achievements in battle.[52] The profusion of titles and the unsystematic nature of awards of tarkhan status reflected the difficulty of the Muscovite state's task of consolidating the diverse statuses that rulers of various parts of Bashkiria had used before 1552. Perhaps the best measure of tsarist officials' perceived need to build a loyal elite in Bashkiria can be found in Moscow's instructions to local officials. Central officials routinely admonished their agents in Bashkiria to treat Bashkirs with caution rather than hostility. They reaffirmed Bashkir land rights on a number of occasions, suggesting their awareness of the need not to offend the local population.[53]

We know much less about the relationships of religious elites with the Muscovite state, which says something about the Muslim elite and the Muscovite state's priorities in extending tsarist authority to the region. Collectively referred to as the *ulama*, members of the learned Muslim elite of the region defied straightforward categorization. As R. Stephen Humphreys writes, "they are neither a socio-economic class, nor a clearly defined status group, nor a hereditary caste, nor a legal estate, nor a profession."[54] The ulama included the most educated part of Muslim society, and the purpose of the group was to interpret Muslim law. Although typically equated with Christian clergy in Russian minds, the status and role of Muslim clerics differed substantially. Whereas Christian clergy comprised a separate estate status group with particular privileges and obligations, Muslim clerics never were a status group.[55] The men who led prayers, interpreted Muslim law (the sharia), and in general carried out any religious duty were typically referred to as *mullahs* in Russian sources, or as *abyzs*, a word favored in, though not unique to, Bashkiria. Over time, Russian sources became more specific and more consonant with uses in the Islamic world outside the Russian Empire. For instance, the word "imam," or "leader of Friday prayers," became a formal title in 1788 with the creation of the Orenburg Muhammadan Ecclesiastical Assembly. Most important for our purposes, imams were elected by their congregations and remained part of the estate from which they came, even after election. Until the arrival of the Orenburg Expedition in 1735, the post of imam was completely unregulated by the tsarist state, which appears to have known almost nothing about them or their activities. The most accomplished and respected interpreters of Islamic law acquired the title of *akhun* or akhund as early as the seventeenth century.[56] In the 1730s, for instance, Ivan Kirilov reported to Empress Anna Ivanovna that there were ten akhunds in all Bashkiria, a number he thought should be reduced to four.[57]

CHANGING ADMINISTRATION AND BASHKIR REBELLIONS

Even modest efforts to transform patterns of governance in the region provoked hostility and caused the Muscovite government to retreat. The consolidation of authority in the Romanov dynasty after 1613 and the incorporation of Ukraine in 1654 gave the tsarist state new confidence and freed more resources to address empire-building in the east. The new attention set the context for a series of armed clashes between tsarist forces and the population of Bashkiria in the late seventeenth and early eighteenth centuries that suggested new tendencies in Muscovite governance. Bashkir uprisings of 1662–1664, 1681–1684, and 1704–1711 have been treated at length by Soviet and post-Soviet historians as indications of Bashkiria's gradual incorporation into the empire and of Bashkir resistance to colonial oppression.[58] Most of all, however, the uprisings demonstrate the limitations on tsarist authority.

Three factors—pressure on Bashkir landholdings, a financial crisis, and especially the entry of a new group, Kalmyks, into the area south and east of Bashkiria in the 1630s—precipitated conflict in 1662–1664.[59] The tsarist government built fortresses, encampments, and monasteries in Bashkiria's northwest on land that had traditionally been Bashkir hereditary lands. A failed monetary reform and poor harvests caused central officials to increase taxes and to pressure tax collectors to be more zealous in their duties.[60] The diplomatic and strategic demands of war with Poland and with its ally, the Khanate of Crimea, further stressed Muscovite finances and military forces, and it threatened an important shift in Bashkir-Muscovite relations. Bashkirs and Kalmyks competed for the best pastureland, and each side plundered the other's villages. Generally, Muscovite officials sided with Bashkirs in such disputes, and Muscovite support for Kalmyks was inconsistent.[61] Eager to win Kalmyk support for its military campaigns against Crimea, however, Moscow began to show greater favor to Kalmyks against Bashkirs. In June 1661, Kalmyk leaders agreed to dispatch cavalry to Crimea. In return Kalmyks demanded that the Russians work to end Bashkir raids. The Muscovite government agreed. The Muscovite government gave Bashkirs a "firm order" not to attack Kalmyk camps. The Ufa military governor received instructions to search Bashkir villages for Kalmyk property and to return it to them. Bashkir "bandits" should be punished with death.[62] These Muscovite policies differed sharply from Bashkirs' agreements with Moscow in the sixteenth century. Bashkirs had sworn loyalty to the tsar in exchange for protection against their enemies and a promise to leave Bashkir customs untouched. Seizing property and people as part of a successful raid was an accepted practice on the steppe and in Bashkir customary law. Moscow also agreed to allow Kalmyks to graze their herds on Bashkir land, which violated the principle of hereditary landholding.[63] Moscow's alliance with Kalmyks demonstrated its unwillingness to defend its Bashkir allies. The prohibition on raids against Kalmyks also cut Bashkir elites off from a major source of wealth. Muscovite actions struck at the heart of the Bashkir-Muscovite relationship.

In July 1662, Bashkirs responded in a manner entirely consistent with past patterns of Bashkir relations with their sovereigns. Bashkirs combined with Maris and Tatars in groups of up to a thousand to strike at the Russian presence, mostly the fortresses east of the Ural Mountains.[64] They attacked monasteries, destroyed villages, and took captives. Dissatisfied with their sovereign, they did what they had done in the past—they sought a new one. Divisions among Bashkir elites caused them to pursue various possibilities. Some collaborated with the sons of Kuchum, the last Siberian khan. Those in Bashkiria's south had greater opportunities to do what nomads often did when faced with inhospitable circumstances: as many as eight thousand fled to Kalmyk lands. Negotiations also took place with the khan of Crimea. In Bashkiria's north, armed clashes were more intense. The Ufa military governor accused Bashkirs of having "betrayed the great sovereign" by going to their eternal enemies, Kalmyks, and to Kuchum's heirs.[65] Moscow sent punitive expeditions from Kazan and from Tobol'sk to take hostages, to burn villages, and to suppress the rebellion.[66] After two years of intermittent violence, the Muscovite government confirmed Bashkir privileges. The tsar's officials agreed to replace a military governor particularly hated by Bashkirs, issued instructions that tax collectors must not abuse those paying iasak, and stated that Bashkirs only needed to return Kalmyk property if it was still at hand. Bashkirs must, in return, take an oath of loyalty to the tsar. Most of all, the Muscovite government issued a decree that reaffirmed Bashkir hereditary landownership. Bashkirs could neither sell nor rent their hereditary landholdings to outsiders.[67] These guarantees and the lack of a viable alternative sovereign ended the rebellion in October 1664.

After 1664, Muscovite officials increased the tsar's servitors in Bashkiria from 400 to 1,615, but this did not prevent renewed violence in 1681. Efforts to expand the power of the Orthodox Church and to convert Muslims to Christianity appear to have caused Bashkir discontent. In 1680, the Muscovite state began to attack Muslim landholding and noble status—Muslim princes (*murzas*) received financial incentives for converting to Christianity.[68] The following year, the tsar decreed that baptized Muslims whose land had been taken away could have it returned, but those who remained Muslim received no such protection.[69] A 1682 church council in Moscow called for a more intense effort to spread Christianity and to fight sectarianism. As part of this effort, the church aimed to strengthen its presence locally in Ufa and in other areas by creating many new bishoprics.[70] In 1682, a law legalized the seizure of Muslim Tatars' lands and its distribution to baptized Tatars. Such actions exceeded any previous proselytizing and indicated a greater desire to intervene in local affairs than Muscovy had previously shown, even if the church's presence in Bashkiria remained small.[71]

In 1680, there were few Muslim princes and few Muslim serf owners in Bashkiria, however, so the new legislation had little effect there, even if it rightly raised alarms about Muscovite intentions. Bashkirs joined Kalmyks, Maris, and Chuvashes in large-scale rebellion against Russian authority in Ufa and Kazan Provinces in the spring of 1682. Violence centered on Osinsk Doroga in Bashkiria's north.[72] In response, the new co-tsars, Ivan and Peter, issued a charter in July 1682 rebutting "false rumors" to the effect that "Muslims (*Basurmanov*) were led to cities to be christened in the Orthodox faith against their will." No such Christianization policy existed, the co-tsars assured the local population.[73] The charter divided the government's opponents: some stood down, and others continued to fight. After the government mobilized Cossacks and soldiers from Kazan to suppress the rebellion, the two sides struggled inconclusively until 1684, when large-scale violence ceased. In addition to the retreat on conversion, after the uprising the relocation of noble servitors to Ufa and the distribution of service lands essentially stopped. Ufa only received a bishop in 1799.[74]

Intermittent clashes between the government and the population from 1705 to 1711 showed a similar pattern to those of the previous century. Preoccupied with the Northern War against Sweden, Peter I demanded more revenue from all parts of the empire. In an effort to squeeze more out of Bashkiria, in 1701 responsibility for all tax collection shifted from Ufa to the Kazan military governor and the chancellery of the Kazan Palace (*Prikaz Kazanskogo Dvortsa*). In 1702, Kazan's military governor sent tax collectors to Ufa with instructions to collect taxes in arrears from 1701 as well. Whereas Ufa's officials had recognized the right of Bashkirs to travel to the capital to address the tsar's men themselves, Kazan's officials denied them that right. The Ingrian Chancellery, created by Peter to increase state revenue and administered by Peter's favorite Alexander D. Menshikov, worked to introduce seventy-two new burdens on the local population, including the confiscation of five thousand horses, taxes on grain mills and horses, and the surrender of fishing rights and land.[75] These demands accentuated the economic stress on Bashkiria's population.[76] In 1704, Bashkirs took up arms to resist efforts to extract taxes and horses.[77] Over the next six years, periods of conflict involving thousands of troops on each side alternated with concessions from the state and the return of calm. As Bashkirs had in previous uprisings, they sent envoys to other potential sovereigns as far away as Istanbul to express their desire to transfer their allegiance.[78] In 1708, Bashkir rebels linked up with those led by the Don Cossack Kondraty Bulavin until the latter's defeat in 1709. Finally, in 1710, Kalmyks switched to energetic support for the Russian side. They and punitive detachments sent by Russian authorities quashed the uprising in 1711.[79] Divisions among Bashkir leaders contributed to its collapse.

As Bashkirs had done in previous uprisings, they insisted on the privileges granted them over the previous century and a half. In 1705, some petitioned: "in past years charters of the Great Sovereign were sent to us that no additional exactions would be placed on us, hereditary lands would not be taken, and our faith would not be violated as long as we live."[80] Imperial officials in Kazan were divided on whether Bashkir status ought to be respected. Some wanted to use force; others sought negotiations. Peter's commissars in Kazan, charged with collecting taxes, argued that their activities were not the problem. Kazan commissar S. Varaksin wrote to Peter's close aide Menshikov that Bashkir "banditry" had started in Ufa "not because of taxes and not because of exactions but in order not to be under the great sovereign ruler's hand and they sent emissaries to the Turks, to the sultan, and to the khan in Crimea to request that they unite with them."[81] If Kazan governor B. N. Sheremetev and his successor, P. I. Khovanskii, had simply used sufficient force against Bashkirs, Varaksin argued, they would have been subdued. Instead, Sheremetev advocated "traditional methods of pacifying Bashkirs." He opened negotiations with them and freed from prison some Bashkirs arrested by Kazan authorities.[82] Sheremetev's replacement, Khovanskii, pursued a similar policy of calming Bashkirs by restoring their previous privileges. Khovanskii had promised concessions and managed to get Bashkirs to swear oaths of loyalty in 1708.

Even after the uprising had largely ended, some officials in Kazan sought harsh measures to subdue Bashkiria on a permanent basis. Kazan governor P. M. Apraksin wrote to his influential brother, Admiral F. M. Apraksin, to get the tsar's permission to organize a campaign against Bashkiria, to which thousands of Kazan Province's taxpayers had already fled. He sought to prevent such flight and to bring Bashkirs to "real subjecthood, to make them real tribute payers." Apraksin could not endure such "antagonistic, disobedient domestic scoundrels" acting as they did toward such a "celebrated and great monarch" as Peter. Bashkirs lived "incomparably richly" and "without any humility" in a "promised land, on many thousands of *versts*."[83] Peter's permission to campaign against Bashkiria never came. The tsar continued to move more cautiously with respect to Bashkiria than many of his officials desired. When Peter introduced the soul tax (*podushnaia podat'*) in 1718, it did not apply to Bashkiria. In 1721, the imperial senate sent Graf Golovkin to investigate the actions of Kazan officials during the Bashkir uprising of 1705–1709. Golovkin traveled to Ufa and sent back a petition from Bashkirs, who stated that they promised to "serve according to their faith just as their grandfathers and fathers served in bygone days," to pay "any sort of tax," to "return fugitive people," and not to accept fugitives anymore. However, these Bashkirs then described how officials from Kazan had demanded five thousand horses and unprecedented taxes and backed up their demands by burning villages and killing people.[84] The senate concluded that Kazan officials were responsible for provoking Bashkir unrest.[85] Peter's willingness to ignore the desire of some officials to force Bashkirs to surrender their status seems to have been motivated by his desire to get into the Asian trade that had so enriched maritime powers to Russia's west, such as the Netherlands and Great Britain. Peter and his closest advisors already were looking beyond Bashkiria to the Kazakh steppe and to Central Asia as a step toward the goal of Asian empire. As Peter I told diplomat and translator for the College of Foreign Affairs Kutlu-Mukhammad Tevkelev, when Tevkelev returned from the Persian campaign in 1722, Peter would spend millions to bring only one Kazakh horde into "exact subjecthood," if only one would "commit itself to be under the protection of the Russian Empire."[86] A violent assault on Bashkiria would only make Kazakhs and other peoples suspicious of the Russian Empire and provoke them to ally against it.

The pattern of Bashkir rebellion followed by negotiation and the imperial state's efforts at accommodation became so familiar that, by the 1720s, Bashkirs did not even have to take up arms, only to discuss doing so, in order to get imperial authorities to confirm the status quo.[87] In 1726 and 1727, Lieutenant General Chekin in the Kama River basin and Prince Golitsyn in Kazan sent word to St. Petersburg of trouble in Bashkiria. Members of the Bashkir estate, including several clerics, a senior cleric or akhund, and Bashkir warriors from volosts in Bashkiria's southeast and northeast had approached Kalmyk and Kazakh leaders, proposing that the groups join forces to "wage war on Russian cities" and to "kill Russian people" in the spring of 1728. The Bashkirs claimed to be able to assemble a force of about fifteen thousand warriors. Imperial officers feared that the alliance of "steppe peoples" could overwhelm the empire's forces and destroy cities and fortresses on the frontier. They asked for and received reinforcements.[88]

In addition to the military preparations, however, in July 1728 a contingent of thirty-two Bashkirs led by one Iarkei Ianchurin arrived in Moscow to present a petition with their grievances and to meet with officials from the College of Foreign Affairs. The Bashkir delegation requested that Bashkirs be "kept gently," that no officials be allowed to offend them, and that all officials "act according to the charters granted to them by the ancestors of His Imperial Majesty." The Bashkir delegation insisted that no tax be imposed on them other than iasak. The military governor should dispense justice among Russians according to the emperor's law, but among Bashkirs legal proceedings should be conducted as they had been in the past without "needless interference and formality." Taxes collected by the military governor should be collected without the need for bribes. If the emperor would protect Bashkirs from "insults" and taxes (*nalog*), then Bashkirs would serve the emperor "faithfully, as their fathers and grandfathers served them," pay iasak, turn over all "Russian fugitives," and not accept members of other peoples. The Bashkirs also wanted the current Ufa military governor, Andrei Likhachev, who took bribes and refused them passports to travel to Moscow, to be replaced with their former military governor, Ivan Bakhmetev. They wanted to be protected from Chuvashes and Meshcheriaks who used force to take possession of Bashkir land, and they requested to be able to pay their taxes in Ufa, not Kazan.[89] In a series of decrees issued in 1728 and 1729, the Supreme Privy Council granted Bashkirs all of their demands, except their choice for military governor.[90] Ufa Province was separated from Kazan for good.

The particular timing of Bashkirs' talk of rebellion may have had much to do with the reception their demands received. Peter the Great had died only a few years before, in 1725, and only the crowning of Empress Anna in 1730 stabilized central authority. In 1730, Kazan governor A. P. Volynskii again advocated attacks on Bashkir status. Although Volynskii argued that Bashkirs were Muslim and thus by nature hostile to Christians, his primary concerns were fiscal and political. The low rates of taxation in Bashkiria had caused the flight of as many as a hundred thousand of Kazan's taxpayers to the east. For this reason, Volynskii sought to mount a campaign against Bashkir enemies, the Kazakhs and Karakalpaks. War against the two peoples could be used to mobilize Bashkir men and horses. It would also provide a pretext to send officers and surveyors to purchase Bashkir horses, to provide intelligence on the Bashkir population, and to build fortresses. Once the campaign against Bashkir enemies had been concluded, the tsar's forces could turn on Bashkirs and force them to pay more taxes. The taxes would provide a disincentive for flight to Bashkiria, pay for imperial troops stationed there, and provide income to the state.[91] Volynskii's plan, like those of previous Kazan governors, was left unrealized. Bashkirs largely thwarted Muscovite authorities' efforts to reshape the local political and fiscal regime. Even Peter the Great, more interested in expansion to the west and south, avoided a decisive confrontation with Bashkiria's population.[92]

MAKING A STATUS GROUP

Although Bashkirs fought to make the Muscovite state maintain the key terms of its original swearing of allegiance and largely succeeded, Bashkirs' position and that of the population of the region as a whole slowly changed through engagement with tsarist law and institutions. Conflicts that occurred every two decades or so in the late seventeenth century resulted in violence but also in greater legal recognition of Bashkir privileges. In the words of Petr Rychkov, an eighteenth-century official and historian of the region, "from olden times Bashkirs were something like nobles, they had various privileges over others."[93] The crucial moment for Bashkirs was the uprising of 1662–1664, which resulted in recognition of Bashkir hereditary landholdings and prohibited the enserfment of Bashkirs. Permanent ownership distinguished Bashkir landholding from the conditional landholding that had become prevalent among Russian nobles and service Tatars in the Kazan region. Bashkir collective landholding continued to be considered hereditary landholding even after Peter the Great combined hereditary landholdings elsewhere with conditional landholdings under the term "real estate" (*nedvizhimoe imenie*).[94] Some Bashkir clan chronicles specifically claimed that charters recognized their land rights as early as the sixteenth or seventeenth centuries.[95] Furthermore, while peasants in the empire found their mobility restricted after 1649, most Bashkirs received protection from enserfment. A few were enserfed in the course of the seventeenth century, but generally as punishment for participation in uprisings. Rychkov calculated that there were only thirty-five Bashkir serfs in 1699.[96] The right to own land collectively and protection from enserfment were crucial in an agrarian economy featuring servile labor, even if they did not equate Bashkirs with nobles, who could own land and serfs individually. Bashkirs' hereditary landownership represented an exception to trends toward the concentration of land in noble hands and an increasingly rigid serf regime that prevailed in the empire.

Bashkir privileges extended also to the realms of taxation and military service. Despite the increasing presence of the tsar's administration, Bashkirs, on average, paid iasak of twenty to fifty kopecks in the seventeenth and early eighteenth centuries.[97] Bashkirs also had to provide services such as the maintenance of roads and transportation. Between 1704 and 1711, state officials increased taxes, such as that on fishing, and levied new ones, such as those on livestock, windows, and marriages. Since roads were few and mail service lacking until the 1730s, however, such taxes affected few. Peter's new taxes brought in little revenue. The "marriage tax" on Muslims brought in only thirty-four to sixty-seven rubles per year in the 1720s.[98] By contrast, the non-Bashkir population paid a tax of about eighty kopecks on average and bore similar burdens of service as they did elsewhere in the empire. Whereas Peter the Great's military machine increasingly conscripted thousands of Russian commoners into service, only particular segments of the Bashkir population, tarkhans and their retinues, served. In the 1720s, state officials sought to extend military conscription to Bashkir and non-Bashkir populations of Bashkiria alike, but this effort failed. Bashkirs bore one other burden characteristic of the steppe—in times of strife, Russian officials held some Bashkirs, often tarkhan*s*, as captives, or *amanaty*. From the uprising of 1662–1664 to the Bashkir frontier war of 1735–1740, Russians held from a dozen to about fifty hostages near Ufa in order to assure Bashkir compliance with state demands.[99]

By the early eighteenth century, imperial policy intersected with Bashkirs' assertions of their interests to produce a status group that enjoyed collective hereditary landownership, avoided servile labor, paid the distinctive iasak, and had limited military service obligations. This meant, essentially, the codification of earlier political and fiscal policies of the tsar's predecessors in the east. In formally codifying these practices, however, the Russian state transformed them. Steppe political practices became elements of estate status that legally distinguished Bashkirs from their neighbors. Bashkirs had become a privileged estate group unlike any other.[100]

Bashkir engagement with Muscovite authority began to change Bashkir conceptions of land use. A number of Bashkir chronicles reflect a connection between swearing allegiance to the tsar, recognition of Bashkir landownership, and the division of that land among subunits of the tribe, typically called *tiubas*. One Iurmat chronicle mentions the vast undivided land that Bashkirs possessed, and another stresses that much of the land came to the Iurmat clans when they received permission from the tsar's men to take the land that Nogais had abandoned.[101] Iurmat, Burzian, Tam'ian, Kypchak, Ming, and Iriakte chronicles specify that the land was then measured and marked off.[102] Other chronicles date this process to Alexei Mikhailovich's reign (1645–1676) or to the time his sons Ivan and Peter ruled together (1682–1696).[103] The period of Bashkir uprisings from the 1660s to the 1680s saw a pattern of the demarcation of land to smaller groups of Bashkirs.[104] Charters that codified Bashkir rights appeared with increasing frequency in government archives in the late seventeenth and eighteenth centuries, demonstrating Bashkirs' increasing consciousness of tsarist law and procedure.

MIGRATION, STATUS, AND CULTURAL DIFFERENCE

Tsarist officials understood little of cultural and ethnic groupings in the region. Bashkir status did not necessarily coincide with Bashkir cultural or ethnic identity. The emergence of Bashkirs as a privileged status group caused people to move to Bashkiria and often into the Bashkir estate. Less privileged subjects of the tsar fled to Bashkiria in search of more land, less onerous tax obligations, and greater distance from Muscovite authorities. Finnic- and Turkic-language speakers from the former Khanate of Kazan, such as the Maris, Udmurts, Mordvas, and Tatars, resettled in Bashkiria in growing numbers in the sixteenth and seventeenth centuries.[105] Movement from Kazan province to Bashkiria accelerated in the first decades of the eighteenth century, when the demand for taxes and service to support Peter the Great's wars made flight to Bashkiria even more attractive. Authorities in Kazan condemned the flight of Kazan residents to Bashkiria and accused Bashkirs of at least tolerating it and often encouraging it. Since Bashkirs owned most of the land, all others rented it from them—at least in principle. In-migrants were known as pripushchenniks, or "those let in." To the state, and likely to Bashkirs too, pripushchenniks were distinguished not by their culture or ethnicity but by the terms of their land use and their legal status. Pripushchenniks who had a written agreement to use Bashkir land were called Teptiars, a status group found only in Bashkiria. Such agreements specified the amount of land allotted to Teptiars and obligations they would discharge in exchange for it. The number of Teptiars was about 8,400 in 1725. Their numbers grew substantially in the eighteenth century.[106]

Two closely related groups of migrants to Bashkiria, Meshcheriaks and service Tatars, were discussed above as part of Bashkiria's elite. They swore allegiance to the tsar in the sixteenth century and carried out military service thereafter. Some had taken part in the Muscovite conquest of Kazan in 1552. Typically they served in lieu of paying taxes. By the 1720s, the number of Meshcheriaks and service Tatars in Bashkiria had grown to about 2,200 males.[107] Perhaps the largest non-Bashkir group in Bashkiria was the *Bobyls,* or landless peasants. They typically were of the same status in their home region as in Bashkiria. They paid Bashkir hereditary landowners rent or simply squatted on Bashkir land. They could be of any ethnic group of the Volga-Urals region. Finally, by the early eighteenth century, a significant population of serfs owned by the crown, monasteries, and nobles had formed in Bashkiria. They tended to be located on the northwestern and northeastern parts of Bashkiria, where Bashkir landholding was not as great as in Bashkiria's center and south. Serf numbers remained small in the early eighteenth century. A tax census in the 1720s found 3,472 male crown peasants and 687 male serfs owned by nobles.

Overall, by the early eighteenth century, historians estimate that approximately 260,000 Bashkirs lived in Bashkiria, along with 50,000–60,000 migrants.[108] Migrants brought change to Bashkiria since they practiced settled agriculture, something that few Bashkirs did. Tatars and Russians also engaged in trade to a greater extent than Bashkirs.

Those who moved to Bashkiria had a strong incentive to move into the Bashkir estate, too. Group boundaries remained porous and state record-keeping rudimentary. This provided a possibility for those who were not members of Bashkir clans to enter them. Marriage was one way to do so for those who shared Bashkirs' Islamic faith. Bashkir-Tatar marriages appear to have been common, so much so that the state tried to ban them in the 1730s. Animist peoples in close proximity with Muslims could become Islamized as well and therefore join Bashkir communities. Others underwent a process of *usynovlenie,* or adoption, and thus became part of the Bashkir status group. The Ming chronicle specifically mentions a Mari who was "registered as a son" of a clan member.[109] *Aimaks* or *Tiubas*—sub-groups of Bashkir clans in the northeast and south of Bashkiria, respectively—included those identified as Sarts, Kalmyks, Nogais, Meshcheriaks, and Turkmen, suggesting that members of these groups had become part of Bashkir hereditary landowning clans.[110] The Iriakte chronicle, for instance, notes, unhappily, that Kalmyk, Chuvash, and Mordva laborers had taken advantage of the death of clan leader Isian-khan to enter his *iurta,* or in this sense, his lands.[111] Since nationality was not a meaningful category in eighteenth- and nineteenth-century imperial politics, however, the ethnic or national composition of an estate group remains largely unknowable.

The fate of Tatar-speaking, Muslim nobles who moved to Bashkiria in the seventeenth through nineteenth centuries demonstrates movement among status groups. Historian I. R. Gabdullin has traced, with varying degrees of precision, 583 Tatar families with origins in areas from southeast of Kazan to Kasimov, located just 150 miles southeast of Moscow, who served the tsar from the fifteenth to the nineteenth centuries. Of these 583 families, 179, or about 30 percent, had at least one branch settle in Bashkiria. Of these, at least eleven families emerged with Bashkir status. Others regained their noble status, entered the Meshcheriak or Teptiar estate groups, or became state peasants.[112] At the time of Catherine the Great's Legislative Commission of 1767–1768, Bashkir petitions discussed Sarts, members of a Muslim group in Central Asia, and Kalmyks who had come to Bashkir communities as youths or as refugees and later acquired Bashkir status.[113] People who considered themselves Bashkirs could also be subject to imprecise classification. The Iriakte chronicle notes one part of the clan had been registered as "iasak-paying Tatars" for unknown reasons.[114] Such evidence indicates how the Bashkir estate's privileges within the imperial system caused people to seek to become Bashkirs, and thus the estate group was not identical with an ethnic group.

The movement of Tatar nobles and servicemen into the Bashkir estate was part of a broader shift in the treatment of Muslim elites in the eighteenth century. Aggressive efforts to restrict Muslims and convert them to Russian Orthodoxy accompanied Peter's conflicts with the Ottoman Empire.[115] Efforts to "monopolize the sacred" and further "absolutist state-building" also invigorated missionary work.[116] Attacks on Muslim ownership of estates and serfs that had begun in 1680 became much more serious in 1713. Petrine legislation in November 1713 announced that Muslims who had service landholdings or hereditary landholdings must convert to Orthodoxy within six months or lose their land and serfs. A flood of petitions from Tatar servitors caused the government to modify the law two years later to allow those who did not convert to keep their homes and lands, but the loss of serfs that had been threatened since the 1680s now took place.[117] Gabdullin has identified sixty-four families of Tatar Muslim servitors who lost serfs or land after the 1713 decree. Very likely, there were others.[118] In any case, in 1719, Peter specified that Tatars and other non-Russians in Ufa County and Kungur County in Siberia not be baptized "against their will" and that a priest the non-Russians accused of baptizing inorodtsy by force be investigated.[119] Nonetheless, such policies indicated a growing interest in increasing state resources and reducing the flexibility and diversity of the empire's political and social structures that Peter's protégés pursued in earnest after his death.

Tsarist rule in Bashkiria and the movement of people from the Kazan region to Bashkiria that accompanied it stimulated change in Bashkirs' ways of life. The delineation of land among Bashkir tribes that took place after Bashkirs swore allegiance to Ivan IV made it more difficult to move herds great distances, causing Bashkirs west of the Urals to begin a gradual shift from nomadic to semi-nomadic pastoralism.[120] In the seventeenth century Bashkirs typically paid iasak in beaver pelts or honey. This motivated Bashkirs to develop hunting and beekeeping skills.[121] Bashkiria's north had been subordinate to and was linguistically and culturally closer to Kazan, so the north felt the change of rulers in 1552 in that city most directly. The path to Siberia lay in Bashkiria's north, and thus, through the 1730s, most migrants to Bashkiria settled there. The influx of people had a mixed effect on the local population. They could be a burden, since some simply squatted on Bashkir land without paying any rent. The Bashkir delegation to Moscow in 1728, for instance, complained that in-migrant Chuvashes, Meshcheriaks, and other peoples had caused "ruin and damage" to them.[122] In other cases, Bashkirs could benefit from in-migrants by collecting rent from them or by using them for labor. In either case, the flow of people to Bashkiria pushed Bashkirs in the northwest toward settled agriculture. A relatively more dense population disrupted the movement of herds in the summer, making semi-nomadic pastoralism less attractive. In-migrants practiced settled agriculture, providing Bashkirs an example of how to make it work.[123] Sources suggest that Bashkirs began growing hay in the late seventeenth century, indicating a greater commitment to agricultural pursuits.[124] Bashkirs' stated interest in reducing customs taxes on products they brought to Kazan also suggests that the proximity of the city stimulated Bashkir trade in lumber, honey, beeswax, and furs.[125] The growing population also put pressure on forests and caused Bashkirs' turn toward agriculture in Bashkiria's north.[126]

The presence of iron ore in the Ural Mountains, which drew state-sponsored mines and factories, began to change life in Bashkiria's north during the reign of Peter I. Peter's military ambitions and conflicts with Sweden, a leading supplier of iron ore to Russia, drove a search for new sources of metal. The state sponsored the construction of three factories east of the Ural Mountains. Later, in the 1720s, seven more would be built, bringing 28,000 serfs fixed to the factories from central Russia. Including their families, they made up a significant portion of the region's population.[127] Nonetheless, although few of the native local population worked in factories, the factories affected the population substantially. Substantial amounts of land were assigned to each factory, much of it coming from Bashkir landholdings. This, combined with the factories' tremendous demand for wood, drove many Bashkirs from animal husbandry into the mountains, where they hunted, fished, kept bees, and trapped furs. The Muscovite conquest of Kazan, intentionally and incidentally, brought settled agriculture, trade, and even industry to northern Bashkiria.

CONCLUSION

Bashkiria entered the empire under different circumstances than Kazan had only a few years before. Kazan's conquest acquired great importance as a decisive defeat of a people who had a social structure generally like Moscow's but practiced Islam. Unlike Bashkirs, Kazan Tatars had an elite that owned serfs and controlled land on an individual basis, and they practiced settled agriculture. Moscow worked to apply the Muscovite social and political system, including a large Russian Orthodox Church, service landholding, and, in the seventeenth century, serfdom to Kazan. But Kazan was the easternmost place where this pattern predominated. Russian imperialism east of Kazan largely lacked a powerful church establishment, extensive service landholding, the extensive use of proprietary serfs, or all three.

Bashkiria's incorporation showed a different side of Muscovite empire-building. The tsar inserted himself and his state into the patterns that had long regulated political life on the steppe. In the context of an expanding empire, however, these practices acquired new meanings. They created a legally distinct status group. The payment of iasak in exchange for use of the khan's land became Bashkir hereditary, collective landownership. The status of Bashkiria's tarkhan elite was consolidated, and the number of its members expanded as they began to fight the tsar's wars. Until the eighteenth century, the tsarist state continued to interfere in the lives of Bashkiria's residents little more than its predecessors had. Missionaries converted few of Bashkiria's Muslims, and the laws responsible for enserfing Russia's peasants did not apply to Bashkirs. Disagreements over taxation and security caused conflict between Bashkiria's population and its sovereigns, but they had done so before the tsar became padishakh, too. The tsar offered Bashkirs and especially their elites a stake in the empire, albeit a relatively modest one, at relatively little cost to them in taxation and with little interference in their affairs. In Bashkiria before 1730, Muscovite rulers sought to exact tribute much more than they "sought the stable control of population and resources."[128]

Bashkiria's treatment reflected a basic lack in Muscovy of a "crusading ideology." As Paul Bushkovitch has written, Eastern Orthodoxy from Byzantium to Muscovy lacked the drive to "ensure religious uniformity by conversion" or expulsion that characterized the Catholic West after the eleventh century.[129] Bashkiria's geographic position and the local population's way of life also had much to do with how the region and its population were treated. Muscovite and imperial Russian power were always perceived as fragile in the southeast. As late as the 1770s, the empire could not control the mass movement of Kalmyks, for instance. Officials in Moscow and then in St. Petersburg sought to win Bashkirs to their side rather than risk a major confrontation that would be costly at least and possibly futile. Moreover, unlike the settled, agrarian population to Bashkiria's west, Bashkirs could always flee farther away. Bashkirs' ability to exit the empire made imperial officials interested in building the loyalty of local elites. The language of Muscovite charters to Bashkirs and Bashkir petitions to the tsar reads much like a negotiation, leading to a bargain with which both sides could live. Russian sources show a fear of losing control of the region, which made Muscovite officials more willing to negotiate the Bashkir relationship with the state.

In the broader context of Muscovite expansion in the sixteenth and seventeenth centuries, the Bashkir case is most similar to that of the Don Cossacks to the west and south. Both groups remained legally distinct within the empire, and, as Brian Boeck has argued, bore relatively fewer state demands than most

Slavs save the nobility. Bashkirs, like Cossacks, were part of the relatively privileged periphery that drew those fleeing the higher taxes and serfdom of central regions.[130] Muscovite officials granted privileges to groups on Muscovy's margins to extend Muscovite influence and to draw the loyalty of people who might fight Moscow, flee, or serve a rival state. In the seventeenth century, Bashkirs were relatively less privileged than Cossacks, who did not have to provide hostages and received trade rights and an annual subsidy from the tsar.[131]

In its Western borderlands, Moscow faced states such as Poland, Lithuania, and Sweden that were more economically developed and militarily at least its equal. For these reasons, tsarist officials offered more in exchange for loyalty. For instance, officials allowed the Zaporozhian Sich—the Cossack center that swore allegiance to Moscow in 1654 in order to gain an ally in its struggle with Poland—greater levels of autonomy than they did the former Kazan Khanate in the east. The greater similarity of social structure between Muscovite Russia and its western rivals also meant that it was easier for Moscow to recognize the noble status of western groups than those in the east. When Moscow conquered territory including the city of Smolensk from Poland-Lithuania in the mid-seventeenth century, Moscow guaranteed the property rights and privileges of the nobles and townsmen, even if some three hundred were exiled to the eastern borderlands, including Ufa.[132] By the eighteenth century, the Polonized nobility in the western borderlands had largely merged with the Russian nobility. Similar practices took place in the Kazan region in the sixteenth and early seventeenth centuries, but in the seventeenth century, the Muscovite state granted imperial elites such as tarkhans in the east fewer privileges and succeeded less in introducing elites from the metropole there than it did in the west. Moving from status to faith, religious differences existed between Russian Orthodox and Catholics in the western borderlands, but there were more options for negotiating the differences between two Christian faiths than between Islam and Russian Orthodoxy. Thus, the Union of Brest in 1596 created a hybrid Uniate Church that recognized the authority of the Pope but maintained largely Orthodox rituals.[133] It is difficult to imagine a hybrid of Russian Orthodoxy and Islam.

Indeed, the Muscovite approach to Bashkiria resembles more Eurasian rather than European patterns. East of Kazan, Moscow embraced the political, social, and cultural ecology of the steppe. Like its contemporary rivals Qing China and the Ottoman Empire, with whom it negotiated, traded, and fought in the seventeenth century, the Muscovite state sought to control territory and trade over vast areas populated by people of different ways of life and faith. Muscovite officials were used to dealing with settled agriculturalists, and their strategies of administration and tax collection were designed for that purpose.

Confronted with the need to administer a distant region such as Bashkiria where there were fewer potential servitors, tsarist officials embraced previous practices of tribute in exchange for land use, religious toleration, and recognized status in ways their predecessors had. Muscovites made no pretense that Bashkiria was like Muscovy's core. Even as serfdom increasingly bound the empire's peasantry, Muscovite authorities never sought to bind Bashkirs. Efforts to convert the tsar's subjects to Russian Orthodoxy had little effect among Bashkirs, whose practice of Islam strengthened in this period as Tatar clerics fled Russian rule in Kazan for the relative freedom of Bashkiria.

As Peter Perdue has argued, the Chinese, Russian, and Ottoman Empires displayed "many common patterns as they expanded across Eurasia." Each empire succeeded not by following "rigid religious ideologies" but because "they pragmatically mixed together multiple traditions."[134] Muscovite officials skillfully practiced steppe diplomacy and drew on a Mongol heritage of horsemanship and political institutions. A crucial aspect of the pragmatism of all three empires before the eighteenth century was the practice of creating legal and administrative distinctions between the settled core of the empire and the nomadic or semi-nomadic steppe frontier. Nomads were often dangerous and threatening, but they were not "animals or natural forces."[135] Nomads could be a source of revenue and essential supplies such as horses, and they could be used to extend the influence of the empire. All three empires, therefore, created different juridical and administrative regimes for them—they mapped their "administrative and legal structures to the ethno-cultural patchwork of the region."[136] The most formal such differentiation occurred in China during the Qing Dynasty in the seventeenth century and took the form of the "Banner System."[137] Banners were complex institutions that combined especially military, but also social, economic, and political functions. Nomadic Mongol forces were organized into banners in 1635 and distinguished from Manchu banners and later Han Chinese banners. Those in banners were distinguished by a "raft of special legal and occupational privileges that further accentuated the separateness of the Han from the Manchu socio-military caste."[138] The treatment of Mongols in law remained distinctive until the end of the Qing dynasty.[139]

In a somewhat similar manner, the nomadic and semi-nomadic population of the Ottoman Empire received distinct treatment in law. Until the last decade of the seventeenth century, the Ottomans "had neither the means nor the intention to permanently settle or discipline" nomadic tribes. Instead, they opted to classify them in their existing situations.[140] Since they were mobile, they were not subject to the same local authorities. Their administrative units were not territorial but based on tribes and clans themselves. Ottoman administrators typically relied on tribes to identify their own leaders, whom the central government then recognized. Nomads were exempt from many taxes imposed on sedentary farmers.[141] After 1689, the state used incentives and force to make nomads settle, but due to the nomadic possibilities for movement the state's and nomads' "relationship was complex and exhibited bargaining and incentives on the part of both participant groups."[142] Muscovite Russia followed a pan-Eurasian pattern in distinguishing sedentary from nomadic and semi-nomadic subjects.

The Muscovite Russian encounter with Bashkirs before 1730 certainly must not be perceived as harmonious. Tensions and violence, hostage-taking, and raids characterized the steppe. Three Bashkir rebellions in this period indicate persistent hostility. Bashkirs had certain understandings of their relationship with the tsar and his officials. When the tsar's men violated those understandings, Bashkirs rebelled. The tsar's officials then reaffirmed such things as Bashkir collective landownership, taxation, and other obligations. A tense peace was then restored, at least for a while. The fact that already in the seventeenth century the tsar could mobilize Bashkirs to fight in wars as distant as Poland and against another Muslim power, such as the Ottoman Empire, suggests that collaboration often characterized Russian-Bashkir relations, if to a lesser degree than conflict.

This state of affairs was predicated in part on the great expanse and small population of the steppe. As long as nomads could fight or, at least in principle, flee, settled states had an incentive to continue the bargain. By the late seventeenth century, however, indications of a more difficult future appeared. The open, fluid space of Eurasia was demarcated. The Treaty of Nerchinsk of 1689 drew a clear boundary between Muscovite and Chinese empires for the first time.[143] Closer to Bashkiria, the boundary between the Ottoman and Russian Empires was drawn in 1704.[144] Although neither directly affected Bashkiria, these events were important early signs of a state system that resisted the mobility of peoples. In the sixteenth and seventeenth centuries, tsars mostly sought to establish authority on the steppe, to become padishakhs. Only in the 1730s, when Peter's protégés turned their attention to Bashkiria as the key to the empire's expansion to the south and east, did Bashkirs learn that their padishakh would be different from any who had come before.

2

ABSOLUTISM AND EMPIRE
1730–1775

RELATIONS AMONG BASHKIRS and imperial authorities had deteriorated by the mid-1730s. In order to build an empire in Asia, in 1734 two men, Ivan Kirilov and Kutlu-Mukhammad Tevkelev, had received permission from Empress Anna to construct a city named Orenburg. Unlike Ufa, which was on the site of a former Nogai stronghold, Orenburg was something new. Many Bashkirs felt that building a city on Bashkir land violated their understandings of imperial authority. Iusup Arykov—batyr, mullah, and volost elder—wrote to Vasilii Tatishchev, director of state industries in the Ural Mountains, in the summer of 1736. He asked "why had [the Russians] broken their promises," persecuted Bashkirs, and shown them such a lack of mercy? Bashkirs such as Arykov sought to continue the politics of rebellion and negotiation that had characterized the region from the time Bashkirs swore loyalty to Ivan IV in the 1550s. Arykov wrote, "We, Bashkir peoples (*bashkirskie narody*), our fathers, grandfathers, and great grandfathers, came to the sovereign as subjects by our own will, abandoning our khans."[1] If tsarist authorities would deal with Bashkirs as they had previously, then "we [Bashkirs] would be slaves as previously." If not, Bashkirs were prepared to give up their lives. If the empress no longer honored agreements with Bashkirs, some wanted to reject subjecthood and find another sovereign just as they had once rejected Nogai rule in favor of the tsar. Bashkirs took to arms against Kirilov and Tevkelev's project.

As Bashkirs began to discover, the nature of authority in the Russian Empire had changed. Peter I, "the Great" (reigned 1682–1725), embraced Western absolutism and rejected the Eurasian steppe pattern of sovereignty. Peter's great respect for the West meant that for most of his reign, he and his officials thought about Bashkiria primarily when it came time to collect taxes. Only late in Peter's reign did Bashkiria capture his imagination. Having concluded that much of British and Dutch power depended upon their profitable trade with the East,

Peter began to explore means to extend Russian influence toward China, Khiva, Bukhara, and Persia. Bashkiria lay precisely on the path from Moscow to the Orient.² After Peter's death, men who had worked with him sought to realize his vision of Asian empire. They did so with great confidence. When one of Peter's protégés, Ivan Kirilov, arrived in Bashkiria in 1734 at the head of the Orenburg Expedition to build the city that would be Russia's gateway to Asia, he assumed that Bashkirs would show the same loyalty to Empress Anna that they had to Peter in wars not only against the Christian Swedes and Poles but also against the Muslim Turks and Crimean Tatars. Bashkirs did not. The expedition's relations with Bashkiria's residents then degenerated into five years of war.

In an effort to manage the situation, first Kirilov and then his successors introduced Peter's absolutist understandings of empire. They subordinated local prerogatives to the "undivided, unlimited, undiluted dominion of the tsar-emperor."³ The Bashkir War of 1735–1740 changed how Bashkiria was integrated into the empire. Imperial officials built a city and forts, introduced new principles of landownership sought to control religious practice, and changed the nature of taxation. They sought to sort loyal Bashkirs from disloyal ones and Bashkirs from Meshcheriaks, Maris, Chuvashes, and Udmurts who had moved to Bashkiria. They sought to introduce elections of volost elders in rebellious areas but largely abandoned strategies to bring about the cooperation of local elites through privileged tarkhan status. In the 1750s, signs of "enlightened" strategies of governance appeared that emphasized greater knowledge, humane values, and commerce. Yet these influenced policy only in a marginal way. Absolute rule of Bashkiria meant vigorous administration and force when necessary.⁴ Tsars and their officials demanded a much more intensive and persistent loyalty than that which had previously sufficed.

The Petrine absolutist model of empire failed dramatically in Bashkiria. Peter's heirs undermined the institutions and practices by which he and his predecessors had governed Bashkiria, yet they did not build a new order that could legitimize imperial rule and make it stable. By the 1770s, imperial authority nearly completely collapsed in the Pugachev Rebellion. Bashkirs became known as wild and insubordinate. This chapter will examine how Bashkiria fit into the Petrine worldview, why changes in imperial governance came so rapidly, and why they led to such violence.⁵

PETER'S PROTÉGÉS

When expansion into Bashkiria began in earnest in the 1730s, Peter's mark lay heavily on the enterprise. Peter I no longer defined the Russian tsar by his "most pious" nature in Muscovite fashion; instead, he recast his and the state's image in terms of "Western myths of conquest and power." In keeping with Peter's identification with a Roman imperial model, he accepted the title *imperator* from the senate in 1721, turning the *tsarstvo*, or tsardom, into an *imperiia*, or empire.[6] Peter and his officials emphasized the absolute character of the emperor's rule, by which the people must obey the sovereign's orders, laws, and statutes "without objection."[7] This vision of monarchical authority had clear implications for territories and peoples that had distinctive compacts with central authority. Respect for local rights, liberties, or privileges hinged upon the recipients' unconditional loyalty to the emperor. Once Russian power was established in non-Russian territories to Russia's west, Petrine ideology might be, as James Cracraft argues, "vague in its requirements, fairly tolerant (at least initially) of diversity, and open-ended."[8] Peter journeyed west to learn and led his armies west to move his empire's borders closer to centers of innovation. By contrast, Peter had less interest in eastern peoples. He believed that Russia had a civilizing mission in the East and made no guarantees to Islam of the sort he made to Christianity. Indeed, for most of the eighteenth century, the empire was relatively less tolerant of diversity in its eastern borderlands than in its western ones.[9]

Peter shaped the lives and careers of the men most responsible for introducing his vision of empire to Bashkiria. They combined Peter's interest in military arts, curiosity about the empire's economic and human potential, and powerful ethic of state service. Ivan Kirilov (1695–1737), who planned Orenburg and led the expedition to build it in 1734, was a priest's son of modest origins who began his career as a clerk for the inspector of the senate. Peter made Kirilov a hereditary nobleman and secretary of the senate, where Kirilov observed Peter firsthand.[10] Vasilii Tatishchev (1686–1750), who succeeded Kirilov as leader of the Orenburg Expedition in 1737, was of higher birth than Kirilov. Through military service and education abroad he developed skills as diverse as metallurgy and geography and wrote a monumental history of Russia. In the introduction to the latter work, Tatishchev made clear his debt to Peter: "everything that I possess: ranks, honor, an estate, and above all else, reason, I possess solely because of the kindness of His Majesty. Had he not sent me to foreign lands, had he not used me in important affairs, had he not encouraged me with his kindness, I could not have obtained any of these things."[11]

Ivan Nepliuev (1693–1773), who served as Orenburg's military governor from 1742 to 1758, was from a distinguished but impoverished noble family. He entered Peter's world in 1715 when he was sent to school to learn mathematics. Several years later he distinguished himself in an examination conducted in the emperor's presence, so Peter appointed him to supervise ship construction in St. Petersburg.[12] In 1721, Peter appointed Nepliuev ambassador to the Ottoman

Empire, a post he held for thirteen years. He became governor of Orenburg Province in 1742.

Although Peter's three protégés favored big ideas, they lacked the diplomatic experience on the steppe necessary to translate them into an Asian empire. Kutlu-Mukhammad Tevkelev (1674–1766) provided such experience. Members of Tevkelev's family had served Moscow for three generations, so Kutlu-Mukhammad's appearance as a translator for Peter the Great in the Turkish and Persian campaigns of 1711 and 1722–1723 is not surprising.[13] In 1734, Tevkelev took the name Aleksei Ivanovich and became Kirilov's second in command on the Orenburg Expedition. Whether he converted to Orthodoxy remains controversial.[14] Taking the name of Peter I's father, the pious Aleksei Mikhailovich, would typically indicate that he had.[15] Yet Tevkelev continued to be identified as a Muslim and a murza, while serving in Bashkiria's administration and as a Russian diplomat to the Kazakhs until the early 1760s.[16]

Tevkelev's diplomacy with the Kazakhs placed him at the center of efforts to expand Russian influence. Before his death in 1725, Peter had recognized that Kazakhs were the "key and gate" to Asia. Russia could communicate with Asian countries only through territory over which the nomadic pastoralists drove their livestock.[17] In 1730, Empress Anna set as a goal the Kazakh Middle Horde's acceptance of subject status. Two years later, Tevkelev proposed construction of a fortress at the mouth of the Or River where it meets the Iaik River in order to achieve this goal. Kazakhs did not want to surrender hostages to the Russians, a traditional strategy for ensuring loyalty. Tevkelev suggested that a judicial body with representatives from each Kazakh clan be created at the fortress, supposedly to adjudicate Kazakh affairs and to collect iasak. These representatives could serve as de facto hostages in case Russo-Kazakh relations turned sour. The fortress could protect caravan traffic to Central Asia. If Kazakhs became hostile, the fortress could be used to cut them off from summer pastures. In the event that Kazakhs, Kalmyks, or Bashkirs—all "wild and thoughtless" peoples—became an enemy, Tevkelev argued, the other two peoples could be used to pacify the third.[18]

Tevkelev's 1732 proposal for a fortress in Bashkiria culminated in the building of the city of Orenburg.[19] Historical accounts typically find pragmatic motivations for Orenburg's construction, such as the need to defend against nomads' attacks, to divide and rule the native peoples, or to increase trade with Central Asia.[20] When Ivan Kirilov proposed the construction of Orenburg to Empress Anna in March 1734, he also made clear much grander ambitions. Kirilov placed the Russian Empire's conquest of Central Asia among the great imperial endeavors in world history, such as those of Alexander the Great in Asia and the Spanish in America.[21] Where Tevkelev called for the building of a fortress, Kirilov called for construction of a city. Where Tevkelev had written of increasing trade with Khiva and Bukhara, Kirilov drew a picture of gold, silver, and gems flowing to Russia from Asia. Kirilov compared the founding of Orenburg with the Dutch founding of Batavia in the south Pacific that had made the Dutch wealthy.[22]

Kirilov's proposed expedition, influenced by European examples, included men of science such as botanists, geologists, and cartographers as well as an artist and a historian. Perhaps the most striking element of Kirilov's proposal, however, addressed the empire's relations with native peoples. Kirilov intended to do more than divide and rule. He persuaded the empress that Asia's riches could be had using only a modest number of Russian forces. Alexander the Great, he argued, provided a precedent for the rapid expansion through Asia using "foreign Asian" forces more than "European" ones. Bashkir tarkhans, along with pripushchenniks—those "let in" to Bashkir volosts such as Meshcheriaks, Tatars, Chuvashes, and Maris—could be used to build and secure Orenburg at minimal cost. Bashkirs had been "secured in subjecthood" by no more than a small garrison in Ufa, yet they had served reliably even against the Muslim Turks and Crimean Tatars. Why would not Bashkirs and others serve as agents for Russian expansion?[23] Kirilov would vastly expand the award of tarkhan status and the freedom from paying iasak that went with it to those who served as allies in empire-building. Such a policy meant an expansion of the practice of previous khans in Bashkiria. Since each tarkhan typically brought with him an entourage of as many as several hundred men, Kirilov expected to enlist twenty thousand men in the construction of the new city. Local peoples, "foreign ones" for whom "no one would grieve," could be used to "expand and enrich the state" at no risk to the empress's "own people."[24] Subjecthood would unite Asian peoples with the empress and make Orenburg a springboard for the empire's rapid spread through Central Asia.

The diverse forces used to build an empire in Asia would be matched by the diversity of peoples recruited to develop trade in Orenburg. Kirilov proposed a policy of toleration that would draw merchants from Khiva, Bukhara, India, Armenia, and Europe to the new city. Such merchants would not be taxed for several years. Justice would be carried out for each people "according to its own laws and customs." Each people should be assigned a particular quarter of the city, and the state should construct a stone mosque. At the same time, schools should be built for Bashkir, Kazakh, and other orphans to raise them "in the law of Christianity and the Russian language."[25] Kirilov's vision was rooted in Western conceptions of rule founded in natural law—what is known in Europe as cameralism—that Peter had introduced. As Marc Raeff has written, cameralism meant an effort to tap the "spiritual, human, and material resources" of a country in order to increase the state's wealth and power and to promote the prosperity of society as a whole.[26] The people's "general welfare" (*obshchaia pol'za*) or "general well-being" (*obshchee blago*) became an official justification of monarchical rule.[27] Toleration in Orenburg would benefit the entire empire.

Empress Anna approved Kirilov's project on May 18, 1734, and preparations began for the Orenburg Expedition. Anna promoted Kirilov to the rank of state councilor and Kutlu-Mukhammad/Aleksei Tevkelev to the rank of colonel.[28] After meeting with the empress on June 15, 1734, the two leaders departed for Bashkiria with key military and technical personnel assigned to the expedition. Kirilov gathered military units from Kazan in October. Finally, he arrived in Ufa on November 10, 1734. Kirilov used the winter to survey and describe Bashkir lands, where possible, and to recruit the tarkhans whom he expected to aid in the construction of Orenburg.[29] State officials' lack of knowledge of the local population hindered his efforts. No one in the provincial chancellery knew how many tarkhans there were. By the end of February 1735, however, Kirilov wrote to the empress that he had confirmed as tarkhans 773 of the best local Bashkirs as well as recruiting service Tatars and Meshcheriaks.[30]

After months of preparations, the expedition finally departed Ufa for the planned location of Orenburg at the conjunction of the Or and Iaik Rivers in April 1735. That spring, Bashkir elders "from all dorogas" met and agreed to resist Kirilov's efforts. The expedition's beginning was inauspicious. Even before it departed Ufa, Vasilii Tatishchev, director of state industries in the Urals, and Platon Musin-Pushkin, the governor of Kazan, had warned of Bashkir hostility to Kirilov's plans. Kirilov ignored them. Kirilov camped only six miles from Ufa and waited for troops under Lieutenant Colonel Chirikov from the Trans-Kama line to join his force. Instead of Chirikov, two Bashkirs caught up with him. A Bashkir elder in St. Petersburg had informed Nurushev, a Bashkir elder in Bashkiria, and others of Kirilov's plans. Nurushev had sent envoys to Kirilov to express opposition to the expedition. Kirilov decided to continue anyway. After two months of waiting in vain for reinforcements, he set out for the Or River. Three companies of dragoons, 150 Ufa Cossacks, 100 Ural Cossacks, and 600 Ufa Meshcheriaks made up the core of his force. Of the 773 Bashkir tarkhans in which he had placed so much confidence, only 100 had shown up.[31]

THE BASHKIR WAR, 1735–1740

The expedition's situation quickly deteriorated. Three thousand Bashkirs descended on Chirikov's troops, killing Chirikov and sixty others and taking forty-six carts of supplies. On August 6, 1735, Kirilov finally arrived at the site about 330 miles from Ufa that he had specified for Orenburg's foundation.

Nine days later he laid the foundations of the city in a ceremony attended by Kazakh leaders. But he was far behind schedule, and his troops were on short rations due to the loss of supplies. As Kirilov had moved toward Orenburg's site, resistance to the expedition had spread. One thousand Bashkirs attacked Menzelinsk, and Bashkirs burned other outposts. As officials in St. Petersburg learned of the scope of resistance, they first ordered Kazan governor Musin-Pushkin to reinforce the emperor's troops and then created a Bashkir Commission commanded by Lieutenant General Alexander Rumiantsev to restore imperial authority.

Kirilov's plan to create an Asian empire on the order of Alexander the Great's had collapsed into a bitter struggle to maintain the tsar's authority in Bashkiria. Kirilov had fundamentally misunderstood the basis of Russo-Bashkir relations and the implications of Orenburg's construction. He interpreted the ability of Ufa's small garrison to secure Bashkirs in subjecthood as indicative of Bashkirs' fundamental loyalty. He quickly learned that Bashkirs were loyal not *despite* the small presence of the tsar's forces but rather *because of* this small presence. As long as the emperor's troops occupied a relatively small piece of land previously held by the Nogai Horde and did little to intervene in Bashkir affairs, Bashkirs considered the empire's presence legitimate.[32] Bashkir resistance had Islamic roots, as well. It took place in the context of the movement of Tatar mullahs from Kazan to Ufa, where they fled to avoid Russian Orthodox missionary activity. Clerics from Kazan invigorated Muslim institutions in Bashkiria. The major madrasa Sterlibash, located south of Ufa, was founded in 1720. A number of the uprising's leaders were Muslim clerics.[33]

Once the clashing conceptions of authority had become clear, Kirilov advocated a very different approach than he had previously. In September 1735, Rumiantsev, head of the Bashkir commission, sought to engage "the Bashkir people (*narod*), religious leaders, elders, and people of all ranks" in discussions that would lead to Bashkirs' return to loyal subjecthood. Shortly thereafter, as many as five hundred Bashkirs sent a delegation of fifty-sixty Bashkirs to speak with Rumiantsev. Kirilov rejected such negotiations. Bashkirs must be punished for their banditry, he argued. They must be brought to "fundamental and complete subjecthood to the Empress."[34] A negotiated end to Bashkir uprisings—the emperor's concessions in exchange for Bashkirs' collective acceptance of responsibility and renewed avowals of loyalty—no longer sufficed. In keeping with Petrine notions of sovereignty, the emperor's subjects could not accept their subject status conditionally. Bashkir resistance must be completely crushed. Kirilov recommended that a line of forts be built to surround Bashkiria and to cut it off from Central Asia. All Bashkir men captured "in banditry" were to be executed, their homes destroyed, and their livestock seized. Men who voluntarily surren-

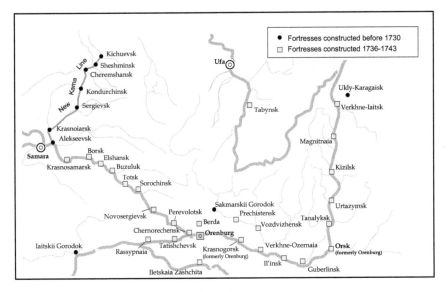

MAP 2.1. Russian fortress construction in Bashkiria, 1736–1743.

dered, along with male children, were to be exiled to the Baltic region. Rebels' wives and daughters were to be "distributed to whomever wants to take them."[35] Kirilov believed that if Bashkir resistance were not eliminated, "Russian infamy would spread to all of southern Asia." All there would proclaim themselves "not subjects, but independent."[36] Empress Anna, along with leading proponents of Petrine absolutism such as Feofan Prokopovich, V. P. Tatishchev, and A. P. Volynskii, supported such a firm response.

After Kirilov died of consumption in April 1737, Tatishchev replaced him as head of what was now called the Orenburg Commission. Tatishchev continued to insist on surrender without conditions. He had written to Bashkirs of Siberian Doroga in June 1736: "It is known to the entire Russian state and to all neighboring people that you are under the power and authority of the Russian sovereign not by your free will, not by voluntary agreement, but by the strength of Russian arms." If some of the previous freedoms were honored, it was due only to the "generosity of Russian sovereigns." Bashkirs were incorrect to call the mercy of tsars "peace" since only agreements "between equal sovereigns and states" could be called peace.[37] On other occasions, Tatishchev offered a few minor concessions, but Bashkirs' complete capitulation remained the guiding principle for imperial officials.

Conflicting interpretations of the Bashkir-Russian relationship set the stage for nearly five years of war.[38] Both sides suffered large numbers of casualties.

Bashkirs used their skill on horseback and knowledge of local terrain to cut Russian supply lines and attack isolated outposts before retreating to the mountains or forests. After Bashkirs cut off supplies to the Orenburg encampment late in 1735, for instance, one of the tsar's detachments lost five hundred men to hunger and frostbite. The intensity of fighting varied substantially depending on the time of year. From late spring to autumn, when they could easily find pasture for their horses, Bashkirs fought most aggressively. Resistance nearly disappeared when winter came and fodder was in extremely short supply. The empress mobilized increasing numbers of troops and artillery and brutally suppressed Bashkir resistance. Tevkelev was responsible for some of the harshest treatment of Bashkirs. When Tevkelev thwarted an ambush of his camp in one village, he and his men executed one thousand men, women, and children by sword or gun and incinerated five hundred others in storehouses. The village was then burned to the ground.[39] Russian forces also used starvation as a weapon. Tevkelev ordered that only Bashkirs who capitulated could buy grain.[40] He earned a reputation as an "executioner" during the Bashkir War that lived long in Bashkir memory.[41]

The forceful assertion of unconditional sovereignty did not eliminate the need to administer parts of Bashkiria that had been pacified. Since Kirilov had assumed that imperial authority was well established before 1735, he had devoted little attention to elaborating it in his Orenburg project. When Kirilov and Rumiantsev met in December 1735 to do so, the result had an improvised feel. The discussions at this meeting, however, became law on February 11, 1736. Kirilov expanded the presence of the tsar's men through the creation of a line of twenty-three forts and redoubts stretching nearly from the Volga in the west to the Orsk River on the eastern slope of the Urals. These, in essence, moved the trans–Kama River defense line forward a few hundred miles and separated Bashkirs from Kazakhs and Central Asia.[42] Officials allocated to each fortress land within anywhere from six to more than thirty miles surrounding it, causing Bashkirs to lose over one million des. by the 1750s.

Wartime exigencies produced many of the February 11, 1736, decree's thirty-three points. For instance, Bashkirs were forbidden to carry weapons, and blacksmiths were banned.[43] In other respects, however, the decree had influence long after violence had ended. The decree's authors primarily sought to create a loyal elite in Bashkiria and to give it a firm basis in landholding. The decree sought to separate Meshcheriaks who had fought with the tsar's men from Bashkirs and award them Bashkir land "for their loyalty and service." Assigning the land of Bashkir rebels to loyal pripushchenniks dispossessed Bashkirs and made loyalty the crucial category for landholding. Teptiars and Bobyls did not receive land, but they no longer had to pay Bashkirs rent. Tatar "service murzas," who had lost land and status or even been impressed into service harvesting and transporting lumber in 1718, could be freed from such service and from the soul tax "in exchange for such a show of loyalty (*vernost'*)." The politics of loyalty informed a key aspect of the law of February 11, 1736—the identification of Bashkir land as a commodity that could be sold on the market. State officials deemed previous prohibitions on the sale of Bashkir land "extremely not useful." The decree enabled nobles, officers, and loyal Meshcheriaks to purchase and receive title to Bashkir land.[44] This represented a marked change from past practices in Bashkiria, where few land transactions had taken place.[45] Before the war, Tatars and others such as Maris, Chuvashes, and Udmurts who moved from Kazan lands to Bashkiria in order to avoid taxes and Russian Orthodox missionaries had a motivation to move into the Bashkir estate. As the empire's administration sought to punish rebellious Bashkirs and reward loyal supporters, members of such groups had a reason to avoid being counted as Bashkirs. They could now, in principle anyway, seek rewards from the state for their loyalty. Both the state and non-Bashkirs now had a motive for sorting the population into non-Bashkir status groups. In the years that followed, we see Teptiars, Meshcheriaks, and others specifically addressed in law.

The imperial government sought to control Bashkiria's civil and religious administration, too. The government introduced the election of elders—subject to the state's confirmation—in areas where Bashkirs had rebelled. Kirilov also sought to appoint four Muslim akhunds, senior Muslim religious leaders, one for each doroga, with the akhund's loyalty as the key factor in his selection. The construction of mosques would be allowed only with official permission. In order to combat the spread of Islam to Bashkirs perceived to be weaker in their faith, new laws forbade Kazan Tatars to marry Bashkirs without permission from the Kazan governor.[46] Kirilov intended the 1736 law to reduce greatly the basis of Bashkir opposition. He argued that a "strict and consistent" policy toward Bashkirs could lead them to a position comparable to that of "Kazan and other Tatars."[47] These laws represented a fundamental break with previous state policy toward Bashkirs. Both Muscovite and Bashkir sources had stated previously that Bashkirs who swore allegiance to the tsar received rights to land and noninterference in Bashkir religious life. Building forts deprived Bashkirs of their land, as did land sales.

Bashkirs resisted greater imperial intervention by long-established means: armed struggle, negotiations with imperial officials, and approaches to other leaders as possible alternative sovereigns with whom they could join forces. Since the empire's representatives refused to accept Bashkir conditions for surrender, negotiations proved fruitless. Discussions with Abulkhayir khan of the Kazakh Lesser Horde (*zhuz*) about his becoming the Bashkirs' sovereign initially seemed promising. Abulkhayir had even married a Bashkir woman.[48] In the end, however, Abulkhayir never committed his Kazakhs to support the Bashkirs. He and many notables of the Lesser Horde had sworn allegiance to Empress Anna in 1731 because the Russian Empire could provide greater security and more possibilities for trade. The Kazakh leadership did not want to risk alienating the empress.[49] With the collapse of Kazakh support, the Bashkir position grew truly desperate. Several major Bashkir leaders capitulated in the summer of 1738. By autumn, only a single one, Bepenia Trupberdin, continued to fight. It is unclear whether he voluntarily surrendered in October 1738 or whether other Bashkirs forced him to turn himself in. Tatishchev had him interrogated and then executed. Tatishchev reported Bashkiria's pacification to St. Petersburg in January 1739. Bashkirs had delivered a large number of horses to Russian authorities as punishment, agreed to transfer land to Meshcheriaks and Chuvashes who supported the empress, and no longer attacked Russian forts.[50]

Tatishchev took advantage of the quiet to continue Kirilov's efforts to build the empress's authority. Tatishchev proposed that Orenburg be moved to a new, less swampy site that would provide better access for merchant traffic and closer sources of wood. What had been Orenburg became the city of Orsk, and Orenburg was relocated about 95 miles to the west.[51] Tatishchev and L. Ia. Soimonov, head of the Bashkir Commission, revived Kirilov's proposal to conduct a census that would allow officials to know Bashkiria's true human and economic resources. Tatishchev was less favorable to Kirilov's policy of granting tarkhan status liberally. He concluded that capable elders simply could not be found among loyal Bashkirs, so he proposed forming a Cossack-like organization among them instead. The government would appoint a "Bashkir colonel" who would work with officials and scribes selected by Bashkirs and confirmed by the governor. Such a plan would, Tatishchev believed, organize Bashkirs' "military energy" in support of the state.[52]

Although Tatishchev's proposal had a future in Bashkiria, he himself did not.[53] By January 1739, Tatishchev had clashed with, arrested, or reassigned local officials including Kirilov's father-in-law, naval officer P. I. Bakhmetev, who had joined the Orenburg Expedition in order to establish a flotilla on the Aral Sea. Tatishchev did not succeed in pushing out Tevkelev, however. Tevkelev traveled to St. Petersburg to denounce Tatishchev to Empress Anna's favorite, Biron.[54] Tevkelev's criticisms of Tatishchev's management of Bashkir affairs and the construction of Orenburg were persuasive among his superiors, who were undoubtedly frustrated by the difficulty and cost of suppressing the Bashkir uprising. Biron had Tatishchev relieved of his command for "irregularities, attacks, and extortions."[55] With the appointment of an army general, V. A. Urusov, to replace Tatishchev, the commission acquired a more purely military cast.[56]

Urusov's appointment also marked a return of Nogai authority in a way. His family had descended from a Nogai bei whose sons had entered the tsar's service in the early sixteenth century.[57]

Opposition to a census Urusov sought to carry out in spring 1740 prompted one last wave of Bashkir resistance. Some Bashkir elders opposed the census because they rightly suspected that it would allow imperial officials to make Bashkirs pay the soul tax—the higher rate of tax paid by those in the empire's core areas. Bashkirs prevented the census's successful completion before Urusov died in July 1741, but the frontier war was over. The war had devastated Bashkiria's population. Official figures put the number of Bashkir casualties at 9,438 killed, 3,101 exiled to Baltic regiments and the navy, 6,300 women and children distributed, 11,282 horses collected in fines, and 396 villages destroyed. According to Tatishchev, more than 60,000 people had been executed or died of hunger.[58] Considering that the Bashkir population probably numbered no more than 260,000 before the war, this was an economic and demographic disaster. The war intensified the implications of loyalty in Bashkiria. Violence caused many Bashkirs to join the empress's forces. Bashkir rebels attacked villages of those loyal to the empire, and loyal Bashkirs fought for the empress and sought to persuade Bashkir rebels to surrender. As the war wound down, the head of the Bashkir Commission reported that Bashkirs comprised nearly 40 percent of the approximately 11,000 troops at his disposal.[59] Tsarist forces succeeded in introducing the empress's unchallenged authority, but imperial authority depended almost entirely on brute force.

The 1735–1740 war had tremendous effects on the Bashkir status group and on the region as a whole. The Bashkir population declined over the next several decades and did not fully recover until nearly the end of the century, when it reached perhaps 275,000.[60] The construction of nearly fifty forts by 1750 reduced Bashkir landholdings and cut Bashkir herds off from the Central Asian steppe, leading to a further reduction in nomadic pastoralism.[61] Yet agriculture spread only slowly—as late as 1767, Petr Rychkov noted little interest in agriculture among Bashkirs in Bashkiria's south. Even in a good year, Orenburg produced only about one-tenth of the grain it required. Therefore, imperial officials welcomed the flow of migrants who practiced agriculture and who could supply more than 10,000 imperial service men to staff Orenburg and the new fortresses.[62] The effort to differentiate Bashkir and non-Bashkir groups based on loyalty continued after the war. According to the first published information on the population of Bashkiria, which appeared in 1743, Ufa Province had a population of 412,080. Of those, 120,000–130,000 were "inorodtsy"—Teptiars, Meshcheriaks, Tatars, Maris, and others—and 75,185 were Russians, indicating non-Muslim Slavs.[63] Higher rates of taxation in the Kazan region and attacks on Islam there continued to make Bashkiria attractive to non–Russian Ortho-dox populations. Kirilov's policy of February 11, 1736, which sought to transfer Bashkir land to those without it, only increased the flow of people to Bashkiria, even if imperial officials sought to get them to pay the soul tax.[64]

The effects of war on Bashkiria's administration are difficult to assess fully. The increased imperial presence resulted in greater production of informa-tion, such as the census mentioned above. Such initiatives made it appear that imperial officials better understood Bashkiria and could bring order to it. In the short term, however, the war brought chaos and destruction. Bashkirs be-came so poor that they sold their children rather than see them starve.[65] The large-scale loss of life undoubtedly wreaked havoc on the Bashkir elite. Even before the war, Bashkirs from one volost could live all over Bashkiria, while members belonging to different volosts and different family units could live in the same village. Deaths of tribal leaders and the loss of great expanses of land to fortresses and in-migrants made larger tribal units unsustainable. The de-struction of villages put many Bashkirs on the move, further confusing Bashkir political organization. The confusion made iasak more difficult to collect and complicated efforts to supervise Bashkir communities.[66] Force had ended open resistance to imperial authority, but imperial officials, Bashkirs, and the local population as a whole would face the cost for years to come.

IVAN NEPLIUEV IN ORENBURG

The Bashkir War proved hazardous for those charged with bringing the em-pire to Bashkiria. Of the three leaders of the Orenburg Expedition/Commission who served in its first six years, two died in office and the third suffered politi-cal disgrace. Urusov's successor, Ivan I. Nepliuev, contrasted sharply with his predecessors. Nepliuev's mother's family included some of the most important leaders of the Old Belief. Nepliuev himself was deeply religious, though to all appearances he participated in the official church.[67] Nepliuev also possessed ex-tensive experience within the Muslim world. In 1721, he became the first regular Russian representative to Constantinople in a decade and was a talented student of Ottoman affairs.[68] Empress Elizabeth appointed him head of the Orenburg Commission as a sort of exile in 1741.

When Nepliuev arrived in Bashkiria in 1742, the entire Russian enterprise in Bashkiria resembled the city of Orenburg itself—it rested on weak foundations and was only half built. The principles of administration sketched by Kirilov in the February 11, 1736, decree remained largely on paper.[69] Even the location of Orenburg needed improvement. Based on engineers' reports, Nepliuev argued successfully that Orenburg ought to be relocated once more, about 30 miles up the Iaik River to where it meets the Sakmarsk River. There the city would have a better strategic position and be closer to sources of wood and grain. Orenburg had found its permanent location. In March 1744, Nepliuev persuaded authorities in St. Petersburg to form Orenburg Province, or *guberniia*, with Orenburg as its center, uniting civil and military power in his hands and nearly all areas inhabited by Bashkirs into four counties (*uezds*). Nonetheless, much work remained to make the region stable and well-integrated into the empire. As historian Iurii Smirnov has written, Nepliuev succeeded in large part because he combined the distinguishing qualities of his predecessors. He had Kirilov's drive, Tatishchev's administrative ability, and Urusov's ability to win people to his point of view, along with the flexibility of a former diplomat. Nepliuev continued to rely upon Tevkelev to manage Muslim affairs and diplomacy among Kazakhs.[70] Nepliuev sought to make imperial authority normal and accepted in Bashkiria through policies regarding Bashkir administration, religion, land, taxation, and tarkhan status.

Since few of Kirilov's policies that became law on February 11, 1736, had taken effect, after 1740 Nepliuev sought to restructure Bashkir administration in part by effecting previous plans and in part through his own initiatives. Most of all, he and his officials sought to sort loyal Bashkirs, Bashkir tarkhans, and Bashkir elders from those that had fought against imperial forces during the war. Nepliuev proposed a law of August 20, 1739, that specified rebellious tarkhans and elders should be stripped of their privileges and rebellious Bashkirs not be allowed to take those positions, though doing so was difficult due to the fact that records on tarkhans had been lost in a fire. The law also was intended to undermine financially rebellious Bashkirs. Teptiars, Bobyls, and Meshcheriaks who had paid land rent to rebellious Bashkirs now need not pay it and could move to empty land formerly held by rebels; only loyal Bashkirs would still be owed rent.[71] Nepliuev petitioned to void other laws that he considered onerous, impractical, or unnecessary, such as the ban on blacksmiths (who could produce weapons) and a prohibition on carrying weapons. Now that Bashkirs had been pacified and fortresses surrounded Bashkiria, a repeat of the recent rebellion was unlikely.[72] In 1742, Vice-Governor P. D. Aksakov imposed new military obligations—Bashkirs would have to provide two thousand men for service every year. Previously, Bashkir tarkhans had served in the tsar's campaigns, but not on a regular, obligatory basis.[73]

Nepliuev sought to organize and regularize Bashkir elders. As it was, the title "Bashkir elder" did not have consistent meaning—some elders presided over several volosts while others were subordinate to other elders.[74] Nepliuev ordered that information be collected on the number of Bashkir volosts, the names of their elders, and the number of households in them. The differences between the sixty volosts identified in the 1740s under Nepliuev and the thirty-four identified by Rychkov in 1755 suggests that the former was counting some mix of volosts and tiubas, subunits of volosts, while the latter counted only the larger volosts.[75] The difference between these counts likely indicates the fluid nature of Bashkir society in the mid-eighteenth century and different motives for Russians' efforts to understand it. Political concerns were more important to imperial officials such as Nepliuev than a precise description of Bashkir society. Nepliuev sought to identify loyal members of the Bashkir elite who would carry out his instructions, work to prevent rebellious behavior, and uphold the empire's laws. In order to do so, he specified smaller units of administration. More units of administration meant more elders to lead them and, it was hoped, a larger group of Bashkirs connected to the empire's administration. Officials began to apply a term with European roots, "command" (*komand*), to these smaller units of administration, rather than the Bashkir word "tiuba."

Nepliuev expected elders to discharge some traditional functions, such as resolving disputes and offenses among members of their commands according to Muslim law, the sharia. Cases of theft, however, needed to be sent to imperial authorities in the "city."[76] This specified the use of Muslim law in questions of family and inheritance, while serious crimes were to be resolved by officials in the new fortresses and towns.[77] Most functions that Nepliuev assigned to elders involved the maintenance of order. Nepliuev sought to implement the election of Bashkir elders envisioned by Kirilov, though those who had fought against the tsar's forces would not be included. Over the next fifteen years, he extended this organization to Meshcheriaks. Nepliuev instructed elders to issue passports to control Bashkirs' movement and issued them formal seals in order to do so. Elders were instructed to be loyal (*vernym*) and to maintain in "obedience and loyalty" all who were subordinate to them, too. They were to do all of this without giving offense to their subordinates and without taking bribes, because elders "knew about the laws of Her Imperial Majesty" and knew that "all cases, small and great" would be judged equally. Elders were fined for any offenses, without exception.[78] The elders, in essence, were to become lower-level imperial officials, but without the salaries or privileges usually given to those who carried out the empire's interests. Lacking income from the state, elders' use of their positions to extract resources from their commands would seem the only source of revenue available to them.

Until the abolition of iasak in favor of the salt tax in 1754, imperial policies toward Bashkirs varied relatively little after the war of 1735–1740. Most of all, local government under Nepliuev sought to draw the Bashkir elite into the imperial elite, with no substantial change in the status of its members. The primary development with respect to status was the effort to separate out non-Bashkir, non-Russians from Bashkir communities. Groups such as Tatars, Meshcheriaks, and Teptiars started to acquire features of separate status groups with their own land. Prohibitions on Bashkir marriages to Tatars and efforts to prevent "Tatars from calling themselves Bashkirs" for tax purposes were intended to reinforce status differences.[79]

When the full scope of Bashkir opposition had become clear, Kirilov had begun to see Islam as a source of hostility and took measures to control it. To some extent, such measures reflected broader concerns about Islam at the time. Increasingly aggressive efforts to restrict Muslims and convert them to Russian Orthodoxy accompanied Russia's conflicts with the Ottoman Empire during Peter I's reign, marking a break with earlier precedents.[80] Officials considered conversion a way to ensure the loyalty of the empire's non-Christian peoples.[81] Efforts to promote conversion to Russian Orthodoxy peaked after Peter's death with the establishment of the Agency of New Convert Affairs in the 1730s.[82] Priests and staff of the agency promoted conversion to Russian Orthodoxy in the provinces of Kazan, Astrakhan, Nizhnii Novgorod, and Voronezh. The Bishop of Kazan led government efforts to destroy 418 of 536 mosques in Kazan Province.[83]

Under Nepliuev, however, Bashkiria remained largely immune to the anti-Islamic activities of the Agency for New Convert Affairs. The flight of Muslim believers and clerics from more intense persecution in Kazan invigorated Islamic practice in Bashkiria. Practical considerations explain much of Bashkiria's exceptionalism. Violent conflict had only recently ended in the province, and officials had no interest in reigniting it. Yet more than pragmatism was at work. As pupils of Peter I, both Kirilov and Nepliuev thought in cameralist terms of how they could best advance state interests. With the Bashkir War's end, Nepliuev pursued a return to Kirilov's vision of Orenburg as a diverse society that had been a feature of his initial project for the city's construction. Nepliuev and Tevkelev worked to make Orenburg a haven for Muslim traders. In the 1740s, for instance, Tevkelev had approved the request of a Bukharan merchant to build a mosque in Orenburg and provided financial support for it.[84] By 1752, a total of 220 people, mostly from Central Asia and Persia, had received privileges to trade in Orenburg.[85] In 1744, Nepliuev received permission to create what became known as Seitov Posad in Russian or Kargala in Tatar, an almost exclusively Muslim city located about twelve miles north of Orenburg. The city received its name from that of Sagid Khaialin, a Kazan Tatar who received a charter to invite up to two hundred Kazan Tatars to Kargala. There they could build a mosque and receive freedom from military conscription in exchange for conducting trade. Kargala became crucial to the development of commerce in Orenburg and to the empire's influence in Central Asia. Writing early in the twentieth century, Muslim religious leader Rizaetdin ibn Fakhretdinov cited Kargala's founding as the first sign of "officially recognized national [Muslim] religious life" since the fall of Kazan.[86]

At the same time Nepliuev's administration supported Muslim traders, it struggled against missionary campaigns. In 1744 the Ufa provincial chancellery argued that the logic supposedly guiding policy in Kazan—that new converts to Russian Orthodoxy needed to be protected from Muslim influence—had little relevance in Ufa Province since so few converts lived there.[87] In 1751, Nepliuev wrote to the senate to criticize Tobol'sk Metropolitan Syl'vestr for attempting to compel eleven Bashkirs in western Siberia to convert to Christianity. As a result of Nepliuev's complaint, the senate established a commission in Orenburg to resolve disputes between secular and religious authorities.[88] The persecution of Old Believers in Nepliuev's own family might have motivated his resistance to efforts to achieve religious uniformity by force. As Russia's ambassador to Constantinople, he would have been aware of the *millet* system, according to which non-Islamic religious communities received recognition and substantial autonomy in religious affairs from the Ottoman state in exchange for paying higher taxes than the sultan's Muslim subjects.[89] Whatever the case, in the 1740s and 1750s, Bashkiria was a place where Muslims could largely avoid the anti-Islamic endeavors tsarist officials pursued elsewhere.

Nepliuev's relatively tolerant policy toward Islam preserved a key aspect of early Russo-Bashkir relations. Policy regarding land and taxation changed. Reassigning Bashkir land, making it a salable commodity, and eliminating iasak undermined the crucial aspect of Bashkir-Russian relations—that the Bashkirs would retain their land in exchange for paying iasak. Nepliuev's tenure as Orenburg governor saw the beginning of what would be a transfer of more than five million des. of land to imperial officials and military men. Strengthening the empire's position in Bashkiria required a loyal group of men who would serve the empress and carry out the government's designs. In the minds of state officials, many Bashkirs had demonstrated a lack of loyalty through rebellion in 1735–1740. So, after 1740, state officials acted to redistribute land from its opponents in the Bashkir War to those who had demonstrated their loyalty to the empress and could perhaps put land to productive use.[90] A senate decree authorized the distribution of "empty steppe lands" to the permanent ownership of nobles, officers, Cossacks, and civilian officials in August 1743.[91] What precisely "empty steppe land" meant is unclear. Considering the number of Bashkirs who died or fled in the war years, much land must have been left without identifiable owners. It did not remain so for long. Since most of the empress's men in Bashkiria served in the military, officers were the most common recipients of land grants ranging from 115 des. for a lieutenant in one of the newly constructed fortresses to 500 des. for the captain of a regiment or 1,420 des. for Orenburg's commander. Civil administrators received substantially less.[92]

Since the decree of February 11, 1736, had made land a commodity that could be bought or sold, industrious men often used some mix of money, influence, alcohol, and fraud to amass vast estates. By the end of the eighteenth century, Kutlu-Mukhammad/Aleksei Tevkelev's family held 216,905 des. of land, mostly in Belebei County of Ufa Province and in Samara and Viatka Provinces. Some land had been purchased. Kutlu-Mukhammad/Aleksei acquired some by having himself forcibly registered as a Bashkir and then taking Bashkir hereditary landholdings for his own use. The Tevkelevs also acquired 766 serfs by 1795.[93] The family of I. L. Timashev, the director of customs in Orenburg, acquired 162,196 des., most of it near Orenburg. The newly land-rich included some Muslims, such as Meshcheriak elder R. U. Ianyshev, who acquired 69,623 des., and murza I. Chanyshev, who acquired substantial holdings in Sterlitamak County.[94] Nepliuev and the Ufa vice-governor P. D. Aksakov sought to slow the pace of land sales, but to little avail.[95] By the century's end, nobles held 571 estates, totaling 2,548,841 des.[96] Mine and factory owners were the other major beneficiaries of new land policy. After 1740, Nepliuev actively promoted private factory construction in the southern Urals, and industry expanded rapidly.[97] Of the fifty-eight factories built in Bashkiria in the period from the 1730s to the 1790s, forty-nine were built in the 1740s and 1750s. By 1762, Ural mines and factories accounted for 70 percent of the empire's iron production and 90 percent of its copper production.[98] Some Bashkirs were specifically encouraged to participate in mining. One Bashkir mine owner, Ismail Tasimov, was even active in the creation of the Petersburg Mining Institute in 1773.[99] Overall, industrial development allowed factory owners to acquire large amounts of land, often for little money. They occupied 3,902,928 des. by the end of the century. Factory owners cut down local forests so rapidly that in 1770 central authorities approved Orenburg governor Reinsdorp's request to halt factory construction.[100]

Less privileged Meshcheriaks, Teptiars, and Bobyls proved much less successful in acquiring land, even though Kirilov's decree of February 11, 1736, and Nepliuev's policies promised that they should receive the land of Bashkir rebels.[101] Meshcheriaks stopped paying Bashkirs rent but awaited government action to confirm their ownership of the land. On at least two occasions, state officials sent men to map Bashkir rebels' land in order to prepare its transfer to Meshcheriaks. In neither case, however, did officials confirm Meshcheriaks' title to the land. Bashkirs protested efforts to deprive them of land, causing local officials to inform St. Petersburg that the transfer of Bashkir land might have "bad consequences."[102] Policies regarding land that emerged from the Bashkir War proved a source of confusion into the next century.

The large-scale losses of land certainly undermined Bashkir semi-nomadic pastoralism, but Bashkirs remained in control of a large amount of land, some 13,742,465 des. in 157 parcels in 1798.[103] Since new elites' land acquisitions usually did not come with serf labor to work them, the newly acquired land's productivity was uncertain. The distributions provided an incentive for the empress's servitors to come to the region, but only a modest number did so. Few not directly involved in governing Bashkiria benefited, and the empire's presence rested on a small, privileged minority of both Russian Orthodox and Muslims. The elaboration of a system of private property for favored servitors and nobles, however, expanded Bashkiria's noble elite. At the same time, distinctions among Bashkirs and closely related groups such as Teptiars and Meshcheriaks became more marked. Distinctions in legal estate status began to develop locally much as they did in the empire as a whole, but with characteristics particular to Bashkiria.[104]

Just as the government altered long-standing policies regarding land tenure in Bashkiria, it transformed taxation by eliminating iasak that Bashkirs had paid to their sovereigns as far back as the Mongols. In the 1740s and 1750s, the tsar's officials undertook a sustained effort to assimilate Bashkiria's population into the more demanding obligations in the empire's core. The primary goal of eliminating iasak, a type of tax found only in the empire's border regions, seems to have been to increase state revenue, since the imposition of other obligations on Bashkirs and other peoples accompanied the move. Secondarily, elimination of iasak made Bashkirs' tax obligations more similar to those prevalent in the empire's central regions. New tax policies affected the non-Bashkir, non-Russian population first. In 1747, Teptiars' and Bobyls' iasak was equated with the soul tax. In doing this, the government sought to make the flight of the non-Orthodox to Bashkiria less attractive. In May 1747, Teptiars and Bobyls resisted the larger obligation. They were joined by some Meshcheriaks who had supported the empire in the Bashkir War and had been free from direct taxation but now had to pay taxes equal to those of Bashkirs. A clash of troops with Tatars, Maris, and Meshcheriaks near Birsk resulted in seventy fatalities and a hundred arrests.[105] Soon change came to Bashkirs, too. In 1754, Nepliuev proposed that Bashkirs' iasak be eliminated in favor of their inclusion in the state's salt monopoly. Bashkir elders had indicated, Nepliuev wrote, that they would rather pay official prices for salt than pay iasak. That the treasury would gain "incomparably more" funds from the sale of salt (at a price of forty kopecks per pood) than it did from iasak undoubtedly figured prominently in Nepliuev's thinking. In March 1754, the senate accepted Nepliuev's proposal and abolished iasak for Bashkirs and Meshcheriaks.[106] Tsarist officials also introduced new postal taxes and labor obligations to support communications among fortresses in Bashkiria.[107]

Taken together, these changes substantially increased the state's burden on Bashkirs and made their obligations more similar to those of other groups. Nonetheless, even the increased tax burden borne by Bashkirs left them and Meshcheriaks in privileged positions vis-à-vis other residents of Bashkiria and of the empire as a whole. Officials estimated that the Bashkir iasak amounted to, on average, twenty-five kopecks per household as late as the 1740s and 1750s. The tsar's subjects in central regions paid the poll tax, according to which each peasant male paid seventy kopecks and each townsman eighty kopecks. In a discussion of arrears in the payment of iasak in 1745, Nepliuev told Bashkir elders that Bashkirs ought to be ashamed of failing to pay such a light tax.[108] Others paid nearly the same salt tax as Bashkirs and Meshcheriaks but paid the poll tax as well. Bashkirs were still hereditary landowners and had more land than other peoples in Bashkiria, and elsewhere, did. In the decree repealing iasak, state officials restated that Bashkirs would continue to own their land as they previously had. This gave Bashkirs a sense of their own distinctive estate status. Orenburg governor D. V. Volkov noted in 1763: "every and even the most base Bashkir considers himself something of a nobleman like a Ukrainian Cossack; each thinks that he owns his own land, granted by Tsar Ivan Vasil'evich to his ancestors for service."[109]

Officials sought to reinforce estate distinctions in other ways, too. Officials recognized that the Bashkir estate was diverse and its boundaries porous. Tax legislation specified that the non-Orthodox who had long lived in Bashkiria were "generally called Bashkirs," but "in their number [are] found" Meshcheriaks, Udmurts, Maris, and Chuvashes.[110] Diversity was not a problem in itself, but it had problematic fiscal implications. Since members of the Bashkir estate paid less in taxes than those who paid the poll tax, state officials sought to keep non-Bashkirs from joining it. A 1761 decree called for a census of Tatars, Maris, and Chuvashes, to identify those who had left Kazan Province and resettled in Orenburg Province so they could be removed from Bashkir volosts in which they dodged the poll tax. For similar reasons, legislation aimed to limit marriages between Tatars and Bashkirs by taxing at higher rates those who married without official permission.[111] In sum, state officials eliminated Bashkirs' paying iasak in exchange for land while maintaining their distinctive status with respect to other peoples.

RENEWED RESISTANCE

After the Bashkir War of the 1730s, imperial officials could force Bashkirs to accept the emperor's absolute sovereignty, but Bashkirs and members of other local status groups, such as Teptiars, still regarded the new order as a fundamental change in the relationship of the state with those it governed. They resisted such changes. The well-documented uprising of 1755, typically described as either Bashkir or Islamic, was both. The perception that the state had betrayed its obligations could be articulated in both a Muslim and a specifically Bashkir vocabulary.

Meshcheriak Mullah Batyrsha Aliev was the person most identified with the 1755 uprising. Batyrsha became an imam and a teacher in a madrasa located in a Meshcheriak village north of Ufa in 1749. His knowledge of Muslim law and reputation for fairness brought him to prominence. In early 1755, Batyrsha learned that Bashkirs in Nogai Doroga planned to act against the government in May. Batyrsha began to agitate among Muslims in favor of an uprising by all four dorogas. At the same time, he was nominated for the open position of official akhund of the Siberian Doroga.[112] Local officials' offer of a position of honor to a man planning an uprising against the empire demonstrates the state's weak connections with and poor understanding of the Muslim ulama.

Batyrsha called for an uprising on July 3, 1755, but Bashkirs in the south of Bashkiria chose not to wait.[113] On May 15, 1755, they killed a party of Russians sent to find clay and stones for a porcelain factory.[114] A few days later Bashkirs attacked a postal station, officials, and military units, halting Orenburg's communications with fortresses to its east. Nepliuev reacted swiftly. He dispatched 1,300 troops with instructions to spare neither Bashkir dwellings nor "Bashkirs themselves, their wives and their children."[115] He instructed the akhund of Orenburg to denounce the uprising and to rally loyal Muslims to support the state.[116] Bashkir resistance to imperial rule in Bashkiria's south grew. As more troops were brought to bear on the disturbances, in August and September more than a thousand Bashkirs and their families fled south to the Kazakh steppe. Elsewhere in Bashkiria, plans for concerted action against the government failed to develop.[117] Batyrsha proved a reluctant leader. Having heard of loyal Bashkir elders' support for the state, Batyrsha fled into the forest. After about one month of hiding, Batyrsha was captured and sent to Shlisselburg Fortress on the Baltic Sea. Sporadic unrest continued in Bashkiria's southeast until late in 1755, but the chance for a broader uprising had passed.

Batyrsha may have disappointed as a rebel leader, but he proved quite capable of explaining his motivations in a vivid letter he wrote to Empress Elizabeth while he was in prison. The key issue at stake in the rebellion was nothing less than the legitimacy of the empress's—the "padishakh's"—authority. Based in large part on Islamic political thought regarding the nature of just rule, Batyrsha argued that when the padishakh's authority made religious practice possible, protected Muslims, and levied agreed-upon obligations, then the Koran forbade violation of her authority.[118] Batyrsha stated that earlier he had routinely implored his fellow Muslims to respect the empress's authority since she and her officials allowed Muslims to practice their faith in "safety and security." Batyrsha now concluded that imperial authority no longer served such a purpose. The Russians' "evil deeds have exceeded all limits," he wrote.[119]

Missionary efforts were a major cause of Muslims' resentment. Batyrsha's volost lay close to Kazan Province, where attacks on Islam were most intense. However, conversion was only one issue among several. Batyrsha argued that tsarist officials demanded from the people obligations to which they had not been subject "according to ancient rules." Russians abused Muslims, took their property, insulted and beat them, and raped their women. Russians forced people to purchase salt from the state. Muslims' efforts to seek justice "in the fortresses," as they had been instructed, became occasions for further abuse. Muslims' own elders were complicit in such abuses, Batyrsha contended. Elders did not pray to Allah. In order to keep elders' favor, Muslims had to provide alcohol, honey, and women to them. In sum, the people received no "justice and mercy" from the empress's officials. Batyrsha especially criticized the region's governors, identified as "*mirza* Kutlumet" or "General" Tevkelev and "Chief" Nepliuev. Faced with an illegitimate imperial authority, Batyrsha argued that, according to Muslim law, Muslims must unite to replace the authority of "unbelievers." Even as Batyrsha identified sources of Muslims' common cause against the state, his letter made clear that tensions between religious and secular leaders had doomed the uprising. "The people are divided into two parts," Batyrsha wrote. Members of the ulama were quite receptive to calls to resist, but elders with the backing of the Russian administration showed little interest in rebellion.[120]

The uprising did not threaten imperial power the way the Bashkir War of 1735–1740 had, but officials still had reason to take the disturbances and Batyrsha's critique seriously. Batyrsha had earned official respect, and Meshcheriaks had provided crucial support for the government in the Bashkir War. Many Meshcheriaks' willingness to attack the tsar's forces showed the breadth and depth of hostility to the state. The modesty of reforms after the uprising is therefore striking. In some areas, the practice of Islam became somewhat easier. Muslims in Kazan, Nizhnii Novgorod, and Siberia were allowed to build mosques once again in villages with at least 200–300 Muslim males and few converts to Russian Orthodoxy. Two aggressively anti-Muslim churchmen were reassigned.[121] Otherwise, proposals to address discontent in Bashkiria were minor, including the elimination of the postal tax and some reductions in service obligations.[122] The impact of other policies, such as one permitting priests, merchants, Cossacks, and others to buy and convert Muslim and animist peoples in the southeastern borderlands, is unclear, since few Muslims converted in Bashkiria.[123] Imperial officials showed little concern about the fragility of their authority.

THE ENLIGHTENMENT IN BASHKIRIA

In the 1750s, new ideologies of governance typically associated with the Enlightenment entered Russia from the West and began to change how officials in Bashkiria thought and wrote about the region's peoples. Although innovation is usually associated with Catherine II's reign (1762–1796), important elements of new thinking emerged earlier. State servitors did not reject Petrine cameralism —state power remained paramount. Rather than Peter's stress on coercion and control, however, leading Russian officials emphasized the need to release "untapped human and material resources."[124] German and Austrian cameralist thinkers who argued that the "strength of a country depends upon the size of its population" attracted supporters in the Russian Empire.[125] Beginning in the 1750s, physiocratic thought coupled the importance of population with that of agriculture. Physiocrats stressed the need for a country to produce an agricultural surplus that could be exported and to develop markets rather than to focus nearly exclusively on state revenues. In Russia, the establishment of banks and the elimination of internal tariffs were concrete signs of such new thinking. The first efforts to gather systematic knowledge about Bashkiria's population and geography and to assimilate it intellectually into the empire accompanied new approaches to governance.[126]

The new thinking had two somewhat unlikely spokesmen in Bashkiria: those who had served the longest, Tevkelev and Rychkov. When Empress Elizabeth promoted Nepliuev to a position in St. Petersburg in 1758, Tevkelev and Rychkov discharged the functions of Orenburg governor. Tevkelev became Russia's first Muslim major-general and appears to have continued directing the administration's relations with the Muslim population as he had for the previous quarter-century.[127] Rychkov had been born into a merchant family in Russia's north in 1712 and then apprenticed with English merchants in Moscow. He took a position as translator and bookkeeper for the St. Petersburg Customs House, which Ivan Kirilov directed. When Kirilov organized the Orenburg Expedition, he appointed Rychkov as its bookkeeper. Rychkov impressed his superiors with his competence and was rewarded with hereditary noble status in 1743. Rychkov read foreign publications, and he became the first corresponding member of the Academy of Sciences in St. Petersburg in 1759 and a member of the Free Economic Society in 1765.[128]

In 1759, Tevkelev and Rychkov produced an analysis of the empire's policy toward Bashkirs' neighbors, Kazakhs, that reflected both their firsthand experience and their sense that the human potential of Kazakhs must be considered in making policy. Non-Russian peoples such as Kazakhs were now considered to have a human nature, a collective quality of mind, which could be understood and transformed.[129] In addressing whether to encourage Kazakhs to remain near the empire's border or to drive them deeper into the steppe as some military officials desired, Tevkelev and Rychkov argued that Kazakhs ought to be kept close at hand. This policy, they believed, accounted not only for the actions of native peoples but for their "humanity and level of development." The two men noted how difficult it was to change the "customs and ingrained sense of community in an entire people." The surest way to administer "newly subject peoples" and to direct them toward the "state interest" was to respect their customs and to practice "fairness and moderation." Kazakhs had already fallen in love with trade. Tevkelev and Rychkov believed that this policy would cause them to give up their nomadic lifestyle and settle on the land. The two men contrasted Kazakhs with Bashkirs. Since no effort had been made to observe and inculcate "humanity and obedience befitting a subject" in Bashkirs, they remained in a coarse and wild state.[130] Historian Ricarda Vulpius identifies the memorandum of Rychkov and Tevkelev as a key document reflecting the Russian Empire's development of a "civilizing mission," in which the imperial elite saw the Russian people as part of a "universal civilization" which in time could eradicate "wildness" and "barbarism."[131]

Imperial authorities' new emphases became clearer in Bashkiria during the reign of Catherine II. She presented herself as a "*philosophe* on the throne" who would bring justice and material benefits to her people through her enlightened and benevolent rule. Yet the east was far from Catherine's first priority. Until the Pugachev uprising in 1773, the empire's rapid expansion southward left few resources for its eastern region. Administrative initiatives came from Bashkiria itself. The governors of Orenburg in the 1760s all used the language of the Enlightenment to express their ideas for change. Debates over how to make imperial rule in Bashkiria stable and prosperous reveal two different strands in Enlightenment thought regarding human differences. An enlightened approach to the incorporation of Bashkirs could mean creating conditions that would allow them to grow from nomadic pastoralists into productive subjects of the empire who tilled the soil and obeyed the law. It could also be used to find that Bashkirs hindered the full development of the empire's power and ought to be deprived of their land for the greater good of humanity.

Dmitrii V. Volkov, one of the closest advisors to Catherine's late husband, Peter III, advocated the first position.[132] With the overthrow of Peter III on June 28, 1762, Catherine had appointed Volkov Orenburg's vice-governor as a type of exile. When Volkov wrote to Catherine in May 1763, he approached administration of the peoples of the steppe from the perspective of population and physiocratic economics. Like Tevkelev and Rychkov in 1759, he favored a new policy of benevolent engagement rather than force to win the sympathy of native peoples.[133] Volkov espoused Enlightenment notions of human agency and progress more vividly than Tevkelev and Rychkov had. In 1763, Volkov told Kazakh khan Nuraly that if Kazakhs accepted subject status, the empress would provide food and fuel to make "summer in the winter and winter in the summer." She would lead Kazakhs on the path of development that all peoples, including Russians, had undergone.[134] Such faith in human progress, however, only served as an introduction to subjects that most concerned Volkov—law, trade, and agriculture. Volkov considered the extension of law and promotion of settled agriculture necessary to make Russian authority effective. Extending the reach of the law, Volkov believed, could be achieved in part with proper leadership. The Orenburg governor must be physically impressive and a military man, since there were "no people other than military [people] here." Volkov's ideal governor would dispense justice among the non-Orthodox quickly and would punish corrupt subordinates.[135]

Volkov considered the development of agriculture to be most fundamental. "Where fields are ploughed, there homes are built," he wrote, and "where homes are built there is quiet and the power of law."[136] The development of agriculture, in turn, required the spread of commerce and of the grain trade. Trade drew all parties involved into a system of peaceful exchange. Volkov believed that Bashkirs, in particular, could benefit from participation in the grain trade; they were "not so wild." Bashkirs, seeing the profit that could be made from trade, would start to practice settled agriculture rather than semi-nomadic pastoralism.[137] Trade would promote the region's well-being and benefit the entire state.[138]

Volkov made specific proposals for the integration of Bashkirs through trade and settled agriculture. To improve the grain trade, Volkov recommended that export tariffs be cut in half and the price of salt be reduced. To improve Bashkir agriculture, he recommended that Bashkirs be permitted to hire labor and that the number of Bashkir blacksmiths be allowed to increase. If Bashkirs were to farm rather than fight, they needed to be able to produce enough agricultural implements to make farming possible. Volkov also recommended that Bashkirs ought to be released from military service. One in eight adult males served on the Orenburg line in the summer. Such service was incompatible with agriculture.[139] These fairly specific proposals, however, would have meant a fundamental transformation of Bashkir relations with imperial authority. Reducing taxes threatened to cut state revenues. Allowing Bashkirs to hire laborers, who would be mostly non-Bashkirs and often non-Muslims, meant potentially reducing the isolation of the Bashkir estate. Permitting blacksmiths meant that the nature of Bashkir-Russian relations had changed from armed confrontation to peaceful trade. Changing Bashkir military service potentially affected the empire's security. Before any of Volkov's proposals could become law, Catherine recalled him to St. Petersburg.

Appointed in 1764, Prince Avram Putiatin advocated the second position—that Bashkirs ought to be expropriated for the good of the region. He shared Volkov's goal of assimilating Bashkiria into the empire through agriculture. The agriculturalists would not be Bashkirs, however. Putiatin argued that Orenburg Province was "useless to the state" since Bashkirs occupied it without bearing "any sort of fruit." In Putiatin's view, the land of Orenburg Province had long been "wild" or simply lain empty. It did not belong to anyone in particular and thus was the property of the Crown. The Bashkir people, "empty-headed and inclined to impertinence," ought to be told specifically that they never had had land in "eternal ownership." Putiatin wanted to survey Bashkiria's land and to rationalize landholdings. Then, Putiatin could settle "Great Russian people" in the region in order to bring "desirable benefit to humankind."[140] Great Russians would overwhelm Muslim and newly baptized populations, which he considered "wavering in loyal subjecthood" and "dangerous," and instruct Bashkirs in tilling the soil and in "other Great Russian customs."[141] Putiatin's project repudiated Bashkir hereditary landholding and would have demarcated Bashkir lands at the family rather than the clan level. His predecessors had associated loyalty with landholding, but that loyalty had been demonstrated by actual fighting for the tsar. Putiatin, for the first time, associated loyalty not with actions taken for or against the tsar but with cultural characteristics.

Neither Volkov's nor Putiatin's proposals became law. Enlightened ideas of Volkov's variety were too great a departure from the tsar's fiscal-military regime.[142] Nor did central authorities embrace Putiatin's vision of dispossessing the Bashkirs. Eliminating Bashkir landownership threatened to provoke unrest in a region that had seen plenty in previous decades, and there was no surplus of "Great Russian" nobles and peasants eager to establish estates and till Bashkiria's soil. The demarcation and sale of "empty" land to nobles enacted in 1770 under Putiatin's successor, Reinsdorp, marked a step in the direction of resettlement as a means to agricultural development, but this was the only significant such policy adopted before the Pugachev Uprising in 1773.[143] The 1760s were more productive of ideas for the incorporation of Bashkiria as a productive part of the empire than of new laws that specified how this would take place.

TARKHAN STATUS AND AN UNPRIVILEGED ELITE

New tax policy eroded the social hierarchy built upon the granting of tarkhan status to free Bashkir elites from the payment of iasak. No part of the new salt tax decree exempted tarkhans from the salt monopoly. This rendered the primary privilege given to tarkhans essentially meaningless, even if the title continued to exist into the nineteenth century.[144] Petr Rychkov wrote in 1767 that

"From olden days, tarkhans were something like a Bashkir nobility. They had various privileges over others, but now there is almost no difference other than title alone. They only deem themselves the best, natural-born serving people."[145]

As the tarkhan declined in importance, the state relied increasingly on volost elders and, to a lesser extent, Muslim religious leaders to serve as intermediaries between it and the region's population. By the 1760s, elders were expected to be literate in Turkic and to have some acquaintance with the empire's laws. Elders had substantial power over members of their communities. They specified who had to appear for service on the Orenburg line each summer; assigned the community's land and resources among its households; and were responsible for maintaining order. Some took advantage of their position to allocate themselves the best land or sometimes even to sell land without the approval of the community.[146] By 1773, 113 volost elders, each with one or two assistants, served the state.[147] Yet elders enjoyed neither the privileges of the empire's nobility nor the authority of the empire's administrators. Elders occasionally received valuable gifts, medals, or payments for their service, but they earned no salary. Bashkir elders did not acquire the most important sources of wealth in eighteenth-century Russia—the ownership of land and of the serf labor necessary to profit from it.

State officials also appointed Muslim religious leaders, akhunds, in each of the four dorogas with an eye toward promoting the administration's influence. Akhunds tended to be selected from among the most senior and influential Meshcheriak mullahs, though Bashkir elders began to advance their own candidates by the 1760s. As we saw above, akhunds could apply Muslim sharia law in cases regarding the family, such as marriage, divorce, and inheritance, while imperial authorities applied the tsar's law to crimes, debts, and property matters.[148] Local mullahs and *azanchis* (those who call the faithful to prayer) were elected by their communities and supposedly confirmed by the provincial chancellery, but there is little evidence that the chancellery actually did so.[149] Instead, influential akhunds had the most to do with selecting or at least approving Muslim clerics, interpreting sharia law, and settling disputes among Muslims.[150] Mullahs served as instructors in the Muslim faith and as leaders of religious services. They were freed from the obligations of ordinary Bashkirs, but other than some appointed akhunds, Muslim clerics appear to have had even looser bonds with the empire's administration. The relationship between elite and nonelite Bashkirs in the second half of the eighteenth century could be tense, as we saw in Batyrsha's letter to Catherine II, yet imperial officials had not drawn the loyalty of the Bashkir elite firmly to the empire. As Fania Shakurova has written, "the stability of their [Bashkir elites'] power to a large extent depended on Bashkir society, rather than from rulers above."[151]

Violence, loss of land, and political changes in the decades after the Bashkir War kept Bashkir society in a state of flux. Bashkir volosts in the south and east showed the least change, since they faced less pressure from colonization and were on the border with the Kazakh steppe to the south. In Bashkiria's center, north and northwest, Bashkir volosts broke down into smaller tiubas that corresponded more closely to an individual community rather than a larger tribal unit. Sometimes differences among Bashkirs drove some to another volost or to form their own, smaller tiuba.[152]

Bashkirs showed no great inclination to sow crops, but the demand for grain for the towns of Ufa and Orenburg and for workers in the Urals factories caused some Bashkirs to turn to grain production. Areas of agricultural production expanded from the northwest of Bashkiria to its center, just north and south of Ufa, and near factories on the eastern slope of the Urals. Bashkirs took to agriculture reluctantly for several reasons. They derived most of what was necessary to sustain themselves from animal milk, meat, and hides, which they could also trade with settled neighbors.[153] By the 1760s, their herds of horses had recovered from the devastation of the Bashkir War in 1735–1740 and from the disturbances of 1755. An ordinary Bashkir might have a herd of thirty to fifty horses, while the wealthiest Bashkirs might own as many as two thousand horses, some of which they brought to market.[154] Annual service on the Orenburg defensive line also served as an impediment to growing grain. Each year, 2,000–2,500 Bashkirs were called to serve. Bashkir communities had to provide food, weapons, and two horses to outfit a warrior. Since service ran from May until the first snow, it took men far from home at just the time they would be needed to raise crops. In case of war, more Bashkir men would be mobilized —531 Bashkirs and another 519 Meshcheriaks to fight Prussia in the Seven Years' War, more than 7,000 to stop the flight of Kalmyks in 1771, and 3,000 against Poland later in 1771.[155] Emphasis on Bashkirs as a militarized estate in a century featuring multiple Bashkir uprisings created a reputation of Bashkirs as a warrior people. Military service became the primary connection with the imperial state for a group tied to a particular piece of land in the east and forming a distinct social status group. Soon, however, they would be fighting against some of the same officers who led them into the tsar's wars.

THE PUGACHEV REBELLION AND THE COLLAPSE OF THE EMPEROR'S AUTHORITY IN BASHKIRIA

The Pugachev Rebellion of 1773–1775, the last large-scale collective action in the empire's east until the twentieth century, demonstrated imperial authority's fragility and the state's tenuous connections with local elites. The rebellion is generally identified with its leader, Emelian Pugachev, and defined as either Cossack or peasant in nature. Without a doubt, it began as a Cossack uprising and ended as a broad rebellion against serfdom that affected an area from Kazan in the north to the shores of the Caspian Sea in the south and from Tambov in the west to the eastern slopes of the Ural Mountains. The majority of those who fought the empress's forces were not Cossacks, however, and many who participated in the rebellion were neither serfs nor threatened with serfdom. Muslims in general and Bashkirs in particular played crucial roles in the rebellion. Without their participation, the uprising would most likely have remained the localized, Cossack mutiny that the empire's leadership initially considered it to be.[156] The rebellion resulted from the combined discontent of frontier populations undergoing incorporation into a centralizing absolutist regime.[157] Absolutism backed by force was the essence of imperial authority in Bashkiria. When military forces were stretched thin, what was initially a modest challenge became sufficient to bring the emperor's authority crashing down in all but the fortress cities of Ufa and Orenburg.

The rebellion had its roots in the discontent of the Iaik Cossacks. The Iaik Cossacks originated in the fifteenth century as a diverse group in flight from the Muscovite state who settled along the Iaik River on the southern and western edges of Bashkiria.[158] They made their living by fishing and by raids along the Caspian Sea, often alongside the Don Cossacks. The Muscovite government gradually incorporated the Iaik Cossacks into a system of frontier defense, building a fort at Gurev where the Iaik meets the Caspian.[159] The government gave the Cossacks ammunition, artillery, and a monopoly on fishing in the Iaik River. In exchange, Iaik Cossacks accepted the tsar's sovereignty, paid a fixed sum for fishing rights, and manned fortifications along the Iaik under the leadership of an elected ataman. By the 1760s, central authorities began to intervene more directly and forcefully in Cossack affairs.[160] Although Cossack leaders prospered, ordinary Cossacks' situations deteriorated. The government forced Cossacks to buy salt from state stores at fixed prices—a substantial burden, since salt was needed to preserve the catch of fish. Since the government was under pressure to mobilize manpower to fight the Turkish War (1768–1774), Cossacks feared that they would be made part of the regular army. Since most Iaik Cossacks were religious dissenters—Old Believers—such a move threatened them with being forced to shave their beards, to cut their hair, and to endure military discipline.

Emelian Pugachev and a few of his associates began the rebellion. Pugachev was born into a Don Cossack and Old Believer family in 1740. He fought in the Seven Years' War, but after his return he hid among Cossacks in the Iaik region to avoid paying the fine imposed on mutinous Cossacks the previous year.

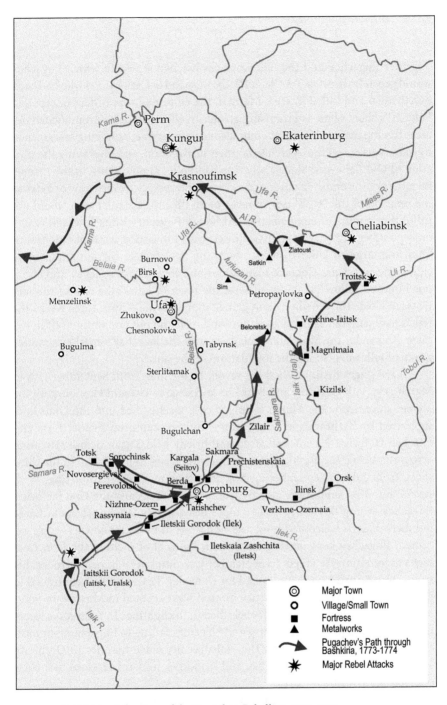

MAP 2.2. Bashkiria at the time of the Pugachev Rebellion, 1773–1775.

Together Pugachev and the Iaik Cossacks hatched a plan in which Pugachev would proclaim himself Tsar Peter III, the husband of Catherine II who had been overthrown and killed in 1762. Many in the empire's lower orders interpreted Peter III's short reign as promising greater freedom, since he promulgated decrees freeing the nobility from compulsory state service, removing serfs owned by monasteries and the church from their jurisdiction, and improving the situation of Old Believers. Since Catherine had no legitimate claim to the throne, members of the empire's lower orders could interpret her overthrow of Peter as the removal of the "true" tsar in favor of an illegitimate ruler who would not fulfill the promise of emancipation. Although Pugachev himself was illiterate, on September 17, 1773, he and his followers began to issue a series of manifestos. They first targeted Iaik Cossacks, promising to eliminate corrupt and abusive elders and to restore Cossack institutions and freedoms. Pugachev and about one hundred followers set out to seize the town of Iaitsk, the seat of the Iaik Cossack Host. The rebellion soon gained momentum. Within three weeks the rebels had gathered as many as a thousand men and put Orenburg itself under siege. Alexander Pushkin later exclaimed over the fact that Pugachev's motley group of followers "shook the foundations of the state!"[161]

Three stages distinguished the revolt. In the first, from September 1773 to March 1774, Iaik Cossacks and Bashkirs laid siege to Ufa and Orenburg. In the second stage, from late March to July 1774, Pugachev fled into the Urals and, supported by Bashkirs and Ural factory workers, captured smaller forts and attacked factories. He then attacked and briefly held Kazan before retreating across the Volga. His Bashkir troops largely returned to Bashkiria. In the third stage, from July to September 8, 1774, Pugachev renewed the uprising. With several hundred supporters, mostly from the Cossacks and the Ural factories, Pugachev swung down the Volga's more heavily populated west bank. Large numbers of serfs welcomed him, and hundreds of noble landowners were executed. Pugachev kept moving south with the goal of inciting the Don Cossacks to join him. He failed. In September 1774, hunted by imperial troops, his supporters turned him in and asked for clemency. Peasant rebels continued to operate well into 1775, but Pugachev himself was executed in Moscow in January 1775. In all, twenty thousand rebels died in the fighting. The empress's forces had managed to prevent Orenburg and Ufa from falling to Pugachev, but most of Bashkiria was devastated by the violence; 295 noble families in Orenburg Province suffered due to Pugachev and his forces, and 277 received monetary compensation for their losses.[162]

Bashkir elites and religious leaders declared support for Pugachev even before the siege of Orenburg.[163] They seemed to see in his movement a force that would protect their lands and religious freedom while reducing their tax and service burdens. Under interrogation by the secret committee investigating the uprising, Pugachev later recalled that Bashkir elder Kinzia Arslanov brought a detachment of 500 men to the rebellion by early October and eventually 5,000 troops in all. By the end of 1773, Bashkir detachments arriving in Pugachev's headquarters numbered 10,000–12,000 men, one-third to nearly one-half of the estimated 25,000–30,000 rebels.[164] Others fought in the siege of Ufa and elsewhere. Muslim mullahs constituted 44 of 120 men named as officers of Pugachev's "Military College," making them a substantial portion of the uprising's leadership.[165] Administrators in Ufa confirmed overwhelming support for Pugachev among non-Russians: 77 of 86 Bashkir elders, 37 of 40 Meshcheriak elders, and nearly all Bashkir households helped him in some way.[166] More of the local population appears to have supported the rebels than had fought the empress's forces in the war of 1735–1740 and the uprising of 1755, indicating an erosion of the imperial state's position among non-Russians over a forty-year period.

Bashkir support for Pugachev must be measured against the government's unsuccessful efforts to recruit local opposition to him. Bashkirs and Meshcheriaks responded in small numbers to Orenburg governor Reinsdorp's order to defend Orenburg and fled or joined the rebels at first sign of Pugachev's success. As the situation became more difficult, Kazan governor von Brandt called on Kutlu-Mukhammad/Aleksei I. Tevkelev's son, the sixty-six-year old Iusup/Osip Tevkelev. Tevkelev reassured von Brandt that he could restore Bashkir zeal for the fight against Pugachev since "he was of one religion with them."[167] Instead, most of Tevkelev's force of four hundred Tatars and Bashkirs went over to Pugachev's side, and Tevkelev himself was captured and executed.[168] Rychkov survived the six-month siege of Orenburg, but his estate was plundered and burned and his eldest son died in battle against Pugachev's forces.[169] Only Pugachev's capture in September 1774 enabled the government to regain the initiative in Bashkiria. In that month Catherine's favorite Grigorii Potemkin informed Bashkir leaders that if the Bashkirs did not "pacify themselves" before October he would send twenty thousand troops to lay waste to their land. By October 1774, all but six Bashkir elders had capitulated.[170] Salavat Iulaev's capture on November 25, 1774, ended organized resistance.[171]

What made Pugachev, as Peter III, so attractive to Bashkirs and to the rest of Bashkiria's population? Pugachev seemingly promised his supporters everything they could have wished, but he varied his promises slightly to reflect the particular interests of the groups that he addressed.[172] "Peter Fedorovich's" first decree to the Bashkirs highlighted promises of land, water, and forests but also included "faith and your law" to the list of what Bashkirs would receive, indicating a concern for religious freedom that did not appear on decrees aimed at the Cossacks. More broadly, Pugachev promised to free Bashkirs from state-imposed burdens so they could live "like steppe animals." A second decree appears to have been intended for Muslims in the Nogai and Siberian Dorogas. It made fewer promises, but salt and religious freedom featured prominently among them.[173] Marc Raeff has written that the ideology of the Pugachev rebellion mixed traditional and "modern Petrine notions of authority." Pugachev stated he would make Iaitskii Gorodok his "Petersburg" and was depicted in "neoclassical profile" and armor in the fashion of Peter the Great.[174] Freedom and the service state would seem difficult to reconcile, since the Petrine service state intervened in the lives of the emperor's subjects to a greater extent than that of his predecessors. Bashkir acceptance of Pugachev makes sense in terms of Bashkir understandings of the emperor's authority. A substantial proportion of the Bashkir elite did not reject service to the empire as long as imperial officials preserved traditional patterns of taxation, religious freedom, and minimal state interference in Bashkir communities. Pugachev's promise to abolish Orenburg Province further answered Bashkir desires to return to the status quo prevailing before the 1730s. In essence, Bashkirs found in Pugachev the alternative sovereign they had sought since the wars of 1735–1740.

CONCLUSION

Pugachev's rebellion marked the near-collapse of an effort to bring Bashkiria fully under the tsar's authority that had begun four decades before. Bashkir leaders continued to try to bargain the terms of their inclusion in the empire, but Kirilov, Tatishchev, and imperial officials in St. Petersburg sought to introduce a new set of rules informed by notions of imperial sovereignty borrowed from the Roman tradition. With the war's end, the empress's representatives, most notably Ivan Nepliuev, set about largely dismantling the basis of Bashkir incorporation into the empire that had prevailed since the 1550s. Nepliuev preserved one key aspect of the pre-1735 arrangement: he blunted missionary activity and anti-Islamic campaigns that raged fiercely to Bashkiria's west. This reduced hostility toward imperial authority even if policies in neighboring Kazan Province still gave cause for Muslim alarm. Other than questions of faith, however, change was sweeping. Nepliuev and his officials introduced a market in land and distributed Bashkir land to servitors, forts, and factories. Bashkirs saw their distinctiveness and privilege eroded. After 1754, they paid the salt tax rather than iasak, which they associated with their landownership and status. Tarkhan status, though not annulled, lost significance. The elite had status as local volost elders and occasionally as official akhunds or mullahs, yet, lacking regular support, state salaries, or noble status, they had little investment in the imperial system. Native elites in Bashkiria lost privileges and received little in return. Ordinary Bashkirs faced new obligations such as the salt tax, a closer Russian presence in the line of forts constructed starting in the 1730s, and loss of land. Under such pressure, larger tribal structures broke down. Fewer Bashkirs could practice semi-nomadic pastoralism, especially in the north and west. The new vision of *grazhdanstvennost'* or "civilizing mission" reflected imperial officials' efforts to engage Enlightenment thinking in Europe but affected Bashkiria very little. As Volkov wrote, there were only military men in Orenburg Province, so it is no surprise that the use of force prevailed in local governance. Bashkirs fought back and acquired a reputation as wild and rebellious.

The powerful presence of the military was clear in many border regions from Siberia to the North Caucasus and Ukraine. Under Peter I, the destruction of Cossack settlements was as violent as the attack on Bashkiria, or more so.[175] Nonetheless, why was this period in Bashkiria so bloody, featuring not only the everyday violence of empire but two large-scale clashes with a population that had long before sworn allegiance to the tsar? Bashkiria was a particular flashpoint in the mid-eighteenth century because, geographically and socially, it fell between two poles of Russian imperialism. As Andreas Kappeler and others have pointed out, where imperial officials encountered a native elite that they could understand as something like a nobility, they sought to co-opt that elite by making it part of the Russian nobility. Such an ennobled elite would share in the privileges that service to the tsar-emperor brought. Farther east where the empire recognized no such elite among Siberian hunters and gatherers, it most often neglected to make one, turning the population into nonprivileged, tribute-paying subjects.[176] During and after Peter I's reign, the variation between the empire's east and its west intensified. In the empire's south and west, local elites, be they Crimean Tatar murzas, Polish shliakhta, or Baltic German nobles, had their social status recognized and received privileges from the tsar's empire similar to those that they previously had received from the Ottoman Empire or Polish or Lithuanian kingdoms. For instance, when Peter and his armies took what is now Estonia from Sweden in 1710, he promised to preserve intact and even to extend the rights and privileges of the Lutheran Church.[177] In Bashkiria, the tsarist state pursued first one and then the other strategy. It first sought to bring Bashkirs into the empire by permitting the practice of Islam and through the extension of privileges such as hereditary landholding and tarkhan status. Kirilov seemed intent on avoiding an analogue of the devastation of Native Americans by the Spanish Empire when he planned to build Orenburg as the basis for an Asian empire. When Kirilov's efforts proved an insufficient basis for empire in Asia, he moved in the opposite direction. Bashkiria's governors sought to undermine Bashkir privileges in an effort to apply Petrine absolutist principles. The abruptness of the change led to bitter disappointment on both sides.

The differences in treatment of the empire's east and west reflect Peter and his officials' reorientation from Eurasian models to European ones. The Ottoman Empire remained a major rival of the Russian Empire and would remain one until the end of the Old Regime. As the references to the Dutch and Spanish Empires in Kirilov's Orenburg Expedition indicate, however, after Peter, Western empires dominated imperial officials' imaginations. Peter had sent many officials who brought the Russian Empire to Bashkiria abroad to study in Europe, where they learned to measure Russia against European models. Before the eighteenth century, the Muscovite empire in Bashkiria seemed relatively moderate compared to European empires. Ideologists of the Muscovite conquest of Kazan represented the victory as part of a divine mission, but not so strongly as did the sixteenth-century Spanish. Religious "crusading enthusiasm" motivated Spanish rulers Ferdinand and Isabella to attack the Kingdom of Granada in 1482. In 1499, after final victory, the Spanish forced all Muslims to convert to Christianity or to leave.[178] Even the zeal to turn Muslims into Christians apparent in Kazan in the 1550s became less intense in the following decades and was scarcely evident in Bashkiria.[179]

Russian treatment of property in land also differed from Western models. The English belief that their mastery of the demarcation and use of property entitled them to land that Native Americans left "empty" had no equivalent in the sixteenth-century Russian Empire. The English and to a large extent the French promoted the principle of *res nullius,* which in Roman law meant that all "'empty things' were the common property of all mankind until they were put to some, generally agricultural, use." The first person to make use of land became its owner.[180] Ivan's charters to Bashkirs, with their emphasis on tribute in exchange for being left largely alone, stand in vivid contrast to such policies. Before the 1740s, Muscovy sent tax collectors to Bashkiria, not agriculturalists. Tsarist officials wanted the local population to stay put and to pay iasak rather than trying to exterminate it or drive it away.

By mid-eighteenth-century standards, however, Russian imperial rule in Bashkiria seems unlike Europe in the greater harshness with which it sought to apply the social and fiscal systems of the center. In India, both the French and the British very much worked with local elites.[181] As Linda Colley and others have argued, eighteenth-century British officials in India were acutely aware of their small numbers and relied overwhelmingly on the cooperation of native leaders for administration and native commoners for their army.[182] In the New World, the French maintained a middle ground in which they cooperated in trade and worked with natives to undermine the British.[183] In the eighteenth century, the Spanish in the New World encouraged intermarriage with local elites and sometimes derived status from such unions.[184] In Bashkiria, on the other hand, the tsarist empire went from one extreme of inserting itself into the pattern of governance characteristic of the Kypchak Khanate's successor states, as we saw in chapter 1, to an effort to assert absolute authority in Bashkiria and eliminate most of what had made previous relations acceptable to the local population. As a result, the large-scale use of force had to be repeated fewer than forty years after the first war in Bashkiria. Only after the suppression of the Pugachev rebellion did the imperial regime at the highest levels—from Catherine on down—pay sustained attention to Bashkiria and begin to establish a new basis for imperial authority.

3

EMPIRE OF REASON

1773–1855

IN ORDER TO win support among Kazakhs and to build loyalty among her Muslim subjects, Catherine II (the Great) appointed Akhund Mukhamedzhan Khusainov to the position of mufti, the head of the new Orenburg Muhammadan Ecclesiastical Assembly, in 1789.[1] Mufti Khusainov's speech at the official opening of the OMEA in December 1789 emphasized that Muslims could become privileged members of the empire's elite due to Catherine's policies of toleration, support of Islamic institutions, and acceptance of Muslims as nobles: "The Russian (*rossiiskii*) son celebrates that Catherine reigns over him. . . . But who is this lover, devotee of happiness? Is it really only he whom the Evangelist's spirit directs? Those who think so, do not think correctly. The sagacious mother does not consider various faiths, just loyalty of the heart."

Khusainov urged Muslims to respect "the common good and tranquility."[2] Privately, Khusainov wrote to St. Petersburg to explain in Islamic terms the legitimacy of a Christian empress's rule over Muslims and the need for Muslims to honor their oaths of loyalty.[3] Members of the Muslim elite could become "sons of the empire" and participate in Catherine's "Age of Gold." New institutions for Bashkirs followed the new institutions for Muslims. In 1798, imperial officials organized Bashkiria into eleven Bashkir, five Meshcheriak, five Orenburg Cossack, and two Ural Cossack cantons.[4] The cantonal system (*kantonnaia sistema*) built upon a half century of Bashkir military service by creating regionally defined units led by Bashkir officers, who would organize Bashir service and much of Bashkir life as well. The new institutions' effectiveness showed itself in 1812, when Orenburg governor-general Volkonskii included Bashkirs when conveying Alexander I's invitation to "all loyal (*vernopoddannykh*) sons of the Russian Empire" to defend it against Napoleon. More than ten thousand Bashkirs responded to the call.[5]

In the quarter-century after Pugachev, Catherine II and her officials in Bashkiria undertook measures designed to govern Muslims in general and Bashkirs in particular more effectively. They sought to bring calm and order by giving Muslim and Bashkir elites a greater stake in the imperial system than they had previously. Catherine's reforms dramatically changed Bashkiria. The Pugachev Rebellion would be the last major disorder there until the twentieth century. Already by the 1830s, Orenburg governor Perovskii could "play sultan" by calling his summer retreat a kochevka after Bashkir summer encampments. Loyal Bashkirs served as guards at Perovskii's kochevka, and Bashkir performers sang native songs to guests from as far away as Europe. Perovskii also initiated construction of a complex of buildings and a mosque, known as a caravanserai, which would serve as a headquarters for Bashkir military units. Bashkirs had become sufficiently reliable that they could be displayed to the emperor, as they were in his visit to Ufa in 1824. This chapter will explain Bashkiria's transformation from a center of rebellion to a relatively calm region where imperial authority had become normal and accepted.

Catherine II had much to do with this change. Pugachev may have been a pretender, but the actual empress had taken the throne in a coup against her husband and had no legal claim to it either. Catherine II's need to legitimate her rule motivated her desire to balance respect for precedents, especially those of Peter I, with her own distinctive self-presentation. She made no retreat from the absolutism of Peter and his protégés: the empress was the source of law, and her authority must not be questioned. She shared her predecessors' cameralist views that the ruler and state administration should be "the driving force of an active and interventionist policy covering all facets of public life."[6] Even as she styled herself as Peter's heiress, however, she transformed his model of rule. She fashioned herself as a "philosophe on the throne"—an enlightened ruler who would bring justice and prosperity to her people through rational rule—rather than as a military commander.[7] Cameralist thought expressed in an Enlightenment idiom—what Robert Crews has described as "enlightened cameralism"—allowed the empress and her officials to imagine an empire run according to the dictates of reason.[8] To some influential thinkers, governing according to reason meant that space and people ought to be organized as productively as possible.[9] Administrative uniformity was important—similar people and places ought to be treated in similar fashions. But administrative uniformity could be accompanied by relatively greater tolerance for cultural and religious diversity rather than by the forced pursuit of homogeneity. The empire's ethnographic diversity became an element of its greatness.[10]

Themes of enlightened rule over a diverse population by agents of the emperor continued through the reigns of Catherine's son Paul I (reigned 1796–1801) and of her grandsons, Alexander I (reigned 1801–1825) and Nicholas I (reigned 1825–1855). To be sure, the international political environment changed greatly in this period. Even before Catherine died in 1796, the French Revolution and the notion of popular sovereignty complicated an "enlightened" ruler's claims to know best the people's welfare. Ideas from abroad challenged administrators of a multinational empire and gave rise to the ideology of "official nationality." The government's primary goal in Bashkiria, however, remained the creation of effective administrative institutions and the incorporation of diverse elements rather than the homogenization of the population. Alexander I's introduction of ministerial government indicated invigorated aspirations for systematic, rational administration. Alexander's officials considered major reforms to Bashkir landholding and military service. The final subordination of the Kazakh Hordes to imperial rule from the 1820s to the 1840s decreased the importance of Bashkir military service and turned imperial officials' attention to civil organization of Bashkirs. Nicholas I's men in Bashkiria continued to promote the practice of Islam and to introduce elements of European "civilization," such as sedentary agriculture and education. The process of state and social formation, begun in the 1770s and lasting to the 1850s, created a multiethnic, multiconfessional political elite. This elite aimed to introduce European values and rational administration that would make the tsar's subjects more obedient and extract more resources from Bashkiria. By using an often-crude system of military command toward rationalizing ends, however, Nicholas I undermined the very idea of the empire of reason. Nicholas I's death in 1855 and the empire's disastrous Crimean War demonstrated vividly the limitations of this approach and its great cost to the local population.

CATHERINE AND THE MAKING OF A MULTICONFESSIONAL ELITE

The first priority of Catherine's administration in Bashkiria was to eliminate the capacity of an illiterate Cossack such as Pugachev to shake the empire's foundations. In a region with an overwhelmingly Muslim population and few Russian speakers, Catherine and her officials pursued two goals. First, Muslim elites must receive recognition, privileges, and a place in the empire's hierarchy so that they would become reliably loyal to tsarist authority. Second, members of the empire's elite must be drawn to the region from the empire's center. In the empire's core, noble landowners administered justice among their serfs, collected taxes, and helped determine who served in the empire's army. Without landowning nobles, what Vice-Governor Volkov had called "military men" and the force they could mete out were nearly all that conveyed the empress's power to Bashkiria.

Religious toleration was perhaps the most important practice Catherine and her officials used to build a diverse elite in Bashkiria. Following cameralist thinkers, Catherine thought mostly of toleration's benefits to the state—religious faith provided a beneficial moral influence on a ruler's subjects, promoted "peace and security," and helped make "useful citizens, good soldiers, and loyal subjects."[11] In 1773, on the eve of the Pugachev Rebellion, Catherine issued a decree "on the toleration of all creeds" that affirmed Muslim religious practice in more sweeping language than before. She approved a request to build two stone mosques in Kazan, arguing: "As the Most High God tolerates all faiths, languages, and creeds, then Her Majesty, [proceeding] from the very same principles, corresponding to His Holy will, is pleased also to allow this, desiring only that love and harmony always reign among subjects of Her Majesty."

The assertion of the secular state's authority over Orthodox Christian religious affairs was key to Catherine's policy. Orthodox Christian ecclesiastical officials henceforth were not to enter into Muslim affairs but instead present such matters "for the consideration of secular authorities."[12] As was the case for rulers in much of Europe, Catherine's concept of religious toleration was limited.[13] She issued no general manifesto on toleration that applied to all faiths. Catherine's legislation maintained that Russian Orthodoxy was the "true Flock of the Faithful."[14] Islam could be practiced, not proselytized. Yet in the east, Catherinian toleration ended the attempt to enforce the elite's religious uniformity, which had been evident in Peter I's effort to strip Muslim nobles of their land and serfs and in the policies of other absolutist rulers since Louis XIV's revocation of the Edict of Nantes in 1685.[15] Imperial officials in Bashkiria took the empress's intentions seriously. They sought to limit the church's efforts to convert Muslims.[16]

Even limited toleration made possible further efforts to incorporate Muslims into the empire. In 1776, certain Tatars and Bashkirs were freed from the soul tax and were permitted to own factories, to engage in trade, and to migrate within the empire.[17] In 1784, Catherine decreed that "princes and murzas of Tatar origins" could regain the privileges of a Russian (*rossiiskii*) nobleman if they could provide written proof that their ancestors had been ennobled. All should enjoy the same privileges, regardless of their "clan or law."[18] Fifty-six service Tatar families identified by Il'dus R. Gabdullin had their noble status restored between 1790 and 1802.[19] As a result of the 1784 law, Bashkiria had a substantial concentration of Muslim nobles. In the second half of the eighteenth century, 14 of the 150 families newly registered in Ufa's Noble Assembly were Muslim.[20] In 1789, Kutlu-Mukhammad/Aleksei Tevkelev's daughter-in-law, for instance, petitioned successfully for her family's inclusion in the Ufa noble assembly.[21] Muslims remained quite underrepresented in the nobility—they comprised more than half of Ufa's population but only 10 percent of the newly ennobled families and far less than that of nobles altogether. Some Muslim nobles had lost their lands and lived little better than peasants. Nonetheless, coming as it did on the eve of Catherine's Charter to the Nobility of 1785, which freed nobles from compulsory service and corporal punishment, the 1784 decree allowed a significant number of Muslims to share in the benefits of Catherine's reign.[22] Bashkiria's elite began to acquire status more like that of elites in the empire's core, while statuses particular to Bashkiria, such as tarkhan and batyr, largely fell out of official use.[23] In 1821, Orenburg military governor Petr Essen decided that tarkhans should have Bashkir rather than noble status.[24]

As Catherine's officials worked to build a Muslim elite in Bashkiria, they sought to bring nobles from the center. Catherine's provincial reform, promulgated in 1775, created the Ufa and Simbirsk governor-generalship headquartered in Ufa seven years later. The reform demarcated the region in the manner of central Russia for the first time—the doroga disappeared as a territorial unit. The new territorial division greatly increased the number and status of state servitors in Bashkiria, and it increased the region's connections to Catherine's court, with its European style and cultural norms.[25] Ten counties (*uezdy*) were created, each with seven positions in the Table of Ranks.[26] Before 1782, Bashkiria had been led by a governor of the seventh rank in Orenburg. Now Ufa received a governor-general of the third rank. The first two men Catherine appointed to the post, General Iakobii (served 1781–1784) and Baron Osip Igel'strom (served 1784–1792 and 1796–1802), reflected the cosmopolitanism of tsarist servitors in the eighteenth century. Iakobii was the son of a Pole who had immigrated to Russia in 1711.[27] Igel'strom, a Baltic German nobleman who could not write Russian, was a protégé of Catherine's favorite Grigorii Potemkin. Igel'strom made a great impression on his contemporaries. One official described him as "amorous, bellicose, hot-tempered, clever, polite in society and intolerably proud, generous and at the same time scrupulous." A senatorial review praised him for following state rules in an "extremely literal" fashion.[28]

The prominence of men such as Iakobii and Igel'strom and the Charter to the Nobility's creation of the noble assemblies in 1785 invigorated social life in otherwise sleepy provincial towns. New positions improved chances for a family's social advancement through marriages to rising servitors. These factors drew noblemen to Bashkiria in substantial numbers. Nobles acquired large expanses of sparsely populated land from Bashkirs either through deception or by purchase at very low prices. The prominent nineteenth-century writer Sergei Aksakov discussed his own family's move to the region in his 1856 semi-autobiographical novel *The Family Chronicle*. His grandfather, a noble landowner in Simbirsk Province on the Volga, had seen his lands divided by marriages to the point that his holdings were, in essence, collectively run. He moved east in order to restore his independence.[29] Land and opportunity drew approximately 150 noble families to Ufa Province alone in the second half of the eighteenth century.[30] Bashkiria became the easternmost region of the empire that had a substantial noble landowning population. Although smaller in number and less wealthy than nobles in much of the empire, local noblemen staffed the region's administration and sent their children to the region's schools. Some became bearers of European culture.

THE FORMATION OF MUSLIM INSTITUTIONS

Catherine's policy of toleration, her interest in creating an elite that could manage distant parts of her empire, and foreign policy considerations motivated the formation of Muslim administrative institutions in the 1780s. With the initiative of Baron Igel'strom, imperial policy changed from tolerance of Muslim religious institutions to the active promotion of Islam. Igel'strom had been responsible for the integration of the Khanate of Crimea into the empire after its annexation in 1783. Igel'strom ensured that Crimean Muslim clerics retained their social and economic status and provided them with annual salaries in exchange for their support of the tsar rather than the Ottoman sultan. When Catherine appointed Igel'strom to Bashkiria, he confronted a situation that differed substantially from that in Crimea. Following Ottoman fashion, Muslim clerics in Crimea were drawn from a hereditary estate, while those in Bashkiria could be from any estate. Clerics in the Volga-Urals region held a great deal of power, but there was no mufti, and there were so few *waqf* properties (Muslim religious endowments) that no rules regarding them existed.[31] If Igel'strom wanted institutions in Bashkiria with which to regulate the tsarist administration's interactions with Muslims, he would have to create them.

Shortly after Igel'strom arrived in Ufa in 1785, he did just that. He became an enthusiastic patron of Islam. He requested permission to construct mosques and bilingual schools in order to use Islam to "civilize" Kazakhs and to bring them closer to the empire.[32] In May 1786, he celebrated the opening of a large, state-sponsored mosque in Orenburg. He scheduled the opening for a Friday when many Kazakhs would be in the city and sacrificed an animal "in an oriental fashion" for three hundred guests at a lunch that followed.[33] The Ottoman declaration of war on the Russian Empire in September 1787 made diplomacy with Kazakh leaders more urgent. In early 1788, Igel'strom learned from Muslim spies that Ottoman diplomats were active in Bukhara and that the khanate was preparing for war against Russia.[34] Faced with the task of securing the Orenburg military line, which stretched 1,650 miles from the Tobol River in western Siberia to the Caspian Sea, Igel'strom sought to compete with Bukhara and its Ottoman allies for the allegiance of Kazakhs. He issued a statement denying any religious basis for Muslims' conflict with Russia because Catherine allowed the free observance of the "Muhammadan law," supported Muslim clerics, and built mosques.[35]

New Muslim institutions emerged from this competition among the Russian empress, the Bukharan khan, and the Ottoman sultan. On May 31, Igel'strom convinced the State Council of the need to confirm Muslim teachers, imams, and akhunds in their posts and proposed that a commission established in Ufa certify their qualifications.[36] In September 1788, Catherine approved legislation that called for the creation of an "Ecclesiastical Assembly of the Muhammadan Creed."[37] Above all, Igel'strom and Catherine created the Ecclesiastical Assembly in an attempt to limit the number of clerics and reduce foreign influence on local religious elites.[38] According to an official in Igel'strom's administration, the assembly would "cut off intrigues of the Bukharans . . . among the simpleminded Russian Muslims."[39] The assembly was to make sure that all Muslim religious officials were loyal and "of good conduct" by testing prospective clerics' knowledge of Muslim law and ritual. Those who passed the examination were sent to the provincial administration for confirmation of their status. In order to combat the influence of foreign clerics, each candidate had to present a certificate from local police officials demonstrating that he resided in the place where he sought to be an imam.

The assembly's role beyond testing and confirming clerics remained vague and sometimes contradictory in Igel'strom's legislative projects. He specified the appointment of a mufti but did not elaborate on his qualifications. Law required that the assembly's three judges (variously *chlens, zasedatels, kaziis,* or *kadiis* in Cyrillic, or *qādīs* in Tatar) be loyal Kazan Tatar mullahs, but he specified neither their selection nor their relationship with the mufti. Igel'strom gave the assembly power to resolve issues including "circumcision, marriage, divorce, and servitors of the mosque" according to sharia law, yet in subsequent articles he insisted that marriage law among local Muslims must be made like that "observed among European countries" and restricted the assembly's authority over the building and staffing of mosques.[40] Igel'strom mandated that all the assembly's written matters be in both Russian and Tatar. Despite the assembly's jurisdiction over all Muslims of the eastern part of the empire, the assembly was subordinated to the Ufa governor-general. The mufti and officials of the assembly received state salaries, but ordinary clerics mostly served without salaries or benefits. Over time, the institution became known as the Orenburg Muhammadan Ecclesiastical Assembly, or OMEA. With its opening, the imperial state acquired access to a crucial sphere of Muslim life.[41] As Robert Crews points out, Igel'strom intended that the OMEA would decide cases involving Muslim religious law and would enforce clerical discipline in a manner similar to the Orthodox Church.[42] Although inspired by the example of the Orthodox Church and influenced by religious administration in the Ottoman Empire and Bukhara, imperial officials created something novel in the OMEA. For instance, the senate allowed the election of three judges from among the Kazan Tatars, subject to the confirmation of Kazan's provincial governor.[43] No Russian Orthodox clergy or bishops were elected.

Neither all Muslim elites nor all imperial officials in Bashkiria favored Igel'strom's policies toward Islam. Khusainov's appointment divided Muslims. Some completely rejected the assembly as an illegitimate intervention of imperial officials into Muslim life.[44] Others accepted the institution in principle but rejected the leadership of Mufti Khusainov as corrupt and arrogant. He had many opponents among educated Muslims and imperial officials.[45] In December 1788 one of Igel'strom's subordinates, Colonel D. Grankin, claimed that Khusainov had collected oaths of support for the empress in 1786 only through deceit and bribery. Kazakhs were "so wild," Grankin argued, that they almost never worshiped in mosques.[46] Igel'strom vigorously denied such allegations. Many border troops and their leaders believed that there was "no other way to cope with Kazakhs than to kill them," Igel'strom wrote, and such military men disliked him since he had acted to curb the troops' excesses.[47]

The belief that imperial institutions and practices could transform people lay at the basis of Catherine's and Igel'strom's policies. Igel'strom agreed with the empress that the art of serving as governor-general consisted "not only in ruling everything with force and military power" but in achieving respect for the government through a sufficiently "gentle and firm" application of the law that "even the wildest peoples acquire trust in the good of the empire."[48] Muslim elites must be made to identify with the Russian emperor rather than with Bukharan or Ottoman authority by use of legal, religious, and cultural means. By 1800, the assembly had confirmed 1,900 men in religious posts, and the assembly's leadership acquired some privileges within the empire's evolving system of estates. Mufti Khusainov was allowed to buy Bashkir land and to own serfs, for instance.[49]

The OMEA gave Muslims an institution whose officials spoke their own language and thus provided the tsarist state with a Muslim face. The OMEA promoted a uniform interpretation of Muslim law through examinations for the position of imam, defined the boundaries of the religious community, and "took upon itself the traditional role of Islamic states: the enforcement of the sharia."[50] In the Russian Empire as in British India, Muslim jurists determined that regimes that permitted the function of Islamic legal procedure—daily prayer in mosques, celebration of religious feasts, and pilgrimage to Mecca—could be considered part of *dar al-Islam*, the house of Islam, and thus were legitimate.[51] In the decades after the OMEA's founding, some Muslims did begin to identify with the empire even if the assembly had "superficial" ties with mosques and "modest" resources, and many mullahs remained active without official confirmation.[52]

BASHKIR CANTONAL ADMINISTRATION

As important as imperial officials' relationships with Muslim clerics were, Igel'strom believed that Bashkir support was essential to maintaining the vast Orenburg military line. So, in 1789 he began to draw upon local precedents—the organization of Cossacks—to begin to develop what became known as the cantonal system of Bashkir administration. As introduced in 1798, cantonal administration refashioned Bashkirs as a militarized estate group that provided a relatively inexpensive way to staff the border separating the empire from Kazakhs and Central Asia. At the same time, military organization would better control Bashkirs, shift Bashkir communities from clan toward territorial organization that reflected the empire's administrative divisions, and systematize Bashkirs' military service. Igel'strom promoted cantonal administration as a way to draw on Bashkir military traditions but to redirect Bashkirs' martial energy toward the empire's rivals, while preserving Bashkirs' connection to their land and their distinctive legal status.

Efforts to rationalize and territorialize Bashkir organization came first. Bashkir volosts had long proven themselves resilient to the imperial state's intervention. In the mid-eighteenth century, however, pressure from in-migrants and lives lost in military conflicts caused the volost structure to begin to break down into smaller units, called tiubas in Bashkir, which Nepliuev had called commands (komands). These units were not territorial but tribal in organization. A Bashkir might live in the command of one elder but come from a different clan and have land rights in that clan's command.[53] Such a system served the needs of Bashkirs, but it did not provide the steady source of recruits and taxes that Governor-General Igel'strom required. Wealthy Bashkirs took advantage of diffuse authority to avoid service and sent in their places poor men who often lacked sufficient horses, weapons, and food.[54] Such recruits provided little security. In an effort to mobilize Bashkir troops more systematically and to receive better men, Igel'strom enumerated Bashkir and Meshcheriak households and fixed their locations in particular commands, which he now called *iurtas*, the word typically used for a nomadic tent. Igel'strom insisted that iurtas correspond to the empire's territorial division into provinces and counties. Iurtas that fell into more than one county were divided, increasing their number from 110 to 153.

Cantonal administration created a corps of Bashkir and Meshcheriak officials to help fix the nomadic or semi-nomadic population in the new territorial units. Igel'strom established the canton head (*nachal'nik*) as the leader of each of eleven Bashkir and five Meshcheriak cantons, situated between the Russian province and the Bashkir iurtas. Cantonal administration meant the creation of more than four hundred positions, including iurta elders and their assistants, who were freed from taxation and labor obligations but only began to receive salaries in 1840. Members of the cantons were supposed to elect canton heads and iurta elders, whom the military governor would then confirm. The extent to which the electoral principle actually was followed is not clear since many positions passed from father to son. Initially, imperial officials favored men who had demonstrated loyalty to the empire by working with it to suppress Bashkir rebellions in the eighteenth century, but not exclusively so.[55] The state thus reinforced the power of Bashkir elites and those of Meshcheriaks too, placing most Bashkirs and Meshcheriaks under the control of a man approved by the imperial officials and subject to a military officer in the emperor's army. Imperial administrators used the cantons to assign a man from one clan to lead the tiuba of another. Clans still existed, but reshuffling Bashkir leaders eroded clan cohesion. As one Russian administrator wrote, "the solidarity of the people was destroyed" and "uprisings were made inconceivable."[56]

Bashkirs and Meshcheriaks became a military force much like the Cossacks. There were many more Bashkir soldiers than Cossacks in Bashkiria, however, and Cossacks served on the Orenburg military line at higher rates than Bashkirs and Meshcheriaks did. Bashkirs and Meshcheriaks also lacked a permanently mobilized regiment.[57] Igel'strom ordered that canton heads and iurta elders gather every year with information on the number of men between the ages of twenty and fifty under their command. They must select Bashkirs for service on the Orenburg line "systematically" rather than simply choosing the poorest and least influential village members. One soldier would be drawn from about every four or five households, depending on the demand for troops. The soldier's iurta had to provide him with a horse, food, and equipment, worth a total of twenty-five to seventy-five kopecks per person, that would allow him to serve on the Orenburg line. Canton heads, iurta elders and their families, and Muslim clerics were exempt from service. The imperial administration gave cantonal leaders considerable powers to control canton members' movements, pursuing a dream of Kirilov and Nepliuev. Bashkirs required permission from the iurta elder to move within the canton and permission from canton heads to move within the province.[58] The tsarist state thus reconstituted the Bashkir service elite, moved Bashkirs from a clan to a territorial and political organization, and made them a more reliable military formation under better state control. Bashkir and Meshcheriak men would staff fortresses on the Orenburg line dividing the region from Central Asia at little cost to the state treasury.

AFTER CATHERINE

Although Catherine II's son Paul I (1796–1801) rejected much of what she held dear, his brief reign did little to change the pattern of elite formation and institutional development established before her death in 1796. Paul even reappointed Igel'strom as governor-general in Ufa, though he instructed Igel'strom on how to govern in a much more specific and often condescending style than his mother had.[59] Structural administrative changes resulted from officials' desires to move the border farther south and east. In 1796, the seat of the Ufa and Simbirsk administration shifted to Orenburg, which lay closer to the frontier. In 1802, Ufa became a provincial center with a civilian governor subordinate to a military governor in Orenburg. The military governor continued to have great authority in Bashkiria. He was responsible for the region's military forces, for the Bashkir cantons, and for conducting diplomacy in Central Asia.

In this administrative configuration Bashkiria experienced the reign of Paul's son, Alexander I (1801–1825). By 1801, the French Revolution had complicated representations of the tsar's authority and challenged the Russian Empire militarily. Alexander sought to reconcile Russia's autocracy and the challenge from France in two ways. First, he introduced governmental reforms intended "to centralize his administration and make it a more efficacious tool for change."[60] The "ministerial reform" that endeavored to introduce rational, hierarchical, and systematic government modeled on the structure of Napoleonic France was most notable in this respect. Alexander and his leading officials, such as Mikhail Speranskii, sought to transform "the personal power of officials" administering the provinces "into power vested in institutions."[61] The elites invited into Catherine's golden age now were often expected to don a uniform in state service. Second, after Napoleon's invasion of Russia in 1812, Alexander's "gaze rose to the heavens," and he "began to strive for the spiritual rather than the earthly betterment of his subjects."[62]

Imperial officials' growing concern for the spiritual betterment of Alexander's subjects became clear in the increased institutional presence of both Russian Orthodoxy and Islam in Bashkiria and in their stronger connections to St. Petersburg. In 1799, even before Paul I's assassination, a bishopric opened in Ufa. A seminary followed in 1800, although rapid growth in church construction did not occur until the 1820s.[63] Muslim institutions also acquired closer ties to the imperial center. In 1803, the OMEA ceased to report to the Orenburg military governor and became subordinate directly to the chief procurator of the Holy Synod, the lay leader of the Orthodox Church, until the Main Administration of Religious Affairs of Foreign Confessions was created in 1810. The number of mosques in Bashkiria grew rapidly and continued to dwarf the number of churches.[64] As the size and constituencies of the OMEA grew, so did Muslim clerics' responsibilities and the mufti's status. An 1804 decree permitted clerics to regulate marriage laws, including polygamy, and inheritance. Alexander I decreed that only the senate, the empire's highest court, would judge allegations against Mufti Khusainov.[65] The OMEA continued to participate in the enforcement of spiritual discipline that Alexander I valued highly.

BASHKIRS AND LAND

The desire for an empire of reason under Alexander I is nowhere clearer than in land policy. The Charter to the Nobility and the rise of a money economy in the eighteenth century brought a greater need to demarcate and record landholdings. State officials also sought to increase the utility of land by putting it in the hands of those who would make the best use of it. Toward this end, Alexander, guided by his "unofficial committee," decreed in December 1801 that all subjects of the emperor other than serfs could own real property. For the first time, the land of the realm ceased to be the monopoly of the tsar and his ruling class.[66] Many other groups could now enjoy the type of hereditary landowning that Bashkirs had been afforded. The General Survey, begun in 1766, was intended to survey and demarcate all the empire's land. Bashkiria's pattern of landownership needed straightening out at least as much as that in any other part of the empire. As discussed in chapter 2, Kirilov's decree of February 1736 allowed nobles, officers, and Meshcheriaks to purchase Bashkir land and had promised the land of disloyal Bashkirs to loyal Meshcheriaks, Teptiars, and service Tatars. Provincial officials had endeavored to resolve such claims at least five times, but without success.[67] Bashkiria's administration simply was not up to regulating land transfers. Nobles and servitors also took advantage of Bashkirs' unfamiliarity with the market to purchase vast tracts of vaguely demarcated land for next to nothing, using gifts, intimidation, and alcohol to expedite the process. Bashkirs sometimes sold the same parcels of land to more than one person, leaving titles unclear. Some nobles resold land without titles, further muddying ownership. A morass of land claims had to be resolved.

In discussions of how to rationalize landholding and to introduce firm notions of property, a shift in imperial officials' perceptions of Bashkirs became clear. For the first time since the 1730s, officials argued that Bashkir interests ought to be protected. When the question of including Bashkir land in the General Survey arose in the 1790s, Bashkirs petitioned for exemption and asked that surveyors demarcate their land only from that of others. Since Bashkirs owned large amounts of land but had few other resources, the survey—funded by a tax on owners of land surveyed—would impose a great burden on them. Baron Igel'strom concurred that the survey's cost to the Bashkirs indeed would be great and that "in deference to their nomadic lives" Bashkir land should be marked off only from "outside owners." In 1824, the government found for Bashkirs in all cases where non-Bashkirs lacked proper title to the land and dropped efforts to reward loyal supporters in the war of 1735–1740.[68] The state's priority was the integrity of Bashkir hereditary landholding.[69] Imperial officials did not forget Bashkirs' past propensity to rebel, but Bashkir actions in the first half of the eighteenth century no longer determined how they would be treated in law.

The state's new paternalism toward Bashkirs and their lands became evident in 1818 legislation that forbade the sale of Bashkir land. A government that valued rational order and control no longer tolerated the chaotic transfer of Bashkir land. According to Senator Obrezkov, who was sent to inspect Orenburg province in 1810, Bashkirs' "bad morality" and "penchant for strong drink" had caused them to sell tens of thousands of des. of land for a pittance. Bashkirs' situation had deteriorated to the point that they might not have sufficient land to support their service on the Orenburg line. Obrezkov proposed that Bashkirs be allowed to sell substantial quantities of land only with the military governor's approval. Obrezkov's concern was for the state's interest, not for the tsar's Bashkir subjects, but his statement called into question the utility of dispossessing the Bashkirs. When General Essen became Orenburg's governor-general in 1818, he took Obrezkov's ideas a step further. Observing that endless arguments over landownership overwhelmed local authorities, he proposed a complete ban on Bashkir land sales.[70] The senate granted his request fairly quickly in October 1818, even though he was thought to command little respect or influence in St. Petersburg.[71]

The Bashkir contribution to the war against Napoleon in 1812 and Alexander I's visit to Bashkiria in 1824 showed the great extent to which perceptions of Bashkirs and their place in the empire had changed since the Pugachev Rebellion. Regular Bashkir military service on the Orenburg line had begun in 1754. Typically, 5,000–6,000 men appeared for service annually. Bashkir military service continued even in times of political turmoil. The military mobilized 7,000 Bashkirs to Prussia and Poland in the early stages of the Napoleonic war. Alexander I's June Manifesto calling on his subjects to defend the fatherland against Napoleon was translated into Chagatay and announced in mosques. Bashkirs and Meshcheriaks eventually contributed 10,000 men, each with two horses, to Alexander's army that defeated Napoleon. Observers as varied as Englishman Sir Robert Wilson and Russian composer Sergei Glinka wrote of Bashkirs' eagerness to defend Russia and their performance in battle.[72] The Bashkir contribution to the all-imperial mobilization against Napoleon looms large among Bashkir contributions to the empire. Nearly a century later, when Bashkir man of letters Mukhametsalim I. Umetbaev identified "Dark and Light Days of the Bashkir People," the Bashkir contribution to the empire's victory was prominent among the "light days."[73] Bashkirs had fought with the emperor's forces before, but never in the numbers and effectiveness that they showed against the French.

Alexander I's trip to Bashkiria in September 1824, in turn, demonstrated his concern for the region and its people. Alexander reviewed Cossack and Bashkir troops in Orenburg, praising the cleanliness and neatness of their ranks.[74] On his way from Orenburg to Ufa, Alexander lunched in a Bashkir village, where he sampled the Bashkir "national dish," *bisbarmak*—the meat of a colt prepared with fat, onions, and garlic—and recommended it to his entourage. Although the visit demonstrated both Alexander's fallibility and the occasional failure of his subjects to observe protocol, a member of his suite, D. K. Tarasov, wrote that Alexander loved the region's residents, in whom he noted "a particular original-ity." People expressed their loyalty to the monarch and rapture at his visit by traveling hundreds of miles to be in his presence and to kiss the ground over which he passed.[75] Rebelliousness no longer defined Bashkirs, and Bashkiria was no longer a distant land. Both were constituents of the empire and the subject of central authorities' concern.

NICHOLAS I

Nicholas I, whose long reign (1825–1855) began with the Decembrist Revolt, became best known for his role in suppressing the revolutions of 1848 abroad, smothering dissent at home, and promoting "Official Nationality"—"Orthodoxy, Autocracy, and Nationality (*narodnost'*)." Officials during Nicholas's reign certainly sought to preserve autocracy, bolster Orthodoxy, and introduce national ideas that Russian intellectuals debated. Yet state policy in the east was neither fundamentally conservative, nor exclusively Orthodox, nor ethnically national. Nicholas's reign showed important continuities with his predecessors' with respect to co-opting non-Russian elites and fitting them into the empire's hierarchy of estates, supporting Islam, and creating rational, systematic administration that could integrate Bashkiria firmly in the empire. Officials presented Russia as an empire in which all peoples had a place. Stepan Shevyrev, an influential proponent of Official Nationality, articulated the mission of the Ministry of Education:

> To bring education in our fatherland under the law of state unity; to encompass in this education, as its great center, the fundamental Russian people, and at the same time to include together with it peoples of different languages and religions which are linked to us by means of the state union and which as radii join the central core of the Russian people.[76]

At the local level, Nicholas I's officials sought to include Bashkiria's peoples in the empire's social system and administration to an unprecedented extent.

The administration of faith played a large role in the effort to draw men into the empire's elite and to build institutions which could bring rational governance and order to the eastern borderlands. The OMEA continued to regulate Islamic practice, acquiring more resources and central direction in order to do so. Beginning in 1828, mullahs had to collect information on births, deaths, marriages, and divorces in all Muslim communities and record them in metrical books, giving clerics the same function that Orthodox clergymen acquired in 1724.[77] In 1829, legislation instructed Muslim clerics to collect a thirty-kopeck marriage fee and forward it to the OMEA, providing the institution with a small income. In 1832, when the Main Administration of Religious Affairs of Foreign Confessions became a department in the Ministry of Internal Affairs, the OMEA became subordinate to it. The OMEA's staff grew in number, its procedures were codified, and it continued to interpret sharia as a means to regulate family life.[78] Muftis continued the process of incorporating the empire into Muslim religious practices. Mention of the tsar in Friday prayers, known in Islam as "the right of *khutba*," became institutionalized at the time of Nicholas I's elevation to the throne. An imam's inclusion of a ruler in the khutba signified his recognition that the ruler's political authority was legitimate, while omission of a ruler signified nonrecognition of that leader's legitimacy.[79] Khusainov's successor, Gabdessaliam Gabdrakhimov, a man regarded as much more devout and better respected by scholars than Khusainov, called upon Muslims to give thanks to God for the tsar and to pray for him every morning and night as well as every Friday in the mosque.[80] By the 1840s, the requirement that imams receive official confirmation seems to have become a normal part of Islamic life.[81]

In 1848, the tsarist administration took steps to make the OMEA's Muslim clerics more similar, if not equal, in status to Russian Orthodox clergy by granting privileges previously given only to clerics in Bashkir cantons. Minister of State Domains Count Kiselev noted that, despite the policy of religious toleration initiated by Catherine II and Muslim clerics' "extremely high level of influence" among Muslims, the government had "no way of tying [the clerics] more closely to the state." Subjecting all but the highest members of the Muslim clerisy to corporal punishment and conscription had "inculcated a wholly disagreeable disposition" toward Russian authority. Therefore, in 1849, Kiselev proposed that Muslim clerics receive the personal exemption from corporal punishment and conscription that Orthodox clergy and their families enjoyed. Some officials remained suspicious of Kiselev's plan, but the State Council ratified his proposal in 1850.[82] Under Nicholas I, central officials aimed to anchor tsarist authority more firmly in Bashkiria by extending estate privileges found across the empire to local Muslims. Muslims continued to have their noble status restored under Nicholas, though at lower rates than under Alexander I.[83] In 1843, Muslims were permitted to become hereditary Honored Citizens (*pochetnye grazhdane*).[84]

At the same time, changes in Bashkiria's strategic position and perceptions of Bashkirs caused some imperial officials to begin to question the need for a distinctive Bashkir status. The dissolution of the Kazakh Middle Horde in 1822 and the Smaller Horde in 1824 decreased the military importance of Bashkir service on the Orenburg line. At the beginning of the 1830s, officials began to emphasize not Bashkirs' rebelliousness and military utility but their morality. Minister of the Emperor's Court Petr M. Volkonskii, who had jurisdiction over three Bashkir cantons, wrote that Bashkir morality was "rotten to the extreme." He considered "laziness, perfidy, and cunning" to be Bashkirs' innate qualities.[85] Orenburg governor-general Pavel Sukhtelen (served April 1830–March 1833) echoed Volkonskii's appraisal, writing that Bashkirs were "immoral, but clever people" with "no loyalty to the government." Bashkirs' lack of morality showed itself most in a plague of horse theft. As sales of Bashkir land to inmigrants broke up large expanses of land necessary for semi-nomadic pastoralism, some found it more profitable to steal horses than to grow crops. According to Volkonskii, in three counties alone Bashkirs had stolen 29,000 horses over ten years. Sukhtelen could not see how such banditry could exist in "a well-run state."[86]

Such concerns stimulated discussions of Bashkirs as a *people* and reform of their status at the highest levels of government. Behind consideration of reform lay the belief that proper legal and administrative arrangements could make Bashkir service correspond to the empire's new strategic position with respect to Central Asia and improve Bashkir morality. Emperor Nicholas established a "Committee for the Review of Proposals on the Administration of Bashkirs" in 1831 under the State Council's authority. The committee included Volkonskii and some of the emperor's most distinguished servitors, such as its chairman, Viktor Kochubei, a member of Alexander's "unofficial committee"; Mikhail Speranskii, author of a reform of Siberian administration in 1822; the minister of interior; and the minister of justice. Committee members showed respect for established practices of Bashkir administration. Chairman Kochubei sought to avoid provoking rebellion among people "of another faith" in an area where "calm" had been preserved with "so little effort."[87] The committee confirmed that Bashkirs owned their land—they would not try to identify and dispossess Bashkir rebels after ninety-six years. But Bashkir land did not bring "the state any sort of benefit" due to Bashkirs' nomadic life, and Bashkir landholding needed to be addressed.[88] Officials now perceived Bashkirs' relationships with their neighbors differently, too. Eighteenth-century officials had considered Bashkirs different from and often hostile to Kazakhs. The Bashkir Committee now concluded that Kazakhs were quite like Bashkirs in "morals, customs, and faith."[89] The general staff concluded that Bashkirs were a "half-wild people" who, "like all Muhammadans," did not believe in the actions of a "Christian government." Bashkirs were so "infected with fanaticism" that the slightest dissatisfaction inclined them to rebellion.[90] Other officials simply lumped Bashkirs together with the other non-Slavic peoples as "Asiatic." Such perspectives and labels were not new, but they found fuller expression here than they had before.

Committee members believed that Bashkirs' morality and productivity would increase and their hostility would decrease if their distinctiveness as an estate status group were reduced. Prince Volkonskii wrote that the state must "weaken in [Bashkirs] the opinion that they make up a particular people."[91] This meant applying to Bashkirs statuses characteristic of the empire as a whole. Minister of Finance Egor L. Kankrin argued that

> Unity and uniformity of administration are the sole means for managing the affairs of so extensive a state as the Russian Empire. Any [exception] without extreme necessity, hampers the conduct of government and is even harmful to private persons. . . . Orenburg Province does not present circumstances that require a special type of administration.[92]

This approach to Bashkirs differed from that shown by Bashkir Committee member Speranskii in the 1820s, when he wrote a statute for the administration of Siberian peoples and Kazakhs.[93] Bashkir Committee members considered the morals of a people such as Bashkirs, who had been the tsar's subjects for much longer than Siberian peoples or Kazakhs, in more urgent need of correction. The committee sought to minimize differences between them and other peoples.

The Bashkir Committee did not, however, advocate abrupt action. It concluded that over the next fifty to sixty years, "Bashkir" ought to become a civil estate subject to the same soul tax and military service obligations as Kazan Tatars, while Bashkirs who lived close to the military line should merge with the Cossacks. Bashkirs in military service could attain noble status in order to ensure "obedience and tranquility" among them.[94] Landholding lay at the heart of committee members' visions of Bashkir status. If Bashkirs were to become subjects of the emperor on the same terms as other subjects, they needed appropriate parcels of land on which to practice agriculture and the example of people who knew how to farm. Permitting Bashkirs to sell their land once again would lead to less nomadic pastoralism and to more contact with Russian agriculturalists, would "soften the wildness" of Bashkir "morals," and would root them in the empire's social order.[95] The senate decree issued on April 10, 1832, sought to balance the redistribution of Bashkir land to in-migrants with the preservation of Bashkirs' own landholdings. The law ended the 1818 ban on Bashkir land sales but recognized Bashkirs as owners of "all those lands that had indisputably belonged to them." In order that land sales not harm Bashkir communities, paternalistic measures limited Bashkirs' ability to alienate their land. Bashkir land sales had to be approved by two-thirds of volost residents, and Bashkir volosts had to retain at least 40–60 des. of land per soul. If a volost lacked 40 des. per soul, none of its land could be sold. Legislation introduced the position of communal representative (*poverenny*) to help arrange land sales and to balance the influence of elders on land transactions. Finally, one-third of the sum received from sales of Bashkir land constituted "communal capital," often referred to as "Bashkir capital." The Orenburg military governor, the "guardian of Bashkirs and keeper of their welfare," could use Bashkir capital to help those who suffered from fire or accidents, to educate Bashkir youth, and to maintain cantonal administrations.[96] The committee of ministers addressed horse theft separately, giving the Orenburg governor-general authority to conscript Bashkir and Meshcheriak horse thieves or to exile them to Siberia.[97]

In the end, despite Bashkir Committee members' stated desire to reduce the distinctiveness of Bashkir status, their legislation left Bashkirs in military cantons with their particular administration. When Sukhtelen died in early 1833, the Bashkir Committee instructed his replacement, Vasilii A. Perovskii, to plan for broader reform of Bashkir administration. Perovskii demurred, arguing that reform on a grand scale was premature. He opted for "not such shining, but more reliable improvements."[98] He preferred that Bashkirs remain a military estate.[99]

PLAYING THE ROLE OF SULTAN

Indeed, Perovskii had little incentive to seek reform. Thanks to "Bashkir capital" and the continued existence of Bashkir cantons, Orenburg governors commanded many more human and financial resources than their predecessors had only a few decades before. According to a military officer in Orenburg, Nikolai G. Zalesov, military governors distant from the imperial capitals possessed "extraordinary authority" and tremendous financial and material resources for which they were accountable to no one. So, a man charged with bringing the empire of reason to Bashkiria could also "play the role of sultan in his area."[100] The "sultans" who dominated Orenburg for most of Nicholas's reign were Perovskii (governed 1833–1842, 1851–1857), who led Russian forces in an unsuccessful campaign against Khiva in 1839, and Vladimir A. Obruchev (governed 1842–1851), who had distinguished himself in actions against Turkey and in Poland in 1828–1831. Perovskii played the role of sultan to the fullest.[101] A subordinate later described Perovskii as a bachelor who had "a broad Slavic nature in the full sense of the word, with all its qualities and defects." He captivated Orenburg society with his generosity and with the grand balls he hosted. He recruited to serve in Orenburg talented, cosmopolitan young men, such as Vladimir Dal', a Lutheran of Danish and German descent who, while in Orenburg, learned the Tatar language and began to collect materials that would make up part of his monumental Russian dictionary.[102] To avoid the summer heat in Orenburg, Perovskii invited Bashkir canton heads, their subordinates, members of Orenburg society, visiting dignitaries, and scholars to stay at what he called his kochevka—a Bashkir nomadic summer encampment—about sixty miles from the city. There he furnished elaborate meals to the sounds of Bashkirs playing traditional instruments. Perovskii was popular among Bashkirs, for whom he put on festivals, horse races, and banquets in order to attract them "to the Russian state."[103] Perovskii described to the tsar his admiration of Bashkirs' "martial qualities: they are quick, agile, outstanding horsemen; they know neither fear nor fatigue, and blindly follow the will of commanders." He designed himself a frock coat in a Bashkir style.[104] Ivan V. Chernov, who was familiar with Orenburg governors from the 1830s until the end of the century, wrote that Pervoskii showed "solicitude" toward the Bashkirs unlike the "belittling" of those who came before and after him. He called Perovskii the best, smartest governor of them all.[105] Obruchev, by contrast, enjoyed a reputation as honest, but "despotic, petty, and extremely short-tempered." He ended Perovskii's lavish subsidy of local social life, and the "best of the intelligentsia" departed. Obruchev wanted to turn Orenburg society to a "more moral path" through modest and sedate social events. His real love, like that of his emperor, was the military parade ground—he held military parades on Sundays and all holidays.[106]

Men serving in Bashkir and Meshcheriak cantons became essentially a pool of labor that Orenburg administrators could exploit for their own purposes rather than for the cause of enlightened administration. Perovskii was particularly enterprising in his use of local resources to support his plans for the

FIGURE 3.1. "Campement de Bachkirs," from Charles de Saint-Julien,
Voyage pittoresque en Russie (Paris, 1852), 320.

province and his own needs. For instance, Perovskii built three potash factories
that burned wood from Bashkir land to produce potassium compounds for agricultural purposes. The three factories generated 100,000 rubles annually, all
under Perovskii's control.[107] Perovskii's campaign of 1839 that failed to defeat
the Khanate of Khiva at the fortress of Ak Mechet' required 8,000 Bashkirs,
causing Perovskii to enlist approximately twice as many Bashkirs as usual—one
of 5.5 men served rather than the one of 11 men in the two previous years. This
high level of service became routine in the 1840s under Obruchev. As fewer
Bashkir and Meshcheriak men were needed to serve on the Orenburg line, they
more frequently reported for demanding labor service. Under Perovskii in the
1830s, typically 70 percent of Bashkir men served on the Orenburg line. By contrast, in the 1840s, only about 15 percent of Bashkirs served on the line; the
remaining 85 percent reported for labor duty.[108] One of Bashkirs' most grueling
duties was to provide Orenburg with wood for heating. Bashkirs had to cut and
haul wood to a river, where they worked whole days in icy water floating logs to
the provincial capital. Local authorities then sold the wood for great sums. The
result, Zalesov recalled, was the stripping of forests, the despoilment of rivers,

and the "terrible ravaging of Bashkiria." Under Obruchev's frugal ways, funds from the sale of Bashkir lands went to the treasury, and Bashkirs "were turned completely into Negro-workers."[109]

Orenburg governors-general Sukhtelen, Perovskii, and Obruchev exploited Bashkir labor and money to construct major public buildings that demonstrated imperial grandeur and their own "sultanic" authority. Their sponsorship of mosque and church construction indicated continuities with Catherine's policy of toleration. Bishop Mikhail, who arrived in Ufa during Sukhtelen's tenure, considered Ufa a "suburb of Moscow" that should resemble Moscow as it had looked before Peter the Great. With Sukhtelen's support, Mikhail replaced the existing cathedral at the edge of Ufa with a new stone one in the town center, initiated construction of twenty-six churches, renovated the men's monastery, and began construction of a women's monastery. Ufa, however, would not resemble pre-Petrine Moscow. In 1830, Mufti Gabdessaliam Gabdrakhimov opened Ufa's first mosque on land in the center of Ufa, not far from Bishop Mikhail's cathedral.[110] Minarets joined bell towers over Ufa. When Bishop Mikhail asked Perovskii for assistance with missionary activity, Perovskii responded coldly.

> I am neither a bishop nor a missionary, but a military governor. My business is to maintain calm and order and [to ensure] that existing state laws and order not be violated in any way. The matter of the propagation and affirmation of the Christian faith belongs to the pastors of the Church, . . . and there must not be interference [in it] of any other authority.[111]

Perovskii invited Konstantin Thon, the designer of the massive Church of Christ the Savior in Moscow and a creator of the "national style" in church architecture, to design a building for the Orenburg Noble Assembly.[112] The building hosted local and touring performers who brought the latest European musical and theatrical culture to the steppe. Perovskii also sought to renovate the city of Orenburg. In 1835, he created a commission to survey the buildings and homes in Orenburg. Those deemed dilapidated were to be torn down and replaced by their owners with structures according to Perovskii's plans.[113]

Perovskii enthusiastically sought to create a Bashkir national style of architecture when he determined to build a "public Bashkir coach inn" or "caravanserai" to house Bashkir and Meshcheriak cantonal administrators required to be in Orenburg on official business.[114] Perovskii first requested from a Kazan architect a design as close as possible "to Asiatic taste," but he found that "even the mosque looks too much like a Christian cathedral."[115] Perovskii then turned to architect Alexander P. Briullov, who had renovated portions of the Winter Palace's interior, to design the building. In 1838, construction began just outside Orenburg on a complex of buildings that could accommodate twenty officers

FIGURE 3.2. "Main Mosque in Ufa from Sluchevskaia Hill. (Mufti's residence)"
Photograph by Sergei Prokudin-Gorskii, 1910. Library of Congress, Prints &
Photographs Division, Prokudin-Gorskii Collection, LC-DIG-prok-10553.
Orenburg mufti Gabdessaliam Gabdrakhimov successfully petitioned for
permission to construct the mosque and a residence for the mufti in 1827.
It was completed in 1830.

and up to a hundred troops. It included office space for the Bashkir administrative, medical, and support staff, a kitchen, a library, and an archive. An
octagonal mosque stood in the complex's large central courtyard. At one end
of the square, two-story structure stood a minaret nearly thirty-nine meters
high. Briullov modeled the mosque on a *tirme*—the elder's tent that stood at the
center of a Bashkir summer encampment. The mosque's design notably lacked
the mihrab, or apse, that typically indicates the direction of Mecca.[116] The mufti
selected verses from the Koran to be written on the walls in Arabic script. In
September 1846, Obruchev celebrated the opening of the mosque. The event,
Obruchev stated, showed Muslims the state's commitment to toleration: "The
government, watching over the welfare of peoples of all faiths professed in the
empire, cares about the well-being of their temples, desiring that everyone devote himself to the rules of his religion as the source of good deeds." The local

Мечеть въ Караванъ-Сараѣ.

FIGURE 3.3. Mosque in the Caravanserai, Orenburg. *Trudy Orenburgskoi Uchenoi Arkhivnoi Komissii,* vol. 18 (1907), opposite page 82. The mosque is part of a complex of buildings built to serve as a headquarters for Bashkir military units. Prominent St. Petersburg architect Alexander P. Briullov designed the mosque to resemble the elder's tent that stood at the center of a Bashkir summer encampment. The eight-sided mosque lacks the mihrab, the niche in the mosque that typically indicates the direction of Mecca. The mosque, with its thirty-nine-meter minaret, was completed in 1846.

military leadership attended a Muslim prayer service in the mosque. Russians, Bashkirs, and representatives from the Kazakh Hordes gathered for horse races, wrestling matches, and a military parade including Muslim peoples in native dress. The day featured a "banquet characteristic of Asiatics."[117] Both the caravanserai and the mosque in Ufa set in stone that Bashkirs and Muslims were constituents of the empire.

MAINTAINING ORDER AND SHAPING LIVES

Under Nicholas I, the imperial state's interventions to rationalize Bashkir life were the most forceful and far-reaching yet. Led by Perovskii, tsarist officials created an increasingly centralized military administration that aspired to regulate Bashkirs' political, social, and economic life. In 1834, Perovskii created the Bashkir-Meshcheriak Host out of the twelve Bashkir and five Meshcheriak cantons. Canton heads, instead of reporting directly to the governor-general, now had an additional military officer supervising them. Bashkirs were transferred from civil to military courts, with a special official appointed to sort out land disputes.[118] In 1836, the host was divided into six "guardianships" subordinate to the host's commander. Bashkir guardians were typically Russian-speaking staff officers assigned to supervise the cantons' moral and economic status. Assisted by a scribe and a translator, they monitored and reported disorders, adjudicated minor criminal matters, and worked to improve the economy and tax collection in the cantons. The institution of the guardian showed the influence of military colonies, an effort started by Alexander I to create orderly and prosperous rural settlements through the application of military discipline.[119]

After these moves increased military control over the cantons, in the 1840s and 1850s the cantons were subdivided to reduce further the power of Bashkirs to resist imperial officials' plans. By 1856, the Bashkir Host included 28 cantons and 394 iurtas, supervised by nine guardians. The number of iurtas in some cantons as much as doubled, and the staff at the cantonal level and below totaled 680 positions, including scribes, translators, and assistants.[120] The new, smaller iurtas bore little relation to the older volosts. Elders of the smaller iurtas, which often included members of various clans, were oriented toward the state that they served rather than their standing in their clans. The breakdown of clan ties between Bashkirs and their political elite made organized rebellion much less likely.[121] As an officer in the Bashkir administration later wrote, "in the half century before 1840, Bashkirs were made into peaceful and loyal subjects" of the tsar.[122] As Bashkir administrative units were broken down, imperial officials amalgamated Bashkirs with other groups to reduce Bashkir particularity and simplify administration. Whereas in the eighteenth century, the imperial state had sought to distinguish groups according to how they served, it now sought to unite diverse peoples into larger status groups. State officials began to switch Bashkir and Meshcheriak cantons distant from the fortified line from military service obligations to taxable status.[123] In 1855, imperial officials included Teptiars and Bobyls in the taxpaying cantons and renamed the Bashkir-Meshcheriak Host simply the Bashkir Host. All in the host would now be called Bashkirs unless there was a "need to distinguish the origins of people," in which case they should be called "Bashkirs from Meshcheriaks, Teptiars or Bobyls," and so on.[124]

The imperial administration's desire to rationalize non-Russian communities and to co-opt non-Russian elites came together in secular educational

FIGURE 3.4. Caravanserai Square, Orenburg. From a postcard, early twentieth century. The building of the Nepliuev Cadet School is in the upper left. The school was established in 1825. The building shown was constructed in 1872. The Bashkir caravanserai is in the upper right. Completed in 1846, the complex included the headquarters of the Bashkir Host.

programs for Muslims. Alexander I's government had opened a university in Kazan to increase the educational level of officials. Bashkiria did not receive a university, but plans for the region's most prestigious educational institution culminated in the opening of a military school in 1825. The Orenburg governor-general at the time, Petr K. Essen, asserted that the school would promote "rapprochement" of "Asiatics" with Russians, "instill in Asiatics love and trust in the Russian government," and provide "this distant land with bureaucrats" for military and civil service. In order to achieve "rapprochement," the school admitted the sons not only of officers and servitors in Orenburg but also of Kazakhs, Bashkirs, Meshcheriaks, and Tatars.[125] The school's first class contained twenty students—ten Muslims and ten non-Muslims. In 1840, Perovskii formally recognized the school's dual mission by renaming it the Nepliuev Cadet School, dividing it into "European" and "Asiatic" parts, and gaining for the school's graduates special rights to enter service. The school's curriculum included religious studies (Russian Orthodox and Islamic), reading and writing in the Russian, Tatar, Persian, and Arabic languages, history, science, and mathematics.[126] In 1832, a girls' section of the school was opened to educate daughters of military servitors. The school fulfilled its purpose to create a small bilingual elite that could become military officers, staff the civilian bureaucracy, and serve as imperial intermediaries, even if conditions at the school were difficult because directors skimmed funds intended to support students.[127] In all, more than seventy Bashkirs and Meshcheriaks completed the program.[128] As the Nepliuev Cadet School drew non-Russians to the empire, it also drew the empire toward non-Russians by officially recognizing and teaching non-Russian languages and cultures.

The Nepliuev Cadet School was one part of a broader effort to prepare elite Muslim youth to serve as scribes, elders, and bilingual administrators in the Bashkir Host. In the 1840s, Bashkirs were also granted sixteen places in the Moscow Military Academy. To address shortages of personnel who could provide medical care to the Muslim population and to draw Bashkirs closer to Russians, Military Governor Sukhtelen sent four Russian-literate Bashkirs to Kazan University in 1832. Mufti Gabdrakhimov wrote a fatwa supporting this policy.[129] In 1836, Perovskii expanded and formalized it. The Bashkir-Meshcheriak Host's administration began to sponsor up to twenty men to study at the Kazan *Gimnasium* with the goal of placing them eventually in the Kazan University Medical School. After a number of men ended up studying Oriental languages, students were forbidden to switch from medicine to any other discipline.[130] The number of Muslim students from Bashkiria at Kazan University remained small—ten to twenty annually—as some slots went unfilled. Even fewer successfully completed the program.[131] Still, the Bashkir administration introduced higher education, Western medicine, and new careers to a population that had previously lacked them.

Service, noble status, and education combined to create a small but influential Muslim elite in Bashkiria in the mid-nineteenth century. The most central element of status was service. Cantonal administration became the means for many Bashkir and Meshcheriak canton heads, iurta elders, and their families to receive salaries and privileges such as exemption from active military service, freedom from corporal punishment, and even noble status.[132] Such opportunities for enlightenment often came at the expense of ordinary Bashkirs, however. Because Bashkir canton heads and iurta elders served without salaries before 1834, squeezing ordinary Bashkirs for resources was a way of life. Canton heads could take bribes for resolving legal disputes and for protecting Bashkir men from service on the Orenburg line. As Leila Tagirova puts it, "a canton head would not be able to hold onto his post without 'bribery and corruption.'" Some supplemented this income through other economic activity. By 1834, only three Bashkir canton heads had managed to become individual landowners, since converting Bashkir collective landownership to one's own purposes was difficult. Many more Bashkir canton heads owned gristmills or potash factories (42 percent in 1834) than land (16 percent). After Bashkir canton heads began to receive salaries of 185 rubles, 90 kopecks in 1840, they shifted from mills and factories toward landowning.[133] Noble status proved a common reward for canton heads. By 1850, 590 Bashkirs and 69 Meshcheriaks who served as army officers in the fourteenth and twelfth levels of the Table of Ranks had earned noble status, even as state officials sought to limit Bashkir movement into the nobility after 1845.[134] Much more than Bashkir elders in the eighteenth century, the status of Bashkir canton heads derived from the tsarist administration rather than from traditional prestige or support from ordinary Bashkirs.[135]

The cases of the Sultanov, Umetbaev, and Syrtlanov families illustrate how one's position in Bashkir cantonal administration could lead to social advancement. The Sultanov family joined the nobility in the period 1818–1832 when one family member served as head of the eleventh Bashkir canton. This favored one of its members, Mukhamed'iar, for enrollment in Kazan University. Mukhamed'iar dropped out of the university but later became the Orenburg mufti from 1885 to 1915. Ishmukhamet Umetbaev was an ordinary Bashkir from the eighth canton who began service in 1819. His knowledge of the Tatar language and some Russian landed him a position as scribe to the head of the canton. In 1836, he himself took over as the canton's head. In 1861, Umetbaev received the order of St. Stanislav, third class, for his service, and he entered the Ufa nobility in 1865. His military rank helped him place his son, Mukhametsalim, in Orenburg's Nepliuev Cadet School in 1852. Mukhametsalim succeeded as a student of Russian, Persian, and Tatar languages. He eventually became a translator for the OMEA as well as a writer, a translator of Pushkin into Turkic languages, and a collector of Bashkir folklore.[136] Shaikhgard Syrtlanov, born in 1801, became head of the twelfth canton in 1837, served with distinction, and became a nobleman in 1865. He was a neighbor of the Tevkelev family, and his eldest son, Arslanbek, married the daughter of Ishmukhamet Umetbaev. His son Shakhaidar graduated from the Nepliuev Cadet School in the 1860s and served as prefect of Samarkand after the Russian conquest of that city. Shakhaidar returned to Belebei County after falling out with Turkestan governor-general von Kaufman in 1873. Shakhaidar first served under Orenburg governor-general Kryzhanovskii, then in the zemstvo, and finally as a deputy to the first State Duma.[137] His son Galiaskar, born in 1875, graduated from the Aleksandrovskii Military-Juridical Academy and then served as a military lawyer in St. Petersburg and assistant to the military prosecutor in Kiev. In 1861, another Kazan University graduate, Akhmet'ian Abdiev, graduated from the Petersburg Medical-Surgical Academy and became the first Bashkir Doctor of Medicine in the Russian Empire.[138]

Muslim nobles not of Bashkir origin joined Bashkirs in using imperial educational institutions as the basis for careers in the imperial system. Mukhammedakram M. Biglov's and Mirsalikh Bikchurin's families both had their noble status restored under Catherine II. This status helped them to enroll in the Nepliuev Cadet School. The combination of status and education enabled Biglov to become a land captain and chairman of the Belebei County zemstvo in the 1870s. Bikchurin taught Eastern languages at the Nepliuev Cadet School for thirty years, published a Tatar textbook, and earned the rank of general.[139] Others from prominent families made use of educational opportunities to build careers in military, state, or public service.

Certainly not all Muslims or Bashkirs who served in the Bashkir administration attained such success, and they remained poor relative to nobles not of Bashkir or Muslim origins. The combination of service, status, and education in Bashkiria, however, allowed a non-Russian elite to live relatively well. Their households had multiple buildings with glass windows and bathhouses, along with barns for storage and for keeping horses. They cooked and served on copper utensils and ate from porcelain dishes stored behind glass in cabinets.[140] One Bashkir canton head, Mirgaliautdin Reziapov, left an estate worth 300,000 rubles, including two potash factories and six gristmills, when he died in 1851. Mukhametsalim Umetbaev's father, who had become a canton head in 1836, left a more modest 2,500 rubles of real estate when he died in 1861.[141] Beyond the everyday, Bashkir canton heads at times would receive valuable gifts as rewards for service and, in a few cases, had an audience with the emperor or participated in prestigious events such as the "Royal Hunt" near Moscow that marked Alexander II's coronation in 1856.[142] Bashkir canton heads' prosperity is also evident from the fact that most, 63 percent, had more than one wife—a privilege only wealthy men could afford.[143] Bashkir elites' family connections helped to stabilize their positions and to increase their wealth. Over the period 1798–1834, 63 percent of Bashkir and Meshcheriak canton heads came from families of cantonal elites, and most married into families of other canton heads. Mukhametsalim Umetbaev, for instance, married Bibigabida, the daughter of canton head Reziapov.[144] The most enlightened of the cantonal elite spoke Russian and Tatar, as well as other languages such as Persian and Arabic, while only the rare exception was illiterate. During the period of cantonal administration, a largely hereditary Bashkir and Muslim governing elite formed in Bashkiria, one that used its position to gain wealth and reproduce its success. One commentator who identified himself as a Bashkir wrote in the journal *Sovremennik* (The contemporary) in 1863: "At the end of the past century, in the Bashkir midst petty officials appeared, and their number gradually multiplied, composing a sort of special caste (*osobuiu kastu*). . . . Out of religious persons formed a new, likewise gradually multiplying caste. In such a manner, the people (*narod*) was left by itself."[145] Ordinary Bashkirs and Muslims benefited little from the prosperity of the elite. They were the ones paying the bribes to and enduring abuse from the elite. They complained frequently about it.

Imperial officials did not simply seek to govern Bashkirs; they sought to transform and rationalize life in Bashkiria. Imperial officials quite explicitly believed they were extending the benefits of European—not specifically Russian—civilization to what they perceived as backward, Asiatic Russia. The Bashkir Host's efforts to restructure and rationalize Bashkir life intruded deeply into Bashkirs' lives. For a century, imperial officials had discussed making Bashkirs give up semi-nomadic pastoralism in favor of settled agriculture in order to make them more governable and productive. Before 1798, however, when Bashkirs did settle and practice agriculture, it was due to the loss of land to nobles and factories or to the loss of people and livestock in wars and rebellions, and their suppression. Bashkirs who had lost their herds or had them confiscated by imperial officials had no reason to migrate. With the creation of the Bashkir-Meshcheriak Host and the introduction of guardians in the 1830s, the imperial state for the first time had the apparatus to attempt to force Bashkirs to practice settled agriculture. Legislation in 1836 that created the post of guardian specified that guardians should "endeavor to have [Bashkirs] acquire a taste for proper agricultural activity and household management."[146] Perovskii was reluctant to try to transform Bashkir life in such a way, arguing that "The order of nomadism is not some sort of skill, founded on whim; to abolish it—means to destroy an entire people's economy."[147] Perovskii's successor, Obruchev, who took over in 1842, had no such hesitations. He pursued a number of strategies to force Bashkirs to practice agriculture. Obruchev gave stern warnings that Bashkirs would be severely punished if they sought to take their herds to distant pastures at times when sowing and harvesting hay or grain was required.[148] Canton heads, their staffs, and Bashkir guardians received instructions from the commander of the Bashkir Host to assign plots of land to particular Bashkirs, to instruct them in the three-field system, and to follow carefully their progress. In 1845, Obruchev ordered Bashkir cantons to grow seventy-two pounds of grain per person. In 1850, Obruchev raised the target to ninety-six pounds per person. Bashkirs were also instructed to grow vegetables and potatoes.

Cantons in Bashkiria's north and northwest and in the older agricultural centers around Menzelinsk and Birsk posed few problems. According to a survey in 1846, their residents all practiced settled agriculture. In the southern and southeastern parts of Bashkiria, however, the situation was quite different. In Orenburg Province east of the Urals, over 90 percent of the population of the fourth and sixth cantons, and over 80 percent of the population of Sterlitamak County, south of Ufa, were still considered semi-nomadic. These were the areas to which officials devoted the greatest attention and had the fewest results. When a similar survey was conducted in 1854, the overall number of semi-nomadic Bashkirs had dropped from 47.4 percent in 1846 to 42.8 percent in 1854. These overall numbers hide some substantial statistical variations, however. The population of the fifth canton, around Cheliabinsk, somehow went from 83.5 percent semi-nomadic to fully settled in only eight years. Other heavily semi-nomadic cantons in 1846 either showed little change or even saw increases in semi-nomadic pastoralism.[149] Pressure on Bashkirs to settle and to practice agriculture seemed to show success where semi-nomadic pastoralism was fading anyway. Officials' efforts were much less effective in areas where Bashkirs still practiced semi-nomadic pastoralism extensively. The cultivation of potatoes and vegetables grew fairly slowly, despite efforts to educate Bashkirs through demonstration gardens and the distribution of seeds.[150]

The physical reconstruction of Bashkir villages accompanied attempts to make Bashkirs sedentary, demonstrating the broad rationalizing drive underlying the new policies. Obruchev's effort to transform Bashkir villages was part of Minister of State Domains P. D. Kiselev's broader initiative in the 1830s to rationalize rural Russia and was also likely inspired by the military colonies first created in the 1810s.[151] Previously, as Pavel Nebol'sin recounted in 1854, "Bashkir villages in steppe cantons were absolutely not as orderly as we see now." Huts clung to creeks and streams, no matter how winding they were. Streets almost did not exist—they were uneven and curvy little alleys, "like labyrinths," that were difficult to pass through. Courtyards and gates were lacking.[152] Since seminomadic Bashkirs moved easily and often, they had established many villages in the previous few centuries only as places to spend the winter. A lack of European-style order in such villages is, therefore, not surprising. In 1843, Obruchev ordered that Bashkir settlements must be rebuilt on a grid pattern with houses twenty-two meters apart. Forges and bathhouses must be built away from farmsteads on the banks of a river or lake. Settlements in inconvenient locations were moved to more favorable places. By 1847, 515 villages had been redone. By 1850, nearly 30,000 new homes had been built, greatly increasing Bashkirs' living space. Smaller villages were consolidated into larger ones, making it easier for state officials to supervise Bashkirs effectively. One Bashkir, Usman syn Ishmukhameta, recalled in his memoirs that in 1842 he and his brother agreed to move back to the village where their deceased father had been registered. His own village later disappeared.[153]

Bashkir canton heads received instructions to make all Bashkir housing conform to Obruchev's plan. Their subordinates must monitor the cleanliness of streets, courtyards, rooms, and even the clothing of residents.[154] State inter-vention extended inside the home in other ways, too. At one point the Bashkir Guardianship learned that some Bashkir children suffered burns each year in stoves built low to the ground. Small children left unattended could accidentally fall in and be burned to death. So, the Bashkir Guardianship ordered Bashkirs to get rid of their low stoves and replace them with new "Holland stoves." Bash-kirs were unable to build the new stoves and were left in the cold. More children froze to death in the winter than had burned using the old stoves.[155] In another case, the Bashkir Guardianship sought to combat a syphilis epidemic by estab-lishing a hospital near the center of the outbreak. It did so by commandeering the huts of several Bashkir families, leaving young and old homeless.[156]

Policies aimed at rationalizing Bashkir life caused controversy even among Russian speakers. One observer wrote that the government's efforts to intro-duce order and agriculture had softened Bashkirs' former "unbridled and will-ful morals."[157] Others, such as Vasilii Grigor'ev, an official in the border admin-istration, opposed efforts to transform Bashkir life in such ways. To Grigor'ev, attempts to rationalize Bashkir lives simply made them worse. Semi-nomadic pastoralism was not compatible with growing cereals. Growing wheat required them to be at their winter quarters to sow seeds at just the time when cattle-raising dictated that they be farthest away. If Bashkirs remained near their win-ter quarters all year, their herds would suffer from lack of pasture. In trying both to grow grain and to raise cattle and horses Bashkirs did neither very successfully, which ruined their economies and left many poor and hungry.[158] Land surveying and sales to in-migrants reduced the size of Bashkir holdings, also making it difficult or impossible for Bashkirs to practice pastoralism as they had in the past. As a result Bashkirs often lived off land sales rather than agrarian pursuits. Overall, the ability of imperial officials to transform the way of life of hundreds of thousands of people in a few decades is questionable. Chernov, who served in the Bashkir military command, writes that in reality, Bashkirs did not change their way of life much, since "all measures [to do so] remained on paper."[159]

Even when well-intentioned initiatives did not cause death, Bashkirs greet-ed them with suspicion. In 1835, after several poor harvests threatened the region with famine, both the Bashkir Host and civilian authorities ordered all Bashkir, Meshcheriak, state peasant, and Teptiar settlements to construct grain storage facilities in order to prepare for future shortfalls. Constructing and filling grain stores burdened poor communities and particularly puzzled Bashkirs, who raised cattle and produced little grain in the first place. Sketches of the proposed facilities showed crossbeams and supports in the form of a cross, raising fears among some Muslims that the state intended to use the project as a cover for church construction. Some Russian Orthodox state peasants feared that the storage facilities were intended to house a rumored "Senator Medvedev," who, they feared, would become their new owner. The combination of such fears provoked an uprising of a total of 40,000 men, according to Perovskii, with most disturbances concentrated in the north and northeast of Orenburg Province. State peasants, Bashkirs, and Meshcheriaks attacked iurta elders who agreed to build the storage facilities and tore up agreements to do so. Perovskii mobilized Cossack troops and the Bashkir-Meshcheriak Host to put down the rebellion.[160]

For all the burdens Bashkirs bore in the period of cantonal administration, their numbers grew rapidly. At the time of the tenth tax census (*reviziia*) in 1857, the number of male and female Bashkirs reached 544,843, roughly twice their number at the end of the eighteenth century. Over the same time, European Russia grew by 46.3 percent. What explains this rapid, higher than natural growth? Much of it had to do with the relative stability of Bashkiria in the period of cantonal administration. Labor for the military governor and patrol on the Orenburg line were burdensome, but they were easier to endure than violent clashes every generation. Paying bribes to a cantonal administrator was unfair, but an effective bribe might make an imperial official less inclined to use force and could perhaps enable a Bashkir to obtain some relief in difficult times. Pressure to settle and grow crops could be destabilizing, but increased food supplies supported a larger population. The Orenburg fortified line cut Bashkirs off from the Kazakh steppe but also prevented the kinds of raids and clashes that cost lives and cattle.[161] Compared to the horrors of the eighteenth century, it was better to be a Bashkir in the nineteenth century.

The attractiveness of Bashkir status relative to that of serfs and state peasants also explains the growth in the Bashkir population. Rail G. Kuzeev estimates the non-Bashkir, non-Russian population at roughly 415,000, meaning there were many Teptiars, Meshcheriaks, and Tatars who lived among Bashkirs. The formation of a single Bashkir Host brought non-Bashkirs into one administrative structure. Since Bashkir status remained desirable due to the amount of land Bashkirs still owned and to the fact that Bashkirs did not pay the soul tax, many Turkic-speaking, Islamized people entered the Bashkir estate. As Nebol'sin wrote in 1852, many Tatars, Kazakhs, Kalmyks, and Meshcheriaks served along with Bashkirs in Bashkir cantons: "they all, in the sense of being persons of military estate, are called Bashkirs."[162] Bashkir estate and Bashkir ethnicity remained two different categories. Living in close proximity and serving together, diverse groups mutually influenced each other. In the first half of the nineteenth century, existing estate groups consolidated and, to an unknown extent, cultural and ethnic groups did too.

CONCLUSION

In the eighty years after Pugachev and his forces devastated Bashkiria, enlightened cameralism had transformed Bashkiria's place in the empire. Where the application of Petrine absolutism had produced major rebellions every two decades, the period 1775 to 1855 saw only one of modest size in 1835. Catherine II, her son, and her grandsons largely achieved their desire to identify and reward loyal servitors across their realm. Men and women of culture came to Bashkiria who could convey the dynasty's vision of the empire to the tsar's subjects. In a predominantly Muslim region, Catherine's policies of limited toleration made it possible for local elites to participate in governance even if not all were eager to do so. Reforms increased the presence and prestige of local officials, who became more closely connected with the empress. In Bashkiria, estate status also proved crucial in creating a Russian Orthodox and Muslim elite that, while not large, had sufficient cultural power, linguistic ability, and resources to compel their co-religionists to accept imperial authority.

If Enlightenment ideas powerfully influenced imperial governance, the militarized quality of administration also defined the period. Bashkir and Meshcheriak cantonal administration fit these groups into the empire through military service. This allowed local men to achieve power as servitors of the tsar and in some cases to earn salaries and to advance in service to levels that qualified them for noble status. Although not many Bashkirs and Muslims achieved such status, the possibility of doing so increased the attractiveness of working with rather than fighting imperial authority. Bashkir contributions to the war against Napoleon marked a turning point in official attitudes toward Bashkirs and Bashkiria's Muslims in general. Rebelliousness no longer defined them; they merited concern and, in some cases, protection. By going to a village and eating "national" cuisine, Alexander, in effect, recognized them as constituents of empire. Major estate groups and religious confessions had their cultures represented in administration as well as in stone and wood used to make churches, the noble assembly, mosques, and the caravanserai.

During Nicholas I's reign, Enlightenment and military influences converged in an effort to remake Bashkir society. With Bashkirs' greater recognition as the emperor's subjects rather than rebels came greater expectations. Bashkirs ought to have the same sense of loyalty to the emperor that others had. The attitudes of some leading statesmen regarding the need to improve Bashkir morality in 1832 were reflected more broadly in literature, such as Alexander Pushkin's *The Captain's Daughter* (1836). In Pushkin's novel of love in the time of the Pugachev Rebellion, he identified Bashkirs as one of the most threatening of Orenburg province's "semi-barbarian peoples." Because of Bashkirs' "frequent revolts, their ways unaccustomed to law and civilized life, and their instability and cruelty," they could only be kept under government control through "constant surveillance."[163] Bashkirs experienced imperial power in their lives to a much greater extent than ever before. Organized in military cantons headed by guardians who had tremendous power to "rationalize" their way of life, Bashkirs felt pressure to practice settled agriculture and even to move their homes and to make them more European. In the 1850s, the state sought to make the region more manageable by consolidating status groups. Through co-optation of elites and control of Bashkir communities, imperial authority greatly increased its power and stability in Bashkiria. As imperial officials relied increasingly on native elites to administer Bashkirs, the status of those elites grew. Ordinary Bashkirs, however, became a pool of exploited labor at the bidding of the military governor. Perovskii commissioned prominent architects to build structures that brought Orenburg prestige, but at the expense of poor Bashkirs.

Imperial officials used military organization and guardians to intervene much more forcefully in Bashkir life than in the lives of peoples to Bashkiria's east and south. The 1822 Statute on the Inorodtsy, or aliens, regularized the status of the tsar's Siberian subjects. The statute was the product of Mikhail Speranskii, who shared the German romantic view that "laws should reflect the spiritual, and intellectual needs of the people as defined by history and tradition," and of Gavriil S. Baten'kov, a Siberian native who also believed that imperial administration should take into account the history and physical conditions of Siberia's peoples.[164] The new statute classified Siberia's population into three groups, according to their "civic education and present way of life": those who were settled in towns and villages; those who were nomadic, occupying different places according to the season; and those who wandered. Settled aliens were equal in law with the other subjects of the tsar of the same estate, usually merchants or state peasants. Nomads were supposed to carry on as clans that owned their own territory, paid iasak in fur, and paid land taxes as well. Wandering inorodtsy paid no taxes other than iasak and kept their lands collectively without subdivisions. Particularly educated and organized peoples, such as the Trans-Baikal Buriat, had a "Steppe Duma," which would represent them before the Russian provincial administration.[165] As Yuri Slezkine writes, the principle guiding governance of nomads and wandering inorodtsy was "indirect rule with as little Russian interference as possible."[166] The Bashkir estate was similar in some ways to that specified for settled and nomadic inorodtsy with respect to landholding, but otherwise Bashkirs were much more enmeshed in the system of taxation and military service characteristic of the empire's core areas. Administration of Bashkirs reflected the goals of state officials, most of whom did not hesitate to direct Bashkirs firmly toward these goals.

To Bashkiria's south, in 1844, a "Statute on the Administration of the Orenburg Kirghiz," or Kazakhs as they are now called, showed differences both from
the Siberian inorodtsy and from Bashkirs. Unlike the Bashkir estate, Kazakhs
were free from military conscription, and their land was under the jurisdiction of the Ministry of Foreign Affairs. Native courts, with jurisdiction over
all but major crimes such as treason, murder, and inciting people to rebellion,
had a more prominent role in Kazakh areas than in Bashkir areas. In 1868, new
laws specified that the state owned all land occupied by Kazakhs and gave it to
them for collective usage, which differed from Bashkir hereditary landownership. Unlike Siberian inorodtsy, Kazakh sultans and heads of Kazakh auls were
appointed by the government and subordinate to the Border Commission in
Orenburg.[167]

The similarity of approaches toward the integration of two very different
peoples, Jews and Bashkirs, highlights the centrality of agriculture and military
service. Bashkirs and Jews practiced different faiths, spoke different languages,
and were concentrated in different parts of the empire—Bashkirs in the east
and Jews in the western borderlands. Much of the Jewish population was classified in the petty urban estate based on their largely mercantile occupations
and lived in cities or small towns, while Bashkirs rarely did so. Neither Jews nor
Bashkirs were enserfed, however, and state officials emphasized settled agriculture and military organization as means to make them more like other subjects
of the tsar. Imperial officials' desire to promote agriculture among Jews and
Bashkirs derived in large part from Enlightenment thought that emphasized
agriculture as the one truly productive economic activity. Beginning with the
Statute on Jews of 1804, Jews were allowed to purchase uninhabited agricultural land and encouraged to farm.[168] In 1850, as part of a "sorting" (*razbor*)
of Jews into groups considered "useful" or "not useful," Jews who expressed a
desire to transition to agriculture would receive money and an exemption from
taxation and conscription. The "selection" was never fully carried out, but the
Nicholaevan government set in motion an increase in the number of Jews who
practiced agriculture, much as officials sought to make Bashkirs into settled
agriculturalists.[169]

Even more than his brother Alexander I, Nicholas I held the "fervent and
unswerving belief in the superiority of the military life and the conviction that
no problem was insoluble if approached through the army."[170] Both Bashkirs
and Jews were organized in military cantons, but the structure and objectives
of the cantons differed greatly. Nicholas I sought to organize parts of the Jewish
population into military settlements or "cantons" that his brother Alexander
I had started, mostly for state peasants. Under Nicholas, Jewish boys, were removed from their families and marked as "fatherless" rather than following

their fathers into the military as did other groups of cantonists, most of whom were state peasants. Jewish cantons were not territorial and had a specifically missionary intent. Nicholas I and his officials pressured commanders of Jewish cantons to convert Jews to Russian Orthodoxy. Motivated by force and financial incentives, 30–40 percent of roughly 50,000 Jewish cantonists converted while in the ranks.[171] By contrast, the military made no significant effort to convert Bashkirs while they served in cantons. As we have seen, Perovskii even built a mosque for Bashkirs. In keeping with the greater acceptance of Islam in the empire and with Bashkir success in military service, some Bashkirs achieved noble status, while proposals for granting noble status to Jews were not realized.[172]

Bashkiria's relative calm in the period 1775–1855 contrasted sharply with the situation in western and southwestern parts of the empire. In the very decades in which cantonal administration brought Bashkirs into the empire's military structure, the empire's forces suppressed two Polish uprisings, in 1830 and 1863, and were locked in a devastating and violent war against Caucasian peoples. Polish resistance to the Russian Empire has been called the empire's "first national movement."[173] As such, it too represented something new and different from unrest in Bashkiria in the eighteenth century. By 1855, if anyone in Europe knew about the empire's Muslim peoples, they likely knew not the Bashkirs but dashing and rebellious Caucasian peoples, and Imam Shamil in particular.[174] The violence of the Caucasian War was similar to, though much more prolonged than, the Bashkir War of 1735–1740. Confronted with disagreements among Russian officials about whether to use little more than brute force to get Caucasian peoples to submit unconditionally or to apply policies informed by Catherine's enlightened cameralism, Nicholas I firmly favored force in the Caucasus.[175]

French thinkers and French models of governance provided reference points for imperial administration during the eighty-year period in which Catherine, her son, and grandsons ruled. Russian imperial officials modeled much, from the ministerial system of government introduced in 1804 to the uniforms Russian soldiers wore, on French state practices. As early as the 1750s, French physiocratic ideas of the centrality of agriculture informed projects to move Bashkirs in the direction of settled agriculture. Imperial officials worked to realize these visions with new vigor in the 1830s. French Enlightenment notions of religious toleration powerfully influenced Catherine's articulation of such ideas. Despite Russian emperors' vehement rejection of so much of the French Revolution and what it stood for, in the nineteenth century, Alexander I followed the "model of the Napoleonic state and established a centralized bureaucratic body for the administration of the tolerated confessions."[176] Napoleon made the military model for civilian administration particularly influential.

He "exalted the image of military leader as the exemplar of all virtue." Romanov rulers embraced the military ideal as well.[177] Russian emperors rejected quite emphatically key elements of the nineteenth-century French state, such as the notions of equality before the law for males, of the sovereignty of the people, and of secular administration. However, they at least tried to apply Enlightenment notions of order and centralized administration to civilian and especially military affairs. Nicholas I's reign saw tensions between aspirations to enlightened governance and the maintenance of the estate system and religious administration in an acute form. An emperor committed to conserving the empire's political order even if it meant cutting imperial elites from education in Europe sought to bring enlightenment to Bashkirs through new educational institutions. Nicholas presided over the large-scale, rational reconstruction of Bashkir villages while he oversaw the construction of a mosque in the caravanserai in Orenburg. Nicholas I's empire simultaneously embraced new models of governance based on reason and order and older models based on social hierarchy in a manner similar to Napoleonic France, although the relative weight of the new and the old differed in the two cases.[178] The military was key to both regimes.

Military administration maintained order among the local population better than previous strategies had but proved unable to alter Bashkirs' deteriorating economic conditions as semi-nomadic pastoralism became less and less viable. The failure of the military organization of society in Bashkiria was part of a much larger failure of the Russian military itself in Crimea. In the forty years after Bashkir troops marched into Paris with the Russian army, Russia's status among Europe's great powers reached its apogee. This changed in the months after British, French, and Ottoman forces landed on the Crimean Peninsula in September 1854. Facing shortages of munitions, carrying inferior weaponry, and displaying questionable tactics, the Russian Army fairly quickly proved unable to defend its own territory. Failures on the battlefield suggested broader, systemic problems of "incompetence, corruption, and backwardness."[179] Russia's international standing crashed, and Nicholas I, the "Gendarme of Europe," himself died in March 1855. The Great Reforms that followed his reign represented yet another fundamental effort to recast the empire.

4

PARTICIPATORY EMPIRE
1855–1881

MUKHAMETSALIM UMETBAEV, SON of a Bashkir canton head and translator for the Orenburg Muhammadan Ecclesiastical Assembly, recalled February 4, 1877, as a day of celebration. The akhund presiding over prayers that Friday at Ufa's main mosque called the attention of those present to Mufti Salim-Girei Tevkelev, the great-grandson of Kutlu-Mukhammad/Aleksei Tevkelev. When Tevkelev turned to face the crowd, the crowd was struck by the extraordinary red ribbon with stars he wore. The emperor had awarded Tevkelev the Orders of St. Stanislav and of St. Anna, first class.[1] The mufti then spoke.

> Muslims! I thank the Most High for his favor; preserve our Sovereign in the future. I convey my thanks to all of you. No way can I think that this honor belongs to me alone; I am obliged, Lord, to the Muslim community of the entire empire. I hope, in the future, that your descendants, too, will forever enjoy peace and pray for the tsar with thanks, and that your love and good feeling will belong to him.

At this, the mufti shed a tear, and "the crowd around him was rather touched as well." Ufa's Muslim community greeted the mufti's honor as "joyous news" and congratulated each other upon it.[2] Mufti Tevkelev's high status within the empire's elite received further confirmation by his presence at Alexander II's twenty-fifth jubilee in 1880 and by virtue of his invitation to the coronation of Alexander III in Moscow in 1883.[3] By the early 1880s, Tevkelev was in his seventies, and he requested to be allowed to retire due to illness. Yet when he heard a rumor that he might be replaced by someone he considered unsuitable and unpopular, he reacted angrily. He wrote to the minister of internal affairs: "I, as a Russian nobleman, for the common good, eagerly agree to continue service."[4] He did so until his death in 1885.

Tevkelev's tenure as mufti, 1865–1885, largely coincided with the Great Reforms, which began with the emancipation of the serfs in 1861 and ended with

Alexander II's assassination in 1881. Alexander II had granted Tevkelev the Orders of St. Stanislav and of St. Anna for his efforts to bring to life reforms in Muslim education and military service. These reforms were part of a far-reaching search during Alexander II's reign (1855–1881) for more effective means to mobilize the empire's resources and to compete with European rivals. The Crimean War, 1853–1856, had ended with the Russian Empire's humiliating defeat at the hands of the British, French, and Ottoman Empires. When Alexander II looked to the West for inspiration for his reforms, he saw a different Europe than Catherine II had. During the ascendency of liberal capitalism after 1848, European rulers identified themselves with "liberal, humanitarian values" and "civilized government."[5] European governments "needed the loyalty of a wider range of communities and interests" even if the propertied expected to lead in political life and society. Most political leaders believed civil life ought to be regulated by "well-established rules."[6] Nearly all countries in Western Europe had ended servile labor and expanded the vote.

Alexander II and his officials responded to this challenge from the West with reforms that came to define his reign. The first and most important reform, the abolition of serfdom in February 1861, freed twenty million serfs from subordination to their noble masters. Judicial reform, the creation of zemstvos—units of local self-administration—in 1864, the municipal reform of 1870, and the reform of military service in 1874 were needed to govern a population that was no longer servile.[7] But reformers also intended participation in zemstvos, juries, and military service to increase social responsibility, economic initiative, and loyalty. Such institutions would school the tsar's adult male subjects in the government and its values, much as an expanding network of schools would educate children to comprehend and contribute to the empire.

A universalistic thrust and an emphasis on participation characterized Great Reform legislation. Officials sought to identify and to elaborate principles of imperial governance and to apply them to the empire's diverse population. Representatives from nearly all parts of the population were supposed to partake of what Yanni Kotsonis describes as "a participatory, civic ethos and a sense of commitment (*grazhdanstvennost'*)."[8] Officials sought to create a political system that no longer rested on a hierarchy of those who commanded and those who passively obeyed. Instead, to be truly loyal the tsar's subjects should understand the goals of the tsarist state and actively support them, even if Emperor Alexander continued to rule without formal limitations on his authority.[9] After 1856, it was no longer sufficient for only elites to understand and show loyalty to the empire and its values. Much lower strata of the social hierarchy needed to do so as well. The Great Reforms made possible the halting emergence of the vision, if not the realization, of what Charles Tilly has called a "national state"—not a homogenous nation-state, but a state featuring central-ized rule of an undifferentiated population with a civic basis.[10] Or, as Alexander P. Bezak, the Orenburg governor-general during the years 1860–1865, put it, re-forms would concentrate authority in the hands of the governor-general, break down the isolation of groups in local society, and "gather the population into a common mass."[11]

The universalistic aspirations behind the reforms were only partially real-ized. The particularism of the estate order imprinted itself heavily on legisla-tion. Imperial officials remained deeply ambivalent about the prospect of po-litical transformation that might reduce the state administration's power, and they recognized limitations in the tsarist system's ability to consolidate legal statuses. So, the reforms created a more common civic order and simplified the estate system even as they maintained and at times reinforced legal and cultural particularities. The result was an institutional and legal structure that incorpo-rated groups with officially recognized and officially constituted differences of estate status, religion, and culture.[12]

Bashkiria's population featured such great diversity that any aspiration to create a "common mass" posed a powerful challenge to the ideals and imple-mentation of the Great Reforms. Many of Bashkiria's residents, including Bash-kirs, were organized into a militarized estate, which was far from a promising basis for participation in civilian political life. Nonetheless, officials showed confidence that the region's peoples were sufficiently developed to participate in the reforms that officials considered essential to the region's prosperity. To one degree or another, central authorities introduced to Bashkiria all the Great Re-forms: serf emancipation, zemstvo local self-administration, legal reform, and universal male military obligations. In a diverse former borderland, however, more geographically specific changes not generally considered Great Reforms, such as reforms of Bashkir status, changes in Muslim religious administra-tion, and new educational policies toward non-Russians, were also key parts of the state's effort to create loyal and productive subjects of the emperor. The challenge of reforming Bashkiria caused imperial officials to value men such as Tevkelev and Umetbaev, who knew the Russian language and the imperial bu-reaucracy well and could serve as intermediaries between imperial authorities and the Muslim and Bashkir population.

The optimism about reform in Bashkiria expressed in the press largely matched the confidence of officials. The relaxation of censorship following Nicholas's death in March 1855 opened discussion of what should be done in Russia in general and regarding non-Russian groups in particular to unprec-edented levels of openness (*glasnost'*) and passion.[13] Bashkirs, their potential, and their fate became one of many subjects of press commentary. Already in

1861 a small notice in Moscow's *Vestnik promyshlennosti* (Herald of industry) regarding the production of agricultural implements in a Bashkir village was enough to set off an impassioned debate about how to govern Bashkirs.[14] In the 1860s, articles in central newspapers expressed considerable hope that Bashkirs would become loyal, productive subjects of the tsar. In 1864, *Sankt-Peterburgskie vedomosti* (St. Petersburg gazette) declared, "Bashkirs are a distinctive nationality (*natsional'nost'*)," but asserted that differences between them and other rural residents existed only because Bashkirs before 1863 had been "put by the previous legal framework in a distinctive position." These distinctions could

> very quickly fade in the most natural way with the new legislation. The natural, most wonderful abilities of Bashkirs are their inquisitiveness, receptiveness, and great ambition—the gratification of which a Bashkir will not refuse even to part with the laziness inculcated in him by circumstances. A Bashkir can very quickly regenerate the essence of such characteristics that have made them useful members of the state and develop the incalculable riches of Bashkir land. It is only necessary to use such elements wisely and to direct them conscientiously.[15]

Even a less enthusiastic publication wrote of the "softening of Bashkir morals" over the previous decades.[16] Notable here is the discussion of Bashkirs not as an estate group but as a coherent people, one whose natural development previous laws had inhibited but that the state could now direct toward the prosperity of the empire as a whole.

By the 1870s, much of this early optimism had faded. Bashkirs accepted their new legal status without difficulty, and by the 1870s some influential Bashkirs and Muslims served in zemstvos. The change from military supervision to relative autonomy was often chaotic, however. Military administration may have been harsh, but, after the abolition of the cantons, officials and the introduction of a market in land proved quite able to dispossess Bashkirs. Within a few decades, journalists and writers developed an image of Bashkiria that was far from bright.

The reason for the darkness in Bashkiria depended on one's politics. Vasilii Florinskii, a doctor, ethnographer, and educational official in Kazan and Western Siberia, wrote in 1874 that Bashkirs' poverty had only increased since the Statute on Bashkirs. Poverty made them vulnerable to disease, their population would drop, and they were "doomed to die out." Due to Bashkirs' "ethnicity (*narodnost'*)" and "Asiatic habits," improving their economic conditions and prosperity was "hardly possible." As "Bashkir-Muslims" they would lose out in the struggle for existence with Russian peasants, even if Bashkirs practiced settled agriculture, received favorable treatment from authorities, and had rich land. For Florinskii, Bashkirs' only hope was assimilation (*sliianie*) with the

Russian population "by way of language, Russian literacy, and religion."[17] Critics of the tsarist state, on the other hand, continued to see Bashkirs as essentially able to be loyal, productive subjects of the emperor. To the extent that Bashkirs were poor and suffered, it was because officials exploited and abused them. The populist journalist Gleb Uspensky described corruption, specifically forgery, as the source of Bashkiria's problems. Bashkiria's officials and Russian migrants falsified documentation to deprive Bashkirs of their land. According to Uspensky, forgery was "a seed that was first carried from the depths of our fatherland to the virgin soil of Bashkir land. Its shoots grew and ensnared the mutual relations of people of a predatory society." Under the protection of imperial institutions, forgery wove itself "into a unified, dark, dense . . . scandal."[18] Due to this scandal, Orenburg governor-general Kryzhanovskii and even Minister of the Interior Valuev resigned in disgrace in 1881. This chapter will argue that the Great Reforms transformed Bashkiria and brought it closer to the empire's core. At the same time, the liberalization of land policy impoverished Bashkirs and made them come to represent the downtrodden victims of empire in the minds of many members of the intelligentsia.

BASHKIRIA IN THE 1860S: NO LONGER REMOTE, BUT HUNGRY

The 1860s were in some ways an opportune time to reform Bashkiria's administration. Bashkiria was no longer a political borderland. In 1859, the steppe to Bashkiria's south and east was transferred from the jurisdiction of the Ministry of Foreign Affairs to that of the MVD, indicating Bashkiria's transition from the empire's frontier to its interior.[19] Bashkiria's increased distance from potentially hostile borders decreased the region's strategic importance and made it difficult to justify Bashkirs' military administration. New means of communication made it easier for people, ideas, and goods to arrive. In 1858, steamship service first connected the city of Ufa via the Belaia River with Kazan, the Volga River, and Moscow.[20] The urban population remained small, with only 13,419 people in Ufa and 9,882 people in Orenburg in 1850, and primarily in military roles, with 25 percent of Ufa's male population and 34 percent of Orenburg's in service. Population grew steadily, however. The city of Ufa had doubled in size by 1886.[21] As Bashkiria became more secure and attractive, more landowning nobles and land-tilling peasants migrated to the region.

At the same time, famine and disease struck the region hard in the early 1860s. Several dry years in a row, 1860–1862, caused crop failures. In 1862, a particularly cold and snowy spring gave way to a hot and dry summer. Tens of thousands of Bashkir horses, cattle, and sheep died, especially south and east of the Urals. Weakened by hunger, the local population was particularly vulnerable to a typhus epidemic that struck Russia in this period. In the winter of 1865–1866, as much as 25–45 percent of the population of some villages died, and 11 percent of the population of Orsk and Orenburg counties perished.[22] New governor-general Nikolai Kryzhanovskii used "Bashkir capital"—funds raised from Bashkir land sales, labor for the state, and taxes—to provide relief, but the Bashkir population suffered greatly. The combination of famine and disease, coming just when the reforms began to be introduced, accentuated the belief of some officials that the Bashkir way of life was unsustainable.

BASHKIRIA'S GREAT REFORMS

Serf emancipation was the cornerstone of the Great Reforms. By 1860, if Russia sought to be considered a European country, serfdom had to go. Alexander II issued the "Statute on Peasants Departing Servile Dependence" on February 19, 1861, which initiated the freeing of Russia's serfs. Privately owned serfs received their freedom from the February 19 statute, though its implementation was delayed by two years. Over the next five years, serfs attached to factories and mines, serfs of the emperor's court, and state peasants received their freedom. "Peace mediators" worked with nobles and former serfs to implement the emancipation. As a result, in Bashkiria officials created 641 village communes and 110 volosts, each with an elected elder and his staff. Peasants gained greater control over their communities as well as personal freedom and collective property rights. In the end, emancipation went far toward consolidating peasants into an overall category of "rural resident" while retaining the power of estate institutions to allocate land, regulate movement, and collect taxes.[23] Since serfs of all categories and state peasants made up only 229,251 people of Bashkiria's population of over three million and very few Bashkirs were enserfed, reform of the region required that issues other than serfdom be addressed.

Governor-General Alexander A. Katenin brought an ambitious agenda for reform of Bashkir administration when he came to Orenburg in 1858, but death cut short his tenure in June 1860. His successor, Alexander P. Bezak, was most responsible for bringing Bashkiria into high-level discussions of reform. Bezak was a less generous host than the well-liked Katenin, who had "unified all of Orenburg society" through weekly social events. Bezak sponsored only official receptions and holiday balls. Locals considered Bezak, an artillery commander who had distinguished himself in the Turkish war of 1828–1829 and the Polish uprising of 1831, "small-minded and stingy" and prone to load officials with written assignments. Bezak replaced nearly all senior officials with his own people, as most new governors-general did.[24] Then he devoted himself "exclusively to the idea of the civil improvement of the vast Orenburg region."[25]

A letter from Minister of War Dmitrii Miliutin, a chief architect of the Great Reforms, focused the minds of Bezak and his subordinates on reforming Bashkir administration, but Miliutin left the details to Bezak and his local officials.[26] Bezak identified the diversity of Bashkiria's institutional structure as the central problem that imperial officials needed to address. He alternated between blaming particularistic administration and blaming particular peoples, the inorodtsy and primarily Bashkirs, for Orenburg's failure to fulfill its great economic potential.[27] The tsar's subjects needed to be more than loyal; they needed to be economically productive. For Bezak, state institutions grew organically from the people. The complexity of one reflected that of the other. Orenburg was a

> frontier region that formed gradually from various ethnic groups [*narodnostei*] sharply differing one from another in origins, language, religious confession, way of life, and level of civic development. All these diverse elements required peculiarities in administration corresponding to their essence or purpose, and, as a consequence, various branches of administration that did not depend on one another formed in the province.[28]

Four major types of administration, each responsible for a specific part of the population, existed in the region: the civilian provincial administration in Ufa and the Bashkir, Cossack, and Kazakh military administrations centered in Orenburg. Additionally, peasants were governed by estate, court, and mining administrations.[29] The presence of different administrations aroused "the artificial antagonism of closely related estate groups and tribes." Such differences, Bezak argued, were expressed "not so much in the people's way of life as much as in the division of authority." The diversity of estate groups and complexity of local administration impeded Orenburg's economic development. Bashkirs, in particular, were "alienated by their rank (*zvaniem*) and administrative position from the rural estates of civil administration." This caused them to "see themselves as a tribe having a different purpose from other estates." Having made a strong case for the importance of administration, however, Bezak concluded by focusing on Bashkir culture. The "very character of the Bashkir tribe (*plemeni*)," its "Asiatic laziness and irresponsibility," he wrote, hindered Orenburg's development.[30] Artificial distinctions that the Bashkir administration had fostered only contributed to this problem.

In order to resolve these economic and social problems, Bezak advocated a more rational and simple administrative and legal order. Bezak sought to combine the Bashkir and Cossack military estates with other populations under one common set of administrative, police, and legal institutions in order to reduce their isolation and "gather the population into a common mass."[31] Orenburg province's great size also had to be reduced if officials were to intervene effectively in local life. The Orenburg governor-general's jurisdiction covered 525 miles from east to west and 360 miles from north to south. Even after being divided into separate Orenburg and Ufa Provinces as Bezak proposed, Orenburg would be the fourth-largest province in European Russia.

Shortly after the issuance of the Emancipation Manifesto of February 19, 1861, Bezak formed a committee, in which Bashkirs participated, to develop a legislative proposal that would elaborate his views of a common civic order. The proposal recommended that Bashkirs eventually become a taxpaying estate subject to the same laws as other "rural residents" under the Emancipation Manifesto's terms. This recommendation, first made by the 1832 Bashkir Committee, would allow Bashkir men to farm more effectively since they would no longer spend much of the agricultural season performing military service on the distant Orenburg line or mandatory labor in the city of Orenburg. Bashkir iurtas would be equivalent to peasant volosts, and, like other peasants, Bashkirs would elect their elders instead of having the governor-general appoint them.[32] Bashkirs would be subject to civilian courts unless they were serving in the military. They would be free to enter into different estates, to engage in trade and industrial activities, and to enroll in merchant guilds.

Bezak's legislative proposal would create a common order in large part by making Bashkir landholding and the Bashkir elite's status more similar to those of other parts of the population. Bezak and his committee assumed that Bashkirs would remain hereditary landowners, but they would be able to sell land more easily.[33] The 1832 prohibition on the sale of Bashkir land below forty des. per soul meant that small Bashkir villages that most needed to turn from nomadic pastoralism to agriculture could not sell their land. Such land, in the hands of Bashkirs, became "dead capital" that simply reinforced their "wildness and idleness."[34] Bashkirs should also be able to divide their land from that of their iurta and sell it.[35] Bashkir land sales would draw from elsewhere in the empire migrants and "capitalists" who could make better use of Orenburg Province's rich soil and give Bashkirs models to emulate. The Bashkir elite would also become more like those of other groups: all Bashkir military officers who reached the appropriate rank would receive hereditary or personal noble status.[36] Bashkir assimilation had a legal and administrative meaning to Bezak. The governor-general believed that Muslim "fanaticism" existed among Bashkirs but did not consider it a threat to the state.[37]

If this first part of Bezak's legislative project stressed Bashkirs' inclusion in the civic order, the second part made clear Bezak's ambivalent, even contradictory, attitude toward Bashkir potential. Bashkirs might be suited to the new civic order, but the administration must tightly control movement toward that order because Bashkirs were "so far from acceptance of full civic consciousness" that any new measure must be introduced only in the most favorable situation. Bashkirs ought to remain temporarily under military jurisdiction and have some labor obligations in Orenburg. Their administration required "correct and sound knowledge of local circumstances and of the people's character" that only current officials possessed. The transfer to civil administration had to be done slowly, even secretly, to preserve the province's tranquility.[38]

When Bezak's superior Dmitrii Miliutin, the minister of war, submitted the project, the Committee of Ministers enthusiastically greeted the prospect of drawing Bashkirs into the empire's emerging civic life. The ministers' language demonstrates how easily they saw an estate status group as a "people" and state structures as flowing organically from the needs and characteristics, though, notably, not from the will of that people. The minister of finance commented that the government had waited thirty years for the head of Orenburg Province to present a plan for turning Bashkirs toward civic consciousness, but that Bezak's predecessors had been too timid. Minister of Justice Zamiatin wrote that Bashkirs had opposed the Bashkir Host's military organization when it had been imposed in 1834 since it did not "flow from national (*narodnoi*) life." If the Bashkir Host received civil organization and their "national (*narodnye*) forces" were turned toward agriculture, industry, and trade, they would benefit the Bashkir people and the entire region. Bezak's reforms would free Bashkirs from "administrative tutelage," provide a necessary broadening of their "civil rights (*grazhdanskikh prav*)," and enable them to participate in "independent, juridical, and social activity."[39] All agreed, without enthusiasm, on the need to proceed slowly and maintain military supervision over Bashkirs until new institutions could be formed. Although they used concepts of "civil rights" and "independent activity," ministers contrasted these ideas to military command and tutelage rather than using them to articulate a concept of citizenship.

Latent tensions between universal and particular principles became overt when Bezak's project reached the desk of the emperor's chancellery for Baron Modest Korf's review. Korf seized on Bezak's ambivalence regarding Bashkirs' readiness for inclusion in the empire's new civic order, arguing that the project's first part recognized Bashkirs neither as a military host nor as a "particular people" but only as "part of the population of the Russian Empire," as "part of the Russian people," that must be subject to the same laws. The project's second part produced a very different impression. Not only were existing laws separating Bashkirs from other status groups (*sostoianii*) left in place, but the project also displayed the principles of administrative tutelage, supervision, and interference from government officials in an extreme form.[40] Since "administrative tutelage" often fit most easily with imperial administration, Korf feared that the proposal's "tutelary" elements would overwhelm those emphasizing greater equality and social independence. Moreover, keeping Bashkirs under military jurisdiction would inhibit "assimilation of Bashkirs, in their internal organization, with other estates" and would make of the "tribe" almost a state within the state. Korf's commentary resulted in part from his desire to separate substantive law from administrative law so that procedural details would not bury legal initiatives. He also believed that a reformulated project would better achieve its ultimate goals: the development of "independent social life" among Bashkirs, their freedom from government tutelage, and their conversion to civil organization.[41]

In response to Korf, Bezak stressed the transitional nature of Bashkir administration. Since Bashkirs were "semi-wild" and "alien" from "civic consciousness," continuity had to be preserved in order to prevent confusion about the new laws.[42] In the end, Korf conceded to Bezak on all but the manner in which the administrative law would be elaborated. Korf seemed unconvinced, but he did not insist on the point against the governor-general given his local knowledge. Korf's intervention, however, had the effect of pushing the State Council to emphasize the universalistic dimensions of the law rather than allowing particularities of administrative control to appear paramount.

Bezak saw his plans become law in the form of three decrees. First, Tsar Alexander II issued the "Statute on Bashkirs" in May 1863. This statute represented a dramatic change in Bashkir status, as fundamental for them as emancipation had been for serfs in 1861. According to the statute "the inorodtsy known by the name Bashkir, Meshcheriak, Teptiar, and Bobyl . . . receive civil organization as free rural residents."[43] Bashkirs and their neighbors received all rights permitted peasants in 1861. They could enter into contracts, acquire property, run industrial and merchant establishments, enter trades, and change estate statuses, as appropriate. Like other rural residents, they were organized into village societies under the leadership of elected *starostas*. These societies, in turn, were subordinate to district societies under the leadership of elected elders (*starshina*).[44] Second, on May 31, 1865, the emperor signed legislation dividing Orenburg in two, creating Orenburg and Ufa Provinces. Ufa Province received the greater share of the former Orenburg Province's population (61.9 percent) and nobility (61.6 percent) and included the counties to the west of the Urals. The new Orenburg Province included the portions beyond the Urals and further south.[45] Third, legislation of July 2, 1865, formally eliminated Bashkir cantons, transferring the Bashkir administration from military to civilian control.[46] At the same time, the Bashkir elite was equated with the Russian nobility as a whole: Bashkir officers received hereditary nobility or personal nobility as indicated by the Digest of Laws. Ishmukhamet Umetbaev, the father of Mukhametsalim mentioned above, and a number of other Bashkirs were ennobled at this time.[47] Bashkir Muslim clerics were subordinate to the general statute on Muslim clerics. Two years later, the shift from military to civilian life was reinforced further. Minister of War Dmitrii Miliutin sponsored a decree that prohibited "Asiatics" such as Bashkirs, Kazakhs, and Kalmyks "who are still at a low level of civic consciousness (*na nizkoi stepeni grazhdanstvennost'*)" from receiving "military ranks" and other "exclusively military decorations and distinctions." Emphasis on military achievements, the decree stated, "promotes the maintenance among the population of martial inclinations, when a healthy policy requires, on the contrary, that the government, with all its strength, school these peoples in a peaceful life and lead them to civil development (*k razvitiiu grazhdanskomu*)."[48] Sixty-seven years after Bashkirs found their place in the empire as a military estate, central officials emphatically rejected military organization in favor of the civil principles of the empire's core. The rejection of particular arrangements for the local population extended to military education, too. Between 1863 and 1867, the Nepliuev Cadet School's separate "Asiatic" division was folded together with the "European" division to create one curriculum for all. Vacancies were no longer set aside for Bashkir, Tatar, and Kazakh boys, and European languages replaced "Eastern" ones.[49]

As the statute incorporated Bashkirs into the general institutional and legal structure of the empire, it also preserved sources of Bashkir particularity and gave them legal recognition. Bashkirs remained hereditary landowners who retained communal ownership rights to their land. The governor-general maintained responsibility for limiting land sales so that Bashkirs would still own forty des. per male and for regulating Bashkir land disputes with pripushchenniks.[50] Bashkirs could, in principle at least, convert their portion of communal land into their own private property, something peasants could not do. In important respects the statute respected "local custom"—meaning Islamic sharia law in Muslim areas. The statute prohibited clerical participation in communal elections, but Muslim villages selected their own mullahs and decided whether to build or to repair mosques, unlike Russian peasant villages, which had priests assigned to them. The guardianship of Bashkir orphans and the disposition of property among Bashkir heirs also continued to be "guided by their local customs." In villages where a court "established by local custom" already existed, there it was maintained.[51] This meant that disputes among Bashkirs in which no more than a hundred rubles were at stake and which did not involve a crime remained within the jurisdiction of traditional law. Bashkirs remained largely in control of who made up their volosts, since they controlled the addition of Bashkirs to and the discharge of Bashkirs from Bashkir communities. Bashkirs also paid a lower tax than other peasants.

KRYZHANOVSKII, LAND, AND MIGRATION

Bezak would not be the man to implement his legislative initiatives. The energy he showed in bringing the Great Reforms to Orenburg Province resulted in his assignment to the more populous and strategically important province of Kiev at the end of 1864. His replacement, Nikolai A. Kryzhanovskii, was his nephew and a fellow artillery officer, but their similarities largely ended there. Where Bezak was formal and a taskmaster, a local observer described Kryzhanovskii as "kind." Kryzhanovskii had served in the Caucasus, in the siege of Sevastopol during the Crimean War, and in Warsaw and Vilnius. He demonstrated the suspicion of Islam and of non-Russian, non-Orthodox populations one might expect of a Russian official who had been wounded fighting the Turks in Crimea and who arrived fresh from battling the Polish uprising of 1863. He made security his overwhelming concern. Although Kryzhanovskii's firm advocacy of "strong-arm methods of rule" may have been traditional in Turkestan, the intensity of his hostility to Islam was something of a departure for an Orenburg governor-general.[52]

Kryzhanovskii's approach to governance during his long tenure in Orenburg, from 1865 to 1881, reflected his arrival at a time of famine and disease among Bashkirs and just after his recent service in the wars of empire. He took the privation among Bashkirs that prevailed upon his arrival—an exceptional if not unique occurrence—as proof that the Bashkir way of life produced poverty and disease. Upon consultation with officials in Orenburg, he wrote to St. Petersburg to advocate vigorous action to address Bashkirs' problems: (1) to dispossess Bashkirs of land so as to make "the continuation of their nomadic life impossible"; (2) to take measures to make sure that land sold by Bashkirs ended up in the hands of Russian peasants, "who have the experience to have a beneficial influence on them"; (3) after final survey of Bashkir land had reduced their landholding, to "strengthen agriculture among them not by force, but naturally"; (4) to remove "any petty tutelage of officialdom" from Bashkirs, to make them hereditary landowners with full rights, and to give them "self-administration on common principles"; and (5) to disseminate among them primary education and Russian literacy, remove schools from the exclusive control of "religious persons," gradually reduce the number of mullahs, and require Bashkirs to know the Russian language.[53] Kryzhanovskii believed that only by making Bashkirs like other peoples in the empire could the pathologies he saw upon his arrival be avoided.

Kryzhanovskii believed that Bashkirs could become similar to other peoples in the empire if there were more of those other people to serve as models for Bashkirs. He elaborated on the statute in order to realize the goal his predecessor Putiatin had advanced nearly a century before—the transfer of Bashkir land to those who could make it more productive. Kryzhanovskii argued that Orenburg's economic development required the settlement of a "Russian element" that would introduce more advanced agricultural practices. These would influence the Bashkir "way of life" in the direction of settled agriculture, increasing the land's productivity and the region's usefulness to the state.[54] Kryzhanovskii mixed the language of property and inclusiveness characteristic of the Great Reforms with older notions of estate particularity and concern about the influence of Islam that had grown in the wake of the Crimean War.[55] He argued that restrictions on Bashkir land sales ran contrary to recognition of Bashkirs as "landowners with full rights" and should be eliminated. Bashkir land ought to be surveyed and divided off from that of pripushchenniks, so that it could be sold more easily.[56] He also argued that the transfer of Bashkirs from military to civil administration warranted a change in the amount of land that Bashkirs held. Where parcels of land owned by Bashkirs were sufficiently large—more than forty des. per soul according to the seventh tax census— Bashkir pripushchenniks of military estates ought to receive thirty des. and those of civilian estates fifteen des. In such places, fifteen des. should be held "in reserve" for those living in areas with too little land to make such a division. Such a plan, according to Kryzhanovskii, would allow Bashkirs to remain landowners while permitting their pripushchenniks to have property they could defend too. Bashkirs' new civilian status also meant that they were free to sell more of their land. They only had to keep fifteen des. instead of thirty. Despite the language of reform and property rights, Kryzhanovskii's proposal left an opening for continued state intervention in Bashkirs' and pripushchenniks' communal affairs. A total of one-third of the value of the land sale would be assigned to the "communal capital" of the villages involved. Communal capital could support projects the state deemed useful, such as the maintenance of a village's grain reserves or schools. The emperor signed Kryzhanovskii's proposal into law on February 10, 1869.[57]

Orthodox and Muslim nobles took advantage of market forces and Bashkirs' lack of mastery of the law to further Kryzhanovskii's goals. They bought Bashkir land for next to nothing. Others essentially stole land through manipulation and deceit. A land fever developed that one local observer likened to "gold fever" during the California gold rush.[58] Meanwhile, Kryzhanovskii worked to ensure that sufficient people were available to settle the land. He convinced the central administration to permit unregistered migrants who had long lived in Orenburg and Ufa Provinces to settle there permanently.[59] Shortly thereafter, Kryzhanovskii introduced a policy intended to develop a Russian landholding elite. Central authorities approved legislation in June 1871 that was intended to improve the position of "educated landowners" and to attract men "who [would] be recognized as useful." The law permitted retired officials and officers to purchase parcels of state land of 150 to 2,000 des., much of it from Bashkirs, at very favorable prices. By 1881, 293 men had purchased land in this manner. Many of them were servitors of high rank in the local administration. The emperor granted Kryzhanovskii 6,294 des.[60] Many later resold their land at great profit, often to peasant migrants from central Russia.

REFORMS OF MILITARY SERVICE, LOCAL SELF-ADMINISTRATION, AND JUSTICE

The transfer of Bashkirs from military to civil administration coupled with increased migration to Bashkiria prepared the basis for the extension of the Great Reforms. The first and last of the major reforms—the emancipation of the serfs in 1861 and the military reform of 1874—applied to all Orenburg Province when they did to the rest of the empire. The reforms of local administration and justice, by contrast, proved more difficult to effect since they relied more on educated and professional men to staff them. These reforms took place in Bashkiria well after they did in central provinces and were not enacted throughout the entire region.

In 1874, the extension of military service obligations to all men, with the major exceptions of men in Siberia and Central Asia, was perhaps the clearest example of the universalizing thrust of the Great Reforms and, in the words of Josh Sanborn, the "forming of a national compact."[61] In essence, the military service obligations defined which men officials considered sufficiently loyal and capable to defend the empire. In preparing for reform, Minister of War Miliutin wrote in 1870: "General obligatory participation in military service, uniting in ranks of the army men of all estates and all parts of Russia, presents the best means for weakening tribal differences among people, the correct unification of all forces of the state, and their direction towards a single, common goal."[62] In keeping with Miliutin's vision, rather than conscripting a certain number of men for periods up to twenty years, the state subjected many more men to conscription for a shorter term of six years. Depending primarily on the level of education a man had, this service commitment could be reduced to as little as six months. Officials such as Bezak and Kryzhanovskii were confident that Bashkirs had reached a sufficient level of civic consciousness that they could be subject to the new military service requirements. A supplement to the January 1, 1874, decree that introduced the reform specified that Bashkirs and Teptiars would not be exempt from service as inorodtsy to Bashkiria's east and south were.[63]

Bashkirs resisted the new military obligations more than they had the end of cantonal administration. Some feared that if they served as ordinary soldiers they would become ordinary peasants, the link between land and service would be broken, and they would lose their land. Bashkirs resisted the new law by taking advantage of the state's need for information to enforce it. In order for men of the proper age to be drafted, their birth dates had to be known. Village imams kept metrical books in which births and deaths were recorded. In March 1874, some imams in Ufa Province resisted military authorities by claiming not to have metrical information. Resistance became more intense in Perm Province to Ufa's north, where imams incited their communities to reject conscription. On instructions from the minister of internal affairs, Orenburg mufti Salim-Girei Tevkelev traveled to the affected areas and confronted the imams. Tevkelev recommended that four imams and one akhund be stripped of their positions, six be suspended, and others receive stern reprimands. The mufti toured rebellious areas with the Perm governor and explained the new statute.[64]

Perhaps in part due to this resistance, military officials amended the law in a way that made clear their ambivalence toward Bashkirs' full inclusion in imperial service. A decree of July 6, 1874, created a special irregular cavalry squadron for 250 Bashkir conscripts from Orenburg Province who maintained their "traditional lifestyle" and displayed their skill as horsemen.[65] The experiment seemed to work. The following year the squadron doubled in size to make a division, and it doubled again in 1878.[66] Yet Bashkir irregular cavalry units remained controversial within the military hierarchy. One officer wrote that Bashkirs were natural-born soldiers whose horses were "hardy and simple." The squadron meant the return of a "splendid martial tradition." Service also helped Bashkir men learn Russian.[67] Another officer disagreed. He argued that the squadrons were unfair because such soldiers served only twenty-eight months, whereas other conscripts served up to six years. Furthermore, Bashkir soldiers in the squadrons showed little knowledge of Russian, were poor marksmen, and had "neither acquired soldierly appearance nor mastered military spirit."[68] Bashkir irregular units' abolition in 1882 suggests that the latter viewpoint prevailed. The units were a transitional solution that reflected anxiety over Bashkirs' military role after their distinctive arrangements, the cantons, had been abolished. Now all Bashkir men served under the same conditions as other men trusted to defend the empire.

Service in local units of self-administration, zemstvos, differed greatly from service in the military but was also a crucial part of the new civic order. Introduced in most of European Russia in 1864, zemstvo assemblies' activities were legally limited to local social welfare causes, such as the development of schools and postal services, and medical, veterinary, and agronomical assistance. Yet zemstvos also had a broader mission. They were supposed to bring privileged and nonprivileged groups together in order to educate the latter in civic life. Both officials and political activists attributed considerable importance to zemstvos. Elections were organized in part by land ownership rather than strictly by estate status, which distinguished them from other institutions. Since zemstvos had legally recognized responsibilities distinct from those of the state administration, some have interpreted them as an early, if partial, deviation from autocratic principles and as the cradle of noble liberalism and civil society in Russia.[69]

Zemstvos were absent from the empire's western borderlands, Siberia, and Turkestan since they required a substantial population of educated, cultured, and Russian-speaking men, preferably nobles, to provide the nucleus of zemstvo leadership. Some officials in Orenburg Province also were reluctant to put members of the Bashkir elite into positions where they could influence other peoples. Governor-General Kryzhanovskii had no such reservations. He argued in favor of including Bashkirs among zemstvo deputies and concluded that Bashkirs must participate equally in zemstvo elections.[70] In 1875, eleven years after zemstvos were introduced in central provinces, this view, along with growth in the number of Ufa's landowners facilitated by the redistribution of Bashkir land, convinced the MVD that the province was ready for zemstvos. In autumn of 1875, an assembly was convoked in each of Ufa's six counties. These bodies elected representatives to the provincial zemstvo that met later that year in the city of Ufa. Orenburg Province, with its smaller population of noble landowners, did not receive zemstvo institutions until 1913.

To be sure, zemstvos did not constitute a fully democratic and representative system. The electoral franchise favored the primarily Russian Orthodox noblemen who owned large estates and who already ran parts of the province virtually as personal fiefdoms. Such men often used their power to assess zemstvo taxes disproportionately on the peasants. Ufa's zemstvos were known for their backwardness and inactivity for their first twenty years.[71] Nonetheless, zemstvo institutions were one place where men of different estate statuses, ethnicities, and religions met. More Muslims participated in Ufa zemstvos than in other zemstvos in the empire for a number of reasons. The law stipulated that Bashkir and Muslim populations should participate in the zemstvos equally with Russian peasants. Since the Muslim population made up slightly more than half of Ufa Province, it had substantial representation in zemstvo assemblies.[72] The Muslim nobles whose status was restored under Catherine II or who had earned nobility through service in the Bashkir cantons gave Ufa Province more Muslim nobles than elsewhere in the empire. The availability of Bashkir land enabled some of these nobles to acquire the land necessary to support their status. Muslim representation fell far short of being proportional to their presence in the population, but by the 1880s it was considerable, as we will see in chapter 5. Despite the flaws and shortcomings of the zemstvos, they provided a forum for Bashkirs and Tatars to engage questions facing local society.

Much as imperial officials intended units of local self-administration to school the population in civic affairs, imperial officials intended reform of judicial procedure to inculcate a notion of justice and law that would increase the empire's prosperity and overcome differences among estate status groups. Independent courts with professional justices, juries, argumentation, and a professional bar replaced a system in which judicial procedure had been slow, opaque, and generally protected the "power, interests, and prestige of administrative authorities."[73] Official ambivalence about the new institutions, however, resulted in the maintenance of separate courts for clergy, the military, and, most important, the peasantry.[74]

In a similar manner, administrators in Bashkiria saw judicial reform as a means to integrate the region into the empire's core and to replace a society divided by estate and religious confession with one of subjects more equal before the law. Governor-General Bezak declared Bashkirs ready for the legal reform in 1865, arguing that the "level of maturity of Bashkirs with respect to the apprehension of the new civic principles of administration and law" gave hope for the "more or less peaceful" implementation of the planned reforms. He even stated that Bashkir participation in volost courts exceeded that of other rural residents.[75] Kryzhanovskii also considered judicial reform essential. Writing to the minister of justice, he denied that introducing the legal reform in an area "where there are many diverse ethnicities (*narodnostei*) just beginning to grasp the principle of civic consciousness" would result in major problems. As part of the effort to apply to all ethnicities "common principles of administration" that had begun with the "Statute on Bashkirs" and reform of Cossack administration in the 1860s, Bashkirs were now "fully subordinated" to the "common laws of the empire." Bashkirs, he argued, differed little from other rural residents in any way other than their agricultural practices. To separate them from the general population with respect to judicial institutions would be a mistake, Kryzhanovskii believed, since this would contradict all the administration's aspirations to elevate these "inorodtsy to a common level."[76] Cossacks, when not in active service, he added, also now made up a civil estate and merited the reformed legal institutions. In short, Ufa and Orenburg Provinces and their populations had become like those of central Russia with respect to administration and status. They should not differ in the administration of justice. Ufa zemstvo assemblies eagerly called for judicial reform, passing resolutions to that effect in their opening sessions in March 1875 and repeating them over the next two years.[77]

Central officials rewarded local officials and elites' efforts in a limited way on May 2, 1878, when the emperor signed a decree introducing only the lowest level of the new system, justices of the peace, to Ufa and Orenburg Provinces.[78] Justices of the peace had jurisdiction over peasant allotments, inheritance, and misdemeanor crimes.[79] Zemstvo assemblies elected justices, and a few Muslims served in that capacity.[80] The reform left customary law in the hands of volost courts. Thus, Muslim courts based on the sharia, known as the "*treteiskii courts*," could continue to handle matters such as inheritance. Neither a circuit court (*okruzhnyi sud*) nor a judicial chamber (*sudebnaia palata*), which adjudicated more serious matters and served as the appellate court for the circuit courts, was introduced in Bashkiria. Local residents had to travel to Kazan or Saratov for these courts.[81] Juries and a professional bar also went lacking locally in the 1878 legislation. Unlike the case of zemstvos, local officials and elites were largely disappointed in their efforts to have Bashkiria integrated into the new legal system. By the mid-1870s, some central administrators grew dissatisfied with the new courts' ability to uphold the administration's interests and were loath to expand reformed judicial institutions and bring greater homogeneity to the empire's "multiple regimes of justice."[82]

REFORM OF CONFESSIONAL AND EDUCATIONAL INSTITUTIONS

The effort to find common principles to govern a diverse population faced particular challenges where differences of language, culture, and faith separated the tsar's subjects from his officials and groups within society from one another. For this reason, changes in religious and educational institutions accompanied the Great Reforms in diverse regions such as Bashkiria. Religion and education were key areas in which officials and elites wrestled over what exactly would unite or divide the empire.

With respect to Muslim administration, change in personnel substituted for change in law as a means to include the Muslim community in the empire's civic life. Orenburg mufti Gabdulvakhid Suleimanov, a man of uncertain religious education and an authoritarian style of administration, died in 1862 during the height of discussions of reform.[83] Orenburg governor-general Bezak proposed Salim-Girei Tevkelev, a retired army officer, as a candidate for mufti. Tevkelev's appointment indicated a growing skepticism about Muslim clergy among imperial officials.[84] Imperial officials' one major change in the OMEA's legal mandate to emerge from the reform era reinforced this shift in state policy. The MVD removed the Kazakh steppe from the OMEA's jurisdiction in order to "weaken the influence of Muslim propaganda" and Tatar influence on Kazakhs.[85] Yet Tevkelev's appointment also demonstrated imperial officials' increased interest in using Muslim elites to promote Russian language acquisition and participation in the empire's secular institutions as ways to integrate Muslims in the post-reform era.

Muftis before Tevkelev had religious training and served as Muslim clerics, even if they were not the most prominent interpreters of Islamic law. None before Tevkelev had been born a nobleman or had enjoyed high status within Russian-speaking society. Now Orenburg governor-general Bezak rejected candidates who knew Islam well but who lacked a "general education" without which they could "hardly exceed a literal interpretation of the Koran." The government could scarcely hope to find in such persons advocates of a rapprochement between Muslims and Russians, Bezak asserted. Bezak saw several advantages in Tevkelev's appointment. In addition to being the great-grandson of Kutlu-Mukhammad/Aleksei Ivanovich Tevkelev, Salim-Girei was also a wealthy nobleman and owned three thousand des. of land. Salim-Girei was not a Muslim cleric, but he had completed the pilgrimage to Mecca and Medina in 1852. He had been educated in elite military schools and had made a career in the army. His loyalty to the emperor was unquestioned.[86] Tevkelev enjoyed high status in Russian-speaking society, having served as marshal of the nobility in Samara Province. Tevkelev would be an effective executor of state policy who could overcome the "harmful influence of the mullahs" and integrate Muslims into the empire's secular administration.[87] Support from, or at least the acquiescence of, influential Muslims in the capital whose interests intersected with those of imperial administrators also helped Tevkelev win the post.[88] By the appointment of Tekelev, imperial officials indicated their greater faith in noble status than in religious confession as a predictor of loyalty to the emperor.

Mufti Tevkelev confronted Orenburg governor-general Kryzhanovskii and other local officials who initially sought to reform the OMEA but then attacked it and Islam.[89] Kryzhanovskii proposed that Muslims pay a tax for practicing their faith, that a large mosque in Orenburg be closed, and that Muslim schools be closely regulated. He also proposed that an imperial official be appointed to the OMEA to monitor its work, that Russian literacy be required of judges, and that the OMEA conduct its correspondence in Russian.[90] In 1872, Ufa civil governor Sergei Ushakov proposed that the MVD close the OMEA. Ushakov argued that the very existence of a Muslim religious institution strengthened Muslims' "consciousness of their ethnic and religious unity" and secured "the inviolability and vitality of their religious delusions."[91] Tevkelev's opinion provided an important counterweight to such views.

Kryzhanovskii found only modest support in St. Petersburg for the attack on mullahs and Islam he had argued for upon taking office in 1865. Encouraged by Tevkelev, Minster of Internal Affairs Valuev and his successor, Alexander Timashev, rebuffed Kryzhanovskii and Ushakov because they feared that their proposals would give rise to "secret mullahs" not under state supervision.[92] Timashev, with his reputation for conservatism, might seem an unlikely supporter of the muftis, but he had deep roots in the Orenburg region. Timashev's ancestors had acquired a great deal of land in Orenburg Province in the eighteenth century, and his father had been the Orenburg Cossack ataman during Nicholas I's reign.[93] Timashev's approach to Islam reflected relatively tolerant local patterns more than Kryzhanovskii's approach did. The fact that Mufti Tevkelev's aunt had eloped with a relative of Timashev's and converted to Christianity does not seem to have prevented the two men from working together.[94] In some cases, Tevkelev addressed Kryzhanovskii directly. In 1876, Russia's declaration of war against the Ottoman Empire gave rise to fears in Russian-speaking society that Turkish agents would provoke the empire's Muslims to rise up in support of the Ottomans.[95] As tensions mounted, Mufti Tevkelev wrote to Kryzhanovskii in order to condemn "absurd rumors" that caused Russian hostility toward Muslims and, Tevkelev argued, could lead to horrible conflicts of the sort that took place between Jews and Orthodox Christians in Odessa. The mufti urged Kryzhanovskii to work to prevent anything that could "harm the good relations among nationalities (*natsional'nostiami*)."[96] Tevkelev's view did not always prevail, however. When in 1866 Tevkelev asked police officials to distribute a fatwa requesting that Muslims carefully observe all rites of their religion, Kryzhanovskii convinced Valuev that making Russian police "confirm and distribute Muslim law (sharia)," driving people to the mosque and supporting "fanaticism," made "a mockery of Russian authorities." Valuev wrote to Tevkelev that the OMEA was not to involve other administrative organs in its activities.[97] The OMEA could police Islamic practice but not promote it.

When the practice of Islam was not in question, however, Tevkelev strongly supported efforts to include Muslims in the reformed political order. Mufti Tevkelev's fatwa in support of the March 1870 regulations on the education of Muslims in the Russian Empire's east stressed the importance of Russian literacy in understanding "civil authority." He asked,

> how will you ask for bread from a Russian if you do not know Russian? How will you ask for favors, how will you defend yourself in court, how will you ask for leniency in punishment, attention to your village, to your house, to your land, to taxes, to obligations, if you do not know the language in which the court operates, . . . [the language of] the administration, . . . [and the language] in which are written . . . rules for your welfare, prosperity and relief?

Learning Russian did not threaten Muslim faith. Tevkelev reasoned that respect for the tsar should extend to all his subjects since both Muslims and Christians were "children of our common father of the Fatherland."[98] Tevkelev captured well how imperial elites conceived the role of Russian literacy in the empire's reformed institutions.

In Nicholas I's empire, inculcating Russian-language literacy in the tsar's subjects had not been a priority. When the state demanded little more than the payment of taxes, the provision of recruits, and the observance of basic criminal laws, Russian-language literacy was unnecessary. Only certain members of a non-Russian-speaking elite or a few translators and scribes needed to know Russian in order to instruct other non-Russians. The Bashkir cantonal administration only began to establish schools for Bashkir youth in 1858.[99]

By contrast, participation in a common civic order rested on the ability of the emperor's subjects to communicate with state officials and with each other. In the era of reform, officials began to promote the Russian language as the primary means to create loyal subjects by inculcating in them the values and goals of the empire's leadership. Beyond that, how extensive Russian language acquisition should be, how Russian should be taught, and what values Russian ought to convey proved controversial. The tsar's subjects could use Russian in different ways. Those whose mother tongue was not Russian could learn it as a language of state and for certain limited purposes but maintain their native languages in most social life. Alternatively, people could use Russian in most social domains, limiting native-language use to their homes, neighborhoods, or religious institutions.[100] Or, language acquisition could be the first step toward full assimilation into Russian culture. If, as many officials believed, the Russian language was to be used in more than a limited way, what values should be taught? Should Russian culture, Russian Orthodoxy, or other values unify the empire?

Multiple conceptions of education, literacy, and their social roles emerged in debates over the empire's laws on the education of non-Russians in 1870. Dmitrii A. Tolstoi, the minister of education from 1866 to 1880, led discussions of how education could make possible the "rapprochement" of non-Russians with the "native" Russian population in the late 1860s. Tolstoi sent assistants to review the British educational system in India and French efforts in Algeria.[101] Ministry of Education (MNP) officials and educators such as the influential Konstantin D. Ushinskii shared the emphasis of German romantic philosophers on language as the crucial element of national consciousness.[102] Tolstoi believed that the Russian language had an almost magical ability to draw non-Russians toward the state and to assimilate them into Russian culture. Guided by MNP's experience with Jews, he argued that the state should demand that non-Russians learn the Russian language "because the Eastern origin and the Mohammedan faith in no way exempt Tatars from the general state structure." Tolstoi believed that the Russian language constituted "that imperceptible yet real connection that will gradually draw Tatars toward the state center—toward Russia, . . . where there is a connection of word and understanding, there arises simultaneously a connection of thought and conviction, and tribal estrangement weakens."[103] The extent of the assimilation envisioned varied, as indicated by the use at times of the word *sblizhenie* ("making near" or "rapprochement"), and at other times *sliianie* ("blending" or "assimilation"). But MNP officials tended to look toward the full assimilation of non-Russians into Russian national culture.

Discussions of non-Russian education sponsored by Tolstoi culminated in the MMP's regulations of March 1870. Tolstoi's goal for the education of non-Russians was their "Russification (*obrusenie*)" and "assimilation with the Russian people" on the basis of Russian-language education.[104] To this end, the ministry planned a network of bilingual schools for non-Russians in which the Russian language would be taught. These became known as Russian-Tatar schools, Russian-Bashkir schools, and so on, depending on which non-Russian group predominated in a given area.[105] Considering officials' assimilationist ambitions and their negative view of Islam, their treatment of the Muslim faith was quite careful. To dampen suspicion that the schools masked missionary activity, curricula would allow time for Muslim religious instruction in the native language of the primary group present.[106] The regulations allowed some use of non-Russian languages in instruction and foresaw the training of native, non-Russian teachers.[107] In order to reach students unable or unwilling to attend a primary school, MNP opened Russian-language classes in Muslim primary and secondary schools, the maktabs and madrasas.

The 1870 regulations, however, also showed the influence of Nikolai Il'minskii. Il'minskii, an influential missionary and educator from Kazan, worked closely with Tolstoi but had his own vision of a universal principle for the educational system: Russian Orthodoxy. Il'minskii believed that Russian Orthodoxy was both the key to salvation and the key principle that ought to unite the empire. To Il'minskii, the primary reason for teaching non-Russians lay "not in Russian language, but in the development of common human conceptions, moral principles and convictions, and Russian sympathies." Russian sympathies and moral content—derived from Russian Orthodoxy—could take any linguistic form.[108] Il'minskii advocated native-language instruction for non-Russians and even created written languages for peoples without them. The use of native languages would break down non-Russians' resistance to Orthodox teachings by preserving non-Russians' ethnicity (*narodnost'*), "which was so dear" to them.[109] Il'minskii suggested, however, that educational materials prepare students for future study of Russian by using the Cyrillic script to write non-Russian languages, as in Il'minskii's own schools. In the 1870 regulations, Tolstoi conceded to Il'minskii's emphasis on religion. Baptized non-Russians who lived more or less isolated from Russian society would receive a bilingual education focused on religion after Il'minskii's fashion. They would also receive native-language instruction until they could master Russian.

Still another interpretation of language instruction and its ultimate goals became clear later that year when discussion of the 1870 regulations shifted to Bashkiria. Orenburg governor-general Kryzhanovskii convoked a special commission to consider how to develop non-Russian schools in Bashkiria in keeping with the new educational regulations. The commission included the governor-general, the director, and an inspector of Orenburg's schools as well as Sultan Seid-Khan Dzhantiurin, a Kazakh and an official for special assignments to Kryzhanovskii, and Shakhaidar Syrtlanov, the son of a former head of a Bashkir canton, who served as a peace mediator in Orenburg. Kryzhanovskii supported the assimilation of non-Russians, and so it is no surprise that instruction in Russian and preparation for enrollment in Russian secondary schools would be the primary task of Bashkiria's schools. However, the commission's recommendations also reflected the views of Kazakh and Bashkir representatives. For them, learning Russian had neither the national implications it did for Tolstoi nor the religious importance it held for Il'minskii. Like Mufti Tevkelev, Dzhantiurin and Syrtlanov had achieved positions of status in part through their knowledge of the Russian language, but speaking Russian did not make them ethnically Russian. The two men prompted the commission to recommend that schoolteachers be of the same people as their students so that education would "not touch the original nationality of the students."[110] Whereas imperial educators considered Russian-language instruction key to Russian nationality, Dzhantiurin and Syrtlanov had a more practical conception of language acquisition. Russian was the empire's lingua franca, and Russian literacy was necessary to participate in the empire's culture and institutions.

Efforts to implement the 1870 regulations in Bashkiria underscored differing conceptions of the role of language in the post-reform civic order and differing levels of non-Russian command of Russian language. A supplement to the 1870 regulations sought to require Russian literacy eventually for all who served as imam or in a zemstvo, city duma, or village administrative position.[111] In order to ascertain the suitability of such a law, the MNP and MVD solicited information from police and local officials on the time necessary for non-Russians in lower-level administration to master Russian. Responses to the

circular indicated the great variety of official views of the non-Russian population's linguistic ability and potential. One peace mediator questioned the Min-
istries' categories: local Bashkirs and Meshcheriaks were not the same as the
"Tatar-Muslims" mentioned in the circular. A few peace mediators reported
that Bashkir village elders already knew Russian or would learn it readily if
asked. Others claimed that local populations actively resisted studying Russian
since it violated religious law. Some asserted that Bashkirs avoided service in
public positions, while another claimed Bashkirs eagerly sought such service.
One wrote that such a law should be promulgated immediately, another that
a delay of less than twenty-five years was impractical.[112] A few correspondents
posed the question: if non-Russians must be literate in Russian, what about the
Russians themselves? One correspondent reported that Bashkir village elders
were literate in Russian but Russian ones were not![113] No consensus existed regarding Muslims' ability to learn Russian and their potential as subjects of the
tsar. All those surveyed agreed that substantial difficulties impeded application
of such a law.

Such complexities did not intimidate educational officials. In 1872, a four-
class Tatar Teachers' School and the first Russian-Bashkir school opened in Ufa
Province. In 1874, central administrators increased the ministry's formal authority by creating the post of inspector of Russian and non-Russian schools
and by giving the MNP formal jurisdiction over all Muslim confessional schools.
Given the ministry's small staff and large geographical jurisdiction, the MNP's
supervision of Muslim schools remained a formality. The Kazan Educational
District, to which Orenburg and Ufa Provinces (among others) were subordinate, was larger than France.[114]

The creation of the Orenburg Educational District (Orenburgskii Ucheb-
nyi Okrug, hereafter OUO) in 1875 increased the ability of the center to transfer
MNP's particularly nationalist, assimilationist policies from the western borderlands to Bashkiria. Petr A. Lavrovskii, the OUO's first curator, had been a
professor of Slavic culture at Kharkov University. He had overseen the transformation of the Warsaw Central School into the Russified Warsaw University
in the 1860s.[115] Like Governor-General Kryzhanovskii, he saw relations among
groups in Bashkiria through the lens of the Russo-Polish conflict, which was
more national in nature, more intense, and more violent. In Lavrovskii's inau-
gural address, he presented the assimilation of non-Russians as central to the
OUO's mission. A vast quantity of "indigenous peoples" of completely "alien
origins" surrounded the "newly arrived element"—Russians. Religion and language separated natives from the Russian milieu to the point that they had
nearly opposite "understandings of the orders of state, social, and private life."
Natives, Lavrovskii argued, either ignored principles of life introduced by the

Russians "as Christians and Europeans" or rejected them outright. "Between us and them," he said, only an external connection existed—"the unity of state power" maintained by force. A school was a weapon that would overcome natives' "age-old ignorance and religious fanaticism" and bring "diverse elements into a unity of common interests and sympathies with state power and the dominant people"—the Russians. Russians had to make the natives "citizens of the Russian tsardom, sympathizing with all its true interests."[116] In essence, Lavrovskii argued that to be a truly loyal subject of the tsar one had to have particular cultural characteristics, which was an idea little developed in a diverse region such as Bashkiria. Discussions of Russian-language instruction in the Great Reform era made clear the simultaneous emergence of a Russifying, national educational project in MNP along with secular and Russian Orthodox conceptions of a multinational polity that members of the Muslim elite and Il'minskii envisioned very differently.

THE PLUNDERING OF BASHKIR LAND AND
THE END OF THE GOVERNOR-GENERAL

The dramatic fall of Orenburg governor-general Kryzhanovskii in 1881, the abolition of his position, and the resignation of the minister of internal affairs provide the best evidence of the shift from a regime based on a militaristic hierarchy of command and obedience to a more inclusive, participatory civic order. When officials appeared to abuse Kryzhanovskii's policies aimed at transferring Bashkir land to agricultural migrants, discussed above, traditional petitions and an expanded press made possible a "scandal" that resulted in Kryzhanovskii's removal. A century earlier, Kryzhanovskii's efforts to separate Bashkirs from their land in order to strengthen the local elite and administration would have raised few eyebrows among officials, even if not all agreed on such a strategy. In the reform era, however, Kryzhanovskii's actions acquired new implications. The scandal started in a traditional manner, with Bashkir petitions protesting the loss of their land through improper land deals and the local administration's participation in such deals. At least a few local landowners wrote to Petersburg of the dangerous, potentially explosive situation that the land policy had produced. By 1878, these petitions caused the government, with the support of Kryzhanovskii, to mandate that the sale of Bashkir land occur only by way of public trade and in properly surveyed parcels. The upper ranks of the local administration were given the ability to annul improper purchases of Bashkir land.[117]

Such action failed to quiet discontent. By 1880, the central press took up the cause of Bashkirs in ways inconceivable before 1855. In 1880, articles began

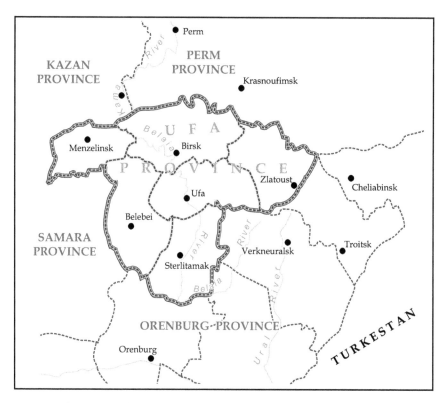

MAP 4.1. Ufa Province after 1881.

to appear in *Nedelia* (The week) and *Golos* (The voice) that exposed and criticized the practices of the Orenburg governor-general and the Ufa provincial
administration. In particular, Petr Dobrotvorskii, a peace mediator in Birsk
and Belebei Counties, became a frequent author of articles in the central press.
Some of Dobrotvorskii's pieces came to the attention of Count Mikhail Loris-
Melikov, the chair of the Supreme Executive Commission, and to Emperor Alexander II himself.[118] The senate directed Mikhail E. Kovalevskii to Ufa and
Orenburg to investigate accusations of corruption.[119] A number of central newspapers followed Kovalevskii's inspection closely in early 1881.[120] According to
Golos, the inspection had provoked "a terrific commotion" among "local ruling
classes." The editor was not surprised, since "in Russia there is hardly another
place like Ufa Province, where the law is so slighted." Bashkirs gathered by the
hundreds to present petitions to Kovalevskii for the return of their land.[121]

Kovalevskii reported abuses of land policy to St. Petersburg. The local
administration had tolerated numerous shady deals in which Bashkirs were

convinced to sell their land at absurdly low prices. Local administrators had joined in the plunder, too. Instead of surveying Bashkir land, separating off allotments above the 30-des. norm, and distributing them to Bashkirs and their pripushchenniks with small parcels, local administrators took the land for themselves or gave it to their friends. After Kovalevskii's inspection a few land deals were annulled, but Kovalevskii considered returning all illegally gotten Bashkir land impractical since migrants had already settled on much of it. In 1882, a new law forbidding the sale of Bashkir lands except to the state and to peasant communes slowed the sale of Bashkir land. Peasants also paid higher prices than the landowners had, from eight to fifteen rubles per des.

The inspection had the greatest effect on the local administration. In 1881 Kryzhanovskii and much of his administration were stripped of their positions, and the governor-general's post itself was eliminated.[122] Orenburg's governor became a civil figure who no longer had authority over Ufa Province's governor. Petersburg also felt the scandal's effects. Although Minister of Internal Affairs Petr Valuev had not personally received Bashkir land, a special commission accused him of participating in the distribution of land to high-ranking bureaucrats. Alexander III suggested that Valuev retire, and he did so late in 1881.[123]

Alexander II's assassination in the midst of Kovalevskii's investigation overshadowed discussion of the scandal, but the plundering of Bashkir land did not fade from Russian memory. The case of Bashkiria became firmly rooted in literature and political thought that were critical of the autocracy. During the 1880s, Bashkiria became the subject of numerous notes in so-called thick journals. In 1887, a land surveyor in the local peasant administration, Nikolai Remezov, wrote a book-length exposé of the politics of land in Bashkiria entitled *Essays from Wild Bashkiria: The True Story in a Fairytale Land*.[124] In 1889, prominent populist writer Gleb Uspensky published a series of articles in *Russkie vedomosti* (The Russian gazette) about his journey to the region.[125] Remezov and Uspensky, along with other writers critical of Ufa's and Orenburg's administrations, identified Bashkiria as one of the empire's most backward areas. In doing so, these writers with populist sympathies inverted the established cultural meaning of the imperial administration. Rather than casting the administration as a source of enlightenment and progress that would civilize "wild" natives and make the region more like European Russia, Remezov argued that its "wild" behavior made Bashkiria less civilized.[126] He and other writers depicted the local administration as a dark force.

Leo Tolstoy's 1886 short story "How Much Land Does a Man Need?" set in Bashkiria, rendered the event as a fable. In the story, a peasant, Pakhom, owns considerable land and rents more. He builds a small fortune but wants more land. He hears that Bashkir land can be acquired cheaply and goes to Bashkiria to acquire as much land as he can for as little as possible. A crafty Bashkir elder offers him a deal. For a thousand rubles, he can buy as much land as he can walk around in a day. If he does not make it back to where he started, however, he loses his money and gets no land. Pakhom covers a great distance, but as the sun sets, he fears he will not make it back to his starting point and starts to run. He succeeds in completing the circle as the sun sets but drops dead of exhaustion. His servant buries him in a six-foot grave, indicating how much land Pakhom needs. The story is a metaphor not only for the mindless expansion of empire, as Alexander Etkind has suggested, but, more specifically, for the greediness of Bashkiria's administrators. In their greed to separate Bashkirs from their land, they lost not their lives but their positions and the post of governor-general itself.[127]

BASHKIR POPULATION AND ESTATE

Despite the loss of land, the Bashkir population as a whole continued to grow rapidly in the period from 1850 to 1897, the year of the empire's first census, from roughly 500,000 in 1850 to 1.3 million in 1897. As in the first half of the century, this represented a higher growth rate than in the rest of European Russia over the same time period, despite famine and disease in the 1860s and the taking of Bashkir land in the 1870s. Again, the reason for this was not the particular prosperity of Bashkirs or remarkable fertility but the attractions of Bashkir estate status. As mentioned in chapter 3, in 1855 Teptiar units were joined to the Bashkir-Meshcheriak Host to create simply the Bashkir Host. All related peoples in Bashkiria now fell under the same administration. As the cantonal administration was dissolved, the particular status of Bashkir hereditary landowners, votchinniks, was maintained. Bashkir hereditary landowners after 1863 were supposed to receive thirty des. of land in communal ownership. Meshcheriaks and Teptiars who had served in the cantons received thirty des. of land that they could use but did not own. Meshcheriaks and Teptiars who were not in cantonal service but considered civil (*grazhdanskie*) persons received use of fifteen des. of land. Those who were not Bashkir hereditary landowners were considered "new Bashkirs" (*novobashkiry*). Since no clear cultural or linguistic boundaries separated the groups, Meshcheriaks and Teptiars merged with Bashkirs. When asked in the 1897 census what their "native language" was, they answered Bashkir. They took advantage of the dual nature of Bashkir identity, estate status and ethnicity, to become Bashkirs. Contemporaries were aware of this fact. Physician and local statistician Nikolai Gurvich wrote in 1877 that "the merging of Meshcheriaks with Bashkirs is an ethnographically completed fact, against which any sort of administrative or fiscal

motives for separation are powerless."[128] The number of Teptiars and Meshcheriaks recorded fell as the number of Bashkirs rose. Mikhail Rodnov has used
documents produced in land disputes to trace how members of particular villages were "service Tatars" in the 1710s, Meshcheriaks or Teptiars in the 1790s,
and "Bashkirs from the Meshcheriaks" in the 1860s.[129] As members of groups
culturally close to Bashkirs joined the core of Bashkir hereditary landowners,
the estate grew in size.

If we move from the aggregate to the level of Bashkir communities, the
Great Reform era was not so great for Bashkirs. Local officials, noblemen, factory owners, and even staff at local schools took Bashkir land, and Bashkirs
received little in return. The combination of officials intent on taking their land,
the legal means they had to do so, and the influx of migrants from central Russia
eager to acquire land posed a greater challenge than ever before. Bashkir land
had been surveyed before, but as we saw in the previous chapter, the Great Survey of the late eighteenth and early nineteenth centuries marked Bashkir land
off from that of others but did not demarcate Bashkir land into smaller parcels.
In less than a decade, 1869–1878, 851,938 des. of land—often the most productive
—was taken from Bashkirs, about one-fifth of their total holdings.[130] As many
as 100,000 were forced to move.[131] The land grab destabilized the area and made
Bashkirs seem so vulnerable that one influential cleric in Ufa, Zainulla Rasulev,
urged "local Muslims to cease all communication with Russians."[132] The parcels
of land Bashkirs had left were reduced. The land survey that took place from
1869 onward for the first time demarcated collective and individual Bashkir
hereditary landholdings from one another.[133] Many Bashkirs were left with parcels of land too small to graze herds of livestock. Animal husbandry declined
rapidly. Earlier in the nineteenth century a Bashkir with twenty or thirty horses
had been considered relatively poor. By the 1890s such a person was considered
wealthy.[134] In one county in southern Perm Province for which data by estate
category are available, the number of horses per household fell from 3.5 to 1.5
from 1849 to 1890. Bashkirs still practiced semi-nomadic pastoralism, but almost exclusively in areas to the east and south of the Urals. Animal husbandry
declined especially rapidly in Bashkiria's southwest. In contrast to the rapid decline in livestock, Bashkir agricultural production grew only gradually.[135] Especially in the mountains, Bashkirs hunted and fished to supplement their diets,
kept bees, and sold honey at local markets. Others harvested forest products or
worked in mines in the Urals. Several thousand worked in cities.[136] Bashkirs
eked out a living as best they could and rented their land to migrants from central Russia. They acquired a reputation as lazy and unproductive subjects of the
emperor. The optimism that had accompanied the Great Reforms was largely
spent by the 1870s.

CONCLUSION

The scandal over Bashkir land and the fall of the governor-general in 1881 highlights the great extent of Bashkiria's transformation during the Great Reform era. Indeed, the influence of reforms can be seen in particularly high relief in a former borderland region where the hierarchy of command and obedience that characterized Nicholaevan Russia was particularly intense. Bashkirs went from a militarized estate group subordinate to the army's hierarchy to civilian administration. Bashkirs now elected their elders rather than having them appointed. In place of military justice, they had their native "*treteiskii* courts" confirmed for minor offenses and civilian courts for more serious offenses. They, in principle and often in practice, participated in zemstvos equally with Russian peasants and occasionally even saw their fellow Muslims and Bashkirs in leadership positions. Bashkir men, along with Meshcheriaks and Teptiars, went from military and labor service obligations in cantonal administration to the payment of taxes and military service obligations like those of other men of the empire. Some members of the elite received more recognition from high officials than ever before, with many Bashkirs becoming nobles and Mufti Tevkelev receiving honors from the emperor himself. The Great Reforms made possible the participation in the cause of empire as never before, even if this participation remained within the framework of absolutism. The Great Reforms went far toward realizing their goals as articulated by Korf: "independent social life," freedom from tutelage, and conversion to civil organization.

The consolidation of estate statuses and the simplification of the social structure are unmistakable. Despite Bezak's stated goal of creating a "common mass," however, imperial officials seemed reluctant to eliminate estate groupings that had long rendered the population manageable and to which many people were attached. The reformers recognized lower levels of Bashkir courts as necessary, for instance. The limited reform of the region's judicial institutions reinforced the notion that Bashkiria was not yet suited for the legal structure of central Russia. Bashkir resistance to providing the metrical registration necessary to move them from cantonal service to universal military obligations demonstrated an attachment to what had worked in the past and, as it turned out, a reasonable fear of what changing landownership patterns held in store. The empire in Bashkiria remained a society defined by legal status, or *sosloviia*.

If we consider the empire as a whole, the effect of the Great Reforms was not at all universal. The reforms were not applied everywhere. Zemstvos, for instance, were initially introduced only in the thirty-four provinces of the empire's core. As mentioned above, Ufa's neighbor Orenburg did not convoke zemstvos until 1913. In 1887, the State Council discussed introducing them to the Baltic provinces but concluded that no matter how skillfully self-administration were organized, it would be entirely in the hands of the German nobility. Zemstvos were only introduced in nine provinces in the western borderlands in 1911, and three provinces were not included in the legislation at all. Jewish zemstvo participation was restricted in another way: No more than one-third of a zemstvo assembly could be Jewish. Such a restriction did not apply to Muslims. By 1914, zemstvos functioned in 43 of 84 provinces of the empire, not including Finland and Poland, and included about two-thirds of the empire's population.[137] The key element, as shown in the case of the Baltics, was the presence of Russian-speaking nobles that central officials considered sufficiently loyal to fulfill the goals for the reform.

In a similar manner, as the Great Reforms made Bashkir men's obligations and political possibilities more like others in the empire's core, they made Bashkir military obligations more different from those of inorodtsy located to the east, to the south, in the Caucasus, and in the western borderlands. Non-Russian men in Siberia, Central Asia, and the Caucasus were not subject to the 1874 statute on military service. Turkestan's first governor-general, von Kaufman, thought Central Asian men "lacked enough trustworthiness (*blagonadezhnost'*) to fulfill the task of defending Russian interests."[138] So, Bashkirs, after some delay, were included in such reforms, while Kazakhs, with whom Bashkirs shared the steppe and at times fought, were not included. Governor-General Kryzhanovskii argued in the 1860s that Kazakhs' level of "civic development," nomadic lifestyle, and ignorance of Russian life and language, along with the lack of suitable social groups for service in the zemstvo or as justices of the peace, made the reforms impossible.[139] The differential application of the Great Reforms in essence increased the imperial dimension of Russia, where different populations had different forms of governance. One boundary between these two portions of the empire ran along Ufa Province's border.

In the mid-nineteenth century, Russia looked to the two most successful European empires as models, as shown by Minister of Education Tolstoi's research into educational systems for Muslims in the British and French empires.[140] Russian imperial practices certainly reflected those of their European rivals and, in 1853–1856, their military opponents in the Crimean War. This was especially true of French Algeria. After France's initial conquest in 1830, French observers blamed the poor state of Algerian agriculture on the "supposed ignorance, indolence, or nomadism" of the Arabs, just as Russian observers of Bashkirs had.[141] In the first few decades of French rule, French officials confiscated arable land and sold it or gave it to desired colonists. This at times meant restrictions on land transactions to prevent speculation. In 1863, policy shifted. Emperor Louis-Napoleon definitively rejected the "despotic rights of Grand Turks" (i.e.,

the Ottoman rulers) to Algerian land and "declared the tribes of Algeria owners of all the lands they had traditionally and permanently occupied." The same
legislation divided native land into property that could be alienated and broke
tribes down into village communes, administered by a village assembly.[142] After
1863, French settlers acquired land primarily through purchases.[143] The Warnier
Law of 1873 in French Algeria effectively abolished all forms of collective ownership of land, making it clear that French policy aimed to redistribute land from
natives to colonists rather than to protect native property.[144] Through various
means between 1861 and 1881, colonists acquired 905,000 hectares of land. Already by 1870, large losses of land left Algeria's tribes with few defenses against
disease and famine, causing 20 to 25 percent of Algerian Muslims to perish in
the mid-1860s.[145] The state confiscated another 574,000 hectares in the wake of
the 1871 Kabiliya uprising and claimed more than a million hectares as part of
the public domain.[146] This was relatively more intensive land loss than Bashkirs
experienced in similar ways and over a similar time, roughly one million des.,
or 1,092,000 hectares, though losses were tremendous in both places.

Beyond the crucial factor of landholding, the Bashkir experience in the
Russian Empire, while difficult, was not as destructive as that of natives of Algeria. The approach of the Russian Empire after the scandalous dispossession
of Bashkirs in the 1870s, as we will see in the next chapter, indicated a greater
Russian interest in continued Bashkir landholding. In a similar fashion, the appointment of Salim-Girei Tevkelev, a man without religious training, indicates
Russian imperial officials' mistrust of Muslim clerics. But it was nothing like
the attack on Islam undertaken by the French in Algeria, where French officials
worked to inhibit the movement of pilgrims, exiled religious leaders, and gave
free rein to Christian missionaries in parts of the country.[147] None of these policies held in Bashkiria.

With the exception of the field of education, specific discussions of foreign
models are largely absent from deliberations of policy toward Bashkirs in the
1860s and 1870s. They may have existed but not been noted in the documentary
record. In other respects, though, the absence of such deliberations is not surprising. By the 1860s, Bashkiria was not considered a colony in the way Algeria
was, and it had not been for nearly a century. Bashkirs fought in the empire's
wars, Russian-speaking administrators governed the region, and native Bashkir and Muslim noblemen held positions of power in society. The question for
imperial officials was, how could Bashkiria be incorporated into a reformed,
more westernized administration? To answer this, imperial officials did not
need to study specifically colonial practice; the broader question was how to
organize governance, people, and resources so that the empire could compete
better with European powers.

In facing this challenge, the Russian Empire faced a similar challenge to that faced by the Ottoman Empire and the Habsburg monarchy. All three empires bordered on Europe, had fought both with and against Europeans in the nineteenth century, and pursued reform to compete better with European rivals. The three empires moved in the same direction, toward "systematic government with fuller participation of the population" and an end to servile or slave labor.[148] They did not proceed at the same pace, however. Reforms in the Ottoman Empire from 1829 to 1856 were intended to make male Ottoman subjects equal in all matters—including dress, taxation, and military service—for the first time, and to provide equal access to state schools and state employment. The Tanzimat reforms of 1839 also promised justice and an end to corruption. In 1876, Sultan Abdülhamid II issued a constitution and convened a parliament.[149] Habsburg ruler Franz Joseph II abolished serfdom in 1848, created an elected parliament in 1861, offered male subjects citizenship, divided his realm into Austrian and Hungarian halves, and emancipated the Jews.[150] The Great Reforms did not match the ambition of similar reform projects in the Ottoman Empire or Habsburg monarchy.

Nonetheless, the Great Reforms were Russia's solution to the challenge of liberalizing political systems in the West in the second half of the nineteenth century. If the Great Reforms did not go as far toward Europe's creation of a society of autonomous individual citizens who exercised popular sovereignty, neither did they fully embrace market capitalism and nation-building. This had great implications for the native peoples of Bashkiria. Tsarist administrators used the market and bureaucratic measures to dispossess many Bashkirs. As the results of such policies became clear, however, the government punished administrators and backed away from the most excessive measures, at least temporarily. In a similar way, Russian educational administrators led by Tolstoi sought to use the inculcation of Russian language as a tool for the Russification of Bashkiria's population in the cause of building a more homogenous state, but the Russian state's agenda was more limited. Years after Muslim primary schools were formally placed under the jurisdiction of the Ministry of Education, no one even knew how many there were, much less imposed regulations on them. The Great Reforms represented an experiment in associating diverse peoples without a vision of short-term assimilation and the elimination of differences. It was a delicate balancing act, to be sure, one that would be tested further when Tsar-Emancipator Alexander II no longer ruled.

5

THE EMPIRE AND THE NATION
1881–1904

MUKHAMETSALIM UMETBAEV'S WRITINGS show the wide range of responses to the Great Reforms in Bashkiria. In 1882, he spoke in the Ufa County zemstvo in favor of greater support for native-language Muslim education. The government had long "concerned itself about the enlightenment of us Muslims, subjects of the Russian Empire, through the sciences," he stated, but little progress had been made. Muslims boys in Russian-language schools looked on religion "as a last subject," when according to sharia law the teachings of the Koran are "the first subject and secular sciences second." Many Muslims saw Russian-language education without prior knowledge of a native language not as "enlightenment, but only as Russification (*obrusenie*)." Umetbaev considered this unfortunate. Since many "European sciences" had been translated from Eastern to European languages long ago, "European sciences" could be translated back into "Eastern languages." Umetbaev asked the zemstvo to fund translation of textbooks into Tatar for use by Muslims.[1]

Umetbaev's appearance demonstrated the potential for zemstvos to serve as a forum in which Muslims could present their needs to Russians, to other Muslims, and even to animists. In at least some small ways, Muslim interests could be served. The zemstvo agreed to fund mullahs to serve as teachers of Islam in Russian-language schools, even though it declined to translate textbooks into Tatar. The language Umetbaev used is also indicative of how Muslims formulated the question of Muslim education. Muslims were subjects of the Russian Empire just like others. They needed to study "European sciences" just as Russians did. If religious differences were respected, Muslims would study European sciences with zeal and success. Umetbaev was a Bashkir, but his expressed interest here was in Islam, and the language into which he sought to have books translated was Tatar. Bashkir remained a subordinate identity to Islam, and both could be constituent elements of the Russian Empire. Reformed institutions could serve as the basis for a new empire that would better reflect the desires of the tsar's subjects, Muslim and Orthodox.

If Umetbaev's zemstvo statement suggested criticism of state policies, other activities and writings demonstrate that he very much identified with autocracy and was a loyal servitor of Alexander III. Umetbaev translated and helped prepare an Arabic prayer in gold calligraphy for Alexander III, and he travelled to Moscow with Mufti Tevkelev to present it at Alexander III's coronation in May 1883.[2] Late in life, in 1904, Umetbaev wrote a poem entitled "Shikaiat," or "Complaint." In it, he criticized the despoiling of Bashkiria and lauded the tsar for appointing Ivan N. Sokolovskii as Ufa's governor to save it. "Into a country once abounding with cattle, bees, and forests," Umetbaev wrote, industrialists and merchants had come "under the protection of army and law." They drove off nearly all the cattle, floated the timber downriver to Astrakhan, and drove the bees away. Merchants partnered with foreign merchants—"Germans"—to leave nothing for the villagers.

> Hauling off treasure, they left their ways,
> Going behind our backs to hurt us,
> To ruin custom and law,
> To make each live by their rule.

For Umetbaev, the autocracy worked to save Bashkiria:

> In eradicating the pernicious,
> In restoring truth and light,
> The government is forever mighty,
> God grant the Tsar long life!

> With that goal he appointed,
> As Governor of Ufa,
> General Sokolovskii, a friend of truth and good,
> Known to the world as Ivan Nikolaevich!

> Oh, friend of righteousness and good,
> Fear neither truth nor enemy,
> Restore for the ages rights,
> Law and honor and truth forever![3]

The poem is remarkable for its description of how Bashkir land sales and thefts, along with migration to Bashkiria, had made the Bashkir way of life untenable. Even more striking is Umetbaev's description of Ivan Sokolovskii as the defender of truth and right. Sent to Ufa to restore order after Governor Bogdanovich's assassination in 1903, Sokolovskii became notorious for the sort of iron-fisted administration that Minister of Internal Affairs Viacheslav Pleve pursued and that enraged educated society in Ufa. Umetbaev's poem underscores his powerful feeling that reformed administration had damaged Bashkir land and culture and that firm, autocratic authority could restore prosperity to Bashkiria.

This chapter explores tensions between order and reform and between Russian nation-building and the maintenance of a diverse empire from Alexander III's accession to the throne in 1881 until the eve of the Revolution of 1905. Viewed from Bashkiria, the policies of Alexander III represented a restoration of order after the chaos and controversy caused by the plundering of Bashkir lands. Moreover, trains running on the railroad that connected Ufa to Moscow in 1888 brought with them new ideas as well as new goods and people. Officials from the western borderlands who arrived to head the Orenburg Educational District, headquartered in Ufa and the Ufa Archdiocese, called into question the capability of non-Russian, non-Orthodox men to be fully loyal subjects of the emperor. From the 1890s forward, however, Muslims and non-Muslim elites began to use reformed institutions to mobilize against Russifying central authority. New approaches to Muslim education and participation in imperial society became, by 1905, important issues that made evident new impulses toward activism and more cosmopolitan conceptions of the body politic. The assassination of the governor in 1903 and the zemstvo's confrontation with central authorities made Ufa Province one of the most turbulent in the empire. How Ufa Province's politics recast what it meant to be a loyal subject of the emperor will be our focus in this chapter.

Even before Alexander II's death, the spirit of the Great Reforms had begun to wane. The 1863 uprising in Poland, the 1866 attempt on Alexander's life, and the growth of political opposition had deeply shaken the confidence of imperial administrators and the emperor himself in the reformed order's ability to bring political stability and economic prosperity.[4] Relaxation of censorship and increased participation in political life seemed to breed disenchantment and to whet some appetites for more extreme change rather than fostering loyalty to the emperor and sympathy for state goals. Alexander II's heir, his son Alexander III (reigned 1881–1894), developed a very different ideology of rule. Rather than appealing to European ideals that would win the affection of the emperor's subjects, Alexander III promoted a Russian national idea combined with effective autocratic authority as principles that would forge a powerful empire. National ideas entered political life with force in the 1860s, when publicists such as Michael Katkov articulated a Russian nationalist, statist view, according to which centuries of "historical life" had developed in Russia "one dominant nationality" and "one dominant language."[5] In the 1870s, Slavophile and pan-Slavic authors echoed Katkov's emphasis on the nation but rejected his faith in the bureaucracy in favor of religion and Russian culture as the crucial foundations for the national spirit. Konstantin Pobedonostsev, Alexander III's tutor and chief procurator of the Holy Synod (1880–1905), brought Katkov and the Slavophiles together with Alexander. Pobenostsev's vision of autocratic power united with the Russian nation through the Russian Orthodox Church influenced Alexander greatly. This had major implications for imperial rule. As Richard Wortman has written, "the idealized conception of the empire shifted from a multinational elite serving the Westernized European emperor to an Orthodox, ethnically Russian elite, serving the Russian tsar." The government became a "Russian master subjecting lesser peoples of the empire." After Alexander's death in 1894, his son and heir, Nicholas II (reigned 1894–1917), maintained his father's emphasis on Russianness and pure autocracy until the end of the Old Regime, even if Nicholas II stressed an "unspoken and spiritual bond with the people" rather than the Orthodox Church and governmental institutions.[6]

Although the effort to Russify the empire was often vaguely formulated, sometimes contradictory, regionally specific, and expressed in multiple vocabularies, central authorities' emphasis on Russianness and pure autocracy greatly affected the diverse region of Bashkiria. Russianness or Russification meant the consolidation of power in institutions that would represent the interests of ethnic Russians and Orthodox Christians, whose language and faith would be the basis for the empire. The national idea provided a framework for struggle over who would be privileged in the polity and who would not. It provided a language with which to define one's opponents and appeal to central authority in defense of one's interests. Russification policies may have made few non-Russians into Russians, but they did make many non-Russians realize that, indeed, they were not Russians and pushed them to formulate a response. Furthermore, it is difficult to separate Alexandrine national ideology from the counter-reforms in the period 1881–1905. The promotion of a specifically Russian national idea implied an attack on the principles of civic inclusion and participation characteristic of the Great Reforms, since the nascent civic order required the participation of representatives of a diverse population that expressed diverse viewpoints and interests. Legislative initiatives before 1905 emphasized instead police power, such as that provided by the "Temporary Regulations" of 1881, and, secondarily, the estate principle, such as that reflected in the appointment of noble "land captains" to administer the countryside beginning in 1889.

For most of the period 1881–1905, the primary institutions for disseminating Russian national ideas in Bashkiria were, not surprisingly, the Orthodox Church and the educational bureaucracy. Yet these institutions' local agents—many of whom had experience in the empire's west—often differed from each other regarding the relative role of Orthodoxy and the Russian language in Russian nationality. Moreover, local study of official efforts to foster Russianness in the east shows its limitations and contradictions. The legacy of Great Reforms and earlier nonnational practices remained strong. Until the turn of the century, even local governors seemed to perceive less of a threat from non-Russians than did central officials, churchmen, and educational officials. Since local governors had as their primary charge the maintenance of stability and economic prosperity, they seemed less inclined to change their modus operandi with local society in general and with prominent Muslims in particular. Only in 1903 did the killing of striking workers and the assassination of Ufa Province's governor mark a new wave of political violence in the empire and sharpen the divide between autocracy and local elites.

RAILROADS AND MIGRATION

The region's growing population and new means of transportation changed the task confronting local officials. In 1888, the Samara-Ufa railway connected Ufa directly with Moscow. Two years later the line extended to Zlatoust in the Ural Mountains and thereafter across Siberia. Ufa Province was no longer remote. Even before the railway opened, thousands of workers arrived to build it. Within a decade, the Samara-Zlatoust railway workshops located in Ufa employed more than a thousand workers. The population of Ufa nearly doubled between 1886 and 1897, reaching a total of 49,275. In the 1890s, the number of factories employing more than sixteen workers increased by 82 percent and the number of workers by three times. Ufa still lagged behind other areas in economic activity, but it had taken on the trappings of a city, with improved roads, some electricity (1898), a water system (1901), and labor conflicts.[7] The railway brought an increased flow of migrants to rural parts of Ufa Province as well. In the thirty-six-year period between emancipation and 1897, 190,944 people migrated to Ufa Province, according to official statistics. Officially registered migrants thus made up about one-tenth of the province's population.[8] Moreover, Kryzhanovskii's simple division of Great Russian migrants from non-Russian local "elements" proved inadequate to describe the diverse stream of people arriving in Ufa. In 1894, for instance, a group of about one thousand Latvians arrived in the city of Ufa. Their resources were exhausted, and they could not make it to Siberia, their intended destination.[9] The large-scale introduction of people of different cultures and religions intensified educators' and the Orthodox hierarchy's perception that they must build institutional connections with the migrants to prevent the spread of harmful ideas.

RUSSIAN ORTHODOXY'S MISSION IN UFA PROVINCE

In Bashkiria, the Russian Orthodox Church began to attack the Great Reforms as secular and foreign to Russia's traditions even before 1881. Local churchmen sought to drive secular and Muslim influences from the public sphere in order to establish Orthodox and, by extension, Russian dominance. To make their appeals for support from central institutions more effective, churchmen argued that Muslim opposition to church programs threatened the integrity of the empire. The church's attack on the Great Reforms and advocacy of a Russian Orthodox nation became apparent locally upon the appointment of Nikanor (Bobrovnikov) as Ufa's bishop in 1876. Historian Alexander Polunov has described Nikanor as a "despotic and conservative 'prince of the Church'" as well as an "outstanding phenomenon" due to his talents as an administrator, preacher, and writer.[10] Born in the town of Mogilev in the empire's west, Nikanor had served as the rector of the Kazan Spiritual Academy and as bishop of Aksaisk in the Don region.[11] He had solid connections in St. Petersburg, maintaining an extensive correspondence with Chief Procurator of the Holy Synod Konstantin Pobedonostsev.[12] John Strickland has identified Nikanor as one of the key early proponents of "clerical Orthodox patriotism" and the conception of Russia as the "new Israel"—a community of believers chosen by God. As such, Strickland writes that Nikanor "had elaborated a vision of how a nation-specific providence brought Orthodox Russia to the leading position in world-historical development, a position formerly occupied by ancient Israel. And, provided its people preserved the national faith, they would continue to occupy this position forever."[13] Nikanor fused Orthodoxy with the Russian national spirit to assert a sort of religious nationalism. In such a scenario, the tsar ideally governed as an apostle-like leader of Holy Rus'. The Great Reforms, inspired by secular ideas imported from the West, threatened the decline of the national spirit, which Nikanor saw as his task to reinvigorate.

Nikanor's activity as Bishop of Ufa makes clear the force and conviction with which he pursued the renewal of Russia's national spirit. On long trips over poor roads to review his bishopric, Nikanor became convinced that both elements of what he called the "state-religious" structure were in dire need of reinforcement. The state had ceased to defend the interests of the church. "Secular society" and local administrators from the governor on down were "indifferent to the dissemination and affirmation of the Christian faith." If a local police or military man attended church services at all, he was often a Pole or a German who had no respect for Orthodoxy.[14]

Nikanor argued that the state's abandonment of the church was nowhere more evident than in the state's treatment of non-Russians. In essence, Nikanor defended the Petrine absolutist rule that had characterized the mid-eighteenth century in Bashkiria. Nikanor believed that the Russian Empire was a "live organism" that had grown for a thousand years through "conquests and assimilation." In Nikanor's view, central officials demonstrated their lack of understanding of this central fact when an uprising of Tatars in Kazan Province spread throughout the region in 1878–1879. Ufa governor Vladimir Levshin responded by trying to calm the rebels through persuasion and palliative measures. Kazan governor Nikolai Skariatin, however, "like a courageous Russian warrior-ruler," went to the site of the uprising, "saw and conquered." He flogged about twenty rebels, "in the ancient fashion, in the Russian fashion," and pacified the entire region.[15] "The Petersburg intelligentsia, Petersburg jurisprudence, and Petersburg officialdom," however, had criticized Skariatin. The senate sent Senator Mikhail Kovalevskii to investigate. In Nikanor's opinion, by insisting on legality "of the newest cut in foreign fashion," Kovalevskii had weakened the Russian Orthodox position. Kovalevskii had given a push backward to the historical truth "of the right of predominance in the local area of the Russian Christian element over the alien, in previous times openly hostile . . . Tatar element." In place of Russian domination by force, Nikanor argued that Kovalevskii sought to establish the "ideal, English, American, juridical justice" intended by the Great Reforms. Nikanor believed that the end of traditional, "warrior-ruler" governance resulted in unrest and made possible defections from the Orthodox Church to Islam and sectarianism.[16]

The church's share of the "state-religious structure" did not escape Nikanor's wrath. His tours about the province convinced him that the "simple Russian people" (*narod*) did not know its faith. Nikanor attributed Orthodoxy's weakness to poor work by church personnel and to the church's inadequate institutional presence. Some village priests did not read or even own a Bible and made no attempt to fulfill church rites.[17] Nikanor expressed the greatest anger, however, at a priest whose lack of engagement was such that in nine years he "had not noticed" whether those in his parish spoke Russian. The province's large expanse and rapidly growing population contributed to these problems. Nikanor questioned how a priest who had four thousand people in his parish or was responsible for people twenty-five to fifty-five miles away could possibly have much influence on them.[18]

Through Nikanor's correspondence with Konstantin Pobedonostsev, he sought to bring central pressure to bear on local administrators. He helped to convince Pobedonostsev that church construction must increase.[19] In all, Nikanor won synod approval for thirty-five new priests, primarily in areas with substantial non-Russian populations, in growing towns, and in areas with new settlements. Twenty-eight churches were built in the province during Nikanor's seven-year tenure, compared to only ten in the eleven years preceding his arrival.[20] Nikanor also prioritized missionary work among animist peoples and formally baptized Tatars. For these programs, Nikanor relied heavily on the work of Kazan missionary Nikolai I. Il'minskii, who placed his students as priests and teachers in Bashkiria's missionary schools.[21] Nikanor established the Ufa

Missionary Committee in 1878 to invigorate missionary activity, which had been "purely nominal."[22] Nikanor began to focus attention on the organization of parish life through the creation of parish councils of trustees (*popechitel'stva*). The idea of creating councils originated in the late 1850s and early 1860s as a means to stimulate the "independence and autonomous activity of parish communities" and to support priests financially.[23] Finally, Nikanor established a journal, *Ufimskie eparkhial'nye vedomosti* (The Ufa eparchial gazette), which provided a means for him to communicate with both clergy and laity.

After Nikanor left to become bishop of Kherson in 1883, his successors continued his effort to strengthen Russian Orthodoxy and to identify the Orthodox Church as a Russian national institution. Bishop Dionisii (Khitrov), who replaced Nikanor, made missionary work a top priority. In 1840, at the age of twenty-two, Dionisii had gone to Iakutsk as a missionary. He remained there for the next forty-three years. While in Ufa, Dionisii presided over explosive growth in the local Russian Orthodox Church. In all, Dionisii presided over the construction of 127 churches and expanded missionary schools from four to forty during his thirteen-year tenure (1884–1896). Of all the churches in the province in 1897, about half (50.85 percent) had been built in the preceding twenty years.[24] Dionisii's tenure as bishop of Ufa also featured a massive expansion of church-supervised parish schools (*tserkovno-prikhodskie shkoly*) and literacy schools (*shkoly gramoty*), which had been nearly nonexistent in Ufa before Pobedonostsev made them one of his fundamental causes as chief procurator of the synod in the 1880s.[25] By the time the Statute on Parish Schools had become law in 1884, sixty-eight were operational in Ufa Province, although in the long run they tended to be less well-funded and less popular than MNP and zemstvo schools.[26] Institution building in this period enabled the Orthodox Church to enter into the lives of the province's population more than before.

Efforts to build Orthodox authority in Bashkiria meant not only building churches and religious schools but attacking what the church perceived as its enemies. In 1867, the Kazan archbishop had called attention to the growing power of a "Mohammedan Spirit" in the Volga-Urals region.[27] Such ideas interacted with the experience of local missionaries to fuel a new level of concern about a Muslim threat. Belebei County was a center of difficulties for the Orthodox. Priest Andrei Petrov's correspondence with Nikolai Il'minskii regarding Islam in Belebei illustrates the church's central interest in depriving Muslims of influence in civic life. Il'minskii had trained Petrov in Kazan and then assigned him to the town of Bizhbuliak, a largely Chuvash village in Belebei. Petrov wrote that Chuvashes in a nearby town had recently come under the influence of Muslim mullahs from a madrasa in Sterlibash, located across the county border in Sterlitamak.[28] In his letters to Il'minskii, Petrov noted the comparative weakness of Orthodoxy in Ufa. In Kazan, Petrov wrote, Muslim Tatars had to work quietly, knowing that they stood "face to face" against "that all-powerful Russian might." In Ufa, one felt a "lack of Russian authority," of "Russian spirit," and of churches, which led to the "dominating spirit of Islam."

Petrov's statements drew on themes used at the very center of power in St. Petersburg. Petrov asserted that "Orthodoxy, tightly merging with Russian ethnicity (*narodnost'iu*)," served as one of the primary bases of the Russian state principle. That principle collapsed in the local context, however. Muslims and non-Russians abounded "in everything, in the cities and even in the sphere of state service." Petrov wrote that there were "no Russians" in Ufa, only "Poles, Yids, and Germans." The rare Russian doctor or police official had become "cosmopolitan" in his attitudes. Petrov believed that Catherinian toleration and the Westernizing ethos of the Great Reforms had helped Muslims win converts. Orthodox officials showed respect to clerics in keeping with "some sort of abstract common human rights," according to which "the division of all humanity living on the earth into separate states would not be possible" and neither the Ottoman nor the Russian-Orthodox empires could exist. Petrov blamed the situation in large part on the OMEA, which had strengthened in Muslims a consciousness of their "power and independence." Muslim missionary activity would enable the "non-Orthodox, non-Russian population of the empire" to form a "theocratized state within the Russian State, hostile to the Russian empire."[29]

In two letters to Pobedonostsev, Il'minskii drew upon Petrov's complaints regarding the Muslim presence in zemstvos to suggest that Muslims had created a "Muslim tsardom" in Ufa. Il'minskii described how Bashkir Shakhaidar Syrtlanov, a nobleman and Belebei zemstvo chairman, had "seized power in Belebei" and directed it "to the detriment of the education of non-Russian Christians." "Standing as if before the fateful gates" not long before his death, Il'minskii stated his alarm over the situation: "In Ufa province Muslims comprise a service, agricultural, and landowning class—of the intelligentsia, but nonetheless Tatar patriots on a Muslim basis. The Ufa area is truly a Muslim tsardom: in the administration, and especially in the zemstvo and in society Muslims are strong, strong and clever."[30] He then suggested that support for Sterlibash clerics extended as far as Petersburg. "Your Petersburg Muslims," Il'minskii wrote, support the apostasy of the Chuvashes "in the name of freedom of conscience and other ideas so seductive for our cosmopolitans." Il'minskii asked Pobedonostsev to warn higher authorities of the Muslim threat. Il'minskii's retelling of Petrov's struggle with the clerics and the local officials refined Petrov's argument for the political importance of Muslim activism. Religion alone did not unite the Muslims in Ufa's administration and zemstvos.

Muslims were "Tatar patriots on a Muslim basis" who lacked loyalties to the tsar and the Russian Empire. The use of an ethnonym indicated that the Muslims were loyal to a cultural complex identified as Tatar that differed from but was built upon Islam. Pobedonostsev became the advocate of Il'minskii's ideas in St. Petersburg.

THE ORENBURG EDUCATIONAL DISTRICT AND RUSSIFICATION

While the Orthodox Church promoted church-building and missionary work, the Orenburg Educational District (OUO) continued to emphasize the inculcation of Russian language and culture. The MNP built schools in the period 1875 to 1905 for both non-Russians and Russian speakers in an attempt to spread Russian literacy and further the state's interests. The number of secular schools—those not run by the church or Muslim religious leaders—in Ufa Province grew by more than four times during this period, from 293 in 1870 to 1,320 in 1900. The number of students grew even faster, by almost seven times.[31] The school network's growth helped produce an increase in Russian literacy rates among Ufa men drafted into the military from 4.4 percent in 1867 to 18.7 percent in 1900. Yet only 6.5 percent of the literate had completed primary school, indicating that the educational system's reach remained quite limited.[32] Many students left school as soon as they achieved fundamental literacy, which limited schools' ability to convey Russian culture more broadly.[33] Meanwhile, secondary schools also did little to promote national consciousness. Before 1900, the MNP's curriculum discounted the cultivation of Russian national identity in favor of classical languages, the study of which Minister of Education Tolstoi thought would discipline young minds and keep them away from oppositional politics.[34]

Bilingual schools that were created in the wake of the legislation of 1870 to produce a rapprochement between non-Russians and the state satisfied no one. In 1884, the number of Russian/non-Russian schools in Ufa Province had grown to over ninety, but state officials believed the schools taught the Russian language poorly and featured too much involvement by non-Russian teachers. In 1887, for instance, the Ufa director of primary schools argued that students who attended bilingual schools or Russian classes attached to Muslim confessional schools could read only a little and understood no spoken Russian, so the schools should be closed as failures.[35] Meanwhile, educational officials did not record the ethnicity of students, so some students whose first language was Russian attended nearby schools meant for non-Russians and, presumably, studied non-Russian languages. Muslims, as Umetbaev suggested, often believed that the schools were insufficiently Muslim and too closely connected to what they perceived as the Russian state's missionary goals. Nonetheless, the number of bilingual schools grew over time, from 96 in 1880 to 248 in 1900, as did the number of students in them, from 1,841 to 10,009.[36] This caused some officials and zemstvo activists to hope that increased funding would lower Muslim resistance to the schools. In the meantime, however, schools seemed to have little success in promoting Russian language and culture.

The process of making the empire's schools more "Russian" began only at the century's turn. Minister of Education Nikolai Bogolepov wrote in 1899 that teachers and parents had begun to decry the "dry formalism and bureaucratic character of gimnasiums and *realschules*." Schools neglected "Russian language, Russian history, and Russian literature," which robbed them of "a vital, national character."[37] Bogolepov's successor, Petr Vannovskii, limited the study of classical languages in favor of Russian language, geography, and science.[38] The curator of the OUO and his top officials introduced changes to Bashkiria's schools in autumn of 1901. Henceforth teachers were to focus on aspects of "universal history" closely connected with events in Russian history, such as the work of Cyril and Methodius and the history of Napoleon. In order to "make the school national," the literature of the fatherland was made fundamental, and Russian history would no longer be only a minor subject. A conference of Russian language and history teachers in 1901 echoed this approach.[39] After 1900, as never before, students in the gimnasium would receive grounding in their "fatherland's" history and geography.

Japan's declaration of war on Russia on January 26, 1904, added the task of mobilizing for war to schools' efforts to cultivate Russianness. The mobilization motivated educational officials to promote patriotism founded upon knowledge of the fatherland, its history, and its mission. Toward this end, officials instructed secondary school staffs to undertake special lectures intended to make clear the true meaning of the war. In order to help guide those who gave the special lectures, the OUO's district inspector issued a circular that put the war in a broad historical context. The district inspector argued that the current war was the continuation of an old conflict with "little-cultured, porous, ethnographic elements (Finns and Mongols)" on Russia's eastern and southeastern border and the beginning of war against "the development of pan-Mongolism," which posed a "terrible danger for Christianity and European civilization." The circular thus identified the Japanese threat as a contemporary equivalent of the "Tatar-Mongol" threat from the thirteenth and fourteenth centuries. Moreover, educational officials wrote Russia into the Europe's Christian, civilizing mission while distinguishing Russian imperialism from the excesses of Western imperialism. Educators argued that Russia practiced a softer, more humane imperialism than European powers. Russia's relations with native populations were "eternally Christian-brotherly" and "kindhearted." Even less-cultured peoples received "all the civil rights of native Russian people." By contrast, Western European countries, especially England, conquered for the benefit of their industrial capitalists, treated subject populations harshly, and derived vast profits from their colonies.[40] Educational officials' understanding of this mission among the "wild, less-cultured" eastern peoples had the effect of making Others out of about half the educational district's population. This fact was not lost on some in the region. Police picked up rumors that the Japanese emperor was a Tatar and that he would give land to Bashkirs if the Japanese won.[41]

MVD officials in St. Petersburg and especially their subordinate local governors showed little concern about the Muslim and Tatar threats cited by religious and educational officials. State bureaucrats and local elites remained much more committed to conceptions of the imperial polity that transcended nation. The MVD and its local governors had to maintain order and to increase economic prosperity. Local officials in so ethnically and religiously diverse a place as Ufa had incentives to rely on elites of all types in fulfilling their missions. Unless members of the local elite threatened public order, local governors considered them loyal subjects of the tsar. Ufa governors' responses to complaints of Muslim influence in local life make this clear. In 1883 local educational officials complained to Dmitrii Tolstoi, appointed minister of internal affairs the previous year, that the Belebei zemstvo paid Muslim clerics to provide religious instruction in Russian-Tatar and Russian-Bashkir schools but did not pay Orthodox clergy for religious instruction. In 1887 the MNP raised the question of Muslim power once again because Kutlu-Mukhammad Tevkelev (Mufti Tevkelev's nephew) had become Belebei marshal of the nobility and thus the head of the school council that supervised the county's Russian Orthodox schools. In neither case did Ufa governor Petr Poltoratskii share the concern of educational officials. Poltoratskii pointed out that, according to law, Bashkirs and other Muslims participated in zemstvo institutions on the same basis as Russian and Russian Orthodox subjects of the tsar. Unless the zemstvo statute was amended to include limits on non-Russian participation such as those intended to reduce the Jewish presence in city Dumas in the western borderlands, he could not prevent Muslims from having a majority in the Belebei zemstvo and a near-majority in the Sterlitamak zemstvo.[42] Poltoratskii did not see Muslims as a threat, however. He stated that Tevkelev had done nothing to cause him to suspect that Tevkelev pursued "any tribal or religious goals" to the detriment of the interests of Orthodoxy and of the Russian population. Tevkelev retained his position, but the law was changed so that the marshal of the nobility's responsibilities with respect to Russian Orthodox education fell to an MNP official in the event a Muslim was elected marshal.[43] In the end, the new zemstvo statute of 1890 did not specifically limit Muslim participation, but the governor could easily use his ability to appoint peasant electors to reduce Muslim representation. Poltoratskii was confident that his ability to override zemstvo actions prevented assertions of Muslim authority.[44]

The MVD and Poltoratskii's successor, Governor Lev E. Nord, handled Bishop Dionisii's and Il'minskii's complaints of Muslim influence in Ufa in a similar manner. Minister of Internal Affairs Ivan N. Durnovo forwarded to Ufa governor Nord a memo from Pobedonostsev containing Il'minskii's complaint regarding a "Muslim tsardom" in Belebei County and the Belebei zemstvo's failure to pay Orthodox clergymen who provided religious instruction in schools. Nord reduced Il'minskii's dramatic complaint to flat bureaucratic prose. Nord pointed out that the Belebei zemstvo's failure to pay salaries was common and reflected the poor state of zemstvo coffers. Nord gave no sense that Muslims threatened missionary schools or his authority. Finally, Nord indicated that he could eliminate any future attacks on missionary activity through use of his powers to limit Muslim representation. According to article 87 of the zemstvo statute of 1890, the governor could annul zemstvo measures that did not "correspond to general state interests and needs."[45] Governors perceived no threat to their power from Muslim participation in political life and asserted that they had sufficient power to eliminate such a threat if it arose. In response to church and educational officials' demands, they denied the ill intentions of individual Muslims and worked under the assumption that Muslims fit within imperial institutions, if in a somewhat reduced role.

BASHKIR LAND AND STATUS

In the wake of the "land fever" and scandal that cost Kryzhanovskii his post as Orenburg governor-general in 1881, Alexander III and his officials, in keeping with his ruling ideology, reasserted state control and estate principles against disruptive market forces. The state did not try to restore the status quo ante in Bashkiria. Only a fraction of the land taken from Bashkirs through improperly documented transactions, some 140,000 des. of roughly 600,000 des. (according to government figures), was returned to its original owners.[46] New legislation continued to recognize Bashkir hereditary landowners' rights to their land, but Bashkirs could not sell that land on the open market. They could only sell it to the state or to peasant communes, not noblemen, merchants, or townspeople.[47] In the 1880s, the state also sought to demarcate Bashkirs from their neighbors and from other estates. Bashkir lands were surveyed so that Bashkir land might finally be separated from that of Bashkir pripushchenniks, the mostly non-Russian, non-Orthodox peoples whose fate had long been tied to that of Bashkirs. This separation was largely achieved by the late 1890s.[48] Bashkir hereditary landowners were largely consolidated into land parcels reduced in size but more homogenously Bashkir, both in the estate and ethnic meaning of the words, than before. As Bashkirs were separated more clearly from others with whom they had shared land, so too were they separated from those who had left the estate for the nobility. In 1884, "princes," merchants, and townspeople living on Bashkir land but lacking formal deeds, 1,982 in all, were separated off from Bashkir communities even though they did not differ "according to way of life and type of occupation" from peasant landholders.[49] Mukhametsalim Umetbaev wrote that as a nobleman, he had to resist those telling him he should not be concerned with burdens placed on ordinary Bashkirs since he was not one of them.[50] Myriad complexities in population remained, but the structure of estate status in Bashkiria became simpler and more similar to that applied elsewhere in the empire.

Nevertheless, during the 1880s Bashkirs' economic situation deteriorated markedly. Stories of Bashkir poverty appeared frequently in both the central and local press. Loss of land in the previous two decades left many Bashkir communities with considerable landholdings, yet the semi-nomadic pastoralism of their past had become difficult to sustain as migrants crowded their traditional pasturage. Crop failures that affected almost all of Bashkiria and provoked famine in 1891–1892 also took their toll. In both Ufa Province and neighboring Orenburg Province, tax arrears soared to more than three times the annual obligation.[51] Some Bashkirs took to settled agriculture, but most found it easier to rent land to migrants than to work it themselves. Bashkiria's native peoples were caught between older ways that were no longer tenable and newer agricultural practices to which they adapted slowly.

Two aspects of Bashkir landownership continued to cause conflicts and legal disputes as well as arrears in land tax payments, becoming the subject of discussion in the State Council in 1898. First, restrictions on Bashkir land sales established in 1882 had brought them to a halt in Ufa Province and slowed them greatly in Orenburg Province. Yet the flow of migrants to Bashkiria continued unabated, and it even accelerated after the railroad connected Ufa to Moscow in 1888. In-migrants hungry for land resorted to renting land instead of buying it and sometimes even rented land that was supposed to support Bashkir hereditary landowners themselves. Second, Bashkir land had been demarcated from that of pripushchenniks, but it was distinguished from that of other hereditary landowners only in rare cases. So, legal disputes, complaints to peasant administrators, and even armed clashes persisted among Bashkirs and between Bashkirs and those to whom they sold or rented land. Even when conflicts of interest were absent, assembling as many as two thousand or more Bashkir heads of household spread over as many as one hundred miles so that the legally required two-thirds of them could agree to have their land surveyed and parceled out among themselves proved difficult. The legislation of 1882 had, in principle, prevented noble and merchant groups from buying Bashkir land, but now problems arose with the rental of Bashkir land. Some Bashkir parcels still had as much as 148, 161, or 381 des. of land per soul, far more than Bashkirs could work. Settlers who rented from Bashkirs, on the other hand, lacked the stable land tenure that ownership could provide and often had to rent land at high prices from merchant intermediaries who used their deep pockets and local knowledge to rent Bashkir land at low prices.[52] Settlers renting land often took advantage of vague agreements and unspecific boundaries to take more land than rental agreements allowed. This left Bashkirs to pay taxes on land that they did not in fact control. Add various "lawyers" who sought out such conflicts in order to bring legal action, and a physical, juridical, and fiscal mess resulted. Neither the administration, nor the zemstvo, nor Bashkirs themselves knew which land belonged to whom. The confusion over landownership complicated Bashkir land use, facilitated improper land deals, distorted taxation, and impoverished Bashkirs.

The State Council's answer to the confusion resulting from previous efforts to regulate Bashkir land was to regulate it more. In 1898, the State Council again permitted Bashkirs to sell or to rent land only to the state or to peasant communes, and the latter could buy no more than 15 des. of land and rent no more than 30 des. per person. The provincial administration was supposed to evaluate land transactions for fairness to both parties. Noble land captains were charged with overseeing the process. The two most important parts of the law, however, involved the surveying of land. Whereas before surveying land was to be voluntary upon approval of two-thirds of those involved, now a commission would survey Bashkir land and divide it from that of other Bashkirs *unless* two-thirds of the heads of households in the relevant settlements voted not to have their land surveyed. This required Bashkirs to take action if they sought to maintain the status quo rather than when they sought to change it. The second major point greatly favored settlers who rented land from Bashkirs. If Bashkirs agreed to rent land to peasant settlers but refused either to renew the agreement when it expired or to sell land to the peasant settlers, they had to compensate settlers for all their expenditures on structures and any improvements they made to the land.[53] These two provisions meant that the state could force the survey and demarcation of Bashkir land even when a village did not want to have its land surveyed and essentially forced Bashkirs to sell or rent land to settlers.

MUFTI SULTANOV, THE ORENBURG MUHAMMADAN
ECCLESIASTICAL ASSEMBLY, AND REFORM ISLAM

Differences between religious and educational officials who sought to build a Russian Orthodox nation of some sort and those in the MVD who needed to govern a diverse population became clear in attitudes toward the Orenburg Muhammadan Ecclesiastical Assembly (OMEA). Churchmen such as Petrov who considered the OMEA implacably hostile to state interests called for its abolition. Officials in the secular administration weighed this concern against the need to influence Muslim society in order to foster loyalty and to promote Russian as a lingua franca for the empire. These two positions emerged when Mufti Tevkelev's death in 1885 necessitated the appointment of a new mufti. The eventual choice, Mukhamed'iar Sultanov, lacked Tevkelev's stature and prominence in Russian-speaking society. His family had been ennobled through service in Bashkir administration, but he was not as wealthy as Tevkelev. He had attended Kazan University but had to drop out for health reasons.[54] He also lacked a religious education that could make him a prominent interpreter of Islamic law. Nikolai Il'minskii urged the appointment of Sultanov as Tevkelev's successor precisely because of Sultanov's comparative lack of stature and purported weak will.[55] Dmitrii Tolstoi, the person most responsible for appointing a mufti, had a different perspective. Tolstoi agreed that the mufti should be a "loyal and faithful executor" of the government's plans and should not possess "Muslim fanaticism." But Tolstoi did not want a weak mufti, either. He required a mufti who could promote the state's interests among Muslims and spread Russian literacy. Ufa governor Poltoratskii felt that Sultanov's education and ability made him among the most prominent members of his faith, while other officials described him as a capable and respected figure.[56] On Tolstoi's recommendation, Tsar Alexander III appointed Sultanov mufti on January 2, 1886.

The mufti's importance resulted in part from the rapid growth of his jurisdiction in the last thirty years of tsarist rule. Rather than restricting the practice of Islam, the administration made it easier in the late imperial period. The late nineteenth century saw a great increase in the number of mosques. In 1886, a State Council resolution made it somewhat easier to open a mosque by reducing the number of village residents required for approval of mosque construction from two hundred males listed in the tenth tax census of 1857 to two hundred males actually living in a village. Echoing Catherine's statement of toleration, the resolution stated that such legislation corresponded to the "animating intention of the government—to ensure people of foreign faiths living within the empire the greatest possible freedom in the satisfaction of their spiritual needs without detriment to the state Church."[57] Muslims in Ufa rapidly took advantage of the law to open mosques. By 1891, the Ufa governor reported that there were 1,452 mosques in the province, about 200 of which had been built in the first three years after the new law.[58] The city of Ufa's first madrasa, Usmaniia, opened in 1887. The number of mosques and clerics in the OMEA's jurisdiction grew steadily, from 4,053 mosques with 6,553 clerics in 1868 to 5,230 mosques with 8,312 clerics in 1908.[59] The number of Muslim primary schools, maktabs, appears to have grown rapidly as well. With more than four million Muslims under its jurisdiction, the OMEA had a large and growing constituency.

Even as central officials sought a strong mufti and allowed rapid growth of Muslim institutions, it sought to exert greater control over Muslim administration. On July 16, 1888, the MNP issued rules that required all OMEA judges to possess Russian skills equivalent to those of secondary school graduates; required all "higher parish clergy" (akhunds and *khatyps*—imams officially licensed to give the Friday sermon) to have skills equivalent to those of primary school graduates; and insisted that all village clerics be able to speak and to read Russian. The law became effective in 1891.[60] Within months of announcing the policy in 1888, the OMEA had received one hundred petitions in protest. Even OMEA judges initially rejected the new rules. The centrality of Arabic to the practice of Islam and the association of the Russian language with missionary activity caused some Muslims to regard the rules as an attack on Islam and a step toward forced conversion. Next, rules of July 10, 1892, mandated that printed books approved by a censor rather than handwritten manuscripts be used as texts in Muslim schools. Finally, teachers in maktabs and madrasas were required to be subjects of the tsar trained within the empire rather than foreigners or subjects of the tsar trained abroad.[61] Since Muslim schools relied heavily on foreign materials and many of the most learned Muslim teachers studied abroad as part of their training, these rules had great potential to disrupt confessional schools.

Overall, however, these policies had limited effects. Several popular Muslim teachers who initially had been fired were later reinstated. In 1894, the MVD annulled the policy banning those trained abroad from teaching positions.[62] Censors approved a total of sixty-two textbooks of foreign origin and prohibited two. Sultanov did not demonstrate great zeal in urging clerics to comply with the new rules.[63] The OMEA's three judges at this time began to sign their names in Russian script, and the governor of Kazan Province claimed that the law increased the number of Muslims studying Russian in Muslim secondary schools.[64] Petitions by clerics and the signatures on them were usually in Tatar, however, so mullahs' mastery of Russian can be questioned. Nonetheless, Sultanov clearly gained favor among St. Petersburg officials for his work. In August

1888, the tsar awarded Mufti Sultanov the Order of St. Stanislav, first class, for the latter's "participation in the education of Muslim clergy." Ufa governor Poltoratskii later recommended that Sultanov receive another medal for his work to overcome Muslim resistance to the 1897 census.[65] When the mufti sought to have his son admitted to military school in Orenburg, Minister of Internal Affairs Ivan Durnovo urged military authorities to approve Sultanov's request since educating his son "in the Russian spirit" would serve as a good example for other Muslims.[66] The State Council also strengthened the mufti's position within the OMEA by allowing the mufti to recommend the OMEA's judges to the MVD rather than having them elected.[67]

Much as the OMEA held an ambiguous position within the tsarist administration, its place in the Muslim community was also complicated. The last half-century of Romanov rule featured intense competition over the nature of Islam and what some perceived as the need for Muslim reform. Beginning in the 1880s, Muslims such as Crimean Tatar Ismail Bei Gasprinskii, influenced by intellectual currents within Islam globally, criticized the backwardness of Muslim life in the empire. Gasprinskii argued that contemporary residents "of Bakhchisarai, Kazan, or Kasim and others" presented a "material and intellectual picture of the time of Ivan Groznyi, Ermak, and Choban-Girei," characterized by a stale atmosphere of immobility and stagnation.[68] Reformers sought to use "new method" (*usul-i jadid*) education to renew Muslim life. The term at first described a phonetic method for teaching Muslim youth how to read Arabic pioneered by Gasprinskii in 1884 in the Crimea. Students learned the sounds of each Arabic letter and then studied their combinations rather than studying syllables and words through rote memorization. In reformed schools, words and phrases from students' native languages often were used to facilitate the mastery of Arabic phonetics. *Jadid* innovations extended beyond the method of Arabic-language instruction. Students in elementary schools began to study their native languages, arithmetic, geography, and calligraphy. The best jadid secondary schools also introduced the study of Russian language, the history of Islam, and secular sciences such as algebra, geometry, and chemistry.[69] The centrality of the new schools to reform was such that reformers became known as jadids.

Reformist currents began to penetrate Muslim educational practices in Bashkiria in the 1880s. Shortly after Khairulla Usmanov became the imam of Ufa's central mosque in 1888, he became a defender of reform. He gradually introduced jadid methods into the madrasa Usmaniia attached to the mosque. Usmaniia became a center for the spread of the "new method" in the province.[70] In the 1890s, the OMEA became a vehicle for portions of the Muslim elite who pursued jadid reforms, even if the OMEA never was on the cutting edge of reform efforts.

The interest of Mufti Sultanov in Muslim reform would seem, perhaps, unexpected. As discussed above, Il'minskii and others supported his candidacy precisely because "national demands" seemed beyond him. Furthermore, the policy of appointing the OMEA's judges seemed to have been aimed at preventing the election of men who would advocate Muslim causes in the OMEA. Nonetheless, beginning in the 1890s, Mufti Sultanov used his influence to appoint several reform-minded clerics to the OMEA. Sultanov appointed Gabderashid G. Ibragimov as an OMEA judge in 1893. Ibragimov served only briefly, however, before departing for Istanbul, where he was influenced by Muslim reformer Jamal ad-Din al-Afghani and wrote a pamphlet critical of Russian administration of Muslims. After Ibragimov was deported back to Russia, arrested, and then freed, he became a publisher in St. Petersburg, an instigator of Muslim cooperation with the Kadet party, and a principal organizer of Muslim conferences in 1905–1906. In 1901, Mufti Sultanov recommended a book by Ibragimov for use at prayer meetings.[71] Prominent Muslim religious thinker Rizaetdin Fakhretdinov left a greater imprint on the OMEA. The son of an imam, Fakhretdinov became an OMEA judge in 1891 and remained in that capacity until 1906. During his tenure, he produced a multivolume bio-bibliography of prominent Muslims in the Volga-Urals region and published widely on religious questions, on the role of women in Muslim society, and on Muslim education.[72] Both men were interested in religious reform to produce a more "pristine" Islam that would reinvigorate Muslim society and make it compatible with "Western concepts of freedom, equality, and progress."[73] Translator and publicist Umetbaev had been appointed to the clerical staff of the OMEA in 1887 and served until his retirement in 1901. In addition to promoting native-language Muslim education in the Ufa County zemstvo, he collected Bashkir folklore, contributed to Russian newspapers, and translated Pushkin into Tatar for Gasprinskii's journal. Other prominent Muslim reformers became judges, including Khasangata Gabashi, who served in the OMEA from 1895 to 1899 and 1908 to 1915.

Sultanov's instructions (*nakazy*) themselves began to reflect the conceptions of Muslim reformers. His instructions to imams in 1897 and 1898 argued that village imams needed to work for the spiritual and moral improvement of Muslims as well as for their economic prosperity. In addition to calling for the proper discharge of religious obligations, in 1897 the mufti urged imams to appeal to Muslims clearly and in their native language, avoiding Arabic and Persian words incomprehensible to common people.[74] The following year Mufti Sultanov wrote to the imams that it was clear to him "that we, Muslims, with every passing day lag behind other peoples, going counter to progress." In Sultanov's eyes, Muslims had settled into "ignorance, stagnation, coarse morals, carefree laziness," and "a lack of desire to work." In sum, he noted that the "complete depravity of the morals of our people" led to poverty, drunkenness, prostitution, criminality, and in the end, "the fall of religion, nationality, trade, and industry." The mufti called upon clerics to exert all possible influence on Muslims through sermons and the words of the Koran and the hadith, or sayings of the Prophet.[75]

The range of religious thought among Russian Orthodox Christians and Muslims was wider than can be considered here. Conservative members of the ulama continued to value Islamic tradition of the old rather than the new variety, and they attacked jadids or denounced them to imperial authorities. Allen Frank and Michael Kemper have questioned the depth of support among Muslims for innovation. But Bashkiria's greater connections to the changes in Russian society and Islamic and European society abroad introduced a pattern of transformation evident in both local Christian and Islamic traditions. Both Russian Orthodox and Muslim elites sought to establish more direct and meaningful connections with their co-religionists. They sought to make the faithful understand and act in accordance with the tenets of their faiths in new ways. Both Orthodox Christians and Muslims did so within imperial institutions.

THE ZEMSTVO FROM COUNTER-REFORM TO ACTIVISM

The heated rhetoric of religious and educational leaders in Ufa regarding Muslim influence was not without some basis. In the 1880s, as jadid ideas invigorated Muslim intellectual life, Muslims achieved their peak of influence in the zemstvos. They made up 16 to 18 percent of the provincial assembly, and in overwhelmingly Muslim Belebei county, Muslim deputies ranged from approximately 30 percent to more than 50 percent of the total in 1887.[76] Leadership in the zemstvos often showed considerable continuity from pre-reform Bashkir institutions. In Belebei county, two Muslims, Abussugud Akhtiamov and Shakhaidar Syrtlanov, served as chair of the zemstvo board for three terms in all, from 1881 to 1891. Akhtiamov was the son of an akhund in a Meshcheriak canton. He completed the Kazan University Law Faculty, served as an official for special assignments for the Ufa governor, and worked as a lawyer. As discussed in chapter 3, Shakhaidar Syrtlanov's father had been head of a Bashkir canton. Shakhaidar had graduated from the Nepliuev Cadet School, served in Turkestan, and owned 2,200 des. of land.[77] The two men had made their careers with the help of institutions created in the first half of the nineteenth century to draw Muslims into imperial life.

There is little evidence that Akhtiamov and Syrtlanov, or anyone else for that matter, saw zemstvo service as an effective means to improve life in Ufa Province throughout the 1880s. While this could be said of other provinces,

Ufa zemstvos were particularly moribund. In 1882, one observer wrote that a "dead chancellerism" reigned in Ufa zemstvos that was no better than that in any state department.[78] Tax revenues collected by zemstvos in Ufa increased only about 1.6 percent per year, among the slowest of any zemstvo. Before 1895, on average only two zemstvo schools opened in the province each year.[79] Other than Umetbaev's speech, quoted at the start of this chapter, there was little sense that the zemstvo could or even should play a role in Muslim education in particular.[80]

The counter-reform of 1890 made the zemstvo an even less promising forum for political activism. Article 87 of the new zemstvo statute put zemstvos more firmly under the thumb of local governors. The introduction of land captains appointed by the governor in 1892 gave the nobility new estate-based power. Since governors now appointed zemstvo deputies from the peasant estate, they could easily use their power to make the bodies more compliant. Ufa governor Nord used the 1890 zemstvo statute to appoint Russian Orthodox peasants rather than Muslims to zemstvo electoral assemblies, reducing the presence of the latter. The 1890 zemstvo statute, for instance, ended Muslim predominance in the Belebei zemstvo assembly. The statute reduced the overall size of the provincial assembly from 42 to 28 and that of the Belebei assembly from 32 to 30. Muslim representation in the provincial zemstvo assembly decreased to only 3 percent in 1903 and to just less than 20 percent in the Belebei assembly, where Muslims had held a majority.[81]

In the 1890s, however, zemstvo activity increased substantially in Ufa, and in the empire as a whole, for a number of reasons. Central and provincial state administrators seemed incapable of managing the rapid social and economic change characteristic of the decade. Severe famine that devastated the Volga-Urals region in 1892, for example, demonstrated to many that autocratic government could not provide for the population. The zemstvo played a major role in famine relief efforts, and the crisis provoked calls for expanded zemstvo work in education and agronomy. Opposition to the state's tariff policies, which generated capital for railway construction and industrialization at the expense of agriculture, discontented noble landowners who dominated the zemstvos.

Ufa zemstvos' resistance to autocratic prerogatives and Russifying policies expanded in a number of ways. In the mid-1890s, the zemstvo developed a comparatively lively politics. After several years of struggle between "right" and "left" factions within the provincial zemstvo, the provincial board came under the control of leftists in 1900 and remained so to varying degrees until 1917. Zemstvo expenditures increased, and the board first proposed such measures as the creation of a periodical publication, small credit operations, and the expansion of educational programs and medical services. The number of professional employees such as agronomists, doctors, and statisticians grew substantially. Ufa became one of a number of provinces in which relations between the governor and the zemstvo grew tense as zemstvo activists began to call for a greater voice in affairs of state. Following the lead of the Tver zemstvo, the Ufa zemstvo addressed the emperor on the need to have the "voice of the people's needs" known. Conflicts between Governor Nikolai A. Bogdanovich and Ufa's zemstvos began in 1895. After the turn of the century, the governor removed the chairman of the provincial zemstvo and refused to confirm zemstvo board members.[82]

Zemstvo activists derived their legitimacy from their ability to meet perceived popular needs better than the state could. Local zemstvos rejected MNP's emphasis on schools as instruments of Russian Orthodoxy and Russification. Whether religious or secular authorities would control schools became a crucial question. After the 1892 famine, zemstvos became increasingly reluctant to support church schools of any sort. When state officials nearly quadrupled support for church schools in 1896, many zemstvo activists believed that church schools became, in effect, state schools funded by the central government that no longer merited zemstvo support. Ufa's provincial zemstvo cut off funding for them.[83] Polemics over parish and zemstvo schools reflected in part a competition for funds between systems that did not differ greatly in function.[84] Yet the Ufa zemstvo embraced educational reformers' arguments that parish schools pursued chiefly religious and moral instruction rather than "educational tasks." Critics accused church schools of excessive study of Old Church Slavonic and singing. They argued that "even the most pious songs" could not "drive away the shadow of popular ignorance."[85] Reformers sought not so much to eliminate religion from the curriculum as to limit the authority of the church in educational matters and to make religious education a discrete subject rather than schools' central mission. Reformers considered schools sponsored by zemstvos and the MNP better able to further the goal of enlightenment.

At about the same time that Ufa zemstvo activists embraced secular control of Russian-language schools, they became interested in jadid reform in Muslim schools. Reform of Russian education often was motivated by concerns similar to those of jadids and shared some sources.[86] Zemstvos included educators and Russian Orthodox and Muslim activists who emphasized new pedagogical methods and the expansion of women's education. Russian Orthodox and Muslim reformers argued that greater attention to vernacular languages and practical skills would make schools more relevant and attractive. Reformers of both faiths sought to reconcile religious instruction with secular sciences. They developed techniques such as phonetic language instruction and aimed to systematize curricula and improve the physical condition of schools.

In the 1890s, zemstvo elites in Ufa Province intensified the development and support of educational programs to bridge the divide between enlightened and ignorant as well as between Russians and non-Russians. The number of zemstvo-supported schools increased 67 percent in only six years from 1894 to 1900. Spending on education rose faster than the zemstvo budget as a whole.[87] In 1898 a group of left-leaning provincial zemstvo deputies, including future provincial zemstvo chairman Petr Koropachinskii, the "Red Prince" Viacheslav Kugushev, and prominent Muslim nobles Kutlu-Mukhammad Tevkelev and Shakhaidar Syrtlanov, formed a bloc that identified the spread of education as the "most immediate task of the zemstvo." Only Tevkelev and Syrtlanov were Muslim, but Koropachinskii and Kugushev also had cosmopolitan roots. Koropachinskii descended from a Polish Catholic nobleman exiled from Smolensk to Bashkiria in the seventeenth century.[88] Kugushev descended from a Tatar service family that had converted to Russian Orthodoxy, and he still occasionally wore Tatar-style clothing around his estate.[89] The left liberal bloc initiated discussion of universal education in 1901 and 1902. At about the same time, the zemstvo began to address education for non-Russians. In 1898 and 1902, Tevkelev and Syrtlanov moved that the provincial assembly should petition MNP to establish a Tatar Teachers' School in Ufa modeled on one in Kazan.[90] The MNP turned it down. The provincial zemstvo also allocated five hundred rubles for the publication of Tatar-language brochures on legal, agricultural, medical, scientific, historical, and literary subjects, to be selected by a commission of native speakers.[91] After Muslim resistance to the 1897 census, Governor Bogdanovich supported zemstvo funding for Muslim education as a way to reduce the ignorance of "Muslim masses" and to make them more responsive to their clerics and to local authorities.[92]

On the whole, zemstvo achievements with respect to Muslim education remained few. Very likely, the weak Muslim presence in both the provincial and county assemblies played a role in zemstvos' lack of strong initiatives. Both Tevkelev and Syrtlanov enjoyed substantial stature in zemstvo work, but they raised neither national nor religious issues with great frequency.[93] The 1890s brought a growing sense that the zemstvo needed to participate more in the region's political, economic, and social life. Zemstvo activists drew upon currents of reform in both Orthodox, Russian-speaking and Muslim, Tatar-speaking cultures in developing programs that emphasized native-language instruction. The effects of this approach became clear mostly after 1905, however.

BASHKIRS AS SUBJECTS OF CONCERN

Despite the poor economic condition of the Bashkir population by the 1890s and Bashkir resistance to census takers, the all-imperial census of 1897 captured the process of Teptiar and Meshcheriak identification as Bashkirs discussed in chapter 4.[94] Based on census data, Rail G. Kuzeev gives the empire's Bashkir population as 960,000–1,010,000 in 1897. It would not exceed that level until the 1950s.[95] The continued influx of migrants and pressure on Bashkir land-holding continued to cause Bashkirs to give up semi-nomadic pastoralism. By 1900, Bashkirs in Bashkiria's northwest—about 45 percent of the Bashkir population—had long practiced settled agriculture and had a way of life close to those of Kazan Tatars and Russians. Another 22 percent of the population, that in northern Belebei County, northern Sterlitamak County, and the non-mountainous west of Zlatoust and Ufa Counties, had fairly recently shifted to settled agriculture. About 12 percent, mostly in Ufa Province's mountainous regions, drew their sustenance from animal husbandry and forest products. Only in southern Orenburg Province and east of the Urals did animal husbandry predominate and some semi-nomadic pastoralism remain.[96] As we saw in chapter 4, Bashkirs adjusted to new agricultural practices with difficulty.

The deterioration of Bashkirs' economy made them a subject of concern for Bashkirs and local administrators alike. In 1898, Ufa governor Bogdanovich wrote to influential figures who would have some knowledge of Bashkirs' situation in order to ask their advice on how to improve Bashkirs' lot. In a letter to Mukhametsalim Umetbaev, Bogdanovich noted his "extremely sad conclusion" that "the native population of the province are Bashkir hereditary landowners [who], owning a vast expanse of land, find themselves in an extremely poor economic situation, significantly worse by comparison with the well-being of other migrant ethnic groups and undoubtedly requiring special administrative concern." According to the governor, the situation had reached the point that among the "native population of the region had appeared indications of dying out." Some areas had witnessed a decrease in population against the number of residents recorded in the tenth tax census of 1857.[97] The governor's request for Umetbaev's opinion on the Bashkir situation is especially notable for his identification of Bashkir landowners as the native people of the region, one whose claim to the land tied them to it and tied them together as an ethnic group (*narodnost'*). The governor collapsed Bashkir estate status and Bashkir ethnicity together. One might think that imperial officials would not be too upset over the gradual disappearance of Bashkirs. Local governors such as Kryzhanovskii had stated decades before that the introduction of a "Russian element" was the key to the region's future prosperity and advocated the dispossession of Bashkirs. After 1881, the autocracy presented the Russians as the top of the empire's hierarchy. If the native owners of much land were "dying out," introducing Russian settlers would be that much easier, and the local economy would improve as a result. Certainly other expanding states in North America or Australia showed little official concern about the dying out of native populations.

Concern about the "dying out" of Bashkirs indicates officials' belief in the need to preserve the empire's diverse population.

Umetbaev's ten-page, single-spaced reply to the governor mixed nostalgia for the cantonal system of administration and calls for stronger administration with concern for Bashkir education. As one might expect from the son of a Bashkir canton head, Umetbaev saw the end of the cantonal system of militarized administration as part of the problem facing Bashkirs. Since the elimination of the Bashkir cantons, a "party of the strong and destructive" had formed in Bashkir communes with the elder at its head. The strong manipulated land sales and rentals so as to maximize their own profit and to impoverish the weak. Bashkirs' impoverishment also resulted from their rapid turn from nomadic pastoralism to settled agriculture, which left them accustomed neither to the crafts necessary to practice sedentary agriculture nor to the "arts of Europeans." Umetbaev lamented the loss of firm authority that had characterized Bashkir cantons, when heads such as his father could corporally punish those who plundered land and forests and could force those under them to practice the three-field system of crop rotation if necessary. At the same time, canton heads had been forbidden to profit from Bashkir land sales and rentals upon pain of losing their posts. Umetbaev also stressed education. His experience as a student in the Nepliuev Cadet School and as a teacher in a Sterlitamak madrasa had shown him that Bashkir youth were quite capable of mastering languages, sciences, and practical skills. If the state stripped schools of all missionary intentions, he argued, Bashkir education would succeed. The zemstvo, he believed, had an important role to play in developing schools in which Bashkirs would learn skills necessary for their economic prosperity.[98] In Umetbaev's call for stronger authority he showed himself in tune with the guiding idea of Alexander III's reign, evident in the poem quoted at the start of the chapter, while his emphasis on education showed his desire for Bashkirs' improvement.

Governor Bogdanovich's investigations of Bashkir status and how it could be reformed to prevent the Bashkir people from dying out reflected a shift of conceptions. By the time consideration of Bashkirs reached the State Council in 1902, officials assessed Bashkir potential very differently than Umetbaev had. Officials argued that the "backwardness and complete lack of culture of the Bashkir tribe" required a new approach to their administration. Russian administrators identified the cause of Bashkir "laziness and carelessness" and that of other "Eastern non-Russians" with confidence: Islam. The number of mosques and religious servitors had grown rapidly over several decades. In the opinion of state officials, two things were required to raise the "intellectual and moral level" of Bashkirs. First, Bashkirs' legal distinctiveness must end and the general laws on the peasantry be applied to them. This would provide greater possibilities for Russian officials to regulate the disposition of Bashkir land, its allocation within the village, and its sales to outsiders; to eliminate imams from the disposition of inheritances; and to facilitate the entry of non-Bashkirs into Bashkir villages.[99] Second, the sale of Bashkir lands should be used to finance general and specialized schools for Bashkirs that would improve them intellectually and provide practical skills necessary for them to make a living. New vocabulary for describing the Bashkirs accompanied these familiar proposals for greater in-migration and education. Officials referred to Bashkirs as an "ethnic group" (*narodnost'*) and as "aborigines" in addition to the more traditional "people" and "tribe."

This effort to end Bashkirs' particular status, to subject them more directly to Russian officials, and to change their culture through education would seem a perfect example of Russification and one that fit well with state priorities. In November 1904, however, the State Council rejected these proposals. It did so in part because it seemed "inexpedient" to apply to Bashkirs a set of laws on the peasantry that was slated for reform in the near term anyway. But the council also acted out of a respect for the estate distinctiveness of Bashkirs and out of fears that efforts at reform might provoke disturbances at a time when war with Japan required all to focus on the struggle with the external enemy. Equating Bashkirs with peasants entailed an "abrupt violation of the firmly formed order in the Bashkir way of life" that might provoke displeasure in "the dark, non-Russian milieu."[100] Although tsarist officials had offered a diagnosis of both the defects in Bashkir status and the need for reform, the time was not right for potentially destabilizing changes in the treatment of Bashkirs. The time never would be right. Bashkirs retained their particular status until 1917.

A key part of the 1898 legislation on Bashkirs, the survey of Bashkir land, went forward. The survey proved deeply unpopular, and Bashkirs resisted it. The new land survey was intended to complete the division of Bashkir land among Bashkir communities; separate Bashkir land from that of settlers, of nobles formerly of the Bashkir estate, and members of other estates; and settle land disputes between Bashkirs and Bashkir pripushchenniks. The survey marked a decisive turning away from the emphasis on Bashkir property characteristic of the Great Reform era. Ufa governor Bogdanovich warmly greeted the 1898 legislation for opening more land to agriculturalists from the empire's central provinces.[101] Bashkirs felt very differently. They viewed the new law as an unprecedented and unjust effort to take their land. The Ufa Survey Commission was responsible for ninety parcels of Bashkir land totaling 3,968,204 des. They managed to accomplish their work over a period of fourteen years.[102] Sorting out a century of land transactions and claims was a formidable task, one that required resolving disputes among Bashkirs and between Bashkirs and non-Bashkirs. Bashkirs were inclined toward legal action over the survey. Of 123 cases surrounding the survey Bashkirs brought to the senate, 84 percent were rejected.

The specification that land be parceled according to the eighth tax census of 1815 proved a sore point for Bashkirs, who could not see why a later, tenth tax census (1857) was not used.[103] When one village in Ufa County simply refused to participate, Governor Sokolovskii, sent his aide Shakhaidar Syrtlanov, the former zemstvo chairman, to investigate. Syrtlanov acknowledged the intransigence of Bashkirs but used the case to critique the Russian administrator, in this case the local land captain. He wrote to the governor that "Bashkirs are not the kind of people (*narod*) that immediately yields to the admonition of authority, they even consider this as a mark of a lack of seriousness," brought about by the fact that state officials had misled them in the past.[104] Bashkirs simply did not want the survey to take place and needed to be convinced that they had no choice in the matter. Ufa's governor eventually called out troops to assist surveyors in completing the most difficult cases.[105]

KILLING WORKERS AND A GOVERNOR

Even before the confrontation with Bashkirs was resolved, a much more bloody one took place in Ufa Province. With the extension of what would become the Trans-Siberian Railroad to the city of Zlatoust, 125 miles east of Ufa, in 1890, Bashkiria participated in the empire-wide growth of industrial production as well as in social tensions that accompanied it. In March 1902, managers of a state armaments factory in Zlatoust introduced new account books. This change had taken place calmly at other factories nearby but precipitated a massive disturbance in Zlatoust. On March 12, the town was essentially in the hands of workers. Governor Bogdanovich hurried to the scene, and a peaceful resolution seemed possible. When negotiations failed, however, the governor warned the crowd that he would authorize force if it did not disperse. When a verbal warning proved ineffective, Bogdanovich asked the military commander to use force. The troops fired three warning shots, but the crowd either did not hear them or did not believe the troops would actually fire on the crowd. The soldiers did, and in moments twenty-eight people lay dead. Seventeen people later died of their injuries, and another eighty-three sustained nonfatal wounds.[106] The killing of Zlatoust workers became a rallying point for radical opponents of the tsarist state locally and across the empire.[107] Even an Ufa nobleman, zemstvo activist, and land captain, A. A. Planson, blamed police errors for the loss of life.[108]

The governor himself was "profoundly depressed" by what had transpired. A socialist revolutionary working in the railway workshops ended Bogdanovich's misery two months later by shooting him while he walked in Ufa's main park.[109] The Zlatoust events and the governor's assassination put Ufa at the forefront of political tension in the empire.

The assignment of Ivan Sokolovskii to replace Bogdanovich as governor late in 1903 greatly intensified educated society's conflicts with the local administration. Minister of Internal Affairs Viacheslav Pleve clearly intended that Sokolovskii use Pleve's favored style of harsh policing to restore order in Ufa. The resulting conflict between the zemstvo and governor prompted zemstvo historian Boris Veselovskii to write that "hardly in any other zemstvos except for Tver's did this conflict have such a tense and protracted character."[110] Sokolovskii asserted that the governor must be the "unifying authority in the province" and its "master." Whenever the governor had exhausted attempts to prompt the zemstvo to do its job, he should be allowed to do it by administrative means. Sokolovskii believed that governors should permanently possess the powers that they normally wielded only in a situation of "reinforced security" (*usilennaia okhrana*).[111] Sokolovskii did not view labor relations as the central obstacle to order. Rather, local zemstvos "served as the breeding-ground and refuge for ill-intentioned people" who sought to "harm the existing state order" and to spread political propaganda.[112] Zemstvos became the focus of his punitive actions. Sokolovskii rejected zemstvo leaders whom he considered unreliable.[113] He shut down the zemstvo statistical bureau, calling it "the primary cadre of revolutionary agitators" in the province.[114] He sought to apply "severe measures" to zemstvos, noble assemblies, and social organizations "completely without regard to estate status" or "level of development."[115] Minister of Internal Affairs Pleve welcomed Sokolovskii's severe approach to zemstvo activity. After Pleve's assassination in June 1904 and the tsar's appointment of the more conciliatory Petr D. Sviatopolk-Mirskii as minister of internal affairs, relations between the zemstvo leadership and Sokolovskii improved little.[116] Sokolovskii's efforts to control the zemstvo spawned further resistance to administrative power, consolidated the left wing in local politics, and set the stage for the clash of autocratic power with mobilized society that commenced in 1905.

SERGEI WITTE AND THE NATURE OF IMPERIAL AUTHORITY

At its very center, however, the imperial state was divided on the nature of state power after the turn of the century. Senior officials such as Sergei Witte believed in autocratic authority, too, but held that it should be articulated differently. Witte believed the state's power would increase if reasons for religious and social groups to be alienated from it were reduced. The key to state authority lay not in the harsh police power and antagonism between educated society and the state that Pleve advocated but in the state's stronger connections with all of the tsar's subjects and, as Witte put it, the "identical relations of all with the state."[117] Before 1905, these ideas inspired officials to explore religious toleration and the elimination of some legislation that discriminated against the peasantry. In 1900, for instance, Witte opposed plans to respond to the 1898 Andijan uprising in Turkestan by attacking the influence of Muslim clerics. Witte wrote to Minister of War Aleksei N. Kuropatkin that "toleration (*terpimost'*) of the Muslim religion and trust in the good intentions of Muslims" lay at the core of state policy. This principle, Witte argued, "led to the recognition of Muslims' full equality with other subjects of the Empire, ensured them freedom to perform their religious obligations and non-interference in their internal life."[118] On February 26, 1903, Nicholas II promised to guarantee his subjects of non-Orthodox and non-Christian faiths the "free practice of their faiths" and religious worship according to their rituals. This promise proclaimed toleration as a fundamental principle in the empire but indicated no concrete changes in policy. The tsar's decree dated December 12, 1904, advanced matters further. The decree called for a review of laws regarding Old Believers and non-Orthodox and non-Christian subjects with an eye toward eliminating any constraint in religious life not directly established in law. The decree suggested changes in state policy specifically intended to improve the situation of the non-Orthodox.[119] In late 1903, a "special commission" under the leadership of Witte sought to make the tsar's subjects' relationship to the state more similar in other ways. The commission recommended that peasants be allowed to convert their communal land into private property in an effort to "eliminate the peasantry's isolation in civil and personal law according to estate status." The following year, lower orders were exempted from corporal punishment.[120]

By 1905, Witte's approach to toleration won out over the hostility of Orthodox churchmen. The Committee of Ministers under Witte's direction stressed the importance of toleration to increasing the reach of the state. Past efforts to convert people of non-Orthodox religions to Orthodoxy had resulted in substantial groups that were "unyielding" in their resistance to the church or who had "apostasied from Orthodoxy." Such persons were Orthodox only in name. They could not openly practice their real religion, but they refused to practice Orthodoxy or have Orthodox clergy minister to them. Such people were "left entirely without religion." Beyond the "moral suffering" experienced by such people, the Committee of Ministers focused on the fact that they were "deprived of essential civil rights": their births, marriages, and deaths were generally not registered in metrical books, since only officially recognized religious leaders recorded such information. People without official religions did not have legally recognized marriages or legitimate children and therefore were deprived of firm property rights.[121] The committee resolved that persons who practiced a faith other than Orthodoxy should be allowed to join officially the sect or religion that they actually practiced. Witte presented the state's new approach to religious faith as essential to the vitality of the Russian Orthodox Church, which, he argued, the state had smothered since the time of Peter I.[122] Witte invited St. Petersburg Metropolitan Antonii (Vadkovskii) to deliberate with the committee, and he became the most prominent church leader of a group who believed that the church must be free to govern itself according to the canons of Russian Orthodoxy without secular, bureaucratic interference.[123]

The Manifesto of April 17, 1905, developed by the Council of Ministers and issued by the tsar, reflected the views of Witte and Metropolitan Antonii. The recognition of the right to leave the Orthodox faith was the manifesto's major innovation. The law stated explicitly that leaving Orthodoxy for another Christian confession or dogma would not be prosecuted. The new law also permitted apostasy into a non-Christian faith, though to a more limited extent. Persons who were registered as Orthodox but professed a non-Christian faith to which they or their ancestors belonged could now officially ask to be removed from registration in the Orthodox faith. The decree also strengthened the position of Old Believers and their clergy.[124] In practice, the decree of April 17, 1905, and the manner in which it was issued left ample room for confusion regarding its meaning and implementation.[125] Nonetheless, as Sergei Witte noted, one could "temporarily not execute" or "curse" decrees on toleration, but they could not be destroyed. "It was as if they were engraved in the hearts and minds of the vast majority of the population that makes up Great Russia."[126]

CONCLUSION

The tension evident between Witte's and Pleve's designs for autocratic authority reveals much about the complexities of the period 1881 to 1904. Witte's reforms seemed to recapture some of the universal thrust of the Great Reforms. He was less attached to estate status as an organizing principle than Great Reformers had been, however, and more interested in establishing a new relationship of the state with religious faith and religious institutions. He sought a sort of great reform of religion that had been noticeably absent in the Great Reform era. Pleve's insistence on forceful police power represented a continuation of the effort of Alexander III and his officials to restore order in the empire that had been so grievously violated by Alexander II's assassination. Before the turmoil of the first years of the twentieth century, this effort required increased reliance on the nobility in particular. However, as zemstvo activists, often from the nobility, mobilized in the late 1890s onward, estate status gave way to police power and force. Witte and Pleve, each in his own way, demonstrated skepticism about the power of estate status to order imperial life.

Both approaches emanating from St. Petersburg had potential to disrupt local life in the early years of the twentieth century. Previously, ministers of internal affairs and the Ufa governors subordinate to them, such as Nord, Poltoratskii, and Bogdanovich, endeavored above all to maintain order and to develop the empire's resources. The Great Reforms had reduced the distinctiveness of statuses particular to Bashkiria, but governors continued to rely on members of the noble estate such as Tevkelev, Umetbaev, Syrtlanov, and Sultanov to help administer Bashkiria's diverse population. When Russian Orthodox churchmen attacked Tevkelev, for instance, Poltoratskii and Nord exhibited no concern over Tevkelev's loyalty. Muslim nobles served as aides and informal consultants to the governors. Faced with the prospect of the dying out of the Bashkirs, Bogdanovich reached out to Umetbaev regarding ways to preserve the Bashkirs as a people. Far from creating a "Muslim tsardom," men such as Syrtlanov, Tevkelev, Sultanov, and Umetbaev had spent their lives working for the interests of the imperial state, which largely overlapped with their own interests. They identified with the imperial state and remained loyal to it. They sought to use state institutions to advance what they considered the interests of Muslim and Bashkir people at the same time. Umetbaev's simultaneous embrace of Muslim education and zemstvo service and praise of Sokolovskii makes sense in this context. Syrtlanov's ability to work with even so harsh a governor as Sokolovskii shows a similar reconciliation of firm autocratic authority with personal loyalty and advocacy for Bashkir interests.

At the same time, the educational and religious establishments, the OUO and the local bishopric, brought a disruptive new cultural and religious agenda to Bashkiria. Men such as Nikanor came from the western borderlands, where the struggle with Poles and Catholics was particularly intense. Such officials called into question the ability of Muslims and Bashkirs to serve the emperor loyally. They asserted that nationality or religious confession, or some combination of the two, was necessary to serve fully the interests of a state that they identified as Russian and Orthodox. As we saw in chapter 3, Nicholas I's officials had first formulated official nationality in the 1830s, but its key feature was the Russian people's love of its sovereigns. In the 1880s, by contrast, Pobedonostsev and others placed the Russian Orthodox Church, Russian language, and a specifically Russian tsar at the center of the national idea. Churchmen and educational officials may not have Russified many of the tsar's subjects, and even supporters of the policy differed over what Russianness meant. But the process had begun by which the tsar's subjects understood themselves to be members of national groups and understood that belonging to such a group had political implications. Rather than creating order and reliably loyal subjects, efforts to strengthen and centralize authority in the hands of Russian speakers and the Russian Orthodox Church proved disruptive and contributed to a broad mobilization of society against autocracy that became clear in Ufa Province already by 1903. For the most part, however, unrest came to Bashkiria from outside. As the strike and violence in Zlatoust showed, along with the governor's assassination, the railroad had made Bashkiria part of the empire's core and brought with it the conflicts that divided the empire.

Over the past two decades, historians of the empire's western borderlands writing in English and Russian have convincingly called into question the coherence, consistency, and systematic nature of efforts to Russify the population of the western borderlands.[127] Nonetheless, efforts to increase the influence of language, faith, and culture in the west were much more powerful than in Bashkiria. Policies such as bans on publishing in Polish and Ukrainian (1876), efforts to introduce Russian in Catholic religious services, confiscation of the land of Catholic monasteries and of Polish noble estates, and the firing of Polish teachers in favor of Russian speakers undertaken in the empire's west after 1863 had no equivalents in the east.[128] As we have seen, efforts to control Muslim religious life and to increase the influence of Russian and Russian Orthodox culture were less ambitious and showed little success. Il'minskii's system of education for non-Russians invigorated Russian Orthodoxy among some non-Russians in the Volga-Urals region, but almost all of those were animist peoples and early Muslim converts to Russian Orthodoxy. Nikanor, Il'minskii, and the priests they trained and supervised may have condemned Muslim influence, but they had little success in eliminating it. Local governors took action to limit Muslim participation only when pressed. They seemed confident that the power accorded them by the counter-reforms was more than sufficient. The MNP's expansion of its efforts to cultivate Russianness expanded beyond Russian literacy only around the turn of the century and then focused on secondary institutions that enrolled few non-Russians.

Clashes of Russians with non-Russian groups, such as pogroms against Jews in the western borderlands, were lacking in the east as well. Despite the growing attention given to Islam, imperial officials simply did not perceive Muslims as posing the type of threat that Catholics and Jews did in the western borderlands. In the west, the presence of Great Power rivals just across the border from Russia, and the presence of the same national communities on both sides of the border, intensified concerns about foreign influence and invigorated efforts to combat it. The fact that Jews had entered the empire more recently than Muslims made their status more vexed in the minds of imperial officials. For all the concern of Russian Orthodox churchmen and Russian nationalists, Muslims had a long history with Russian rule that moderated some of the more alarmist reactions to their mobilization. Poles, who had violently clashed with the tsarist state as recently as 1863, were in a much higher category of concern as well.

Clearly, however, efforts to enforce order and strengthen the state affected the entire empire, not just the western borderlands. Domestic concerns reinforced international ones. Across the empire, Alexander II's assassination seemed to indicate to many imperial officials that the reformed order, with its Western-style justice, self-administration, and military service, had brought little benefit to the emperors' subjects but had been obtained at great cost. In Bashkiria, the introduction of market forces to the distribution of Bashkir land brought chaos, illegality, and Bashkir poverty. In this respect, we can see the counter-reform in Bashkiria in the same light as developments in the Ottoman Empire and the Habsburg monarchy. Each in its own way spent the last quarter of the nineteenth century reacting to reforms undertaken earlier in the century. As Karen Barkey writes, "In the creation of a central official nationalism, the Habsburgs, Russians, and Ottomans worked with different material but toward a similar goal, a transition to a modern imperial model infused with national imagery and identity." They also all used schools, the press, and state institutions to mobilize the population in their support.[129] Sultan Abdülhamid II (reigned 1876–1909) prorogued parliament not even a year after it had opened. It remained closed until after he was deposed. The sultan favored technocratic development more than Alexander III did: Articles written at his behest emphasized progress and presented him as "an Ottoman Peter the Great," an ancestor whose example Alexander III did not embrace. But both rulers used faith, whether Islam or Russian Orthodoxy, to bolster their authority. Abdülhamid II "made a point of reviving the caliphate, a symbol of Ottoman Islamic dominance," and sought to knit "together the Muslim elements of the empire into a cohesive new core of identity."[130] They also both used police power and censorship to stifle dissent.

The Habsburg situation was more complicated. Franz Joseph II never rejected the representative institutions created after 1848, nor was promoting a German national monarchy a real option. Yet the dynasty emphasized the emperor's piety and used institutions such as the press and schools to create support for the dynasty, whose very existence seemed an anchor against the uncertainties of modern capitalism. In other ways, the reaction against modern social developments was pushed on the dynasty itself, such as when Franz Joseph II had to confirm the election of an anti-Semitic, Christian Socialist mayor of Vienna in

1898. The rejection of late nineteenth-century developments evident in Umet-baev's poem that opened this chapter expressed itself in different forms in differ-ent places. Each empire that lived in the shadow of its Western rivals countered reform in some manner. In the first decade of the twentieth century, the tension between reform and order would be increasingly difficult to manage.

6

EMPIRE IN CRISIS
1905–1907

THE ZLATOUST STRIKE, the killing of workers, and the assassination of Governor Bogdanovich made Ufa one of the most conflicted provinces in the empire before 1905.[1] That year brought a much more disruptive politics to the empire as a whole and to Ufa Province in particular. Shortly after Nicholas II issued his Manifesto of October 17, 1905—granting his subjects freedom of speech, assembly, and conscience and promising them personal inviolability and a new state Duma—Ufa governor Boleslav Tsekhanovetskii authorized a public demonstration.[2] The crowd on October 19, 1905, made a striking impression. Eight to ten thousand of the city's 75,000 residents—what Tsekhanovetskii called "nearly the entire city"—came to Ufa's Ushakovskii Park out of curiosity at this "extraordinary, exceptional spectacle of a new character." The crowd's diversity was as impressive as its size. Containing members of the intelligentsia, "simple people," students, women, workers, petty bureaucrats, officers, and soldiers, the crowd made clear the meaning of the manifesto to a wide variety of city residents. For the first time, Tsekhanovetskii wrote, freedom of speech and assembly were "brought to life."[3]

The Revolution of 1905 and the Manifesto of October 17 brought mass politics to Ufa and to much of the rest of the empire. In the greatly expanded political realm of 1905, people who had never been expected to articulate views of how the empire should be governed now did so. In this novel, largely unforeseen context, discussions of loyalty and of who should be included in the imperial polity moved from bureaucratic and zemstvo meeting rooms to the street and to the newly energized and partially freed press. In these realms, traditional categories of estate and religious confession took on new meanings and helped shape the new politics. But categories of loyalty and nationality also acquired widespread relevance and did not always correspond to established hierarchies of estate privilege and faith. The divide between loyal "patriots" and suspect "revolutionaries" ran through nearly all social groups and local institutions, including the nobility, the workers, the zemstvo, and even the local administration. Elections to a new, all-imperial representative body, the State Duma, which were intended to draw together the empire's population, instead made clear the fragmentation within the polity.

The emperor and the state administration very much participated in this new politics. Indeed, the continued viability of state power at times seemed to rest upon expressions of patriotism. Donald Rawson has described Nicholas II's issuance of a February 18, 1905, decree calling on "persons of good will from all estates and statuses, everyone to his calling and in his place, to unite in harmonious assistance to Us," as an "unprecedented appeal by a Russian monarch, who presumably had no need to appeal for loyalty."[4] The form of loyalty most commonly expressed in 1905–1907 consisted of allegiance to the tsar, active endorsement of the tsar's decrees, and participation in the empire's reformed political order.[5] After the events of 1905 and early 1906, officials and political actors of all sorts promoted active allegiance as necessary to overcome deep fissures in political life that the revolution had made apparent. Though such appeals were not entirely new, they found new means of expression in the large-scale production and distribution of "patriotic" pamphlets and the staging of lectures. The loyalty state officials and political elites most often promoted was not, at its core, specific to any estate, religious confession, class, or national group. At the same time that inclusive appeals for loyalty became more widespread, however, other activists rejected the politics of patriotism altogether, and an ethnically exclusive concept of loyalty became increasingly common and important. As Charles Taylor has argued, the cultivation of active support is a defining feature of the modern state, one closely connected to the emergence of nationalism.[6] In Bashkiria, political mobilization brought with it a pervasive concern with nationality. As a local newspaper observed, "a geographical understanding of 'fatherland' is being replaced by an ethnographic understanding of 'people (the Russian people).'"[7] Some "patriots" began to assert that members of certain groups could not be fully loyal to the tsar. In street demonstrations and pamphlets, Jews and Poles were identified as the primary enemies of autocracy despite their very small numbers in the province.[8] With the institution of identification by nationality (*natsional'nost'*) of voters in elections to the Third Duma in 1907, categorization by nationality formally entered local politics.[9]

In this context, perceptions of Muslim political participation changed. Before 1905, Orthodox churchmen stoked fears of Muslims as enemies of Orthodoxy and the state, but secular authorities did not regard them as particularly threatening. Ufa nobleman and land captain A. A. Planson described Muslims and animists alike as living "with Russians like brothers," working for Russia's betterment, and as "loyal children of their mother—Russia (*Rossiia*)."[10] In 1905, Muslim elites did not play a particularly visible role and were not initially associated with revolutionary disturbances.[11] As Muslims assembled to articulate collective interests after October 1905 and especially during elections to the first State Duma in Ufa, however, Muslim elites became more prominent. Some Russian political actors began to consider Muslims to be of questionable loyalty and having a particular spirit and political aspirations that separated them from others within the empire. Muslims became a suspect nationality.[12]

This chapter will focus fairly tightly on the events of 1905 in the city of Ufa and the provincial State Duma elections that followed. The revolution was primarily an urban event in Ufa Province. Since few Bashkirs lived in the city, Bashkirs did not play a key role in the events of 1905. Despite the influx of migrants over the past century, Ufa Province's peasants had more land than did peasants in central and western regions of the empire. Moreover, Bashkir land was free from redemption payments that former serfs and state peasants had to make, so these two major causes of unrest were largely absent. The survey of Bashkir land that had begun in 1898 and was not yet finished in parts of the province motivated some unrest in Bashkir villages. Other agrarian disturbances, with the exception of the burning of an estate in Menzelinsk County, were isolated and not severe.[13] The momentary collapse of the governor's authority in Ufa, however, had implications for the entire province.

ACTIVE MOBILIZATION AND MASS POLITICS

In 1905, connections between radical workers and radical members of educated society in the zemstvo and the City Duma strengthened oppositional movements. The local Social Democratic Party Committee consisted chiefly of members of the zemstvo board, and zemstvo employees directed a committee responsible for propaganda among railway workers. Under the influence of Viacheslav A. Kugushev and of other zemstvo activists from the nobility, a number of people under police observation worked for the zemstvo board as clerks, insurance agents, agronomists, teachers, and statisticians. Alexander D. Tsiurupa, later Lenin's commissar of food supply, worked on Kugushev's estate from 1902 to 1912.[14] The alliance of members of educated, propertied society with manual workers is key to understanding the events of 1905.[15]

After Bloody Sunday, January 9, 1905, when soldiers fired on a crowd of peaceful marchers in St. Petersburg, a wave of demonstrations and strikes spread throughout the empire. On January 12, 1905, more than two hundred students and members of the intelligentsia met in a large hotel in Ufa to stage an informal political meeting or "banquet" that would unite the city's democratic opposition. Police promptly broke up the event.[16] A strike of students at the Ufa gimnasium was one 1905's first major demonstrations locally. Demonstrations of clerks (April 23) and of three hundred workers and male and female students occurred on May 1. In May and July, strikes at the Katav-Ivanovskii factory in the Ural Mountains and at the railroad shop in Ufa saw about 1,600 and 2,000 workers, respectively, walk off the job.[17] In May 1905, Governor Sokolovskii was shot and severely wounded while at a local theater. By mid-1905 the local administration confronted a political society largely united in hostility to the political order. Until October 1905, however, the administration and police successfully contained political action. Specific groups of students, workers, or zemstvo activists pressed their demands, but political opposition remained fragmented.

The situation changed in October. On October 7, workers in the Samara-Zlatoust railway workshops and depot struck in response to a call issued in Moscow.[18] On October 14, strike leaders summoned Governor Boleslav P. Tsekhanovetskii, who had replaced Sokolovskii late in the summer, to the railway workshops to present their demands. The two thousand or more men in the workshops removed their caps in respect for him, but demands considered political, such as the right to assemble and freedom of speech, had begun to supplement workers' insistence on better pay and working conditions. Tsekhanovetskii attributed this change to the presence of one "Nikolai Ivanovich," a Social Democrat and "professional agitator" whose full name was unknown.[19] Having reached an impasse with the workers, the governor departed. The railway workers then began to march toward Ufa's center, singing "revolutionary songs" and carrying red flags. Troops soon confronted the workers, who retreated.[20] On October 14 and the following days, unrest in Ufa expanded beyond the railway workshops. Factory workers, store clerks, and provincial zemstvo and City Duma employees all ceased to work. Both boys' and girls' schools closed due to disorder within them. These groups produced a local version of the general strikes that had brought the capitals to a halt and set the stage for demonstrations on a much greater scale than before.[21]

Almost as soon as railway workers came to lead local opposition to autocracy, divisions appeared among them over their strike's goals. Strikes prompted some in the railway workshop to respond with a display of support for the state and tsar. Two railway contractors and Old Believers, Grigorii Busov and Klementii Laptev, began to organize a "circle of Russian patriots" composed of railway workers who supported "economic" strike demands but who found either their "monarchist" or their religious beliefs incongruent with the strike leadership's demands. They opposed revolutionaries led, in their opinion, by "Jews and Poles."[22] The clash between patriots and revolutionaries intensified after Busov and Laptev asked two priests at a church overlooking the railway workshops to have a meeting at which workers could present their economic demands and profess their loyalty to throne and church. At the meeting, the priests accepted economic demands from several hundred workers and administered a traditional oath of loyalty to the tsar. People "belonging to various strata of society," including a number of students, came upon the meeting and began to mock the assembled workers, shouting "Why do you turn to God? [It is] better to join us. We are more reliable than your God." Workers attacked the students. Several were beaten, and one person, described as a Jewish student or a Jewish dentist, died of his wounds.[23]

This violence polarized many city residents against those who had committed it and the police, who appeared to support it. The governor claimed to have insufficient forces to control the situation. The local garrison's commander took ill and did not leave his room, Ufa's vice-governor was on leave in Moscow, and the province had no mounted troops—Cossacks—until December 1905.[24] Between October 15 and 18, attacks on city residents by unknown persons strengthened convictions that police were unable or unwilling to maintain residents' security or even took part in the violence themselves. The local administration's apparent inability to prevent violence cast doubt on the legitimacy of the governor's authority. Residents increasingly sought to take matters in their own hands.

The October Manifesto's sudden appearance in Ufa on October 18 provided the basis for truly mass demonstrations. The tsar declared "civic freedoms" without having notified governors in advance. Tsekhanovetskii interpreted the manifesto as sharply curtailing his legal authority to prohibit demonstrations. This, along with the governor's uncertainty that his limited forces could impose order, caused him largely to surrender the streets. The governor ordered troops to avoid confrontations with crowds in order to prevent deaths that could incite popular anger. The October Manifesto greatly expanded the political mobilization in Ufa. People bowed to the governor as he handed them copies of the manifesto. As news of the manifesto spread, it became cause for celebration. The governor had two large national flags unfurled that had been "almost wrapped up in storage." Many homeowners copied this gesture. Led by workers, students, and members of the intelligentsia, residents of petty urban estates paraded about the city. Despite the cold, people threw open windows to hail the moment. Some cried with joy.[25] The manifesto, by granting civil liberties, gave the tsar's subjects a greater stake in the political order and increased the number of people who actively identified with the tsar and state. Its publication ended strikes locally, with the exception of that of the railway workers. In this manner, the manifesto changed the nature of political mobilization. Collective actions after its issuance no longer primarily took the form of strikes or demonstrations in particular occupational or institutional contexts but of actions by comparatively more equal persons in public spaces.

As the manifesto made legal large public gatherings of people from diverse statuses and occupations, it provided grounds for fracturing the polity along new lines. Before October 17, one could be, in essence, for the autocracy or against it. Now, Ufa featured three politically active camps: one that opposed the tsar's authority in nearly any manifestation, one that supported the post–October 17 order, and one that rejected the manifesto and preferred unreformed autocracy. On October 18 and 19, the governor was under siege from three sides, especially regarding the maintenance of order. Late on October 18, Nikolai Ivanovich and a large group of railway workers gathered before the governor's house to demand that he protect city residents from violence. Speakers in the City Duma denounced violence, attributed it to persons paid by the police, and called for a popular militia—a "Commission for the Protection of Public Security"—to defend city residents. The governor even faced opposition from members of his own administration who perceived his failure to suppress demonstrations by force as capitulation to revolution. Lower-level administrators rejected his interpretation of the manifesto, and on October 18, some began to suggest that the governor was a "traitor."[26] Tsekhanovetskii, however, felt compelled to retreat further. In response to death threats against two police officials, Tsekhanovetskii relieved them of their duties in order to protect them and to show his objectivity regarding criticism of the police.[27] The governor felt obligated to give permission for a public demonstration the following day.

Revulsion at violence, the weakness of the governor's authority, and the October Manifesto combined to bring about the unprecedented public demonstration on October 19 described at the beginning of the chapter. The long list of social types identified as present at the demonstration, from members of the intelligentsia to "simple people," indicates the broad range of social groups involved in the political mobilization. The roof of a summer theater's pavilion provided a rostrum for an array of orators, including Nikolai Ivanovich, to demand that the inviolability of persons be respected. The governor participated in the demonstration essentially as a spectator. Tsekhanovetskii agreed with the Ufa mayor's request that he guarantee publicly the security of Ufa residents because he thought such a statement would help gain the confidence of moderate and conservative elements. Rather than coming across as authoritative, the governor seemed to submit to the crowd's will and to Nikolai Ivanovich. The physical layout of the pavilion did much to give this impression. To speak from the top of the pavilion, as others did, required one to climb to the roof. The governor did not deem this possible. So, he passed his statements promising that the police would protect city residents and that soldiers would be kept in their garrisons up to Nikolai Ivanovich, who announced them to the crowd. Nikolai Ivanovich pressured the governor to close all drinking establishments in Ufa, and Tsekhanovetskii agreed to do so. Nikolai Ivanovich became the governor's spokesman, in effect. Then Tsekhanovetskii left the demonstration. He later expressed regret at his decisions on October 19 since they "had not produced the desired effect of calming the population."[28]

Tsekhanovetskii's apparent concessions to the crowd on October 19 mobilized members of his own administration against him. The account of Nikolai N. Zhedenev, an assistant to the governor for special assignments, emphasized that the governor had bowed deeply "before all sorts of rabble." Zhedenev asserted that the crowd sang "revolutionary songs" in the presence of the governor and that Tsekhanovetskii even shouted "death to the tsar" along with it. Zhedenev claimed that the governor endorsed the printing of the demonstration's resolutions calling for freedom to strike, equal rights for all nationalities, and the arming of a popular militia.[29] Zhedenev and his colleagues believed that Tsekhanovetskii had betrayed the tsar and the dignity of his office. One land captain present at the demonstration was said to have aimed his revolver at the governor before being restrained by his colleagues.[30]

The eclipse of the governor's authority on October 19 provided a new impetus to political mobilization. Since the governor seemed unable to direct events, others moved in to fill the vacuum of authority. The demonstration suggested that power was in the hands of those who could mobilize people in the city's parks and streets. The governor soon regained the initiative, however, when statements by Nikolai Ivanovich tested popular interpretations of freedom of speech. The governor heard on the evening of October 19 that Nikolai Ivanovich had uttered "criminal words, insulting to the religious and monarchical feelings of the people" in a speech earlier in the day. The crowd had let the remark pass. However, at a demonstration the next day, October 20, one worker asked Nikolai Ivanovich whether the announcement of freedom permitted one to say outrageous things regarding the tsar and the Orthodox Church. Nikolai Ivanovich somewhat awkwardly apologized for his remark, but his statement made a very "bad impression" on the public, according to the governor. Many present were "monarchists and deeply religious people" who perhaps supported the October Manifesto but were uncomfortable with Nikolai Ivanovich's vehement criticism of the tsar. Tsekhanovetskii perceived a shift in sympathy away from Nikolai Ivanovich toward the administration and a narrower interpretation of the October Manifesto. The governor decided to attempt to end the public meetings that he thought the "parties of disorder" had misused. On the evening of October 20, Tsekhanovetskii had military patrols march about the city beating drums and breaking up demonstrations.

Tsekhanovetskii's turn toward restoring order did not satisfy his opponents within his administration. They sent a telegram to the minister of the tsar's court and to the assistant minister of internal affairs denouncing Tsekhanovetskii's actions and asking for permission to relieve the governor of his duties. Guided by a law that prohibited collaboration with traitors to the emperor, the governor's opponents declared their loyalty and willingness to die for the sovereign and requested permission to defend their "life and property from armed revolutionaries." They felt confident that loyal troops would support them. According to one account, nearly the entire staff of the provincial administration, the governor's chancellery, and several land captains signed the telegram.[31] The administrative opposition then pressured local leaders of the noble estate, the Ufa provincial and county marshals of the nobility, to support what amounted to a coup against the governor.

The administrators soon realized the limits of their influence. Marshals refused to endorse the administrators' telegram, an action that the telegram's authors considered evidence that bonds of estate solidarity proved more powerful than their influence as local officials. According to Zhedenev, Ufa's mayor did not enjoy a good reputation among the marshals, but the marshals still felt it necessary to accept the mayor's repentance for getting "carried away by the revolution." Since, in the marshals' words, the mayor "is our nobleman," the marshals "could not fail to believe him." The governor had prevailed upon "the noblemen of the revolutionaries and Muslims" to telegraph St. Petersburg denying the officials' statements' veracity and supporting the governor.[32]

Establishing more enduring order required a broader mobilization in support of the local administration. Initiative for such a mobilization came on October 21, when "citizens of petty urban estates and of the working class" asked Tsekhanovetskii to approve their request to mount Ufa's first mass "patriotic, loyal demonstration" the following day, October 22. Several thousand people marched through Ufa, singing the national anthem and carrying portraits of the tsar, national flags, and icons. Marchers "from all classes of the population" converged on Ufa's central cathedral, where they participated in a prayer service. The governor joined the service at an appointed time. When asked why "authorities" tolerated "public reviling of His Majesty," the governor climbed on a table to explain himself. The governor told the crowd he had stood alone. Although half of the crowd at the prayer service had heard Nikolai Ivanovich criticize the tsar, no one had said a word. The governor had considered it poor service to the tsar to allow blood to be shed by people who had the right to assemble. As soon as he saw this freedom misused, he had moved to restore order. He finished his speech with a loud "hurrah" for the tsar that the crowd enthusiastically repeated. A soldier proposed a cheer for the governor, which the crowd answered with an extended cry.[33] This was a turning point: The governor perceived his authority to depend upon the crowd's support. That the governor, the tsar's representative in Ufa, felt compelled to stand on a table to explain himself to demonstrators would have been difficult to imagine even a few weeks before.

The success of the "patriotic" demonstration on October 22 inspired "several honored citizens" to organize a still larger one the following day. Two processions of several thousand persons carrying portraits of the tsar, banners declaring "God Save the Tsar," and national flags moved from churches at opposite ends of the city. The marchers told those they encountered to remove their hats to show respect for the tsar's portrait. All did so, which leftists took as a sign that the people were not on the side of the revolution.[34] More than 10,000 people converged finally on the governor's house. The governor led a loud "hurrah" for the tsar, and the crowd sang the national anthem. The crowd hushed as the governor read a telegram of loyalty to the tsar, then broke out into hurrahs and the national anthem once again. The demonstration had an ethnically and religiously diverse dimension to it. One lady of society "with a German name" (Baumgarten) asked the governor to take the hand of a "Russian woman," and the governor marched with her.[35] Some Tatars in the crowd invited it to proceed to the residence of Mufti Mukhamed'iar Sultanov. The mufti offered a cheer for the tsar, and then he himself received an ovation. The crowd moved on while the governor accepted the mufti's invitation to rest a moment and have a cigarette.[36]

The dangers inherent in mass mobilization soon became clear. While the crowd stopped at the mufti's, Ufa's police chief informed the governor that a man had been killed. The incident occurred at a prayer service in front of a cathedral where the day's patriotic demonstration had begun. A young worker named Kaulin, drunk and barely able to stay on his feet, apparently fell or lurched suddenly, causing the pole of his banner to strike sharply a portrait of the tsar. Many in the crowd believed the sound to be a rifle shot and thought that Kaulin had fired upon the tsar's portrait. They attacked Kaulin savagely. According to rightist accounts, men and women, Tatars and Orthodox, participated in beating Kaulin. When police intervened, they found only a "formless, bloody corpse."[37] The crowd's rage continued. Nikolai Pashkin, a lawyer, homeowner, and City Duma deputy, had watched with horror as the crowd beat Kaulin to death. Minutes later, Pashkin angrily rebuked a group that had participated in the murder. The group surrounded Pashkin, calling him "one of the politicians" among those who shot at the tsar's portrait. The group beat and trampled Pashkin until he was a "bloody mass without human shape."[38] When Matvei Rukker, a man identified as a Jew and Pashkin's friend, questioned the crowd over beating an innocent man, several soldiers beat Rukker to death.[39]

Upon hearing of the three murders, the governor called out troops. They managed to save a zemstvo statistician from death at the hands of the crowd.

Once again, fatal violence catalyzed political action. On October 24, the governor used the murders as justification for a complete ban on political demonstrations. On October 26, the governor and the procurator first called meetings with "monarchist" or "patriotic" leaders and then with opposition leaders, "revolutionaries," to pressure them to cease violence and demonstrations.[40] Tsekhanovetskii relied primarily on police and troops when he moved to reassert his authority in October. The support of traditional social leaders, the marshals of the nobility, also played a large role in his efforts to restore order. Yet, notably, he did not move to end demonstrations until he felt popular sentiment turn against the "revolutionaries," until representatives from society organized "patriotic" demonstrations, and after several deaths had shown many Ufa residents that uncontrolled violence could result from political struggle. The crowd's expression of support in patriotic demonstrations helped the governor maintain power against those on the right and the left who either sought a return to the pre-October order or considered it insufficiently reformed.

The governor and local administration succeeded in preventing further mass demonstrations after Pashkin's and Rukker's murders. Political struggle continued, however, in the central press and in local railway workshops. Tsekhanovetskii, Ufa noblemen, and their opponents within the local administration led by Zhedenev exchanged letters on the pages of St. Petersburg's *Novoe vremia* (The new time) and *Moskovskie vedomosti* (The Moscow gazette) in November 1905. Two of Zhedenev's articles, one entitled "The Ufa Sedition," received considerable exposure.[41] Zhedenev also presented his account to the Russian Monarchist Party in Moscow and to Minister of Internal Affairs Petr N. Durnovo.[42] Two weeks later, on December 5, Durnovo removed Tsekhanovetskii from office. Zhedenev had helped bring about the removal of Tsekhanovetskii that he and others had sought in October.

The last major political mobilization of 1905, the December railway strike, had many characteristics of pre-October mobilizations in that the strikers had very limited success in expanding the strike beyond their workshops. Some students and workers at a large Ufa factory joined the railway strikers, but zemstvo employees did not. By December, moreover, differences among workers had taken institutional form. The "circle of patriots" that formed after the October 14 confrontation of railway workers with the governor and soldiers had become the "Patriotic Society of Workers and Other Employees of the Railway Workshops of the Ufa Station" (hereafter Patriotic Society) under Busov's leadership and probably under the direction of the local administration. The violence following the "patriotic" demonstrations in Ufa caused Social Democrats in the workshop to begin to arm themselves and to form a "militant detachment." The Social Democrats' (SDs') leader, Ivan S. Iakutov, a metal worker in the assembly shop, had such great influence that SDs were often called "the party of Iakutov."[43]

As a result of these divisions, on December 7, when the railway shop joined the general strike that had been initiated in Moscow, those workers who did not support it went home, while those who did met in the assembly shop. According to witnesses, the number who left, called "patriots," greatly outnumbered Social Democrats, by approximately 1,200–1,400 "patriots" to only 300–400 SDs in the "party of Iakutov."[44] The local administration, its garrison reinforced with Cossacks, quickly moved against the strikers. Workers wounded nine police and soldiers, one fatally, and eighteen workers were arrested in a confrontation at the workshops. The strikers got some revenge on December 26 when acting governor Kelenovskii was severely wounded in an assassination attempt, but this led only to the declaration of a state of "extraordinary security" that was used to break the strike on December 29. Without the broad mobilization of urban society that had accompanied the October strike, railway workers were isolated and defeated. Political violence remained a part of Ufa life for at least the next two years, but it took the form of individual attacks on officials, "expropriations," or the robbery of trains and banks.[45]

CONCEPTIONS OF PATRIOTISM AFTER DECEMBER 1905

The suppression of the railway strike and the declaration of "extraordinary security" made the civic freedoms promised in the October Manifesto seem all but dead. Tsekhanovetskii was gone, and crowds no longer filled Ufa's streets and parks. Although police power maintained order, the administration's reliance on the popular will was still fresh in the minds of officials and political elites. Moreover, the political violence of late 1905 made deepening fissures in the polity abundantly clear. Political actors of various types and, most important, state officials themselves, undertook large-scale efforts to win the allegiance of the tsar's subjects and to overcome divisions that cut through nearly all institutions and social groups. The tsar's decrees, the October Manifesto, and the disturbances that followed had legitimized and provided precedents for appeals to loyalty from persons not connected to the state administration, or connected to it only indirectly. As a result, after October, varied and sometimes contradictory appeals for loyalty competed for influence in Ufa.

The Patriotic Society described above was among the most visible "patriotic" organizations. Perhaps because its leaders, Busov and Laptev, received help from "administrative officials" and were located in the railway workshops, the Patriotic Society positioned itself not as a militant, "black-hundred" group but as an inclusive cultural organization. "Faith, Tsar, and Fatherland" were the society's fundamental principles, and its slogan was "in loyalty to the native land is our strength." The program greeted the October Manifesto as a gift from the tsar. Closer to home, the Patriotic Society sought to reduce drunkenness, to oppose strikes, to improve the condition of labor, and to satisfy workers' moral and spiritual needs—goals that indicated its opposition to the "revolutionaries" in the railway workshops.[46] Newspaper accounts estimated attendance at the society's meetings at between eighty and one hundred workers.[47]

The Patriotic Society's political opponents identified it with the violent right wing of the demonstrations in October and argued that only pressure from the administration had pushed them to make the society's appeals less violent. The account of Zhedenev, a lower-level official, makes clear the presence of aggressively, ethnically exclusive notions of loyalty within the administration itself. In denouncing the participation of non-Russians in politics and social life, Zhedenev echoed the alarmist writings of churchmen such as Dionisii and Petrov nearly two decades before. Throughout Zhedenev's text, he identifies his and his like-minded colleagues' opponents by ethnonyms that are supposed to explain their disloyalty, but he addresses Muslims very little. Jews were the most prominent "enemy" group. Under the anti-Semitic Sokolovskii, according to Zhedenev, "Ufa province was free of these parasites." Zhedenev labeled leaders of the revolutionary movement and Nikolai Ivanovich in particular as Jews; Tsekhanovetskii was considered sympathetic to Jews. The pamphlet does not dwell on Tsekhanovetskii's actual support for Muslims. He gave Muslims in state service four days of leave to observe Ramadan, which started on October 17. Poles were the other commonly cited disloyal element. Zhedenev described Governor Tsekhanovetskii as a "devout Pole" who, "out of love for his motherland, desire[d] the breakup of the Russian empire in order to restore Poland on its ruins."[48] Zhedenev claimed wide popular support for anti-Polonism. He stated that the crowd chanted: "Death to the traitor! Death to the governor! Death to the Pole!" after it murdered Pashkin.[49] A zemstvo congress's recognition of the movement for Polish autonomy on September 12, 1905, probably provided the most immediate reason that Poles' loyalty came into doubt—Zhedenev wrote that Tsekhanovetskii was ecstatic about the zemstvo congress's resolutions.[50] The prominence of the issue of Polish autonomy during a time of political unrest helped associate the two events in the minds of rightists. Anti-Polonism had older sources in the region, too. After the Polish uprising of 1831, some Polish rebels were exiled to Orenburg and over the next decade were accused of a conspiracy against the state. In 1905, the far right consistently used the language of nationality to describe threats to the state. Opposition to the tsar became identified with sympathy for a "foreign" nationality and the fragmentation of Russia.

Ethnic difference in itself is not necessarily more or less divisive than religious difference, of course, but the use of ethnonyms associated the dangers faced by the state in 1905–1907 with a specific kind of particularism, one predicated on autonomy or sovereignty and separation from the empire rather than one that reflected traditional tensions among religious groups.

Others on the right echoed Zhedenev's attitude toward non-Russian groups but added violent resentment of the noble estate. One leaflet, an "Appeal of the Monarchist Russian (*Rossiiskogo*) Society to the Russian People," fixated on the empire's disintegration. Traitors had "sold Russia (*Rossiia*), Finland, and Poland to the Jews"; "Finland and Sweden [*sic*] [had] already separated from the empire." The appeal linked the empire's dissolution explicitly to a lack of Russians in positions of authority.

> Where is Russian authority[?] . . . All Mother Russia is filled with Poles, Yids, Finns, Swedes, and Germans . . . who of the authorities in Ufa is Russian? No one. Starting with the governor and ending with his lackey—all are Poles. On the railroad Dopatto, Keller and other Poles, Germans, Swedes, and Jews stage strikes. It is a second Poland, and not Ufa.

In response, the appeal called for the "Russian people" to defend the tsar by beating "Yids," "bloodthirsty zemstvo robbers," and "educated youth." This appeal's authors shared with Zhedenev and his colleagues a belief in the necessity of "Russian" authority. However, because this appeal called for the beating of Petr Ginevskii, the chairman of the Ufa County zemstvo whom Zhedenev praised for his conservative influence, its authors do not appear to be those behind the Patriotic Society.[51] The Monarchist Russian Society identified the noble estate as treasonous and equated educated society's power with a return to noble domination. The authors asked their audience to "Remember, how our grandfathers and great-grandfathers cringed at the arbitrariness of the lords . . . how the lords, just after the wedding, took our wives and daughters with them on the first night . . . Would you like, brothers, to fall under the terror of aristocratic arbitrariness again?" The Monarchist Society's appeal thus combined the notion that traitorous non-Russians dominated the administrative apparatus with older resentments of estate privilege and notions of masculine honor.

In the aftermath of the Revolution of 1905, Ufa's left, which had a strong presence among zemstvo City Duma delegates and employees as well as the press, generally rejected the use of "patriotism" in its appeals.[52] Ufa's Social Democrats energetically waged war in print, issuing leaflets meant to expose the "patriots" as pawns of the police and administration who offered "Yids" and "Poles" as enemies in order to distract the masses. Jews and Poles, SDs argued, were as oppressed as the "benighted people." Social Democrats sought to direct the masses along class lines, arguing that police, the priests, and "patriotic" leaders oppressed and exploited people of all types.[53] Social Democrats mocked suggestions that the socialists sold out Russia, Finland, and Poland, asserting that non-Russians simply wanted to be left alone. A June 1906 leaflet, written to denounce government reprisals against workers, called for equality of all faiths and an end to oppression based upon nationality.[54] Ufa's left-liberal paper used the term "patriot" ironically. The newspaper frequently asserted that "patriotism" served merely as a cover to protect railway workers accused of theft and corruption. One local writer argued that the time for patriotism had passed and was giving way to new forces such as the "international proletariat" and "new broad, enlightened, truly human feelings of universal brotherhood and the equality of people."[55] The relative strength of the patriots and revolutionaries is difficult to determine, but "progressive elements" and left-liberal Kadets, including some Muslims, soundly defeated Busov and others associated with the "patriotic" parties of the right who stood for election to the State Duma from the city of Ufa.[56] In order to achieve greater success in elections to the Second Duma, Busov and other monarchist activists reached out to Muslims. Busov wrote that the Union of the Russian People "has the closest tie with Muslims and considers them our brothers." Two Muslims were among the top three finishers in the preelection campaign for the "monarchist, Octoberist, and moderate Muslim" list to stand for election to the Duma, but the monarchists went down to defeat again.[57]

After October, the state administration from St. Petersburg down to the county level undertook a novel and massive effort to win support from the population through lectures and the distribution of pamphlets, leaflets, and newspapers. Previous tsarist administrations had recognized the power of the printed word, but their dealings with the press occurred "only in negative terms," such as censorship and sanctions. Sergei Witte and Petr A. Stolypin, his successor as chairman of the Council of Ministers, by contrast, had an activist conception of the press and sought to win over public opinion.[58] On the local level, Ufa's governor as of January 1906, Alexander S. Kliucharev, coordinated efforts to influence the tsar's subjects' minds. The predominant form of allegiance promoted by Ufa's administration was inclusive and sought to unite all in support of the tsar but without the violence associated with Busov and the Patriotic Society.[59]

The relative emphases on loyalty to the tsar and to the fatherland sometimes distinguished different actors within this consensus. Kliucharev called for the creation of county committees that would assist the government in restoring order and opposing "enemies of the fatherland." The committees sponsored public lectures in cities and distributed 40,000 pamphlets and as many as 150,000 leaflets, some of which were in Tatar.[60] The county committees' primary goals were the "proper" explanation of the October Manifesto and of the workings of the

State Duma. Speakers included priests and others who addressed topics such as "What is personal freedom and for what is it necessary?" and "[Our] Brothers the Poles."[61] Rural administrators—land captains—and police officials sometimes also took initiative in the distribution of printed material. The Sterlitamak county police superintendent, for instance, requested permission to distribute a leaflet authored by the governor that would help the police combat enemies of the "Tsar and Motherland." The superintendent wrote to the governor that the police were the only ones who did not "run under the red flag" when the tsar and motherland were being abused "by all . . . its enemies," including Russians and representatives "of other nationalities (*natsional'nostei*)."[62]

The governor suggested that the state build upon these initiatives in the form of a wide network of "truly popular schools" with "ideologically patriotic teaching personnel."[63] The political leadership sought to convey their understanding of the new political system and to counteract interpretations of it that had produced disturbances and hostility toward non-Russians. Reform and new institutions, combined with the power of the popular will demonstrated in the October crisis, fed the perception among officials that the people must be made to understand and actively support the state.

STATE DUMA ELECTIONS AND PERCEPTIONS OF MUSLIMS

Muslims occupied an ambiguous position in the events of 1905. Even persons most aggressively exclusive in their conception of loyalty lacked a strong, consistent identification of Muslims as an "enemy" group in 1905. Rightist accounts identified the mufti and a Muslim servitor in the provincial administration, Akhmet-Sultan Teregulov, as loyal and mentioned them favorably.[64] In this respect, the right wing in Ufa was similar to its counterparts in the capitals. In 1907, the Union of the Russian People created an organization with the name "The Muslim Union of the Russian People from the Kazan Tatars." The organization aimed to assist in the construction of mosques and Muslim schools.[65] It indicated the success of the incorporation of Muslim institutions into the imperial administration. Although Zhedenev accused Tsekhanovetskii of conspiring with Muslim marshals of the nobility, Tevkelev and Sultanov, to "form a Muslim state from Ufa province and those surrounding it," these portions seem tacked on to his narrative. Zhedenev's earlier newspaper accounts did not contain such an argument.[66] When Zhedenev wrote critically of Muslims, their status as members of the intelligentsia or nobility was decisive.

The tsar's concession of creating an elected legislative body, the State Duma, made more urgent the task of cultivating loyalty among Muslims. Although the State Duma's authority was limited and the electoral system was an indirect one, hopes for it were high in many circles.[67] The province's Muslim population proved most able to make use of the elections to mobilize politically. The reaction of some prominent Russians to Muslims' striking success illustrates how political mobilization began to change perceptions of political groups.[68] The Islamic faith may have remained the cultural content of the group identified as Muslim in 1905–1906, but, to some, new institutions and political practices gave Muslim organizational efforts more threatening implications.

The question of Muslim participation in Duma elections did not receive much attention before elections began. Muslim goals seemed modest. Muslim leaders had discussed the need to have two of the province's ten seats reserved for Muslims to ensure that they would be represented. A number of the local electoral assemblies strove for proportional representation. By the time the provincial electoral assembly met in March 1906, Muslims' electoral success surprised everyone. Non-Muslims predominated among workers (4–0) and landowners (26–9), but only narrowly so among urban electors (15–11). In the largest curiae, electors from the peasant-dominated volosts, Muslims outnumbered "Russians" by a margin of more than two to one (54–25). This gave them an absolute majority among electors, 74–70, with two Mari electors rounding out the assembly. Some Muslims now argued that Muslims should hold all ten of Ufa's places in the Duma, since Muslims would be less likely to be elected from places with smaller, more scattered Muslim populations and fewer Muslim landowners. Other Muslim leaders, anxious to maintain alliances they had developed with non-Muslim leftists, rejected such a motion. In the end, Muslim and non-Muslim leaders agreed that six Muslim and four Russian deputies would represent the province—a split that gave Muslims a bit more representation than would have been proportionate to their presence in the province's population—and that the Muslims could veto the non-Muslims selected. A few Russians who resented Muslims' show of power walked out of the assembly in protest.[69] Those non-Muslims elected included one peasant and three zemstvo activists with reputations for treating Muslims fairly.

How were Muslims so able to dominate the electoral process? Muslims had three ingredients essential to electoral success: They were the largest group in Ufa's population, they had a significant landowning nobility favored by the electoral system, and they had an elite capable of organizing political activity. The presence of Muslim nobles such as Tevkelev, Dzhiantiurin, and others, and the ennoblement of Bashkirs through service, gave Muslims in Ufa greater representation in all four convocations of the Duma. Ivan Zhukovskii, a wealthy Russian nobleman and one of the province's leading Kadets, had a different explanation for Muslim success. He blamed the state for the preponderance of Muslim electors. Since the local administration did not consider Muslims a threat and believed Muslims were concerned primarily with "matters of faith and nationality (*natsional'nosti*)" and not "politics," it permitted Muslims to assemble and allowed Muslim agitators to circulate freely. "Russian people," on the other hand, always found themselves "under suspicion." Ufa's elections were conducted while the province had only recently (March 9) been shifted from a state of extreme security to heightened security.[70] Russian activists were denied permission to speak or were even arrested.

More important to Muslim success, according to Zhukovskii, were Muslims' intensive organizational efforts. Muslims were particularly obsessed with "tribal" and religious questions and with defending their "blood interests." Zhukovskii acknowledged that each tribe had a right to defend its interests but held that these should not be allowed to counter "common-state interests." Muslims had introduced "dissension and tribal separation" into questions of state and had taken advantage of their strong position to usurp the rights of Russians.[71] Elections also clearly showed weaknesses and divisions among people assumed to be Russians. Zhukovskii argued that Russian nobles and members of the intelligentsia could not agree on a wide range of issues. Moreover, much of the "Russian" group turned out not to be Russian at all. Among "native Russians" and migrant groups in the region—Ukrainians, Latvians, Germans, and others —no agreement was possible. The only thing unifying peasants was a lack of trust in estates and classes above them in the social order.[72] Zhukovskii condemned conflict on a "tribal basis" and concluded with a call for supranational unity. By focusing on "tribal" difference and blood ties, Zhukovskii called attention to Muslims as fundamentally different from Russians not only in a religious sense but in a blood or ethnic sense. After 1905, the content of Muslim group interests may not have changed substantially—they continued to define themselves religiously—but new means to express these interests—the ballot box and the press—gave their activity new implications to some observers. They had acquired the characteristics of a nationality, a political formation that threatened to divide the local elite and perhaps the entire empire in the manner rightist politicians had attributed to Poles and Finns. Thus Zhukovskii and others could describe individuals as "of the Muslim ethnicity (*narodnosti*)."[73]

Who were these Muslims Zhukovskii identified as motivated only by their "blood interest?" The Muslims who represented Ufa in the First Duma were primarily those elite Muslims most invested in the imperial system. Abussu-gud Akhtiamov, discussed in chapter 3, had completed the Juridical Faculty at Kazan University and served as an aide to the Ufa governor in the 1870s, as chairman of the Belebei Zemstvo, and as honorary secretary of the OMEA. Salim-Girei Dzhantiurin, a descendant from a Kazakh khan, completed the Physics and Math Faculty of Moscow University and served as a justice of the peace and a land captain. Shakhaidar Syrtlanov, discussed in previous chapters, was the son of a Bashkir canton head and nobleman who graduated from the Nepliuev Cadet School and then served nine years in the military in Turkestan. Upon his return to Ufa, he served in the Belebei zemstvo—as chairman from 1887 to 1891—and then as the Ufa governor's senior official for special assignments. Kutlu-Mukhammad Tevkelev, the former mufti's nephew, had graduated from the prestigious Corps of Pages in St. Petersburg and had served in the military, in the Ufa zemstvo, and as Belebei marshal of the nobility. Sakhipzada Maksiutov was a grain and leather merchant and zemstvo activist educated in Kazan's four-class Russian-Tatar School. Though he is most often identified as a Tatar, his origins are unclear, and he came from a very diverse Teptiar, Tatar, and Bashkir district in Birsk County. Only one of Ufa's six Muslim deputies, Iamaletdin Khuramshin, an akhund, had been trained exclusively in Muslim confessional schools.[74] In all, deputies from Ufa constituted six of twenty-five Muslim deputies to the First Duma and seven of thirty-six Muslim deputies to the Second Duma—the largest Muslim delegation from any single province in the empire.[75] Two Muslims were also elected from Orenburg Province to the First Duma—Shagisharif Matinov, an akhund and honored citizen from the Bashkir estate, and Mukhammed-Zakir Ramiev, a poet, Tatar merchant, and owner of a gold-mining operation in the Urals who had been born in Ufa Province. Muslim electoral success in Ufa was a product of local Muslims' successful integration into the imperial system.

As some Muslims entered the State Duma, however, others left administrative institutions to pursue opportunities provided by the relatively more open public sphere after 1905. The MVD's subordinate institutions in Ufa had never featured a large number of strong Muslim voices, but this became even more the case after 1905. In 1905, Rizaeddin Fakhretdinov left his post as a judge in the OMEA to edit the Tatar-language publication *Shura* (Council) in Orenburg and to devote his time to literary pursuits made possible by the greatly expanded Tatar-language book trade. The following year, Salim-Girei Dzhantiurin resigned to become the director of a major Muslim madrasa, Galiia. He was a deputy from Ufa to the first two State Dumas. The governor retained a Muslim, Akhmet-Sultan Teregulov, as an assistant, but he lacked Dzhantiurin's stature. Movement into the State Duma and into positions in Muslim education and the press indicates the creation of a new kind of public after 1905.[76]

Bashkiria's representatives used the State Duma as a forum to articulate Bashkir interests, among other interventions. Until 1905, political thought among Muslims had developed primarily in the city of Kazan. It had emphasized either Islamic faith or the Turkic language as an organizing principle. Ufa Province's Duma deputies advanced Bashkirs as people united by shared experience and culture. Shakhaidar Syrtlanov spoke in the Second Duma of Bashkirs' acceptance of Russian sovereignty, which indicated that "this is not a conquered people." He specifically noted the charter from Ivan IV to Bashkirs granting them their land. He also cited Bashkirs' service in Russia's wars and as members of the Bashkir cantons.[77] In the Second Duma, a Bashkir from Orenburg Province, Shakhbal Seifitdinov, stressed that Bashkirs had long been loyal subjects of the tsar. He spoke favorably of the cantonal system of administration, when, in his view, cantonal leaders were Bashkirs themselves and defended Bashkirs' interests. Representatives from Ufa and Orenburg Provinces summarized the history of confiscations of Bashkir land since the 1860s and presented Bashkirs' request that their land be returned to them. In the Second Duma, a Tatar deputy from Ufa, Kalimulla Khasanov, stated that if, in the view of Stolypin's government, "private property is really inviolable, then Bashkir land must likewise be inviolable."[78] The essential points suggested in these speeches were that Bashkirs were the native people of the region with a recognized right to the land, that their entry into the Russian state was voluntary, that Bashkirs needed to be led by Bashkirs to protect their interests, and that Bashkirs had demonstrated through military service their commitment to fulfilling their obligations.

THE STATE DUMA AND NATIONALITY

Expressions of Bashkir national identity in the Duma accompanied the growing national organization of the Duma itself. Even before 1905, nationality had become an operative category in political practice. As political scientist John Slocum has argued, decrees on religious toleration "indicate an erosion in the official equation of Russianness and Orthodoxy and a growing tendency toward protecting the interests of subjects of Russian nationality regardless of their religious affiliation."[79] Nationality became a category in other realms, too. In June 1904 new legislation on migration specified that "only persons of native Russian origins and Orthodox confession" were allowed to migrate to Central Asia and the Caucasus.[80] Elections to the First State Duma in 1906 expanded the importance of nationality. In the areas of the empire that had zemstvos, elections to the first two convocations of the Duma in 1906 and in early 1907 took place using a system of curiae organized by estate status and property-holding. Ufa Province had zemstvo institutions, so its electoral system resembled those of central Russia. In non-zemstvo regions in the empire's periphery, however, elections were arranged to give Russians greater representation than their non-Russian neighbors and often greater representation than Russians had in central regions.[81]

The division of the polity into national groupings became even more evident after the emperor closed the Second State Duma on June 3, 1907. Nicholas II cited the substantial participation of non-Russian delegates as a primary cause for his disappointment with the institution. Nicholas II decided that non-Russians should not have decisive voices in "purely Russian" questions.[82] The electoral system for the Duma's third and fourth convocations reduced representation from the countryside and from non-Russian regions. The new electoral law specified that preliminary electoral meetings could be segregated by estate and nationality (*natsional'nost'*) where appropriate. When Ufa's zemstvos compiled lists of eligible voters, they included the category of nationality as well as estate status, place of residence, and the voters' land holdings. Identification according to nationality does not seem to have come easily to Ufa. By the time elections to the Fourth Duma in Ufa Province took place in 1912, national classifications were still not consistent among its six counties. Some with Muslim surnames were listed as Muslims in Belebei County, as Bashkirs in Birsk County, and as Tatars in Menzelinsk County. A few who owned land in more than one county were listed by different nationalities in the different counties. The nationalities of others were not specified.[83] The tsar had declared nationality to be of great importance to the functioning of the Duma. What exactly this meant was not yet clear in the center and even less so locally.[84] Nonetheless, in the empire's east, the formal use of nationality to categorize political participants and to segregate electors was unprecedented and directly connected to political mobilization.

CONCLUSION

The October Manifesto, the crisis of authority, and Duma elections transformed political life in Ufa. Politics moved out of a relatively narrow sphere of state offices, zemstvo assemblies, and schools and became a mass phenomenon. Administrative officials and political elites perceived a need to mobilize the population's active support rather than counting on passive obedience to authority. As the perceived importance of popular loyalty grew, new forums for expressing one's loyalty opened, and means of displaying one's allegiance acquired new importance. Large, unprecedented, and sometimes violent public demonstrations challenged Ufa residents of all types to figure out what "revolutionary" or "patriotic" groups represented and whether to join one. People signified their support by traditional means such as the swearing of oaths and by carrying the tsar's portrait, a national flag, or a red flag. Some sang the national anthem and others "revolutionary" songs such as "La Marseillaise." Although such banners had been raised before and such songs had been sung, they had never been done in the same spaces, on the same scale, or with the same consequences. Who could be loyal and what should be the focus of one's loyalty became contentious issues.

The most common patriotism that emerged from 1905 to 1906 was ethnically and religiously inclusive. Although it was associated with the Orthodox Church and the Russian tsar, these connections were only vague. Anyone, with the possible exception of the Jews, could be considered loyal. Poles and Germans, Muslim and Orthodox were identified as loyal at different times in descriptions of the events of 1905–1906. At the same time, an exclusive, ethnic conception of political allegiance became more vital in the post-1905 context. Some "patriots" began to claim that people to whom they applied certain ethnonyms could not be fully loyal to the tsar and to the fatherland. They attacked as disloyal and "revolutionaries" men who had served in the administration or in prominent social positions such as marshal of the nobility. Being Jewish or Polish no longer meant simply that one would not support Orthodoxy but rather that one sought to separate from the empire and thus destroy it.

These phenomena in Ufa echoed similar phenomena in the western borderlands, but with less intensity. The much lower level of violence in Ufa's revolution of 1905 differentiated Ufa from regions further east in Siberia and in the western and southern borderlands. Thousands died in conflicts in the south Caucasus between the local population and tsarist police and soldiers, and in clashes between Azerbaijani Muslims and Armenians in Baku. Hundreds died in uprisings in the Black Sea port of Odessa at the hands of police and soldiers and of so-called Black Hundreds who carried out pogroms against Jews. In the Baltic Provinces, punitive expeditions to suppress agrarian disturbances claimed two thousand lives and resulted in seven hundred more death sentences.[85] As Faith Hillis has shown, the politics of nationality had much deeper roots in southwest Russia. Whereas in the western borderlands the revolution reinvigorated political violence previously seen in pogroms following Alexander II's assassination in 1881, 1905 brought such hostilities to Bashkiria for the first time in over a century. In Kiev, twenty-seven died, hundreds were wounded, and Jewish business and homes were destroyed in large numbers.[86] By contrast, six deaths and three death sentences in all of Ufa Province indicate the relatively low level of violence in the region.[87] The imperial state did not rule with the same heavy hand, and local religious and national groups simply lacked the antagonism that appeared elsewhere. Both in Ufa and in the western borderlands, however, similar processes were at work. The polity fragmented according to whether one remained loyal to the tsar, to the reformed order promised by the October Manifesto, or to some political form based on a vision of "universal brotherhood." These loyalties often became identified with nationality. To both the tsar system's supporters and its opponents in both the east and the west, the empire became fragmented into an empire of nationalities after 1905.[88] Which nationalities would be included and what role they should play in imperial politics remained unresolved. Collaboration across ethnic and confessional divides was tested by efforts to use concepts of nationality and religion to homogenize the political elite and increase central control.

It would be tempting to see the Revolution of 1905 in Ufa Province as the local manifestation of a series of revolutions that affected Eurasia: the December 1905 constitutional revolution in Iran, the 1908 Young Turk Revolution in the Ottoman Empire, and the October 1911 Xinhai Revolution in China. Despite the tensions evident locally as early as 1903, however, and unlike seventeenth- and eighteenth-century unrest in Bashkiria, the Revolution of 1905 in Ufa was closely connected to developments in the center. Revolution arrived by railroad with news of Bloody Sunday in St. Petersburg in January and with the railway strike and October Manifesto later in the year rather than being sparked by events in other Turkic, Islamic, or Asian areas. Bashkir and Muslim populations in Ufa participated relatively little in the Revolution of 1905.

The Revolution of 1905 in the empire as a whole shared characteristics with the revolutions in its neighbors. All four involved a revolt in a country linguistically and religiously different from most Europeans and against rulers whose vacillations between reform and repression left it weakened and vulnerable.[89] Most revolutionaries in each country aspired to some sort of constitutional rule. Nonetheless, important differences remain. As Jürgen Osterhammel has written, the Revolution of 1905 in Russia featured greater, more intensive popular participation than the others, uniting, as we have seen, wide swaths of the urban and rural populations. The military remained largely loyal to the Romanov dynasty but struck decisive blows against rulers in China and the Ottoman Empire. Religious elites remained among the most zealously loyal to Nicholas II, while Sh'ia clerics comprised an important force for revolution against the shah in Iran. All four revolutions came in the wake of military or political failures, but the Chinese, Iranian, and Ottoman revolutionaries were motivated by the desire to create states that would better stand up to Western imperialism, while unrest in Russia resulted from the failure of imperialist policies of its own in the Far East.[90] Most of all, the same Russian emperor, Nicholas II, held power at the start of unrest and when it ended in 1907. Nicholas II managed to rally support among the military, clergy, and bureaucracy and tolerate sufficient concessions to remain very much the emperor, particularly in his own mind. How he and imperial officials would manage the forces set in motion by the revolution remained an open question.

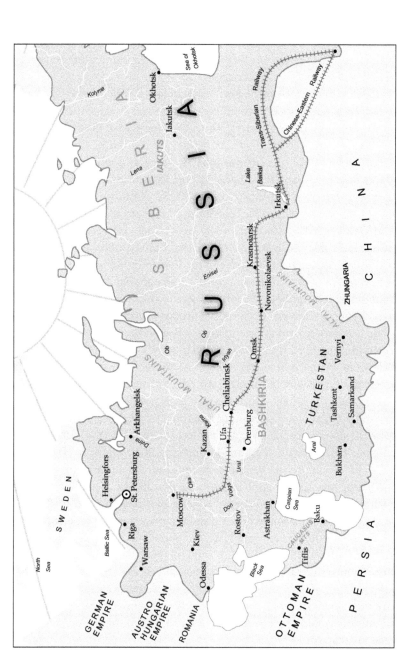

MAP 7.1. The Russian Empire in 1914.

7

EMPIRE, NATIONS, AND MULTINATIONAL VISIONS

1907–1917

IN THE WINTER of 1915–1916, twenty-five-year-old Akhmed-Zeki Validov, a political activist and future leader of the Bashkir movement for autonomy, was summoned to St. Petersburg. The Muslim Fraction in the State Duma, which had been as large as thirty-three members in the Duma's second convocation, had been cut to six due to imperial officials' efforts to reduce non-Russian representation. Validov considered the head of the Muslim Fraction, Kutlu-Mukhammad Tevkelev—nephew of the late Orenburg mufti, wealthy noble landowner, and zemstvo activist—"a brave and knowledgeable man." But Tevkelev recognized that members of the Muslim Fraction had mostly secular education and experience. They lacked detailed knowledge of Muslim affairs. So the fraction called on areas with substantial Muslim populations to send representatives to assist in its work. At the end of 1915, a meeting of Muslim society in Ufa decided to send Validov to St. Petersburg. Tevkelev graciously introduced Validov to the Duma leadership and ministers at various receptions and social events in the capital. Validov found meeting the "Petersburg aristocracy" through Tevkelev interesting. However, "these people had no clue: their principal activity was games of chance, which I hated. This class, doomed to extinction, lived only by reminiscences and dreams."[1]

Validov wrote with the benefit of hindsight, but his picture of the Muslim Fraction tells much about how imperial officials conceived the role of Muslims in imperial affairs. Half of the six members of the Muslim fraction—Tevkelev, Gaisa Enikeev, and Ibniamin Akhtiamov—were noblemen. Four were born in Ufa Province.[2] Their estate status and social prestige had helped them and their families integrate into the imperial system, where they represented their communities in the State Duma. As much as they were welcome at receptions in the capital, however, the state that they served sought to minimize their influence. Kutlu-Mukhammad Tevkelev's great-great-grandfather had conquered Bashkiria. Tevkelev was left to play cards and remember, in Validov's account.

The empire was very much alive in 1915, and estate still mattered. Since 1905, however, estate and religion had not been sufficient to mark political loyalty, and different conceptions of the polity complicated conceptions of what should be the object of loyalty. Different forms of nation drew the loyalty of some in the empire, but the question of whether that nation would be based on language and culture or religion divided Russian Orthodox and Muslims alike. Various national visions of the empire had adherents in Bashkiria, and tensions among these visions remained evident well into the First World War. The particular population and politics of Ufa Province, however, produced a vision of empire less evident in the center. Many members of Ufa Province's Russian Orthodox and Muslim elites collaborated to promote a vision of the empire as a place in which diverse peoples could find support for their national identities within a multinational state. This view was most apparent locally in zemstvos and their staffs. Even after the local administration excluded Muslims from the zemstvos, local elites continued to work together to promote native language instruction, the publication of materials in languages other than Russian, and extracurricular or "adult" educational programs in native languages. The multinational vision had analogues in the Kadet Party's effort to build support among non-Russians by supporting autonomy for non-Russian nationalities. The Kadet view was a minority position in the center, whereas it dominated Ufa's zemstvos and Duma delegation. Moreover, the province's left-leaning political elites also drew on Social Democratic influences.

The outbreak of the First World War in August 1914 intensified the competition among differing local visions of the empire. The initial surge of patriotic fervor accentuated calls for the reinvigoration of loyalty to the tsar and the empire. At the same time, the mass migration of peoples from the west of the empire catalyzed the formation of Polish, Latvian, and other mutual aid societies and catalyzed national thinking among local elites. The Russian Orthodox Church portrayed the war as a test sent from God, and charismatic Bishop Andrei brought together church and school officials for the cause of Russian nationalism. This coalescence of Russian nationalism took place roughly simultaneously with that of Bashkir nationalism, and neither left much of a place for the emperor. In the core of Bashkiria, the last decade of imperial rule witnessed not a shift from empire to nation but the crystallization of national, multinational, and cosmopolitan visions of the body politic.

STOLYPIN AND REFORM

Even Nicholas II and Petr Stolypin, chairman of the Committee of Ministers and minister of internal affairs from 1906 until his assassination in September 1911, held different visions of the empire. Nicholas II harkened back to a pre-Petrine dynastic-imperial model in which the tsar was connected with his subjects in an almost mystical union. This union largely transcended state institutions and was mediated by his own version of Russian Orthodoxy, which left non-Russian, non-Orthodox peoples with an inferior, if any, role in the empire's politics.[3] As a committed monarchist, Stolypin obviously shared many of Nicholas's priorities. Stolypin is well-known as the man who used force to suppress the Revolution of 1905. Police and military tribunals executed at least 2,700 people in 1906 and brought an end to the cycle of strikes and political disturbances. Beyond restoring order and centralizing state power, however, Stolypin sought fundamentally to restructure imperial authority so as to root the state in property-owning individuals loyal to the state and to the emperor himself. More than his predecessors, Stolypin perceived that state power depended on "the attitude of the people toward the government" and surveyed public opinion as expressed in zemstvos.[4] Upon assuming duties as minister of internal affairs in April 1906, Stolypin pursued reforms that would include more of the population in civic life and shift the state's focus from large collective estates and religious institutions to direct connections with individuals more equal in law than before.[5]

At the core of Stolypin's political initiatives lay three that greatly affected life in Bashkiria. First, Stolypin sought to reduce the power of estate distinctions to shape peasants' lives and to integrate them better into the empire's civic life. In October 1906, the tsar supported Stolypin's attempt to end "the segregation of the peasant estate from other classes of the population."[6] Nicholas II issued a decree that eliminated some of the most obvious laws that discriminated against peasants.[7] Peasants could enter the civil service, higher education, or the clergy. The law reestablished direct peasant voting in zemstvo elections that had ended in 1890 and allowed peasant property owners to vote in the landowner's curia in zemstvo elections. Second, Stolypin is perhaps best known for his agrarian reforms, which aimed to replace peasant communal landholdings with private property in the hands of individual proprietors. This would give peasants a stake in the civic order that he hoped would make them respect state laws and other people's property more than many had in 1905–1906.[8] The most important decree in this regard was that of November 9, 1906, which allowed each peasant head of household holding a communal allotment of land—often divided into as many as one hundred strips and interspersed among other communal land—to receive one coherent piece of land that he could cultivate as his private property. Progress on the consolidation of land in private ownership was slow but significant.[9] The reforms met considerable resistance from both ends of the political spectrum, however. Stolypin had to have the emperor issue them as a decree because the State Duma would not pass them.

Third, Stolypin initially embraced religious toleration but deemphasized it as he sought to appease Nicholas II and the empire's political right. Stolypin intended to build upon the April 17, 1905, Manifesto on Toleration by easing restrictions on non-Orthodox subjects of the tsar. Stolypin's ministry submitted fourteen bills to the Council of Ministers between September 1906 and February 1907 that specified how people could change religions and removed legal disadvantages resulting from a person's religion. Nicholas II, however, opposed toleration in general and greater freedoms for Jews in particular.[10] Nicholas's opposition caused Stolypin to withdraw the bills that would have implemented the decree on toleration.[11] Instead, Stolypin issued circulars that limited some discriminatory measures against Jews. In the period 1905–1910, Stolypin also defended the rights of petitioners to convert under the terms of the law and instructed civil authorities to cease measures that would slow or prevent apostasy.[12] As long as a person was registered in some recognized faith and subject to its moral influence, the secular state should not concern itself with which faith a person practiced.[13] Privately and sometimes publicly, Russian Orthodox clergy blamed Stolypin for the policy of religious toleration. One missionary argued that Stolypin "was constantly working against Orthodoxy."[14] As Stolypin increasingly needed to find support from conservatives in the Duma early in 1909, religious toleration faded as a priority "in favor of more resolute support for the Orthodox Church."[15]

Stolypin's approach to non–Russian Orthodox political activism was more severe. The Young Turk Revolution in the Ottoman Empire in 1908 alerted the officials to potential threats from political reformers in an Islamic milieu. Concern over Muslim political activism largely followed events in Istanbul.[16] Stolypin and MVD officials sought to locate and oppose any indications of a "pan-Islamic" threat, since political opposition on a religious basis was incompatible with Stolypin's statist conception of the empire's organizing principle.[17] Stolypin considered the "struggle between Orthodox-Russian and Muhammadan-Tatar principles" to be "not a religious struggle" but a "state (*gosudarstvennaia*), cultural one."[18] The central administration pursued a policy of separating the mass of Muslims as a religious community in a multiconfessional state from the deeds of religious-nationalist politicians who transgressed the limits of accepted conduct. Such a strategy proved difficult to execute.

In keeping with officials' suspicions of Muslim activism, the central state administration sought to reduce non-Russian, non-Orthodox participation in the State Duma. The overall number of Muslim representatives in the Duma increased from twenty-five in the First Duma to thirty-six in the Second Duma. After the emperor closed the Second Duma on June 3, 1907, arguing that non-Russians should not have decisive voices in "purely Russian" questions, Muslim representation in the State Duma declined sharply. Only eight Muslim deputies were elected to the Third Duma and six to the Fourth Duma. As the number of Muslims in the Duma decreased, the importance of Ufa's Muslim representation increased. The relatively large number of Muslims and of Muslim landowners in Ufa Province meant that Ufa Muslims made up a considerable proportion of Muslim deputies from the empire as a whole. Nearly one-fourth of Muslim deputies in the Second Duma were from Ufa. After central officials worked to reduce Muslim representation, Ufa Muslims made up half of the small Muslim Duma contingents in the Third and Fourth Dumas (elected in 1907 and 1912).[19] Kutlu-Mukhammad Tevkelev was the only Muslim elected to all four Dumas, and he served as chair of the Duma's Muslim Fraction in the last two. Without the election of Muslim nobles from Ufa Province, the fraction would have nearly disappeared.

THE MVD AND REFORMS IN UFA PROVINCE

The fate of the reforms in Ufa showed the limited reach of St. Petersburg officials. The implementation of Stolypin's reforms in Ufa Province fell to Governor Alexander S. Kliucharev and his local administration. Kliucharev's tenure in Ufa, from 1906 to 1911, brought continuity to the province over which three governors had presided in the previous three years. Kliucharev represented something of a compromise between the styles of his two predecessors. Kliucharev more vigorously worked to suppress political activism than Tsekhanovetskii had, but he antagonized educated society less energetically than Sokolovskii had.[20] Kliucharev implemented Stolypin's agrarian reforms, but with little zeal. Stolypin's reforms showed fewer results in Ufa than elsewhere in the empire. By late 1916, in the empire as a whole, 10.7 percent of peasants tilled consolidated landholdings as private property. In Bashkiria only a bit more than half that number did—5.8 percent. The law of November 9, 1906, did not even apply to Bashkir hereditary landowners because the Statute on Bashkirs gave Bashkirs the right to convert their share of the commune's lands to private property in 1863, but they rarely did so. Neither did Bashkirs, fearing that large-scale land reorganization was merely a pretext for expropriation, show much willingness to consolidate their lands after 1906.[21] The left-leaning local political elite showed little enthusiasm for agrarian reform with its emphasis on breaking down communal organization in favor of private property.

Other than Kliucharev's fervent anti-Semitism, he and his local administration displayed little interest in matters of faith.[22] The governor's passivity in religious affairs reached such an extent that Petersburg officials questioned his enforcement of the law.[23] Instead of making decisions as to which formally

FIGURE 7.1. "General View of the Bashkir Village Ekh'ia." Photograph by
Sergei Prokudin-Gorskii, 1910. Library of Congress, Prints & Photographs
Division, Prokudin-Gorskii Collection, LC-DIG-prok-10643.

Russian Orthodox subjects who wanted to convert to Islam could do so (because they had ancestors who were Muslim and practiced Islam themselves),
as the Manifesto on Toleration required, in June 1907 Kliucharev simply agreed
to let Ufa Bishop Khristofor (Smirnov) and local priests help judge the "inner
consciousness" of those who petitioned to convert.[24] But Kliucharev also down-
played the local significance of a "pan-Islamic" union of the empire's Muslims,
which Russian Orthodox religious figures considered a threat to the integrity of
the empire. In 1909, Kliucharev reported that Ufa's Muslims had not welcomed
pan-Islamic propaganda and had remained loyal.[25] Kliucharev minimized the
significance of conversion. He pointed out that the number of people who returned to Islam had declined year by year, from 2,578 in late 1905–1906 to 1,145 in

1907 and then to only 585 in 1908, and that converts had been only superficially Orthodox. They did not differ "in an ethnographic and cultural respect from true followers of Muslim religion."[26] Kliucharev had his hands full maintaining stability in a time of unrest, agrarian transformation, and a booming urban population—the city of Ufa's population more than doubled in sixteen years, from 49,275 in 1897 to 108,280 in 1913.[27] He showed little concern for religion.

Stolypin's agrarian policies and his efforts to reduce estate distinctions undermined Bashkir distinctiveness and caused Bashkirs to lose land despite the relatively limited success of reform. Now all peasants had the right to own land as hereditary property, which made common what had been a quality of the Bashkir estate.[28] An MVD circular of October 6, 1910, allowed Russian peasants to be registered in Bashkir communes, marking a dramatic break in imperial law regarding Bashkirs. Ufa governor Kliucharev wrote that this rule, along with the famine that hit the region in late 1911, caused many people who did not live in Bashkir settlements or, in some cases, did not even practice agriculture at all, to buy large amounts of Bashkir land "exclusively with the goal of profit" from its later sale.[29] Central administrators interested in finding land on which to settle peasants from crowded regions in central Russia identified Bashkir land as a target for settlement. Alexander V. Krivoshein, the leading official of the Peasant Land Bank and Stolypin's close associate, wrote in 1907 that he considered it desirable for the bank to buy up Bashkir land for the government's purposes. In all, Bashkir hereditary landowners lost 222,000 des. of land in Ufa Province and another 300,000 des. in Orenburg between 1905 and 1915.[30] Much of that land was resold to in-migrants to Bashkiria. Migration administrations along the railroads counted 43,885 new settlers in Ufa Province and 65,574 in Orenburg Province from 1904 to 1914. Many more migrated by other means. Stolypin's administration may have failed to restructure peasant landholding and rural society, but it was more successful in undermining Bashkirs as an estate group. In important respects, reform such as that contemplated by the State Council in 1904 (see chapter 4) was not necessary to erode the Bashkir estate. Post-1905 reforms undercut what had made Bashkirs most distinctive.

The survey of land for those "let in" to Bashkir land, the pripushchenniks, the expansion of property rights, and consequent reduction in Bashkir estate distinctiveness contributed to what historian Mikhail Rodnov calls a large scale "de-Bashkirization" of Bashkiria's population. Those "let in" to Bashkir communities, who had identified with the Bashkir estate in the nineteenth century, were now separated from Bashkir hereditary landowners. Those who wanted to acquire Bashkir land could fairly easily purchase it without needing to enter the Bashkir estate through adoption or marriage. The result was a movement away from identification as Bashkir. Rodnov traces the process from the all-imperial census of 1897 through a local agricultural census of 1912–1913 and 1917. In the three counties Rodnov examines in particular, Birsk, Belebei, and Ufa, he finds dramatic changes in nationality. Some Finnic peoples such as Maris, who had identified as Bashkir, now returned to calling themselves Maris. Likewise, Meshcheriaks returned to that status. The ethnonym Tatar did not gain much in popularity; rather, the categories of Mari, Meshcheriak, and Teptiar grew sharply in number. In Belebei County, for instance, the overall population increased from 427,344 in 1897 to 638,748 in 1917. The number of Bashkirs decreased from 232,676 to 184,878, while Teptiars increased from 6,889 to 138,781 and Meshcheriaks increased from 2,602 to 40,258.[31] Overall, those less committed to Bashkir status identified in other ways. Significantly, however, Rodnov found great stability among Bashkir hereditary landowners. Extremely few changed their identification in this period. They continued to own a great deal of land—61 percent of all agricultural land in Birsk County, for instance. As the Bashkir estate declined in number, Bashkir hereditary landowners became a more coherent group.

ZEMSTVO ALTERNATIVES

The sense of revolutionary possibility that invigorated zemstvo activity in 1905 soon evaporated as Stolypin and his local administrators fought to suppress oppositional politics. Under pressure from the governor, zemstvos avoided confrontations that had led to the removal of leading provincial zemstvo activists in 1905 and 1906. Nonetheless, neither the zemstvo leadership nor its goals fundamentally changed in the post-revolutionary period. The Ufa zemstvo remained one of the empire's most liberal: Petr Koropachinskii was the only provincial zemstvo chairman with Kadet (left-liberal) sympathies in the empire after the elections of 1906.[32] He chaired the zemstvo board continuously until February 1917. The noble reaction that occurred in other provinces had little force in Ufa.[33] Koropachinskii struck a careful balance. He relied upon men inside and outside the zemstvo more politically leftist than himself. For instance, leading zemstvo activist Viacheslav Kugushev employed Lenin's future commissar of food supply, Alexander Tsiurupa, on his estate for years.

Zemstvo leaders imagined the state very differently than Stolypin. Zemstvo elites sought to integrate Russians and non-Russians alike into a state that recognized national and religious diversity but transcended them. Much more than Stolypin, zemstvo leaders conceived of Russian as the empire's lingua franca but envisioned the basis of the state as fully multinational rather than ethnically Russian or Orthodox. The criterion for political inclusion would be a command of enlightened values that zemstvo activists considered universal.

Zemstvo leaders considered differences between the educated and the ignorant to be the fundamental social divide, not those between Orthodoxy and Islam or Russian and Bashkir. Zemstvo activists sorted various groups according to their level of enlightenment, but they felt obliged to teach *all* the province's population the language of politics so they could participate fully in the post-1905 civic order. The first issue of a short-lived Ufa zemstvo newspaper explained that politics was the "art of governing a country" and that State Duma and zemstvo elections made the people themselves "politicians."[34] The new civic order would not only tolerate but even promote non-Russian, non-Orthodox languages and cultures as crucial to the elite's enlightenment project.

Ufa zemstvo leaders sympathized with zemstvo constitutionalists who sought to ally with leaders of non-Russian groups in elections to the first State Duma and appealed to non-Russians by making cultural self-determination part of their program. The Ufa zemstvo's work with Muslim leaders was a local manifestation of this alliance.[35] The Ufa zemstvo leadership's conception of the integration of different cultures was also influenced by Muslim thinkers such as Crimean Tatar Ismail Bei Gasprinskii, who in the 1880s wrote of the "moral, spiritual assimilation" of Muslims into civic life on the basis of "national individuality, freedom and self-administration" rather than the "blood" or "chemical unity" of assimilation and Russification.[36] The zemstvo elite's approach to the education of non-Russians was not typical of the empire. Zemstvos in other areas with Muslim populations, such as Kazan and Simbirsk, did not encourage native-language instruction. Some experts noted the effectiveness of the Ufa zemstvo's approach to non-Russians, but it did not become a widely emulated model.[37] Ufa's particular population and the relatively high status of Muslim elites there produced distinctive educational practices.

Such practices became evident in December 1905 when the provincial zemstvo responded favorably to two petitions from Muslims regarding educational funding. Khairulla Usmanov, akhund of Ufa's largest mosque, appealed to the zemstvo for funds to finish a new madrasa, arguing that Muslims bore tax obligations equally with the Russian half of the province's population but received little in return.[38] An akhund from Birsk County petitioned that students in the village's Russian-Bashkir school be able to study their native language equally with other subjects. Muslim deputy Syrtlanov endorsed Usmanov's argument: the zemstvo did nothing at all for the Muslims, even though they made up the majority of taxpayers.[39] The zemstvo board also firmly supported native-language instruction. The zemstvo leadership asserted that "the right to study a native language and grammar alongside the state language" was a "right so basic and fundamental" for "every citizen of our diverse empire" that no one questioned it. The March 26, 1870, decree that mandated instruction in Russian was "an ancient relic of Russifying aspirations."[40] Although only two deputies were Muslim and the entire zemstvo board was Russian Orthodox, the zemstvo voted to spend three thousand rubles to finish the madrasa and approved the proposal for instruction in native languages parallel with Russian in Russian-Bashkir schools.

Since the zemstvo board endorsed only schools that taught Russian, both existing state schools and those supported by the zemstvo may seem to have promoted Russification. Yet the zemstvo board, Muslim zemstvo deputies, and Muslims who came before the assembly in 1905 all perceived a difference between the zemstvo's and the MNP's approaches. The perceived difference reflected the importance of bilingual education and of supervisory authority over a school. Instruction in Russian alone meant that a student would become Russian politically and culturally, since that student would have no support for a cultural identity other than a Russian one. The zemstvo's promotion of Russian allowed Muslims to acquire the linguistic skills necessary to participate in the empire's political and social life but also the support necessary to develop their own cultures. Moreover, if Muslim religious leaders helped to supervise schools, Muslims would not fear that their children were targets for conversion and Russification.[41] Russification was more a question of cultural and political power than of language, as the attitude of Validov made clear. In his memoirs, Validov describes his desire to learn Russian so that he could be certified to teach school but also his aversion to enrolling in the Kazan Teachers' Seminary, which had been created to prepare non-Russians to be teachers and to draw Muslims to Christianity. So, Validov hired a Russian teacher at the seminary to teach him privately in the evening.[42]

By 1908, the central government was moving toward universal education, which intensified debate over Muslims' role in local educational institutions. Should Muslims and animist non-Russians who did not speak Russian be integrated into the projected school system, and on what terms? In order to address this question, Koropachinskii sought out members of the Muslim intelligentsia to provide guidance for the all-Christian zemstvo board. In conjunction with the school commission's report on universal education in 1908, Koropachinskii asked Ibragim Akhtiamov to report on the place of Muslims in the school system. Akhtiamov was the son of State Duma deputy Abussugud Akhtiamov and a member of Ufa's Social Democratic party. He had attended St. Petersburg University and been expelled from Kazan University for participation in a student protest.[43] Akhtiamov's report declared that the province's Muslim population "unconditionally should be included in the school network"—Muslim boys within a ten-year period and Muslim girls at an unspecified point in the future. Akhtiamov called for a type of school that would give Muslims a "fundamental knowledge not only of Russian but also of the pupils' native language."[44] In 1909, the zemstvo board asked the OMEA leadership about the Bashkir and Tatar population's readiness for inclusion in universal education. The OMEA leadership replied that Muslims were as ready as Russians for inclusion and emphasized the need for native-language instruction to attract Muslims.[45]

A conference Koropachinskii convoked in May 1911 on the education of non-Russians in order to prepare a report for the All-Zemstvo Congress on Education in Moscow in August 1911 illustrates well the difference between the Ufa zemstvos' approach to Muslim education and those of both state officials and Kazan Muslims. Fully half of those present at the first meeting of Koropachinskii's conference were representatives of the "Muslim intelligentsia" and Muslim teachers.[46] Only two employees of the OUO attended. Conference participants all agreed that school plans had educational rather than assimilationist or missionary goals as their objective. All who spoke at the conference condemned the State Duma's legislative project requiring teachers to be Russian and Christian. Ufa zemstvo deputies and employees sought to incorporate Muslims more firmly in state- and zemstvo-sponsored schools and to organize the schools according to nationality and religion whenever possible. Since a primary school teacher was "almost the sole bearer of culture" to the local population, that teacher should be a "fellow national and fellow believer." Conference participants agreed on the importance of the Russian language to the Muslim population. Akhtiamov argued that the Russian language was "the sole means to join the common culture."[47]

Before long, however, disagreements became evident among Ufa's contingent; two State Duma deputies from Kazan, Sadritin Maksudov and Gaisa Enikeev; and representatives of the local educational district, A. A. Liubimov and A. V. Leont'ev. Ufa and Kazan participants disagreed regarding the exclusivity of Muslim schools, the education of Muslim girls, and the value of the "old-method" maktab. Kazan's Maksudov and Enikeev had worked in the State Duma to exclude Muslim confessional schools from the projected school network. They wanted Muslim schools to remain ethnically and religiously distinct and urged great care in including Muslim girls in educational programs.[48] Ufa delegates rejected old-method Muslim schools and showed little concern about their possible demise. Representatives of the MNP defended ministry policy, arguing for limited native-language education and for the incorporation of Muslims into the state-run educational system. The path to education in secondary schools required a mastery of Russian. More usage of a native language meant less knowledge of Russian.

These discussions revealed different conceptions of Muslim education and different views of Muslims' role in the empire's civic life. By stressing the importance of the old-method maktab and the creation of native-language teachers' schools, Maksudov and Enikeev advocated the separation of Muslim society from Orthodox Christian and Russian-speaking society on both religious and linguistic bases. Officials of the MNP took the opposite approach. They rejected exclusively Muslim schools and tolerated only limited native-language instruction in order to integrate Muslims into the empire's Russian-language culture. Ufa activists pursued a third way: to incorporate Muslims into a statewide system of compulsory education on a secular basis, but with extensive native-language instruction.[49] Participants from Ufa believed Muslims should be strongly connected to a common Russian-language culture but advocated native-language instruction to strengthen secular, non-Russian cultures, too.

The Ufa zemstvo's conception of a multinational educational system found its most thorough elaboration in extracurricular education programs—literally "outside of school" (*vneshkol'noe*) education—such as libraries, literacy programs, and local cultural centers.[50] Zemstvo extracurricular educational programs illuminate its leaders' vision of using visible institutions to weave a network of "invisible threads" connecting each individual with the political life of the empire and uniting Russians and non-Russians. Because the MNP under Lev A. Kasso (served 1910–1914) moved aggressively to reduce or eliminate zemstvo influence over schools, the provincial zemstvo created a department of education in 1910 to address every facet of educational activity outside of the school curriculum.[51] By 1911 zemstvos funded 850 libraries in primary schools, six libraries for zemstvo employees, the publication of books in non-Russian languages, Sunday schools, slide shows, and the publication of *Sel'sko-khoziaistvennyi listok* (The agricultural leaflet). Beginning in 1912, the zemstvo developed extracurricular programs with a new urgency, stimulated, in part, by resolutions of the all-zemstvo congress that extracurricular education was "no less valuable than school education and equally necessary." Ufa zemstvo leaders projected an ambitious system of "people's houses" and "reading huts." Provincial and county institutions would include a museum with a laboratory, a workshop, a library, and an auditorium. People's houses in cities featured a cinema intended to fight the negative influence of private theaters. At the district level, the zemstvo would provide a "people's house" for every 15,000 people in the province. Finally, village "reading huts" would have courses, lectures, and a library, all supervised by a zemstvo organizer. All these institutions would serve all of the province's population. The provincial zemstvo's department of education called it "strange" to set up cinemas, museums, and people's houses separately for Russians and for non-Russians as the Ufa County zemstvo desired.[52] If a district's population was exclusively non-Russian, then books in the district library must be primarily in the same non-Russian language. If the population

FIGURE 7.2. "Bashkir Woman in National Costume." Photograph by Sergei Prokudin-Gorskii, 1910. Library of Congress, Prints & Photographs Division, Prokudin-Gorskii Collection, LC-DIG-prok-10657.

of a district was mixed, the books should be mixed. Muslim females would use the same facilities as males, since zemstvo leaders believed that the "seclusion of women" and the veil would disappear with the "development of culture."[53]

The zemstvo followed the principle that the educational activities of a group should be managed by a person familiar with the language and culture of that group. Therefore, the zemstvo appointed persons with a command of local languages to be directors of extracurricular education in predominantly non-Russian districts.[54] Two Muslims who achieved prominence in work for the Ufa zemstvo were Gumer Teregulov and Mirsaid Sultan-Galiev. Both had graduated from the Tatar Teachers' School in Kazan and were associated with the Social Democratic Party. Teregulov became the head of non-Russian education in the

zemstvo's department of education in the middle of 1913 and served in that capacity until at least 1916.[55] Sultan-Galiev, a future member of the Commissariat
of Nationalities under Stalin, became district head of non-Russian education in
Sterlitamak County.[56] Lectures by Sultan-Galiev and by other Tatar speakers
on hygiene, temperance, and economic issues were well attended and received
notice in the Russian-language press. Muslim employees played a key role in
building support among their co-religionists for libraries and people's houses.
Sultan-Galiev boasted that the library he opened in Sterlitamak County, "the
first people's Tatar-language library in Russia opened by a zemstvo," enrolled
four hundred readers within its first three weeks.[57]

BASHKIR NATIONALISM

At the same time issues of Muslim education began to concern zemstvo activists, a specifically Bashkir national idea found expression locally. Before 1905,
Muslim intellectuals in Kazan and in other cities in the region debated how
their community should be defined. These debates over collective identity were
multifaceted and complex, resembling debates among the Russian-speaking,
Russian Orthodox population on the nature of Russianness and the role of Russian Orthodoxy in the empire. Local Muslims could see themselves primarily
as Muslims and as part of an empire-wide and even international Islamic community. At the same time, Muslims could emphasize the regional dimension of
community identity as it derived from Bulgar origins—the idea that all Volga-
Urals Muslims had originally been and remained linked by common origins
in the city of Bulgar, the ruins of which were located south of Kazan near the
Volga River and whose population encountered Islam in the tenth century.[58]
Others argued instead that the Turkic language and culture ought to unite the
empire's Muslim Turkic peoples, since it provided a type of nationalism that coincided better with contemporary European types of nationalism—often based
on a common language and liberalism. A small group of local Muslims rejected
Muslim and Turkic national concerns. They linked the future Turkic Muslims
to oppositional movements active among Russian speakers, most notably either
Marxist-inspired Social Democracy or agrarian socialism in the form of the
Socialist Revolutionary Party. Such thinking appears to have been somewhat
more prominent in Ufa than in other parts of the region. Scholars debate the
relative influence of these conceptions of the Muslim and Turkic community.[59]

In the mobilization of 1905–1907, a Bashkir national idea developed alongside the broader Muslim and Turkic ideas of community. It first found public
expression for a large audience in the State Duma, as we saw in chapter 6. Duma
deputies from Ufa and Kazan spoke of Bashkirs not as an estate group but as

a people who had been granted land by the tsar and who had fought for the empire. Deputies decried the loss of Bashkir land and called on the government to honor its original bargain with Bashkirs, in which they received land for loyalty. This would mean protecting Bashkir landholding and supporting Bashkirs as they shifted from semi-nomadic pastoralism to settled agriculture. By 1908, Bashkir national ideas found expression in the Tatar-language press. In a manner similar to what Umetbaev had written before 1905, writers stressed the poor state of Bashkirs. One wrote:

> The majority of our Bashkir people, particularly when compared with other peoples, are poor and unskilled, lazy and naked. . . . Because of such ignorance, we are selling the land left us by our fathers and grandfathers to the Khokhols [a derogatory term for Russians] for very low prices. What a miserable state this is. Because of such ignorance, for one day's pleasure, we gather up [and give away] our children's lifelong well-being.[60]

Bashkir writers did not look to existing imperial institutions to come to the aid of Bashkirs, as Umetbaev had, but called upon Bashkirs to overcome their "dark ignorance" and to unite as a people to protect their land rights and increase their prosperity. In 1909, Mullah Mönir Hadiev from Cheliabinsk, east of the Urals, wrote a series of articles in the Orenburg journal *Shura* (Council) that he intended as a national history demonstrating that Bashkirs had the territory, history, language, culture and literature to make a nation. At the core of the Bashkir national idea, for Hadiev, was land. Bashkirs had lived on the land before the tsar's men arrived, and only after they swore loyalty to the tsars did all sorts of migrants—Meshcheriaks, Maris, Chuvashes, and finally Russians—arrive.[61] Bashkir ties to the land, which had originated in the sixteenth century and made Bashkirs into an estate group, now stood at the center of efforts to define Bashkirs as a nation.

Akhmed-Zeki Validov, whom we met at the start of this chapter, became the most prominent Bashkir political leader. Although he had as much Teptiar or Meshcheriak ancestry as Bashkir, he firmly embraced the Bashkir idea. Validov initially was drawn to the reformist intellectual circles of his extended family. He studied in Orenburg and Kazan and worked closely with Tatar- and Russian-speaking scholars in the latter city. His early writings emphasized the Turkic connections among the region's population. Over time, however, family connections among Bashkirs and Kazakhs and his travels to Turkestan caused him to begin to focus on their common experience of Slavic colonization and loss of land. Validov's first work was a history of Turkic peoples that was well received by leading pan-Turkic thinker and activist Galimdzhan Ibragimov. Already by 1913, however, Validov's interest in particularly Bashkir themes emerged. He published an ethnography of the Burzian tribe of Bashkirs, emphasizing the group's preservation of Turkic culture and military prowess. He argued that "very rich Bashkir folklore becomes impoverished under the influence of Tatars and Russians."[62] His turn from scholarship to political activism and promotion of Bashkir interests came in the fall of 1915. He writes in his memoirs: "It seemed to me that there could not be a separate Bashkir policy. I thought that in the historical struggle, in territorial questions, in the matter of the struggle with Russian settlers, we [Bashkirs], Kazakhs, and Kirghiz had common problems. Turkestan must be united."[63] The political implications of such thinking grew in the fall of 1915, when Validov met "prominent Muslim nobleman" Shakhaidar Syrtlanov; his son Galiaskar, a prominent attorney; and Salim-Girei Dzhantiurin, a Kazakh who claimed descent from Chinggis Khan. All three were active in Ufa politics, and represented the province in the State Duma. During the Revolution of 1905, according to Validov, Galiaskar and Dzhantiurin had defended the notion of autonomy for Eastern Turks or what they called, according to Validov, "simply 'Muslims.'" Having become interested in the idea of autonomy, Validov read the works of an early advocate of Siberian autonomy, Grigorii Potanin, and exchanged correspondence with him. Dzhantiurin, whose ancestors had fought the Russians in alliance with Bashkirs, was sympathetic to Bashkir interests. Validov shared Potanin's letters with Dzhantiurin and stated that after Siberian autonomy had been realized, "the autonomy of Bashkiria could be joined to it."[64] Dzhantiurin agreed and, apparently, recommended that Validov be sent to Petersburg to work with the Muslim Fraction of the Duma. Since Dzhantiurin was married to a cousin of the fraction's leader, Tevkelev, his opinion carried considerable weight.

EDUCATING THE NATION

Local representatives of the MNP expressed a vision of education's role that contrasted sharply with the visions of zemstvo activists and Bashkir nationalists alike. Educational administrators sought more than simply the acquisition of a state language; they insisted that students become conscious of their connections to their fatherland and identify with the culture of the dominant Russians. Educational officials' attention to the state and to Russian culture often seemed even to overshadow the image of the autocrat.[65] "Nationalizing" schools of the OUO began in earnest in June 1912, when OUO Curator Feodor N. Vladimirov called the OUO's staff to a "congress" to discuss primary schools. Discussions focused on the need to make primary education a greater cultural, national, and moral force. Schools must be responsive to the population rather than being bookish and "cut off from life." National education meant the inculcation of values using new strategies often borrowed from western European models. District Inspector Mikhail A. Miropiev, one of the congress's main speakers, cited favorably French social psychologist Gustave Le Bon, who opposed French colonial schools predicated on the "underlying sameness of peoples and thus leading to assimilation" because such schools would "gradually kill national feeling in a country."[66] With no sense of irony, Miropiev quoted a German ped-agogue to buttress his view that Russian primary schools must be "founded on the national principle" and must strive to develop a "burning love for the Fatherland."[67]

Educational officials outlined ways to develop patriotism, national pride, and love for the tsar at the educational congress, over the next several years in school curricula, and in the pages of the new, official journal, the *Vestnik oren-burgskogo uchebnogo okruga* (*Herald of the Orenburg Educational District*).[68] Curator Vladimirov believed that "national consciousness and national pride" must be reinforced through prayers, imperial and religious holidays, songs, and verse. Russian history and geography thoroughly suffused with "national feel-ing" provided essential means for establishing a school on national principles.[69] Students must be made to identify with "the great historical mission of Rus-sia," which included serving as "the bulwark for Europe against attack from Asian peoples" and carrying "to Asia the principles of European education and culture."[70] Educators advocated "fatherland studies" (*otechestvovedenie*) and "studies of the native land" (*rodinavedenie*) as means to enable all students to imagine themselves as part of the empire.[71] Finally, in order to turn patriotic feelings into masculine support for the fatherland in the tense environment be-fore the First World War, District Inspector Miropiev advocated military train-ing for schoolboys. Education should prepare young men to fulfill the tasks of citizens, which included defending a "united, indivisible Russia" "to the last drop of blood."[72]

As educational officials worked to create national education, they turned against non-Russian cultures and bilingual education. By including nomads, Islamic, and Asian peoples as historical enemies of Russia, OUO officials placed about half of the province's population outside the national mission. Vladimirov and Miropiev were deeply skeptical of bilingual education. Vladimirov made his career in Polish regions of the empire where Il'minskii's system of education had no equivalent.[73] Vladimirov believed that bilingual education retarded the "as-similation of small non-Russian groups with Russians," introduced "never before extant written languages and literature," instilled in non-Russians "their national particularity," and isolated them.[74] In the west, the empire struggled against movements for self-determination, according to Vladimirov. In the east, tsarist administrators had actually helped *create* them. In most areas, non-Russians acquired few Russian skills. In one area Bashkirs not only failed to learn Russian, Russians living among them had begun to speak Bashkir![75] District Inspector Miropiev argued that when Il'minskii died, the "brightly burning religious fire" of his system went out.[76] Now non-Russian teachers had ruined Il'minskii's system by demanding special textbooks and pursuing national self-determination. Miropiev and Vladimirov interpreted Il'minskii's bilingual education as essentially a religious, missionary effort that was no longer useful. Patriotism could no longer be expressed through non-Russian languages.

In the end, the congress resolved to eliminate bilingual schools in favor of Russian-language schools in which Russians and non-Russians would study together under teachers who knew little or nothing of non-Russian languages. These resolutions marked a break with forty-two years of official pedagogical practice. Native language became a tool to be used as sparingly as possible rather than a vehicle by which "Russian sympathies" could be taught to non-Russians. The OUO leadership rejected native-language instruction more aggressively than the MNP's officials in the center did.[77] The OUO officials considered the Russian nation the basis of the imperial state. Native-language programs might be necessary in the short term, but they at best slowed the tsar's subjects' assimilation into the Russian nation and at worst threatened to separate non-Russians from the dominant culture.

THE ORTHODOX CHURCH AND TOLERATION

Where OUO educators in Ufa seized upon the national principle as the basis for educational programs, the Russian Orthodox Church emphasized faith as the core of Russianness. Faith transcended language. Native-language instruction and institutions strengthened the church by making its teaching accessible to those whose first language was not Russian. Church officials feared that even limited legislation on toleration challenged the church's dominance. Their fears were not without basis. The Manifesto on Toleration gave life to Protestant sects, such as the Baptists, which had not been recognized previously as a force in the province. Toleration made possible expansive interpretations of religious freedom, such as Belebei Marshal of the Nobility Kutlu-Mukhammad Tevkelev's supposed announcement that "now freedom is given to all, and baptized Tatars may freely convert to Mukhammadism."[78]

The church struggled against support for religious toleration in zemstvo assemblies. In December 1907, the Sterlitamak County zemstvo resolved to stop providing free transit for Orthodox clergy since it could not also afford to provide free passage to Muslim, Jewish, and Old Believer religious leaders. The decision outraged one priest, who was amazed that "Orthodox religious servitors" were equated "with Mukhammadan mullahs!" in an "Orthodox Russian tsardom."[79] Finally, the Manifesto on Toleration and revolutionary politics revealed important differences of opinion between the church's leadership and the "black clergy" who served in the parishes.[80] One priest, Ivan Gromov, tried to convert to Islam in 1907.[81] Two others, Nikolai Krasnov and Vladimir Beliaev, were accused of agitating for revolutionary parties in elections to the third State Duma in 1907. Krasnov had Muslim support for his candidacy.[82]

Alarming local events and instructions from the Holy Synod in Petersburg provoked local churchmen, like clergy across the empire, to seek to place the church at the center of life in the empire. Local clergy presented Russian Orthodoxy as more than a means to salvation and the official religion of the empire: it was the will of the people. The process of invigorating Ufa's Orthodox community took several forms. The most essential involved making the church more accessible to its flock. Between 1898 and 1914, the number of parishes in Ufa Province expanded from 331 to 488. In 1914 alone, twenty-three stone and twenty-nine wooden churches were under construction. Although the province's population also was growing rapidly, increased numbers of churches and parishes reduced the distance of Orthodox Christians from their priests.[83] Following the Holy Synod's instructions, Ufa church leaders also sought to make parish life more vital and to eliminate the church's "superfluous formalism and lifelessness."[84]

The desire to make Orthodoxy central to imperial society became clear in the local church's missionary activity after 1905. Although a provincial missionary committee had existed since 1887, the Manifesto on Toleration caused its lay leader, Nikolai A. Gurvich, to convoke the diocese's first missionary "congress" in early 1906.[85] Any attempt at a rapprochement between Russians and non-Russians required their mastery of the fundamental element of "Russian nationality—Orthodoxy." Like Nikolai Il'minskii, local churchmen sought to use non-Russians' language and culture to spread Orthodoxy.[86] Schools for non-Russians should not attempt their "Russification" (*obrusenie*). The diocesan journal declared that "the only true and efficacious path" for propagating Christianity among the non-Russians" was "a school with the teaching of sacred subjects in the native language" even if school inspectors sought to require Russian-language instruction.[87] Local missionaries also sought to organize parishes and parish schools along national lines by moving each non-Russian priest or teacher to a non-Russian parish or school "of corresponding nationality, and a Russian to a Russian parish."[88]

Strengthening Orthodoxy proved complicated, however. In the view of the Holy Synod, the Ufa diocese did not respond quickly enough to the challenge of apostasy and seemed to lack the personnel necessary to do so. In October 1908,

Nafanial (Troitskii), the vicar-bishop of Tambov Province, replaced Khristofor. In April 1909, the synod condemned nearly all aspects of the diocese's operation and stressed the "lack of energy" of Ufa missionary activity. Nafanial responded by making missionary affairs the "primary subject of his concern." He renewed the Missionary Committee's membership and established regular missionary courses. He requested the appointment of a vicar bishop, who would assume responsibility for all educational and missionary affairs.[89] Rather than providing Nafanial with an assistant, the synod replaced Nafanial himself with Mikhei (Alekseev), the bishop of Tambov.[90] Mikhei proved no more successful. He retired after only twenty months as bishop and was little missed by members of educated society.[91] Despite Khristofor's, Nafanial's, and Mikhei's efforts, the Holy Synod believed that the Ufa church had failed to unify and invigorate the Orthodox community.

THE ORENBURG MUHAMMADAN ECCLESIASTICAL ASSEMBLY AND MUSLIM REFORM

Whereas religious toleration proved threatening to the Orthodox Church, toleration invigorated Islam and OMEA operations. The official conversions to Islam that the decrees made possible, about 4,500 in Ufa by 1909, represented only a small fraction of the province's more than 1.3 million Muslims. More striking was growth in the size of the clerisy and religious institutions. On average, nearly twice as many men took the OMEA's examination to become a mullah each year after 1905 than before. These men staffed a growing number of mosques—the number within the OMEA's jurisdiction increased by nearly 15 percent, from 4,908 to 5,640, between 1908 and 1910 alone.[92] Muslim schools grew rapidly in number as well.[93] With more than four million Muslims under its jurisdiction, the OMEA had a large and growing constituency. By 1909, the city of Ufa itself had five mosques.

In the context of discussions of religious toleration, OMEA officials sought to invigorate Muslim practices and institutions much as the Russian Orthodox Church sought to invigorate Orthodox Christianity. Although Mufti Sultanov at first seemed reluctant to address reform of Muslim institutions, in 1905 Witte instructed him to convoke a meeting to discuss Muslim issues and to report the results to St. Petersburg.[94] Sultanov organized an Ulama Council (a meeting of Muslim scholars and authorities) in April 1905 at which OMEA judge Rizaetdin Fakhretdinov presented a draft proposal for reform of the OMEA. Fakhretdinov considered the OMEA "an intermediary between the government and the people" and "an interpreter of the [needs of the] latter."[95] As adopted by the Ulama Council, Fakhretdinov's project argued for the expansion of the OMEA's jurisdiction to include Sunni Muslims of the Kazakh steppe and of the north Caucasus. By arguing for the election of the mufti, akhunds, and village mullahs without the influence of "government bureaucrats" and for the creation of nine *majlises*—intermediate Muslim administrative bodies—on the level of the province or county, Fakhretdinov's project sought to make the OMEA more responsive to the Muslim population. Furthermore, all administrative matters were to be conducted in Tatar rather than in Russian, which would only be used as necessary to communicate with other parts of the tsarist administration. Fakhretdinov's proposals indicated the triumph of the principle of religious community over linguistic diversity.[96]

The petition produced by the Ulama Council, which emphasized Muslims' demands to use their own textbooks regardless of where they were produced and to publish newspapers and journals, was not immediately granted. Nor was its request to elect the mufti. According to Musa Ia. Bigeev, a prominent religious thinker and writer in St. Petersburg, the Ulama Council marked the beginning of a Muslim political movement. Gabderashid Ibragimov and others organized Russia's First All-Russian Muslim Congress in August 1905.[97] During and after the Revolution of 1905, Muslim clerics mobilized, too. In 1907, they petitioned St. Petersburg to be equal in status and privileges with Russian Orthodox clergy. Clerics argued that they served "fatherland and government" and instilled in their parishioners loyalty to the tsar but received neither salaries nor anything else in return.[98] Muslim women became active as well. Toward the end of 1907, the first Muslim women's society was registered in Ufa, pursuing the cultural, educational, and moral improvement of Muslim women.[99]

As Muslim demands exceeded those traditional to confessional administration, central bureaucrats began to perceive Muslim institutions differently. Islam became a religious-national force that threatened the empire's security and unity. The suspicion of Petersburg officials included the OMEA. At a "Special Conference on Matters of the Muslim Faith" convoked in 1906 in order to bring the empire's laws into accord with the April 17, 1905, Manifesto on Toleration, some proposed that ethnicity or nationality be mobilized to counter the OMEA's religious authority. One official, Vladimir P. Cherevanskii, argued that concentrating authority over the Muslim faith as well as over marriage, family, and inheritance law in the OMEA, as Fakhretdinov and others had proposed, would create a "state within a state," a "Muslim Rome." He proposed that the state break up the OMEA along territorial lines and that "those ethnicities that have their own histories" receive their own Muslim administrations.[100] The advocacy of ethnicity as a counterweight to religious unity marked an important shift in thought on the OMEA's organization, even if conference participants could not agree on how to counter Muslims' "aspiration to unification."[101] Officials from

Petersburg and from the Volga-Urals region at another special conference four years later, in 1910, argued that the Revolution of 1905 had initiated among Muslims and "fanatical" clerics the "identification of religion with nationality in the Tatar meaning of this last word." Muslims advanced a "religious nationalism" that was "in opposition to the common European principles of tribal nationalism" and pushed Muslims toward "religious-national separatism."[102]

Such concerns prompted the MVD to order an inspection of the OMEA in June 1910. The MVD official in charge, Ivan M. Platonikov, confirmed many of his superiors' fears. The OMEA had become a battleground for conservative and progressive camps of the Muslim community, and progressives appeared to be winning. Local authorities praised the mufti's conduct in the Revolution of 1905, but since then the influence of Tatar "populists" had become evident.[103] One OMEA judge was a "fervent proponent of pan-Turkism," and one staff member "fully shared the views of the pan-Islamists." Sympathy for "nationalist" goals pervaded the institution. The OMEA did not sufficiently monitor its clerics and did not punish those who failed to pray for the tsar. It published a journal, *Maglumat* (Information), which expressed "Tatar nationalist" ideas and whose editors included Khasangata M. Gabashi, a supporter of the Muslim Fraction in the State Duma.[104] Perhaps most important, the OMEA had begun to support new-method schools that taught secular subjects. In conclusion, Platonikov argued that the OMEA had become "a Muslim-Tatar institution" that had put itself "on a manifestly illegal path, incompatible with the mission of the Russian state." In effect, Platonikov argued that a state institution, the OMEA, no longer served state interests.[105]

THE PURGE OF MUSLIM ZEMSTVO DEPUTIES

Governor Kliucharev shared Stolypin's skepticism of Muslim political activity. Kliucharev sought to exclude Muslim influence from the province's political life. In doing so, the governor marked not only his differences with the zemstvo but also a decline in the importance of estate status as a regulator of political participation after 1905. Reforms in peasant status in 1906 restored direct elections from the peasant curiae. This reform, combined with the general Muslim mobilization for Duma elections, increased Muslim influence in zemstvos. The Muslim membership of the provincial zemstvo grew from about 6 percent in 1906 to approximately 15 percent in 1909.[106] Muslims made up nearly half of the deputies elected to the Belebei zemstvo in 1909. Muslim activism provoked the suspicion of provincial authorities. In response, the governor began to make the zemstvos more reliably "Russian" institutions in a manner similar to Stolypin's reduction in Muslim participation in the State Duma. In 1909,

Governor Kliucharev eliminated those who promoted Muslim interests from the Belebei zemstvo leadership, regardless of whether they were Muslim or noble. He explained to Stolypin that Muslims had united with leftist Russians to form a "Kadet-Muslim bloc" in the Belebei County zemstvo. In order not to be cut off from this "bloc," Russians were "required to concede much to the Muslims in their purely national demands." Muslims elected to public positions had sought "to force Russian monarchists out of public positions" and "to realize Tatar-national demands at public expense." The governor refused to confirm the elected zemstvo board, including Ibragim V. Teregulov and three Russian-Orthodox men whom the governor accused of having Muslim sympathies. Allowing Teregulov to take a zemstvo position would only "strengthen the Muslim element to the direct detriment of Russian affairs."[107] Instead, the governor appointed nobleman Vasilii I. Bunin as chairman and a bailiff, a peasant, and a former schoolteacher as board members. None of the latter three was a nobleman, met the property qualification to serve in his position, or had much zemstvo experience. One board member was a Muslim deemed reliable, indicating a split within Muslim representation in the county assembly. Stolypin requested permission to confirm the appointments from Nicholas II, since Stolypin himself did not have the legal authority to do so. The move startled the noblemen of Belebei. Even a Russian nobleman who supported Bunin wrote to Stolypin to express his outrage.[108] Where elections had produced a zemstvo board that could mediate ethnic and religious differences, the governor sacrificed estate and property-holding criteria in order to appoint a board that reaffirmed imperial interests against Muslim interests.

Late in 1911, Petr P. Bashilov, a man somewhat more conciliatory to educated society and Muslims, replaced Governor Kliucharev. Nevertheless, Bashilov further reduced the power of Muslims in the Ufa zemstvos. Even after Kliucharev refused to confirm the Belebei County board in 1909, three members of the Muslim noble Enikeev family and two members of the Muslim noble Teregulov family had been elected to the Belebei County assembly from the first curia. The county zemstvo assembly, in turn, had selected four Muslims out of a total of five men to represent the county in the provincial assembly. In 1912, Vasilii Bunin successfully petitioned to reduce the Belebei assembly's Muslim membership by challenging the qualifications of notable Muslim families. Teregulovs and Enikeevs had held land in common as long ago as the eighteenth century. Individually, their holdings were not large, but together 149 heads of household from the two families controlled more than 7,300 des. of land. As many as one hundred participated in the first curia for zemstvo elections, and they usually sympathized with the zemstvo left.[109] In 1912, the local administration initially allowed the families to participate in elections in the first curia.

Eleven of eighteen deputies elected from the curia were Muslim. The senate, upon Bunin's petition, denied Enikeevs and Teregulovs the right to participate in the first curia's elections because they did not have proper documentation for their landholdings and annulled the elections. In new elections, without Enikeevs and Teregulovs in the first curia, Kutlu-Mukhammad Tevkelev was the lone Muslim nobleman and the lone liberal elected. He resigned as a zemstvo deputy in protest. Elimination of the Muslim nobility from the county zemstvo greatly reduced the Muslim presence in the provincial assembly. Only 6 percent of the provincial assembly was Muslim (two of twenty-eight deputies).[110] Although 47 percent of those chosen to represent volosts were Muslim, this did not translate into influence in the noble-dominated provincial assembly.[111] Overall, the Muslim presence in the provincial assembly declined to what it had been before 1906.

MOBILIZATION FOR WAR

The Russian Empire's declaration of war against Austria-Hungary and the German Empire on August 2, 1914, initially seemed to reinforce more inclusive sentiments than had been apparent in the governor's interventions in zemstvo politics. The local newspaper noted that organizations and people as diverse as the zemstvo, the City Duma, merchants, townspeople, nobles, Muslims, Old Believers, and Jews worked together to aid the wounded.[112] The war was indeed a common effort. Many Muslims served in the military—ten at the rank of general.[113] In reports to St. Petersburg, Ufa governor Bashilov emphasized, in particular, the fervent support of Muslim religious leaders for the war effort. Muslim clerics in the city of Ufa included special prayers for a Russian victory on the Friday after the declaration of war. In Ufa's central mosque, the akhund declared that any "nation (*natsiia*) can only exist when it loves its fatherland, when with truth and justice it serves its Tsar." Since the enemy had attacked "our motherland—Russia (*Rossiia*)," all Muslims had the duty to sacrifice their property and lives to defend Russia. The akhund's speech closed with a loud "hurrah," and then those present staged an impressive "patriotic demonstration" in the city.[114] Muslim populations in the province expressed similar sentiments.[115] Mufti Sultanov also instructed Muslim clerics to support the war effort. "Russia is dear and beloved to us Muslims, as it is to all other ethnic groups (*narodnostiam*) living in it; to preserve and defend Russia from any enemy is our sacred duty, as it is of all other ethnic groups in it."[116] Two of Ufa's State Duma deputies, Kutlu-Mukhammad Tevkelev—the leader of the Muslim Fraction—and Ibniamin Akhtiamov, were late to the Duma session that approved the declaration of war on Germany, but they inserted a statement in a

Petersburg newspaper the next day that stated Muslims would "fight the enemy together with the Russian people until the end."[117] Substantial indications that Muslims, among others, did not universally support the war effort receive little attention. For instance, the governor considered September 1914 disturbances in Birsk, Sterlitamak, and Belebei that involved hundreds of Tatar, Bashkir, and Russian conscripts as not political in nature and due entirely to local circumstances regarding provisions.[118]

Just as mobilization for war provided space to express loyalty to the tsar and country, it provided political actors of all types with a much greater impetus to attempt to realize their varied visions of what the empire should be. The wartime experience did not change officials' and local elites' perspectives so much as it pushed them to articulate their views with greater energy and urgency. As the autocracy proved unable to win the war and began to lose legitimacy, differences among rival conceptions of the civic order began to matter more.

The war's outbreak gave zemstvo elites a greater opportunity to communicate their vision of a multinational state throughout the province. As men went off to war, the desire for information about their fate and the course of battle dramatically increased demand for the printed word. Demand also grew for lectures on the war's background, its geography, its combatants, and the technology used.[119] In the fall of 1914, the provincial zemstvo resolved to open twenty-eight intermediate and 108 lower-level libraries and substantially increased funding for extracurricular programs. The zemstvo published pamphlets on the war to support lecturers and added war news to the agricultural journal.[120] In 1916, the MNP even encouraged extracurricular programs. The ministry's new leader, Pavel N. Ignat'ev, proclaimed it the duty of all the country's intelligentsia to reinforce "the general patriotic upsurge that now characterizes the popular spirit." He called for public lectures on the war, history, geography, and Russia's allies, among other subjects.[121]

Zemstvo goals for extracurricular educational work did not directly contradict those of the minister of education, but evidence suggests that zemstvo activists' interpretations of what their audience should fight for varied from those state officials might have preferred. A conference held in August 1915 on extracurricular education in Zlatoust County, for instance, planned a lecture series on Russia's "common culture," which focused on "the history of economic life, the more important factor of the history of culture." This interpretation supported the materialist conceptions of history held by some of the state's critics. Zlatoust activists also proposed that history lectures interweave Tatar history with the history of Russia in general, rather than making local Islamic peoples invisible or important primarily as subjects of conquest.[122] Publications and lecture topics notably omitted the tsar as the object of patriotism.[123]

At the very least, the lectures lent themselves to the advancement of the left-liberal or socialist inclinations of many zemstvo activists rather than to patriotic mobilization in defense of tsar and fatherland. This may have motivated continued official suspicion of zemstvo enlightenment projects. In 1915, Governor Bashilov recommended that wounded army officers be appointed as zemstvo librarians.[124]

County zemstvos, which bore responsibility for funding primary schools, also began to support Muslim education. Pressured by Muslim constituents to support Muslim schools, but prohibited from establishing the type of schools that the Muslims wanted, two county zemstvos began to fund Muslim confessional schools directly. In 1913, the Birsk County zemstvo authorized 10,000 rubles in support of madrasas and maktabs, more than twice the amount provided to Orthodox Church schools.[125] In 1914, the Menzelinsk County zemstvo voted to allocate a total of 14,700 rubles for Muslim confessional schools but refused the bishop's request for 2,850 rubles for Russian Orthodox schools.[126] The Menzelinsk assembly intentionally funded only Muslim schools that gave up the old method of instruction in favor of the "phonetic method" favored by jadid reformers.[127] Zemstvo decisions to support Muslim education indicated a growing tendency among some zemstvo deputies to view themselves as representatives of all the people, not just those of a particular national or religious group. In a debate over the archbishop of Ufa's request for support for parish schools, a Russian Orthodox board member of the Ufa County zemstvo stated in 1914 that from the zemstvo point of view "all must be equal—the Orthodox, and the Muslims, and the Jews—and there must be no question of religious conflict."[128] Many influential zemstvo activists assumed that ethnic and religious differences existed among the population and would continue to exist but that institutions of self-administration must relate to different groups more equally.

THE ORENBURG EDUCATIONAL DISTRICT
AND EDUCATION ON A NATIONAL BASIS

While zemstvo activists built on prewar trends toward multinational inclusion, the educational administration's investment in national education received more intensive development upon the outbreak of the war.[129] Identification with the Russian people became more important than identification with the state or with the tsar. In 1915 the OUO's chief inspector, Miropiev, issued a manifesto of sorts in the form of an article and pamphlet entitled "The Necessity of Basing the Russian School on National Principles."[130] In Miropiev's opinion, war provided an opportunity for the Russian people to realize its national mission, even a kind of national redemption, as it united against the Germans and the Turks. When the Russians finally proved victorious, the country could finally begin to live "fully its own national life," a life that first various Asian peoples, then various European enemies and especially Germans under Peter I, and more recently Russia's own "stepchild," the inorodtsy, had denied it. Since Peter I's time a "deep abyss" had opened between the intelligentsia and the people. The intelligentsia was torn from its national roots and Europeanized, while the people looked with scorn at the intelligentsia that it considered hostile to everything national. Russia's intelligentsia and bureaucracy were "distinguished by dead, lifeless formalism," which ruined "the motherland until this day." Since their animating force lay in the West, Russia's schools also had a soulless formalism to them. Russia would only prosper intellectually, morally, and economically when enlightenment was founded on "our national principles, on our marvelous and rich language, on our deeply national and strongly patriotic feelings, on our Russian particularities and national bases, on our much-suffering history, on the complete and many-sided knowledge of our fatherland."[131] Only when a healthy nationalism rather than a "soulless cosmopolitanism" and socialism spread throughout the entire Russian people would Russia realize its potential. Miropiev's manifesto made no reference to the tsar, indicating a turn from the autocracy toward Russian nationalism. Miropiev argued that education of non-Russians must have the sole goal of the "assimilation" (*sliianie*) of "all minor non-Russian ethnic groups" with the "strong spirit and culture" of neighboring peoples. The rejection of the state in favor of the Russian nation left little room for non-Russians, and the administration became more ethnically exclusive in its organization.[132] Miropiev's thorough, public condemnation of the bureaucracy and its lifelessness is striking coming from one of the most highly placed bureaucrats in the local educational administration. The presence of such populist, antibureaucratic attitudes within the bureaucracy itself gives powerful indication of the extent to which even tsarist officials had begun to abandon the imperial state idea.

THE CATEGORIZATION AND RELIEF OF REFUGEES

Even as Miropiev wrote his manifesto, wartime exigencies ran contrary to the notion that the empire's east could become part of a Russian nation. The flow of refugees, deportees, and prisoners from the war zone made the province's population even more diverse. As the German army moved through Russian Poland in early 1915, millions of the tsar's subjects fled east ahead of it. Intent on eliminating populations the military considered unreliable, officers deported others, especially Poles and Jews, from border regions.[133] Most relocated to places closer to their homes than Ufa. As relief resources became overtaxed, however, refugees continued eastward. By the end of 1915, the last year for which we have statistics, officially 71,108 refugees had settled in Ufa Province and another 53,054 in Orenburg Province.[134] Unregistered refugees and those arriving in 1916 and after would push these statistics substantially higher. Ufa's governor reported that 228,000 refugees had entered his province in 1915.[135]

The movement of refugees eastward catalyzed the formation of national organizations in the eastern borderlands. Before the war, charitable organizations had formed according to religious criteria to aid students and the poor.[136] Efforts to support refugees from the western borderlands gave a national accent to such efforts. From the start of the war, authorities in the center organized refugee relief along national (*natsional'nye*) lines. The state, overwhelmed by the war effort, proved unable to provide food, housing, and supplies to displaced persons. So it ceded, often uneasily, responsibility for refugees to national organizations.[137] The all-imperial Committee on the Registration of Refugees in Petrograd included members from Polish, Latvian, Lithuanian, Jewish, and Armenian national organizations. When the committee developed forms for registering adult refugees, it did not require that refugees provide their estate status or religious confession. The forms' primary categories were nationality (*natsional'nost'*) and profession (*professiia*).[138]

Refugee relief efforts in Ufa reflected the example of those in the center. Since the state could not provide social welfare, local officials relied upon zemstvos and national (*natsional'nye*) organizations to do so.[139] Polish, Jewish, and Latvian organizations registered their "fellow tribe members" and used funds from the provincial council on refugees to find them housing and food. In addition, these national organizations raised their own independent funds primarily to perform "cultural-enlightenment work" outside the mission of the provincial council on refugees. Nationality became a key factor in whether one received aid, how much one received, and who provided it. Though few Muslims fled the western borderlands, Muslim philanthropic organizations played a similar role to "national" organizations with respect to relief for wounded Muslim soldiers and for Muslim families that lost male members and their labor power to the army.

BISHOP ANDREI, THE CITY OF GOD, AND RUSSIAN NATIONALITY DURING WARTIME

Efforts to organize Russians along national lines occurred as a reaction to the war and to the growth of non-Russian organizations. Bishop Andrei (Ukhtomskii) was the principal intellectual and organizational force behind the creation

of a Russian national organization, the Eastern-Russian Cultural Enlightenment Society, in early 1916. Andrei's arrival in February 1914 brought a vigorous
man to lead the church.[140] Andrei had become a specialist on missionary work
among non-Russian groups as vicar bishop of Kazan Province and as bishop of
Sukhumi, in the North Caucasus. Andrei made it his mission to unite and to
expand Orthodox society in Ufa as well. In Andrei's address upon his arrival
in Ufa in February 1914, he distanced himself from the political right wing by
condemning the activity of "an influential political party," interpreted in the
press as the Union of the Russian People, because it "entirely forgot to speak of
the Church."[141] A local newspaper declared that Ufa had acquired "an uncom-
mon, lively, bishop" who was "sensitive to questions of contemporary life." The
editorial writer did not agree with all of what Andrei said, but nevertheless he
considered Andrei's arrival "a phenomenon worthy of close attention" from society.[142] Andrei later earned sympathy from educated society by being among
the most aggressive critics of Rasputin. Andrei denounced the Siberian "holy
man" both publicly and privately, in Ufa and in the central press. He publicly
urged the tsar to remove Rasputin from his court.[143] Andrei's energy, prolific
writing, and open, accessible style contrasted sharply with those of his predecessors and attracted many to his mission.

Andrei succeeded in invigorating Orthodoxy where his predecessors had
failed. He focused his efforts on reform of the Church's basic unit, the parish.[144]
Local parishes had to be given legal status, he argued, like that the Manifesto
on Toleration granted to Old Believers, so Orthodox parishes could manage
their own financial affairs without having to "beg eternally for . . . handouts
from Petrograd for any trifle."[145] Andrei advocated the election of parish clergy,
which marked a decisive break with nearly two hundred years of church history
and distinguished him from other clergy. The powerful sense of community
and clerical authority among Old Believers helped convince Andrei that the
elective principle would eliminate a major weakness of Orthodox parishes—
that parishioners little "knew and therefore little loved their priests." In April
1916, Andrei published rules for the selection of head priests in Ufa's churches.[146]
Andrei's introduction of the elective principle without the synod's permission
was one of the issues that caused central church authorities to consider his
ouster.[147]

Andrei achieved considerable success, at least initially, in achieving a rapprochement between church and zemstvo. In 1914, Andrei sought the renewal of
zemstvo support for church schools that had ended eighteen years earlier. Five
of Ufa's six county zemstvos allocated at least modest sums to Bishop Andrei
for support of the schools. Even "Red Prince" Viacheslav Kugushev noted the
"exceptional" nature of Andrei's request, stating the "personality of the author

is so attractive and has gained such deep sympathy in local society that we cannot hesitate before this."[148] Andrei soon discovered the limits of his willingness to work with educated society and the zemstvo, however. Try as he did to unite society with the church, Andrei faced opposition from secular-minded Russian-speaking zemstvo activists and from Muslims who had no interest in doing anything "under the cross." Andrei considered it outrageous that the Menzelinsk County zemstvo rejected his request for 2,850 rubles for Orthodox Church schools but allocated 14,700 rubles for Muslim schools. He castigated the Menzelinsk deputies for their lack of knowledge of Islam and decried their action as "completely reckless, senseless liberalism." "There are limits even to religious toleration," he wrote. Andrei attacked Russian-speaking zemstvo deputies as either false Christians or secret Muslims. He claimed that Muslim religious education corrupted Muslims and asserted that Muslim families were characterized by incest.[149] The bishop's statements provoked an outcry among Muslims that reached the national press. Andrei also clashed with zemstvo deputies over extracurricular education. Andrei complained to the synod that zemstvo reading rooms were schools for "atheism and political nihilism" and recommended that they be turned over to priests.[150] He denounced the conduct of extracurricular education to the minister of internal affairs as "in a spirit absolutely against the Russification (*obruseniiu*) of the region." He characterized the activity of two Teregulov brothers in zemstvo employ as a "project of Islamization."[151] Andrei rejected plans initiated by officials in St. Petersburg to promote Muslim loyalty to the empire, arguing the state could not compete with the Muslim press for the attention of the Muslim population. For Andrei, Muslims were the enemy of Russian Orthodoxy, and the church needed to reform in order to respond to this threat.[152]

Andrei's efforts to invigorate the Russian Orthodox Church, to increase its influence, and to mark the boundaries between Orthodoxy and other faiths lay behind his interest in creating a Russian national organization. His concern over the fate of refugees in Ufa Province provided the final impetus. In the course of his work on refugee aid, Andrei came into contact with the Western-Russian Society in Petrograd, which provided funds for the relief of Russian refugees, and with Bishop Anastasii of Kholm and Liublin's All-Russian Society for the Care of Refugees. Concerns about Russian refugees seem to have motivated Andrei to promote the cultural development of Russians.[153]

Writing in the diocesan journal, one of Andrei's priests, Nikolai Kontsevich, justified what became the Eastern-Russian Cultural Enlightenment Society. Kontsevich bemoaned the "helplessness of the Russian person" living on the borderlands of the Russian state. Jews, Germans, Latvians, Poles, and Armenians all had "national (*natsional'nye*) organizations" which vigilantly looked after their "fellow tribe members." "Only Russian people for some reason do not bother to create their own organization for the defense of Russian interests," wrote Kontsevich. The helplessness of Russians left without a protector became a standard theme in subsequent descriptions of the Eastern-Russian Society. According to Kontsevich, Russians could no longer live among non-Russians and non-Christians as they had before, because doing so had made them "outcasts in their own home." Russians had their own interests, and no one else would "study," "explain," and fight for them.[154] Russians could not turn for help to the government. Its representatives were guided by "general norms of law" that addressed "subjects of the Russian state in general regardless of their nationality (*natsional'nosti*)." Since no state help would be forthcoming, Russians on the borderlands must show "initiative, unite, and organize mutual aid. *It is necessary to create a national Russian society,* which would guard the spiritual and material interests of the Russian population, which would unite all the intellectually engaged workers for the good of Russian people of a given region." The Eastern-Russian society was meant to be just such a "national society."[155]

The Eastern-Russian Society's first meeting took place on February 1, 1916. Bishop Andrei acknowledged the influence of the Western-Russian Society, whose charter the Eastern-Russian Society had nearly copied. The speakers at the society's first session—a priest, a professor, the director of the Orenburg Educational District, the inspector of primary schools in Ufa, and an Old Believer—give some sense of the organization's intended constituency. It sought to overcome the divisions between the church, the educational administration, and the intelligentsia. It sought to include those kept out of religious organizations due to their adherence to dissident sects of Orthodoxy. In so doing, the society sought to overcome the split between proponents of linguistic and religious conceptions of Russianness. It signified a consolidation of forces in the name of a nation that had been lacking. The meeting appears to have been small, however. Andrei bitterly explained that the "vast majority" of Russians were too busy with their card games or at the local movie house.[156] Nonetheless, the group's members considered their unity a great step forward.[157]

Andrei fitted the creation of the society firmly into a religious mission. All "our public spiritedness, [and] also the private life of our Russian person, must be constituent parts of one great city of God" according to St. Augustine. Nonetheless, Andrei clearly meant the society to be a secular organization—he stated that he would "speak on earthly subjects; therefore I will speak in an earthly, non-spiritual language, I will speak almost in a lay fashion." He warned that he would be "repeating the words of others," by which he meant the words of his teachers, "our great Slavophiles."[158] Andrei applied Slavophile thought to his predominantly non-Russian milieu. Andrei argued that non-Russians feared

Russians but did not love them. Since Russians lacked a cultural spirit, the Russian state governed non-Russians only through a "cult of force." Non-Russians saw in Russia a "nation" that did not respect its faith or its people's customs. Structuring his remarks around lengthy quotations from Nicholas Danilevskii, Ivan Aksakov, and Nikita Giliarov-Platonov, Andrei blamed the cult of force and lack of spiritual culture on two hundred years of German influence on the Russian state. Peter the Great had begun a process by which Russia's "common interests" were killed. Russian ethnicity (*narodnost'*) was "scorned, spat on, trampled, [and] beaten." The "administrative-police" influence on Russian culture resulted in spiritual emptiness and socialism. The people could not wait for the government to act. The realization of the Slavophile program was necessary to make Russian culture healthy again. Andrei had in mind freedom of the "honest printed word," "freedom of mutual aid and of various cooperatives," and especially "freedom of the Church."[159] Andrei argued that if Russians made vital their "cultural mission" and realized it in "social life," then strength in "political relations" and in "relations with our smaller ethnic groups" would follow. The spiritually invigorated Russian nation that Andrei envisioned would not dominate the non-Russians through force and might but rather overwhelm them with its spiritual power and guide them in a brotherly manner. The tsar was notably absent in Andrei's vision of a revitalized Russia. Although one could conceive of a role for a tsar in such a system, the source of authority was the people and the Russian nation. One year before Nicholas II abdicated, both religious and educational leaders in Ufa quietly rebelled against the imperial state in the name of the Russian people. Whether the people would follow them was another matter.

CONCLUSION

Akhmed-Zeki Validov's depiction of the noble estate in the last days of the empire shows the benefit of hindsight. Looking back from beyond 1917, as Validov did, the empire's hierarchy of men whose status and privileges reflected their loyalty to the emperor, and who would use that status to influence their communities, seemed anachronistic and doomed. On the eve of the Revolution of 1917, however, estate remained a key element of imperial order. As we have seen, Ufa's Muslim Duma deputies remained largely of noble status. In a number of cases, families of Duma deputies—Akhtiamovs, Dzhantiurins, Syrtlanovs, and Tevkelevs—were the same that had helped govern Ufa Province and Bashkiria for more than a century. The system of estates created a cohort of noblemen of Muslim and Bashkir origins who were literate in Russian and could move in imperial society. Bashkir privileges and especially landholding had become less distinctive, but Bashkir status remained. Reform meant that peasants were not completely an estate apart, but they maintained distinctive legal institutions until nearly 1912 and lacked full property rights until 1917. Religious distinctions still mattered greatly too.

Nonetheless, the Revolution of 1905 was a decisive moment in the empire's governance, even in a region such as Ufa that experienced much less violence and unrest than elsewhere. The tsar's authority was so deeply shaken that political actors of all sorts sought to find new bases for imperial authority. The use of estate to reward and structure loyalty no longer sufficed. The politics of loyalty required a much deeper commitment. One had to support imperial authority actively. The tsar's officials would consider status and property ownership in judging loyalty, but demonstrations of loyalty or patriotism were crucial. The closing of the Second State Duma in June 1907 and its replacement by an electoral system meant to make it more responsive to "Russian national interests" were key markers of change. In Ufa, the effort to remove Muslims and those deemed sympathetic to Muslims from the Belebei zemstvo demonstrated how the attitude that informed Duma electoral policy spread throughout the imperial system. The removal of Teregulovs and Enikeevs, members of Muslim noble families who had been in the region since at least the eighteenth century and served as a stabilizing influence in a century of Bashkir rebellions, marked a turn from estate status distinctions toward a more narrow understanding of who could be a faithful servitor of the emperor.

After imperial visions tottered in 1905, the following decade witnessed the simultaneous emergence of nationalism of various sorts as a new focus of loyalty. Since the Great Reform era, members of Russian Orthodox and Muslim communities had debated whether faith or language ought to be at the core of collective identity. Sectarian divides among Orthodox and Old Believer and the very different ways of life of settled Tatars and semi-nomadic Bashkirs also inhibited the coalescence of national groups. Most of all, however, the local population had little motivation for national identification before 1905. As long as estate and religious hierarchies of elites loyal to the emperor held sway, nationalism had little constituency. The crack in imperial authority in 1905 and the mass politics that accompanied it meant that political elites now had to appeal to a broader public. Nationalism proved a way to articulate a collective interest, and old elites now had to engage new constituencies. Thus, as Bashkir estate status declined in importance, a Bashkir national idea grew. Muslims became a nationality rather than a confessional group that fit into imperial institutions. More striking than non-Russian, non-Orthodox Christians pulling away from the imperial idea, even bureaucrats such as Miropiev and churchmen such as Bishop Andrei began to use national language to describe the emerging political community. Both men outlined visions of a state without any mention of the tsar. Since the central state essentially ceded refugee support to national organizations, the polity in the empire's east became much more nationally identified.

The introduction of nationalism only complicated efforts to articulate a coherent concept of the empire. Many people active in 1905 remained committed to the imperial idea and to the tsar as the head of the empire. The most important contribution of the local elite centered around the zemstvo in Ufa was a belief in a sort of Enlightenment universalism. Both political conviction and the need to get elected in a very diverse province motivated Ufa zemstvo leaders to support bilingual education on a secular basis and to involve Muslims in deliberations over the fate of non-Russian education. In an important way, zemstvo activists resembled Orthodox churchmen who believed that national languages and cultures could be means to spread a set of ideas. However, zemstvo activists drew their common values from the Enlightenment rather than from Christianity. The consistency and scope of Ufa elites' vision of integrating Muslims and animist peoples into a common culture and educational system that encompassed at least major local linguistic groups distinguished it from the positions of elites in the rest of the empire. The viability of such ideas must not be exaggerated. Mostly noble zemstvo leaders could develop such notions in large part because of their positions of privilege, and they paid for educational programs with money taxed from often poor peasants and workers who likely would have preferred to be able to spend it themselves.

In important ways, the immediate prewar and wartime experiences of empire had the effect of making Ufa Province more like other parts of the empire. Stolypin decisively shifted policy initiative to the center. Governors in the Great Reform era such as Bezak and Kryzhanovskii had had substantial input in the application of reforms to their jurisdictions that Kliucharev and Bashilov lacked after 1905. The profusion of special congresses called by Stolypin's administration to address questions of education and faith indicates an effort to put questions of imperial diversity regarding various regions into the same frame.[160] The vast mobilization to fight the First World War brought the empire together to an unprecedented degree. The great movement of peoples set in motion by the war accelerated the process of nationalization of Bashkiria's population also observed elsewhere in the empire. Social and political transformations of wartime integrated the region into the empire's core as never before.

At the same time, war clearly affected the empire's west much more than its east. Ufa Province experienced none of the intensive violence and destruction characteristic of the empire's southern and western borderlands. Located far from the frontlines, Ufa avoided the massive death and destruction characteristic of the borderlands with opposing empires. The province remained under civilian rule for the duration of the war. Its population never faced the expropriations, deportations, ethnic cleansing, and genocide that military activity and administration effected in border regions.[161] If the border regions became "shatterzones" of empire, Bashkiria knew no such shattering experience before 1917.[162]

The Russian Empire's immediate prewar and wartime experiences of parliamentary politics, nationalization, and centralization echoed those in Russia's chief imperial neighbors and rivals. The effort to reduce the Muslim presence in the State Duma after 1907 must be considered in the context of how unusual it was for members of non-predominant racial or religious groups to be in parliaments at all. Only in the Ottoman Empire were non-predominant groups represented in all-imperial bodies more than in the Russian Empire. The first postrevolutionary elections of 1908 resulted in proportional representation for the empire's non-Turkish communities.[163] But if the initial results of Ottoman elections better reflected the diversity of the Ottoman population, subsequent elections excluded non-Muslims and non-Turks even more dramatically than the Russian Empire excluded Muslims and non-Russians. The Habsburg monarchy lacked one predominant national group but had a lively, sometimes raucous national politics already in the nineteenth century. Muslims remained an exception to this pattern. No Bosnian Muslims served in parliament in Vienna or Budapest after Bosnia's annexation in 1908. On the whole, though, these three empires, however briefly and at times reluctantly, diverged from European precedents by reflecting imperial diversity. By contrast, the first black African elected to the French parliament, Blaise Diagne, took his seat only in February 1914, and in Britain, only two South Asians were elected to parliament before the First World War.[164]

The First World War brought with it administrative centralization and the emergence of national thinking across Europe. In the Ottoman Empire, the Committee of Union and Progress after the Revolution of 1908 centralized administration, cancelled privileges of non-Turkic Muslim groups, and demanded that all citizens put their Ottoman identity above all others. At the same time, the "difference between 'Ottoman' and 'Turkish' became increasingly blurred."[165] Greek, Bulgarian, and Armenian nationalisms intensified as the empire's center became more Turkic, and Arab and Albanian nationalisms began to grow. In the Habsburg monarchy, German, Czech, and Hungarian nationalism grew as well, even as the dynasty and imperial institutions sought to remain "beyond nationalism" to a greater extent than the Romanov dynasty did.[166]

The wartime experience of nationalization in Ufa Province echoed more intense processes closer to theaters of war. All sides at war used national ideas to erode loyalty to empires and to intensify national movements on the other side of the front.[167] As Ariel Roshwald has written, by 1917, "the Great War was leading to a rapid escalation of nationalist sentiments, activities and expectations across . . . East Central Europe, the Russian Empire, and the Middle East."[168] German military commanders in conquered lands to Germany's east categorized populations by ethnicity and developed "enlightenment" programs that included native-language instruction.[169] Germans used emigrés from the Russian Empire to agitate among Muslim prisoners of war against the empire and to fight for the Ottomans.[170] As the war dragged on, with millions losing their lives and others struggling to feed themselves adequately, the horrors of the war undermined the legitimacy of Habsburg and German rulers. The war set in motion a struggle for succession within Russia's neighboring empires and within the Russian Empire itself.

Conclusion

A STRUGGLING WAR EFFORT and unrest in St. Petersburg caused Nicholas II to abdicate in February 1917. Nicholas II viewed the First World War as a trial sent by God and agreed to step aside if it would speed the fatherland's victory.[1] The "fatherland" had become more important than the tsar. With the monarchy's collapse, the institution to which Bashkirs had sworn loyalty in the 1550s, and which had provided political continuity thereafter, disappeared. By the twentieth century, however, what had been a fairly straightforward agreement by Bashkir clan leaders to be loyal, and to pay tribute in exchange for land and help protecting it, had changed. What had been a collection of clans living beyond Muscovite defensive lines was now conceived by tsarist officials and Bashkirs themselves as a Bashkir estate and even a national group. An area that had been administered by an island of military servitors in a sea of non-Russian-speaking, non-Christians now had a civil administration, a very diverse population, and a location on the eastern edge of "European Russia." In the course of 365 years, Bashkirs and Bashkiria had been integrated, and had integrated themselves, into the core of the world's largest land empire.

To build and sustain imperial rule, officials needed to create subjects whose loyalty would be drawn to the tsar. Officials had to connect people to the will of the sovereign in order to weave a diverse population into a coherent polity. Imperial officials used a variety of strategies to do so. This book has focused on estate status, force, religious confession, and nationality. From the sixteenth century to the empire's end, estate status was a crucial dimension of imperial rule. Estate status was fundamentally political and legal.[2] Imperial authorities used estate status to assign privileges and obligations meant to identify and reward those who supported the empire. Whether privilege meant freedom from taxation, the ability to own land and serfs, access to positions of authority locally, or getting one's son into an educational institution, estate created a tie between ruler and ruled and elevated the privileged subject within the hierarchy of imperial subjects. The imperial state did not just order existing differences;

241

it created new differences among the tsar's subjects in order to build ties of loyalty. In Bashkiria, estate status differentiated Bashkirs from other subjects of the tsar. Bashkirs' hereditary landownership, their ability to make the imperial state recognize it in principle, and the relatively large size of their landholdings made them distinctive until the end of the Old Regime, even as Bashkirs lost much land in practice. At the same time, imperial authorities differentiated elite Bashkirs from other Bashkirs. In the seventeenth century, the tsar continued the practice of granting tarkhan status. In the eighteenth century, imperial officials broke down larger tribal structures to create an elite oriented toward imperial service. The militarized cantonal system of administration created a Bashkir elite of canton heads and iurta elders who used their status to enrich themselves and even enter the all-imperial nobility. A number of important families used that status to remain influential in local self-administration and eventually in State Duma service. Bashkirs retained their particular status until 1917, even if Stolypin's agrarian reforms and allowing Russians to register in Bashkir communities made hollow key elements of what had distinguished Bashkirs.

Based on the example of Kazan's violent conquest in 1552, it is easy to see imperial expansion as beginning with force and ending with assimilation into the empire. Russian expansion in Bashkiria followed a different pattern. Whether Bashkirs' entry into the empire was "voluntary" is debatable, since unstable politics on the steppe seem to have left Bashkir elites little choice but to work with the tsarist state. Nonetheless, substantial violence was rare before the mid-seventeenth century. When Bashkirs perceived that their relationship with imperial authority had been violated, Bashkirs and the tsar's men fought each other. Before the 1730s, this violence continued until the two sides came to terms, according to which the tsar typically affirmed Bashkir status and Bashkirs agreed to return to loyal subjecthood. Only in the Bashkir War of 1735–1740, more than 150 years after Bashkir elites swore allegiance to the tsar, did violence come to dominate the relationship between Bashkiria's population and the tsarist state. The war devastated and divided those in the Bashkir estate over a five-year period. Many Bashkirs joined forces with the tsar to fight fellow Bashkirs. Violence, however, was simply too costly to rely upon continually and over large portions of the population. It was also too destructive of people and of the region's prosperity. Bashkiria's population took decades to recover from the war of the 1730s. Such violence was not repeated in Bashkiria, nor was a repetition necessary to demonstrate the tsar's power.

Religious faith or "religious confession" remained a central category according to which the empire's diversity was defined until 1917. For the tsar's subjects, religion could be a means to salvation, a grounding for morality, or a source of community. For imperial officials, it was also a means to understand, to categorize, and to govern the tsar's subjects and to accommodate differences among them.[3] The great importance of religious institutions for the integration of Bashkiria cannot be denied. The period of greatest stability in Bashkiria, roughly 1780–1905, coincided with the period when local religious and secular leaders both maintained strong connections to imperial authority, which sought to accommodate Islam.[4] In many respects, the relationship between political authority and religious communities in Bashkiria lay at the very foundation of the policy of religious toleration in the east as a whole. The region's strategic importance on the borderland with Central Asia and its often hostile and violent relations in the 1730s and 1740s provided an incentive for Orenburg governor-general Nepliuev to prevent the introduction of the most harsh and disruptive Russian Orthodox missionary activity when such activity was at its height in neighboring Kazan. Policies such as Nepliuev's prefigured legislation creating the OMEA in 1788 and the "confessionalization" of the empire. Toleration made possible the entry of some Muslims into noble status after 1784. Confessional administration was territorially and temporally limited, however. Before the 1735–1740 Bashkir War, imperial administrators had contact with Muslim clerics, but this relationship was largely informal and little documented. After 1736, such relationships continued to lack formal elaboration and regulation, representing more a desire to intervene in Islamic life than an ability to do so. Only with laws establishing the OMEA in 1788 did the imperial state develop this means of confessional administration. Even then, it took decades for Islamic institutions to acquire the ability to record metrical information and the power to confirm clerics within their jurisdiction. The arrangements arrived at in Bashkiria never extended into Central Asia.

As important as religious confession was to imperial governance, it was often only one element of political conflict and not always the central one. Bashkir rebellions of the seventeenth and eighteenth centuries seem to have had more to do with Bashkir's perceived lack of Muscovite support against Kalmyks, abuses by local officials, increased tax burdens, loss of land, and the empire's lack of effort to cultivate local elites than attacks on Bashkirs' faith. Muslim clerics at times led resistance in the wars and uprisings of the eighteenth century, such as Batyrsha's role in 1755. Yet the support of lay leaders had the greatest influence on the ability of the local population to shake imperial authority. Bashkir elders did not support the 1755 uprising, and it was short-lived. They largely supported Pugachev in 1773, and imperial power nearly collapsed altogether.

By the twentieth century the confessional state was in crisis. The confessional structure that had shaped Russia's engagement with Islam no longer satisfied the emperor and his top officials. The meaning of religious confession changed during the crisis of 1905. Central officials perceived Islam as a threat to the empire's integrity and no longer fully trusted the mufti to serve their purposes. The appointment of Mukhamed'iar Sultanov, a nobleman of Bashkir origins, as Orenburg mufti in 1886 indicated Bashkir integration into the religious elite. Yet Sultanov's frustrated efforts to retire made clear the limits of religious institutions in integrating the local population after 1905. Mufti Sultanov turned sixty-three in 1901 and was in poor health. He asked permission to retire. The minister of internal affairs promised him a substantial pension, but only if he continued to serve. Imperial officials could find no candidate for mufti whom they considered reliable but who also enjoyed prestige and influence among Muslims. Mufti Sultanov would die in office in June 1915. By then he had become a relic of a time when officials believed they could find an influential Muslim in the Volga-Urals region to serve as their chief intermediary with Muslim society.[5]

By the late nineteenth century, religious confession became increasingly identified with nationality in the view of imperial officials, who often considered nationality a more important element of political life. As Paul Werth has pointed out, imperial officials had long associated religion "with belonging to one or another ethnic community": Orthodoxy was "the Russian faith," Islam was the "Tatar faith," Lutheranism was the "German faith," Catholicism was the "Polish faith," and so on.[6] When the Great Reforms provided new possibilities for Muslim participation in civic life, churchmen, many of them with experience in the western borderlands, saw Muslim participation as itself a threat to the Russian cause, which they defined religiously. Orthodox churchmen denied the possibility that Muslims could be loyal subjects of the tsar while offering a new center of loyalty—the Russian Orthodox nation. With the establishment of the Orenburg Educational District in 1875, educators, also experienced in the battle against Polonism in the western borderlands, embraced a Russian national mission for schools in the region. War against Japan and the Revolution of 1905 intensified the national dimension of religious and educational officials' thought and activism. The near collapse of imperial authority in 1905, combined with electoral politics, provided spaces and media for Muslims to mobilize and to articulate their interests. When they did so, some imperial officials considered them a nationality and referred to them as such. Identification of Muslims as a nationality attributed to the Muslim community coherence and political aspirations that challenged the integrity of the empire.

Russian, Tatar, and Bashkir national ideas emerged as forces in local politics after 1905. They provided a new locus for political loyalty even if disagreements raged among Muslims and Russian Orthodox alike over what should be the core of the nation: language, religion, or, in the case of Bashkirs, language, religion, and landholding. The emergence of Bashkir nationality from within the institutions of empire is striking. Although they had been an estate group, that estate group was porous and culturally complex. People of different cultural backgrounds drawn by Bashkir estate privileges joined the estate through marriage or adoption but identified with other groups as Bashkir fortunes worsened in the late nineteenth century. Yet by the First World War, in the press and from the podium of the State Duma, a Bashkir national idea emerged from Muslim and broader Turkic senses of community. Daniel Schafer summarizes well the key elements of Bashkir national ideology: the Bashkirs' "nomadic past, a history of rebellion against Russian authority, corporate rights to land, the semi-autonomous canton system," and "the Bashkir Host."[7] All these elements were in place by 1917. Perhaps equally striking, however, was the pervasiveness of national ideas among Russian educational bureaucrats, who denounced the bureaucratic state in favor of a Russian national state after 1905, and Russian Orthodox Church officials, who embraced a Russian nation that left little role for the tsar, the defender of the Orthodox Church. By the time the emperor resigned for the good of the fatherland, even many of his own officials looked toward the nation, not the tsar, as the highest object of loyalty. Threads that had connected imperial officials to the tsar had frayed.

The power of a particular type of cosmopolitan thinking distinguished the region as well. Local elites on the border of European and Asian parts of the empire maintained a commitment to recognize formally and to serve more equally a diverse population. Influential members of the Russian Orthodox and Muslim elites mobilized together in the early twentieth century. They defined their enemies as the tsarist state and the backwardness of common people rather than each other. They collaborated on the creation of educational programs to enlighten all the province's population. Native-language educational programs were central to this project of enlightenment, which would encompass everything from museums, cinemas, and libraries to reading huts and periodical publications. When possible, such programs would be led by those of the same faith and language as the people for whom programs were intended. The use of reason, morality, notions of equality, and rational economic practices could be conveyed in any language or culture. All must learn Russian as the lingua franca of a new, multinational public realm, but their own cultures must also be preserved. Such an approach to diversity was suited best not to a nation-state or to an empire but to a multicultural state of citizens. The idea of a population united by civic ties remained surprisingly vital until 1917, even if the privileged, noble elite that predominated in the zemstvos was unable to bridge hierarchical divides and bring such a polity into existence.

As potential members of an estate group, a religious group, or a national group of one kind or another, and at times the target of state violence, Bashkirs embodied the many complexities of the empire's body politic over its last 365 years.

The shifts in identification described by Mikhail Rodnov, among others, in the early twentieth century are evidence of that fact.[8] Bashkirs made clear the legacy of various efforts to sort and order the population in a manner that would identify loyal subjects and connect them to the emperor. Shifts in strategy and lack of neat categories are characteristic of all empires, for which social science categories developed in the West seem inadequate or fit awkwardly. Imperial officials used all these categories to identify loyal subjects and to establish a hierarchy of imperial subjects under the rule of the tsar. The empire collapsed when none of them sufficed to connect the population to the tsar.

SITUATING BASHKIRIA IN THE RUSSIAN EMPIRE

Although Bashkiria's particular qualities made it unlike any other part of the empire, analysis of what made it so can help us map the geography of imperial rule in regions to its east and west, and in the empire's western and southern borderlands as well. Although Bashkir elites began to swear allegiance to Ivan IV shortly after the fall of the Khanate of Kazan, their experience differed greatly from Kazan's. Moscow's violent conquest of Kazan Khanate took place shortly after Grand Prince Ivan IV had been newly crowned "tsar," and the Russian Orthodox Church deemed that conquest an Orthodox one. For 170 years, Bashkiria remained too distant for Muscovite power to conquer militarily. So, Moscow did much to integrate the Kazan region into the empire in the period 1552–1671 but did not even really try to integrate Bashkiria until the 1730s.[9] Kazan featured institutions characteristic of the empire's core, such as service landholding and conscription, serfdom, and the head tax, beginning in the 1720s while Bashkiria did not. As late as the twentieth century, Kazan society was considered more "black"—influenced by church clergy—than Ufa society. The Bashkir estate was more like that of another neighbor, the Cossacks. Before 1865, both Bashkirs and Cossacks exchanged military service for land rights, and until the suppression of the Pugachev uprising, Bashkirs and Cossacks fought side by side. The greater cultural distance between the imperial center and Bashkirs than between the imperial center and the Cossacks had already become crucial in the eighteenth century, however.

If regions to the west of Bashkiria, such as Kazan, were fully integrated into the empire's core, areas to Bashkiria's east and south, Siberia and Turkestan, were not. The latter two regions, with their vast spaces and relatively sparse populations, acquired distinctive legal status starting in 1822 with the Statute on Inorodtsy, or aliens. Administration of the Bashkir estate was similar in some ways to that specified for the settled and nomadic inorodtsy with respect to clan administration and landholding. But the military obligations borne by members of the Bashkir estate differed substantially, especially after 1798. Military service made it possible for some men of the Bashkir estate to leave it to join the nobility, and Muslim nobles not from the Bashkir estate served as an elite as well. Although Siberia and the Kazakh steppe had nobles in state service and Kazakh sultans received noble status, noble landowning never took root in these regions, which meant they were not drawn into the culture of the imperial capitals as Bashkiria was. A noble elite was notably absent in Siberia. The noble elite in Baskiria figured prominently in the region's future when Great Reforms were introduced to Bashkiria but not to Siberia.

To the south of Bashkiria, in 1844, a Statute on the Administration of the Orenburg Kirgiz, or Kazakhs as they are now called, showed differences both from Siberian inorodtsy and from Bashkirs. Unlike the Bashkir estate, Kazakhs were not subject to conscription, and the Ministry of Foreign Affairs had jurisdiction over their land. Native courts had a more prominent role. In 1868, new laws specified that all land occupied by Kazakhs was state-owned and given to them for collective usage, which differed from Bashkir hereditary landownership.[10] Unlike the Siberian inorodtsy, Kazakh sultans and heads of Kazakh *auls* were appointed by the government and subordinated to the Border Commission in Orenburg.

When imperial forces reached farther into Central Asia in the 1860s and that region was administered as Turkestan, what Vladimir Bobrovnikov calls "military-popular" governance was the norm.[11] Russian military governors administered, but all matters "not having a political character" were granted to "those elected from among the people (*narod*) itself, applying to it customs and morals."[12] The authority of the OMEA was not extended to Central Asia. As Alexander Morrison has pointed out, such regions remained under a "militarized administration" until the end of the empire.[13] In Turkestan, imperial officials interfered relatively little in local life and showed much less inclination to integrate the local population into the pattern of administration prevalent in the empire's core.

Imperial officials did not make legal status and landholding in Bashkiria just like that in the empire's core, nor did Bashkiria's institutional arrangements differ from those in the empire's core as greatly as those in areas to its east and south. By the nineteenth century, Bashkiria had a noble elite much like that of Kazan, but with many more Muslim nobles. Taxation and conscription of Bashkirs differed from that of the population of Kazan until the 1870s. Bashkiria marked the easternmost movement of landowning nobles and the easternmost non-Russian, non-Russian-Orthodox population that, by the 1870s, imperial officials considered sufficiently loyal and capable to fight for the tsar. These differences show the great variety of administrative arrangements that persisted in the empire's east well into the twentieth century. The empire remained a space where imperial officials governed a diverse population in different ways.

THE RUSSIAN EMPIRE: EAST AND WEST

Scholars have identified different patterns of imperial expansion in the empire's east and west, and the imperial center's relationship with local elites is central to such analyses.[14] In all parts of the empire, however, imperial officials sought to lure local non-Russian elites to the service of the tsar, often while simultaneously threatening or actually employing force. As Karen Barkey points out in her comparative observations on the Ottoman and Russian Empires, in the Russian Empire "the service nobility, which was relatively open to newcomers, established a tradition of incorporation into the state elite that the state could then use as its bargaining tool."[15] Strategies for integration are best conceived as a continuum of force and reward. The concept of bargained incorporation can help us understand empire building in the east and the west as long as we keep in mind that the bargain was not between equals and often involved the threat of, or actual recourse to, costly force when a bargain remained elusive. Imperial officials sought to win over local elites so as to minimize the need for such force.[16]

The key difference between the empire's east and its west, then, was one not of strategy but of geopolitical context. The Russian Empire lacked major rival states in the east until the distant Chinese border. In the west, Russia faced nothing but well-armed rivals, including, at various times, the Ottoman Empire, Poland-Lithuania, Sweden, Prussia, the Habsburg monarchy, France, and a united Germany. In the east, violence could be devastating to local populations in Kazan and Bashkiria, but the lack of large states with powerful militaries meant that large-scale violence needed to be applied only once; after that, violence was employed only episodically and at lower levels. The presence of great power rivals in the west meant that individual servitors had a richer choice of sovereigns to whom they might choose to be loyal. This meant that both extremes of incorporation were practiced. Bargains offered in the western borderlands were more generous than in the east. Individual servitors such as Baltic Germans could rise higher in the imperial bureaucracy in greater numbers than Muslims from the east, and places such as the Baltics, Finland, and even Poland until the 1860s could retain more distinctive social and political systems.

When a bargain could not be struck, however, violence in borderland territories resulted. By the nineteenth century, nationalism in the empire's west made bargains increasingly difficult to achieve. Already in the 1830s, imperial officials pursued repressive measures with respect to Catholicism and Judaism. Force replaced bargained incorporation in such events as the Polish Uprising of 1863 and in the violent suppression of the Revolution of 1905, which was more intense than unrest in the east. Aggressive Russian nationalists who held sway in the southwestern borderlands were much scarcer in Bashkiria.[17] The mass, anti-Semitic populism characteristic of Kiev and Odessa had no anti-Islamic equivalent in Bashkiria.[18] While similar processes were at work in the empire's east and west, different contexts produced different outcomes. In the twentieth century, Russia's western borderlands became a "shatterzone of empire."[19] European Russia's eastern frontier did not.

THE RUSSIAN EMPIRE IN A WORLD OF EMPIRES

Bashkiria's changing place within the empire reflected changes in Russia's place among the world's empires. Before the reign of Peter I (1692–1725), the Muscovite state in Bashkiria was very much a Eurasian empire like its predecessors. A pattern of distinctive administrative arrangements for settled and nomadic peoples was common as far east as China, where the Qing Dynasty created a "banner" for governance of nomadic peoples that drew on Mongol influences also evident in Bashkiria.[20] Only with Ivan Kirilov's effort in the 1730s to build Orenburg as the forward position for a Russian empire in Asia did explicit comparisons with European empires become prominent. In the 1730s, Kirilov believed Orenburg could do for Russia what Batavia had done for the Dutch, and he stated a desire to avoid in the steppe the violence and desolation that Spanish empire building had done to the New World.[21] Thereafter, Russian imperial officials would measure their empire against European models. Elite understandings of the empire as European reached their apogee under Catherine II and continued under her son and grandsons. The result was an emphasis on ideas of religious toleration, expressed throughout the empire in Catherine's 1773 Decree on Toleration and locally in the opening of the Orenburg Muhammadan Ecclesiastical Assembly in 1789. These were roughly contemporaneous with Joseph II's more categorical Patent of Toleration of 1781. Toleration made possible in both the Habsburg monarchy and the Russian Empire the formal recognition of nondominant religious institutions, which Andreas Kappeler describes as a movement toward "milletization," the Ottoman practice that allowed non-Islamic religious communities to govern their own religious affairs in exchange for the payment of taxes that members of the dominant faith, Muslims, did not pay.[22] At the same time, the French military and administrative structure became a model for Russia and its neighbors.[23] Bashkirs' militarized administration reflected the militarization of government that Russia's emperors drew from Napoleonic France.

The Russian military defeat at the hands of the Ottomans, French, and British in the Crimean War, 1853–1856, however, revealed the distance between Russia and its European rivals. This military failure, against the backdrop of a

European economic and technological surge, changed Russian officials' perception of the empire's standing with respect to Europe. European countries would still serve as models to which Russia would aspire, but Russia would have to reform in order to present itself as European. Russia joined the Ottomans and Habsburgs in playing catch-up with Europeans. All three empires undertook substantial reforms in the mid-nineteenth century. Confronted with revolution in 1848, the Habsburg emperor divided his empire into what amounted to a Hungarian half and an Austrian half, with only his person, a common treasury, a common army, and a foreign ministry uniting them. The emperor also emancipated the Jews. In 1856, Ottoman sultan Abdülmecid I declared all subjects legal equals regardless of religion and reformed the empire's courts to reflect European models. In 1876, his successor, Sultan Abdülhamid II, declared all subjects to be Ottoman citizens, issued a constitution, and convoked a parliament.

The Russian Empire's response to the European challenge was not as extensive as those of the Habsburgs and Ottomans. The Russian emperors never granted a form of autonomy to half of the empire or emancipated the Jews, as Franz Joseph II did. Nicholas II only reluctantly created all-imperial representative institutions and issued a sort of constitution, "Fundamental Laws," in the wake of the Revolution of 1905, decades after the Ottomans and the Habsburgs had. Yet the Great Reforms had powerful effects on Russian imperial rule. Ufa Province received nearly all the Great Reforms as well as the reform of Bashkir status in 1863. These shifted the region to civilian rule and provided ways for locals of all estates and religious identifications to participate in imperial institutions. In Bashkiria, reform-era policy on Bashkir land emphasized the importance of property much as France did in Algeria, to the detriment of the local population in both cases.

The Russian response also differed from the Ottoman and Habsburg ones in that it was a dual one: Russian imperial officials sought to emulate European empires both in their metropoles and in their distant colonies. In their European metropoles, European states sought to make their populations more homogenous and better connect their populations to authority. By doing so, states could mobilize their populations to achieve the greatest state power. Toward such an end, in 1912, Sergei Witte argued for what he called a "national (*natsional'nogo*) state of a certain type" that would increase Russia's power. Witte offered Germany's chancellor Otto von Bismarck as a "true nationalist": a leader who had created a state featuring "religious toleration with respect to non-predominant confessions, even non-Christian, equality of all citizens independent of religious confession and origins, the establishment of relations of the government to all citizens, and of [citizens] among themselves on the basis of stable and identical laws for all." This type of nationalism was the "highest manifestation of love and loyalty to a state."[24] Witte was less impressed by the nationalism of the Ottoman Empire, which he considered more a nationalism of passion and fear than one that increased the state's power. The Ottoman Empire had lost mostly non-Islamic lands in Europe and non-Turkic ones in the Middle East even before the 1908 Young Turk Revolution and became correspondingly more Islamic and more aggressively Turkic at its core.[25] Its peripheries either became independent or became part of other states. After the 1860s, the core of the Russian Empire would be subject to reform in a generally European direction. It remained to be seen which type of nationalism would prevail—one more inclusive and focused on state power or one less inclusive and aimed at specifically Russian greatness.

By contrast, when Russian imperial officials addressed Central Asia, Siberia, and the Far East, they would do so in a manner similar to the way British, French, and German officials regarded their colonies in Africa and Asia.[26] Native populations in Russia's east would remain foreign in important respects, perceived as racially different and unsuited for reformed institutions. In 1865, Russian diplomats presented the conquest of Central Asia to Europe as part of a civilizing mission similar to that of the British in India. Imperial officials did not deem Central Asian men or those of non-Slavic origin in the Far East sufficiently reliable to bear arms for the empire. Military officers would bear the burden of many of the obligations that fell on zemstvos in the empire's core. This type of military rule remained characteristic of much of the empire.[27]

In essence, the Russian Empire embodied at once and in adjacent spaces two forms of governance, what Adeeb Khalid has identified as that of "modern overseas colonial empires" and of "modern mobilizational states." The former were based on the "*perpetuation* of difference between rulers and the ruled," while the latter "tended to homogenize populations in order to attain universal goals."[28] Bashkiria was located geographically just at the point where the two forms of governance met. Bashkiria would be in the European core, but just barely. That is, Bashkiria received nearly all the empire's Great Reforms, plus its own "Great Reform"—the Statute on Bashkirs—by 1875, while regions to Bashkiria's east and southeast would not receive them until much later, if at all.[29] Bashkiria experienced neither the full drive for homogeneity of a European mobilizational state nor the effort to perpetuate difference characteristic of European colonial empires. The distinctive character of the region's movement from Muscovy's eastern borderlands to European Russia makes clear the relevance until 1917 of the conception of Russia as an empire in which distinctive status groups, religious confessions, and nationalities could have particularistic relationships to state authority. After the turn of the twentieth century, leading ministers such as Sergei Witte and Petr Stolypin worked to reduce differences in status among the emperor's subjects. The profusion of special committees and congresses they and others organized on issues such as education and religion after 1905 indicated an effort to systematize and regularize relations with the empire's many diverse regions. But these efforts came in the empire's last decade and marked the limit of efforts to create a national state.

FROM RUSSIAN EMPIRE TO SOVIET UNION

The fall of Nicholas II set in motion forces that resulted in the creation of the Bashkir Autonomous Republic in 1919. In 1917, a fissure in Bashkiria between those who identified with the Kazan Tatars and those who traced their origins to Bashkir tribes came into the open. Bashkir differences from Tatars were clearly marked in the minds of local nationalist elites, even though the Tatar language may have been very close to that which most Bashkirs spoke, Bashkirs and Tatars practiced Islam, and Tatar was the written language of local Muslims in 1917. Muslims who looked toward Kazan advocated cultural autonomy within a democratic Russian state for the empire's Muslims, who in their view formed a cultural-religious community that should have its own legislative, executive, and judicial organizations. Supporters of this view, such as Gumer Teregulov, a former Ufa zemstvo educational activist, believed that organizing all the empire's Muslims would best preserve Muslim strength. They feared that territorial autonomy would produce isolated and politically weak national groups.[30] By contrast, local Bashkir leaders were among the most vocal proponents of territorial autonomy. Akhmed-Zeki Validov argued that there was "not a Muslim nation in Russia."[31] For Bashkir leaders such as Validov, territorial autonomy meant that Bashkir land would be in their political control.[32] No action was taken on the autonomy question before the Bolshevik seizure of power in October 1917, however.

After the Bolshevik seizure of power in October 1917, Bashkiria became a battleground between "Red" Bolshevik and "White" anti-Bolshevik forces. The city of Ufa changed hands four times during the Civil War. Bashkir leader Validov first sided with the Whites. On November 8, 1917, Validov and Sharaf A. Manatov convoked a Bashkir national assembly (*kuraltai*) to declare the territorial autonomy of "Greater Bashkiria," including most of Orenburg and Ufa Provinces and parts of Simbirsk, Samara, Perm, and Viatka Provinces. Governor Perovskii's effort to create a Bashkir style of architecture in the 1830s had clearly succeeded—the *kuraltai* convened in Perovskii's caravanserai near Orenburg. Orenburg fell to Bolshevik forces in January 1918, however, and Whites under Admiral Kolchak turned against Bashkir autonomy in late 1918. Validov began negotiations with the Bolsheviks. In March 1919, a Bashkir nationalist–

Bolshevik agreement resulted in the formation of the Autonomous Soviet Bashkir Republic, the first such constituent of the Russian Federation.[33] This Bashkir Republic was centered in Sterlitamak County in the south of what had been Ufa Province.[34]

Validov soon grew frustrated with the Bolshevik government and especially with its local officials, who saw in the Bashkir national movement former White forces and possibly future enemies. In June 1920, members of Validov's Bashkir government did what local elites had done centuries before when they came into conflict with Russian authorities: they disappeared into the Urals, where a Bashkir insurgency had begun, or fled to Central Asia to continue the struggle for Muslim territorial autonomy.[35] The Bashkir Republic that formed late in 1920 contained few Bashkir leaders, and Bashkirs were a minority of the population.[36] A new "Little Bashkiria," incorporating what had been Ufa, Belebei, Zlatoust, and Birsk Counties of the old Ufa Province, became the Bashkir Autonomous Republic in 1922, with the city of Ufa as its capital. The Bashkir Republic became part of the Soviet Union upon its formation in 1924.[37] The Bashkir Republic's leadership did not remain Russian and Tatar for long. The policy of nativization, or *korenizatsiia*, in the 1920s and early 1930s increased the Bashkir presence in local institutions.[38] The Bashkir Autonomous Republic provided a context for the elaboration of a Bashkir culture. The republic developed a Bashkir literary language and culture and disseminated it through dictionaries, textbooks, newspapers, and histories.[39] The autonomous republic's population remained predominantly non-Bashkir, however.[40]

Bashkiria's prerevolutionary elites influenced subsequent developments in the Bashkir Autonomous Republic and in the Soviet Union as a whole.[41] Certainly, even a superficial examination of elites indicates considerable change after 1917. High-level officials in the local administration and educational district were the first to depart. Noblemen active in public institutions were next.[42] Lower-level zemstvo activists and staff members had a different experience of Soviet power. Ufa's zemstvo professionals, accustomed to zemstvo conceptions of the empire as one composed of national groups united around supranational, enlightened values, took positions in the new Bolshevik regime. Mirsaid Sultan-Galiev, a county director of non-Russian education for the Ufa zemstvo, became the most influential Muslim in the early Soviet period. In 1920, Joseph Stalin promoted Sultan-Galiev to membership in the Small Collegium of the Commissariat of Nationalities, and Sultan-Galiev became an editor of the commissariat's publication *Zhizn' natsional'nostei* (The life of the nationalities).[43] Alexander Tsiurupa, a statistician for the Ufa zemstvo (1897–1901) and agronomist (1905–1917), became people's commissar of food supply in Lenin's government in 1918 and deputy chairman of the Council of People's Commissars,

Sovnarkom (1921–1928).[44] Closer to home, Mikhail I. Obukhov, the head of the provincial zemstvo's education department during the First World War, held a similar position in Ufa during the 1920s.[45] Even some Muslim religious figures managed to work with the new regime. Rizaetdin Fakhretdinov, a former judge of the OMEA, became head of the OMEA's successor, the Ecclesiastical Administration for the Muslims of Russia and Siberia.[46]

Zemstvo professionals and other members of the local intelligentsia could initially work effectively in the Soviet Union, because the province's zemstvos tended to be more left-leaning than those elsewhere in the empire. Moreover, the nationality policies of the early Soviet period would not have seemed odd or unusual to them. The classification of the population by nationality had precedents in the late imperial period. The design and management of programs for non-Russians by people of the same nationality had already become a standard zemstvo practice. Bolsheviks greatly expanded the publication of materials in native languages begun before 1917. In many respects the Bolsheviks took precedents from the imperial period and built upon them, sometimes in ways inconceivable under the Old Regime.[47] The Soviet Union bore the imprint of its imperial predecessor and, in particular, of local elites in Bashkiria who sought to create a state united by principles other than ethnic nationality.

Bashkiria's imprint on successors to the Russian Empire was only partial, of course. By 1917, Bashkiria represented only one part of a massive empire. Narrating the engagement of Turkic, Islamic people with a self-consciously Slavic, Russian Orthodox ruler and his officials from the sixteenth century to the early twentieth century reveals a constant process of debate, conflict, and accommodation regarding how to understand and order people and the territory in which they lived. All distinctive regions, lands, and social groups in the empire were involved in similar processes. The result was the integration of peoples and regions in diverse ways. The case of a sparsely populated territory on the eastern edge of the Muscovite state is very indicative of this process, revealing the threads of empire that sustained a self-consciously imperial Russia for more than two centuries. The case also provides insight into what happened when these threads holding the empire frayed and snapped. By 1917, imperial officials no longer sought the loyalty of all and began to exclude Turkic and Muslim leaders from Bashkiria's elite. All types of residents of Bashkiria pursued new principles on which to build a political order. The result was a very turbulent three-quarters of a century. Nonetheless, Bashkiria's incorporation into the Russian Empire left a powerful legacy, one still evident when Bashkirs declared the sovereignty of Bashkortostan within the framework of the Russian Federation in 1990.

NOTES

INTRODUCTION

1. Petr Koropachinskii, "O nashei gazete," *Ufimskaia zemskaia gazeta*, no. 1 (March 1, 1906): 7.

2. RGADA, f. 16, op. 1, d. 934, ch. 5, ll. 81–82, cited in Danil D. Azamatov, *Orenburgskoe magometanskoe dukhovnoe sobranie v kontse XVIII–XIX vv.* (Ufa: Gilem, 1999), 26.

3. Some exceptions include Michael Khodarkovsky's work, which examines the diplomacy involved in getting steppe peoples to swear allegiance to the tsar and focuses on Kalmyks, Kazakhs, and the Caucasus. See *Where Two Worlds Met: The Russian State and the Kalmyk Nomads, 1600–1771* (Ithaca, N.Y.: Cornell University Press, 1992); *Russia's Steppe Frontier: The Making of a Colonial Empire, 1500–1800* (Bloomington: Indiana University Press, 2002); and *Bitter Choices: Loyalty and Betrayal in the Russian Conquest of the North Caucasus* (Ithaca, N.Y.: Cornell University Press, 2011). Mikhail Dolbilov addresses loyalty in relation to religious faith and nationality in his *Russkii krai, chuzhaia vera: Etnokonfessional'naia politika imperii v Litve i Belorussii pri Aleksandre II* (Moscow: Novoe Literaturnoe Obozrenie, 2010). Article-length treatments include Stephen Velychenko's work on service in the Western borderlands, "Identity, Loyalty, and Service in Imperial Russia," *The Russian Review* 54, no. 2 (April 1995): 188–208; and Aleksandr Kamenskii, "Poddanstvo, loial'nost', patriotizm v imperskom diskurse Rossii XVIII v.: K postanovke problemy," *Ab Imperio* 4 (2006): 59–99. Notable examples regarding other empires include Clifford Ando, *Imperial Ideology and Provincial Loyalty in the Roman Empire* (Berkeley: University of California Press, 2000), and Laurence Cole and Daniel Unowsky, eds., *The Limits of Loyalty: Imperial Symbolism, Popular Allegiances, and State Patriotism in the Late Habsburg Monarchy* (New York: Berghahn Books, 2007).

4. Khodarkovsky, *Russia's Steppe Frontier*, 44.

5. Max Weber, *Economy and Society: An Outline of Interpretive Sociology*, vol. 1, ed. Guenther Roth and Claus Wittich (Berkeley: University of California Press, 1978), 214.

6. R. J. W. Evans, *The Making of the Habsburg Monarchy, 1550–1700* (Oxford: Oxford University Press, 1979), 307.

7. Albert O. Hirschman's work made loyalty an important concept in the social sciences. As Jeremy Adelman and other commentators have indicated, however, it is not the best-elaborated of the three key concepts he uses. Albert O. Hirschman, *Exit, Voice, and Loyalty: Responses to Decline in Firms, Organizations, and States* (Cambridge, Mass.: Harvard University Press, 1970), 76–105; Jeremy Adelman, *Worldly Philosopher: The Odyssey of Albert O. Hirschman* (Princeton, N.J.: Princeton University Press, 2013), 445–446. See also Keith Dowding, Peter John, Thanos Mergoupis, and Mark van Vugt, "Exit, Voice, and Loyalty: Analytical and Empirical Developments," *European Journal of Political Research* 37 (2000): 469–495.

8. William G. Rosenberg, "The Problems of Empire in Imperial Russia," *Ab Imperio* 3 (2005): 453–465.

9. "Differentiated governance" comes from Jane Burbank and Mark von Hagen, "Coming into Territory: Uncertainty and Empire," in *Russian Empire: Space, People, Power, 1700–1930*, ed. Jane Burbank, Mark von Hagen, and Anatolyi Remnev (Bloomington: Indiana University Press, 2007), 25.

10. Lieven uses the term "dilemmas of empire." Dominic Lieven, *Empire: The Russian Empire and Its Rivals* (New Haven, Conn.: Yale University Press, 2000), xi. Frederick Cooper insightfully explicates the nature of this dilemma in "Empire Multiplied: A Review Essay," CSSH 46, no. 2 (2004): 267. Karen Barkey addresses some similar issues using a different vocabulary. See Karen Barkey, *Empire of Difference: The Ottomans in Comparative Perspective* (Cambridge: Cambridge University Press, 2008), 1–27. Ronald Grigor Suny emphasizes hierarchy, inequality, and difference in his analysis of empire. See Ronald Grigor Suny, "The Empire Strikes Out: Imperial Russia, 'National' Identity, and Theories of Empire," in *A State of Nations: Empire and Nation-Making in the Age of Lenin and Stalin*, ed. Ronald Grigor Suny and Terry Martin (Oxford: Oxford University Press, 2001), 25–26.

11. Charles Tilly, "How Empires End," in *After Empire: Multiethnic Societies and Nation-Building: The Soviet Union and the Russian, Ottoman, and Habsburg Empires*, ed. Karen Barkey and Mark von Hagen (Boulder, Colo.: Westview, 1997), 1–11.

12. See Ann Laura Stoler and Carole McGranahan, "Introduction: Refiguring Imperial Terrains," in *Imperial Formations*, ed. Ann Laura Stoler, Carole McGranahan, and Peter C. Perdue (Santa Fe and Oxford: School of Advanced Research Press and James Currey, 2007), 3–44; and Ilya Gerasimov, Sergey Glebov, Jan Kusber, Marina Mogilner, and Alexander Semyonov, "New Imperial History and the Challenges of Empire," in *Empire Speaks Out*, ed. Ilya Gerasimov, Jan Kusber, and Alexander Semyonov (Leiden: Brill, 2009), 3–32.

13. Richard S. Wortman, *Scenarios of Power: Myth and Ceremony in Russian Monarchy*, vols. 1 and 2 (Princeton, N.J.: Princeton University Press, 1995, 2000).

14. On the tendency "to reduce the uneven heterogeneity of imperial experience to a more manageable, one-dimensional diversity of nationalities, regions of empire, or confessions," see Gerasimov et al., "New Imperial History," 24.

15. To cite only some representative works on these themes that have appeared since the collapse of the Soviet Union: Aleksandr Polunov, *Pod vlast'iu ober-prokuror: Gosudarstvo i tserkov v epokhu Aleksandra III* (Moscow: AIRO-XX, 1996); Adeeb Khalid, *The Politics of Muslim Cultural Reform: Jadidism in Central Asia* (Berkeley: University of California Press, 1998); Allen J. Frank, *Islamic Historiography and 'Bulghar' Identity among the Tatars and Bashkirs of Russia* (Leiden: Brill, 1998); Michael Kemper, *Sufis und Gelehrte in Tatarien und Baschkirien, 1789–1889: Der islamische Diskurs unter russischer Herrschaft* (Berlin: K. Schwarz, 1998); Christian Noack, *Muslimischer Nationalismus im russischen Reich: Nationsbildung und Nationalbewegung bei Tataren und Baschkiren, 1861–1917* (Stuttgart: Franz Steiner Verlag, 2000); Robert Geraci, *Window on the East: National and Imperial Identities in Late Tsarist Russia* (Ithaca, N.Y.: Cornell University Press, 2001); Virginia Martin, *Law and Custom in the Steppe: The Kazakhs of the Middle Horde and Russian Colonialism in the Nineteenth Century* (Richmond, Surrey: Routledge Curzon, 2001); Sviatoslav Kaspe, *Imperiia i modernizatsiia: Obshchaia model' i rossiiskaia spetsifika* (Moscow: Rosspen, 2001); Khodarkovsky, *Russia's Steppe Frontier*; Vladimir O. Bobrovnikov, *Musul'mane Severnogo Kavkaza: Obychai, pravo, nasilie. Ocherki*

po istorii i etnografii prava Nagornogo Dagestana (Moscow: Vostochnaia Literatura-RAN, 2002); Paul Werth, *At the Margins of Orthodoxy: Mission, Governance, and Confessional Politics in Russia's Volga-Kama Region, 1827–1905* (Ithaca, N.Y.: Cornell University Press, 2002); Nicholas Breyfogle, *Heretics and Colonizers: Forging Russia's Empire in the South Caucasus* (Ithaca, N.Y.: Cornell University Press, 2005); Robert D. Crews, *For Prophet and Tsar: Islam and Empire in Russia and Central Asia* (Cambridge, Mass.: Harvard University Press, 2006); Jeff Sahadeo, *Russian Colonial Society in Tashkent, 1865–1923* (Bloomington: Indiana University Press, 2007); Il'dus Zagidullin, *Islamskie instituty v rossiiskoi imperii: Mechety v evropeiskoi chasti Rossii i Sibiri* (Kazan: Tatarskoe Knizhnoe Izdatel'stvo, 2007); Vera Tolz, *Russia's Own Orient: The Politics of Identity and Oriental Studies in the Late Imperial and Early Soviet Periods* (Oxford: Oxford University Press, 2011); Marina Mogilner, *Homo Imperii: A History of Physical Anthropology in Russia* (Lincoln: University of Nebraska Press, 2013); and Elena Campbell, *The Muslim Question and Russian Imperial Governance* (Bloomington: Indiana University Press, 2015).

16. Influential interpretations of the estate system include those by Gregory Freeze, "The *Soslovie* (Estate) Paradigm and Russian Social History," *American Historical Review* 91, no. 1 (February 1986): 11–36; Elise Kimerling Wirtschafter, *Social Identity in Imperial Russia* (DeKalb: Northern Illinois University Press, 1997); Michael Confino, "The *Soslovie* (Estate) Paradigm: Reflections on Some Open Questions," CMR 49, no. 4 (October–December 2008): 681–699; Laurie Manchester, *Holy Fathers, Secular Sons: Clergy, Intelligentsia, and the Modern Self in Imperial Russia* (DeKalb: Northern Illinois University Press, 2008); David L. Ransel, "Implicit Questions in Michael Confino's Essay: Corporate State and Vertical Relationships," CMR 51, no. 2 (2010): 195–210; and Alison Smith, *For the Common Good and Their Own Well-Being: The System of Social Estates in Imperial Russia* (Oxford: Oxford University Press, 2014). None of these influential works in English addresses in a sustained way how those who neither spoke Russian nor practiced Russian Orthodoxy fit into the estate system. Natalia A. Ivanova and Valentina P. Zheltova's comprehensive *Soslovnoe obshchestvo rossiiskoi imperii (XVIII–nachalo XX veka)* (Moscow: Novyi Khronograf, 2009), addresses the category of inorodtsy.

17. The literature on estate groups in the Russian Empire is vast. The work most relevant here addresses Jews, inorodtsy, the non-Russian nobility, and Cossacks. Works that address Jews as an estate group include John Klier, *Russia Gathers Her Jews: The Origins of the "Jewish Question" in Russia, 1772–1825* (DeKalb: Northern Illinois University Press, 1986); Michael Stanislawski, *Tsar Nicholas I and the Jews: The Transformation of Jewish Society in Russia, 1825–1855* (Philadelphia, Pa.: Jewish Publication Society of America, 1983); Benjamin Nathans, *Beyond the Pale: The Jewish Encounter with Late Imperial Russia* (Berkeley: University of California Press, 2002); Olga Litvak, *Conscription and the Search for Modern Russian Jewry* (Bloomington: Indiana University Press, 2006); Olga Minkina, *"Syny Rakhili": Evreiskie deputaty v rossiiskoi imperii, 1772–1825* (Moscow: Novoe Literaturnoe Obozrenie, 2011); and Eugene M. Avrutin, *Jews and the Imperial State: Identification Politics in Tsarist Russia* (Ithaca, N.Y.: Cornell University Press, 2010). The category of inorodtsy is examined in Yuri Slezkine, *Arctic Mirrors: Russia and the Small Peoples of the North* (Ithaca, N.Y.: Cornell University Press, 1994); John Slocum, "Who, and When, Were the *Inorodtsy?* The Evolution of the Category of 'Aliens' in Imperial Russia," *Russian Review* 57, no. 2 (April 1998): 173–190; Vladimir O.

Bobrovnikov, "Chto vyshlo iz proektov sozdaniia v Rossii *inorodtsev?* (otvet Dzhonu Slokumu iz musul'manskikh okrain imperii)," in *Poniatiia o Rossii: K istoricheskoi semantike imperskogo perioda,* vol. 1, ed. A. Miller, D. Sdvizhkov, and I. Shirle (Moscow: Novoe Literaturnoe Obozrenie, 2012), 259–291; Ivanova and Zheltova, *Soslovnoe obshchestvo,* 655–718; Kelly O'Neill addresses non-Russian nobles in Crimea. See Kelly O'Neill, "Rethinking Elite Integration: The Crimean Murzas and the Evolution of Russian Nobility," *CMR* 51, no. 2 (2010): 397–417. Some important work on Cossacks includes Shane O'Rourke, *Warriors and Peasants: The Don Cossacks in Late Imperial Russia* (New York: St. Martin's Press, 2000); and Brian J. Boeck, *Imperial Boundaries: Cossack Communities and Empire-Building in the Age of Peter the Great* (Cambridge: Cambridge University Press, 2009).

18. As Khairutdinov points out, a great many Muslim nobles in Ufa Province were "princes in peasant boots" whose level of wealth and culture made them live much more humbly than others of the noble estate. Ramil' Khairutdinov, "Tatarskaia feodal'naia znat' i rossiiskoe dvorianstvo: Problem integratsii na rubezhe XVIII–XIX vv.," in *Islam v tatarskom mire: Istoriia i sovremennost' (materialy mezhdunarodnogo simpoziuma, Kazan' 29 aprelia–1 maia 1996 g.),* ed. Rafael' Khakimov (Kazan: Panoramy-Forum, 1997), 87–90. Nonetheless, many had wealth, prestige, and access to the state that exceeded that of other subjects of the tsar. Kelly O'Neill shows that central authorities made it much more difficult for Turkic, Muslim subjects of the tsar to be recognized as nobles in the mid-nineteenth century than before. O'Neill, "Rethinking Elite Integration," 415–416.

19. Eric Hobsbawm, "Mass-Producing Traditions: Europe 1870–1914," in *The Invention of Tradition,* ed. Eric Hobsbawm and Terence Ranger (Cambridge: Cambridge University Press, 1983), 266.

20. Yanni Kotsonis, "'Face-to-Face': The State, the Individual, and the Citizen in Russian Taxation, 1863–1917," *Slavic Review* 63, no. 2 (Summer 2004): 222.

21. Marc Raeff, "Patterns of Imperial Russian Policy toward the Nationalities," in *Soviet Nationality Problems,* ed. Edward Allworth (New York: Columbia University Press, 1971), 26.

22. In the nineteenth century and especially in the era of national unifications of Italy and Germany, imperial integration is typically labeled "Russification." Edward C. Thaden, for instance, used an influential typology of unplanned, administrative, and cultural Russification. Edward C. Thaden, "Introduction," in *Russification in the Baltic Provinces and Finland, 1855–1914,* ed. Edward C. Thaden (Princeton, N.J.: Princeton University Press, 1981), 8–9. In the early modern period, Michael Khodarkovsky sees the encounter with native peoples on the eastern steppe as a three-part process of identification as an Other, swearing of allegiance, and religious conversion as the "ultimate rite of incorporation." Michael Khodarkovsky, "'Ignoble Savages and Unfaithful Subjects': Constructing Non-Christian Identities in Early Modern Russia," in *Russia's Orient: Imperial Borderlands and Peoples, 1700–1917,* ed. Daniel R. Brower and Edward J. Lazzerini (Bloomington: Indiana University Press, 1997), 10. Elsewhere, Khodarkovsky emphasizes Russia's expansion as a deliberate and consistent process of "centralization and homogenization." Khodarkovsky, *Russia's Steppe Frontier,* 228–229. For a contrasting view, stressing the accommodation of difference in the empire and how difference became an "imperial asset," see especially Jane Burbank and Frederick Cooper, *Empires in World*

History: Power and the Politics of Difference (Princeton, N.J.: Princeton University Press, 2010), 185–218, 251–286. Willard Sunderland stresses the colonial nature of Russian expansion but also emphasizes its ambiguities and complexities. Willard Sunderland, *Taming the Wild Field: Colonization and Empire on the Russian Steppe* (Ithaca, N.Y.: Cornell University Press, 2004). Matthew Romaniello emphasizes the "extremely slow, contingent, and heavily negotiated process" by which Kazan became part of the empire. Matthew P. Romaniello, *The Elusive Empire: Kazan and the Creation of Russia, 1552–1671* (Madison: University of Wisconsin Press, 2012), 15.

23. Mark Bassin, "Geographies of Imperial Identity," in *The Cambridge History of Russia, vol. II, 1689–1917,* ed. Dominic Lieven (Cambridge: Cambridge University Press, 2006), 55–63.

24. Alexander Etkind, *Internal Colonialism: Russia's Imperial Experience* (Cambridge: Polity Press, 2011). On the other hand, colonial policies that encouraged migration to Bashkiria were perceived differently by Russian migrants, who received land, than by Bashkirs, who lost it.

25. On variation in policy toward non-Russians, see Theodore Weeks, "Managing Empire: Tsarist Nationalities Policy," in *The Cambridge History of Russia,* vol. II, 27–44.

26. Jane Burbank, "The Rights of Difference: Law and Citizenship in the Russian Empire," in *Imperial Formations,* 80–81. On the persistence of imperial patterns of administration, see John LeDonne, "Building an Infrastructure of Empire in Russia's Eastern Theater, 1650s–1840s," *CMR* 47, no. 3 (July–September 2007): 581–608; and Alexander Morrison, "Metropole, Colony, and Citizenship in the Russian Empire," *Kritika: Explorations in Russian and Eurasian History* 13, no. 2 (Spring 2012): 327–364.

27. Nathans, *Beyond the Pale,* 11.

28. Andreas Kappeler, *The Russian Empire: A Multiethnic History,* trans. Alfred Clayton (Harlow: Longman, 2001); Geoffrey Hosking, *Russia: People and Empire, 1552–1917* (Cambridge, Mass.: Harvard University Press, 1997); Lieven, *Empire: The Russian Empire and Its Rivals*; Burbank and Cooper, *Empires in World History.*

29. In this respect, I follow the lead of Catherine Evtuhov's work on Nizhnii Novgorod but address the question of imperial diversity to a greater extent and consider a longer chronology. Catherine Evtuhov, *Portrait of a Russian Province: Economy, Society, and Civilization in Nineteenth-Century Nizhnii Novgorod* (Pittsburgh, Pa.: University of Pittsburgh Press, 2011).

30. Yuri Slezine's *Arctic Mirrors* and Willard Sunderland's *Taming the Wild Field* are notable exceptions.

31. Ronald Grigor Suny, *The Revenge of the Past: Nationalism, Revolution and the Collapse of the Soviet Union* (Stanford, Calif.: Stanford University Press, 1993), 23.

32. Andreas Kappeler, "Tsentr i elity periferii v gabsburgskoi, rossiiskoi, i osmanskoi imperiiakh (1700–1918)," *Ab Imperio* 2 (2007): 17–58.

33. Mikhail Avdeev, "Gory," *Otechestvennye zapiski* 79 (1851), cited in M. G. Rakhimkulov, comp., *Bashkiriia v russkoi literature,* vol. 1 (Ufa: Bashkirskoe Knizhnoe Izdatel'stvo, 1989), 203. Konstantin Thon (1774–1881) also designed the Church of Christ the Savior in Moscow, one of the most prominent and influential architectural projects of the nineteenth century.

34. R. G. Ganeev, V. V. Boltushkin, and R. G. Kuzeev, eds. *Istoriia Ufy: Kratkii ocherk* (Ufa: Bashkirskoe Knizhnoe Izdatel'stvo, 1981), 22.

35. Sergei T. Aksakov, *Sobranie sochinenii*, vol. 1 (Moscow: Gos. Izdatel'stvo Khu-dozhestvennoi Literatury, 1955), 83.

36. NA UNTS RAN, f. 22, op. 1, ed. khr. 2, ll. 7 ob.–8, dated February 8, 1904.

37. Avdeev, "Gory"; Aksakov, *Sobranie sochinenii*, 269–272; Mukhametsalim Umet-baev, "Po povodu iubileia Pushkina," *Ufimskie gubernskie vedomosti*, no. 109 (May 27, 1899): 1.

38. It took two centuries after Peter's reign for Bashkiria to become symbolically part of European Russia. Mark Bassin, "Russia between Europe and Asia: The Ideologi-cal Construction of Geographical Space," *Slavic Review* 50, no. 1 (Spring 1991): 1–17; and Charles Steinwedel, "How Bashkiria Became Part of European Russia, 1762–1881," in *Russian Empire: Space, People, and Power, 1700–1930*, ed. Jane Burbank, Mark von Ha-gen, and Anatolyi Remnev (Bloomington: Indiana University Press, 2007), 94–124.

39. Mustafa O. Tuna, "Imperial Russia's Muslims: Inroads of Modernity" (PhD dis-sertation, Princeton University, 2009), 162–185.

40. Peter Golden stresses the importance of Ugric sources for Bashkir ethnogenesis and their Kypchakization under Mongol influence in the thirteenth century and later, whereas Rail G. Kuzeev argues for the importance of the migration of Turkic-speaking people from Siberia and Central Asia. Peter B. Golden, *An Introduction to the History of the Turkic Peoples: Ethnogenesis and State-Formation in Medieval and Early Modern Eur-asia and the Middle East* (Wiesbaden: Otto Harrassowitz, 1992), 262–264, 397–399. Rail G. Kuzeev, *Proiskhozhdenie bashkirskogo naroda: Etnicheskii sostav, istoriia rasseleniia* (Moscow: Nauka, 1974).

41. Frank, *Islamic Historiography*, 42, 67.

42. Aislu B. Iunusova, *Islam v Bashkortostane* (Ufa: Ufimskii Poligrafkombinat, 1999), 23.

43. Bashkir and Tatar share about 96 percent of their words. Kuzeev, *Proiskhozdenie bashkirskogo naroda*, 475; Lars Johanson and Éva Ágnes Csato, eds., *The Turkic Lan-guages* (London: Routledge, 1998), 82, 283. Bashkirs of southern and eastern Bashkiria speak a dialect that is closer to Kazakh and Turkmen. This dialect serves as the basis of the Bashkir literary language. Frank, *Islamic Historiography*, 8–9.

44. Johanson and Csato, *The Turkic Languages*, 166–167.

45. The political organization of Bashkirs before 1230 is not entirely clear, but evidence from Arab and European writers suggests that a union of Bashkir clans existed under the leadership of a khan before the Mongol conquest. *Istoriia Bashkortostana s drevneishikh vremen do nashikh dnei, v dvukh tomakh, vol. 1: Istoriia Bashkortostana s drevneishikh vremen do kontsa XIX veka* (Ufa: Kitap, 2004), 62, 66.

46. David Sneath has called into question two of the fundamental concepts used to understand Central Eurasian societies, clan or *rod* and tribe or *plemia*, as having to do with nineteenth-century efforts to distance European state institutions from "back-ward" tribal and clan organization. Such terminology had great staying power in the region, however. David Sneath, "Tribe, *Ethnos*, Nation: Rethinking Evolutionist Social Theory and Representations of Nomadic Inner Asia," *Ab Imperio* 4 (2009): 80–109.

47. *Istoriia Bashkortostana*, 68–69.

48. Ural Kh. Rakhmatullin, *Naselenie bashkirii v XVII–XVIII vv. Voprosy formiro-vaniia nebashkirskogo naseleniia* (Moscow: Nauka, 1988), 131. David Sneath argues that the lack of blood connections among clan members was typical of nomadic inner Asia. Sneath, "Tribe, *Ethnos*, Nation," 92–93, 97, 100.

49. The origins and meaning of the term *teptiar* are controversial. As R. I. Iakupov and U. Kh. Rakhmatullin point out, the sources for a definitive conclusion regarding the term's origin are lacking. Rakhmatullin, *Naselenie bashkirii v XVII–XVIII vv.*, 202–204. R. I. Iakupov, "Teptiari: K istoriografii voprosa," in *Etnologicheskie issledovaniia v Bashkortostane: Sbornik statei*, ed. Il'dar Gabdrafikov (Ufa: UNTS RAN, 1994), 85–100. Iskhakov argues that Teptiars were of Tatar ethnicity and formed an estate group that drew close to Bashkirs but never completely separated from Tatars. Damir M. Iskhakov, *Istoricheskaia demografiia tatarskogo naroda (XVIII–nachalo XX vv.)* (Kazan: Akademiia Nauk Respubliki Tatarstan, 1993), 33–35.

50. D. M. Iskhakov, *Etnograficheskie gruppy tatar volgo-ural'skogo regiona* (Kazan: Akademiia Nauk Respubliki Tatarstan, 1993), 44–50; Il'dar Gabdrafikov, "Etnokul'turnye rezul'taty migratsionnykh protsessov v severo-zapadnoi Bashkirii (konets XVI–nach. XX v.)," in *Etnologicheskie issledovaniia v Bashkortostane*, 22–28; Dmitry Gorenburg, "Identity Change in Bashkortostan: Tatars into Bashkirs and Back," *Ethnic and Racial Studies* 22, no. 3 (May 1999): 554–580.

51. Iskhakov, *Istoricheskaia demografiia*, 102. R. G. Mukhamedova, *Tatary-mishari* (Moscow: Nauka, 1972), 1–32.

52. Golden, *An Introduction to the History of the Turkic Peoples*, 396–397.

53. Rail G. Kuzeev, comp. and ed., *Bashkirskie shezhere* (Ufa: Bashkirskoe Kniznoe Izdatel'stvo, 1960), 192. Rail G. Kuzeev, Ramil' M. Bulgakov, and Minlegali Kh. Nadergulov, comps. and eds., *Bashkirskie rodoslovnye* (Ufa: Kitap, 2002), 283, 359, 380, 405–407.

54. Gulnaz B. Azamatova, *Integratsiia natsional'nogo dvorianstva v rossiiskoe obshchestvo na primere roda Tevkelevykh* (Ufa: Gilem, 2008), 134.

55. Ivan V. Chernov, *Zametki po istorii orenburgskoi gubernii general-maiora I. V. Chernova* (Orenburg: Orenburgskaia Guberniia, 2007), 67; Ivan F. Blaramburg, *Vospominaniia*, trans. O. I. Zhigalina (Moscow: Nauka, 1978), 298–299.

56. Sergei R. Mintslov, *Ufa: Debri zhizni. Dnevnik 1910–1915* (Ufa: Bashkirskoe Knizhnoe Izdatel'stvo, 1992), 60.

1. STEPPE EMPIRE, 1552–1730

1. Bashkir chronicles may have arisen out of the exogamy of Bashkir clans and from the need to know one's ancestors in order to establish degrees of relation, often going back ten to fifteen generations. The chronicles must be used with great caution since they were frequently written down long after the events they describe. Rail G. Kuzeev, comp. and ed., *Bashkirskie shezhere* (Ufa: Bashkirskoe Knizhnoe Izdatel'stvo, 1960), 5–23.

2. Vadim V. Trepavlov, "'Dobrovol'noe vkhozhdenie v sostav Rossii': Torzhestvennye iubilei i istoricheskaia deistvitel'nost'," *Voprosy istorii* 11 (November 2007): 156. Bulat A. Aznabaev, *Integratsiia bashkirii v administrativnuiu struktury rossiiskogo gosudarstva (vtoraia polovina XVI–pervaia tret' XVIII vv.)* (Ufa: RIO Bashkirskii Gosudarstvennyi Universitet, 2005), 40–41.

3. Regarding internal and external tensions of the Nogai Horde, see Allen Frank, "The Western Steppe: Volga-Ural region, Siberia and the Crimea," in *The Cambridge History of Inner Asia: The Chinggisid Age*, ed. Nicola Di Cosmo, Allen J. Frank, and Peter B. Golden (Cambridge: Cambridge University Press, 2009), 243–244. Vadim V.

Trepavlov, "Nogai v Bashkirii, XV–XVII vv.," *Materialy i issledovaniia po istorii i etnologii Bashkortostana* 2 (1997): 15, 17.

4. The Min, Burzian, Kypchak, Usergan, and Tam'ian chronicles specify that they became subjects of Ivan because of the suffering and insults they received from the Nogai Horde. The Karagai-Tabyn chronicle suggests that tensions among clan members and the khan of Kazan caused them to support Ivan's forces in the struggle with Kazan. Kuzeev, *Bashkirskie shezhere*, 51–53, 71–74, 164–165. See also Abubakir N. Usmanov, *Prisoedinenie bashkirii k russkomu gosudarstvu* (Ufa: RIO Bashkirskoe Knizhnoe Izdatel'stvo, 1960), 86–94.

5. Jaroslaw Pelenski, *Russia and Kazan: Conquest and Imperial Ideology (1438–1560s)* (The Hague: Mouton, 1974), 225–226, 298–300.

6. Kuzeev, *Bashkirskie shezhere*, 111–117. The Burzian, Kypchak, Usergan, and Tam'ian chronicles describe Ivan as agreeing he would not subject Bashkirs to additional obligations without their agreement, not cause them suffering, and not "violate [their] religion." The Iurmat chronicle specifies 1561 as the year in which Muscovite emissaries circulated charters, and it uses similar language to describe them. Kuzeev, *Bashkirskie shezhere*, 29–30, 33–34, 75–76, 78–79, 195–196.

7. *Polnoe sobranie russkikh letopisei, vol. 13: Letopisnyi sbornik, imenuemyi patriarshei ili Nikonovskoi letopis'iu* (Moscow: Iazyki Russkoi Kul'tury, 2000[1904]), 221. The chronicle mentions the arrival of "Bashkirtsy," who, having "bowed their heads" (*dobiv chelom*), "paid iasak" in 1557 (282).

8. Trepavlov, "'Dobrovol'noe vkhozhdenie v sostave Rossii,'" 156. Lowell Tillett, *The Great Friendship: Soviet Historians on the Non-Russian Nationalities* (Chapel Hill: University of North Carolina Press, 1969), 79–80, 300. A 1933 pamphlet published by Petr Ishcherikov, before the "friendship of the peoples" became the official line of the Soviet state, declares the idea of "voluntary joining" of Bashkirs to the Muscovite state a "fairy tale." Ishcherikov emphasizes the coercive nature of the Bashkir entry into the Muscovite state. Petr Ishcherikov, *Ocherki iz istorii kolonizatsii Bashkortostana: Ot zavoevaniia Bashkortostana do epokhi raskhishcheniia bashkirskikh zemel'* (Ufa: Kitap, 2003[1933]), 5.

9. Kuzeev, *Bashkirskie shezhere*, 33.

10. See Rail G. Kuzeev, "O kharaktere prisoedineniia narodov volgo-ural'skogo regiona k russkomu gosudarstvu i nekotorye voprosy ikh srednevekovoi istorii," in *Etnologicheskie issledovaniia v Bashkortostane: sbornik statei*, ed. Il'dar M. Gabdrafikov (Ufa: UNTS RAN, 1994), 63–65.

11. Charles J. Halperin discusses the Nogai's use of "white prince" or "white tsar," arguing that the Nogai response to Muscovite expansion shows "how intimately connected Moscow was to the steppe world." Moscow accepted Nogai recognition, even though "it was not willing to assimilate such assertions into its own titulature, imperial genealogy, or, more broadly, political self-consciousness." Charles J. Halperin, "Ivan IV and Chinggis Khan," *Jahrbücher für Geschichte Osteuropas* 51, no. 4 (2003): 497.

12. Kuzeev, *Bashkirskie shezhere*, 29, 33, 75–76, 78–79, 195–196.

13. *Letopisnyi sbornik, imenuemyi patriarshei ili Nikonovskoi letopis'iu*, 221; Usmanov, *Prisoedinenie bashkirii*, 79. As Michael Khodarkovsky has argued, oaths nearly always meant something different to Muscovite officials than to natives. Moscow saw an oath of allegiance as a pledge of "eternal submission," rather than a peace treaty. Michael Khodarkovsky, *Russia's Steppe Frontier: The Making of a Colonial Empire, 1500–1800*

(Bloomington: Indiana University Press, 2002), 51–56. Soviet historians writing after World War II attributed great significance to the voluntary nature of the Bashkirs' joining (*prisoedinenie*) of the Russian Empire. See Tillett, *The Great Friendship*.

14. On the conquest of Kazan and its antecedents, see Matthew P. Romaniello, *The Elusive Empire: Kazan and the Creation of Russia, 1552–1671* (Madison: University of Wisconsin Press, 2012), 39–43.

15. Sergei Bogatyrev, "Reinventing the Russian Monarchy in the 1550s: Ivan the Terrible, the Dynasty, and the Church," *Slavonic and East European Review* 85, no. 2 (April 2007): 279.

16. William Craft Brumfield, *A History of Russian Architecture* (Seattle: University of Washington Press, 2004[1993]), 122–129.

17. Pelenski, *Russia and Kazan*, 272–273.

18. Romaniello, *The Elusive Empire*, 44–49; Matthew P. Romaniello, "Mission Delayed: The Russian Orthodox Church after the Conquest of Kazan," *Church History* 76, no. 3 (September 2007): 520–521, 539; Andreas Kappeler, *The Russian Empire: A Multiethnic History*, trans. Alfred Clayton (Harlow: Longman, 2001), 27.

19. Janet Martin, "Multiethnicity in Muscovy: A Consideration of the Christian and Muslim Tatars in the 1550s–1580s," *Journal of Early Modern History* 5, no. 1 (2001): 6–23.

20. I have in mind the nature of Muscovite rule in Bashkiria rather than the larger question of the extent to which Muscovite central institutions derived from Mongol or Kypchak Khanate precedents. On this issue, see Donald Ostrowski, *Muscovy and the Mongols: Cross-Cultural Influences on the Steppe Frontier, 1304–1589* (Cambridge: Cambridge University Press, 1998); Charles Halperin, *Russia and the Golden Horde: The Mongol Impact on Medieval Russian History* (Bloomington: Indiana University Press, 1987); and Halperin, "Ivan IV and Chinggis Khan," 481–497.

21. Richard Hellie translates *votchina* as "hereditary estate." I use "land" in order to communicate that Bashkirs owned their lands collectively rather than individually or by family groups. Richard Hellie, trans. and ed., *The Muscovite Law Code (Ulozhenie) of 1649*, pt. 1: *Text and Translation*, in *The Laws of Russia*, series I, vol. 3 (Irvine, Calif.: Charles Schlacks Jr., 1988), 121.

22. Karen Barkey, *Bandits and Bureaucrats: The Ottoman Route to State Centralization* (Ithaca, N.Y.: Cornell University Press, 1994), 9–11. Brian Boeck uses similar language when he identifies the "separate juridical existence" of the Cossacks, the Hetmanate (central Ukraine), and the Baltic German territories (Livonia and Estonia) as "separate deals." Brian J. Boeck, *Imperial Boundaries: Cossack Communities and Empire-Building in the Age of Peter the Great* (Cambridge: Cambridge University Press, 2009), 2.

23. Edward L. Keenan, "Muscovy and Kazan: Some Introductory Remarks on the Patterns of Steppe Diplomacy," *Slavic Review* 26, no. 4 (December 1967): 557–558.

24. Trepavlov, "Nogai v Bashkirii," 13.

25. Usmanov, *Prisoedinenie bashkirii*, 42.

26. Usmanov, *Prisoedinenie bashkirii*, 73–114. Aznabaev, *Integratsiia bashkirii*, 43–44.

27. István Vásáry, "The Golden Horde Term *daruġa* and Its Survival in Russia," in István Vásáry, *Turks, Tatars, and Russians in the 13th–16th Centuries* (Aldershot: Ashgate Variorum, 2007), 188, 195.

28. Trepavlov, "Nogai v Bashkirii XV–XVII vv.," 7.

29. The term "volost" could signify a group of landowners, of people subordinate to the same political authority, and part of the same ethnic or clan grouping, but these meanings did not always coincide. Faniia A. Shakurova, *Bashkirskaia volost' i obshchina v seredine XVIII-pervoi polovine XIX veka* (Ufa: BNT Ural'skogo Otdeleniia RAN, 1992), 42–43, 57.

30. Aznabaev, *Integratsiia bashkirii*, 50–51. Aznabaev notes that Nogai khans, who did not claim descent from Chinggis Khan, did not bestow tarkhan status; the tsar, who claimed to be heir to the Kypchak Khanate, did. The term *asaba* or *athaba* comes from an Islamic legal term signifying "agnates." Allen J. Frank, "Russia and the Peoples of the Volga-Ural Region: 1600–1850," in *The Cambridge History of Inner Asia*, 383.

31. Peter B. Golden, *An Introduction to the History of the Turkic Peoples: Ethnogenesis and State Formation in Medieval and Early Modern Eurasia and the Middle East* (Wiesbaden: Otto Harrassowitz, 1992), 297. See also Thomas T. Allsen, *Mongol Imperialism: The Policies of the Grand Qan Möngke in China, Russia, and the Islamic Lands, 1251–1259* (Berkeley: University of California Press, 1987), 121. George Vernadsky, *The Mongols in Russia* (New Haven, Conn.: Yale University Press, 1953), 102. Devin DeWeese rejects as "anachronistic" the description of Mongol attitudes toward religion as "tolerance," understood as religious indifference or ecumenism. Devin DeWeese, *Islamization and Native Religion in the Golden Horde: Baba Tükles and Conversion to Islam in Historical and Epic Tradition* (University Park: Pennsylvania State University Press, 1994), 100–101.

32. Before the eighteenth century there were four monasteries east of the Kama River. In 1721, a Russian Orthodox religious administration was established in Ufa. It never acquired any substantial weight and soon ceased to exist. N. F. Demidova, "Upravlenie Bashkiriei i povinnosti naseleniia ufimskoi provintsii v pervoi treti XVIII v.," *Istoricheskie zapiski* 68 (1961): 236.

33. R. G. Ganeev, V. V. Boltushkin, and R. G. Kuzeev, eds., *Istoriia Ufy: Kratkii ocherk* (Ufa: Bashkirskoe Knizhnoe Izdatel'stvo, 1981), 18. Bulat A. Aznabaev, *Ufimskoe dvorianstvo v kontse XVI–pervoi treti XVIII vv. (zemlevladenie, sotsial'nyi sostav, sluzhba)* (Ufa: Bashkirskii Gosudarstvennyi Universitet, 1999), 92–93. Trepavlov, "Nogai v Bashkirii," 9, 27.

34. Bulat Aznabaev found only three cases in the entire period 1591–1734 when the Muscovite administration assigned iasak land as service landholding, and those appear to have been the result of agreements with Bashkirs. Of twenty-two cases in which Bashkirs petitioned the state about the wrongful seizure of hereditary lands in the sixteenth and early seventeenth centuries the administration found for the Bashkirs in sixteen cases and for the nobles in four cases. The outcome of two cases was not clear. Aznabaev, *Ufimskoe dvorianstvo*, 99, 113–114.

35. Irek G. Akmanov, *Bashkiriia v sostave rossiiskogo gosudarstva v XVII–pervoi polovine XVIII veka* (Sverdlovsk: Izdatel'stvo Ural'skogo Universiteta, 1991), 48.

36. Roza G. Bukanova, *Goroda-kreposti iugo-vostoka Rossii v XVIII veke: Istoriia stanovleniia gorodov na territorii bashkirii* (Ufa: Kitap, 1997), 50–80.

37. Only a handful of the tsar's men were non-Orthodox or new converts to Orthodoxy, though their numbers grew in the second half of the seventeenth century. In 1638, only ten nobles were recent converts, and three were service Tatars. Aznabaev, *Ufimskoe dvorianstvo*, 39–40, 57, 76–77, 83–87.

38. Aznabaev, *Integratsiia bashkirii*, 72.

39. In the period 1646–1699, nineteen nobles from a list of eighty-three fled Ufa to places unknown. Forty-five noble families disappeared from service lists between 1697 and 1718. Aznabaev, *Ufimskoe dvorianstvo*, 19, 55, 130–135, 156, quoted at 55.

40. Hellie, *The Muscovite Law Code*, 112; N. A. Gurvich, ed. and comp., *Sbornik materialov dlia istorii ufimskogo dvorianstva sostavlennyi V. A. Novikovym v 1879 g., prodolzhennyi i dopolnennyi do 1902 goda vkliuchitel'no, deputatom ufimskogo dvorianstva N. A. Gurvichem* (Ufa: N. K. Blokhin, 1904), 32; V. Lebedev, "Bashkirskie vosstanie 1705–1711 gg.," *Istoricheskie zapiski*, no. 1 (1937): 89.

41. One family, the Kalovskiis, owned 142 serfs. No other nobles owned more than 38. Aznabaev, *Ufimskoe dvorianstvo*, 17–18. In the small size of their holdings and few serfs, Ufa nobles resembled servitors in other border regions in the seventeenth century. Judith Pallot and Denis J. Shaw, *Landscape and Settlement in Romanov Russia, 1613–1917* (Oxford: Clarendon Press, 1990), 33–54.

42. Aznabaev, *Ufimskoe dvorianstvo*, 52.

43. Anvar Z. Asfandiiarov, *Bashkirskie tarkhany* (Ufa: Kitap, 2006), 21–22; Sergei I. Rudenko, *Bashkiry: Istoriko-etnograficheskie ocherki* (Moscow-Leningrad: Akademiia Nauk, 1955), 44.

44. Asfandiiarov, *Bashkiriskie tarkhany*, 15.

45. As late as 1635–1636, only 2,217 Bashkir households paid iasak in Bashkiria. Boris Nolde speculates that the tsar's men in Ufa only managed to collect iasak from areas near Ufa. Boris Nolde, *La formation de l'empire russe: Études, notes, et documents*, vol. 1 (Paris: Insitut d'Études Slaves, 1952), 199.

46. Asfandiiarov, *Bashkirskie tarkhany*, 34, 49; Rudenko, *Bashkiry*, 43.

47. According to Irek G. Akmanov, of the 155 tarkhans mentioned in documents from the 1670s to 1690s, 134 were found in Nogai Doroga. Fires in 1611–1612 and 1759 destroyed the relevant records on the number of tarkhans. Akmanov, *Bashkiriia v sostave*, 27.

48. Nolde, *La formation de l'empire russe*, 202; Asfandiiarov, *Bashkirskie tarkhany*, 42.

49. Aznabaev, *Integratsiia bashkirii*, 118.

50. I. R. Gabdullin, *Ot sluzhilykh tatar k tatarskomu dvorianstvu* (Moscow: R. Sh. Kudashev, 2006), 18; Demidova, "Upravlenie Bashkiriiei i povinnosti naseleniia," 214; Asfandiiarov, *Bashkirskie tarkhany*, 23.

51. Gabdullin discusses the process of resettling service Tatars to Bashkiria. Some service Tatars were identified as Nogai. See Gabdullin, *Ot sluzhilykh tatar*, 47–54.

52. Asfandiiarov, *Bashkirskie tarkhany*, 26.

53. Ustiugov indicates the caution with which tsarist officials were supposed to approach Bashkirs for the collection of iasak. N. V. Ustiugov, "Bashkirskoe vosstanie 1662–1664 gg.," *Istoricheskie zapiski* 24 (1947): 30–110.

54. R. Stephen Humphreys, *Islamic History: A Framework for Enquiry* (Princeton, N.J.: Princeton University Press, 1991), 187. My discussion of Islamic terminology draws on Allen J. Frank, *Islamic Historiography and 'Bulghar' Identity among the Tatars and Bashkirs of Russia* (Leiden: Brill, 1998), 21–28; and Allen J. Frank, *Muslim Religious Institutions in Imperial Russia: The Islamic World of Novouzensk District and the Kazakh Inner Horde, 1780–1910* (Leiden: Brill, 2001), 99–113.

55. Gregory L. Freeze, *The Russian Levites: Parish Clergy in the Eighteenth Century* (Cambridge, Mass.: Harvard University Press, 1977); Laurie Manchester, *Holy Fathers,*

Secular Sons: Clergy, Intelligentsia, and the Modern Self in Revolutionary Russia (DeKalb: Northern Illinois University Press, 2008). Frank, *Islamic Historiography*, 22.

56. On Muslim clerics and scholars through the eighteenth century, see Frank, *Islamic Historiography*, 21–46 and *Muslim Religious Institutions*, 99–113; Michael Kemper, *Sufii i uchenye v Tatarstane i Bashkortostane: Islamskii diskurs pod russkim gospodstvom*, trans. Iskander Giliazov (Kazan: Idel-Press, 2008), 45–109; Nathan Spannaus, "The Decline of the Ākhūnd and the Transformation of Islamic Law under the Russian Empire," *Islamic Law and Society* 20, no. 3 (2013): 202–241; Il'dus K. Zagidullin, *Islamskie instituty v rossiiskoi imperii: Mecheti v evropeiskoi chasti Rossii i Sibiri* (Kazan: Tatarskoe Knizhnoe Izdatel'stvo, 2007), 42–85.

57. Frank, *Muslim Religious Institutions*, 109–110; and Frank, *Islamic Historiography*, 27.

58. Ustiugov, "Bashkirskoe vosstanie," 30–110; Alton S. Donnelly, *The Russian Conquest of Bashkiria, 1552–1740: A Case Study in Imperialism* (New Haven, Conn.: Yale University Press, 1968), 23–26.

59. Aznabaev emphasizes strongly the importance of Muscovite relations with Kalmyks as the cause of the Bashkir uprising of 1662–1664. Aznabaev, *Integratsiia bashkirii*, 102–103. Michael Khodarkovsky treats this last great migration of a people across the steppe in *Where Two Worlds Met: The Russian State and the Kalmyk Nomads, 1600–1771* (Ithaca, N.Y.: Cornell University Press, 1992).

60. Ustiugov, "Bashkirskoe vosstanie," 56–58.

61. Irek G. Akmanov, *Bashkirskie vosstaniia XVII–pervoi treti XVIII v.* (Ufa: Bashkirskoe Gosudarstvennyi Universitet, 1978), 28.

62. Khodarkovsky, *Where Two Worlds Met*, 94–96; Ustiugov, "Bashkirskoe vosstanie," 55.

63. Aznabaev, *Integratsiia bashkirii*, 103–104.

64. Akmanov, *Bashkirskie vosstaniia*, 31.

65. RGADA, Dela i prigovory pravit. Senata po Orenb. Gub., kn. 1/132, l. 135 ob., cited in Ustiugov, "Bashkirskoe vosstanie," 67–68.

66. Akmanov, *Bashkirskie vosstaniia*, 34–35.

67. RGADA, Dela i prigovory pravit. Senata po Orenb. Gub., kn. 1/132, ll. 121 ob.–122, 126–126 ob., 135–136, 138, cited in Ustiugov, "Bashkirskoe vosstanie," 106.

68. Romaniello, "Mission Delayed," 537.

69. PSZRI, series I, vol. 2, no. 867 (May 16, 1681), 312–313; Romaniello, "Mission Delayed," 537.

70. Akmanov, *Bashkiriia v sostave*, 60–61; Ivan Zlatoverkhovnikov, comp., *Ufimskaia eparkhiia: Geograficheskii, etnograficheskii, administrativno-istoricheskii i statisticheskii ocherk* (Ufa: A. P. Zaikov, 1899), 74; Georg Michels, "Rescuing the Orthodox: The Church Policies of Archbishop Afanasii of Kholmogory, 1682–1702," in *Of Religion and Empire: Missions, Conversion, and Tolerance in Tsarist Russia*, ed. Robert P. Geraci and Michael Khodarkovsky (Ithaca, N.Y.: Cornell University Press, 2001), 20.

71. Nolde, *La formation de l'empire russe*, 194.

72. Khodarkovsky, *Where Two Worlds Met*, 118–119; Akmanov, *Bashkirskie vosstaniia*, 44–45.

73. Akmanov, *Bashkirskie vosstaniia*, 47–48.

74. Aznabaev, *Ufimskoe dvorianstvo*, 101–105.

75. Aznabaev, *Integratsiia bashkirii*, 151–156.

76. On the desperate measures to which Bashkiria's population took recourse, including selling members of their family into servile labor, see Michael Khodarkovsky, "Non-Russian Subjects," in *The Cambridge History of Russia, vol. I: From Early Rus' to 1689*, ed. Maureen Perrie (New York: Cambridge University Press, 2006), 534–535; MPIBA, vol. III: *Ekonomicheskie i sotsialnye otnosheniia v bashkirii v pervoi polovine XVIII veka* (Moscow and Leningrad: AN ASSR, 1949), 9–25; A. P. Smirnov et al., eds., *Ocherki po istorii bashkirskoi ASSR*, vol. I, part I (Ufa: Bashkirskoe Knizhnoe Izdatel'stvo, 1956), 132–134.

77. Paul Bushkovitch writes that the Bashkir rebellion is "the only known case of popular revolt over these exactions." Paul Bushkovitch, *Peter the Great: The Struggle for Power* (Cambridge: Cambridge University Press, 2001), 246.

78. Donnelly, *The Russian Conquest of Bashkiria*, 45–46.

79. Khodarkovsky, *When Two Worlds Met*, 147–148.

80. Aznabaev, *Integratsiia bashkirii*, 160.

81. MPIBA, vol. I, 236.

82. Aznabaev, *Integratsiia bashkirii*, 162. Paul Bushkovitch writes that, in pursuing a more conciliatory approach, Sheremetev was carrying out Peter's agenda much more than his own. Sheremetev was harsher in dealing with rebellion in Astrakhan. Bushkovitch, *Peter the Great*, 249.

83. MPIBA, vol. I, 277.

84. MPIBA, vol. I, 108.

85. Aznabaev, *Integratsiia bashkirii*, 157.

86. Ia. V. Khanykov, "Raznye bumagi general-maiora Tevkeleva ob orenburgskom krae i kirgiz-kaisatskikh ordakh: 1762 g.," *Vremennik moskovskogo obshchestva istorii i drevnostei Rossiiskikh* 13 (1858): 15.

87. Nolde, *La formation de l'empire russe*, 215.

88. "Protokol Verkhovnogo Tainogo Soveta, January 31, 1728. Prilozheniia," SRIO 79 (1891): 72–83, quoted at 74, 75.

89. SRIO 84 (1893): 175–177.

90. PSZRI, series I, vol. 8, no. 5,316 (July 27, 1728), 68; no. 5,318 (July 31, 1728), 69–70; no. 5,438 (July 16, 1729), 214; no. 5,473 (October 24, 1729), 232. Nolde, *La formation de l'empire russe* 217.

91. MPIBA, vol. I, 302–306, quoted at 304.

92. In this way, Bashkiria seems an exception to a general pattern in which Peter I's more impetuous instincts were moderated by his aides. John P. LeDonne, "Building an Infrastructure of Empire in Russia's Eastern Theater, 1650s–1840s," CMR 47, no. 3 (July–September 2007): 588.

93. Petr I. Rychkov, "O sposobakh k umnozheniiu zemledel'stva v orenburgskoi gubernii," *Pamaiatnaia knizhka ufimskoi gubernii na 1873*, pt. II, comp. N. Gurvich (Ufa: Tipografiia Gubernskogo Pravleniia, 1873), 8.

94. V. Storozhev, "Votchina," in *Novyi entsiklopedicheskii slovar'*, vol. 11 (Leipzig and St. Petersburg: F. A. Brokgauz i I. A. Efron, 1906), 797–800.

95. Asfandiarov, *Bashkirskie tarkhany*, 54–65.

96. In 1664, the Muscovite state specifically forbade the enserfment of either Bashkirs or Tatars in Bashkiria. Aznabaev, *Ufimskoe dvorianstvo*, 127.

97. Akmanov, *Bashkiriia v sostave*, 55–57.

98. Demidova, "Upravlenie Bashkiriei," 224–226.

99. Akmanov, *Bashkiriia v sostave*, 59; Demidova, "Upravlenie Bashkiriei," 221, 230–233; Asfandiarov, *Bashkirskie tarkhany*, 54–65.

100. Ural Kh. Rakhmatullin, *Naselenie Bashkirii v XVII–XVIII vv.: Voprosy formirovaniia nebashkirskogo naseleniia* (Moscow: Nauka, 1988).

101. Rail G. Kuzeev, Ramil' M. Bulgakov, and Minlegali Kh. Naderulov, comps. and eds., *Bashkiriskie rodoslovnye* (Ufa: Kitap, 2002), 58, 97.

102. *Bashkiriskie rodoslovnye*, 58, 109, 124, 151, 286, 361. Muscovite officials seem to have accepted the boundaries that clan leaders indicated.

103. Some Ming and Bailar clans claimed to have received a land charter from Aleksei Mikhailovich, and the Iumran-Tabynsk clan received its from co-tsars Ivan Alekseevich and Peter Alekseevich. *Bashkiriskie rodoslovnye*, 221, 267, 316, 335.

104. Kuzeev, *Bashkirskie shezhere*, 118.

105. Muscovite sources mention this flow of "Chiuvash and Cheremis" beginning in the 1630s. RGADA, Stlb. Oruzh. Palaty, no. 41,395, l. 49, cited in Ustiugov, "Bashkirskoe vosstanie," 35.

106. Damir M. Iskhakov, *Istoricheskaia demografiia tatarskogo naroda (XVIII–nachalo XX vv.)* (Kazan: Akademiia Nauk Respubliki Tatarstan, 1993), 57.

107. The Muscovite state resettled 100 Meshcheriak and 100 Tatar families to Bashkiria at the end of the 1650s. According to Irek G. Akmanov, the Meshcheriaks and service Tatars originally received salaries but later were granted land. Akmanov, *Bashkiriia v sostave*, 41–42, 48.

108. *Istoriia Bashkortostana*, 184–187, 202. As N. V. Ustiugov points out, the Muscovite state kept records on elites charged with collecting iasak rather than a list of those who paid it. When in 1737 the tsarist state sought lists of iasak payers, none could be found. Ustiugov, "Bashkirskoe vosstanie," 30n2.

109. *Bashkiriskie rodoslovnye*, 283.

110. Rakhmatullin, *Naselenie Bashkirii*, 131; Rudenko, *Bashkiry*, 50.

111. *Bashkiriskie rodoslovnye*, 386.

112. Gabdullin, *Ot sluzhilykh tatar*, especially 54–55.

113. I. N. Kulbakhtin and N. M. Kulbakhtin, *Nakazy narodov Bashkortostana v ulozhennuiu komissiiu 1767–1768 gg.* (Ufa: Kitap, 2005), 117–118.

114. *Bashkiriskie rodoslovnye*, 408.

115. See Michael Khodarkovsky, "'Not by Word Alone': Missionary Policies and Religious Conversion in Early Modern Russia," CSSH 38, no. 2 (April 1996): 278–279.

116. Paul Werth, "Coercion and Conversion: Violence and the Mass Baptism of the Volga Peoples, 1740–55," *Kritika: Explorations in Russian and Eurasian History* 4, no. 3 (Summer 2003): 546–547.

117. PSZRI, series I, vol. 5, no. 2,734 (November 3, 1713), 66–67.

118. Gabdullin, *Iz sluzhilykh tatar;* PSZRI, series I, vol. 5, no. 2,920 (July 12, 1715), 163.

119. PSZRI, series I, vol. 5, no. 3,410 (July 31, 1719), 726.

120. Rail G. Kuzeev, *Istoricheskaia etnografiia bashkirskogo naroda*, 2nd ed. (Ufa: Kitap, 2009), 75.

121. Kuzeev, *Istoricheskaia etnografiia bashkirskogo naroda*, 78–80.

122. SRIO 84 (1893), 179.

123. Ethnographer Rail G. Kuzeev found legends about the importance of immigrants in teaching Bashkirs to grow crops. Since Bashkir agricultural practices are

nearly identical with those of Russians and others from the west, they appear to have been borrowed. Kuzeev, *Istoricheskaia etnografiia bashkirskogo naroda*, 85.

124. Fidail' F. Shaiakhmetov, *Mezhdu velikoi step'iu i osedlost'iu: Protsessy sedentarizatsii Bashkir i rasprostraneniia zemledelia v XVII–XIX vv.* (Ufa: Bashkirskii Gosudarstvennyi Universiteta, 2005), 106–107.

125. *SRIO* 84 (1893), 181.

126. Kuzeev, *Istoricheskaia etnografiia bashkirskogo naroda*, 79.

127. The factories produced cast iron, wrought iron, and smelted copper. Roger Portal, *L'Oural au XVIII siècle: Etude d'histoire economique et sociale* (Paris: Institut d'Etudes Slaves, 1950), 30–33, 80.

128. Charles Tilly, *Coercion, Capital and European States, AD 990–1992*, rev. ed. (Cambridge: Blackwell, 1992), 29.

129. Paul Bushkovitch, "Orthodoxy and Islam in Russia, 988–1725," in *Religion and Integration in Moskauer Russland: Konzepte und Praktiken, Potentiale und Grenzen, 14.–17. Jahrhundert*, ed. Ludwig Steindorff (Wiesbaden: Harrassowitz Verlag, 2010), 137–139.

130. Boeck, *Imperial Boundaries*, 209–210, 246. Peter Holquist develops this point and traces it to the writings of Boris Nolde. Peter Holquist, "Review of Brian J. Boeck, *Imperial Boundaries*," *Journal of Interdisciplinary History* 41, no. 3 (Winter 2011): 462.

131. Boeck, *Imperial Boundaries*, 41.

132. The Cossack elite was granted landed estates and serfs and eventually was transformed into a landowning nobility. Kappeler, *The Russian Empire*, 62, 66.

133. Kappeler, *The Russian Empire*, 61–62, 66; Barbara Skinner, *The Western Front of the Eastern Church: Uniate and Orthodox Conflict in Eighteenth-Century Poland, Ukraine, Belarus, and Russia* (DeKalb: Northern Illinois University Press, 2009).

134. Peter C. Perdue, *China Marches West: The Qing Conquest of Central Eurasia* (Cambridge, Mass.: Belknap Press of Harvard University Press, 2005), 127–128. Matt Romaniello emphasizes that Muscovite Russia mixed Mongol and Byzantine traditions. Romaniello, *The Elusive Empire*, 39.

135. Perdue, *China Marches West*, 543.

136. James Millward addresses China and the Ottoman Empire here, but I would argue that the idea applies to a considerable extent to Russia in the East in the sixteenth and early seventeenth centuries as well. James Millward, "Eastern Central Asia (Xinjiang): 1300–1800," in *The Cambridge History of Inner Asia*, 273. Nicola Di Cosmo argues that the northern China frontier remained "ethnically and culturally distinct and administratively separate from the rest of China nearly to the end of the dynasty." Nicola Di Cosmo, "The Qing and Inner Asia: 1636–1800," in *The Cambridge History of Inner Asia*, 338.

137. Perdue, *China Marches West*, 108.

138. Mark C. Elliot elaborates on these privileges in *The Manchu Way: The Eight Banners and Ethnic Identity in Late Imperial China* (Stanford, Calif.: Stanford University Press, 2001), 197–209. See also Di Cosmo, "The Qing and Inner Asia," 340–342.

139. Millward, "Eastern Central Asia," 274. Dorothea Heuschert, "Legal Pluralism in the Qing Empire: Manchu Legislation for the Mongols," *International History Review* 20, no. 2 (June 1998): 317, 323.

140. Reşat Kasaba, *A Moveable Empire: Ottoman Nomads, Migrants, and Refugees* (Seattle: University of Washington Press, 2009), 21.

141. Kasaba, *A Moveable Empire*, 24, 27.

142. Barkey, *Bandits and Bureacrats*, 121. Dina Rizk Khoury, "Administrative Practice between Religious Law (*Shari'a*) and State Law (*Kanun*) on the Eastern Frontiers of the Ottoman Empire," *Journal of Early Modern History* 5, no. 4 (2001): 305–307.

143. Peter C. Perdue, "Boundaries, Maps, and Movement: Chinese, Russian, and Mongolian Empires in Early Modern Central Eurasia," *International History Review* 20, no. 2 (June 1998): 271.

144. Boeck, *Imperial Boundaries*, 148–149.

2. ABSOLUTISM AND EMPIRE, 1730–1775

1. "Pis'mo vosstavshikh Bashkir Iusupa Arykova s tovarishchami V. N. Tatishchevu s otkazom v priezde dlia prineseniia povinnoi," in *Materialy po istorii Bashkortostana, vol. VI, Orenburgskaia ekspeditsiia i bashkirskie vosstaniia 30-x godov XVIII v.*, comp. N. F. Demidova, ed. N. V. Ustiugov (Ufa: Kitap, 2002), 215–216.

2. Alton S. Donnelly, *The Russian Conquest of Bashkiria, 1552–1740: A Case Study in Imperialism* (New Haven, Conn.: Yale University Press, 1968), 39–40. Petr I. Rychkov, *Istoriia orenburgskaia po uchrezhdenii orenburgskoi gubernii* (Ufa: Goskomnauki Respubliki Bashkortostan, 2001[1759; 1856]), 5.

3. James Cracraft, "Empire versus Nation: Russian Political Theory under Peter I," *Harvard Ukrainian Studies* 10, no. 3/4 (December 1986): 538.

4. Conflict and violence had always been present in Eurasia, of course, but Petrine ideology exalted triumph at arms and the "superhuman force" of the modern army. Richard S. Wortman, *Scenarios of Power: Myth and Ceremony in Russian Monarchy, vol. I: From Peter the Great to the Death of Nicholas I* (Princeton, N.J.: Princeton University Press, 1995), 42–44. Michael Khodarkovsky addresses the shift from "frontier concepts" of rule to "more modern and more European concerns of settling, colonizing, civilizing, and evangelizing the new lands." See Michael Khodarkovsky, *Russia's Steppe Frontier: The Making of a Colonial Empire, 1500–1800* (Bloomington: Indiana University Press, 2002), 5–6, 184–220. Willard Sunderland analyzes the shift to a new imperialism under Peter I, according to which the state sought not only "security and profit, but also worldly glory, scientific knowledge, and the deeper transformation of people and territory." See Willard Sunderland, *Taming the Wild Field: Colonization and Empire on the Russian Steppe* (Ithaca, N.Y.: Cornell University Press, 2004), 46.

5. For a very different assessment of eighteenth-century reforms in Bashkiria, see Bulat A. Aznabaev, *Integratsiia bashkirii v administrativnuiu struktury rossiiskogo gosudarstva (vtoraia polovina XVI–pervaia tret' XVIII vv.)* (Ufa: Bashkirskii Gosudarstvennyi Universitet, 2005), 1–2. Aznabaev argues that, in the 1730s and early 1740s, state officials "formulated optimal principles for the administration of Bashkiria that eliminated the primary reasons for Bashkir uprisings."

6. Wortman, *Scenarios of Power*, 40–41, 63.

7. Cracraft, "Empire versus Nation," 531–532.

8. Cracraft, "Empire versus Nation," 525, 533–535.

9. Yuri Slezkine, *Arctic Mirrors: Russia and the Small Peoples of the North* (Ithaca, N.Y.: Cornell University Press, 1994), 47–53; Khodarkovsky, *Russia's Steppe Frontier*, 192–193; Matthew P. Romaniello, "Mission Delayed: The Russian Orthodox Church after the Conquest of Kazan," *Church History* 76, no. 3 (September 2007): 511–540.

10. Ivan Kirilov, *Tsvetushchee sostoianie vserossiiskogo gosudarstva*, ed. Iu. A. Tikhonov (Moscow: Nauka, 1977[1727]), 8, 12; Donnelly, *The Russian Conquest of Bashkiria*, 59. Willard Sunderland discusses Kirilov as a leading example of Peter I's "new imperialism." Sunderland, *Taming the Wild Field*, 46–48.

11. V. N. Tatishchev, *Istoriia Rossiskaia*, vol. 1 (Moscow and Leningrad: Nauka, 1962), 86–87, cited in Nicholas V. Riasanovsky, *The Image of Peter the Great in Russian History and Thought* (Oxford: Oxford University Press, 1985), 26. Tatishchev wrote a tract in defense of autocratic power in the wake of the coup attempt in 1730. Brenda Meehan-Waters, *Autocracy and Aristocracy: The Russian Service Elite of 1730* (New Brunswick, N.J.: Rutgers University Press, 1982), 140.

12. Riasanovsky, *The Image of Peter the Great*, 44. See also I. I. Nepliuev, *Zapiski, 1693–1773*, reprint with an introduction by Herbert Leventer, ed. Marc Raeff (Cambridge: Oriental Research Partners, 1974[1893]), 103–104. Nepliuev married the daughter of Ivan Panin, a prominent servitor of Peter the Great, and was a distant relative of Tatishchev. Meehan-Waters, *Autocracy and Aristocracy*, 113. *Rodoslovnaia kniga kniazei i dvorian rossiiskikh i vyezzhikh*, vol. 2 (Moscow: Universitetskaia Tipografiia u N. Novikova, 1787), 116–119.

13. V. F. Shakhmatov, F. N. Kireev, and T. Zh. Shoinbaev, eds., *Kazakhsko-russkie otnosheniia v XVI–XVIII vekakh: Sbornik dokumentov i materialov* (Alma-Ata: Izdatel'stvo Akademii Nauk Kazakhskoi SSR, 1961), 31.

14. I. V. Erofeeva, "Sluzhebnye i issledovatel'skie materialy rossiiskogo diplomata A. I. Tevkeleva po istorii i etnografii kazakhskoi stepi," in *Istoriia Kazakhstana v russkikh istochnikakh XVI–XX vekov*, vol. 3, comp. I. V. Erofeeva (Almaty: Daik-Press, 2005), 24–28; Ia. V. Khanykov, "Raznyia bumagi general maiora Tevkeleva ob orenburgskom krae i o kirgiz-kaisatskikh ordakh, 1762 g.," *Vremennik imperatorskogo moskovskogo obshchestva istorii i drevnostei rossiiskikh* 13 (1852): 15; Dmitrii Iu. Arapov, "Pervyi russkii general-musul'manin Kutlu-Muhammad Tevkelev," *SRIO* 153, no. 5 (2002): 34–36. Gulnaz Azamatova, *Integratsiia natsional'nogo dvorianstva v rossiiskoe obshchestvo na primere roda Tevkelevykh* (Ufa: Gilem, 2008).

15. István Vásáry writes of an earlier period that a person bearing a Christian name, such as Vasilii or Grigorii, makes it "certain that he was a Christian" and that "Muslim Tatars bearing a Russian name are unknown." István Vásáry, "Clans of Tatar Descent in the Muscovite Elite of the Fourteenth to Sixteenth Centuries," in *The Place of Russia in Europe and Asia*, ed. Gyula Szvák (Wayne, N.J.: Center for Hungarian Studies and Publications, 2010), 258.

16. *Kazakhsko-russkie otnosheniia v XVI–XVIII*, 41. Tevkelev continued to identify and to be identified by others as a Muslim. It seems that Tevkelev presented a dual identity: he used his Christian name for service purposes but maintained a Muslim identity in his personal life and when working with Muslims. See Azamatova, *Integratsiia natsional'nogo dvorianstva*, 43–44.

17. *Kazakhsko-russkie otnosheniia v XVI–XVIII*, 31; Michael Khodarkovsky clarifies the complexities of Russo-Kazakh relations in the eighteenth century. See Khodarkovsky, *Russia's Steppe Frontier*, 146–156.

18. *Kazakhsko-russkie otnosheniia v XVI–XVIII*, 94–97, 99–101; Khodarkovsky, *Russia's Steppe Frontier*, 155–156.

19. Salavat U. Taimasov, "Rol' orenburgskoi ekspeditsii v prisoedinenii Bashkirii k Rossii (1730-e gg.)," *Voprosy istorii* 2 (February 2008): 145–146.

20. Orenburg's first historian, Petr I. Rychkov, wrote in 1759 that Peter I foresaw the need to protect his empire from the "steppe peoples, living in Great Tatariia," was concerned about Christians falling into "Barbaric hands," and sought to "control" Bashkirs permanently. This has been the dominant interpretation of Orenburg's founding ever since. Rychkov, *Istoriia orenburgskaia*, 5–6.

21. Khodarkovsky and Sunderland address Kirilov's project with somewhat different emphases. See Khodarkovsky, *Russia's Steppe Frontier*, 156–157; Sunderland, *Taming the Wild Field*, 46–48.

22. *Kazakhsko-russkie otnosheniia v XVI–XVIII*, 112.

23. A. I. Dobrosmyslov, ed., *Materialy po istorii Rossii (Sbornik ukazov i drugikh dokumentov, kasaiushchikhsia upravleniia i ustroistva orenburgskogo kraia): 1734 god*, vol. 1 (Orenburg: F. B. Sachkov, 1900), 45; vol. 2, 47; Taimasov, "Rol' orenburgskoi ekspeditsii," 146.

24. *Kazakhsko-russkie otnosheniia v XVI–XVIII*, 112.

25. Dobrosmyslov, *Materialy po istorii Rossii*, vol. 1, 25.

26. Marc Raeff, *Understanding Imperial Russia: State and Society in the Old Regime*, trans. Arthur Goldhammer, foreword by John Keep (New York: Columbia University Press, 1984), 24–31.

27. Cracraft, "Empire versus Nation," 530.

28. *Kazakhsko-russkie otnosheniia v XVI–XVIII*, 114–116.

29. PSZRI, series I, vol. 9, no. 6,721 (April 20, 1735), 508–510.

30. *Materialy po istorii Bashkortostana*, vol. VI, 20, 663. V. V. Vel'iaminov-Zernov, who served in Orenburg in the 1850s, published archival material identifying hundreds of the tarkhans who received their status in late 1734 and early 1735. V. V. Vel'iaminov-Zernov, "Istochniki dlia izucheniia tarkhanstva, zhalovannogo bashkiram russkimi gosudariami," *Zapiski imperatorskoi akademii nauk* 4, no. 6 (1864): 1–47; MPIBA, vol. III, 489–490.

31. *Materialy po istorii Bashkortostana*, vol. VI, 366; Donnelly, *The Russian Conquest of Bashkiria*, 67–68.

32. In his own defense, Kirilov reported to the cabinet in October 1735 that the "best people" from nearby Bashkir volosts had told him that the land on which he began to construct Orenburg had been "empty." *Materialy po istorii Bashkortostana*, vol. VI, 83.

33. Michael Kemper, *Sufii i uchenye v Tatarstane i Bashkortostane: Islamskii diskurs pod russkim gospodstvom*, trans. Iskander Giliazov (Kazan: Idel-Press, 2008), 55; Allen J. Frank, *Islamic Historiography and 'Bulghar' Identity among the Tatars and Bashkirs of Russia* (Leiden: Brill, 1998), 25–26; Danielle M. Ross, "In Dialogue with the Shadow of God: Imperial Mobilization, Islamic Revival, and the Evolution of an Administrative System for the Tatars, Bashkirs, and Mishars of Eighteenth Century Russia" (MA thesis, University of Wisconsin-Madison, 2007), 19–24, 26.

34. *Materialy po istorii Bashkortostana*, vol. VI, 63, 75, 78, 92. The quotation is Rumiantsev's distillation of Kirilov's view.

35. Donnelly, *The Russian Conquest of Bashkiria*, 76–77; N. V. Ustiugov, *Bashkirskoe vosstanie, 1737–1739 gg.* (Moscow-Leningrad: Akademiia Nauk, 1950), 19.

36. Sergei Solov'ev, *Istoriia Rossii s drevneishikh vremen*, vol. 10 (Moscow: Izdatel'stvo Sotsial'no-Ekonomicheskoi Literatury, 1963), 594.

37. *Materialy po istorii Bashkortostana*, vol. VI, 189–190.

38. For a more complete account of the fighting, see Donnelly, *The Russian Conquest of Bashkiria.*

39. Donnelly, *The Russian Conquest of Bashkiria,* 73–74, 80–81, 84; Rychkov, *Istoriia orenburgskaia,* 20.

40. Ustiugov, *Bashkirskoe vosstanie,* 38; Donnelly, *The Russian Conquest of Bashkiria,* 93.

41. Bulat S. Davletbaev, *Bol'shaia Oka: Istoriia sela* (Ufa: Ministerstva Pechati i Sredstv Massovoi Informatsii, 1992), 17. Azamatova, *Integratsiia natsional'nogo dvorianstva,* 56.

42. Donnelly, *The Russian Conquest of Bashkiria,* 171.

43. Rebel groups were to pay a tax of 500 horses, which would make further resistance nearly impossible. Kirilov insisted that each rebel appear and acknowledge his or her guilt individually rather than the group doing so collectively, as had been the pattern. *PSZRI,* series I, vol. 9, no. 6,890 (February 11, 1736), 741–745; Ustiugov, *Bashkirskoe vosstanie,* 36.

44. Different levels of service merited different amounts of land, ranging from 200 des. for elders to 12.5 des. of land for rank-and-file soldiers. *PSZRI,* series I, vol. 9, no. 6,890 (February 11, 1736), 742, 744.

45. Aitugan I. Akmanov, *Zemel'naia politika tsarskogo pravitel'stva v Bashkirii (vtoraia polovina XVI–nachalo XX vv.)* (Ufa: Kitap, 2000), 28–31.

46. *PSZRI,* series I, vol. 9, no. 6,890 (February 11, 1736), 743–744.

47. RGADA Po Kabinetu, kn. 87/1164, l. 23 ob., cited in Ustiugov, *Bashkirskoe vosstanie,* 128.

48. Ustiugov, *Bashkirskoe vosstanie,* 96–97, 106–107; Donnelly, *The Russian Conquest of Bashkiria,* 111–112.

49. Khodarkovsky, *Russia's Steppe Frontier,* 152–159; Donnelly, *The Russian Conquest of Bashkiria,* 114–115.

50. RGADA Po Kabinetu, kn. 106/1183, ll. 11–11 ob., 84–84 ob., cited in Ustiugov, *Bashkirskoe vosstanie,* 123.

51. *PSZRI,* series I, vol. 10, no. 7,876 (August 20, 1739), 867–871.

52. Ustiugov, *Bashkirskoe vosstanie,* 125–128, quoted at 127–128.

53. *PSZRI,* series I, vol. 10, no. 7,876 (August 20, 1739), 867–871. Tatishchev's proposal anticipated the Bashkir cantonal administration introduced in 1798.

54. Iurii N. Smirnov, *Orenburgskaia ekspeditsiia (komissiia) i prisoedinenie zavolzh'ia k Rossii v 30–40e gg. XVIII veka* (Samara: Samarskii Universitet, 1997), 98–100.

55. Nikita Demidov, who built much of the Urals industrial base, complained that Tatishchev had taken bribes. Tatishchev may also have run afoul of the vice-governor of Ufa, P. D. Aksakov, who was well connected at court. R. G. Ignat'ev, *Sud nad Brigadirom Aksakovym* (Ufa: Ufimskii Gubernskii Statisticheskii Komitet, 1875).

56. Koiti Toyokava, *Orenburg i orenburgskoe kazachestvo vo vremiia vosstaniia Pugacheva, 1773–1774 gg.* (Moscow: Arkheograficheskii Tsentr, RGADA, 1996), 60.

57. Vadim V. Trepavlov, "Kniazheskie rody nogaiskogo proiskhozhdeniia," *Materialy i issledovaniia po istorii i etnologii Bashkortostana* 2 (1997): 50–51.

58. Rail G. Kuzeev, *Istoricheskaia etnografiia bashkirskogo naroda,* 2nd ed. (Ufa: Kitap, 2009), 251.

59. Donnelly, *The Russian Conquest of Bashkiria,* 138, 168–169.

60. Kuzeev, *Istoricheskaia etnografiia bashkirskogo naroda*, 248–251.

61. Donnelly, *The Russian Conquest of Bashkiria*, 174–177.

62. Kuzeev, *Istoricheskaia etnografiia bashkirskogo naroda*, 88–89. On the number of servitors in the region, see Donnelly, *The Russian Conquest of Bashkiria*, 169.

63. This is Kuzeev's interpretation of Ufa Military Governor Liutkin's figures. Kuzeev, *Istoricheskaia etnografiia bashkirskogo naroda*, 255. Liutkin's figures are found in V. N. Vitevskii, *I. I. Nepliuev i orenburgskii krai v prezhnem ego sostave do 1758 g.*, vol. 2 (Kazan: Kliuchnikov, 1897), 295.

64. Rychkov, *Istoriia orenburgskaia po uchrezhedenii orenburgskoi gubernii*, 147–148; Vitevskii, *I. I. Nepliuev i orenburgskii krai*, vol. 2, 422.

65. Nepliuev proposed that rather than having the children sold to particular individuals, the government should convert them to Christianity and support them, while educating the boys for military service. It is not clear what came of such children. Vitevskii, *Nepliuev i orenburgskii krai*, vol. 2, 414–415.

66. Faniia A. Shakurova, *Bashkirskaia volost' i obshchina v seredine XVIII–pervoi polovine XIX veka* (Ufa: BNT Ural'skogo Otdeleniia RAN, 1992), 55.

67. His grandfather, Prince Myshetskii, had immolated himself rather than be arrested by Peter I's officials. In 1713, Nepliuev left his pregnant wife and one-year-old son in order to live in a monastery for more than one year. Nepliuev, *Zapiski*, iii–iv, 2.

68. Nepliuev negotiated a treaty with the Ottoman Empire to divide Persia's northwest provinces in 1724. Illness forced him to return to Russian in 1734. Nepliuev was close to Andrei Osterman, who was implicated in a plot against newly crowned Empress Elizabeth in 1741. Nepliuev, *Zapiski*, v–vii.

69. Toyokava, *Orenburg i orenburgskoe kazachestvo*, 61.

70. Toyokava, *Orenburg i orenburgskoe kazachestvo*, 57; PSZRI, series I, vol. 11, no. 8,630 (October 15, 1742), 673–675; Rychkov, *Istoriia orenburgskaia*, 147. Smirnov, *Orenburgskaia ekspeditsiia*, 158, 162.

71. PSZRI, series I, vol. 10, no. 7,876 (August 30, 1739), 870.

72. Vitevskii, *Nepliuev i orenburgskii krai*, vol. 2, 405. Nepliuev and Vice-Governor Aksakov later allowed blacksmiths in Russian settlements and three blacksmiths in Bashkir villages for each of the four dorogas. MPIBA, vol. IV, pt. 2, 459, 461.

73. Farit Kh. Gumerov, ed., *Zakony rossiiskoi imperii o bashkirakh, mishariakh, teptiariakh, i bobyliakh* (Ufa: Kitap, 1999), 79.

74. Vitevskii, *Nepliuev i orenburgskii krai*, vol. 2, 411.

75. Ruf G. Ignat'ev, *Sobranie sochinenii (ufimskii i orenburgskii period)*, vol. IV *1873 g.*, ed. M. I. Rodnov (Ufa, 2011), http://cp809702.cpanel.tech-logol.ru/fr/5/public /Ruf.%20T-IV.pdf, accessed May 20, 2014, 210–212. The publication contains documents Ignat'ev found in a local administration archive in Orenburg Province in the nineteenth century and published in the book *Pamiatnaia knizhka ufimskoi gubernii,* vol. 2, 1873. Rychkov's table from 1755 is found in Rychkov, *Topografiia orenburgskoi gubernii,* 55–59.

76. Ignat'ev, *Sobranie sochineii*, 237.

77. See Danil D. Azamatov, *Orenburgskoe magometanskoe dukhovnoe sobranie v kontse XVIII–XIX vv.* (Ufa: Gilem, 1999), 16–17; Nathan Spannaus, "The Decline of the Ākhūnd and the Transformation of Islamic Law under the Russian Empire," *Islamic Law and Society* 20, no. 3 (2013): 212.

78. Ignat'ev, *Sobranie sochenii*, 213–214, 227, 235, 239–240, quoted at 239–240.

79. *PSZRI*, series I, vol. 12, no. 9,230 (November 26, 1745), 483.

80. As noted in chapter 1, Paul Bushkovitch argues for the lack of an ideal of religious uniformity in Orthodoxy. This changed in the 1730s, at least in the Kazan region, when the drive for conversion intensified. Paul Bushkovitch, "Orthodoxy and Islam in Russia, 988–1725," in *Religion and Integration in Moskauer Russland: Konzepte und Praktiken, Potentiale und Grenzen, 14.–17. Jahrhundert*, ed. Ludwig Steindorff (Wiesbaden: Harrassowitz Verlag, 2010), 139–140.

81. As Peter I sought to make Russia a European power, the presence of large numbers of Muslims and animist peoples increasingly was perceived as a sign of the empire's backwardness. Michael Khodarkovsky, "Not by Word Alone": Missionary Policies and Religious Conversion in Early Modern Russia," *CSSH* 38, no. 2 (April 1996): 278–279.

82. F. G. Islaev, *Islam i pravoslavie v povol'zhe XVIII stoletiia: Ot konfrontatsii k terpimosti* (Kazan: Kazan University, 2001), 60; Paul Werth, "Coercion and Conversion: Violence and the Mass Baptism of the Volga Peoples, 1740–55," *Kritika: Explorations in Russian and Eurasian History* 4, no. 3 (Summer 2003): 546–547.

83. Those who converted received money and relief from taxation and military conscription. Only one mosque was permitted per village, and only in those with purely Muslim populations of at least 200 to 300 males. Khodarkovsky, "Not by Word Alone," 283–284.

84. Kemper, *Sufii i uchenye*, 51, 54–56.

85. Petr I. Rychkov, *Topografiia orenburgskoi gubernii* (Ufa: Kitap, 1999[1762]), 101–102.

86. Regarding Seitov Posad/Kargala, see Grigorii Kosach, "A Russian City between Two Continents: The Tatars of Orenburg and State Power," in *Russia at a Crossroads: History, Memory, and Political Practice,* ed. Nurit Schleifman (London: Frank Cass Publishers, 1998), 44–50; and Rychkov, *Topografiia orenburgskoi gubernii*, 180.

87. *PSZRI*, series I, vol. 12, no. 8,875 (February 20, 1744), 26. See also Frank, *Islamic Historiography*, 30; N. Firsov, *Inorodcheskoe naselenie prezhnego kazanskogo tsarstvo v novoi Rossii do 1762 goda* (Kazan: Universitetskaia Tipografiia, 1869), 424. A 1744 decree limiting mosque construction made no mention of Bashkiria, Ufa, or Orenburg. *PSZRI*, series I, vol. 12, no. 8,978 (June 22, 1744), 157–159.

88. *PSZRI*, series I, vol. 13, no. 9,904 (November 12, 1751), 535–536.

89. Karen Barkey, *Empire of Difference: The Ottomans in Comparative Perspective* (Cambridge: Cambridge University Press, 2008), 109–153.

90. Due to the loss of land records to fire in Ufa in 1759 and imprecise records of land sales, the exact amount of land acquired by the empire's elite cannot be known for certain. Akmanov, *Zemel'naia politika*, 34–35.

91. Akmanov, *Zemel'naia politika*, 24. For unknown reasons, the *Polnoe Sobranie Zakonov Rossiiskoi Imperii* omitted the decree. Judging by references to the law as justification for noble landholding later in the century, however, it appears to have taken effect.

92. Petr I. Rychkov, for instance, received a total of 45 des. of land. Akmanov, *Zemel'naia politika*, 1–32.

93. Tevkelev acquired 38 Bashkir women and minors whose husbands were killed in the Bashkir War. During the Bashkir War, Tevkelev also acquired serfs by declaring

some iasak-paying Tatars fugitives. Azamatova, *Integratsiia natsional'nogo dvorianstva*, 67–76.

94. The average price was 70–80 kopecks per des. Akmanov, *Zemel'naia politika*, 32–43.

95. Shakurova, *Bashkirskaia volost'*, 118–119.

96. There were 212 noble estates in Ufa County. One other county, Buzuluk, located on the western fringe of Bashkiria, contained 120 generally smaller estates. No other county contained more than 50. Akmanov's figures include landholdings in the west and east of Bashkiria that were not included in Orenburg Province in the nineteenth century. Akmanov, *Zemel'naia politika*, 44.

97. PSZRI, series I, vol. 13, no. 10,141 (October 13, 1753), 899–908. Roger Portal, *L'Oural au XVIII siècle: Etude d'histoire economique et sociale* (Paris: Institut d'Etudes Slaves, 1950), 131.

98. Of the 58 factories, 48 were still operating by the end of the century. Donnelly, *The Russian Conquest of Bashkiria*, 156.

99. A. Z. Asfandiarov, *Bashkirskie tarkhany* (Ufa: Kitap, 2006), 93.

100. The concentration of factories in the mountains and their relative isolation limited their interference in Bashkir agriculture and prevented them from dominating local life. A 1753 decree stated that the construction of factories to that point had met with little Bashkir opposition. PSZRI, series I, vol. 13, no. 10,141 (October 13, 1753), 899–901. The Pugachev uprising in 1773 devastated many factories. Portal, *L'Oural au XVIII siècle*, 330–341; Akmanov, *Zemel'naia politika*, 48–52, 98.

101. PSZRI, series I, vol. 10, no. 7,876 (August 20, 1739), 867–871.

102. MPIBA, vol. IV, pt. II, no. 376, cited in Akmanov, *Zemel'naia politika*, 54.

103. RGB, otdel rukopisi, f. 364, kn. 6, d. 1, Matvei Kuz'mich Liubavskii, "Ocherki po istorii bashkirskogo zemlevladeniia i zemlepol'zovaniia v XVII, XVIII, i XIX vv.," l. 12.

104. Alison K. Smith, *For the Common Good and Their Own Well-Being: The System of Social Estates in Imperial Russia* (Oxford: Oxford University Press, 2014), 47–71.

105. *Istoriia Bashkortostana s drevneishikh vremen do nashikh dnei, v dvukh tomakh. Tom 1: Istoriia Bashkortostana s drevneishikh vremen do kontsa XIX veka* (Ufa: Kitap, 2004), 251; N. F. Demidova, "Upravlenie Bashkiriei i povinnosti naseleniia ufimskoi provintsii v pervoi treti XVIII v.," *Istoricheskie zapiski* 68 (1961): 221; Rychkov, *Istoriia orenburgskaia*, 84.

106. PSZRI, series I, vol. 14, no. 10,198 (March 16, 1754), 42–44. Demidova, "Upravlenie Bashkiriei," 225; MPIBA, vol. IV, pt. 2, 426–429; Inga M. Gvozdikova, *Bashkortostan nakanune i v gody krest'ianskoi voiny pod predvoditel'stvom E. I. Pugacheva* (Ufa: Kitap, 1999), 157.

107. Bashkir and Meshcheriak households now paid 21 1/4 kopecks to support postal stations that connected the region's fortresses. Teptiars and Bobyls also had to provide 700 laborers each summer for fortress construction. MPIBA, vol. IV, pt. 2, 432; Gvozdikova, *Bashkortostan nakanune*, 156; MPIBA, vol. IV, pt. 2, 439–440.

108. The precise amount of iasak that Bashkirs paid is difficult to determine since the state did not have a list of Bashkir iasak payers and since elders collected iasak from whole volosts rather than individually. Demidova, "Upravlenie Bashkiriei," 217–218.

109. MPIBA, vol. IV, pt. 2, 427, 457.

110. PSZRI, series I, vol. 13, no. 10,097 (May 7, 1753), 829–830.

111. *PSZRI*, series I, vol. 15, no. 11,214 (March 13, 1761), 664–665; Gvozdikova, *Bashkortostan nakanune*, 160.

112. G. B. Khusainov, ed., *Pis'mo Batyrshi imperatritse Elizavete Petrovne* (Ufa: UNTS RAN, 1993), 72–102; Rychkov, *Topografiia orenburgskoi gubernii*, 185.

113. Portal, *L'Oural au XVIII siècle*, 168–169.

114. Rychkov, *Istoriia orenburgskaia*, 185.

115. Nepliuev, *Zapiski*, 146.

116. He forged the akhund's signature on documents the akhund would not sign. Nepliuev, *Zapiski*, 50–51.

117. A. P. Chuloshnikov, *Vosstanie 1755 g. v Bashkirii* (Moscow-Leningrad: Akademiia Nauk SSSR, 1940), 76–77.

118. Danielle Ross identifies Nazim al-Mulk, Mohammad al-Ghazali, and Badr al-Din ibn Jama'a as three major influences on Batyrsha. Batyrsha, for instance, cited the same Koranic verses as al-Ghazali. Ross, "In Dialogue with the Shadow of God," 49–50.

119. *Pis'mo Batyrshi*, 71, 75.

120. *Pis'mo Batyrshi*, 73–74, 78–79, 88–89, 96, 98.

121. *PSZRI*, series I, vol. 14, no. 10,597 (August 23, 1756), 607–612. In most respects, these policies extended to Kazan the basic approach to Islam that characterized Bashkiria before the uprising. For a contrasting view, see Iskander Gilyazov, "Die Islampolitik von Staat und Kirchen im Wolga-Ural-Gebiet und die Batïr sah-Aufstand von 1755," in *Muslim Culture in Russia and Central Asia from the 18th to the Early 20th Centuries*, ed. Michael Kemper, Anke von Kügelgen, and Dmitriy Yermakov (Berlin: Klaus Schwarz Verlag, 1996), 69–89.

122. *MPIBA*, vol. IV, pt. 2, 439–443.

123. Michael Khodarkovsky, "Non-Russian Subjects," in *The Cambridge History of Russia, vol. I: From Early Rus' to 1689*, ed. Maureen Perrie (New York: Cambridge University Press, 2006), 537.

124. Carol S. Leonard, *Reform and Regicide: The Reign of Peter III in Russia* (Bloomington: Indiana University Press, 1993), 25–26.

125. Roger P. Bartlett, *Human Capital: The Settlement of Foreigners in Russia, 1762–1804* (Cambridge: Cambridge University Press, 1979), 24, 27; Marc Raeff, *The Well-Ordered Police State: Social and Institutional Change through Law in the Germanies and Russia, 1600–1800* (New Haven, Conn.: Yale University Press, 1983), 70–73.

126. Leonard, *Reform and Regicide*, 26–27; on the relationship between commerce and empire in Europe, see Anthony Pagden, *Lords of All the World: Ideologies of Empire in Spain, Britain, and France, c. 1500–1800* (New Haven, Conn.: Yale University Press, 1995). On new thinking about the interrelationships of population, land, and empire in Russia in this period, see Sunderland, *Taming the Wild Field*, 55–95.

127. Khodarkovsky describes Tevkelev as "cogovernor of Orenburg" in the 1750s and notes that Kazakhs regarded Tevkelev as a Muslim. Khodarkovsky, *Russia's Steppe Frontier*, 204. Tevkelev's service in suppressing the Bashkir rebellion of 1735–1740 earned him a promotion to brigadier in 1742. Khanykov, "Raznyia bumagi general maiora Tevkeleeva," 48–49. Arapov, "Pervyi russkii general-musul'manin," 34.

128. Colum Leckey, *Patrons of Enlightenment: The Free Economic Society in Eighteenth-Century Russia* (Newark: University of Delaware Press, 2011), 110–113. Rychkov, *Topografiia orenburgskoi gubernii*, 5–7. Rychkov purchased an estate in Ufa Province near the town of Bugul'ma in 1743. He had an audience with Catherine II in 1767.

129. Ricarda Vulpius sees the usage of *liudskost'* by Rychkov and Tevkelev as indicative of a transformation in understanding of the empire in the mid-eighteenth century. See Rikarda Vul'pius, "K scmantike *imperii* v Rossii XVIII veka: poniatiinoe pole *tsivilizatsii*," in *Poniatiia o Rossii: K istoricheskoi semantike imperskogo perioda*, vol. 1., ed. A. Miller, D. Sdvizhkov, and I. Shirle, trans. V. S. Dubina (Moscow: Novoe Literaturnoe Obozrenie, 2012), 58–59.

130. *Kazakhsko-russkie otnosheniia v XVI–XVIII*, 575–577.

131. See Vul'pius, "K semantike *imperii* v Rossii XVIII veka," 69; Dov B. Yaroshevski, "Attitudes towards the Nomads of the Russian Empire under Catherine the Great," in *Literature, Lives and Legality in Catherine's Russia*, ed. A. G. Cross and G. S. Smith (Nottingham: Astra Press, 1994), 15–24; and Dov B. Yaroshevski, "Empire and Citizenship," in *Russia's Orient: Imperial Borderlands and Peoples, 1700–1917*, ed. Daniel R. Brower and Edward J. Lazzerini (Bloomington: Indiana University Press, 1997), 58–79.

132. Carol S. Leonard identifies Volkov as a moving force behind crucial reforms of Peter III, including the emancipation of the nobility from obligatory state service and a reduction in monopolies and tariffs to promote the development of markets and foreign commerce. Leonard, *Reform and Regicide*, 52–57, 101–109. See also Yaroshevski, "Attitudes towards the Nomads," 15–24; and "Empire and Citizenship," 58–79.

133. *MPIBA*, vol. IV, pt. 2, 446–447; Yaroshevski, "Attitudes towards the Nomads," 21.

134. *Kazakhsko-russkie otnosheniia v XVI–XVIII*, 653.

135. Volkov himself claimed none of these characteristics. John P. LeDonne, *Ruling Russia: Politics and Administration in the Age of Absolutism, 1762–1796* (Princeton, N.J.: Princeton University Press, 1984), 284; *MPIBA*, vol. IV, pt. 2, 446, 451.

136. *MPIBA*, vol. IV, pt. 2, 448, 601; Portal, *L'Oural au XVIII siècle*.

137. *MPIBA*, vol. IV, pt. 2, 456, 461.

138. In the 1740s and 1750s, much of Orenburg's trade consisted of gold and silver. Toyokava, *Orenburg i orenburgskoe kazachestvo*, 68–69.

139. Rychkov, who served in Orenburg's administration until 1768, shared Volkov's vision of Bashkirs as agriculturalists. He did not see any difficulties directing Bashkirs toward agriculture and considered them quite able to overcome their "former coarseness." "Stat'ia Petra Ivanovicha Rychkova o zemledelii v orenburgskoi gubernii (proshlogo stoletiia)," in *Pamiatnaia knizhka ufimskoi gubernii*, part II, comp. N. A. Gurvich (Ufa: Tipografiia Gubernskogo Praveleniia, 1873), 131–136.

140. *MPIBA*, vol. IV, pt. 2, 472.

141. *MPIBA*, vol. IV, pt. 2, 469.

142. Commerce proved no more able to tame an "ancient military ethos" and eliminate hostility in favor of mutual interests and a sense of "common humanity" in the Russian context than it did in Europe. Pagden, *Lords of All the World*, 179–183.

143. *PSZRI*, series I, vol. 19, no. 13,441 (March 30, 1770), 43–45.

144. Vel'iaminov-Zernov, "Istochniki dlia izucheniia tarkhanstva," 47–48. In 1765, there were 443 tarkhan households in Bashkiria. *MPIBA*, vol. 4, pt. 2, 11.

145. Rychkov, "Stat'ia Petra Ivanovicha Rychkova o zemledelii," 132.

146. Gvozdikova, *Bashkortostan nakanune*, 187, 195–200.

147. Gvozdikova includes 653 tarkhans among the elite and estimates that the elite included 1,400–1,500 men. Members of a commune elected the elder, and the Orenburg

governor confirmed him. Bashkir communities favored wealthy elders who had less need to extract bribes from their constituents. Gvozdikova, *Bashkortostan nakanune,* 185–186.

148. Azamatov, *Orenburgskoe magometanskoe dukhovnoe sobranie,* 17–18; Spannaus, "The Decline of the Ākhūnd," 212.

149. Bashkir elders frequently pleaded to be appointed to service on the Orenburg Line so that they could receive regular support. They also presented *nakazy* to Catherine's Legislative Commission in 1767 seeking to receive the military ranks that those serving in the regular army or as Cossack elders did. Gvozdikova, *Bashkortostan nakanune,* 189–190.

150. Spannaus, "The Decline of the Ākhūnd," 215–216.

151. Shakurova, *Bashkirskaia volost',* 67.

152. Shakurova, *Bashkirskaia volost',* 60–67.

153. Gvozdikova, *Bashkortostan nakanune,* 60, 62.

154. Ioann G. Georgi, *Opisanie vsekh obitaiushchikh v rossiiskom gosudarstve narodov,* pt. 2 (St. Petersburg: Akademiia Nauk, 1799), 98.

155. Gvozdikova, *Bashkortostan nakanune,* 148–153.

156. John T. Alexander, *Autocratic Politics in a National Crisis: The Imperial Russian Government and Pugachev's Revolt, 1773–1775* (Bloomington: Indiana University Press, 1969), 10.

157. Marc Raeff has questioned the identification of the rebellion as a "peasant war." Marc Raeff, "Pugachev's Rebellion," in *Preconditions of Revolution in Early Modern Europe,* ed. Robert Forster and Jack P. Greene (Baltimore, Md.: Johns Hopkins University Press, 1970), reprinted in Marc Raeff, *Political Ideas and Institutions in Imperial Russia* (Boulder, Colo.: Westview, 1994), 254. LeDonne argues that the Pugachev Rebellion was the last stand of Cossacks against the advance of serfdom, Bashkirs who wanted to remain nomads in the face of "advancing civilization," and "industrial workers who felt the norms of serfdom were incompatible with their new status." LeDonne, *Ruling Russia,* 20.

158. The Iaik Cossacks themselves were a culturally diverse estate group. "Spodvizhniki pugacheva svidetel'stvuiut . . . ," *Voprosy istorii* 8 (1973), 108.

159. In the wake of the Pugachev Rebellion, Catherine II forbade the term "Iaik" and renamed the river "Ural."

160. My account here follows those of Raeff, "Pugachev's Rebellion," 234–267; and Alexander, *Autocratic Politics,* 44–52. The most extensive account of the uprising is found in V. V. Mavrodin, ed., *Krest'ianskaia voina v Rossii v 1773–1775 godakh: Vosstanie Pugacheva,* 3 vols. (Leningrad: Leningradskii Universitet, 1961, 1966, 1970). See also Gvozdikova, *Bashkortostan nakanune,* and Philip Longworth, "The Pugachev Revolt: The Last Great Cossack Peasant Rising," in *Rural Protest: Peasant Movements and Social Change,* ed. Henry A. Landsberger (London: Macmillan, 1974), 194–256.

161. Alexander Pushkin, *The History of Pugachev,* reprint, with foreword by Orlando Figes, trans. Earl Sampson (London: Phoenix Press, 2001[1833]), 39.

162. Gvozdikova, *Bashkortostan nakanune,* 179.

163. Seven Bashkir elders, including Kinzia Arslanov, met with Pugachev on September 30, 1773. Arslanov told Pugachev that "their entire Bashkir horde" would join him if he sent a decree to them. "Spodvizhniki pugacheva svidetel'stvuiut . . . ," 110. Toyokava

and others have pointed out the contribution of non-Russian nationalities to Pugachev's initial success. Toyokava, *Orenburg i orenburgskoe kazachestvo*, 220.

164. Gvozdikova, *Bashkortostan nakanune*, 279–281; Mavrodin, *Krest'ianskaia voina*, vol. 2, 211.

165. Gvozdikova, *Bashkortostan nakanune*, 502–508; Ross, "In Dialogue with the Shadow of God," 68.

166. Mavrodin, *Krest'ianskaia voina*, vol. 2, 210–216. Over 98 percent of Bashkir households in Kazan Doroga supported Pugachev.

167. Sergei A. Golubtsov, ed., *Pugachevshchina*, vol. 3 (Moscow: Gosudarstvennoe Izdatel'stvo, 1926), 231.

168. Azamatova, *Integratsiia natsional'nogo dvorianstva*, 80.

169. Petr I. Rychkov, "Zapiski Petra Ivanovicha Rychkova," *Russkii arkhiv*, book 3, vol. 10 (1905): 335.

170. Mavrodin, *Krest'ianskaia voina*, vol. 3, 283.

171. Salavat Iulaev became known as a Bashkir hero even before 1917 and was promoted as the Bashkir national hero in the Soviet era.

172. Mavrodin, *Krest'ianskaia voina*, vol. 2, 136–142; "Spodvizhniki Pugacheva svidetel'stvuiut . . . ," 113; *Pugachevshchina*, vol. 1; A. I. Aksenov, R. V. Ovchinnikov, and M. F. Prokhorov, eds., *Dokumenty stavki E. I. Pugacheva, povstancheskikh vlastei i uchrezhdenii, 1773–1774 gg.* (Moscow: Nauka, 1975), 25–28.

173. Aksenov, Ovchinnikov, and Prokhorov, *Dokumenty stavki E. I. Pugacheva*, 23–28.

174. Raeff, "Pugachev's Rebellion," 253–258.

175. Brian J. Boeck, *Imperial Boundaries: Cossack Communities and Empire-Building in the Age of Peter the Great* (Cambridge: Cambridge University Press, 2009), 161, 181–183, 218.

176. Kappeler, *The Russian Empire*, 36–38; the imperial state began some limited efforts to create a new elite in the late eighteenth century. Slezkine, *Arctic Mirrors*, 11–45, 68–69.

177. Cracraft, "Empire versus Nation," 525, 533–535.

178. J. H. Elliot, *Imperial Spain, 1463–1716* (London: Edward Arnold, 1963), 34–41, 299–303. "Crusading enthusiasm" is found on page 34. See also Henry Kamen, *Empire: How Spain Became a World Power, 1492–1763* (New York: HarperCollins, 2003), 14–21; L. P. Harvey, *Islamic Spain, 1250–1500* (Chicago, Ill.: University of Chicago Press, 1990), 324–339; and L. P. Harvey, *Muslims in Spain, 1500–1614* (Chicago, Ill.: University of Chicago Press, 2005), 1–44. On the lack in Eastern Orthodoxy of the concept of "holy war" in a Catholic, crusading sense, see Bushkovitch, "Orthodoxy and Islam in Russia," 138–139.

179. Valerie Kivelson, *Cartographies of Tsardom: The Land and Its Meanings in Seventeenth-Century Russia* (Ithaca, N.Y.: Cornell University Press, 2006), 162–163.

180. Pagden, *Lords of All the World*, 76.

181. Thomas R. Metcalf, *Ideologies of the Raj* (Cambridge: Cambridge University Press, 1997); Maia Jasanoff, *Edge of Empire: Lives, Culture, and Conquest in the East, 1750–1850* (New York: Knopf, 2005).

182. Linda Colley, *Captives: Britain, Empire and the World, 1600–1850* (New York: Anchor Books, 2004).

183. Richard White, *The Middle Ground: Indians, Empires, and Republics in the Great Lakes Region, 1650–1815* (Cambridge: Cambridge University Press, 1991). On the lack of a middle ground in Russia's east, see Khodarkovsky, *Russia's Steppe Frontier*, 227–228.

184. J. H. Elliott, *Empires of the Atlantic World: Britain and Spain in America, 1492–1830* (New Haven, Conn.: Yale University Press, 2006), 81–83, fig. 40.

3. EMPIRE OF REASON, 1773–1855

1. Khusainov was of the Naqshbandi Sufi order. He had studied in Bukhara and was a follower of Fayz Khan, a Naqshbandi shaykh in Kabul. See Hamid Algar, "Shaykh Zaynullah Rasulev: The Last Great Naqshbandi Shaykh of the Volga-Urals Region," in *Muslims in Central Asia: Expressions of Identity and Change*, ed. Jo-Ann Gross (Durham, N.C.: Duke University Press, 1992), 113–114. See also Michael Kemper, "Entre Boukhara et la Moyenne-Volga: 'Abd an-Nasir al-Qursawi (1776–1812) en conflit avec les Oulémas traditionalistes," *CMR* 37, no. 1–2 (January–June 1996): 42.

2. RGADA, f. 16, op. 1, d. 934, ch. 5, pp. 81–82, cited in Danil D. Azamatov, *Orenburgskoe magometanskoe dukhovnoe sobranie v kontse XVIII–XIX vv.* (Ufa: Gilem, 1999), 26.

3. RGADA, f. 16, d. 934, ch. 5, reel 1, ll. 101 ob.–106 ob.

4. A twelfth Bashkir canton was created in 1803. Leila F. Tagirova, *Kantonnye nachal'niki Bashkirii: Natsional'naia regional'naia elita pervoi poloviny XIX veka* (Ufa: UNTS RAN, 2012), 53.

5. Anvar Z. Asfandiiarov, ed., *Materialy po istorii bashkirskogo naroda*, vol. IV (1800–1903) (Ufa: UNTS RAN, 2009), 4–7, quoted at 7. Volkonskii was writing on July 25, 1812.

6. Marc Raeff, "Uniformity, Diversity, and the Imperial Administration in the Reign of Catherine II," in *Political Ideas and Institutions in Imperial Russia*, ed. Marc Raeff (Boulder, Colo.: Westview, 1994), 142–143.

7. On Catherine's ideology of rule, see Richard S. Wortman, *Scenarios of Power: Myth and Ceremony in Russian Monarchy*, vol. 1: *From Peter the Great to the Death of Nicholas I* (Princeton, N.J.: Princeton University Press, 1995), 133.

8. Robert D. Crews, *For Prophet and Tsar: Islam and Empire in Russia and Central Asia* (Cambridge, Mass.: Harvard University Press, 2006), 45.

9. Willard Sunderland, *Taming the Wild Field: Colonization and Empire on the Russian Steppe* (Ithaca, N.Y.: Cornell University Press, 2004).

10. Catherine idealized the personal devotion of native elites to the throne as the principal bond with the empire's expanded elite. Andreas Kappeler, *The Russian Empire: A Multiethnic History* (Harlow: Longman, 2001), 114–115; Wortman, *Scenarios of Power*, vol. 1, 86–88, 135–142.

11. Paul Dukes, ed., *Russia under Catherine the Great*, vol. II: *Catherine the Great's Instruction* (Nakaz) *to the Legislative Commission, 1767* (Newtonville, Mass.: Oriental Research Partners, 1977), 104; Klaus Schreiner, "Toleranz," in *Geschichtliche Grundbegriffe: Historiches Lexikon zur politisch-sozialen Sprache in Deutschland*, vol. 6, ed. Otto Brunner, Werner Conze, and Reinhart Koselleck (Stuttgart: Klett-Cotta, 1990), 505, cited in Crews, *For Prophet and Tsar*, 40–41.

12. PSZRI, series I, vol. 19, no. 13,996 (June 17, 1773), 776.

13. Ole Peter Grell and Roy Porter, "Toleration in Enlightenment Europe," and Michael G. Müller, "Toleration in Eastern Europe: The Dissident Question in Eighteenth-Century Poland-Lithuania," in *Toleration in Enlightenment Europe*, ed. Ole Peter Grell and Roy Porter (Cambridge: Cambridge University Press, 2000), 1–22, 212, 215.

14. W. F. Reddaway, ed., *Documents of Catherine the Great: The Correspondence with Voltaire and the* Instruction *of 1767 in the English Text of 1768* (Cambridge: Cambridge University Press, 1931), 289.

15. Marisa Linton, "Citizenship and Religious Toleration in France," in Grell and Porter, *Toleration in Enlightenment Europe*, 159–160.

16. In January 1789, for example, Orenburg governor-general Osip Igel'strom asked the Tobol'sk Ecclesiastical Consistory to cease efforts to convert Muslims to Orthodoxy since it was causing disturbances in Cheliabinsk and Troitsk counties. Igel'strom sent a Muslim aide to investigate. RGADA, f. 7, op. 2 d. 2753, ll. 1 ob.–2 ob.

17. PSZRI, series I, vol. 20, no. 14,540 (November 22, 1776), 455–462.

18. The only exception to this rule regarded the ownership of Christian serfs, which Muslims were denied. PSZRI, series I, vol. 22, no. 15,936 (February 22, 1784), 50–51. See also Andreas Kappeler, *Russlands erste Nationalitäten: Das Zarenreich und die Völker der Mittleren Wolga vom 16. bis 19. Jahrhundert* (Cologne: Böhlau, 1982), 373. The following year, Tatar nobles in Crimea automatically entered the Tauride Noble Assembly. Marc Raeff, "In the Imperial Manner," in Raeff, *Political Ideas and Institutions*, 165. On the Tatar nobility in Crimea, see Kelly O'Neill, "Rethinking Elite Integration: The Crimean Murzas and the Evolution of Russian Nobility," CMR 51, no. 2 (2010): 397–417.

19. Il'dus R. Gabdullin, *Ot sluzhilikh tatar k tatarskomu dvorianstvu* (Moscow: R. Sh. Kudashev, 2006). Vadim V. Trepavlov, "Kniazheskie rody nogaiskogo proiskhozhdeniia," *Materialy i issledovaniia po istorii i etnologii Bashkortostana* 2 (1997): 38–72.

20. Families listed by Novikov include Avdeevs, Akchurins, Bikchurins, Biglovs, Diveevs, Enikeevs, Mansurovs, Maksiutovs, Suleimanovs, Sultanovs, Teregulovs, and Chanyshevs. N. A. Gurvich, ed. and comp., *Sbornik materialov dlia istorii ufimskogo dvorianstva sostavlennyi V. A. Novikovym v 1879 g., prodolzhennyi i dopolnennyi do 1902 goda, vkliuchitel'no, deputatom ufimskogo dvorianstva N. A. Gurvichem* (Ufa: N. K. Blokhin, 1904), 37–38. According to István Vásáry, the Akchurins (1509) and Enikeevs (1551) entered Muscovite service as early as the sixteenth century. István Vásáry, "Clans of Tatar Descent in the Muscovite Elite of the Fourteenth to Sixteenth Centuries," in *The Place of Russia in Europe and Asia*, ed. Gyula Szvák (Wayne, N.J.: Center for Hungarian Studies and Publications, 2010), 264.

21. Ia. V. Khanykov, "Raznyia bumagi general maiora Tevkeleeva ob orenburgskom krae i o kirgiz-kaisatskikh ordakh, 1762 g.," *Vremennik imperatorskogo moskovskogo obshchestva istorii i drevnostei Rossiiskikh* 13 (1852): 19.

22. Wortman, *Scenarios of Power*, vol. 1, 87–88.

23. Tagirova, *Kantonnye nachal'niki Bashkirii*, 40.

24. Anvar Z. Asfandiiarov, *Bashkirskie tarkhany* (Ufa: Kitap, 2006), 96–97.

25. John P. LeDonne, *Ruling Russia: Politics and Administration in the Age of Absolutism, 1762–1796* (Princeton, N.J.: Princeton University Press, 1984). David Ransel shows the impact of reform on local society in *A Merchant's Tale: The Life and Adventures of Ivan Alekseevich Tolchenov, Based on His Diary* (Bloomington: Indiana University Press, 2008), 98–100.

26. Peter I created the Table of Ranks in 1722 to regulate progress in service and advance into the nobility. John P. LeDonne, "The Territorial Reform of the Russian Empire, 1775–1796: II. The Borderlands, 1777–1796," CMRS 24, no. 4 (1983): 427–428, 432, 455–456.

27. Natal'ia L. Semenova, *Voennoe upravlenie orenburgskim kraem v kontse XVII–pervoi polovine XIX v.* (Sterlitamak: Sterlitamakskii Gosudarstvennyi Pedagogicheskii Institut, 2001), 46–47.

28. LeDonne, *Ruling Russia*, 107, 278, 285–286. LeDonne, "Territorial Reform of the Russian Empire," 427–428; "Zapiski D. V. Mertvogo," *Russkii arkhiv* supplement (1867): 39. RGADA, f. 16, d. 988, l. 3 ob.

29. Sergei T. Aksakov, *Sobranie sochinenii*, vol. 1 (Moscow: Gos. Izdatel'stvo Khudozhestvennoi literatury, 1955), 71–280.

30. Gurvich, *Sbornik materialov*, 37–38.

31. In 1891 only 21 *waqf* properties—books, land, buildings, and small stores—existed in the OMEA's jurisdiction. *V pamiat' stoletiia orenburgskogo magometanskogo dukhovnogo sobraniia uchrezhdennogo v gorode Ufy* (Ufa: Tipografiia Gubernskogo Pravleniia, 1891), 19–20, 34–35.

32. The empress specified that school materials be printed in Russian (*Rossiiskii*) and Chagatay, the literary language used by local Muslims. "Arkhiv Grafa Igel'stroma," *Russkii arkhiv* 24, no. 3 (1886), 355, 358.

33. Those in attendance included two men "of Muslim law" who served under Igel'strom as well as "Tatars, Bukharans, and Khivans." RGADA, f. 16, d. 934, ch. 1, reel 1, ll. 3 ob., 4 ob., 5, 11, 53 ob., 54 ob.

34. RGADA, f. 16, op. 1, d. 934 ch. 2, reel 4, ll. 259 ob., 264, 268 ob., 270 ob., 271; "Zapiski Dmitriia Mertvogo," 43–44; M. M. Kul'sharipov, "Otkrytie dukhovnogo upravleniia musul'man v Ufe," in *Sotsial'no-ekonomicheskoe razvitie i klassovaia bor'ba na iuzhnom urale i v srednem povol'zhe: Dorevoliutsionyi period*, ed. Irek G. Akmanov (Ufa: Bashkirskii Universitet, 1988), 44.

35. RGADA, f. 16, op. 1, d. 934 ch. 2, reel 4, ll. 418 ob.–419.

36. *Arkhiv gosudarstvennogo soveta*, 812. Igel'strom pointed out that Kirilov's laws of February 1736 already provided the legal basis for the appointment of clerics. RGADA, f. 16, op. 1, d. 934 ch. 4, reel 3, ll. 142–144; Michael Kemper, *Sufii i uchenye v Tatarstane i Bashkortostane: Islamskii diskurs pod russkim gospodstvom*, trans. Iskander Giliazov (Kazan: Idel-Press, 2008), 55.

37. PSZRI, series I, vol. 22, no. 16,710 (September 22, 1788), 1107; no. 16,711 (September 22, 1788), 1107–1108; no. 16,759 (April 20, 1789), 20–21. I follow Robert Crews's interpretation of the assembly's "ecclesiastical" rather than "spiritual" nature. See Crews, *For Prophet and Tsar*, 52, 385.

38. On the formation of the OMEA, see Crews, *For Prophet and Tsar*; Azamatov, *Orenburgskoe magometanskoe dukhovnoe sobranie*, 20–30; Allen J. Frank, *Islamic Historiography and 'Bulghar' Identity among the Tatars and Bashkirs of Russia* (Leiden: Brill, 1998), 35–39; Stéphane A. Dudoignon, "Djadidisme, Mirasisme, Islamisme," CMR 37, no. 1–2 (January–June 1996): 16.

39. "Zapiski Dmitriia Mertvogo," 44–45.

40. "Polozhenie o dukhovnom magometanskom sobranii, sostavlennoe simbirskim i ufimskim namestnikom O. A. Igel'stromom," December 4, 1789, and "Proekt polozheniia o kompetentsii dukhovnogo magometanskogo sobraniia, predlozhennyi simbirskim i ufimskim namestnikom O. A. Igel'strom na reshenie imp. Ekaterinny II," December 5, 1789, in MPIBA, vol. V, 563; Alan Fisher, "Enlightened Despotism and Islam under Catherine II," *Slavic Review* 27, no. 4 (1967): 550.

41. Kappeler, *Russlands erste Nationalitäten*, 376.

42. Crews, *For Prophet and Tsar*, 50, 53–54. The Ecclesiastical Assembly was located in Ufa until 1796, when the headquarters of the Ufa military governor's seat shifted to Orenburg and closer to the frontier. The Ecclesiastical Assembly acquired the name "Orenburg Muhammadan Ecclesiastical Assembly" and retained it even after returning

to Ufa in 1802. Danil Azamatov, "Russian Administration and Islam in Bashkiria (18th–19th Centuries)," in *Muslim Culture in Russia and Central Asia from the 18th to the Early 20th Centuries*, ed. Michael Kemper, Anke von Kügelen, and Dmitriy Yermakov (Berlin: Klaus Schwarz Verlag, 1996), 91–112.

43. *pszri*, series I, vol. 33, no. 17,146 (August 17, 1793), 452–454.

44. Kemper, *Sufii i uchenye*, 88. Frank, *Islamic Historiography*, 36–37; M. V. Gainutdinov, "Razvitie obnovlencheskikh idei v tatarskoi obshchestvennoi mysli," in *Problema preemstvennosti v tatarskoi obshchestvennoi mysli*, ed. R. M. Amirkhanov et al. (Kazan: Institut Iazyka, Literatury, i Istorii im. G. Ibragimova, 1985), 41–42.

45. Crews, *For Prophet and Tsar*, 56–57. One of Khusainov's sons caused a scandal by living with a Russian woman and having four daughters out of wedlock. Kemper, *Sufii i uchenye*, 93–94, 98–103.

46. "Zapiski D. Grankina, predstavlennaia kniaziiu G. Potemkinu po povodu administrativnogo ustroistva v Mladshem zhuze," in *Kazakhsko-russkie otnosheniia v XVI–XVIII vekakh: Sbornik dokumentov i materialov*, ed. V. F. Shakhmatov, F. N. Kireev, and T. Zh. Shoinbaev (Alma-Ata: Izdatel'stvo Akademii Nauk Kazakhskoi ssr, 1961), 125, 130.

47. Dov Yaroshevski, "Imperial Strategy in the Kirghiz Steppe in the Eighteenth Century," *Jahrbücher für Geschichte Osteuropas* 39, no. 2 (1991): 223–224; *Arkhiv gosudarstvennogo soveta*, 818, 833, 841.

48. *Arkhiv gosudarstvennogo soveta*, 820.

49. The number of clerics confirmed comes from Kemper, *Sufii i uchenye*, 73. On the mufti's privileges see *pszri*, series I, vol. 21, no. 15,936 (February 22, 1784), 51; vol. 33, no. 16,897 (August 13, 1790), 164–165.

50. Allen J. Frank, "Islamic Regional Identity in Imperial Russia in the Eighteenth and Nineteenth Centuries" (PhD dissertation, Indiana University, 1994), 38; and Allen J. Frank, "Islamic Shrine Catalogues and Communal Geography in the Volga-Ural Region: 1788–1917," *Journal of Islamic Studies* 7, no. 2 (1996): 265–286; Dudoignon, "Djadidisme, Mirasisme, Islamisme," 21–22.

51. Crews, *For Prophet and Tsar*, 86–89. This notion remained controversial. See Kemper, "Entre Boukhara et la Moyenne-Volga," 42; Azade Ayşe Rorlich, *The Volga Tatars: A Profile in National Resilience* (Stanford, Calif.: Hoover Institution Press, 1986), 49–50; Edward J. Lazzerini, "Beyond Renewal: The Jadid Response to Pressure for Change in the Modern Age," in *Muslims in Central Asia*, 151–166; Mahmud Tahir, "Abu-nasir Kursavi, 1776–1812," *Central Asian Survey* 8, no. 2 (1989): 155–158.

52. Crews, *For Prophet and Tsar*, 56, 153. In 1829, only 41 of 107 imams in Kazan Province outside of the city of Kazan were *ukaznye mully*, or official imams. Kemper, *Sufii i uchenye*, 78.

53. As described in chapter 2, *tiuba* and *aimak* (the latter term was more commonly associated with Bashkiria's northwest) were the equivalents of villages and managed land and agricultural resources. A Bashkir could move among different commands fairly easily. Faniia A. Shakurova, *Bashkirskaia volost' i obshchina v seredine XVIII–pervoi polovine XIX veka* (Ufa: Bashkirskii Nauchnyi Tsentr, Ural'skogo Otdeleniia ran, 1992), 75, 117.

54. *pszri*, series I, vol. 25, no. 18,477 (April 10, 1798), 189.

55. Tagirova, *Kantonnye nachal'niki Bashkirii*, 66, 60.

56. The number of Bashkirs living in a canton varied from 4,000 to 30,000, and the number of iurtas or commands in each canton varied from seven to twenty-six. Shakurova, *Bashkirskaia volost'*, 70–71, 77.

57. At the end of the eighteenth century, there were more than three times as many Bashkir and Meshcheriak men under arms (47,866) than Cossacks (14,836). Semenova, *Voennoe upravlenie*, 130, 135, 145.

58. PSZRI, series I, vol. 25, no. 18,477 (April 10, 1798), 191, 193–194.

59. "'Vam krome voli moei dorogi net': Reskripty imperatora Pavla k Orenburgskomu general-gubernatoru baronu O. A. Igel'stromu, 1796–1797 gg.," *Istoricheskii arkhiv* 1 (2003): 180–201, quoting page 193.

60. Wortman, *Scenarios of Power*, vol. 1, 169–170, 193–194.

61. Marc Raeff, *Michael Speransky: Statesman of Imperial Russia, 1772–1839*, 2nd rev. ed. (The Hague: Martinus Nijhoff, 1969), 41–42, 260.

62. Wortman, *Scenarios of Power*, vol. 1, 194–195, 202–203.

63. *Stoletnii iubilei ufimskoi dukhovnoi seminarii* (Ufa: n.p., 1900). The number of churches built did not average one per year in the province until the 1820s, when twenty-nine opened. Ivan Zlatoverkhovnikov, comp., *Ufimskaia eparkhiia: Geograficheskii, etnograficheskii, administrativno-istoricheski i statisticheskii ocherk* (Ufa: A. P. Zaikov, 1899), 221.

64. At the start of the nineteenth century, Orenburg Province had 1,258 wooden and four stone mosques. The number reached 1,932 wooden and seven stone mosques by the 1850s. Aislu B. Iunusova, *Islam v Bashkortostane* (Ufa: Ufimskii Poligrafkombinat, 1999), 55.

65. PSZRI, series I, vol. 31, no. 24,819 (October 18, 1811), 872.

66. John P. LeDonne, *Absolutism and the Ruling Class: The Formation of the Russian Political Order, 1700–1825* (Oxford: Oxford University Press, 1991), 218–222; Ekaterina Pravilova, *A Public Empire: Property and the Quest for the Common Good in Imperial Russia* (Princeton, N.J.: Princeton University Press, 2014), 35.

67. When the issue arose in 1790, Baron Igel'strom argued that the passage of time, transactions, and various government decrees made the question of land redistribution impossible to resolve. Meshcheriaks should keep the lands they already had, and the matter should be closed. RGIA, f. 1167, op. XVI, ed. khr. 310/44, ll. 108–118.

68. Many Meshcheriak, Teptiar, and Bobyl settlements were separated from Bashkir parcels onto "vacant land." RGIA f. 1167, op. XVI, ed. khr. 310/44, ll. 122–123.

69. Matvei Liubavskii notes that Bashkir landholdings remained large through the first half of the nineteenth century. RGB, otdel rukopisi, f. 364, kart 6, d. 1, "Ocherki po istorii bashkirskogo zemlevladeniia i zemlepol'zovaniia v XVII, XVIII, i XIX vv.," ll. 12–14.

70. RGIA f. 1167, op. 16, ed. khr. 310/44, ll. 125, 128–128 ob.

71. Ivan V. Chernov, *Zametki po istorii orenburgskoi gubernii general-maiora I. V. Chernova* (Orenburg: Orenburgskaia Guberniia, 2007), 39.

72. Anvar Z. Asfandiiarov, *Kantonnoe upravlenie v Bashkirii (1798–1865)* (Ufa: Kitap, 2005), 69–73.

73. Möxämätsälim Ömötbaev, "Bashqort khalqïnïng aq häm qara kändäre," in *Yädkär* (Ufa: Bashqortostan Kitap Näshriäte, 1984), 212–213.

74. Wortman, *Scenarios of Power*, vol. 1, 240–241. According to D. K. Tarasov, the local military review went less than smoothly. Commanded to parade before the emperor, soldiers converged in such disorder that Alexander criticized the commander for not having

better control of his troops. D. K. Tarasov, "Vospominaniia moei zhizni: Zapiski pochet-nogo leib-khirurga D. K. Tarasova, 1792–1866," *Russkaia starina*, 3 (March 1872): 359.

75. Tarasov, "Vospominaniia," 360, 363–364.

76. Nicholas Riasanovsky, *Nicholas I and Official Nationality in Russia, 1825–1855* (Berkeley: University of California Press, 1959), 213–214. Nicholas's officials found Russia's distinctiveness in the people's devotion to their sovereigns. Popular devotion "turned the Petrine empire, with its Westernized official culture, into a national institution." Wortman, *Scenarios of Power*, vol. 1, 266, 277, 379–381. Andreas Kappeler notes the relative subordination of national ideas to "the traditional dynastic and estate-based legitimation of the autocratic system." Kappeler, *The Russian Empire*, 252.

77. *V pamiat' stoletiia*, 26; PSZRI, series II, vol. 3, no. 2,296 (September 21, 1828), 839; Abel' E. Ianovskii "Metricheskie knigi," in *Entsiklopedicheskii slovar'*, vol. 37, ed. F. A. Brokgauz and I. A. Efron (Leipzig and St. Petersburg: Brokgauz and Efron, 1896), 201. Regarding metrical books, see Charles Steinwedel, "Making Social Groups, One Person at a Time: The Identification of Individuals by Estate, Religious Confession, and Ethnicity in Late Imperial Russia," in *Documenting Individual Identity: The Development of State Practices since the French Revolution*, ed. Jane Caplan and John Torpey (Princeton, N.J.: Princeton University Press, 2001), 67–82; and Paul W. Werth, "In the State's Embrace? Civil Acts in an Imperial Order," *Kritika: Explorations in Russian and Eurasian History* 7, no. 3 (Summer 2006): 433–458.

78. *V pamiat' stoletiia*, 27; PSZRI, series II, vol. 9, no. 7,351 (August 21, 1834), 827. By 1836, the OMEA's staff had increased to thirteen with a budget of 6,700 rubles in addition to the muftis' and judges' salaries. PSZRI, series II, vol. 11, no. 8,780 (January 15, 1836), 47. In 1835, Muslim clerics received official sanction to decide cases of disobedience of children to their parents, a function of the so-called conscience court (*sovestnyi sud*) for Russian speakers. Such cases were left to the Muslim clergy to resolve "according to their customs and laws." PSZRI, series II, vol. 10, no. 8,436 (September 30, 1835), 991. In 1836, the senate confirmed the right of OMEA clerics to "review and decide according to its law matters of private property arising from wills or the division of property among heirs." PSZRI, series II, vol. 11, no. 9,158 (May 11, 1836), 504. Crews, *For Prophet and Law*, 145–146. Family law was largely the realm left to sharia law in the late Ottoman Empire as well. Noah Feldman, *The Fall and Rise of the Islamic State* (Princeton, N.J.: Princeton University Press, 2008), 81.

79. The inclusion of the ruler in Muslim prayers had a long history. From the second half of the tenth century onward, the leader of Friday prayers inserted after the name of the caliph the name of the current ruler of the Muslim community. Azamatov, *Orenburgskoe magometanskoe dukhovnoe sobranie*, 158; "Khutba," in *Islam: Entsiklopedicheskii slovar'*, ed. L. V. Negria (Moscow: Nauka, 1991), 285.

80. Kemper, *Sufii i uchenye*, 110–125, quoted at 118. "Perevod rechi, proiznesennoi Muftiem Abdussalamom k ego edinovertsam," *Kazanskii vestnik*, no. 9/10 (1826): 148–152.

81. Danielle M. Ross, "From the Minbar to the Barricades: The Transformation of the Volga-Ural 'Ulama into a Revolutionary Intelligentsia" (PhD dissertation, University of Wisconsin–Madison, 2011), 33.

82. Abby M. Schrader, *Languages of the Lash: Corporal Punishment and Identity in Imperial Russia* (DeKalb: Northern Illinois University Press, 2002), 63; PSZRI, series II, vol. 25, no. 23,932 (February 20, 1850), 126.

83. Gabdullin, *Ot sluzhilykh tatar,* 84–292.

84. *PSZRI,* series II, vol. 28, no. 16,599 (March 8, 1843), 121–123.

85. RGIA, f. 1167, op. XVI, ed. khr. 310/44, ll. 2 ob. and 3.

86. RGIA, f. 1167, op. XVI, ed. khr. 310/44, ll. 12, 15, 18 ob.

87. RGIA, f. 1167, op. XVI, ed. khr. 310/44, ll. 231, 235 ob. and 236.

88. RGIA, f. 1167, op. XVI, ed. khr. 310/44, ll. 156–156 ob., 235–235 ob.

89. RGIA, f. 1167, op. XVI, ed. khr. 310/44, ll. 21 ob. and 22.

90. RGIA, f. 1167, op. XVI, ed. khr. 310/44, l. 170 ob.

91. RGIA, f. 1167, op. XVI, ed. khr. 310/44, l. 12 ob.

92. RGIA, f. 1167, op. XVI, ed. khr. 310/44, ll. 200–200 ob.

93. Raeff, *Michael Speransky,* 217–218; Yuri Slezkine, *Arctic Mirrors: Russia and the Small Peoples of the North* (Ithaca, N.Y.: Cornell University Press, 1994), 81–87.

94. RGIA, f. 1167, op. XVI, ed. khr. 310/44, ll. 87–88.

95. RGIA, f. 1167, op. XVI, ed. khr. 310/44, l. 135 ob.

96. *PSZRI,* series II, vol. 8, no. 5,287 (April 10, 1832), 197–198; 6,334 (July 19, 1833), 424.

97. *PSZRI,* series II, vol. 7, no. 5,201 (March 1, 1832), 114–115.

98. I. M. Gvozdikova, ed., *Otchet orenburgskogo voennogo gubernatora V. A. Perovskogo po upraveliniu kraem (1833–1842)* (Ufa: RAN Institut Istorii, Iazyka i Literatury Ufimskogo Nauchnogo Tsentra, 2010), 34.

99. RGIA, f. 1181, op. 15, god 1862, d. 124, l. 515; Chernov, *Zametki po istorii,* 164.

100. Nikolai G. Zalesov, "Zapiski N. G. Zalesova," *Russkaia starina* 114, no. 3 (1903), 275.

101. For an insightful discussion of Perovskii and his family, see Alexander Etkind, *Internal Colonization: Russia's Imperial Experience* (Cambridge: Polity Press, 2011), 150–169.

102. Semenova, *Voennoe upravlenie,* 102. Perovskii hosted from fifteen to thirty people for lunch every day. Chernov, *Zametki po istorii,* 68, 151. A. G. Prokof'eva, G. P. Matvievskaia, V. Iu. Prokof'eva, and I. K. Zubova, eds., *Neizvestnyi Vladimir Ivanovich Dal': Orenburgskii krai v ocherkakh i nauchnykh trudakh pisatelia* (Orenburg: Orenburgskoe Knizhnoe Izdatel'stvo, 2002), 34.

103. Chernov, *Zametki po istorii,* 67; Ivan F. Blaramburg, *Vospominaniia,* trans. O. I. Zhigalina (Moscow: Nauka, 1978), 298–299. When Perovskii returned as military governor in 1851, he created another "kochevka" about 80 miles north of Orenburg. Gvozdikova, *Otchet,* 103.

104. Gvozdikova, *Otchet,* 7, 108.

105. Chernov, *Zametki po istorii,* 129.

106. Zalesov, "Zapiski N. G. Zalesova," no. 1 (1903): 60–61; no. 3 (1903): 282; Chernov, *Zametki po istorii,* 92, 115.

107. Chernov, *Zametki po istorii,* 64.

108. RGIA, f. 1021, op. 1, god 1851, d. 100, ll. 3 ob.–4, 5 ob.–6.

109. Zalesov, "Zapiski N. G. Zalesova," no. 1 (1903): 57.

110. O. V. Vasil'eva, V. V. Latypova, et al., *Doroga k khramu* (Ufa: TsGIA RB, 1993), 81–83; R. G. Ignat'ev, *Episkop Mikhail, byvshii orenburgskii i ufimskii. Po sluchaiu 40 let ot dnia konchiny ego* (Moscow: M. G. Volchaninov, 1898), 28–31, 44, 51–52.

111. Ignat'ev, *Episkop Mikhail,* 53–54.

112. William Craft Brumfield, *A History of Russian Architecture* (Seattle: University of Washington Press, 2004), 397–399.

113. If owners lacked funds to rebuild, they were supposed to receive some compensation from the state and be given land near the city. Chernov, *Zametki po istorii orenburgskogo kraia*, 74.

114. "Gg. nachal'nikam bashkirskikh and meshcheriakskikh kantonov," April 20, 1836, in Rim Z. Ianguzin and Gul'naz B. Danilova, comps., *Karavan-sarai*, 3rd ed. (Ufa: Kitap, 1996), 106–107.

115. Viktor Dorofeev, "Simvol goroda," in *Karavan-sarai*, 69.

116. Dorofeev, "Simvol goroda," in *Karavan-sarai*, 78. See also Baryi G. Kalimullin, *Karavan-sarai v g. Orenburge* (Moscow: Izdatel'stvo Literatury po Stroitel'stvu, 1966), 29.

117. Ianguzin and Danilova, comps., *Karavan-sarai*, 151, 154–156.

118. PSZRI, series II, vol. 9, no. 6,852 (February 26, 1834), 163–164; PSZRI, series II, vol. 12, no. 10,281 (May 27, 1837), 342. Semenova, *Voennoe upravlenie*, 150–151.

119. Wortman, *Scenarios of Power*, vol. 1, 233–234.

120. PSZRI, series II, vol. 31, no. 30,138 (February 4, 1856), pt. 1, 70–71; pt. 2, 26–32.

121. Shakurova, *Bashkirskaia volost'*, 76–77; Tagirova, *Kantonnye nachal'niki Bashkirii*, 53.

122. Chernov, *Zametki po istorii*, 83.

123. By the 1850s, most Bashkirs and Meshcheriaks—200,190 men in volosts distant from the fortified border—paid a tax instead of serving, while 101,126 in areas closest to the frontier with Central Asia continued to serve as they had before. Khamza F. Usmanov, ed., *Istoriia Bashkortostana s drevneishikh vremen do 60-x godov XIX v.* (Ufa: Kitap, 1997), 352–353, 361.

124. PSZRI, series II, vol. 30, no. 29,060 (February 22, 1855), 170–171; no. 29,519 (July 14, 1855), 512; no. 29,769 (October 31, 1855), 641.

125. *Kratkii ocherk istorii orenburgskogo nepliuevskogo kadetskago korpusa* (Orenburg: A. N. Gavrilova, 1913), 4–5. The school had changed names four times by 1917.

126. PSZRI, series II, vol. 15, no. 14,029 (December 6, 1840), 787–791. Chernov, *Zametki po istorii*, 96. In 1862, Orenburg official Grigor'ev took a Kazakh pseudonym, Sultan Mendali Priraliev, to convey Russian officials' hopes for the Nepliuev Cadet School. Grigor'ev's "Priraliev" recalled that Kazakhs learned what Russian students learned and left the institution with the same "development of the mind and heart" as their "comrade Russians." Sultan Mendali Priraliev, "Iz zauralskoi stepi (Pis'ma k redaktoru *Dnia*)," reprinted in *Orenburgskie gubernskie vedemosti*, no. 21 (May 26, 1862), 95.

127. Zalesov, "Zapiski N. G. Zalesova," *Russkoe starina* 114, no. 1 (1903): 47, 49, 51.

128. Asfandiiarov, *Kantonnoe upravlenie*, 155–156.

129. S. Shukshintsev, "Pervye vrachi iz bashkir v orenburgskom krae," TOUAK 11 (1903): 14–16; Chernov, *Zametki po istorii*, 55; Anna Afanas'eva, "'Osvobodit' . . . ot shaitanov i sharlatanov': Diskursy i praktiki rossiiskoi meditsiny v kazakhskoi stepi v XIX veke," *Ab Imperio* 4 (2008): 137.

130. PSZRI, series II, vol. 11, no. 8,771 (January 13, 1836), 35–36; vol. 24, no. 23,616 (October 31, 1849), 142.

131. Historian Saveia Mikhailova writes that at least half of the three dozen "Tatar, Bashkir, and Kazakh" students at Kazan University in the period 1840 to 1861 were

from Bashkiria. Saveia Mikhailova, *Kazanskii universitet v dukhovnoi kul'ture narodov vostoka Rossii* (Kazan: Kazan University Press, 1991), 336–337.

132. Khamza F. Usmanov, *Razvitie kapitalizma v sel'skom khoziaistve Bashkirii v poreformennyi period, 60–90-e gody XIX v.* (Moscow: Nauka, 1981), 31; Fazyl'ian A. Ishkulov, *Sudebno-administrativnaia reforma v Bashkortostane* (Ufa: Kitap, 1994), 55–56.

133. Tagirova, *Kantonnye nachal'niki Bashkirii,* 66, 78, 120.

134. The statute establishing the Order of St. Stanislav of May 28, 1839, specified that those in the Bashkir-Meshcheriak host who received the order only acquired personal, not hereditary, nobility. PSZRI, series II, vol. 14, no. 12,385 (May 28, 1839), 523. Bashkirs who acquired noble status, unlike their Russian Orthodox counterparts, did not have freedom to choose their form of service or elect not to serve at all. A. Ia. Il'iasova's careful research identifies seventeen noble families of Bashkir origins starting with Kucherbai Akchulpanov and his son in 1793 through Mirsalikh Bikchurin in 1868. He writes that no Bashkirs became nobles between 1845 and 1863. A. Ia. Il'iasova, "Osobennosti formirovaniia dvorianskogo sosloviia iz Bashkir," *Vestnik cheliabinskogo gosudarstvennogo universiteta* 38 (2009): 26–32. Tagirova writes that no Bashkirs were ennobled from 1851 to 1865. Tagirova, *Kantonnye nachal'niki Bashkirii,* 45, 126, 128.

135. Tagirova, *Kantonnye nachal'niki Bashkirii,* 68, 86, 104.

136. NA UNTS RAN, f. 3, op. 1, ed. khr. 1, ll. 9–12.

137. On Syrtlanov's service in Samarkand, see Alexander S. Morrison, *Russian Rule in Samarkand, 1868–1910: A Comparison with British India* (Oxford: Oxford University Press, 2008), 143–146.

138. Tagirova, *Kantonnye nachal'niki Bashkirii,* 134; Asfandiiarov, *Kantonnoe upravlenie,* 159–160.

139. Larissa A. Iamaeva, comp., *Musul'manskie deputaty gosudarstvennoi dumy Rossii, 1906–1917* (Ufa: Kitap, 1998), 284, 302–303; Asfandiiarov, *Kantonnoe upravlenie,* 155–156.

140. Tagirova, *Kantonnye nachal'niki Bashkirii,* 80–84. Tagirova's information comes from an inventory of the possessions of Tukhvatulla Utiavov, the only Bashkir elder exiled to Siberia for criminal activity. He had been under investigation twenty times in as many years for everything from bribery to a murder committed by his son. The Orenburg Criminal Court sought to strip him of his post in 1820, but Utiavov's connections and Governor-General Essen kept him in his position. Finally, a new governor, Graf Sukhtelen, ordered him sent to "a distant place" in 1830. Utiavov's ill-gotten gains may have made him wealthier than others, but it is also likely that some of his possessions were removed before authorities could confiscate them.

141. Iu. Absaliamov et al., *Ufimskie pomeshchiki: Tipy istochnikov, vidy dokumentatsii* (Ufa, 2013), 162–163, 165. http://cp809702.cpanel.tech-logol.ru/fr/o/public/Pomeshik.pdf, accessed July 21, 2014.

142. Tagirova, *Kantonnye nachal'niki Bashkirii,* 78–79, 85, 110; Abasaliamov et al., *Ufimskie pomeshchiki,* 163.

143. From 1820 to 1830, 37 percent had one wife, 25 percent had two, 13 percent had three, and 25 percent had four, the most allowed according to local Muslim tradition. Tagirova, *Kantonnye nachal'niki Bashkirii,* 79. By contrast, statistics for Bashkiria as a whole from 1816 indicated only 10.8 percent of Bashkir households in predominantly agricultural areas included multiple wives, and 12.4 percent did in areas where animal

husbandry predominated. Anvar Z. Asfandiiarov, *Bashkirskaia sem'ia v proshlom* (Ufa: Kitap, 1997), 58–59.

144. Tagirova, *Kantonnye nachal'niki Bashkirii*, 77, 119; Abasaliamov et al., *Ufimskie pomeshchiki*, 162.

145. Nazarov, "Zametki bashkira o bashkirakh," *Sovremennik* 99, no. 11 (1863): 58.

146. Fidail' F. Shaiakhmetov, *Mezhdu velikoi step'iu i osedlost'iu: Protsessy sedentarizatsii Bashkir i rasprostraneniia zemledelia v XVII–XIX vv.* (Ufa: Bashkirskogo Gosudarstvennogo Universiteta, 2005), 150.

147. RGIA, f. 1021, op. 1, d. 100, l. 13.

148. Shaiakhmetov, *Mezhdu velikoi step'iu i osedlost'iu*, 173. Perovskii had issued similar instructions in 1834 and 1835. RGIA f. 1021, op. 1, god 1851, d. 100, ll. 12–12 ob.

149. Shaiakhmetov, *Mezhdu velikoi step'iu i osedlost'iu*, 178–181, 256–257.

150. Rim Z. Ianguzin, *Khoziaistvo Bashkir dorevoliutsionnoi Rossii* (Ufa: Bashkirskoe Knizhnoe Izdatel'stvo, 1989), 114.

151. Shaiakhmetov, *Mezhdu velikoi step'iu i osedlost'iu*, 195.

152. P. Nebol'sin, *Rasskazy proezzhego* (St. Petersburg: Tipografiia Shtab Voenno-Uchebnykh Zavedenii, 1854), 250–251; Chernov, *Zametki po istorii*, 119.

153. Minnigali Nadergulov, ed., "Obrazets bashkirskoi voiskovoi memuaristiki XIX veka," *Vatandash* (August 2008), http://www.vatandash.ru/index.php?article=1672, accessed July 18, 2014.

154. Nebol'sin, *Rasskazy proezzhego*, 248; Ianguzin, *Khoziaistvo Bashkir*, 115.

155. Ia. Sakharov, "Zametki otnositel'no zemledeliia v Bashkiria," *Vestnik promyshlennosti* 9, no. 1 (November 1860): 35–36. Sakharov was a pseudonym of Vasilii Grigor'ev. Nathaniel Knight, "Grigor'ev in Orenburg, 1851–1862: Russian Orientalism in Service of Empire?" *Slavic Review* 59, no. 1 (Spring 2000): 74–100.

156. RGIA, f. 1021, op. 1, god 1851, d. 100, l. 22 ob.

157. N. Kazantsev, *Opisanie Bashkirtsev* (St. Petersburg: Obshchestvennaia Pol'za, 1866), 29.

158. Knight, "Grigor'ev in Orenburg"; RGIA, f. 1021, op. 1, god 1851, d. 100, ll. 18–18 ob.

159. Chernov, *Zametki po istorii*, 113.

160. In all, 370 people, including twenty-nine lower-level officers and nine mullahs, were punished for their participation. Sixteen were sentenced to death. *Istoriia Bashkortostana*, 423–425. I. S. Shukshintsev, "Volneniia v Bashkirii v 1835 godu," TOUAK 11 (1903): 97–108.

161. Kuzeev, *Istoricheskaia etnografiia*, 254–255.

162. Pavel I. Nebol'sin, "Otchet o puteshestvii v orenburgskii i astrakhanskii krai," *VRGO*, ch. 4, kn. 1 (1852): 16–17.

163. Alexander Pushkin, "The Captain's Daughter," in *The Collected Stories*, intro. John Bayley, trans. Paul Debreczeny and Walter Arndt (New York: Alfred A. Knopf, 1999), 368. In 1833, Pushkin spent about four months in the area researching the novel and his *A History of Pugachev*.

164. Slezkine, *Arctic Mirrors*, 82–83.

165. This summary follows that of Slezkine in *Arctic Mirrors*, 84–86. Regarding the "Steppe Duma," see Sergey Glebov, "Siberian Middle Ground: Languages of Rule and Accommodation on the Siberian Frontier," in *Empire Speaks Out: Languages of Rational-*

ization and Self-Description in the Russian Empire, ed. Ilya Gerasimov, Jan Kusber, and Alexander Semyonov (Leiden: Brill, 2009), 145–148.

166. Slezkine, *Arctic Mirrors,* 85.

167. Natalia A. Ivanova, and Valentina P. Zheltova, *Soslovnoe obshchestvo rossiiskoi imperii (XVIII–nachalo XX veka)* (Moscow: Novyi Khronograf, 2009), 673–674, 677.

168. Joseph II of Austria promoted agricultural settlements for Jews in Austria-Hungary in 1785. John Doyle Klier, *Russia Gathers Her Jews: The Origins of the "Jewish Question" in Russia, 1772–1825* (DeKalb: Northern Illinois University Press, 1986), 40–41, 138, 153–155.

169. Michael Stanislawski, *Tsar Nicholas I and the Jews: The Transformation of Jewish Society in Russia, 1825–1855* (Philadelphia, Pa.: Jewish Publication Society of America, 1983), 157–159, 168.

170. Stanislawski, *Tsar Nicholas I and the Jews,* 14–15.

171. Olga Litvak, *Conscription and the Search for Modern Russian Jewry* (Bloomington: Indiana University Press, 2006), 18–19, 28.

172. Ol'ga Minkina points out that Jewish deputies received respect under Alexander I, but Jews were not allowed to become nobles. Ol'ga Minkina, *"Syny Rakhili": Evreiskie deputaty v rossiiskoi imperii, 1772–1825* (Moscow: Novoe Literaturnoe Obozrenie, 2011), 140, 220. Benjamin Nathans, *Beyond the Pale: The Jewish Encounter with Late Imperial Russia* (Berkeley: University of California Press, 2002), 72–73.

173. Kappeler, *The Russian Empire,* 216–218.

174. Kappeler, *The Russian Empire,* 179–185.

175. Michael Khodarkovsky, *Bitter Choices: Loyalty and Betrayal in the Russian Conquest of the North Caucasus* (Ithaca, N.Y.: Cornell University Press, 2011), 69–70, 129–130.

176. Crews, *For Tsar and Prophet,* 23. A Russian imperial legislative proposal in 1804 called for the creation of a Jewish Sanhedrin, or grand council. A Sanhedrin never took place in Russia, but Napoleon convoked one in Paris in 1806. Minkina, *"Syny Rakhili,"* 94.

177. Wortman, *Scenarios of Power,* vol. 1, 170, 202, 205–210, 303, quoted at 170. Thierry Lentz, "Imperial France in 1808 and Beyond," in *The Napoleonic Empire and the New European Political Culture,* ed. Michael Broers, Peter Hicks, and Augustin Guimerá (Basingstoke: Palgrave Macmillan, 2012), 30.

178. Jane Burbank and Frederick Cooper, *Empires in World History: Power and the Politics of Difference* (Princeton, N.J.: Princeton University Press, 2010), 229–232.

179. Richard S. Wortman, *Scenarios of Power: Myth and Ceremony in Russian Monarchy, vol. 2: From Alexander II to the Abdication of Nicholas II* (Princeton, N.J.: Princeton University Press, 2000), 20.

4. PARTICIPATORY EMPIRE, 1855–1881

1. Regarding these honors, see L. E. Shepelev, *Tituly, mundiry, ordena v rossiiskoi imperii* (Leningrad: Nauka, 1991), 190–214.

2. NA UNTS RAN, f. 3, op. 1, ed. khr. 2, v. 1, ll. 99–100.

3. *V pamiat' stoletiia orenburgskogo magometanskogo dukhovnogo sobraniia* (Ufa: Tipografiia Gubernskogo Pravleniia, 1891), 45; NA UNTS RAN, f. 3, op. 1, ed. khr. 2, v. 1, l. 260.

4. RGIA, f. 821, op. 8, d. 754, l. 114.

5. Richard Wortman, *Scenarios of Power: Myth and Ceremony in Russian Monarchy*, *vol. 2: From Alexander II to the Abdication of Nicholas II* (Princeton, N.J.: Princeton University Press, 2000), 59. Larissa Zakharova, "Autocracy and the Reforms of 1861–1874 in Russia: Choosing Paths of Development," in *Russia's Great Reforms, 1855–1881*, ed. Ben Eklof, John Bushnell, and Larissa Zakharova (Bloomington: Indiana University Press, 1994), 19–39.

6. John Darwin, *After Tamerlane: The Global History of Empire since 1405* (New York: Bloomsbury Press, 2008), 229–230.

7. Francis W. Wcislo, *Reforming Rural Russia: State, Local Society, and National Politics, 1855–1914* (Princeton, N.J.: Princeton University Press, 1990), 44–45. Reform of municipal governance took place in Bashkiria in 1870 as elsewhere but had less effect, since Bashkiria's urban population was small.

8. Kotsonis notes that that this discussion "ignored the issue of formal citizenship (*grazhdanstvo*)." Yanni Kotsonis, "'Face-to-Face': The State, the Individual, and the Citizen in Russian Taxation, 1863–1917," *Slavic Review* 63, no. 2 (Summer 2004): 222. For a view defining *grazhdanstvennost'* as citizenship, see Dov Yaroshevski, "Empire and Citizenship," in *Russia's Orient: Imperial Borderlands and Peoples, 1700–1917*, ed. Daniel Brower and Edward J. Lazzerini (Bloomington: Indiana University Press, 1997), 58–79.

9. Regarding a related shift from a notion of faith as primarily "a matter of fulfilling religious obligations, accepting legal ascription, and recognizing the church's authority" to faith as "belief and religious conviction," see Paul Werth, *At the Margins of Orthodoxy: Mission, Governance, and Confessional Politics in Russia's Volga-Kama Region, 1827–1905* (Ithaca, N.Y.: Cornell University Press, 2002), 124–146.

10. Charles Tilly, *Coercion, Capital and European States, AD 990–1992*, rev. ed. (Cambridge: Blackwell, 1992), 2–3. Sviatoslav Kaspe articulates a similar understanding of national state, focusing on the Great Reforms and the Polish uprising of 1863 as transformational factors. See Sviatoslav Kaspe, *Imperiia i modernizatsiia: Obshchaia model' i rossiiskaia spetsifika* (Moscow: Rosspen, 2001); and "Imperial Political Culture and Modernization in the Second Half of the Nineteenth Century," in *Russian Empire: Space, People, Power, 1700–1930*, ed. Jane Burbank, Mark von Hagen, and Anatolyi Remnev (Bloomington: Indiana University Press, 2007), 455–493.

11. RGIA, f. 1149, op. 6, god 1865, d. 16, l. 26. On the role of taxation in breaking down the isolation of status groups and the limitations of such efforts, see Yanni Kotsonis, *States of Obligation: Taxes and Citizenship in the Russian Empire and Early Soviet Republic* (Toronto: University of Toronto Press, 2014), 27–54.

12. My formulation has been particularly influenced by those in Jane Burbank, "An Imperial Rights Regime: Law and Citizenship in the Russian Empire," *Kritika: Explorations in Russian and Eurasian History* 7, no. 3 (Summer 2006): 406, 430–431; Valerie Kivelson, *Cartographies of Tsardom: The Land and Its Meanings in Seventeenth-Century Russia* (Ithaca, N.Y.: Cornell University Press, 2006), 11; and Benjamin Nathans, *Beyond the Pale: The Jewish Encounter with Late Imperial Russia* (Berkeley: University of California Press, 2002), 15–17.

13. Elena I. Campbell, *The Muslim Question and Russian Imperial Governance* (Bloomington: Indiana University Press, 2015), 21–32.

14. A local official, Vasilii Grigor'ev, wrote under a pseudonym that the state had no right to try to change a people's way of life. Even intelligent and conscientious bureaucrats scarcely did more good than harm. Ia. Sakharov, "Zametki otnositel'no zemledeliia v Bashkirii i pozharov v Orenburge," *Vestnik promyshlennosti* 1 (January 1861): 29–41. On Grigor'ev, see Nathaniel Knight, "Grigor'ev in Orenburg, 1851–1862: Russian Orientalism in the Service of Empire?" *Slavic Review* 59, no. 1 (Spring 2000): 74–100.

15. "Iz Bashkirii," *Sankt-Peterburgskie vedomosti* 9 (1864): 774.

16. N. Kazantsev, comp., *Opisanie bashkirtsev* (St. Peterburg: Obshchestvennaia Pol'za, 1866), 29.

17. V. M. Florinskii, "Bashkiriia i Bashkirtsy," *Vestnik Evropy* 9, vol. 6 (December 1874): 764–765.

18. G. I. Uspensky, "Ot Orenburga do Ufy," in G. I. Uspensky, *Sobranie sochinenii*, vol. 8 (Moscow: Gos. Izd. Khudozhestvennoi Literatury, 1957), 375–376.

19. N. I. Veselovskii, comp., *Vasilii Vasil'evich Grigor'ev po ego pis'mam i trudam, 1816–1881* (St. Petersburg: A. Transhel', 1887), 185.

20. Steam transport was much faster than nonmechanized river travel. On river transport and the Volga-Urals region's connections to the global economy, see Mustafa Tuna, "Imperial Russia's Muslims: Inroads of Modernity" (PhD dissertation, Princeton University, 2009), 151–167.

21. R. G. Ganeev, V. V. Boltushkin, and R. G. Kuzeev, eds., *Istoriia Ufy: Kratkii ocherk* (Ufa: Bashkirskoe Knizhnoe Izdatel'stvo, 1981), 96.

22. Fidail' F. Shaiakhmetov, *Mezhdu velikoi step'iu i osedlost'iu: Protsessy sedentarizatsii Bashkir i rasprostraneniia zemledelia v XVII–XIX vv.* (Ufa: Bashkirskogo Gosudarstvennogo Universiteta, 2005), 185–186, 262.

23. Orenburg Province noblemen owned 60,280 serfs, private factories had 47,370 serfs, the emperor owned 24,565 serfs, and there were 97,036 state peasants, for a total of 229,251. Bulat S. Davletbaev, *Krest'ianskaia reforma 1861 goda v Bashkirii* (Moscow: Nauka, 1983), 46–47, 63, 75, 89, 103, 107.

24. Vasilii Grigor'ev was one of the few whom Bezak did not replace, but the two men soon had a falling-out. Veselovskii, *Vasilii Vasil'evich Grigor'ev*, 200–205. According to Nikolai G. Zalesov, Grigor'ev's authority declined greatly under Bezak, who did not like influential people around him. N. G. Zalesov, "Zapiski N. G. Zalesova," *Russkaia starina* 114, no. 5 (1903): 35.

25. Petr P. Zhakmon, "Iz vospominanii orenburgskogo starozhila," *Istoricheskii vestnik* 27, 105 (July 1906): 75. Zalesov is at times critical of Bezak as a military commander but considers him "wise as a person and as a civil administrator." Zalesov, "Zapiski N. G. Zalesova," no. 5: 30, 36.

26. Ivan V. Chernov, *Zametki po istorii orenburgskoi gubernii general-maiora I. V. Chernova* (Orenburg: Orenburgskaia Guberniia, 2007), 179–180.

27. RGIA, f. 1263, op. 1, ed. khr. 2906, zh. st. 717–719, l. 351 ob.

28. RGIA, f. 1149, op. 6, god 1865, d. 16, l. 13.

29. Customs and salt administrations had headquarters "more or less" separate from the governor-general's authority, too. RGIA, f. 1149, op. 6, god 1865, d. 16, ll. 13–13 ob.

30. RGIA, f. 1263, op. 1 ed. xr. 2906, zh. st. 717–9, ll. 356, 424. Complaints about diversity of administration were not new. In 1830, General I. F. Pashkevich decried the lack of unity in forms of administration, law, and finance in the Caucasus. Robert Crews,

"The Russian Worlds of Islam," in *Islam and the European Empires*, ed. David Motadel (Oxford: Oxford University Press, 2014), 14.

31. RGIA, f. 1149, op. 6, god 1865, d. 16, l. 26.

32. RGIA, f. 1181, op. 15, god 1862, d. 123, ll. 515 ob., 518; Chernov, *Zametki po istorii orenburgskoi*, 187.

33. Chernov, *Zametki po istorii orenburgskoi*, 186.

34. RGIA, f. 1263, op. 1 ed. xr. 2906 zh. st. 717–719, l. 356.

35. RGIA, f. 1181, op. 15, god 1862, d. 124, l. 518–518 ob.

36. RGIA, f. 1181, op. 15, god 1862, d. 123, l. 517.

37. RGIA, f. 1263, op. 1, ed. khr. 2958, zh. st. 168, ll. 6 ob.–7.

38. RGIA, f. 1181, op. 15, god 1862, d. 123: ll. 564, 571.

39. RGIA, f. 1181, op. 15, god 1862, d. 124, ll. 521 ob., 528–528 ob.

40. RGIA, f. 1181, op. 15, god 1862, d. 124, l. 541. Korf's views here echo those of Vasilii Grigor'ev, who rejected military administration of Bashkirs. Veselovskii, *Vasilii Vasil'evich Grigor'ev*, 066–069.

41. RGIA, f. 1181, op. 15, god 1862, d. 124, ll. 542, 543 ob.

42. RGIA, f. 1181, op. 15, god 1862, d. 124, l. 545.

43. PSZRI, series II, vol. 40, no. 42,282 (July 2, 1865), 753–776. This contains the "Statute on Bashkirs" first published May 14, 1863, supplemented by the Orenburg governor-general on the basis of the State Council's opinion of July 2, 1865.

44. In August 1863, 808 villages and 130 districts (*volostnikh* or *iurtovykh obshchestv*) were formed in Bashkiria. The change from cantons to peasant districts was somewhat tense, but open conflict was avoided. Canton heads feared the loss of their authority, and Bashkirs feared that loss of their lands, enserfment, or even Christianization would result from their change in status. Davletbaev, *Krest'ianskaia reforma*, 109–110; Ivan A. Tukman, comp., *Polozhenie o Bashkirakh* (Ufa: Pechat'nia Blokhina, 1912), 110–111.

45. PSZRI, series II, vol. 40, no. 42,058 (May 31, 1865), 477–482.

46. PSZRI, series II, vol. 40, no. 42,282 (July 2, 1865), 753–776.

47. N. A. Gurvich, ed. and comp., *Sbornik materialov dlia istorii ufimskogo dvorianstva, sostavlennyi V. A. Novikovym v 1879 g., prodolzhennyi i dopolnennyi do 1902 goda vkliuchitel'no deputatom ufimskogo dvorianstva N. A. Gurvichem*, (Ufa: Blokhin, 1904), 42.

48. PSZRI, series II, vol. 42, no. 44,424a (April 2, 1867), 3. Regarding this decree, see Alexander Morrison, "Metropole, Colony, and Imperial Citizenship in the Russian Empire," *Kritika: Explorations in Russian and Eurasian History* 13, no. 2 (Spring 2012): 340–341; Yaroshevski, "Empire and Citizenship," 69–70.

49. In 1886, a "military gimnasium" opened within the school, and it became the best secondary school in the region. In it, students could study Tatar rather than German, and classical languages were eliminated. Marsel' N. Farkhshatov, *Narodnoe obrazovanie v Bashkirii v poreformennyi period 60–90e gody XIX v.* (Moscow: Nauka, 1994), 131–132. *Kratkii ocherk istorii orenburgskogo nepliuskogo kadestskogo korpusa* (Orenburg: A. N. Gavrilova, 1913), 9.

50. The statute specified several limits on Bashkir land sales: The village assembly had to approve and the district administration had to certify them, and the Orenburg governor-general needed to confirm them. PSZRI, series II, vol. 40, no. 42,282 (July 2, 1865), 753–776; P. Shramchenko, "Zemel'nyi vopros v ufimskoi gubernii," *Russkii vestnik* 158 (March 1882): 463–464.

51. PSZRI, series II, vol. 40, no. 42,282 (July 2, 1865), 753–776, cited at 758 and 767.

52. Daniel Brower, *Turkestan and the Fate of the Russian Empire* (London: Routledge, 2003), 27–28.

53. RGADA, f. 1263, op. 1, d. 3,213, ll. 8–9, cited in Shaiakhmetov, *Mezhdu velikoi step'iu i osedlost'iu*, 187.

54. Central authorities feared that easing restrictions on migration would lead to uncontrolled movement that would disturb the social order and the rural economy of central Russia. By contrast, local governors and landowners in comparatively sparsely settled border regions welcomed migrants. N. V. Remezov, *Ocherki iz zhizni v dikoi bashkirii: Byl' v skazochnoi strane* (Moscow: Kushnerov, 1887); Shramchenko, "Zemel'nyi vopros," 449–532.

55. Campbell, *The Muslim Question*, 26–32.

56. Shramchenko, "Zemel'nyi vopros," 465–466.

57. PSZRI, series II, vol. 44, no. 46,750 (February 10, 1869), 148–156.

58. *Orenburgskii listok* (February 15, 1876), cited in Khamza F. Usmanov, *Razvitie kapitalizma v sel'skom khoziaistve Bashkirii v poreformennyi period, 60–90-e gody XIX v.* (Moscow: Nauka, 1981) , 45.

59. PSZRI, series II, vol. 44, no. 46,952 (April 9, 1869), 310; vol. 44, no. 49,230 (February 6, 1871), 89–90.

60. The average price per des. was about 1 ruble, 80 kopecks, when the market price of land varied from 7 to 25 rubles per des. Usmanov, *Razvitie kapitalizma*, 42–43, quoted at 42.

61. See Joshua Sanborn, *Drafting the Russian Nation: Military Conscription, Total War, and Mass Politics, 1905–1925* (DeKalb: Northern Illinois University Press, 2003), 20–62.

62. RGIA, f. 906, op. 1, d. 28, ll. 35–36, cited in Robert F. Baumann, "Universal Service Reform and Russia's Imperial Dilemma," *War and Society* 4, no. 2 (September 1986): 31.

63. Robert F. Baumann, "Subject Nationalities in the Military Service of Imperial Russia: The Case of the Bashkirs," *Slavic Review* 46, no. 3/4 (Fall/Winter 1987): 489–502.

64. TsGIA RB, f. 11, op. 1, d. 263, ll. 32–34, 43, 56–57 ob., 60–61, 64, 69, 70–71, 127.

65. Baumann, "Subject Nationalities," 497; PSZRI, series II, vol. 49, no. 53,706 (July 6, 1874), 17–18. Similar squadrons existed for Caucasian peoples and Crimean Tatars.

66. PSZRI, series II, vol. 50, no. 54,927 (July 21, 1875), 76–77; vol. 53, no. 58,341 (March 30, 1878), 210–211.

67. A. Kvitka, "Zametki o bashkirskom konnom polke," *Voennyi sbornik* 6 (1882): 315, cited in Baumann, "Subject Nationalities," 500.

68. V. Afanas'ev, "O bashkirskom konnom polke," *Voennyi sbornik* 8 (1882): 328–329, 332, quoted at 332, cited in Baumann, "Subject Nationalities," 501.

69. Marc Szeftel attributed "a certain limitation of autocracy" to zemstvo legislation, since the law delegated a limited amount of authority to the bodies. Marc Szeftel, "The Form of Government of the Russian Empire Prior to the Constitutional Reforms of 1905–1906," in *Essays in Russian and Soviet History*, ed. John Shelton Curtiss (New York: Columbia University Press, 1965), 116–119. Terence Emmons, "The Zemstvo in Historical Perspective," in *The Zemstvo in Russia: An Experiment in Local Self-Government*, ed. Terence Emmons and Wayne S. Vucinich (Cambridge, Mass.: Harvard University Press, 1982), 423.

70. Fazyl'ian A. Ishkulov, *Sudebno-administrativnaia reforma v Bashkortostane* (Ufa: Kitap, 1994), 78; TsAOO RB, f. 10, op. 9, d. 22, ll. 39–40, cited in Nikolai I. Leonov, *Burzhuaznye reformy 60–70-x godov XIX v v Bashkirii* (Ufa: Redaktsionno-Izdatel'skii Otdel Bashkirskogo Universiteta, 1993), 5–6.

71. Leonov, *Burzhuaznye reformy 60–70 gg.*, 10–11; Boris Veselovskii, *Istoriia zemstva za sorok let*, vol. 4 (St. Petersburg: O. N. Popov, 1911), 404–417; A. I. Veretennikova, "Zapiski zemskogo vracha," *Novyi mir* 32, no. 3 (March 1956): 209, 219–220.

72. In this respect the Ufa zemstvos included Muslims on a more equal basis than other institutions such as the provincial administration and even the city Duma, where non-Russian representation was limited to one-third of the deputies. Jewish participation in Western zemstvos was also limited to one-third of the total number of deputies.

73. Richard S. Wortman, *The Development of a Russian Legal Consciousness* (Chicago, Ill.: University of Chicago Press, 1976), 238; Jane Burbank, *Russian Peasants Go to Court: Legal Culture in the Countryside, 1905–1917* (Bloomington: Indiana University Press, 2004), 6.

74. Wortman, *The Development of a Russian Legal Consciousness*, 260.

75. TsGIA RB, f. 2, op. 63, d. 13,028, ll. 1–2; d. 3022, ll. 307–310, cited in Ishkulov, *Sudebno-administrativnaia reforma*, 75.

76. TsGIA RB, f. I-11, op. 1, d. 889, l. 4.

77. Ishkulov, *Sudebno-administrativnaia reforma*, 81.

78. PSZRI, series II, vol. 53, no. 58,758 (September 5, 1878), 71.

79. Burbank, *Russian Peasants Go to Court*, 5, 83, 119.

80. A list of county and provincial zemstvo assemblies compiled in early 1893 lists four Muslims as justices of the peace: Akhmetzian Basimov, Sultan Seid-Khan Dzhantiurin, Mustafa Kutlubaev, and Araslan-Ali Sultanov. RGIA, f. 1287, op. 27, d. 2709, ll. 1 ob.–30.

81. Ishkulov, *Sudebno-administrativnaia reforma*, 94, 116, 120, 129.

82. Burbank, "An Imperial Rights Regime," 402.

83. Michael Kemper, *Sufii i uchenye v Tatarstane i Bashkortostane: Islamskii diskurs pod russkim gospodstvom*, trans. Iskander Giliazov (Kazan: Idel-Press, 2008), 126.

84. Crews, *For Prophet and Tsar*, 141, 149.

85. S. G. Rybakov, ed., *Ustroistvo i nuzhdy upravleniia dukhovnymi delami musul'man v Rossii* (Petrograd: Tipografiia S. Samoilova, 1917), 7.

86. He had been decorated for his service in the Turkish war of 1828–1829 and in the suppression of the Polish uprising of 1830–1831. *V pamiat' stoletiia*, 43–45.

87. Azamatov, *Orenburgskoe magometanskoe dukhovnoe sobranie*; RGIA, f. 821, op. 8, d. 601, ll. 73, 85–85 ob., 86; the quotations from Bezak are located on 73.

88. Tevkelev's status in the eyes of tsarist administrators caused some Muslim scholars, such as Khusain Faizkhanov, to hope that Tevkelev could advance the cause of reform in Muslim education. Mirkasym Usmanov, *Zavetnaia mechta Khusaina Faizkhanova* (Kazan: Tatarskoe Knizhnoe Izdatel'stvo, 1980), 124–131. Prominent Muslim thinker and akhund Shigabuddin Mardzhani had sought to become mufti, but Il'minskii and the Ufa governor rejected them. They preferred a Muslim with a secular education. Tevkelev and Mardzhani, however, both believed that the mufti could help protect Muslim interests and needed to know Russian in order to improve relations with Russian speakers. Ahmet Kanlidere, *Reform within Islam: The Tajdid and Jadid Movement among the Kazan Tatars (1809–1917), Conciliation and Conflict* (Istanbul: Eren, 1997), 49. Michael Kemper describes Tevkelev as a military man who, like his predecessors except Gabdrakhimov, was "not a spiritual representative of Muslims." Kemper, *Sufii i uchenye*, 127.

89. Paul W. Werth, *The Tsar's Foreign Faiths: Toleration and the Fate of Religious Freedom in Imperial Russia* (Oxford: Oxford University Press, 2014), 144–145.

90. TsGIA RB, f. I-11, op. 1, d., 1110, l. 7. See also Campbell, *The Muslim Question,* 110–112.

91. RGIA, f. 821, op. 8, d. 611, ll. 143 ob.–144, cited in Werth, *The Tsar's Foreign Faiths,* 144.

92. RGIA, f. 821, op. 8, d. 594, ll. 30, 33 ob., d. 601, ll. 143 ob., and d. 616, ll. 49 ob.; TsGIA RB, f. I-295, op. 3, d. 6253, ll. 44, 45, 60 ob., cited in Azamatov, *Orenburgskoe magometanskoe dukhovnoe sobranie,* 101.

93. Daniel T. Orlovsky, *The Limits of Reform: The Ministry of Internal Affairs in Imperial Russia, 1802–1881* (Cambridge, Mass.: Harvard University Press, 1981), 84–93.

94. The elopement is described by Sergei T. Aksakov in his 1856 novel *Semeinaia khronika* (The family chronicle). Sergei T. Aksakov, "Semeinaia khronika," in *Sobranie sochinenii,* vol. 1 (Moscow: Gos. Izdatel'stvo Khudozhestvennoi Literatury, 1955), 269–272.

95. The police lacked staff who could decipher Tatar manuscripts seized in searches, which compounded the confusion. TsGIA RB, f. I-11, op. 1, d. 1076, ll. 1, 6, 15, 17, 58, 66–70.

96. TsGIA RB, f. I-11, op. 1, d. 1076, ll. 24–25, 60, 62, 66–70.

97. TsGIA RB, f. 295, op. 2, d. 1965, l. 175; RGIA, f. 821, op. 8, d. 607, ll. 2, 3, 9, cited in Azamatov, *Orenburgskoe magometanskoe dukhovnoe sobranie,* 166.

98. The mufti also presented justification within Islam for the study of Russian. TsGIA RB, f. I-11, op. 1, ed. khr. 959, l. 60 ob.

99. "Rasprostranenie gramotnosti mezhdu bashkirami," *UGV,* otd. neoffitsial'nyi, no. 14 (April 18, 1861): 60.

100. Political scientists have termed these "unassimilated bilingualism" and "assimilated bilingualism." David Laitin, Roger Peterson, and John Slocum, "Language and the State: Russia and the Soviet Union in Comparative Perspective," in *Thinking Theoretically about Soviet Nationalities: History and Comparison in the Study of the USSR,* ed. Alexander J. Motyl (New York: Columbia University Press, 1995), 129–168.

101. TsGIA RB, f. I-11, op. 1, d. 925, ll. 3, 4; *Zhurnaly ministerstva narodnogo prosveshcheniia,* ch. 147 (1870): 49.

102. K. D. Ushinskii, "Rodnoe slovo," *Pedagogicheskie sochineniia,* vol. 2 (Moscow: Pedagogika, 1988), 108–121.

103. Ministerstvo narodnogo prosveshcheniia, *Sbornik dokumentov i statei po voprosu ob obrazovanii inorodtsev* (St. Petersburg, 1869), 160, cited in John Slocum, "The Boundaries of National Identity: Religion, Language, and Nationality Politics in Late Imperial Russia" (PhD dissertation, University of Chicago, 1993), 139.

104. *Zhurnaly ministerstva narodnogo prosveshcheniia,* 53. The regulations are discussed in Robert P. Geraci, *Window on the East: National and Imperial Identities in Late Tsarist Russia* (Ithaca, N.Y.: Cornell University Press, 2001), 122–125; Wayne Dowler, "The Politics of Language in Non-Russian Elementary Schools in the Eastern Empire, 1865–1914," *Russian Review* 54, no. 4 (October 1995): 516–522; and Stephen J. Blank, "National Education, Church, and State in Tsarist Nationality Policy: The Il'minskii System," *Canadian-American Slavic Studies* 17, no. 4 (Winter 1983): 466–486.

105. France created similarly named "écoles arabes-françaises" in Algeria beginning in 1833, and these might have served as inspiration for the bilingual schools. The Algerian schools were not popular, however. John Ruedy, *Modern Algeria: The Origins and Development of a Nation,* 2nd ed. (Bloomington: Indiana University Press, 2005), 103.

106. Religious classes had to be financed by the local community. Imams could be present in classes to verify the strictly educational and non-missionary purposes of a school. *Zhurnaly ministerstva narodnogo prosveshcheniia*, 59.

107. Farkhshatov, *Narodnoe obrazovanie v Bashkirii*, 41.

108. TsGIA RB, f. I-11, op. 1, d. 924, l. 19 ob.

109. Paul Werth, "From 'Pagan' Muslims to 'Baptized' Communists: Religious Conversion and Ethnic Particularity in Russia's Eastern Provinces," *CSSH* 42, no. 3 (2000): 497–523; Isabelle Kreindler, "Educational Policies toward the Eastern Nationalities in Tsarist Russia: A Study of Il'minskii's System" (PhD dissertation, Columbia University, 1969).

110. TsGIA RB, f. I-11, op. 1, d. 924, l. 31.

111. *Zhurnaly ministerstva narodnogo prosveshcheniia*, 62.

112. TsGIA RB, f. I-11, op. 1, d. 925, ll. 31, 41, 181, 371, 431.

113. Responses pointing out the need for a similar requirement for Russians appear in TsGIA RB, f. I-11, op. 1, d. 925, ll. 37, 24–25 and 46–47.

114. *Istoricheskii ocherk narodnogo obrazovaniia v Orenburgskom Uchebnom Okruge za pervoe 25-letie ego sushchestvovaniia (1875–1899)*, vypusk 1 (Orenburg: I. I. Efimovskii-Mirovitskii, 1901), 16–17.

115. Alexis E. Pogorelskin, "*Vestnik Evropy* and the Polish Question in the Reign of Alexander II," *Slavic Review* 46, no. 1 (Spring 1987): 100.

116. The speech is reproduced in *Istoricheskii ocherk narodnogo obrazovaniia*, 26–29.

117. *PSZRI*, series II, vol. 53, no. 58,487 (May 9, 1878), 332–335; P. I. Liashchenko, *Ocherki agrarnoi evoliutsii Rossii*. Vol. 2, *Krest'ianskoe delo i poreformennaia zemleustroitel'naia politika* (St. Petersburg: Ministerstvo Finansov, 1913), 164–165.

118. Petr Dobrotvorskii, "Moia ispoved'," in P. I. Dobrotvorskii, *V glushi Bashkirii: Rasskazy, vospominaniia* (Ufa: Bashkirskoe Knizhnoe Izdatel'stvo, 1989), 192–193.

119. The instructions to M. E. Kovalevskii appear in the Rare Book and Manuscript Library, Columbia University, Maksim M. Kovalevskii collection, box 4.

120. See, for example, *Golos*, no. 2 (January 2, 1881): 2; no. 11 (January 11, 1881): 2; no. 26 (January 26, 1881): 2; no. 33 (February 2, 1881): 1; no. 34 (February 3, 1881): 2; no. 35 (February 4, 1881): 2; no. 42 (February 11, 1881): 3; no. 43 (February 12, 1881): 3; no. 45 (February 14, 1881): 3; no. 50 (February 19, 1881): 3; no. 51 (February 20, 1881): 4; no. 72 (March 13, 1881): 4; no. 103 (April 15, 1881): 3; *Nedelia*, no. 4 (1881): 130–131, no. 9 (1881): 321–322, and others.

121. *Golos*, no. 72 (March 13, 1881): 4. Kovalevskii refused the petitions. *Golos*, no. 103 (April 15, 1881): 3.

122. Usmanov, *Razvitie kapitalizma*, 48.

123. Pavel A. Valuev, *Dnevnik P. A. Valueva, ministra vnutrennikh del, v dvukh tomakh, vol. 1, 1861–1864*, ed. and comp. Petr A. Zaionchkovskii (Moscow: Akademiia Nauk, 1961), 50–51.

124. Nikolai V. Remezov, *Ocherki iz zhizni v dikoi bashkirii: Byl' v skazochnoi strane* (Moscow: Kushnerov, 1887). See Nikolai V. Remezov, *Ocherki iz zhizni dikoi bashkirii: Pereselencheskaia epopeia* (Moscow: Kushnerov, 1889), and Nikolai V. Remezov, *Ocherki iz zhizni dikoi bashkirii: Sudebnaia oshibka ili sozdannoe prestuplenie?* (Vladivostok: n.p., 1900). After Kovalevskii's inspection, Remezov was pressured to leave Ufa. He ended up working in Vladivostok as an administrative exile.

125. Uspensky, "Ot Orenburga do Ufy," 375–426.

126. In the eighteenth century, by contrast, the term "wild" or *dikii* "became a descriptive synonym of 'alien'." Yuri Slezkine, *Arctic Mirrors: Russia and the Small Peoples of the North* (Ithaca, N.Y.: Cornell University Press, 1994), 58.

127. Leo Tolstoy, "How Much Land Does a Man Need?" in *How Much Land Does a Man Need? And Other Stories*, trans. Ronald Wilks (London: Penguin, 1993), 96–110; Alexander Etkind, *Internal Colonization: Russia's Imperial Experience* (Cambridge: Polity Press, 2011), 6.

128. Rail G. Kuzeev, *Istoricheskaia etnografiia bashkirskogo naroda*, 2nd ed. (Ufa: Kitap, 2009), 263.

129. M. I. Rodnov, "Chislennost' tiurkskogo krest'ianstva ufimskoi gubernii v nachale XX v.," *Etnograficheskoe obozrenie* 6 (1996): 125.

130. Rim Z. Ianguzin, *Khoziaistvo Bashkir dorevoliutsionnoi Rossii* (Ufa: Bashkirskoe Knizhnoe Izdatel'stvo, 1989), 134.

131. Petr P. Zhakmon, "Khishchenie bashkirskikh zemel. (Iz vospominanii orenburgskogo starozhila.)," *Istoricheskii vestnik* 28, 107 (March 1907): 860–874.

132. Danielle M. Ross, "From the Minbar to the Barricades: The Transformation of the Volga-Ural 'Ulama into a Revolutionary Intelligentsia") PhD dissertation, University of Wisconsin–Madison, 2011), 146. Rasulev's political activism and religious innovation brought the hostile attention of imperial authorities, who exiled him to the province of Vologda in 1872. Werth, *The Tsar's Foreign Faiths*, 98–99.

133. RGB, otdel rukopisi, f. 364, k. 6, dela 1, l. 14.

134. Ianguzin, *Khoziaistvo Bashkir*, 143.

135. Dmitrii P. Nikol'skii, *Bashkiry: Etnograficheskoe i sanitarno-antropologicheskoe izsledovanie* (St. Petersburg: Soikin, 1899), 80; Ianguzin, *Khoziaistvo Bashkir*, 138–145. Most agricultural statistics were not broken down by estate category, so data are limited.

136. Nikol'skii, *Bashkiry*, 93–97; Ianguzin, *Khoziaistvo Bashkir*, 162–164. Sergei G. Rybakov, *Muzyka i pesni ural'skikh musul'man s ocherkom ikh byta* (St. Petersburg: Akademiia Nauk, 1897), 20, 281–282; M. D. Kiekbaev, *Bashkiry v gorodakh Bashkortostan: Istoriia i sovremennost'* (Ufa: NUR-Poligrafizdat, 1998), 18–23.

137. Grodno, Kovno, and Vil'no were excluded. Kermit E. McKenzie, "Zemstvo Organization and Role within the Administrative Structure," in *The Zemstvo in Russia: An Experiment in Local Self-Government*, ed. Terence Emmons and Wayne S. Vucinich (Cambridge: Cambridge University Press, 1982), 33–34. Legislation extending zemstos to Orenburg, Stavropol, and Astrakhan excluded Kazakhs and Kalmyks. Morrison, "Metropole, Colony, and Imperial Citizenship," 348.

138. Tomohiko Uyama, "A Particularist Empire: The Russian Policies of Christianization and Military Conscription in Central Asia," in *Empire, Islam, and Politics in Central Eurasia*, ed. Tomohiko Uyama (Sapporo: Slavic Research Center, 2007), 41.

139. TsGIA RB, f. I-11, op. 1, d. 889, ll. 51–51 ob.

140. Vladimir Bobrovnikov also describes the process of mutual study about practices of empire in his work on the Caucasus. Vladimir O. Bobrovnikov, *Musul'mane Severnogo Kavkaza: Obychai, pravo, nasilie. Ocherki po istorii i etnografii prava Nagornogo Dagestana* (Moscow: Vostochnaia Literatura-RAN, 2002), 171–174.

141. Jennifer E. Sessions, *By Sword and Plow: France and the Conquest of Algeria* (Ithaca, N.Y.: Cornell University Press, 2011), 215.

142. Ruedy, *Modern Algeria,* 74–75; Bobrovnikov, *Musul'mane Severnogo Kavkaza,* 174.

143. Ekaterina Pravilova, "The Property of Empire: Islamic Law and Russian Agrarian Policy in Transcaucasia and Turkestan," *Kritka: Explorations in Russian and Eurasian History* 12, no. 2 (Spring 2011): 360.

144. Ian Lustick, *State-Building Failure in British Ireland and French Algeria* (Berkeley, Calif.: Institute of International Studies, 1985), 58; Ruedy, *Modern Algeria,* 81.

145. Sessions, *By Sword and Plow,* 318–319.

146. Ruedy, *Modern Algeria,* 69, 75, 83. A desiatina is about 1.092 hectares and 2.7 acres. Between 1871 and 1885, French colonists in Algeria purchased 377 million hectares of land for 37 million francs, and forest tracts were sold for between 1 and 3 percent of their value. Theodore Zeldin, *France, 1848–1945,* vol. 2 (Oxford: Oxford University Press, 1977), 927. From 1871 to 1900, 1,147,000 hectares of land was simply seized. Lustick, *State-Building Failure,* 57.

147. Julia Clancy-Smith, "Islam and the French Empire in North Africa," in Motadel, *Islam and the European Empires,* 90–111.

148. Jane Burbank and Frederick Cooper, *Empires in World History: Power and the Politics of Difference* (Princeton, N.J.: Princeton University Press, 2010), 364–366.

149. The realization of these promises would, of course, take longer. The parliament was closed and the constitution suspended within a year, for instance. Donald Quataert, *The Ottoman Empire, 1700–1922* (Cambridge: Cambridge University Press, 2000), 63–68; Caroline Finkel, *Osman's Dream: The Story of the Ottoman Empire, 1300–1923* (New York: Basic Books, 2005), 447–451, 488–490.

150. Burbank and Cooper, *Empires in World History,* 365.

5. THE EMPIRE AND THE NATION, 1881–1904

1. *Vestnik ufimskogo zemstva,* god 4, vyp. 4, 22 (1882): 226–228.

2. On Umetbaev's participation in Alexander III's coronation, see NA UNTS RAN, f. 22, op. 1, ed khr. 1, vol. 1, ll. 234–260. The prayer is found on l. 260.

3. NA UNTS RAN, f. 22, op. 1, ed khr. 2, vol. 2, ll. 7 ob.–8. The Russian version of the poem appears in Umetbaev's archives. I thank Diane Nemec-Ignashev and Fred Corney for assistance with the translation.

4. Petr A. Zaionchkovsky, *The Russian Autocracy in Crisis, 1878–1882,* ed. and trans. Gary M. Hamburg (Gulf Breeze, Fla.: Academic International Press, 1979).

5. Martin Katz, *Mikhail N. Katkov: A Political Biography, 1818–1887* (The Hague: Mouton, 1966), 127.

6. Richard Wortman, *Scenarios of Power: Myth and Ceremony in Russian Monarchy, vol. 2: From Alexander II to Nicholas II* (Princeton, N.J.: Princeton University Press, 2000), 164, 237, 366.

7. R. G. Ganeev, V. V. Boltushkin, and R. G. Kuzeev, eds., *Istoriia Ufy: Kratkii ocherk* (Ufa: Bashkirskoe Knizhnoe Izdatel'stvo, 1981), 105.

8. Khamza F. Usmanov, *Razvitie kapitalizma v sel'skom khoziaistve Bashkirii v poreformennyi period, 60–90-e gody XIX v.* (Moscow: Nauka, 1981), 72.

9. A subsequent effort to raise funds for the Latvians marked the beginning of a local Latvian Aid society. TsGIA RB, f. I-11, op. 1, d. 1272, ll. 22, 55, 69, 77, 82.

10. Aleksandr Polunov, *Pod vlast'iu ober-prokurora: Gosudarstvo i tserkov' v epokhu Aleksandra III* (Moscow: AIRO-XX, 1996), 8–9.

11. On Nikanor, see John Strickland, *The Making of Holy Russia: The Orthodox Church and Russian Nationalism before the Revolution* (Jordanville, N.Y.: Holy Trinity Publications, 2013), 73–89. Strickland does not address Nikanor's tenure in Ufa Province or his perspective on Islam.

12. "Perepiska K. P. Pobednostseva," RA 53, no. 4 (1915): 458–473; no. 5 (1915): 68–111; no. 6 (1915): 244–256. Nikanor was transferred in December 1883 to the province of Kherson, the seat of which was the city of Odessa.

13. Strickland, *The Making of Holy Russia*, 75–76.

14. "Perepiska K. P. Pobednostseva," RA 53, no. 5 (1915): 70–71, 75.

15. "Perepiska K. P. Pobednostseva," RA 53, no. 5 (1915): 87–88.

16. "Iz zapisok Arkhiepiskopa Nikanora," RA 47, no. 5 (1909): 48–60; quoted at 45–46, 60.

17. "Iz zapisok Arkhiepiskopa Nikanora," RA 47, no. 2 (1909), 217, 219, 220, 222–226, no. 5 (1909): 26, 29.

18. "Iz zapisok Arkhiepiskopa Nikanora," RA 47, no. 5 (1909): 34–35, 60, 63–65.

19. Pobedonostsev considered 1869 laws restricting church construction "unfortunate." He wrote that Nikanor should "not hesitate to open more parishes." Perepiska K. P. Pobedonostseva," RA 53, no. 4 (1915): 469.

20. Ivan Zlatoverkhovnikov, comp., *Ufimskaia eparkhiia: Geograficheskii, etnograficheskii, administrativno-istoricheskii i statisticheskii ocherk* (Ufa: A. P. Zaikov, 1899), 219–224.

21. Nikanor's inspections of three such schools convinced Nikanor that Il'minskii's missionaries achieved greater success teaching the fundamentals of Orthodox faith, liturgy, and singing to baptized Tatars than a nearby parish school had among its Russian-speaking students. Nikolai I. Il'minskii, *Perepiska o trekh shkolakh ufimskoi gubernii* (Kazan: V. M. Kliuchnikov, 1885), 65, 67.

22. "Iz zapisok Arkhiepiskopa Nikanora," RA 47, no. 5 (1909): 75.

23. RGIA, f. 804, op. 1, d. 470, ll. 86–86 ob., cited in Gregory Freeze, *The Parish Clergy in Nineteenth-Century Russia: Crisis, Reform, Counter-Reform* (Princeton, N.J.: Princeton University Press, 1983), 252. The effort to establish councils throughout the empire was considered a failure already by the late 1860s, which makes Nikanor's commitment to them notable.

24. Ivan Barsukov, *Pamiati Dionisiia* (St. Petersburg: Sinodal'naia Tipografiia, 1902), 98–99. Ufa's population grew rapidly in this period, but church construction outpaced both population growth and church construction in the empire as a whole. Zlatoverkhovnikov, *Ufimskaia eparkhiia*, 217–221, 256–257.

25. The church first created parish schools in substantial numbers in the 1830s, but they were poorly funded. Beginning in 1882, Pobedonostsev made the case for increased state funding for parish schools. By the time he resigned in 1905, there were 42,696 parish schools with nearly two million students in the empire. Thomas C. Sorensen, "The Thought and Policies of Konstantin Pobedonostsev" (PhD dissertation, University of Washington, 1977), 301–329.

26. After peaking at eighty-four in 1893, the number of parish schools fell to fifty-six by 1897. Zlatoverkhovnikov, *Ufimskaia eparkhiia*, 271–273. The push to open schools

regardless of their staffing and financial basis often resulted in weak schools. Some existed only on paper. Polunov, *Pod vlast'iu ober-prokurora*, 88.

27. Elena Campbell, "The Muslim Question in Late Imperial Russia," in *Russian Empire: Space, People, Power, 1700–1930*, ed. Jane Burbank, Mark von Hagen, and Anatolyi Remnev (Bloomington: Indiana University Press, 2007), 322.

28. Sterlibash was one of the most prominent centers of Muslim education in the region. It drew as many as six hundred students from all over the empire. Marsel' N. Farkhshatov, *Narodnoe obrazovanie v Bashkirii v poreformennyi period, 60–90e gody XIX. v.* (Moscow: Nauka, 1994), 59.

29. NA RT, f. 93, op. 1, d. 128v, ll. 42 ob., 43–43 ob.

30. N. I. Il'minskii, *Pis'ma N. I. Il'minskogo k Ober-Prokuroru Sviateishogo Sinoda Konstantinu Petrovichu Pobedonostsevu* (Kazan: Pravoslavnyi Sobesednik, 1895), 408, 412.

31. The student population grew from 12,404 in 1870 to 84,821 in 1900. Farkhshatov, *Narodnoe obrazovanie*, 98. The 1874 military service statute required those who completed primary school to serve only four years instead of six, increasing interest in education. Jeffrey Brooks, *When Russia Learned to Read: Literacy and Popular Literature, 1861–1917* (Princeton, N.J.: Princeton University Press, 1985), 20.

32. Farkhshatov, *Narodnoe obrazovanie*, 108.

33. Ben Eklof, *Russian Peasant Schools: Officialdom, Village Culture, and Popular Pedagogy, 1861–1914* (Berkeley: University of California Press, 1986).

34. See Allen Sinel, *The Classroom and the Chancellery: State Educational Reform in Russia under Count Dmitry Tolstoi* (Cambridge, Mass.: Harvard University Press, 1973); Patrick L. Alston, *Education and the State in Tsarist Russia* (Stanford, Calif.: Stanford University Press, 1969), 81–90.

35. TsGIA RB, f. I-109, op. 1, d. 72, ll. 1–2 ob., 3–3 ob., 4, 7.

36. Farkhshatov, *Narodnoe obrazovanie*, 111.

37. *Sbornik postanovlenii po ministerstvu narodnogo prosveshcheniia*, 1899, no. 528, cited in Alston, *Education and the State*, 140.

38. Latin was dropped from the first and second years and Greek from the third and fourth years of the gimnasium. Alston, *Education and the State*, 162.

39. TsGIA RB, f. I-109, op. 1, d. 151, ll. 6–6 ob., 8–12 ob.

40. TsGIA RB, f. I-109, op. 1, d. 157, ll. 71 ob.–72.

41. TsGIA RB, f. I-11, op. 2, d. 73, l. 22; d. 84, ll. 12–12 ob.; f. I-187, op. 1, d. 90, l. 35.

42. RGIA, f. 1287, op. 27, d. 1303, ll. 1, 3–4 ob.

43. RGIA, f. 1287, op. 27, d. 1497, ll. 20–20 ob. As head of the school council, the marshal of the nobility's duties included agreeing to new schools, closing schools when they were not run properly, removing "unreliable" teachers, inspecting schools, and finding resources for them.

44. In July 1892, Poltoratskii's successor, Nord, wrote to his superiors that he used his ability to select peasant representatives to reduce Muslim participation. RGIA, f. 1287, op. 27, d. 1926, ll. 4–5 ob., 10.

45. RGIA, f. 1287, op. 27, d. 1526, 1–2, 5, 7–12, 14, quoted at 5.

46. This according to a law enacted even before St. Petersburg formally investigated the scandal. PSZRI, series II, vol. 54, no. 59,675 (May 9, 1878), 440–442.

47. Non-peasant landowners could still purchase land by using communes as fronts for purchases or by bribing officials, but acquiring land became more difficult. PSZRI, series III, vol. 2, no. 973 (June 15, 1882), 311–312; no. 974 (June 15, 1882), 312–313.

48. Usmanov, *Razvitie kapitalizma*, 39.

49. The quotation is from RGIA, f. 1152, Gos. sovet, Depart. Ekonomii, op. 10, d. 490, l. 55 ob. PSZRI, series III, vol. 4, no. 1,947 (January 10, 1884), 5.

50. Möxämätsälim Ömötbaev, "Örshäk küpere," *Yädkär* (Ufa: Bashqortostan Kitap Näshriäte, 1984), 99.

51. *Sushchestvuiushchii poriadok vzimaniia okladnykh sborov s krest'ian: Po svedeniiam, dostavlennym podatnymi inspektorami za 1887–1893*, vyp. 1 (St. Petersburg: Gosudarstvennaia Tipografiia, 1894), 50–58. Tax inspectors attributed much of the problem in collection in Ufa Province not to economic problems but to police inactivity, the "extremely poor condition of peasant officials," and chaotic accounting on the volost level.

52. RGIA, f. 1148, op. 12, g. 1898, d. 91, ll. 87, 90 ob., 94 ob., 95, 96, 97, quoted at 96.

53. PSZRI, series III, vol. 18, no. 15,278 (April 20, 1898), 249–254.

54. Sultanov owned a factory and 774 des. of land. He bargained for a salary of 5,000 rubles after he was initially offered 1,572. RGIA, f. 821, op. 8, d. 1068, ll. 10, 41–46.

55. Il'minskii considered it a mistake to have appointed a "rich, authoritative, and influential" noble such as Mufti Tevkelev. Il'minskii, *Pis'ma N. I. Il'minskogo k Ober-Prokuroru Sviateishogo Sinoda*, 2, 64, 175, 177.

56. RGIA, f. 821, op. 8, d. 1068, ll. 4–4 ob., 5a.

57. The only restriction on mosque construction was that the latter not damage the cause of Orthodoxy. PSZRI, series III, vol. 6, no. 4,102 (December 15, 1886), 532.

58. Elena Campbell, *The Muslim Question in Russian Imperial Governance* (Bloomington: Indiana University Press, 2015), 123.

59. Il'dus K. Zagidullin, *Islamskie instituty v Rossiiskoi imperii: Mecheti v evropeiskoi chasti Rossii i Sibiri* (Kazan: Tatarskoe Knizhnoe Izdatel'stvo, 2007), 142–143.

60. PSZRI, series III, vol. 10, no. 7,120 (October 1, 1890), 663–664; *Sbornik zakonov o musul'manskom dukhovenstve v tavricheskom i orenburgskom okrugakh i o magometanskikh uchebnykh zavedeniiakh* (Kazan: P. I. Kidalinskii, 1898), 18–19.

61. The mufti caused the judges to reconsider their decision, and the OMEA as a whole supported government policy in the end. *Sbornik zakonov o musul'manskom dukhovenstve*, 57–58, 191–92. According to the Ufa governor, the Muslim population in general remained indifferent to the new law. *Vsepoddanneishii otchet ufimskogo gubernatora za 1889 goda*, 4.

62. Farkhshatov, *Narodnoe obrazovanie*, 49–50; Danil D. Azamatov, *Orenburgskoe magometanskoe dukhovnoe sobranie v kontse XVIII–XIX vv.* (Ufa: Gilem, 1999), 156.

63. One prohibited book, in Arabic, was deemed hostile to Christian doctrines. The other, a geography book used in Turkish schools, described the Ottoman Empire in detail but had little material on Russia. TsGIA RB, f. I-11, op. 1, d. 1274, ll. 1, 23–24 ob., 29–29 ob.

64. *Vsepoddanneishii otchet ufimskogo gubernatora za 1892 god*, 5.

65. The Ufa governor reported to the tsar that the "overwhelming majority" of clerics had taken active part in the "calming and admonition" of their fellow Muslims. *Vsepoddanneishii otchet za 1897 g.*, 1. NA RT, f. 100, op. 1, d. 13, l. 1; NA RT, f. 101, op. 2, d. 7, ll. 8–9.

66. RGIA, f. 821, op. 8, d. 1068, ll. 89–90, 122.

67. PSZRI, series III, vol. 10, no. 6,512 (January 9, 1890), 5.

68. Ismail Bei Gasprinskii, "Russkoe Musul'manstvo: Mysli, zametki i nabliudeniia Musul'manina," in *Rossiia i vostok*, ed. M. A. Usmanov (Kazan: Fond Zhien, Tatarskoe Knizhnoe Izdatel'stvo, 1993[1881]), 21–22.

69. For an analysis of how educational reform transformed the meaning and transmission of knowledge in Islamic society, see Adeeb Khalid, *The Politics of Muslim Cultural Reform: Jadidism in Central Asia* (Berkeley: University of California Press, 1998). See also Danielle M. Ross, "From the Minbar to the Barricades: The Tranformation of the Volga-Ural 'Ulama into a Revolutionary Intelligentsia" (PhD dissertation, University of Wisconsin–Madison, 2011), 160–219; Mustafa O. Tuna, "Imperial Russia's Muslims: Inroads of Modernity" (PhD dissertation, Princeton University, 2009), 186–244; Azade Ayşe Rorlich, *The Volga Tatars: A Profile in National Resilience* (Stanford, Calif.: Hoover Institution Press, 1986), 92; Dzhamaliutdin Validov, *Ocherk istorii obrazovannosti i literatury volzhskikh Tatar*, vol. 1 (Moscow: Gosudarstvennoe Izdatel'stvo, 1923), 7, 36–37.

70. Farkhshatov, *Narodnoe obrazovanie*, 87.

71. Sebast'ian Tsviklinski, "Islamskaia model' modernizatsii? Zhizn' Gabdrashida Ibragimova v meniaiushchemsia mire (konets XIX–nachalo XX v.)," in *Volgo-Ural'skii region v imperskom prostranstve: XVIII–XX vv.*, ed. M. Khamamoto, N. Naganava, and D. Usmanova (Moscow: Vostochnaia Literatura, 2011), 121–136; Komatsu Hisao, "Muslim Intellectuals and Japan: A Pan-Islamist Mediator, Abdurreshid Ibrahimov," in *Intellectuals in the Modern Islamic World*, ed. Stéphane A. Dudoignon et al. (London: Routledge, 2006), 273–288; Ahmet Kanlidere, *Reform within Islam: The Tajdid and Jadid Movement among the Kazan Tatars (1809–1917), Conciliation and Conflict* (Istanbul: Eren, 1997), 103; Jacob Landau, *The Politics of Pan-Islam: Ideology and Organization* (Oxford: Oxford University Press, 1994), 29–39; Rorlich, *The Volga Tatars*, 107, 235–236; Edward J. Lazzerini, "Gadidism at the Turn of the Twentieth Century: A View from Within," CMRS 16, no. 2 (April–June 1975), 269; Galimdzhan Ibragimov, *Tatary v revoliutsii 1905 goda*, trans. G. Mukhamedova (Kazan: Gos. Izd. TSSR, 1926), 35.

72. Fakhretdinov resigned his post in the OMEA in May 1906 to become editor of the Tatar-language journal *Shura* (Council) in Orenburg and one of the most prominent Tatar-language commentators on religious and public affairs. Mahmud Tahir, "Riza Fahreddin," *Central Asian Survey* 8, no. 1 (1989): 111–115; Rorlich, *The Volga Tatars*, 53–59, 212.

73. Kanlidere, *Reform within Islam*, 26.

74. Orenburgskoe Magometanskoe Dukhovnoe Sobranie, *Sbornik tsirkuliarov i inykh rukovodiashchikh rasporiazhenii po okrugu Orenburgskogo Magometanskogo Dukhovnogo Sobraniia* (Ufa: Gubernskaia Tipografiia, 1905), 132, dated September 6, 1897.

75. *Sbornik tsirkuliarov i inykh rukovodiashchikh rasporiazhenii*, 151–152, dated August 25, 1898.

76. P. N. Grigor'ev, comp., *Sistematicheskii svodnyi sbornik postanovlenii ufimskogo gubernskogo zemstvo za 35-letie 1875–1909 (Uchreditel'naia, 1–35 ocherednye i 1–42 chrezvychainye sessii) v trekh tomakh*, vol. 1 (Ufa: Gubernskaia Tipografiia, 1915), 19–24; Statisticheskii otdel Ufimskoi Gubernskoi Upravy, *Istoriko-statisticheskie tablitsy deiatel'nosti ufimskikh zemstv: K sorokoletiiu sushchestvovaniia zemstv ufimskoi gubernii, 1875–1914*, ed. M. P. Krasil'nikov (Ufa: Pechat', 1915), 226–228.

77. Larissa A. Iamaeva, comp., *Musul'manskie deputaty gosudarstvennoi dumy Rossii, 1906–1917 gg.: Sbornik dokumentov i materialov* (Ufa: Kitap, 1998), 280, 302–303.

78. Boris Veselovskii, *Istoriia zemstva za sorok let*, vol. 4 (St. Petersburg: Popov, 1911), 404.

79. Veselovskii, *Istoriia zemstva*, 404, 417. Birsk County provides a good illustration of the lack of interest in education. The Birsk zemstvo supported twenty-one schools in 1875 and only two more sixteen years later. TSGIA RB, f. 151, op. 1, d. 21, l. 6.

80. *Vestnik ufimskogo zemstva 1882 g.*, god 4, vyp. 4, 21 (1882): 227–228. Two of Birsk County's four Russian-Bashkir schools had only three to five students.

81. *Istoriko-statisticheskie tablitsy deiatel'nosti ufimskikh zemstv*, 226–228. On the zemstvo reform of 1890, see Kermit E. McKenzie, "Zemstvo Organization and Role within the Administrative Structure," in *The Zemstvo in Russia: An Experiment in Local Self-Government*, ed. Terence Emmons and Wayne S. Vucinich (Cambridge: Cambridge University Press, 1982), 43.

82. Bogdanovich removed Leonid Balakhontsev of Birsk County as provincial zemstvo board chairman in 1901 for illegal acts, including creating a zemstvo library. Veselovskii, *Istoriia zemstva*, vol. 4, 405–407, 412, 499; RGIA, f. 1287, op. 25, d. 2441, ll. 1–2 ob., 3–30.

83. Eklof, *Russian Peasant Schools*, 164–165. *Protokoly XXI ocherednogo ufimskogo gubernskogo zemskogo sobraniia 1895 goda*, protocol 4, December 8, 1895 (Ufa, 1896): 18. County zemstvos, which held direct responsibility for primary education, continued to support church schools, but at quite modest levels. *Istoriko-statisticheskie tablitsy*, 286–287.

84. Eklof, *Russian Peasant Schools*, 166–176.

85. N. V. K—vich, "Tserkovno-shkol'noe delo v Rossii," *Vestnik Evropy* 36, no. 5 (September 1901): 228, 231, 237.

86. For instance, according to Rorlich, Kayyum Nasiri of Kazan, the "Tatar Lomonosov," audited courses at Kazan University and became interested in the work of Russian educational reformers such as Pirogov and Ushinskii. Rorlich, *The Volga Tatars*, 66.

87. There were 193 schools in 1894 and 323 in 1900. Grigor'ev, *Ocherk deiatel'nosti*, 104; Farkhshatov, *Narodnoe obrazovanie*, 108.

88. Ia. P. Barsov, "Pervye zaselentsy i pervye nasaditeli Khristianstva i grazhdanst-vennosti v ufimsko-orenburgskom krae," *Ufimskie gubernskie vedomosti*, no. 37 (February 17, 1896): 2.

89. TsAOO RB, f. 9776, op. 2, d. 844, l. 24.

90. *Protokoly XXIV ufimskogo gubernskogo zemskogo sobraniia 1898 goda* (Ufa, 1899), 145, December 22, 1898. Regarding the Tatar Teachers School in Kazan, see Robert P. Geraci, *Window on the East: National and Imperial Identities in Late Tsarist Russia* (Ithaca, N.Y.: Cornell University Press, 2001), 143–150; and Tuna, "Imperial Russia's Muslims," especially 186–244.

91. The zemstvo chairman invited Umetbaev to participate, along with Syrtlanov, Tevkelev, Rizaetdin Fakhretdinov, translator for the district court Gumer Teregulov, and four others. NA UNTS RAN, f. 3, op. 1, ed. khr. 1, l. 357. Due to the events of 1905, the translation project was not undertaken. Grigor'ev, *Ocherk deiatel'nosti*, 134–135.

92. *Protokoly XXIII ocherednogo ufimskogo gubernskogo zemskogo sobraniia 1897 god* (Ufa, 1898), 6–7.

93. Tevkelev held important elective positions within the provincial zemstvo. He was a member of the committee that assessed property for zemstvo taxation and the zemstvo representative to the peasant land bank. Syrtlanov was elected several times to the provincial zemstvo board, including the vice chairmanship. *Ufimskaia zemskaia gazeta*, no. 5 (March 29, 1906): 122.

94. Mikhail I. Rodnov, "Chislennost' tiurkskogo krest'ianstva ufimskoi gubernii v nachale XX v.," *Etnograficheskoe obozrenie*, no. 6 (1996): 126.

95. Rail G. Kuzeev, *Istoricheskaia etnografiia bashkirskogo naroda*, 2nd ed. (Ufa: Kitap, 2009), 289.

96. Kuzeev, *Istoricheskaia etnografiia*, 122–124; Rim Z. Ianguzin, *Khoziaistvo Bashkir dorevoliutsionnoi Rossii* (Ufa: Bashkirskoe Knizhnoe Izdatel'stvo, 1989), 148–149.

97. NA UNTS RAN, f. 3, op. 1, ed. khr. 1, vol. 1, l. 103.

98. NA UNTS RAN, f. 3, op. 1, ed. khr. 1, vol. 1, ll. 102, 105–115.

99. RGIA, f. 821, op. 8, d. 1197: ll. 34–34 ob., 44–48.

100. Petr I. Liashchenko, *Ocherki agrarnoi evoliutsii Rossii*. Vol. 2, *Krest'ianskoe delo i poreformennaia zemleustroitel'naia politika* (St. Petersburg: Ministerstvo Finansov, 1913), 179.

101. *Vsepoddanneishii otchet ufimskogo gubernatora za 1898 goda*, 5; *Vsepoddanneishii otchet ufimskogo gubernatora za 1889 goda*, 2.

102. *Otchet ufimskoi mezhevoi komissii o razmezhevanii bashkirskikh dach, za vremia 1898–1912 gg.* (Ufa: N. V. Sarobkin, 1912), 6–13.

103. *Otchet ufimskoi mezhevoi komissii*, 22, 26.

104. TsGIA RB, f. 10, op 1, d. 2406, ll. 41–41 ob.

105. Salavat Iskhakov, *Pervaia russkaia revoliutsiia i musul'mane rossiiskoi imperii* (Moscow: Izd. Sotsial'no-Politicheskaia Mysl', 2007), 90. Conflicts over the land survey took place in three other places in the province. R. M. Rakhimov, *1905 v Bashkirii* (Moscow: Akademiia Nauk, 1941), 79–80.

106. Mikhail I. Rodnov et al., eds., *Istoriia Bashkortostana vo vtoroi polovine XIX–nachale XX veka*, vol. 1 (Ufa: UNTS RAN, 2006), 233–234.

107. TsAOO RB, f. 1832, op. 1, d. 7, ll. 1–2, "Boinia v g. Zlatoust," dated March 1903.

108. A. A. Planson, *Byloe i nastoiashchee* (St. Petersburg: M. Zarkhin, 1905), 70.

109. Richard G. Robbins Jr., *The Tsar's Viceroys: Russian Provincial Governors in the Last Years of the Empire* (Ithaca, N.Y.: Cornell University Press, 1987), 216–219.

110. Veselovskii, *Istoriia zemstva*, vol. 4, 407.

111. TsGIA RB, f. I-9, op. 1, d. 655, ll. 4–5 ob., 9. The provision for reinforced security was a temporary measure enacted in the wake of Alexander II's assassination but remained an option until 1917. Under reinforced security, a governor could keep citizens in prison for up to three months, impose fines, prohibit public gatherings, exile alleged offenders, transfer cases from criminal to military courts, and dismiss local government and zemstvo employees. This was the more moderate type of heightened security, the others being "extraordinary security" and martial law. Abraham Ascher, *The Revolution of 1905: Russia in Disarray* (Stanford, Calif.: Stanford University Press, 1988), 110.

112. *Vsepoddanneishii otchet o sostoianii ufimskoi gubernii za 1903*, 1, 2.

113. RGIA, f. 1287, op. 25, d. 2691, ll. 2–4, 11–12 ob., 18.

114. TsGIA RB, f. I-9, op. 1, d. 655, ll. 11–12 ob.; Veselovskii, *Istoriia zemstvo*, vol. 4, 407.

115. *Vsepoddanneishii otchet o sostoianii ufimskoi gubernii za 1904 god*, 7.

116. Sviatopolk-Mirskii rejected some of Sokolovskii's actions and told him to "avoid words and expressions" that "insulted the dignity" of zemstvo leaders. RGIA, f. 1288, op. 2, razdel 1904, d. 6, ll. 41–42 ob.

117. Graf S. Iu. Witte, *Po povodu natsionalizma: Natsional'naia ekonomiia i Fridrikh List*, 2nd ed. (St. Petersburg: Brokgauz-Efron, 1912), 4.

118. RGIA, f. 821, op. 125, ed khr. 409, ll. 4 ob.–14 ob., reproduced in Sergei Witte, "Nasha vnutrenniaia politika po musul'manskomu voprosu iavliaetsia vazhnym faktorom politiki vneshnei," ed. Dmitrii Arapov, *Istochnik* 62, no. 2 (2003): 25.

119. *Za pervyi god veroispovednoi svobody v Rossii* (St. Petersburg: Kolokol, 1907), 2, 6; PSZRI, series III, vol. 24, no. 25,495 (December 12, 1904), 196–198.

120. David A. J. Macey, *Government and Peasant in Russia, 1861–1906: The Prehistory of the Stolypin Reforms* (DeKalb: Northern Illinois University Press, 1987), 71.

121. *Zhurnaly komiteta ministrov po ispolneniiu ukaza 12 dekabria 1904 g.* (St. Petersburg: Izdatel'stvo Kantseliarii Komiteta Ministrov, 1905), 157–158.

122. Sergei Witte, "O sovremennom polozhenii pravoslavnoi tserkvi (zapiska S. Iu. Witte)," *Slovo*, no. 108 (March 28, 1905), reproduced in I. V. Preobrazhenskii, comp., *Tserkovnaia reforma: Sbornik statei dukhovnoi i svetskoi periodicheskoi pechati po voprosu o reforme* (St. Petersburg: Tip. E. Arngol'da, 1905), 122–133. Sergei Iu. Witte, *Vospominaniia*, vol. II (Tallinn and Moscow: Skif Aleks, 1994), 345.

123. James W. Cunningham, *A Vanquished Hope: The Movement for Church Renewal in Russia, 1905–1906* (Crestwood, N.Y.: St. Vladimir's Seminary Press, 1981), 52–59. Metropolitan Antonii stated that using force to keep people in the faith was "alien to the very nature of the Church of Christ." *Zhurnaly Komiteta Ministrov*, 159, 160.

124. Houses of worship that had been closed by the state were permitted to reopen, and non-Orthodox communities could register and own property. Sectarian and non-Orthodox religious leaders could be recognized as clergy and exempted from conscription. The decree permitted religious instruction in native languages and allowed orphans to be raised within non-Orthodox communities. PSZRI, series III, vol. 25, no. 26, 126 (April 17, 1905), 258–259.

125. Initially, the legislation caused confusion because it failed to specify the mechanism by which a person could actually leave Orthodoxy for another faith. Only on August 18, 1905, did a circular inform local officials how transfers to another faith should proceed. On May 3, 1905, the Committee of Ministers affirmed that it was illegal for non-Orthodox clergy to proselytize their faiths. TSGIA RB, f. I-9, op. 1, d. 714, ll. 1–2. Regarding the persistence of state regulation of religious identity after 1905 and the continuing inhibitions on registration in a new faith, see Paul Werth, "Arbiters of the Free Conscience: State, Religion, and the Problem of Confessional Transfer after 1905," in *Sacred Stories: Religion and Spirituality in Modern Russia*, ed. Mark D. Steinberg and Heather J. Coleman (Bloomington: Indiana University Press, 2007), 171–199.

126. Witte, *Vospominaniia*, vol. II, 345.

127. Examples include Theodore Weeks, *Nation and State in Late Imperial Russia: Nationalism and Russification on the Western Frontier, 1863–1914* (DeKalb: Northern Illinois University Press, 1996); Mikhail Dolbilov, "Russification and the Bureaucratic Mind in the Russian Empire's Northwestern Region in the 1860s," *Kritika: Explorations in Russian and Eurasian History* 5, no. 2 (Spring 2004): 245–271; Darius Staliunis, "Did the Government Seek to Russify Lithuanians and Poles in the Northwest Territory after the Uprising of 1863–1864?" *Kritika: Explorations in Russian and Eurasian History* 5, no. 2 (Spring 2004): 273–289; and Mikhail Dolbilov and Aleksei Miller, eds., *Zapadnye okrainy rossiiskoi imperii* (Moscow: Novoe Literaturnoe Obozrenie, 2006).

128. Weeks, *Nation and State*, 96–108.

129. Karen Barkey, *Empire of Difference: The Ottomans in Comparative Perspective* (Cambridge: Cambridge University Press, 2008), 292.

130. M. Şükrü Hanioğlu, *A Brief History of the Late Ottoman Empire* (Princeton, N.J.: Princeton University Press, 2008), 130.

6. EMPIRE IN CRISIS, 1905–1907

1. Richard G. Robbins Jr., *The Tsar's Viceroys: Russian Provincial Governors in the Last Years of the Empire* (Ithaca, N.Y.: Cornell University Press, 1987), 216–221; TSAOO RB, f. 1832, op. 1, d. 7, l. 1, dated March 1903.

2. *PSZRI*, series III, vol. 25, no. 26,126 (October 17, 1905), 755–756. Salavat Iskhakov, *Pervaia russkaia revoliutsiia i musul'mane rossiiskoi imperii* (Moscow: Izd. Sotsial'no-Politicheskaia Mysl', 2007), 182.

3. TSAOO RB, f. 1832, op. 3, d. 385, ll. 30–32, "Vospominaniia byvshego gubernatora." The attendance figure comes from Soiuz Russkogo Naroda, *Gosudarstvennaia izmena* (St. Petersburg: n.p., 1906), 40.

4. Donald Rawson, *Russian Rightists and the Revolution of 1905* (Cambridge: Cambridge University Press, 1995), 14.

5. On the ideology of autocracy and the tsar's personal authority, see Andrew M. Verner, *The Crisis of Russian Autocracy: Nicholas II and the 1905 Revolution* (Princeton, N.J.: Princeton University Press, 1990), especially chapter 3.

6. Charles Taylor, "Nationalism and Modernity," in *The State of the Nation: Ernest Gellner and the Theory of Nationalism*, ed. John A. Hall (Cambridge: Cambridge University Press, 1998), 191–218. For discussions of the shift from passive subjecthood to active identification with the state in Russian history, see Yanni Kotsonis, "'Face to Face': The State, The Individual, and the Citizen in Russian Taxation, 1863–1917," *Slavic Review* 63, no. 2 (Summer 2004): 221–246; Peter Holquist, "'Information Is the Alpha and Omega of Our Work': Bolshevik Surveillance in Its Pan-European Context," *Journal of Modern History* 69 (September 1997): 419. On 1905 as a key moment in Russia's "search for modernity" and the implications of the "new political arena" that opened in its wake, see Laura Engelstein, *The Keys to Happiness: Sex and the Search for Modernity in Fin-de-Siècle Russia* (Ithaca, N.Y.: Cornell University Press, 1992).

7. "Voskresnye nabroski," *Ufimskii vestnik*, no. 114 (May 28, 1906): 2.

8. Since the 1897 census did not classify people by ethnicity or nationality, the number of Poles remains elusive. Using the most common categories before 1905, religious confession, Ufa province had 811 Jews and 1,631 Catholics out of a total population of approximately 2,200,000 in 1899. F. A. Brokgauz and I. A. Efron, *Entsiklopedicheskii slovar'*, vol. 35 (St. Petersburg and Leipzig: Brokgauz-Efron, 1902), 93.

9. On the use of ethnicity and nationality before and after 1905, see Charles Steinwedel, "To Make a Difference: The Category of Ethnicity in Late Imperial Russian Politics, 1861–1917," in *Russian Modernity: Politics, Knowledge, Practices*, ed. Yanni Kotsonis and David Hoffman (Basingstoke: Macmillan, 2000), 67–86.

10. A. A. Planson, *Byloe i nastoiashchee* (St. Petersburg: M. Zarkhin, 1905), 41. By contrast, Planson regarded Poles, Jews, and Armenians with hostility.

11. Christian Noack stresses the lack of Muslim radicalism and participation in disturbances in Kazan and Orenburg in 1905. See Christian Noack, "Retrospectively Revolting: Kazan Tatar 'Conspiracies' during the 1905 Revolution," in *The Russian Revolution of 1905: Centenary Perspectives*, ed. Jonathan D. Smele and Anthony Heywood (London: Routledge, 2005), 121, 129.

12. My use of "nationality" follows Rogers Brubaker's definition of the French *nationalité*, an "ethnocultural community, and consequent community of political aspiration,

in the absence of autonomous political organization." Rogers Brubaker, *Citizenship and Nationhood in France and Germany* (Cambridge, Mass.: Harvard University Press, 1992), 98. I would argue that what began as a Muslim movement became, in the context of the late Russian Empire and its institutions, a national movement. In this respect, I follow Christian Noack, who emphasizes that the Muslim mobilization after the 1860s combined ethnic or national and religious characteristics to become a "Muslim nationalism." Christian Noack, *Muslimischer Nationalismus im russischen Reich: Nationsbildung und Nationalbewegung bei Tataren und Baschkiren, 1861–1917* (Stuttgart: Franz Steiner Verlag, 2000), 18–19. Salavat Iskhakov defines Muslim collective action as "religious-cultural" in character. Iskhakov, *Pervaia russkaia revoliutsiia*, 319. On the perception of a Muslim mobilization in the 1905 revolutionary context, see Elena Campbell, "The Muslim Question in Late Imperial Russia," in *Russian Empire: Space, People, Power, 1700–1930*, ed. Jane Burbank, Mark von Hagen, and Anatolyi Remnev (Bloomington: Indiana University Press, 2007), 330–331; and Elena Campbell, *The Muslim Question and Russian Imperial Governance* (Bloomington: Indiana University Press, 2015), 138–144.

13. When the Free Economic Society surveyed Ufa Province regarding the agrarian movement, eight of thirteen respondents replied that there was no local agrarian movement. Four of the other five respondents wrote of the same event in Belebei County—a large-scale cutting of a noble landowner's forest. The other event reported was the burning of a noble estate in Menzelinsk. S. N. Prokopovich, "Priural'skie gubernii," in *Agrarnoe dvizhenie v Rossii v 1905–1906: Obzory po raionam*, ed. V. S. Golubev et al., vol. 1 (St. Petersburg: Tip. Vol'nogo Ekonomicheskogo Obshchestva, 1908), 163–164. R. Rakhimov identifies fifteen Ufa volosts in which police were called to disturbances in 1905, mostly in the province's northeast. None of the incidents was particularly severe or resulted in loss of life. R. M. Rakhimov, *1905 v Bashkirii* (Moscow and Leningrad: Akademiia Nauk, 1941), 110–113.

14. E. E. Pisarenko, "Kadet kniaz' V. A. Kugushev," *Voprosy istorii* 2 (February 1997): 151; TsGIA RB, f. 187, op. 1, d. 44, ll. 80–84 ob., dated October 28, 1902. Leopold Haimson, ed., with Ziva Galili y Garcia and Richard Wortman, *The Making of Three Russian Revolutionaries: Voices from the Menshevik Past* (Cambridge: Cambridge University Press, 1987), 248–255; I. D. Kuznetsov, ed., *Natsional'nye dvizheniia v period pervoi revoliutsii v Rossii* (Cheboksary: Chuvashkoe Gos. Izdatel'stvo, 1935), 152–153.

15. Laura Engelstein argues for the importance of 1905 as part of a "general mobilization of urban society" in *Moscow, 1905: Working-Class Organization and Political Conflict* (Stanford, Calif.: Stanford University Press, 1982).

16. R. G. Ganeev, V. V. Boltushkina, and R. G. Kuzeev, eds., *Istoriia Ufy: Kratkii ocherk* (Ufa: Bashkirskoe Knizhnoe Izdatel'stvo, 1981), 150. The assembly appears to have been part of the "banquet campaign" inspired by the Union of Liberation in late 1904 and early 1905. Banquets were intended to draw oppositional elements together in support of reforms at a time when parties and public assemblies were still illegal. Terence Emmons, "Russia's Banquet Campaign," *California Slavic Studies* 10 (1977): 45–86.

17. S. M. Vasil'ev, L. P. Gnedkov, and T. Sh. Saiapov, eds., *Sbornik dokumentov i materialov o revoliutsionnom dvizhenii 1905–1907 gg. v Bashkirii* (Ufa: Bashkirskoe Knizhnoe Izdatel'stvo, 1956), 24–25, 31–37, 41–42.

18. Henry Reichman, *Railway Men and Revolution: Russia, 1905* (Berkeley: University of California Press, 1987), 194–223.

19. Authorities did not establish the last name of "Nikolai Ivanovich," El'kind, until well after the October days.

20. TsAOO RB, f. 1832, op. 3, d. 385, ll. 7–14, "Vospominaniia byvshego guberna-tora"; Aleksei Kiikov, *Iz bylogo urala: Materialy k istorii revoliutsionnogo dvizheniia na iuzhnom urale i v priural'i, 1905–1916* (Ufa: Izd. Bashkirskogo obl. Biuro Istparta RKP(b), 1923), 21; *1905. Revoliutsionnye sobytiia 1905 g. v g. ufe i ural'skikh zavodakh (Bashrespublika)* (Ufa: n.p., 1925), 12–13; *Gosudarstvennaia izmena*, 28–29.

21. *1905. Revoliutsionnye sobytiia*, 13; *25 let pervoi revoliutsii (Sbornik Istparta Bashobkoma VKP(b) posviashchennyi 25-letnemu iubileiu revoliutsii 1905 goda)* (Ufa: Tipografiia Imeni Dzerzhinskogo, 1930), 25; TsAOO RB, f. 1832, op. 3, d. 385, l. 15; *Gosudarstvennaia izmena*, 15.

22. *Gosudarstvennaia izmena*, 29. Busov later became the head of the local branch of the Union of the Russian People.

23. TsAOO RB, f. 1832, op. 3, d. 385, l. 17; *Gosudarstvennaia izmena*, 30–31; TsAOO RB, f. 1832, op. 4, d. 77, ll. 1–2 ob.

24. TsAOO RB, f. 1832, op. 3, d. 385, ll. 4, 19; A. M. Pankratova et al., eds., *Revoliutsiia 1905–1907 gg. v Rossii: Dokumenty i materialy. Chast' pervaia—Vysshii pod'em revoliutsii 1905–1907 gg. Vooruzhennye vosstaniia noiabr'–dekabr' 1905 goda* (Moscow: Gospolitizdat, 1955), 140.

25. TsAOO RB, f. 1832, op. 3, d. 385, ll. 22–24. Although the white-blue-red tricolor flown in 1905 dated to Peter the Great's reign, the government first ordered the flag to be displayed on holidays in 1883. Only in 1896, in conjunction with Nicholas II's coronation, did a special commission make this flag the "national" (*narodnyi*) flag of the entire empire. V. A. Artamanov, "Flag," in *Gerb i flag Rossii, X–XX veka* (Moscow: Izdatel'stvo Iuridicheskaia Literatura, 1997), 419–463.

26. *Gosudarstvennaia izmena*, 35.

27. Tsekhanovetskii wrote that he himself had been sentenced to death by the "Executive Revolutionary Committee." TsAOO RB, f. 1832, op. 3, d. 385, ll. 30–32.

28. TsAOO RB, f. 1832, op. 3, d. 385, ll. 6, 32–35, 371.

29. *Gosudarstvennaia izmena*, 45–51.

30. *1905: Revoliutsionnye sobytiia*, 14. TsAOO RB, f. 1832, op. 3, d. 385, ll. 383–389.

31. *Gosudarstvennaia izmena* reproduces the telegram in full. *Gosudarstvennaia izmena*, 55–57.

32. *Gosudarstvennaia izmena*, 26, 60, 79.

33. TsAOO RB, f. 1832, op. 3, d. 385, ll. 42–45; *Gosudarstvennaia izmena*, 60.

34. Kiikov, *Iz bylogo urala*, 24.

35. The rightist account follows the governor's closely here, though the governor is said to have participated against his will. *Gosudarstvennaia izmena*, 67.

36. TsAOO RB, f. 1832, op. 3, d. 385, ll. 45–47; *Gosudarstvennaia izmena*, 70.

37. *Gosudarstvennaia izmena*, 67; TsAOO RB, f. 1832, op. 3, d. 385, l. 48.

38. TsAOO RB, f. 1832, op. 3, d. 385, l. 49; Kiikov, *Iz bylogo urala*, 24.

39. *Gosudarstvennaia izmena*, 68; Kiikov, *Iz bylogo urala*, 24.

40. The "monarchist" party included the former head of the telephone network, the secretary of the provincial office on urban and zemstvo affairs, the governor's former senior official of special assignments, a candidate for the post of land captain, Zhedenev, Busov, and Laptev. *Gosudarstevennaia izmena*, 71–72.

41. N. Zhedenev, "Ufimskaia revoliutsiia: Pis'mo k izdateliu," *Moskovskie vedomosti*, no. 305 (November 19, 1905): 2; N. Zhedenev, "Ufimskaia kramola," *Moskovskie vedomosti*, no. 307 (November 21, 1905): 1.

42. Zhedenev, "Ufimskaia kramola," 1. The "Russian Monarchist Party" originated in Moscow shortly after the tsar's appeal for support in February 1905. The organization advocated highly centralized power and unencumbered personal rule by the tsar. Rawson, *Russian Rightists*, 21–33.

43. Kiikov argues that the local administration directed the work of "patriots" in the workshops. Kiikov, *Iz bylogo urala*, 25.

44. The right-wing press in Moscow and Petersburg claimed 1,200 rightists in the railway workshops in Ufa. This figure, also quoted by Kiikov, appears to represent all those who chose not to support the December strike, whether or not they actually belonged to the Patriotic Society. Kiikov, *Iz bylogo urala*, 32; V. Levitskii, "Pravye partii," in *Obshchestvennoe dvizhenie v Rossii v nachale XX-go veka*, vol. III, no. 5, ed. L. Martov, P. Maslov, and A. Potresov (St. Petersburg: Obshchestvennaia Pol'za, 1914), 410.

45. Kiikov, *Iz bylogo urala*, 109–110.

46. The program was printed by the government printing press. TsAOO RB, f. 1832, op. 4, d. 75, ll. 1–2.

47. *Ufimskii vestnik*, no. 117 (June 1, 1906): 3.

48. The head of the state bank's Ufa branch, Kvitsinskii, was also allegedly a Pole who sympathized with the revolutionaries. *Gosudarstvennaia izmena*, 14, 23, 27, 53, quoted at 53.

49. *Gosudarstvennaia izmena*, 67–69.

50. Zemstvo constitutionalists proposed cultural self-determination, federalism, and the decentralization of the empire's administrative structures. When this program threatened to split the zemstvo movement, it was tabled indefinitely. The congress did approve political autonomy for Poland, however, and this proved quite controversial both inside and outside the zemstvo movement. Roberta Thompson Manning, *The Crisis of the Old Order in Russia: Gentry and Government* (Princeton, N.J.: Princeton University Press, 1982), 134–137; "Soveshchanie zemskikh i gorodskikh deiatelei," *Russkii vestnik*, no. 252 (September 16, 1905): 4.

51. TsAOO RB, f. 1832, op. 4, d. 76, ll. 1–2 ob. The leaflet named leading leftists and zemstvo activists; *Gosudarstvennaia izmena*, 22.

52. The type of patriotism Hubertus Jahn describes as "social patriotism, loyalty to the people of the country rather than to a ruler or an ideology" or as "progressive patriotism" was little evident in Ufa in 1905–1906. Those who rejected the "patriotism" of the administration and the right did not use the term at all, or did so ironically. Hubertus Jahn, *Patriotic Culture in Russia during World War I* (Ithaca, N.Y.: Cornell University Press, 1995), 91, 115, 148–149.

53. TsAOO RB, f. 1832, op. 1, d. 20, ll. 1–4, dated November 1905.

54. TsAOO RB, f. 1832, op. 1, d. 20, l. 11, dated June 1906.

55. "Voskresnye besedy," *Ufimskii vestnik*, no. 110 (May 21, 1906): 2; "Voskresnye nabroski," *Ufimskii vestnik*, no. 114 (May 28, 1906): 2; "Voskresnye besedy," *Ufimskii vestnik*, no. 117 (June 1, 1906): 2.

56. "Resul'taty vyborov v ufimskom gorodskom izbiratel'nom sobranii 21 marta," *Ufimskii vestnik*, no. 66 (March 23, 1906): 2.

57. The two Muslims were Sakhipzada Maksiutov, a deputy to the first Duma, and Galliam Mustafin, the editor of a local Tatar newspaper. Iskhakov, *Pervaia russkaia revoliutsiia*, 265.

58. Andrew Verner describes Witte's efforts to both collect information and create governmental newspapers that would influence public opinion. Verner, *The Crisis of Russian Autocracy*, 256–260. Witte's successor, Petr Stolypin, had a similar view of public opinion.

59. This resembles what Jahn calls "conservative patriotism," that designed to preserve the existing "state and power structure." Jahn, *Patriotic Culture in Russia*, 148–149, 176–177.

60. *Vsepoddanneishii otchet o sostoianii ufimskoi gubernii za 1905 god*, 5. TsGIA RB, f. I-11, op. 1, d. 1452, ll. 14, 16.

61. These titles are taken from a list requested by the director of a village "people's tearoom/reading room" in Birsk County. TsGIA RB, f. I-11, op. 1, d. 1452, l. 10.

62. TsGIA RB, f. I-11, op. 1, d. 1452, l. 41. For another example, see TsGIA RB, f. I-11, op. 1, d. 1452, l. 12.

63. *Vsepoddanneishii otchet o sostoianii ufimskoi gubernii za 1905 g.*, 6.

64. Iskhakov, *Pervaia russkaia revoliutsiia*, 175.

65. Sergei A. Stepanov, *Chernaia sotnia v Rossii 1905–1914 gg.* (Moscow: VZPI A/o Rosvuznauka, 1992), 16–17; Iskhakov, *Pervaia russkaia revoliutsiia*, 299.

66. Zhedenev, "Ufimskaia revoliutsiia," 2; Zhedenev, "Ufimskaia kramola," 1. Anti-Muslim sections may have been added after Duma elections and the Second All-Russian Congress of Muslims in St. Petersburg on January 13 and 23, 1906, made awareness of Muslim political demands widespread. *Gosudarstvennaia izmena*, 26, 79.

67. On the electoral process, see Terence Emmons, *The Formation of Political Parties and the First National Elections in Russia* (Cambridge, Mass.: Harvard University Press, 1983), especially 237–379.

68. Regarding how the first State Duma featured "the articulation and discovery of the heterogeneous social and political space of the Russian Empire" more broadly, see Alexander Semyonov, "'The Real and Live Ethnographic Map of Russia': The Russian Empire in the Mirror of the State Duma," in *Empire Speaks Out: Languages of Rationalization and Self-Description in the Russian Empire*, ed. Ilya Gerasimov, Jan Kusber and Alexander Semyonov (Leiden: Brill, 2009), 191–192.

69. Ivan Zhukovskii, "Moim izbirateliam," *Ufimskoi zemskoi gazety* (May 5, 1906): 3–5. Muslims made up 49.9 percent and Russian Orthodox 43.8 percent of the province's population, with Catholics, Protestants, Jews, and animist peoples composing the rest. N. A. Troinitskii, ed., *Pervaia vseobshchaia perepis' naseleniia rossiiskoi imperii 1897 goda*, vol. 65 (St. Petersburg: Tsentral'nyi Statisticheskii Komitet, 1904), vii.

70. *Sovet ministrov rossiiskoi imperii, 1905–1906 gg.: Dokumenty i materialy* (Leningrad: Nauka, 1990), 301–302.

71. Ivan Zhukovskii, "Moim izbirateliam," 3.

72. An observer from Birsk County echoed Zhukovskii's sentiment. "Iz zhizni gubernii," *UGV*, no. 69 (March 28, 1906): 3.

73. Zhukovskii, "Moim izbirateliam," 2.

74. Larissa A. Iamaeva, comp., *Musul'manskie deputaty gosudarstvennoi dumy Rossii, 1906–1917 gg.* (Ufa: Kitap, 1998), 280, 286, 295–296, 302–303, 304–305, 311; Diliara Usmanova,

Musul'manskie predstaviteli v rossiiskom parlamente: 1906–1916 (Kazan: Fen Akademiia Nauk Respubliki Tatarstan, 2005), 554–576; Iskhakov, *Pervaia russkaia revoliutsiia*, 143. Based on census data from 1920, Mikhail Rodnov calculated the nationality of the district from which Maksiutov came as 45.3 percent Teptiar, 31 percent Meshcheriak, and 22.8 percent Bashkir. Mikhail I. Rodnov, *Naselenie ufimskoi gubernii po perepisi 1920 goda: Etnicheskii sostav (Birskii, Zlatoustovskii, i drugie uezdy)* (Moscow: Institut Etnologii i Antropologii im. N. N. Miklukho-Maklaia, 2014), 31, http://static.iea.ras.ru /books/Rodnov.pdf, accessed July 22, 2014.

75. Rustem A. Tsiunchuk, *Dumskaia model' parlamentarizma v rossiiskoi imperii: Etnokonfessional'noe i regional'noe izmereniia* (Kazan: Fen, 2004), 413.

76. Norihiro Naganawa, "Holidays in Kazan: The Public Sphere and the Politics of Religious Authority among Tatars in 1914," *Slavic Review* 71, no. 1 (Spring 2012): 25–48.

77. Iamaeva, *Musul'manskie deputaty*, 20–23.

78. Iamaeva, *Musul'manskie deputaty*, 76–78, 87. Khasanov was born in a Tatar village in Kazan Province. He received his education at the Tatar Teachers' School in Kazan and taught at a Russo-Bashkir primary school in Ufa Province.

79. John Slocum, "The Boundaries of National Identity: Religion, Language, and Nationality Politics in Late Imperial Russia" (PhD dissertation, University of Chicago, 1993), 205–206.

80. *PSZRI*, series III, vol. 24, no. 24,701 (June 6, 1904), 604.

81. Rustem Tsiunchuk provides a comprehensive account of the role religion and ethnicity played in the organization of elections to the first State Duma. Tsiunchuk, *Dumskaia model'*, 72–172. Diliara Usmanova thoroughly examines Muslim representation in all four convocations of the State Duma. Usmanova, *Musul'manskie predstaviteli*.

82. *PSZRI*, series III, vol. 27, no. 29,240 (June 3, 1907), 320, 324. In the last two Dumas, electoral lists often identified potential voters by nationality (*natsional'nost'*).

83. *UGV*, prilozhenie k no. 60 (August 1, 1912); prilozhenie k no. 61 (August 4, 1912). The first two Duma elections were not held in curiae segregated by religion or nationality. *TsGIA RB*, f. I-388, op. 1, d. 4, l. 2.

84. As Yuri Slezkine points out, on the eve of the revolutions of 1917, Russia had "no official view of what constituted nationality." Yuri Slezkine, "The USSR as a Communal Apartment, or How a Socialist State Promoted Ethnic Particularism," *Slavic Review* 53, no. 2 (Summer 1994): 427. Before 1917, statistics on nationality appear to have been based upon a mix of factors, most prominently native language, religion, and "way of life." Juliette Cadiot writes that registration of nationality was done "occasionally and chaotically," without a central definition of terms. Juliette Cadiot, *Le laboratoire impérial: Russie-URSS 1860–1940* (Paris: CNRS Editions, 2007), 63. Peter Holquist demonstrates that by the turn of the twentieth century and in particular after 1905, "ethnicity increasingly became the preeminent category by which military statistics determined the quality and reliability of the population's various elements." Peter Holquist, "To Count, to Extract, to Exterminate: Population Statistics and Population Politics in Late Imperial and Soviet Russia," in *A State of Nations: Empire and Nation-Making in the Age of Lenin and Stalin*, ed. Ronald Grigor Suny and Terry Martin (New York: Oxford University Press, 2001), 111–144.

85. Andreas Kappeler, *The Russian Empire: A Multiethnic History*, trans. Alfred Clayton (Harlow: Longman, 2001): 328–348; James D. White, "The 1905 Revolution in Russia's Baltic Provinces," in Smele and Heywood, *The Russian Revolution of 1905*, 72–73;

Abraham Ascher, *The Revolution of 1905: Russia in Disarray* (Stanford, Calif.: Stanford University Press, 1988), 255, 333–334; Abraham Ascher, *The Revolution of 1905: Authority Restored* (Stanford, Calif.: Stanford University Press, 1992), 248.

86. Faith Hillis, *Children of Rus': Right-Bank Ukraine and the Invention of a Russian Nation* (Ithaca, N.Y.: Cornell University Press, 2013), 169.

87. In addition to the three killed in demonstrations in Ufa, described above, one soldier was killed by demonstrators in December, two Bashkirs in Sterlitamak County were killed by police in 1907, and four revolutionaries were sentenced to death and executed in the same year. I. G. Akmanov et al., eds., *Istoriia Bashkortostana s drevnei-shikh vremen do nashikh dnei*, vol. 1 (Ufa: Kitap, 2006), 53–54, 59, 61.

88. On how the mobilization and electoral politics nationalized the empire, see Hillis, *Children of Rus'*, especially chapter 7.

89. Jürgen Osterhammel, *The Transformation of the World: A Global History of the Nineteenth Century* (Princeton, N.J.: Princeton University Press, 2014), 559–571.

90. Osterhammel, *The Transformation of the World*, 567.

7. EMPIRE, NATIONS, AND MULTINATIONAL VISIONS, 1907–1917

1. Zaki Validi Togan, *Vospominaniia: Bor'ba Musul'man turkestana i drugikh vostochnykh tiurok za natsional'noe sushchestvovanie i kul'turu*, trans. V. B. Feonov, ed. S. M. Iskhakov (Moscow: Moskovskaia Tipografiia, 1997), 108–110.

2. Enikeev was born in Belebei County of Ufa Province but was elected to the Duma first from Kazan Province and then from Orenburg Province. Tatar peasant Gabdul-Latif Baiteriakov was also from Ufa. Larissa A. Iamaeva, comp., *Musul'manskie deputaty gosudarstvennoi dumy Rossii, 1906–1917* (Ufa: Kitap, 1998), 283, 288.

3. Richard S. Wortman, *Scenarios of Power: Myth and Ceremony in Russian Monarchy*, vol. 2: *From Alexander II to the Abdication of Nicholas II* (Princeton, N.J.: Princeton University Press, 2000).

4. Vladimir I. Gurko, *Features and Figures of the Past: Government and Opinion in the Reign of Nicholas II,* ed. J. E. Wallace Sterling, Xenia Joukoff Eudin, and H. H. Fisher, trans. Laura Matveev (Stanford, Calif.: Stanford University Press, 1970), 462. Francis W. Wcislo, *Reforming Rural Russia: State, Local Society, and National Politics, 1855–1914* (Princeton, N.J.: Princeton University Press, 1990), 209. For a survey of zemstvo attitudes, see RGIA, f. 1288, op. 2, 1906 razdel, d. 76, l. 23.

5. On the themes of civic equalization, universal inclusion, and the movement from large collectives to individuals as objects of government focus, see Yanni Kotsonis, "'Face to Face': The State, the Individual, and the Citizen in Russian Taxation, 1863–1917," *Slavic Review* 63, no. 2 (Summer 2004): 221–246; and Kotsonis, "'No Place to Go': Taxation and State Transformation in Late Imperial and Early Soviet Russia," *Journal of Modern History* 76, no. 3 (September 2004): 531–577.

6. David A. J. Macey, *Government and Peasant in Russia, 1861–1906: The Prehistory of the Stolypin Reforms* (DeKalb: Northern Illinois University Press, 1987), 71.

7. PSZRI, series III, vol. 20, no. 28,392 (October 6, 1906), 891–893; Wcislo, *Reforming Rural Russia*, 210–211.

8. On property as the key component of agrarian reform in this period and the limitations of the Stolypin reforms, see Yanni Kotsonis, *Making Peasants Backward:*

Managing Populations in Russian Agricultural Cooperatives, 1861–1914 (New York: Macmillan, 1999), 57–93.

9. By 1914, about 20 percent of peasants had obtained ownership of their land. By late 1916, 10.7 percent of peasant households in European Russia worked land that was enclosed. Khamza F. Usmanov, *Stolypinskaia agrarnaia reforma v Bashkirii* (Ufa: Bashkirskoe Kniznoe Izdatel'stvo, 1958), 74–79; Abraham Ascher, *P. A. Stolypin: The Search for Stability in Late Imperial Russia* (Stanford, Calif.: Stanford University Press, 2001), 158–161.

10. Marc Szeftel, *The Russian Constitution of April 23, 1906: Political Institutions of the Duma Monarchy* (Brussels: Les Éditions de la Librairie Encyclopédique, 1976), 248–250. Hans Rogger takes a skeptical view of Stolypin's commitment to reform of laws restricting Jews. Hans Rogger, *Jewish Policies and Right-Wing Politics in Imperial Russia* (Berkeley: University of California Press, 1986), 92–95.

11. Peter Waldron, "Religious Toleration in Late Imperial Russia," in *Civil Rights in Imperial Russia,* ed. Olga Crisp and Linda Edmondson (Oxford: Oxford University Press, 1989), 113.

12. The potential convert had to be protected against coercion from religious authorities bent on preventing conversion as well as from non-Orthodox clergy who sought to impel Orthodox subjects to apostasy. TsGIA RB, f. I-9, op. 1, d. 714, ll. 13, 14 ob., 19–19 ob., 24, 36–36 ob. When religious gatherings seemed intended to increase the visibility and influence of a particular non-Orthodox sect outside its own membership, however, Stolypin approved restrictions. TsGIA RB, f. I-9, op. 1, d. 714, ll. 26–26 ob. Paul Werth, *The Tsar's Foreign Faiths: Toleration and the Fate of Religious Freedom in Imperial Russia* (Oxford: Oxford University Press, 2014), 241–242.

13. Petr A. Stolypin, "Rech' o veroispovednykh zakonoproektakh," in *Rechi v gosudarstvennoi dume i gosudarstvennom sovete, 1906–1911,* comp. Iu. G. Fel'shtinskii (New York: Teleks, 1990), 183. TsGIA RB, f. I-9, op. 1, d. 714, ll. 25, 36 ob.

14. Gregory Freeze, "Subversive Piety: Religion and the Political Crisis in Late Imperial Russia," *Journal of Modern History* 68, no. 2 (June 1996): 337.

15. Werth, *The Tsar's Foreign Faiths,* 264.

16. Salavat Iskhakov, *Pervaia russkaia revoliutsiia i musul'mane rossiiskoi imperii* (Moscow: Izdatel'stvo Sotsial'no-Politicheskaia Mysl', 2007), 292.

17. Elena Campbell, "The Muslim Question in Late Imperial Russia," in *Russian Empire: Space, People, Power, 1700–1930,* ed. Jane Burbank, Mark von Hagen, and Anatolyi Remnev (Bloomington: Indiana University Press, 2007), 332–337.

18. RGIA, f. 821, op. 8, d. 800, ll. 51–51 ob., cited in Robert P. Geraci, *Window on the East: National and Imperial Identities in Late Tsarist Russia* (Ithaca, N.Y.: Cornell University Press, 2001), 285.

19. Diliara Usmanova, *Musul'manskie predstaviteli v rossiiskom parlamente, 1906–1916* (Kazan: Fen, 2005), 151, 166, 186, 201. See also Rustem Tsiunchuk, *Dumskaia model' parlamentarizma v rossiiskoi imperii: Etnokonfessional'noe i regional'noe izmereniia* (Kazan: Fen, 2004); and Larissa A. Iamaeva, *Musul'manskie deputaty gosudarstvennoi dumy Rossii, 1906–1917 gg.: Sbornik dokumentov i materialov* (Ufa: Kitap, 1998).

20. An MVD report in 1907 identified the Ufa provincial zemstvo as one of only four in the empire where the leading majority identified with parties of the left. Four of Ufa's six counties showed similar sympathies. Generally someone on the "left" was considered

to be to the left of the Octoberist Party. RGIA, f. 1288, op. 2, 1904 razdel, d. 2, May 1907, ll. 1–54.

21. Usmanov, *Stolypinskaia agrarnaia reforma*, 85, 167.

22. Sergei R. Mintslov, *Ufa: Debri zhizni. Dnevnik 1910–1915 gg.* (Ufa: Bashkirskoe Knizhnoe Izdatel'stvo, 1992), 90.

23. In 1909, MVD officials asked Kliucharev to investigate published complaints from Ufa Muslims that Ufa church authorities prevented people from reregistering in Islam. Only then did Kliucharev reassert his authority in the conversion process. TsGIA RB, f. I-9, op. 1, d. 831, ll. 32–32 ob. Werth, *The Tsar's Foreign Faiths*, 242.

24. TsGIA RB, f. I-9, op. 1, d. 714, ll. 7–10.

25. Marsel' Farkhshatov, *Samoderzhavie i traditsionnye shkoly Bashkir i Tatar v nachale XX veka (1900–1917 gg.)* (Ufa: Gilem, 2000), 214.

26. TsGIA RB, f. I-9, op. 1, d. 831, l. 26.

27. Marsel' Farkhshatov, "Ufa," in *Islam na territorii byvshei rossiiskoi imperii: Entsiklopedicheskii slovar'*, vol. 4, ed. S. M. Prozorov (Moscow: Izdatel'stvo Firma Vostochnaia Literatura RAN, 2003), 81.

28. Stolypin's land policies did increase the frequency with which Bashkirs donated land as a *waqf*, or pious endowment. Norihiro Naganawa, "Molding the Muslim Community through the Tsarist Administration: *Mahalla* under the Jurisdiction of the Orenburg Mohammedan Spiritual Assembly after 1905," *Acta Slavica Iaponica* 23 (2006): 118.

29. TsGIA RB, f. 10, op. 1, d. 1,692, ll. 128–129, cited in Usmanov, *Stolypinskaia agrarnaia reforma*, 91.

30. Usmanov, *Stolypinskaia agrarnaia reforma*, 107, 141–142.

31. Mikhail I. Rodnov, "Chislennost' tiurkskogo krest'ianstva ufimskoi gubernii v nachale XX v.," *Etnograficheskoe obozrenie* 6 (1996): 123–131. As Rodnov points out, nationality (*natsional'nost'*) was not a primary focus of the 1912–1913 and 1917 agricultural censuses. For the 1917 census, nationality was not even published. Il'dar Gabdrafikov emphasizes the northwest of Bashkiria, the zone of greatest migration of Tatar, Meshcheriak, Chuvash, Mari, and Udmurt migration, as the area with particularly dynamic ethnocultural processes. Il'dar M. Gabdrafikov, "Etnokul'turnye rezultaty migratsionnykh protsessov v severo-zapadnoi Bashkirii (konets XVI–nachalo XX v.)," in *Etnologicheskie issledovaniia v Bashkortostane: Sbornik statei*, ed. Il'dar Gabdrafikov (Ufa: UNTS RAN, 1994), 21–28.

32. Boris Veselovskii, *Istoriia zemstvo za sorok let*, vol. 4 (St. Petersburg: Popov, 1911), 58.

33. To the extent that the Ufa zemstvo became less radical, this resulted from the governor's actions, not from a change in the attitude of most zemstvo activists. On the zemstvo reaction, see Roberta Thompson Manning, *The Crisis of the Old Order in Russia: Gentry and Government* (Princeton, N.J.: Princeton University Press, 1982); RGIA, f. 1288, op. 2, 1906 razdel, d. 76, l. 23.

34. Entitled "What Is Politics?," the article compared teaching even Russian-speaking peasants the meaning of "politics" (*politika*) to Robinson Crusoe teaching Friday the meaning of a new word. "Chto takoe politika," *Ufimskaia zemskaia gazeta*, no. 1 (March 1, 1906): 10.

35. Manning, *The Crisis of the Old Order in Russia*, 134–135.

36. Ismail Bei Gasprinskii, "Russkoe Musul'manstvo: Mysli, zametki i nabliudeniia Musul'manina," in *Rossiia i vostok,* ed. M. A. Usmanov (Kazan: Fond Zhien, Tatarskoe Knizhnoe Izdatel'stvo, 1993), 29.

37. S. S. Larionov, *Nachal'noe obrazovanie inorodtsev kazanskogo i ufimskogo kraia* (St. Petersburg: Soikin, 1916), 99–100.

38. *Zhurnaly zasedanii ufimskogo gubernskogo zemskogo sobraniia XXXI ocherednoi i XXXVII chrezvychainoi sessii 1905–1906, i doklady upravy* (Ufa: Girbasova, 1906), 378–379.

39. *Zhurnaly zasedanii ufimskogo gubernskogo zemskogo sobraniia XXXI ocherednoi i XXXVII,* 23, 394.

40. *Zhurnaly zasedanii ufimskogo gubernskogo zemskogo sobraniia XXXI ocherednoi i XXXVII,* 384–385. Zemstvo priorities differed among provinces. The chairman of the Kazan zemstvo, N. Melnikov, recalled that he and others in Kazan considered building roads and bridges the zemstvo's primary mission. Rare Book and Manuscript Library, Columbia University. N. Melnikov, "Deviat'nadtsat' let zemskoi sluzhby."

41. NA UNTS RAN, f. 3, op. 1, ed. khr. 1, 113.

42. Togan, *Vospominaniia,* 54–55.

43. Iskhakov, *Pervaia russkaia revoliutsiia,* 81; Leopold Haimson, ed., with Ziva Galili y Garcia and Richard Wortman, *The Making of Three Russian Revolutionaries: Voices from the Menshevik Past* (Cambridge: Cambridge University Press, 1987), 249.

44. P. N. Grigor'ev, comp., *Ocherk deiatel'nosti ufimskogo gubernskogo zemstva po narodnomu obrazovaniiu, 1875–1910 gg.* (Ufa: Pechat' N. F. Delinskogo, 1910), 132–133.

45. Naganawa, "Molding the Muslim Community," 120.

46. *Zhurnaly soveshchaniia pri ufimskoi gubernskoi zemskoi uprave po voprosu o tipe nachal'noi obshcheobrazovatel'noi musul'manskoi shkoly, 23–25-go maia 1911* (Ufa: L. E. Miliukov, 1911), 1–2.

47. *Zhurnaly soveshchaniia pri ufimskoi gubernskoi zemskoi uprave,* 40.

48. *Zhurnaly soveshchaniia pri ufimskoi gubernskoi zemskoi uprave,* 33–34.

49. The Ufa zemstvo's position differed from that expressed at a similar conference in January 1911 in Kazan, which called for Muslim schools that corresponded to the government's criteria. What Koropachinskii described as the "Muslim intelligentsia" had much less influence in Kazan than it did in Ufa. Iakov D. Koblov, *Konfessional'nye shkoly kazanskikh Tatar* (Kazan: Tsentral'naia Tipografiia, 1916), 76–79.

50. I have chosen the term because it indicates all types of education outside of courses at a school, including those aimed at children. Scott Seregny uses the term "adult education" to describe these programs. Scott J. Seregny, "Zemstvos, Peasants, and Citizenship: The Russian Adult Education Movement and World War I," *Slavic Review* 59, no. 2 (Summer 2000): 290–315.

51. *Plan deiatel'nosti ufimskogo gubernskogo zemstva po narodnomu obrazovaniiu utverzhdennyi gubernskim zemskim sobraniem ocherednoi sessii 1912,* 2nd ed. (Ufa: Gubernskaia Tipografiia, 1913), i–ii.

52. *Plan deiatel'nosti ufimskogo gubernskogo zemstva,* 40–41, 43–44, 47, 53–58.

53. "Po voprosu o pravakh sobstvennosti na otkrytiia ufimskim gubernskim zemstvom pri shkolakh narodnykh bibliotek," *VOUO,* no. 7–8 (1913): 53.

54. The zemstvo also began to extend its work to the Mari and Chuvash who were considered less developed by elite members of the zemstvo. "Koe-chto o Cheremise,"

BONO, no. 2 (June 2, 1915): 20; "Polgoda raboty v biblioteke (Zametki zavedyvaiushchogo raionnoi biblioteki)," *Ufimskii vestnik*, no. 83 (April 14, 1914): 3.

55. Kazan gendarmes warned Ufa gendarmes that Teregulov was a Social Democrat who worked for the party newspaper *Ural* in Orenburg. TsGIA RB, f. 187, op. 1, d. 467, l. 147. Teregulov had participated in the first Tatar literary-political circles formed in Kazan in the period 1895–1900. Azade-Ayse Rorlich, *The Volga Tatars: A Profile in National Resilience* (Stanford, Calif.: Hoover Institution Press, 1986), 105–106. According to reminiscences of Ufa Social Democrats, Teregulov translated their publications into Tatar and participated in sessions of the Ufa party committee in 1905. TsAOO RB, f. 1832, op. 3, d. 124, l. 9. Iskhakov, *Pervaia russkaia revoliutsia*, 197.

56. In August 1914, the Orenburg provincial zemstvo created a position similar to that held by Teregulov and appointed Sultan-Galiev to it. Sultan-Galiev never actually assumed his duties in Orenburg, however. *Ufimskii vestnik*, no. 190 (August 27, 1914): 4; I. G. Gizzatullin and D. R. Sharafutdinov, comps., *Mirsaid Sultan-Galiev: Stat'i, vystupleniia, dokumenty* (Kazan: Tatarskoe Knizhnoe Izdatel'stvo, 1992), 398. The number of Muslim employees initially remained small, with between one and three Muslim employees active at the district level or above. *BONO*, no. 1 (1915): 30–31, 35, 43; no. 1 (1916): 67–78.

57. Gizzatullin and Sharafutdinov, *Mirsaid Sultan-Galiev*, 398. Zemstvo non-Russian libraries opened in late 1913 enjoyed similar success. "Inorodcheskie biblioteki," *Ufimskii vestnik*, no. 11 (January 15, 1914): 3. Sultan-Galiev was not always so successful. Gizzatullin and Sharafutdinov, *Mirsaid Sultan-Galiev*, "Pochemu nuzhny narodnye doma?" 40–41, translated and reprinted from *Tormysh* 67 (May 23, 1914), and "Na kogo obizhat'sia?" 41–44, translated and reprinted from *Tormysh* 82 (July 2, 1914).

58. Allen J. Frank, *Islamic Historiography and 'Bulghar' Identity among the Tatars and Bashkirs of Russia* (Leiden: Brill, 1998).

59. Allen J. Frank and Michael Kemper make a strong case for the centrality of Islam and Bulgar to Muslim identity in the region. See Frank, *Islamic Historiography*; Allen J. Frank, *Muslim Religious Institutions in Imperial Russia: The Islamic World of Novouzensk District and the Kazakh Inner Horde, 1780–1910* (Leiden: Brill, 2001); and Michael Kemper, *Sufii i uchenye v Tatarstane i Bashkortostane: Islamskii diskurs pod russkim gospodstvom*, trans. Iskander Giliazov (Kazan: Idel-Press, 2008). For an interpretation emphasizing Tatar nationalism, see Rorlich, *The Volga Tatars*. The Soviet literature stresses the emergence of Socialist Revolutionary or Social Democratic movements among Muslims.

60. Muhammad Sadiq al-Urargani, "Bezneng Khallar," *Din va maghyishat*, no. 4 (1911), 59, cited in Danielle M. Ross, "From the Minbar to the Barricades: The Transformation of the Volga-Ural 'Ulama into a Revolutionary Intelligentsia" (PhD dissertation, University of Wisconsin–Madison, 2011), 411.

61. Ross, "From the Minbar to the Barricades," 412–414.

62. Togan, *Vospominaniia*, 90.

63. Togan, *Vospominaniia*, 106–107.

64. Togan, *Vospominaniia*, 106–107.

65. Jeffrey Brooks describes a growing focus on the empire rather than on the tsar in late imperial popular culture. Jeffrey Brooks, *When Russia Learned to Read: Literacy and Popular Culture, 1861–1917* (Princeton, N.J.: Princeton University Press, 1985), 244–245.

66. M. A. Miropiev, ed., *Zhurnaly zasedanii s"ezda direktorov i inspektorov narodnykh uchilishch orenburgskogo uchebnogo okruga v. g. Ufe, 11–16 iiunia 1912 goda* (Ufa: F. G. Solov'ev, 1913), 51. On Gustave Le Bon, see Tzvetan Todorov, *On Human Diversity: Nationalism, Racism, and Exoticism in French Thought*, trans. Catherine Porter (Cambridge, Mass.: Harvard University Press, 1993), 55–56.

67. Miropiev, *Zhurnaly zasedanii s"ezda*, 72.

68. The journal's circulation grew from 1,200 copies in 1912 to 2,475 copies in 1915. M. A. Miropiev edited it. *vouo*, no. 1 (1915): n.p.

69. Miropiev, *Zhurnaly zasedanii s"ezda*, 64, 172–173. "O merakh k podniatiiu uchebno-vospitatel'nogo dela v nachal'nykh narodnykh uchilishchakh," *vouo*, no. 2 (1913): offits. otdel 187. In their emphasis on history, educational officials in Ufa reflected the interest of the MNP in St. Petersburg. "Programmy i ob"iasnitel'nye zapiski po russkoi i vseobshchei istorii v muzhskikh gimnaziiakh, July 13, 1913," *vouo*, no. 7–8 (1913): offits. otdel 595–596, 602.

70. Miropiev, *Zhurnaly zasedanii s"ezda*, 56, 65.

71. TsGIA RB, f. 109, op. 1, d. 157, ll. 58–59 ob.; *vouo*, no. 1 (1912): nauchnyi otdel 1. Study of the "native land" in Russia was influenced by European models. See Alon Confino, *Nation as a Local Metaphor: Würtemberg, Imperial Germany, and National Memory, 1871–1918* (Chapel Hill: University of North Carolina Press, 1997). Brooks notes the emergence of a new conception of empire and the individual's relationship to it in popular fiction. Brooks, *When Russia Learned to Read*, 244–245.

72. Miropiev, *Zhurnaly zasedanii s"ezda*, 69. Miropiev took his model of masculinity from England. "Oblomovism," a type of sluggishness and indecision, was Russian men's "national, innate vice" and separated Russians from Englishmen with their strong, firm characters. Miropiev, *Zhurnaly zasedanii s"ezda*, 69–70. "Polozhenie o vneshkol'noi podgotovke russkoi molodezhi k voennoi sluzhbe," *vouo*, no. 1 (1912): offits. otdel 12.

73. Vladimirov was born a hereditary nobleman in Mogilev Province and educated at Warsaw University. He had served as a school inspector in the Warsaw Educational District. He personally experienced the violence of the 1905 revolution in Warsaw when some educational administration offices were occupied by armed men. M. Gorbunov, "Fedor Nikolaevich Vladimirov," *vouo*, no. 5 (1913): 309; N. Beliaev, "Pamiati Feodora Nikolaevicha Vladimirov," *vouo*, no. 5 (1913): 310–311.

74. Miropiev, *Zhurnaly zasedanii s"ezda*, 252.

75. Miropiev, *Zhurnaly zasedanii s"ezda*, 235, 247, 251.

76. Miropiev, *Zhurnaly zasedanii s"ezda*, 255.

77. The MNP's regulations on the instruction of non-Russians, issued July 14, 1913, criticized native-language instruction but stopped short of eliminating it. "S pravilami o nachal'nykh uchilishchakh dlia inorodtsev," *vouo*, no. 5 (1913), offits. otdel 394–398; Wayne Dowler, "The Politics of Language in Non-Russian Elementary Schools in the Eastern Empire, 1865–1914," *Russian Review* 54, no. 4 (October 1995): 537.

78. RGIA, f. 796, op. 442, d. 2124, l. 201; RGIA, f. 796, op. 442, d. 2247, ll. 19 ob.–20; Nikolai Egorov, "Otkliki iz eparkhii. Kak inye ponimaiut zakon 17 April 1905," *uev*, no. 7 (April 1, 1906): 483–486.

79. Ioann Khokhlov, "Novye vzgliady i veianiia v sterlitamakskom zemstve," *uev*, no. 2 (January 15, 1908): 92.

80. Gregory L. Freeze, *The Parish Clergy in Nineteenth-Century Russia: Crisis, Reform, Counter-Reform* (Princeton, N.J.: Princeton University Press, 1983), 470–471.

81. In February 1907, Gromov requested that the OMEA register him as a Muslim, petitioned Bishop Khristofor for permission to leave the clergy, called himself Iakh'i Iskanderovich, and started to practice the Muslim faith. RGIA, f. 821, op. 8, d. 1197, ll. 48 ob.; RGIA, f. 796, op. 442, d. 2241, ll. 11 ob.–121.

82. RGIA, f. 796, op. 442, d. 2308; TSAOO RB, f. 1832, op. 4, d. 80, ll. 1–2.

83. The figure for 1898 comes from Ivan Zlatoverkhovnikov, comp., *Ufimskaia eparkhiia: Geograficheskii, etnograficheskii, administrativno-istoricheskii i statisticheskii ocherk* (Ufa: A. P. Zaikov, 1899), 217; the figure for 1914 comes from RGIA, f. 796, op. 422, d. 2677, l. 34 ob.

84. RGIA, f. 796, op. 442, d. 2124, ll. 131–141; "Opredeleniia Sv. Sinoda ot 18 noiabria 1905 g.," *UEV*, no. 2 (January 15, 1906): 66; "Otradnoe iavlenie (iz byta dukhovenstva Bel. U.)," *UEV*, no. 5 (March 1, 1906): 399–400. "Ot redaktsii," *UEV*, no. 1 (January 1, 1906): 12–13.

85. TSGIA RB, f. I-9, op. 1, d. 831, ll. 7–14. N. A. Gurvich was born in the Grodno region of Russian Poland and trained as a doctor in St. Petersburg. He arrived in Ufa in the 1850s and worked as a medical doctor and as head of the provincial statistical committee. In the 1870s, he founded the provincial museum and the city library. "N. A. Gurvich," *Ufimskii vestnik*, no. 115 (May 25, 1914): 5; Mintslov, *Ufa: Debri zhizni*, 84–85.

86. N. Nikol'skii, "K chemu obiazyvaet Vysochaishe darovannaia svoboda sovesti," *UEV*, no. 8 (April 15, 1906): 544–545.

87. RGIA, f. I-9, op. 1, d. 831, l. 121, "Pervyi v ufimskoi eparkhii missionerskii s"ezd (28 fevralia–3-go marta 1906)." Nikol'skii, "K chemu obiazyvaet," 541.

88. "Otradnoe iavlenie," *UEV*, no. 3 (February 1, 1906): 401. "Otchet eparkhial'nogo Komiteta Pravoslavnogo Missionerskogo Obshchestva za 1905 g.," *UEV*, no. 17 (September 15, 1906): 1076.

89. RGIA, f. 796, op. 445, d. 211, l. 211.

90. Igor K. Smolich, *Istoriia russkoi tserkvi, 1700–1917* (Moscow: Izdatel'stvo Spaso-Preobrazhenskogo Valaamskogo Monastyria, 1996), 766.

91. A local newspaper noted the lack of representatives of the administration, city, zemstvo, or military at Mikhei's last service. "K uvolneniiu na pokoi preosv. Mikheia," *Ufimskii vestnik*, no. 3 (January 4, 1914): 3; "Proshchanie episkopa Mikheia s ufimskoiu pastvoiu," *Ufimskii vestnik*, no. 10 (January 14, 1914): 3.

92. Between 1900 and 1904, every year an average of approximately 391 men took the examinations administered by the OMEA. In the next five years, the yearly average nearly doubled to 766. Nearly one thousand men took the exam in 1907 and 1909. RGIA, f. 821, op. 133, d. 625, ll. 18 ob., 28.

93. Ten Muslims and four zemstvo board members identified 1,579 maktabs in 1912–1913. More than one-fifth (348) had opened after 1905. M. I. Obukhov, *Mekteby ufimskoi gubernii* (Ufa: Pechat', 1915), 3–4, 11.

94. According to Salavat Iskhakov, Witte proposed the meeting in response to Bashkir petitions. Iskhakov, *Pervaia russkaia revoliutsiia*, 122–123.

95. Rorlich, *The Volga Tatars*, 57–58.

96. Later in the year, Fakhretdinov and another OMEA judge, Kapkaev, received gold medals "for zeal" (*za userdie*). Iskhakov, *Pervaia russkaia revoliutsiia*, 200.

97. S. G. Rybakov, ed., "Proekt lits vysshogo magometanskogo dukhoventstva o pre-obrazovanii Orenburgskogo Magometanskogo Dukhovnogo Sobraniia, predstavlennyi Orenburgskim Muftiem v 1905 godu," in *Ustroistvo i nuzhdy upravleniia dukhovnymi delami musul'man v Rossii*, ed. S. G. Rybakov (Petrograd: Tipografiia S. Samoilova, 1917), 48–51. Ahmet Kanlidere, *Reform within Islam: The* Tajdid *and* Jadid *Movement among the Kazan Tatars (1809–1917), Conciliation and Conflict* (Istanbul: Eren, 1997), 106.

98. RGIA, f. 821, op. 8, d. 632, ll. 84–86. The document was signed by 103 clerics. Six years later, clerics from Orenburg published a petition to the OMEA in the Tatar newspaper *Vakt* (Time). The clerics asserted that they were "ecclesiastical persons of Russia" who served "equally with Russian clergy for the successful economic, political, and cultural development of our Fatherland." They demanded equal status with Russian Orthodox clergy. TsGIA RB, f. I-187, op. 1, d. 467, ll. 33–34.

99. Iskhakov, *Pervaia russkaia revoliutsiia*, 307.

100. RGIA, f. 1276, op. 2, d. 593, ll. 113, 114. See also Elena Campbell, *The Muslim Question and Russian Imperial Governance* (Bloomington: Indiana University Press, 2015), 146–148.

101. Rybakov, *Ustroistvo i nuzhdy*, 38–40.

102. "Iz istorii natsional'noi politiki tsarizma," *Krasnyi arkhiv* 35 (1929): 112, 116–118. This contains the "Zhurnal osobogo soveshchaniia po vyrabotke mer dlia protivodeist-viia tatarsko-musul'manskomu vliianiiu."

103. RGIA, f. 821, op. 133, d. 625, l. 3 ob.

104. These included criticism of the government's policies regarding Muslim confessional schools and Bashkir lands. RGIA, f. 821, op. 133, d. 625, ll. 44–44 ob., 45–45 ob., 46 ob.–53. Started in 1908, the journal's first editor was Mukhammad-Sabir Khasanov, imam of Ufa's third *mahalla*, or Muslim community, a deputy to the second State Duma. Farkhshatov, "Ufa," 82.

105. RGIA, f. 821, op. 133, d. 625, ll. 54–64, 83.

106. Statisticheskii otdel Ufimskoi gubernskoi upravy, *Istoriko-statisticheskie tablitsy deiatel'nosti ufimskikh zemstv. K sorokoletiiu sushchestvovaniia zemstv ufimskoi gubernii, 1875–1914*, ed. M. P. Krasil'nikov (Ufa: Pechat', 1915), 226–228.

107. RGIA, f. 1288, op. 2, 1909 razdel, d. 25b, ll. 3 ob., 7, 8 ob.–10. The "purely national demands" were for a Muslim school inspector at zemstvo expense and equalization of expenditures on Muslim maktabs and madrasas with expenditures on Russian schools. Ibraghim Teregulov had served as an inspector of students at Kazan University.

108. TsGIA RB, f. 187, d. 451, ll. 20–25, 27–28, 29, 42–43, 66. One of the board members appointed was Bunin's brother-in-law.

109. Individual members of the two families held between 35 and 154 des. each. Members of the Utiashev and Diveev families held additional, much smaller amounts of land. UGV, prilozhenie k no. 60 (1912): 16–19. RGIA, f. 1288, op. 2, 1909 razdel, d. 46, ll. 35–38 ob.

110. Tevkelev was a voting member of the provincial assembly by virtue of his position as Belebei County marshal of the nobility. *Adres-kalendar ufimskoi gubernii na 1915 god* (Ufa: Gubernskaia Tipografiia, 1915), 18.

111. Krasil'nikov, "Itogi zemskoi izbiratel'noi kampanii v ufimskoi gubernii," *Zemskoe delo*, no. 18 (September 20, 1912): 1138. Krasil'nikov called the elections from the districts a success with respect to the representation of "nationality (*natsional'nost'*) and religion."

112. "Ob"ediniaiushchii organ," *Ufimskii vestnik*, no. 179 (August 13, 1914): 3.

113. Il'dus K. Zagidullin, "Osobennosti sobliudeniia religioznykh prav musul'man v rossiiskoi sukhoputnoi reguliarnoi armii v 1874–1914 g.," *Journal of Power Institutions in Post-Soviet Societies*, 10 (2009): 4.

114. Bashilov sent the letter in response to the MVD's request for comment on Muslim attitudes toward the announcement of war on August 2, 1914. All responses to the MVD's inquiries other than those of Saratov, Kazan, and Turkestan confirmed Muslims' loyalty. RGIA, f. 821, op. 133, d. 603, ll. 22, 54–55 ob.

115. *Ufimskii vestnik*, no. 184 (August 20, 1914): 4.

116. RGIA, f. 821, op. 133, d. 603, ll. 65–66 ob. Sultanov issued a similar instruction on November 11, 1914, after the Ottoman Empire entered the war against Russia and sought to win support from Russia's Muslim population. RGIA, f. 821, op. 133, d. 603, ll. 131–132, 49–150, 172, 180.

117. *Ufimskii vestnik*, no. 172 (August 3, 1914): 3. Ibniamin Akhtiamov was expelled from St. Petersburg University in 1899 for participating in a student demonstration, arrested in Moscow in 1901, and arrested in Ufa after that. He was associated with the Party of Socialist Revolutionaries after 1903. Iskhakov, *Pervaia russkaia revoliutsiia*, 81.

118. RGIA, f. 821, op. 133, d. 603, ll. 54–55 ob. Allan Wildman has noted substantially less enthusiasm for the mobilization among lower status groups than among educated society. Allan K. Wildman, *The End of the Imperial Army*, vol. 1 (Princeton, N.J.: Princeton University Press, 1980), 76–80.

119. Leonid Korovin, "Polgoda raboty v biblioteke," *BONO*, no. 2 (June 2, 1915): 17.

120. *BONO*, no. 1 (March 1, 1915): 1–2.

121. "Iz 'ob"iasnitel'noi zapiski k smete ministerstva narodnogo prosveshcheniia na 1916 g.,'" *Zhurnal ministerstva narodnogo prosveshcheniia*, no. 7–8 (1916): 170–176; A. B-ov, "Narodnye lektsii i chteniia o voine," *Petrogradskii zemskii vestnik* (July–August 1916): 65–66, cited in Seregny, "Zemstvos, Peasants, and Citizenship," 297.

122. *BONO*, no. 1 (March 1, 1916): 67–78.

123. Scott Seregny and Hubertus Jahn also note the lack of patriotic identification with the tsar during the First World War. Scott Seregny, "Zemstvos, Peasants, and Citizenship"; Jahn, *Patriotic Culture*; and Hubertus Jahn, "For Tsar and Fatherland? Russian Popular Culture and the First World War," in *Cultures in Flux: Lower-Class Values, Practices, and Resistance in Late Imperial Russia*, ed. Stephen P. Frank and Mark D. Steinberg (Princeton, N.J.: Princeton University Press, 1994), 131–146.

124. Seregny, "Zemstvos, Peasants, and Citizenship," 312.

125. TSGIA RB, f. 151, op. 1, d. 21, ll. 8, 9.

126. *Zhurnaly menzelinskogo uezdnogo zemskogo sobraniia 40-i ocherednoi sessii, zasedanie 17 noiabria 1914 g.*, reprinted in Andrei, *Mneniia ufimskikh zemtsev o tserkovnykh delakh (na osnovanii rechei v uezdnykh zemskikh sobraniiakh 1914 goda)* (Ufa: Gubernskaia Tipografiia, 1915), 32–33.

127. *Ufimskii vestnik*, no. 3 (January 4, 1914): 3.

128. Andrei, *Mneniia ufimskikh zemtsev*, 14, 27.

129. With respect to financial support, however, the war had a different impact. Whereas zemstvos expended greater sums on extracurricular education after 1914, the MNP had less money to fund schools. "O poriadke i usloviiakh otpuska v 1915 g. sredstv na nuzhdy nachal'nogo obrazovaniia," *VOUO*, no. 2 (February 1915): 143.

130. M. A. Miropiev, "Neobkhodimost' obosnovaniia russkoi shkoly na natsional'-nykh nachalakh," *VOUO*, no. 1 (1915): ped. otdel 1–10; no. 2 (1915): ped. otdel 87–96.

131. Miropiev's belief that Russians borrowed too much from German and French educational models did not stop him from quoting German thinker Fichte to the effect that "a good system of social education is the only salvation of Germany." Miropiev, "Neobkhodimost' obosnovaniia," *VUOU*, no. 2 (1915): 95.

132. M. A. Miropiev, "Sushchnost' sistemy obrazovaniia inorodtsev N. I. Il'minskogo," *VOUO*, no. 3 (March 1915): 185–191.

133. On the First World War's impact on ethnicity and forced population movements in the western borderlands, see Eric Lohr, *Nationalizing the Russian Empire: The Campaign against Enemy Aliens during World War I* (Cambridge, Mass.: Harvard University Press, 2003); and Mark L. von Hagen, "The Great War and the Mobilization of Ethnicity in the Russian Empire," in *Post-Soviet Political Order: Conflict and State Building*, ed. Barnett R. Rubin and Jack Snyder (London: Routledge, 1998), 34–57.

134. *Otchet o deiatel'nosti osobogo otdela komiteta Eia Imperatorskogo Vysochestva velikoi kniazhny Tatiany Nikolaevny po registratsii bezhentsev v 1915 g.* (Petrograd: Moskovskaia Khudozhestvennaia Pechatnia, 1916), 49–50.

135. Gatrell estimates that official statistics underreported refugees by about 10 percent. Peter Gatrell, "Refugees in the Russian Empire, 1914–1917: Population Displacement and Social Identity," in *Critical Companion to the Russian Revolution, 1914–1921*, ed. Edward Acton, Vladimir Iu. Cherniaev, and William G. Rosenberg (Bloomington: Indiana University Press, 1997), 544–564; Peter Gatrell, *A Whole Empire Walking: Refugees in Russia during World War I* (Bloomington: Indiana University Press, 1999), 55.

136. *Adres-kalendar ufimskoi gubernii i spravochnaia knizhka na 1910 god* (Ufa: Gubernskaia Tipografiia, 1910), 45–48. See *Otchet orenburgskogo obshchestva popecheniia ob uchashchikhsia musul'manakh: Za 1912 god* (Orenburg: Tipgrafiia Gazety Vakht, 1913); and *Otchet orenburgskogo obshchestva popecheniia ob uchashchikhsia musul'manakh za 1914* (Orenburg: A.A. Khusainov, 1915).

137. On refugees and nationality, see Gatrell, *A Whole Empire Walking*, especially 141–170.

138. *Otchet o deiatel'nosti*, 7, 75. The meaning of nationality was elaborated only by example, Russian, Pole, Lithuanian, Latvian, Georgian, Armenian, and other (*russkii, poliak, litovets, latysh, gruzin, armianin, i proch.*).

139. TsGIA RB, f. I-9, op. 1, d. 1374, l. 52.

140. On Andrei see M. L. Zelenogorskii, *Zhizn' i deiatel'nost' Arkhiepiskopa Andreia (Kniazia Ukhtomskogo)* (Moscow: Terra, 1991); and E. I. Larina, "Episkop Andrei i doktrina ministerstva vnutrennikh del rossiiskoi imperii v 'musul'manskom voprose,'" *SRIO* 155, no. 7 (2003): 212–225.

141. Andrei, "Slovo pri vstuplenii na ufimskuiu kafedru, 14 fevralia 1914," *UEV*, no. 4 (February 15, 1914): 50.

142. "Slovo Episkopa," *Ufimskii vestnik*, no. 50 (March 2, 1914): 3.

143. "O lozhnykh prorokakh sovremmenosti," *Ufimskii vestnik*, no. 57 (March 11, 1914): 2, summarizing an article of the same title in *Razsvet* excerpted in *Birzhevie vedomosti*; Andrei, "O samoderzhavii 'Blagochestiveishego' (Slovo v den' koronovaniia Ikh Imperatorskikh Velichestv 14.5.1916)," *UEV*, no. 10 (May 15, 1916): 336, cited in Zelenogorskii, *Zhizn' i deiatel'nost'*, 22.

144. The question of parish reform was not one that Andrei alone raised. Church figures such as Antonii (Gradovskii) and Antonii (Khrapovitskii) had long argued that the renewal of church life depended both on the restoration of the patriarchate and on the revival of parish life. Metropolitan Antonii (Khrapovitskii), *Pastyrskoe bogoslovie* (Pskov: Izdatel'stvo Sviato-Uspenskogo Pskovo-Pecherskogo Monastyriia, 1994).

145. Andrei, "O tserkovno-prikhodskoi zhizni. (Rech' k chlenam ufimskogo eparkhial'nogo s"ezda dukhovenstva 1916)," *UEV*, no. 19 (October 1, 1916): 637.

146. Andrei, "O gospode vozliublennoi pastve ufimskoi," *UEV*, no. 7 (April 1, 1916): 217. Elections were introduced in 1916. Larina, "Episkop Andrei," 216.

147. P. E. Shchegolev, ed., *Padenie tsarskogo rezhima*, vol. 4: *Zapiski A. D. Protopopova i S. P. Beletskogo* (Leningrad: Gosudarstvennoe Izdatel'stvo, 1925), 288–289.

148. Andrei, *Mneniia ufimskikh zemtsev*, 4–5, 7, 11, 18–19, 23, 27, 46–47.

149. Andrei, *Mneniia ufimskikh zemtsev*, 34–35.

150. RGIA, f. 796, op. 442, d. 2616, l. 32 ob., otchet o sostoianii Ufimskoi eparkhii za 1913 g.; Andrei, "Pis'ma k pastyriam ufimskoi eparkhii. Eshche i eshche o narodnom chtenii," *UEV*, no. 23 (December 1, 1915): 988–989; Bishop Andrei, "O vneshkol'nom rukovodstve vo spasenie," *UEV*, no. 10 (May 15, 1915): 417.

151. GARF, f. 102, osob. otdel, 1916 g., op. 246, d. 74, ll. 223–224 ob., August 2, 1916, reproduced in Larina, "Episkop Andrei," 219–220.

152. Campbell, *The Muslim Question*, 211, 223.

153. RGIA, f. 796, op. 442, d. 2616, ll. 17 ob.–18, otchet o sostoianii ufimskoi eparkhii za 1913 g.

154. N. Kontsevich, "Chego nedostaet russkim liudiam na okrainakh russkogo gosudarstva," *UEV*, no. 1 (January 15, 1916): 51–52.

155. Kontsevich, "Chego nedostaet russkim liudiam," 53.

156. Andrei, "Ob osnovanii vostochno-russkogo obshchestva," *UEV*, no. 4 (February 15, 1916): 131–133.

157. A. Kuliasov, "O znachenii intelligentsii s tochki zreniia derevni i o metodakh eia deiatel'nosti. (Rech' sviashchennika o. A. Kuliasova na pervom obshchem sobranii chlenov vostochno-russkogo kul'turno-prosvetitel'nogo obshchestva 14 maia 1916)," *UEV*, no. 13 (July 1, 1916): 447.

158. Andrei, *O pechal'nykh posledstviiakh russkoi nekul'turnosti i o luchshem budushchem v etom otnoshenie*, 2nd ed. (Ufa: Galanov, 1916), 1–2. In shifting from what John Strickland calls "clerical Orthodox patriotism" toward an explicit embrace of nationalism, Bishop Andrei appears to have been moving in the opposite direction from other prominent clerics, such as V. Beliaev, who wrote that Christians must "struggle against national inclinations" and toward a universal view of the church. See John Strickland, *The Making of Holy Russia: The Orthodox Church and Russian Nationalism before the Revolution* (Jordanville, N.Y.: Holy Trinity Publications, 2013), 246.

159. Andrei, *O pechal'nykh posledstviiakh*, 21–22.

160. Elena Campbell analyzes these many congresses and conferences. See Campbell, *The Muslim Question*, 157–214.

161. A few key works in this literature include Joshua A. Sanborn, *Imperial Apocalypse: The Great War and the Destruction of the Russian Empire* (New York: Oxford University Press, 2014); selections in Omer Bartov and Eric D. Weitz, eds., *Shatterzone of Empires: Coexistence and Violence in the German, Habsburg, Russian, and Ottoman*

Borderlands (Bloomington: Indiana University Press, 2013); Faith Hillis, *Children of Rus': Right-Bank Ukraine and the Invention of a Russian Nation* (Ithaca, N.Y.: Cornell University Press, 2013), 274–284; Peter Holquist, "The Politics and Practice of the Russian Occupation of Armenia, 1915–February 1917," in *A Question of Genocide: Armenians and Turks at the End of the Ottoman Empire*, ed. Ronald Grigor Suny, Fatma Müçek, and Norman M. Naimark (New York: Oxford University Press, 2011), 151–174; Aleksandra Iu. Bakhturina, *Okrainy rossiiskoi imperii: Gosudarstvennoe upravlenie i natsional'naia politika v gody pervoi mirovoi voiny (1914–1917 gg.)* (Moscow: ROSSPEN, 2004); Lohr, *Nationalizing the Russian Empire.*

162. Bartov and Weitz, *Shatterzone of Empires.*

163. M. Şükrü Hanioğlu, *A Brief History of the Late Ottoman Empire* (Princeton, N.J.: Princeton University Press, 2008), 151–152.

164. Alice Conklin, *A Mission to Civilize: The Republican Idea of Empire in France and West Africa, 1895–1930* (Stanford, Calif.: Stanford University Press, 1997), 154–155. The most important representative body in Algeria, the Délégations financières, included 21 Muslims of 69 members, but Muslims were proportionately vastly underrepresented and had little actual influence on the allocation of resources. Muslim representation in Algerian municipal councils was reduced in 1884 to no more than one-fourth of the body, and until 1908, Muslims were appointed, not elected, to department general councils. John Ruedy, *Modern Algeria: The Origins and Development of a Nation,* 2nd ed. (Bloomington: Indiana University Press, 2005), 87. Patrick Weil, *How to Be French: Nationality in the Making since 1789,* trans. Catherine Porter (Durham, N.C.: Duke University Press, 2008), 215–216. Before the First World War, only two South Asians who had emigrated to England, Dadabhai Naoroji and Mancherjee Bhownagree, served in the British Parliament in London. Sukanya Banerjee, *Becoming Imperial Citizens: Indians in the Late-Victorian Empire* (Durham, N.C.: Duke University Press, 2010), 36–74; Antoinette Burton, "Tongues Untied: Lord Salisbury's 'Black Man' and the Boundaries of Imperial Democracy," *CSSH* 42, no. 3 (2000): 632–661.

165. Hanioğlu, *A Brief History,* 166.

166. Istvan Deak, *Beyond Nationalism: A Social and Political History of the Habsburg Officer Corps, 1848–1919* (New York: Oxford University Press, 1990).

167. Mark L. Von Hagen, "The Great War and the Mobilization of Ethnicity in the Russian Empire," in *Post-Soviet Political Order: Conflict and State Building,* ed. Barnett R. Rubin and Jack Snyder (London: Routledge, 1998), 34–57.

168. Ariel Roshwald, *Ethnic Nationalism and the Fall of Empires: Central Europe, Russia, and the Middle East, 1914–1923* (London: Routledge, 2001), 218.

169. Vejas Liulevicius, *War Land on the Eastern Front: Culture, National Identity, and German Occupation in World War I* (Cambridge: Cambridge University Press, 2000), 113–150.

170. Ross, "From the Minbar to the Barricades," 434–442.

CONCLUSION

1. A copy of the original and a translation are available at "Primary Documents: Tsar Nicholas II Abdication Proclamation, 2 March 1917," http://www.firstworldwar.com/source/nicholasiiabdication.htm, accessed August 2, 2010. See also Richard S.

Wortman, *Scenarios of Power: Myth and Ceremony in Russian Monarchy, vol. 2: From Alexander II to the Abdication of Nicholas II* (Princeton, N.J.: Princeton University Press, 2000), 522–523.

2. Influential prerevolutionary historian Vasilii Kliuchevskii wrote that "sosloviia" was "a term of state law and indicates a well-known array of political institutions." Through the granting of rights (*prava*) or the assessment of obligations, "supreme state authority is expressing its will in law. Therefore, an estate division is essentially juridical." Vasilii O. Kliuchevskii, *Istoriia soslovii v Rossii*, 3rd ed. (Petrograd: Literaturno-Izdatel'skii Otdel Komissariata Narodnogo Prosveshcheniia, 1918), 1–2.

3. See especially Paul Werth, *The Tsar's Foreign Faiths: Toleration and the Fate of Religious Freedom in Imperial Russia* (Oxford: Oxford University Press, 2014); Robert D. Crews, "Empire and the Confessional State: Islam and Religious Politics in Nineteenth-Century Russia," *American Historical Review* 108, no. 1 (February 2003): 50–83.

4. Robert D. Crews, "The Russian Worlds of Islam," in *Islam and the European Empires*, ed. David Motadel (Oxford: Oxford University Press, 2014), 37; and Robert D. Crews, *For Prophet and Tsar: Islam and Empire in Russia and Central Asia* (Cambridge, Mass.: Harvard University Press, 2006), 353.

5. In July 1915 Sultanov was replaced by a military imam in St. Petersburg, Mukhametsafa Baiazitov, whose appointment was criticized by Muslim liberals. RGIA, f. 821, op. 133, part a, d. 520, part 1, l. 213; M. I. Rodnov et al., eds., *Istoriia Bashkortostana vo vtoroi polovine XIX–nachale XX veka*, vol. 2 (Ufa: UNTS RAN, 2007), 22.

6. Werth, *The Tsar's Foreign Faiths*, 32–33.

7. Daniel E. Schafer, "Local Politics and the Birth of the Republic of Bashkortostan, 1919–1920," in *A State of Nations: Empire and Nation-Making in the Age of Lenin and Stalin,* ed. Ronald Grigor Suny and Terry Martin (Oxford: Oxford University Press, 2001), 171.

8. Mikhail I. Rodnov, "Chislennost' tiurkskogo krest'ianstva ufimskoi gubernii v nachale XX v.," *Etnograficheskoe obozrenie* 6 (1996): 123–131; Il'dar Gabdrafikov, "Etnokul'turnye resultaty migratsionnykh protsessov v severo-zapadnoi Bashkirii (konets XVI–nach. XX v.)," in *Etnologicheskie issledovaniia v Bashkortostane*, ed. Il'dar Gabdrafikov (Ufa: UNTS RAN, 1994), 21–28; Dmitry Gorenburg, "Identity Change in Bashkortostan: Tatars into Bashkirs and Back," *Ethnic and Racial Studies* 22, no. 3 (May 1999): 554–580.

9. Matthew P. Romaniello, *The Elusive Empire: Kazan and the Creation of Russia, 1552–1671* (Madison: University of Wisconsin Press, 2012).

10. Natalia A. Ivanova and Valentina P. Zheltova, *Soslovnoe obshchestvo rossiiskoi imperii (XVIII–nachalo XX veka)* (Moscow: Novyi Khronograf, 2009), 673–674, 677.

11. On "military-popular governance," see Vladimir O. Bobrovnikov, "Chto vyshlo iz proektov sozdaniia v Rossii *inorodtsev*? (otvet Dzhonu Slokumu iz musul'manskikh okrain imperii)," in *Poniatiia o Rossii: K istoricheskoi semantike imperskogo perioda*, vol. 1, ed. A. Miller, D. Sdvizhkov, and I. Shirle (Moscow: Novoe Literaturnoe Obozrenie, 2012), 280–284; and Bobrovnikov, *Musul'mane Severnogo Kavkaza: Obychai, pravo, nasilie. Ocherki po istorii i etnografii prava Nagornogo Dagestana* (Moscow: Vostochnaia Literatura-RAN, 2002), 171–172.

12. Ivanova and Zheltova, *Soslovnoe obshchestvo*, 675.

13. Alexander Morrison, "Metropole, Colony, and Citizenship in the Russian Empire," *Kritika: Explorations in Russian and Eurasian History* 13, no. 2 (Spring 2012): 347.

14. Marc Raeff differentiated military and diplomatic expansion in the empire's west and northwest from efforts to lure non-Russian elites in the east, and David Laitin, Roger Peterson, and John Slocum argued for the application of the concepts "bargained incorporation" in the west and "predatory expansion" in the east. Marc Raeff, "Patterns of Imperial Russian Policy toward the Nationalities," in *Soviet Nationality Problems*, ed. Edward Allworth (New York: Columbia University Press, 1971), 26–27; David Laitin, Roger Peterson, and John Slocum, "Language and the State: Russia and the Soviet Union in Comparative Perspective," in *Thinking Theoretically about Soviet Nationalities: History and Comparison in the Study of the USSR*, ed. Alexander J. Motyl (New York: Columbia University Press, 1995), 137.

15. Karen Barkey, *Bandits and Bureaucrats: The Ottoman Route to State Centralization* (Ithaca, N.Y.: Cornell University Press, 1994), 14.

16. This bargain is evident even in the wake of a violent conquest such as that of Kazan, where former enemies of the tsar became important military servitors after conquest. Romaniello, *The Elusive Empire*.

17. See Don C. Rawson, *Russian Rightists and the Revolution of 1905* (Cambridge: Cambridge University Press, 1995), 75–106; Robert Edelman, *Gentry Politics on the Eve of the Russian Revolution: The Nationalist Party 1907–1917* (New Brunswick, N.J.: Rutgers University Press, 1980), 49–64; Faith Hillis, *Children of Rus': Right-Bank Ukraine and the Invention of a Russian Nation* (Ithaca, N.Y.: Cornell University Press, 2013). See also V. Levitskii, "Pravye partii," in *Obshchestvennoe dvizhenie v Rossii v nachale XX-go veka*, vol. III, no. 5, *Partii—ikh sostav, razvitie, i proiavlenie v massovom dvizhenii, na vyborakh i v dume*, ed. L. Martov, P. Maslov, and A. Potresov (St. Petersburg: Obshchestvennaia Pol'za, 1914), 372, 405; and Sergei A. Stepanov, *Chernaia sotnia v Rossii 1905–1914 gg.* (Moscow: VZPI A/o Rosvuznauka, 1992).

18. See Heiz-Dietrich Löwe, *The Tsars and the Jews: Reform, Reaction and Anti-Semitism in Imperial Russia, 1772–1917* (Chur: Harwood Academic Publishers, 1993), 206–209. On the development of anti-Semitic mass politics in Kiev, see Hillis, *Children of Rus'*.

19. Omer Bartov and Eric D. Weitz, eds., *Shatterzone of Empire: Coexistence and Violence in the German, Habsburg, Russian, and Ottoman Borderlands* (Bloomington: Indiana University Press, 2013).

20. Peter C. Perdue, *China Marches West: The Qing Conquest of Central Eurasia* (Cambridge, Mass.: Belknap Press of Harvard University Press, 2005), 108.

21. As a result of Kirilov's miscalculation and that of authorities in St. Petersburg, the Orenburg Expedition produced violence similar to that of European colonial rule at its most harsh. On the Russian Empire on the steppe as a European colonial empire, see Michael Khodarkovsky, *Russia's Steppe Frontier: The Making of a Colonial Empire, 1500–1800* (Bloomington: Indiana University Press, 2002), 229.

22. Andreas Kappeler, "Tsentr i elity periferii v gabsburgskoi, rossiiskoi, i osmanskoi imperiiakh (1700–1918)," *Ab Imperio* 2 (2007), 30–31.

23. Catherine's grandson, Emperor Alexander I, introduced a hierarchical and centralized ministerial system of government and made the military parade ground the central representation of monarchical power. Wortman, *Scenarios of Power*, vol. 1, 226.

24. Sergei Iu. Witte, *Po povodu natsionalizma: Natsional'naia ekonomiia i Fridrikh List*, 2nd ed. (St. Petersburg: Brokgauz-Efron, 1912), 4. Whether Witte's conception of the German Empire is an accurate one is, of course, another matter.

25. Kappeler, "Tsentr i elity," 22.

26. Morrison, "Metropole, Colony, and Citizenship," 342. According to Peter Waldron, by the time the First World War broke out, about 60 percent of the empire's population lived in zemstvo provinces, while 40 percent did not. Peter Waldron, *Governing Tsarist Russia* (Basingstoke: Palgrave Macmillan, 2007), 107.

27. Morrison, "Metropole, Colony, and Imperial Citizenship," 347.

28. Adeeb Khalid, "Backwardness and the Quest for Civilization: Early Soviet Central Asia in Comparative Perspective," *Slavic Review* 65, no. 2 (Summer 2006): 232–233.

29. Orenburg only received zemstvos in 1913. L. E. Lapteva, *Zemskie uchrezhdeniia v Rossii* (Moscow: Institut Gosudarstva i Prava RAN, 1993), 122.

30. Serge Zenkovsky, *Pan-Turkism and Islam in Russia* (Cambridge, Mass.: Harvard University Press, 1960), 141–156.

31. Zenkovsky, *Pan-Turkism and Islam in Russia*, 149.

32. Bashkir sources from 1917 demonstrate a particular sensitivity to the loss of lands since 1898. A Bashkir *kuraltai*, or national assembly, resolved in December 1917 that "All settlers who settled in Bashkiria after 20 April 1898 by means of compulsory alienation of land and as a result of various predatory laws and regulations of the tsarist government" should be forced to exchange their land for land of Bashkirs outside of Bashkiria who wanted to relocate within its borders. TsGIA RB, f. 395r, op. 1, d. 7, l. 1 ob., quoted in Daniel E. Schafer, "Building Nations and Building States: The Tatar-Bashkir Question in Revolutionary Russia, 1917–1920" (PhD dissertation, University of Michigan, 1995), 141.

33. Schafer, "Local Politics and the Birth of the Republic of Bashkortostan," 173.

34. A Tatar Autonomous Republic centered in Kazan was created in May 1920. Azade-Ayşe Rorlich, *The Volga Tatars: A Profile in National Resilience* (Stanford, Calif.: Hoover Institution Press, 1986), 138.

35. Daniel Schafer examines this crucial period in his article "Local Politics and the Birth of the Republic of Bashkortostan," 165–190.

36. Schafer, "Building Nations and Building States," 389; Terry Martin, *The Affirmative Action Empire: Nations and Nationalism in the Soviet Union, 1923–1939* (Ithaca, N.Y.: Cornell University Press, 2001), 52–53; Zenkovsky, *Pan-Turkism and Islam in Russia*, 207; Richard E. Pipes, "The First Experiment in Soviet National Policy: The Bashkir Republic, 1917–1920," *Russian Review* 9, no. 13 (October 1950): 318.

37. Autonomous republics retained competence in education, justice, public health, and social security, under the supervision of the Russian Federation. Richard E. Pipes, *The Formation of the Soviet Union: Communism and Nationalism, 1917–1923*, rev. ed. (New York: Atheneum, 1968[1954]), 247–248.

38. Martin, *The Affirmative Action Empire*, 142, 381.

39. Schafer, "Building Nations and Building States," 392; Xavier Le Torrivellec, "Histoire des identités en Russie musulmane: la République du Bachkortostan (1969–2003)" (PhD dissertation, École des Hautes Études en Sciences Sociales, 2006), 163–201.

40. Gorenburg, "Identity Change in Bashkortostan," 561.

41. As Karen Barkey points out, "institutions, elites and associations" play a substantial role in shaping post-imperial nation-building. Karen Barkey, "Thinking about the Consequences of Empire," in *After Empire: Multiethnic Societies and Nation-Building. The Soviet Union and the Russian, Ottoman, and Habsburg Empires*, ed. Karen Barkey and Mark von Hagen (Boulder, Colo.: Westview, 1997), 110, 112.

42. Koropachinskii became the provisional government's commissar after February 1917, but the zemstvos' noble leadership was swept away along with the zemstvo itself in March 1918. Grigorii A. Gerasimenko, *Zemskoe samoupravlenie v Rossii* (Moscow: Nauka, 1990), 220.

43. In 1923, Sultan-Galiev fell out of favor with Stalin and was arrested. On Sultan-Galiev, see Alexandre Bennigsen and Chantel Lemercier-Quelquejay, *Sultan-Galiev: Le père de la revolution tiers-mondiste* (Paris: Fayard, 1986); Pipes, *The Formation of the USSR*, 168–169.

44. TSAOO RB, f. 9776, op. 2, d. 844, l. 24.

45. Scott Seregny, "Zemstvos, Peasants and Citizenship: The Russian Adult Education Movement and the First World War," *Slavic Review* 59, no. 2 (Summer 2000): 315.

46. Crews, *For Prophet and Tsar*, 365.

47. Francine Hirsch examines the development of national ideas and language and their use by Bolsheviks and imperial experts to understand the empire's population before October 1917. Francine Hirsch, *Empire of Nations: Ethnographic Knowledge and the Making of the Soviet Union* (Ithaca, N.Y.: Cornell University Press, 2005), 21–61.

Bibliography

ARCHIVAL SOURCES

Columbia University, Rare Book and Manuscript Library
    Collection of N. Melnikov, autobiography "Deviat'nadtsat' let zemskoi sluzhby"
    Collection of Maksim. M. Kovalevskii collection, box 4
Nauchnyi Arkhiv Ufimskogo Nauchnogo Tsentra Rossiiskoi Akademii Nauk (Scholarly
    Archive of the Ufa Scholarly Center of the Russian Academy of Sciences)
    f. 22   Lichnyi fond M. I. Umetbaeva
    f. 3   Lichnyi fond P. F. Ishcherikova
Rossiiskii Gosudarstvennyi Arkhiv Drevnikh Aktov (Russian State Archive of Ancient
    Acts, Moscow)
    RGADA, f. 7   Secret Chancellery and Secret Expeditions
    RGADA, f. 16   Vnutrenee upravlenie
Rossiiskaia Gosudarstvennaia Biblioteka, Otdel Rukopisi (Russian State Library,
    Manuscript Department)
    f. 364, k. 6, delo 1, Matvei Kuz'mich Liubavskii
Rossiiskii Gosudarstvennyi Istoricheskii Arkhiv (Russian State Historical Archive,
    St. Petersburg)
    f. 733   Departament Narodnogo Prosveshcheniia
    f. 796   Kantselariia Sviateishogo Sinoda
    f. 821   Ministerstvo Vnutrennikh Del, Departament Dukhovnykh Del
                   Inostrannykh Ispovedanii
    f. 1148   Gosudarstvennyi Sovet, Obshchee Sobranie
    f. 1149   Gosudarstvennyi Sovet, Departament Zakonov
    f. 1152   Gosudarstvennyi Sovet, Departament Ekonomii
    f. 1181   Gosudarstvennyi Sovet, Glavnyi Komitet ob Ustroistve Sel'skogo
                   Sostoianiia
    f. 1263   Komitet Ministrov
    f. 1287   Ministervo Vnutrennikh Del, Khoziaistvennyi Departament
    f. 1288   Ministervo Vnutrennikh Del, Khoziaistvennyi Departament
Natsional'nyi Arkhiv Respubliki Tatarstan (National Archive of the Republic of
    Tatarstan, Kazan)
    f. 51   Kazanskaia Sudebnaia Palata
    f. 89   Prokuror Kazanskoi Sudebnoi Palaty
    f. 93   Kazanskaia Uchitel'skaia Seminariia
    f. 142   Kazanskaia Tatarskaia Uchitel'skaia Shkola
Tsentral'nyi Gosudarstvennyi Istoricheskii Arkhiv Respubliki Bashkortostan (Central
    State Historical Archive of the Republic of Bashkortostan, Ufa)
    f. I-9   Ufimskoe Gubernskoe Pravlenie
    f. I-10   Ufimskoe Gubernskoe po Krest'ianskim Delam Prisutstvie

f. I-11   Kantseliariia Ufimskogo Grazhdanskogo Gubernatora
f. I-109   Kantseliariia Popechitelia Orenburgskogo Uchebnogo Okruga
f. I-132   Ufimskaia Gubernskaia Zemskaia Uprava
f. I-151   Birskaia Uezdnaia Zemskaia Uprava
f. I-187   Ufimskoe Gubernskoe Zhandarmskoe Upravlenie
f. I-295   Orenburgskoe Magometanskoe Dukhovnoe Sobranie
Tsentral'nyi Arkhiv Obshchestvennykh Ob"edinenii Respubliki
    Bashkortostan (Central Archive of Social Associations, Republic of
    Bashkortostan)
f. 1832   Istpart
f. 9776   Istpart

PERIODICALS

Biulleten' otdela narodnogo obrazovaniia (Ufa)
Golos (St. Petersburg)
Kazanskii vestnik (Kazan)
Moskovskie vedomosti (Moscow)
Nedelia (Moscow)
Orenburgskie gubernskie vedemosti (Orenburg)
Russkii vestnik (Moscow)
Sbornik russkogo istoricheskogo obshchestva (St. Petersburg)
Sankt-Peterburgskie vedomosti (St. Petersburg)
Ufimskie eparkhial'nye vedomosti (Ufa)
Ufimskie gubernskie vedomosti (Ufa)
Ufimskii vestnik (Ufa)
Ufimskaia zemskaia gazeta (Ufa)
Vestnik orenburgskogo uchebnogo okruga (Ufa)
Vestnik russkogo geograficheskogo obshchestva (St. Petersburg)
Vestnik ufimskogo zemstva (Ufa)
Vestnik Ufy (Ufa)
Zemskoe delo (St. Petersburg)

PUBLISHED PRIMARY SOURCES

Adres-kalendar ufimskoi gubernii i spravochnaia knizhka na 1910 god. Ufa: Gubernskaia
    Tipografiia, 1910.
Adres-kalendar ufimskoi gubernii na 1915 god. Ufa: Gubernskaia Tipografiia, 1915.
Aksakov, Sergei T. "Semeinaia khronika." *Sobranie sochinenii.* Vol. 1. Moscow: Gos.
    Izdatel'stvo Khudozhestvennoi Literatury, 1955.
Aksenov, A. I., R. V. Ovchinnikov, and M. F. Prokhorov, eds. *Dokumenty stavki E. I. Puga-
    cheva, povstancheskikh vlasteĭ i uchrezhdeniĭ, 1773–1774 gg.* Moscow: Nauka, 1975.
Andrei (Ukhtomskii). *Mneniia ufimskikh zemtsev o tserkovnykh delakh (na osnovanii
    rechei v uezdnykh zemskikh sobraniiakh 1914 goda).* Ufa: Gubernskaia Tipografiia,
    1915.
———. "O gospode vozliublennoi pastve Ufimskoi." *Ufimskie eparkhial'nye vedomosti,*
    no. 7 (April 1, 1916): 217–220.

———. "Ob osnovanii vostochno-russkogo obshchestva." *Ufimskie eparkhial'nye vedomosti*, no. 4 (February 15, 1916): 131–133.

———. *O pechal'nykh posledstviiakh russkoi nekul'turnosti i o luchshem budushchem v etom otnoshenii.* 2nd ed. Ufa: Galanov, 1916.

———. "O tserkovno-prikhodskoi zhizni. (Rech' k chlenam ufimskogo eparkhial'nogo s"ezda dukhovenstva 1916)." *Ufimskii eparkhial'nye vedomosti*, no. 19 (October 1, 1916): 630–638.

———. "O vneshkol'nom rukovodstve vo spasenie." *Ufimskie eparkhial'nye vedomosti*, no. 10 (May 15, 1915): 416–419.

———. "Pis'ma k pastyriam ufimskoi eparkhii. Bor'ba s sektantstvom mozhet byt' tol'ko iskrenniiu bez umalchivanii." *Ufimskii eparkhial'nye vedomosti*, no. 11 (June 1, 1915): 458–470.

———. "Pis'ma k pastyriam ufimskoi eparkhii. Eshche i esche o narodnom chtenii." *Ufimskie eparkhial'nye vedomosti*, no. 23 (December 1, 1915): 988–989.

———. "Slovo pri vstuplenii na ufimskuiu kafedru, 14 fevralia 1914." *Ufimskie eparkhial'nye vedomosti*, no. 4 (February 15, 1914): 47–51.

Antonii (Khrapovitskii). *Pastyrskoe bogoslovie.* Pskov: Izdatel'stvo Sviato-Uspenskogo Pskovo-Pecherskogo Monastyria, 1994.

Arkhiv Gosudarstvennogo Soveta. Vol. 1. *Ekaterina II-i, 1768–1796.* St. Petersburg: Tipografiia Vtor. Otdeleniia Sobstvennoi EIV Kantseliarii, 1869.

Asfandiiarov, Anvar Z. ed. *Materialy po istorii Bashkirskogo naroda.* Vol. 4, *1800–1903.* Ufa: UNTS RAN, 2009.

Avdeev, Mikhail. "Gory." In *Bashkiria v russkoi literature.* Vol. 1. Comp. M. G. Rakhimkulov. Ufa: Bashkirskoe Knizhnoe Izdatel'stvo, 1989.

Beliaev, N. "Pamiati Feodora Nikolaevicha Vladimirova." *Vestnik orenburgskogo uchebnogo okruga*, no. 5 (1913): 310–311.

Blaramburg, Ivan F. *Vospominaniia.* Trans. O. I. Zhigalina. Moscow: Nauka, 1978.

Cheremshanskii, V. M. *Opisanie orenburgskoi gubernii.* Ufa: Uchenyi Komitet Ministerstva Gos. Imushchestv, 1859.

Chernov, Ivan V. *Zametki po istorii orenburgskoi gubernii general-maiora I. V. Chernova.* Orenburg: Orenburgskaia Guberniia, 2007.

Dobrosmyslov, A. I. *Materialy po istorii Rossii (Sbornik ukazov i drugikh dokumentov, kasaiushchikhsia upravleniia i ustroistva orenburgskogo kraia). 1734 god.* 2 vols. Orenburg: F. B. Sachkov, 1900.

Dobrotvorskii, Petr. *V glushi Bashkirii: Rasskazy, vospominaniia.* Ufa: Bashkirskoe Knizhnoe Izdatel'stvo, 1989.

Dukes, Paul, ed. *Russia under Catherine the Great.* Vol. II, *Catherine the Great's Instruction* (Nakaz) *to the Legislative Commission, 1767.* Newtonville, Mass.: Oriental Research Partners, 1977.

Egorov, Nikolai. "Otkliki iz eparkhii. Kak inye ponimaiut zakon 17 April 1905." *Ufimskie eparkhial'nye vedomosti*, no. 7 (April 1, 1906): 483–486.

Florinskii, V. M. "Bashkiriia i Bashkirtsy." *Vestnik Evropy* 9, no. 6 (December 1874): 721–765.

Gasprinskii, Ismail Bei. "Russkoe musul'manstvo: Mysli, zametki i nabliudeniia Musul'manina." In *Rossiia i vostok.* M. A. Usmanov. Kazan: Fond Zhien Tatarskoe Knizhnoe Izdatel'stvo, 1993[1881].

Georgi, Ioann G. *Opisanie vsekh obitaiushchikh v rossiiskom gosudarstve narodov.* Pt. 2. St. Petersburg: Akademiia Nauk, 1799.

Gizzatullin, I. G., and D. R. Sharafutdinov, comps. *Mirsaid Sultan-Galiev. Stat'i, vystupleniia, dokumenty.* Kazan: Tatarskoe Knizhnoe Izdatel'stvo, 1992.

Golubtsov, Sergei A., ed. *Pugachevshchina.* Vol. 3. Moscow: Gosudarstvennoe Izdatel'stvo, 1926.

Gorbunov, M. "Fedor Nikolaevich Vladimirov." *Vestnik orenburgskogo uchebnogo okruga,* no. 5 (1913): 309–311.

Grigor'ev, P. N., comp. *Ocherk deiatel'nosti ufimskogo gubernskogo zemstva po narodnomu obrazovaniiu, 1875–1910 gg.* Ufa: Pechat' N. F. Delinskogo, 1910.

———. *Sistematicheskii svodnyi sbornik postanovlenii ufimskago gubernskogo zemstvo za 35-letie 1875–1909 (Uchreditel'naia, 1–35 ochrednyiia i 1–42 chrezvychainyia sessii) v trekh tomakh.* Vol 1. Ufa: Gubernskaia Tipografiia, 1915.

Gumerov, Farit Kh., comp. *Zakony rossiiskoi imperii o bashkirakh, mishariakh, teptiariakh, i bobyliakh.* Ufa: Kitap, 1999.

Gurvich, N. A., ed. and comp. *Sbornik materialov dlia istorii ufimskogo dvorianstva sostavlennyi V. A. Novikovym v 1879 g., prodolzhennyi i dopolnennyi do 1902 goda vkliuchitel'no, deputatom ufimskogo dvorianstvo N. A. Gurvichem.* Ufa: N. K. Blokhin, 1904.

Gvozdikova, I. M., ed. *Otchet orenburgskogo voennogo gubernatora V. A. Perovskogo po upraveliniu kraem (1833–1842).* Ufa: RAN Institut Istorii, Iazika, i Literatury UNTS, 2010.

Hellie, Richard, trans. and ed. *The Muscovite Law Code (Ulozhenie) of 1649.* Pt. 1, *Text and Translation.* In *The Laws of Russia.* Series I. Vol. 3. Irvine, Calif.: Charles Schlacks Jr., 1988.

Ianguzin, Rim Z., and Gul'naz B. Danilova, comp. *Karavan-sarai.* 3rd ed. Ufa: Kitap, 1996.

Ignat'ev, Ruf. *Sobranie sochinenii (ufimskii i orenburgskii period).* Vol. IV, *1873 g.* Ed. M. I. Rodnov. Ufa, 2011. http://cp809702.cpanel.tech-logol.ru/fr/5/public/Ruf.%20T-IV.pdf, accessed May 20, 2014.

Il'minskii, Nikolai I., ed. *Perepiska o trekh shkolakh ufimskoi gubernii.* Kazan: V. M. Kliuchnikov, 1885.

———. *Pis'ma N. I. Il'minskogo k Ober-Prokuroru Sviateishogo Sinoda Konstantinu Petrovichu Pobedonostsevu.* Kazan: Pravoslavnyi Sobesednik, 1895.

"Iz istorii natsional'noi politiki tsarizma." *Krasnyi arkhiv* 34 (April 1929): 107–127; 35 (May 1929): 61–83.

"Iz zapisok arkhiepiskopa Nikanora." *Russkii arkhiv* 47, no. 2 (1909): 209–226; no. 5 (1909): 19–77.

Kazantsev, N. *Opisanie bashkirtsev.* St. Petersburg: Obshchestvennaia Pol'za, 1866.

Khokhlov, Ioann. "Novye vzgliady i veianiia v sterlitamakskom zemstve." *Ufimskie eparkhial'nye vedomosti,* no. 2 (January 15, 1908): 92–94.

Khusainov, G. B., ed. *Pis'mo Batyrshi imperatritse Elizavete Petrovne.* Ufa: UNTS RAN, 1993.

Kirilov, Ivan. *Tsvetushchee sostoianie vserossiiskogo gosudarstva.* Ed. Iu. A. Tikhonov. Moscow: Nauka, 1977[1727].

Koblov, Iakov D. *Konfessional'nye shkoly kazanskikh Tatar.* Kazan: Teatral'naia Tipografiia, 1916.

Kontsevich, N. "Chego nedostaet russkim liudiam na okrainakh russkogo godsudarstva." *Ufimskie eparkhial'nye vedomosti,* no. 1 (January 15, 1916): 51–53.

Kulbakhtin, I. N., and N. M. Kulbakhtin. *Nakazy narodov Bashkortostana v ulozhennuiu komissiiu 1767–1768 gg.* Ufa: Kitap, 2005.

Kuliasov, A. "O znachenii intelligentsii s tochki zreniia derevni i o metodakh eia deiatel'nosti. (Rech' sviashchennika o. A. Kuliasova na pervom obshchem sobranii chlenov vostochno-russkogo kul'turno-prosvetitel'nogo Obshchestva 14 maia 1916)." *Ufimskie eparkhial'nye vedomosti*, no. 13 (July 1, 1916): 440–447.

Kuzeev, Rail G., comp. and ed. *Bashkirskie shezhere*. Ufa: Bashkirskoe Knizhnoe Izdatel'stvo, 1960.

Kuzeev, Rail G., Ramil' M. Bulgakov, and Minlegali Kh. Naderulov, comps. and eds. *Bashkiriskie rodoslovnye*. Ufa: Kitap, 2002.

K-vich, N. V. "Tserkovno-shkol'noe delo v Rossii." *Vestnik Evropy* 36, no. 5 (September 1901): 218–247.

Larionov, S. S. *Nachal'noe obrazovanie inorodtsev kazanskago i ufimskago kraia*. St. Petersburg: Soikin, 1916.

Materialy po istorii bashkirskoi ASSR. Vol. I, *Bashkirskie vosstaniia v XVII i pervoi polovine XVIII vv*. Moscow and Leningrad: Akademiia Nauk SSSR, 1936.

———. Vol. III, *Ekonomicheskie i sotsial'nye otnosheniia v Bashkirii v pervoi polovine XVIII veka*. Moscow and Leningrad: Akademiia Nauk ASSR, 1949.

———. Vol. IV. Part 2, *Ekonomicheskie i sotsial'nye otnosheniia v Bashkirii i upravlenie Orenburgskim kraem v 50–70–x godakh XVIII v*. Moscow: Akademiia Nauk, 1956.

———. Vol. V. Moscow: Akademiia Nauk, 1960.

———. Vol. VI, *Orenburgskaia ekspeditsiia i Bashkirskie vosstaniia 30–x godov XVIII v*. Comp. N. F. Demidova. Ed. N. V. Ustiugov. Ufa: Kitap, 2002.

Mavrodin, V. V., ed. *Krest'ianskaia voina v Rossii v 1773–1775 godakh: Vosstanie Pugacheva*. 3 vols. (Leningrad: Leningradskii Universitet, 1961, 1966, 1970).

Mintslov, Sergei R. *Ufa: Debri zhizni. Dnevnik 1910–1915 gg*. Ufa: Bashkirskoe Knizhnoe Izdatel'stvo, 1992.

Miropiev, M. A. "Neobkhodimost' obosnovaniia Russkoi shkoly na natsional'nykh nachalakh." *Vestnik orenburgskogo uchebnogo okruga*, no. 1 (1915): ped. otdel 1–10; no. 2 (1915): ped. otdel 87–96.

———. "Sushchnost' sistemy obrazovaniia inorodtsev N. I. Il'minskogo." *Vestnik orenburgskogo uchebnogo okruga*, no. 3 (March 1915): 185–191.

———, ed. *Zhurnaly zasedanii s"ezda direktorov i inspektorov narodnykh uchilishch orenburgskogo uchebnogo okruga v. g. Ufe, 11–16 iiunia 1912 goda*. Ufa: F. G. Solov'ev, 1913.

Nadergulov, Minnigali, ed. "Obrazets bashkirskoi voiskovoi memuaristiki XIX veka." *Vatandash* (August 2008). http://www.vatandash.ru/index.php?article=1672, accessed July 18, 2014.

Nazarov. "Zametki Bashkira o Bashkirakh." *Sovremennik* 99, no. 11 (1863): 57–84.

Nebol'sin, P. "Otchet o puteshestvii v orenburgskii i astrakhanskii krai." *Vestnik rossiiskogo geograficheskogo obshchestva*, ch. 4, kn. 1 (1852): 1–20.

———. *Rasskazy proezzhego*. St. Petersburg: Tipografiia Shtab Voenno-Uchebnykh Zavedenii, 1854.

Nepliuev, I. I. *Zapiski, 1693–1773*. Ed. Marc Raeff. Cambridge: Oriental Research Partners, 1974[1893].

Nikol'skii, Dmitrii P. *Bashkiry: Etnograficheskoe i sanitarno-antropologicheskoe izsledovanie*. St. Petersburg: Soikin, 1899.

Nikol'skii, N. "K chemu obiazyvaet Vysochaishe darovannaia svoboda sovesti." *Ufimskie eparkhial'nye vedomosti*, no. 8 (April 15, 1906): 541–546.

1905. Revoliutsionnye sobytiia 1905 g. v g. Ufe i ural'skikh zavodakh (Bashrespublika). Ufa: n.p., 1925.

Obukhov, M. I., comp. *Mekteby ufimskoi gubernii.* Ufa: Pechat', 1915.

Ömötbaev, Möxämätsälim. *Yädkär.* Ufa: Bashqortostan Kitap Näshriäte, 1984.

"Opredeleniia Sv. Sinoda ot 18 Noiabria 1905 g. . . ." *Ufimskie eparkhial'nye vedomosti,* no. 2 (January 15, 1906): 65–67.

Orenburgskoe Magometanskoe Dukhovnoe Sobranie. *Sbornik tsirkuliarov i inykh rukovodiashchikh rasporiazhenii po okrugu Orenburgskogo Magometanskogo Dukhovnogo Sobraniia.* Ufa: Gubernskaia Tipografiia, 1905.

"Otchet eparkhial'nogo Komiteta Pravoslavnogo Missionerskogo Obshchestva za 1905 g." *Ufimskie Eparkhial'nye Vedomosti,* no. 17 (September 15, 1906): 1076–1081.

Otchet o deiatel'nosti osobogo otdela komiteta Eia Imperatorskogo Vysochestva velikoi kniazhny Tatiany Nikolaevny po registratsii bezhentsev v 1915 g. Petrograd: Moskovskaia Khudozhestvennaia Pechatnia, 1916.

Otchet orenburgskogo obshchestva popecheniia ob uchashchikhsia musul'manakh. Za 1912 god. Orenburg: Tipgrafiia Gazety Vakht, 1913.

Otchet orenburgskogo obshchestva popecheniia ob uchashchikhsia musul'manakh za 1914. Orenburg: A.A. Khusainov, 1915.

Otchet ufimskoi mezhevoi komissii o razmezhevanii bashkirskikh dach, za vremia 1898–1912 gg. Ufa: N. V. Sarobkin, 1912.

"Otradnoe iavlenie (iz byta dukhovenstva Bel. U.)" *Ufimskie eparkhial'nye vedomosti,* no. 6 (March 1, 1906): 396–408.

Pankratova, A. M. et al. eds. *Revoliutsiia 1905–1907 gg. v Rossii: Dokumenty i materialy. Chast' pervaia—Vysshii pod'em revoliutsii 1905–1907 gg. Vooruzhennye vosstaniia noiabr'-dekabr' 1905 goda.* Moscow: Gospolitizdat, 1955.

"Perepiska K. P. Pobedonostseva." *Russkii arkhiv* 53, no. 4 (April 1915): 458–473; no. 5 (May 1915): 68–111; no. 6 (June 1915): 244–255.

Plan deiatel'nosti ufimskogo gubernskogo zemstva po narodnomu obrazovaniiu utverzhdennym gubernskim zemskim sobraniem ocherednoi sessii 1912. 2nd ed. Ufa: Gubernskaia Tipografiia, 1913.

Planson, A. A. *Byloe i nastoiashchee.* St. Petersburg: M. Zarkhin, 1905.

"Po voprosu o pravakh sobstvennosti na otkrytiia ufimskim gubernskim zemstvom pri shkolakh narodnykh bibliotek." *Vestnik orenburgskogo uchebnogo okruga,* no. 7–8 (1913): offits. otdel 660–661.

Polnoe sobranie russkikh letopisei. Vol. 13, Letopisnyi sbornik, imenuemyi patriarshei ili Nikonovskoi letopis'iu. Moscow: Iazyki Russkoi Kul'tury, 2000[1904].

Pol'noe sobranie zakonov rossiiskoi imperii. Series I. 45 vols. St. Petersburg: Gosudarstvennaia Tipografiia, 1830.

———. Series II. 55 vols. St. Petersburg: Gosudarstvennaia Tipografiia, 1830–1884.

———. Series III. 28 vols. St. Petersburg: Gosudarstvennaia Tipografiia, 1911.

"Polozhenie o vneshkol'noi podgotovke russkoi molodezhe k voennoi sluzhbe." *Vestnik orenburgskogo uchebnogo okruga,* no. 1 (1912): offits. otdel 12–15.

Preobrazhenskii, I. V., comp. *Tserkovnaia reforma: Sbornik statei dukhovnoi i svetskoi periodicheskoi pechati po voprosu o reforme.* St. Petersburg: Tip. E. Arngol'da, 1905.

"Programmy i ob"iasnitel'nye zapiski po russkoi i vseobshchei istorii v muzhskikh gimnaziiakh, 13 iiulia 1913-go goda." *Vestnik orenburgskogo uchebnogo okruga,* no. 7–8 (1913): offits. otdel 595–605.

Prokopovich, S. N. "Priuralskie guberniia." In *Agrarnoe dvizhenie v Rossii v 1905–1906 gg.: obzory po raionam.* Ed. B. B. Veselovskii et al. Vol. 1. St. Petersburg: Tip. Vol'nogo Ekonomicheskogo Obshchestva, 1908.

Protokoly XXI ocherednogo ufimskogo gubernskogo zemskogo sobraniia 1895 goda. Ufa, 1896.

Protokoly XXIII ocherednogo ufimskogo gubernskogo zemskogo sobraniia 1897 goda. Ufa, 1898.

Protokoly XXIV ocherednogo ufimskogo gubernskogo zemskogo sobraniia 1898 goda. Ufa, 1899.

Pushkin, Alexander. "The Captain's Daughter." In *The Collected Stories.* Intro. John Bayley. Trans. Paul Debreczeny and Walter Arndt. New York: Alfred A. Knopf, 1999.

Reddaway, W. F., ed. *Documents of Catherine the Great: The Correspondence with Voltaire and the* Instruction *of 1767 in the English Text of 1768.* Cambridge: Cambridge University Press, 1931.

Remezov, N. V. *Ocherki iz zhizni dikoi bashkirii: Byl' v skazochnoi strane.* Moscow: Kushnerov, 1887.

———. *Ocherki iz zhizni dikoi bashkirii: Pereselencheskaia epopeia.* Moscow: Kushnerov, 1889.

———. *Ocherki iz zhizni dikoi bashkirii: Sudebnaia oshibka ili sozdannoe prestuplenie?* Vladivostok: n.p., 1900.

Rodoslovnaia kniga kniazei i dvorian Rossiiskikh i vyezzhikh. 2 vols. Moscow: Universitetskaia Tipografiia U. N. Novikova, 1787.

Rybakov, S. G. *Muzyka i pesni ural'skikh musul'man s ocherkom ikh byta.* St. Petersburg: Akademiia Nauk, 1897.

———, ed. *Ustroistvo i nuzhdy upravleniia dukhovnymi delami musul'man v Rossii.* Petrograd: Tipografiia S. Samoilova, 1917.

Rychkov, Petr I. *Istoriia orenburgskaia po uchrezhdenii orenburgskoi gubernii.* Intro. I. Kuchumov and Iu. N. Smirnov. Ufa: Goskomnauki Respubliki Bashkortostan, 2001[1759; 1896].

———. "O sposobakh k umnozheniiu zemledel'stva v orenburgskoi gubernii." *Pamiatnaia knizhka ufimskoi gubernii na 1873.* Pt. II. Comp. N. Gurvich. Ufa: Tipografiia Gubernskogo Pravleniia, 1873.

———. "Stat'ia Petra Ivanovicha Rychkova o zemledelii v orenburgskoi gubernii (proshlogo stoletiia)." In *Pamiatnaia knizhka ufimskoi gubernii na 1873.* Pt. II. Comp. N. Gurvich. Ufa: Tipografiia Gubernskogo Pravleniia, 1873.

———. *Topografiia orenburgskoi gubernii.* Ufa: Kitap, 1999[1762].

———. "Zapiski Petra Ivanovicha Rychkova." *Russkii arkhiv,* book 3, vol. 10 (1905): 289–340.

"S pravilami o nachal'nykh uchilishchakh dlia inorodtsev." *Vestnik orenburgskogo uchebnogo okruga,* no. 5 (1913): offits. otdel 394–398.

Sakharov, Ia. "Zametki otnositel'no zemledeliia v Bashkiria." *Vestnik promyshlennosti 9,* no. 1 (November 1860): 35–36.

———. "Zametki otnositel'no zemledeliia v Bashkirii i pozharov v Orenburge." *Vestnik promyshlennosti 1* (January 1861): 29–41.

Sbornik zakonov o musul'manskom dukhovenstve v tavricheskom i orenburgskom okrugakh i o magometanskikh uchebnykh zavedeniiakh. Kazan: P. I. Kidalinskii, 1898.

Shakhmatov, V. F., F. N. Kireev, and T. Zh. Shoinbaev, eds. *Kazakhsko-russkie otnoshe-niia v XVI–XVIII vekakh: Sbornik dokumentov i materialov.* Alma-Ata: Izdatel'stvo Akademii Nauk Kazakhskoi SSR, 1961.

Shchegolev, P. E., ed. *Padenie tsarskogo rezhima: Stenograficheskie otchety doprosov i pokazanii, dannykh v 1917g v chrezvychainoi sledstvennoi komissii Vremennogo Pravitel'stva.* Vol. 4, *Zapiski A. D. Protopopova i S. P. Beletskogo.* Leningrad: Gosu-darstvennoe Izdatel'stvo, 1925.

Shramchenko, P. "Zemel'nyi vopros v ufimskoi gubernii." *Russkii vestnik* 158 (March 1882): 449–532.

Soiuz Russkogo Naroda. *Gosudarstvennaia izmena.* St. Petersburg: n. p., 1906.

Sovet ministrov rossiiskoi imperii, 1905–1906 gg.: Dokumenty i materialy. Leningrad: Nauka, 1990.

"Spodvizhniki pugacheva svidetel'stvuiut . . ." Trans. Aleksandr Lunin. *Voprosy istorii,* no. 8 (1973): 97–114.

Statisticheskii otdel Ufimskoi Gubernskoi Upravy. *Istoriko-statisticheskie tablitsy deiatel'nosti ufimskikh zemstv. K sorokoletiiu sushchestvovaniia zemstv ufimskoi gubernii, 1875–1914.* Ed. M. P. Krasil'nikov. Ufa: Pechat', 1915.

Stolypin, Petr A. *Rechi v gosudarstvennoi dume i gosudarstvennom sovete, 1906–1911.* Comp. Iu. G. Fel'shtinskii. New York: Teleks, 1990.

Sushchestvuiushchii poriadok vzimaniia okladnykh sborov s krest'ian. Po svedeniiam, dostavlennym podatnymi inspektorami za 1887–1893. Vyp. 1. St. Petersburg: Gosu-darstvennaia Tipografiia, 1894.

Tarasov, D. K. "Vospominaniii moei zhizni. Zapiski pochetnogo leib-khirurga D. K. Tarasova, 1792–1866." *Russkaia starina* 3 (March 1872): 355–388.

Togan, Zaki Validi. *Vospominaniia. Bor'ba musul'man turkestana i drugikh vostochnykh tiurok za natsional'noe sushchestvovanie i kul'turu.* Trans. V. B. Feonov. Ed. S. M. Iskhakov. Moscow: Moskovskaia Tipografiia, 1997.

Tolstoi, Dmitrii, ed. "Arkhiv grafa Igel'stroma." *Russkii arkhiv* 24, no. 3 (1886): 341–371; 480–496.

Tolstoy, Leo. "How Much Land Does a Man Need?" In *How Much Land Does a Man Need? And Other Stories,* 96–110. Trans. Ronald Wilks. London: Penguin, 1993.

Troinitskii, N. A., ed. *Pervaia vseobshchaia perepis' naseleniia rossiiskoi imperii 1897 goda.* Vol. 65, *Ufimskaia guberniia.* St. Petersburg: Tsentral'nyi Statisticheskii Komitet, 1904.

"Tsar Nicholas II Abdication Proclamation, 2 March 1917." http://www.firstworldwar .com/source/nicholasiiabdication.htm, accessed August 10, 2010.

Tukman, Ivan A., comp. *Polozhenie o Bashkiriiakh.* Ufa: Pechat'nia Blokhina, 1912.

Ushinskii, K. D. "Rodnoe slovo." *Pedagogicheskie sochineniia.* Vol. 2. Moscow: Peda-gogika, 1988.

Uspensky, G. I. "Ot Orenburga do Ufy." In *Sobranie sochinenii.* Vol. 8. Moscow: Gos. Izd. Khudozhestvennoi Literatury, 1957.

V Pamiat' stoletiia orenburgskogo magometanskogo dukhovnogo sobraniia. Ufa: Tipo-grafiia Gubernskogo Pravleniia, 1891.

Valuev, Pavel A. *Dnevnik valueva, ministra vnutrennikh del v dvukh tomakh.* Vol. 1, *1861–1864.* Ed. and comp. P. A. Zaionchkovskii. Moscow: Akademiia Nauk, 1961.

"'Vam krome voli moei dorogi net': Reskripty imperatora Pavla k orenburgskomu general-gubernatoru baronu O. A. Igel'stromu, 1796–1797 gg." *Istoricheskii arkhiv* 1 (2003): 180–201.

Vasil'ev, S. M., L. P. Gnedkov, and T. Sh. Saiapov, eds. *Sbornik dokumentov i materialov o revoliutsionnom dvizhenii 1905–1907 gg. v Bashkirii.* Ufa: Bashkirskoe Knizhnoe Izdatel'stvo, 1956.

Vel'iaminov-Zernov, V. V. "Istochniki dlia izucheniia tarkhanstva, zhalovannogo bashkiram russkimi gosudariami." *Zapiski imperatorskoi akademii nauk* 4, no. 6 (1864): 1–47.

Veretennikova, A. I. "Zapiski zemskogo vracha." *Novyi mir* 32, no. 3 (March 1956): 205–232.

Veselovskii, N. I., comp. *Vasilii Vasil'evich Grigor'ev po ego pis'mam i trudam, 1816–1881.* St. Petersburg: A. Transhel', 1887.

Vsepoddanneishie otchety ufimskogo gubernatora.

Witte, Sergei Iu. "Nasha vnutrenniaia politika po musul'manskomu voprosu iavliaetsia vazhnym faktorom politiki vneshnei." Ed. Dmitrii Arapov. *Istochnik* 62, no. 2 (2003): 24–26.

———. *Po povodu natsionalizma. Natsional'naia ekonomiia i Fridrikh List.* 2nd ed. St. Petersburg: Brokgauz-Efron, 1912.

———. *Vospominaniia.* Vol. II. Tallinn: Skif Aleks, 1994.

Za pervyi god veroispovednoi svobody v Rossii. St. Petersburg: Kolokol, 1907.

Zalesov, Nikolai G. "Zapiski N. G. Zalesova." *Russkaia starina* 114, no. 1 (1903): 41–64.

———. "Zapiski N. G. Zalesova." *Russkaia starina* 114, no. 3 (1903): 267–289.

———. "Zapiski N. G. Zalesova." *Russkaia starina* 114, no. 5 (1903): 27–40.

———. "Zapiski N. G. Zalesova." *Russkaia starina* 114, no. 6 (1903): 527–542.

"Zapiski D. V. Mertvogo, 1760–1824." *Russkii arkhiv* supplement (1867): 1–334.

Zhakmon, Petr P. "Iz vospominanii orenburgskogo starozhila." *Istoricheskii vestnik* 27, 105 (July 1906): 73–87.

———. "Khishchenie bashkirskikh zemel. (Iz vospominanii orenburgskogo starozhila.)" *Istoricheskii vestnik* 28, 107 (March 1907): 855–874.

Zhurnaly Komiteta Ministrov po ispolneniiu ukaza 12 dekabria 1904 g. St. Petersburg: Izdatel'stvo Kantseliarii Komiteta Ministrov, 1905.

Zhurnaly ministerstva narodnogo prosveshcheniia. Pt. 147 (1870): 49.

Zhurnaly soveshchaniia pri ufimskoi gubernskoi zemskoi uprave po voprosu o tipe nachal'noi obshcheobrazovatel'noi musul'manskoi shkoly, 23–25 maia 1911. Ufa: L. E. Miliukov, 1911.

Zhurnaly zasedanii ufimskogo gubernskogo zemskogo sobraniia XXXI ocherednoi i XXXVII chrezvychainoi sessii 1905–1906, i doklady upravy. Ufa: Girbasova, 1906.

SECONDARY SOURCES

Absaliamov, Iu. M. et al. *Ufimskie pomeshchiki: Tipy istochnikov, vidy dokumentatsii.* Ufa, 2013. http://cp809702.cpanel.tech-logol.ru/fr/o/public/Pomeshik.pdf, accessed July 21, 2014.

Adelman, Jeremy. *Worldly Philosopher: The Odyssey of Albert O. Hirschman.* Princeton, N.J.: Princeton University Press, 2013.

Afanas'eva, Anna. "'Osvobodit' . . . ot shaitanov i sharlatanov': Diskursy i praktiki ros-siiskoi meditsiny v kazakhskoi stepi v XIX veke." *Ab Imperio* 4 (2008): 113–150.

Agrarnoe dvizhenie v Rossii v 1905–1906. Vol. I. St. Petersburg: Vol'nogo Ekonomicheskogo Obshchestva, 1908.

Akmanov, Aitugan I. *Zemel'naia politika tsarskogo pravitel'stva v Bashkirii (vtoraia polovina XVI–nachalo XX vv.)*. Ufa: Kitap, 2000.

Akmanov, Irek G. *Bashkiriia v sostave rossiiskogo gosudarstva v XVII–pervoi polovine XVIII veka*. Sverdlovsk: Izdatel'stvo Ural'skogo Universiteta, 1991.

———. *Bashkirskie vosstaniia XVII–pervoi treti XVIII v*. Ufa: Bashkirskii Gosudarstven-nyi Universitet, 1978.

Akmanov, Irek G. et al. eds. *Istoriia Bashkortostana s drevneishikh vremen do nashikh dnei*. Vol. 1. Ufa: Kitap, 2006.

Alexander, John T. *Autocratic Politics in a National Crisis: The Imperial Russian Govern-ment and Pugachev's Revolt, 1773–1775*. Bloomington: Indiana University Press, 1969.

Algar, Hamid. "Shaykh Zaynullah Rasulev: The Last Great Naqshbandi Shaykh of the Volga-Urals Region." In *Muslims in Central Asia: Expressions of Identity and Change*. Ed. Jo-Ann Gross. Durham, N.C.: Duke University Press, 1992.

Allsen, Thomas T. *Mongol Imperialism: The Policies of the Grand Qan Möngke in China, Russia, and the Islamic Lands, 1251–1259*. Berkeley: University of California Press, 1987.

Alston, Patrick. *Education and the State in Tsarist Russia*. Stanford, Calif.: Stanford University Press, 1969.

Anderson, M. S. *Peter the Great*. London: Thames and Hudson, 1978.

Ando, Clifford. *Imperial Ideology and Provincial Loyalty in the Roman Empire*. Berkeley: University of California Press, 2000.

Arapov, Dmitrii Iu. "Pervyi russkii general-musul'manin Kutlu-Muhammad Tevkelev." *Sbornik russkogo istoricheskogo obshchestva* 153, no. 5 (2002): 34–36.

Artamanov, V. A. "Flag." In *Gerb i flag Rossii, X–XX veka*. Moscow: Izdatel'stvo Iuridicheskaia Literatura, 1997.

Ascher, Abraham. *P. A. Stolypin: The Search for Stability in Late Imperial Russia*. Stan-ford, Calif.: Stanford University Press, 2001.

———. *The Revolution of 1905: Authority Restored*. Stanford, Calif.: Stanford University Press, 1992.

———. *The Revolution of 1905: Russia in Disarray*. Stanford, Calif.: Stanford University Press, 1988.

Asfandiiarov, Anvar Z. *Bashkirskaia sem'ia v proshlom*. Ufa: Kitap, 1997.

———. *Bashkirskie tarkhany*. Ufa: Kitap, 2006.

———. *Kantonnoe upravlenie v Bashkirii (1798–1865)*. Ufa: Kitap, 2005.

Avrutin, Eugene M. *Jews and the Imperial State: Identification Politics in Tsarist Russia*. Ithaca, N.Y.: Cornell University Press, 2010.

Azamatov, Danil D. *Orenburgskoe magometanskoe dukhovnoe sobranie v kontse XVIII–XIX vv*. Ufa: Gilem, 1999.

———. "Russian Administration and Islam in Bashkiria (18th–19th Centuries)." In *Muslim Culture in Russia and Central Asia from the 18th to the Early 20th Centuries*. Ed. Michael Kemper, Anke von Kügelgen, and Dmitriy Yermakov. Berlin: Klaus Schwarz Verlag, 1996.

Azamatova, Gulnaz B. *Integratsiia natsional'nogo dvorianstva v rossiiskoe obshchestvo na primere roda Tevkelevykh*. Ufa: Gilem, 2008.

Aznabaev, Bulat A. *Integratsiia Bashkirii v administrativnuiu struktury rossiiskogo gosudarstva (vtoraia polovina XVI–pervaia tret' XVIII vv.).* Ufa: RIO Bashkirskii Gosudarstvennyi Universitet, 2005.
———. *Ufimskoe dvorianstvo v kontse XVI–pervoi treti XVIII vv. (zemlevladenie, sotsial'nyi sostav, sluzhba).* Ufa: Bashkirskii Gosudarstvennyi Universitet, 1999.
Bakhturina, Aleksandra Iu. *Okrainy rossiiskoi imperii: Gosudarstvennoe upravlenie i natsional'naia politika v godu pervoi mirovoi voiny (1914–1917 gg.).* Moscow: Rosspen, 2004).
Banerjee, Sukanya. *Becoming Imperial Citizens: Indians in the Late-Victorian Empire.* Durham, N.C.: Duke University Press, 2010.
Barkey, Karen. *Bandits and Bureaucrats: The Ottoman Route to State Centralization.* Ithaca, N.Y.: Cornell University Press, 1994.
———. *Empire of Difference: The Ottomans in Comparative Perspective.* Cambridge: Cambridge University Press, 2008.
———. "Thinking about the Consequences of Empire." In *After Empire: Multiethnic Societies and Nation-Building: The Soviet Union and the Russian, Ottoman, and Habsburg Empires.* Ed. Karen Barkey and Mark von Hagen. Boulder, Colo.: Westview, 1997.
Barkey, Karen, and Mark von Hagen, eds. *After Empire: Multiethnic Societies and Nation-Building. The Soviet Union and the Russian, Ottoman, and Habsburg Empires.* Boulder, Colo.: Westview, 1997.
Barsukov, Ivan. *Pamiati Dionisiia.* St. Petersburg: Sinodal'naia Tipografiia, 1902.
Bartlett, Roger P. *Human Capital: The Settlement of Foreigners in Russia, 1762–1804.* Cambridge: Cambridge University Press, 1979.
Bartov, Omer, and Eric D. Weitz, eds. *Shatterzone of Empires: Coexistence and Violence in the German, Habsburg, Russian, and Ottoman Borderlands.* Bloomington: Indiana University Press, 2013.
Bassin, Mark. "Geographies of Imperial Identity." In *The Cambridge History of Russia.* Vol. II, *1689–1917.* Ed. Dominic Lieven. Cambridge: Cambridge University Press, 2006.
———. "Russia between Europe and Asia: The Ideological Construction of Geographical Space." *Slavic Review* 50, no. 1 (Spring 1991): 1–17.
Baumann, Robert. "Subject Nationalities in the Military Service of Imperial Russia: The Case of the Bashkirs." *Slavic Review* 46, no. 3/4 (Fall/Winter 1987): 489–502.
———. "Universal Service Reform and Russia's Imperial Dilemma." *War and Society* 4, no. 2 (1986): 31–49.
Bennigsen, Alexandre, and Chantal Lemercier-Quelquejay. *Les mouvements nationaux chez les musulmans de Russie: Le "sultangalievisme" au Tatarstan.* Paris: Mouton, 1960.
———. *Sultan-Galiev: Le père de la révolution tiers-mondiste.* Paris: Fayard, 1986.
Betts, Raymond F. *Assimilation and Association in French Colonial Theory, 1890–1914.* New York: Columbia University Press, 1961.
Blank, Stephen. "National Education, Church and State in Tsarist Nationality Policy: The Il'minskii System." *Canadian-American Slavic Studies* 17, no. 4 (Winter 1983): 466–486.
Bobrovnikov, Vladimir O. "Chto vyshlo iz proektov sozdaniia v Rossii *inorodtsev?* (otvet Dzhonu Slokumu iz musul'manskikh okrain imperii)." In *Poniatiia o Rossii: K istoricheskoi semantike imperskogo perioda.* Vol. 1. Ed. A. Miller, D. Sdvizhkov, and I. Shirle. Moscow: Novoe Literaturnoe Obozrenie, 2012.

———. *Musul'mane Severnogo Kavkaza: Obychai, pravo, nasilie. Ocherki po istorii i etnografii prava Nagornogo Dagestana.* Moscow: Vostochnaia Literatura-RAN, 2002.

Boeck, Brian J. *Imperial Boundaries: Cossack Communities and Empire-Building in the Age of Peter the Great.* Cambridge: Cambridge University Press, 2009.

Bogatyrev, Sergei. "Reinventing the Russian Monarchy in the 1550s: Ivan the Terrible, the Dynasty, and the Church." *Slavonic and East European Review* 85, no. 2 (April 2007): 271–293.

Breyfogle, Nicholas. *Heretics and Colonizers: Forging Russia's Empire in the South Caucasus.* Ithaca, N.Y.: Cornell University Press, 2005.

Brooks, Jeffrey. *When Russia Learned to Read: Literacy and Popular Literature, 1861–1917.* Princeton, N.J.: Princeton University Press, 1985.

Brower, Daniel. "Islam and Ethnicity: Russian Colonial Policy in Turkestan." In *Russia's Orient: Imperial Borderlands and Peoples, 1700–1917.* Ed. Daniel Brower and Edward J. Lazzerini. Bloomington: Indiana University Press, 1997.

———. "Russian Roads to Mecca: Religious Tolerance and Muslim Pilgrimage in the Russian Empire." *Slavic Review* 55, no. 3 (Fall 1996): 567–584.

———. *Turkestan and the Fate of the Russian Empire.* London: Routledge, 2003.

Brubaker, Rogers. *Citizenship and Nationhood in France and Germany.* Cambridge, Mass.: Harvard University Press, 1992.

———. "Nationhood and the National Question in the Soviet Union and Post-Soviet Eurasia: An Institutionalist Account." *Theory and Society* 23 (1994): 47–78.

Brumfield, William Craft. *A History of Russian Architecture.* Seattle: University of Washington Press, 2004[1993].

Bukanova, Roza G. *Goroda-kreposti iugo-vostoka Rossii v XVIII veke. Istoriia stanovleniia gorodov na territorii Bashkirii.* Ufa: Kitap, 1997.

Burbank, Jane. "An Imperial Rights Regime: Law and Citizenship in the Russian Empire." *Kritika: Explorations in Russian and Eurasian History* 7, no. 3 (Summer 2006): 397–431.

———. "The Rights of Difference: Law and Citizenship in the Russian Empire." In *Imperial Formations.* Ed. Ann Laura Stoler, Carole McGranahan, and Peter C. Perdue. Santa Fe and Oxford: School for Advanced Research Press and James Currey, 2007.

———. *Russian Peasants Go to Court: Legal Culture in the Countryside, 1905–1917.* Bloomington: Indiana University Press, 2004.

Burbank, Jane, and Frederick Cooper. *Empires in World History: Power and the Politics of Difference.* Princeton, N.J.: Princeton University Press, 2010.

Burbank, Jane, and Mark von Hagen. "Coming into Territory: Uncertainty and Empire." In *Russian Empire: Space, People, Power, 1700–1930.* Ed. Jane Burbank, Mark von Hagen, and Anatolyi Remnev. Bloomington: Indiana University Press, 2007.

Burton, Antoinette. "Tongues Untied: Lord Salisbury's 'Black Man' and the Boundaries of Imperial Democracy." *Comparative Studies in Society and History* 42, no. 3 (2000): 632–661.

Bushkovitch, Paul. "Orthodoxy and Islam in Russia, 988–1725." In *Religion and Integration in Moskauer Russland: Konzepte und Praktiken, Potentiale und Grenzen, 14.–17. Jahrhundert.* Ed. Ludwig Steindorff. Wiesbaden: Harrassowitz Verlag, 2010.

———. *Peter the Great: The Struggle for Power.* Cambridge: Cambridge University Press, 2001.

Cadiot, Juliette. *Le laboratoire impérial: Russie-URSS, 1860–1940.* Paris: CNRS Editions, 2007.

Campbell, Elena. "The Muslim Question in Late Imperial Russia." In *Russian Empire: Space, People, Power, 1700–1930.* Ed. Jane Burbank, Mark von Hagen, and Anatolyi Remnev. Bloomington: Indiana University Press, 2007.

———. *The Muslim Question and Russian Imperial Governance.* Bloomington: Indiana University Press, 2015.

Chuloshnikov, A. P. *Vosstanie 1755 g. v Bashkirii.* Moscow-Leningrad: Akademiia Nauk SSSR, 1940.

Clancy-Smith, Julia. "Islam and the French Empire in North Africa." In *Islam and the European Empires.* Ed. David Motadel. Oxford: Oxford University Press, 2014.

Cole, Laurence, and Daniel Unowsky, eds. *The Limits of Loyalty: Imperial Symbolism, Popular Allegiances, and State Patriotism in the Late Habsburg Monarchy.* New York: Berghahn Books, 2007.

Colley, Linda. *Captives: Britain, Empire and the World, 1600–1850.* New York: Anchor Books, 2004.

Confino, Alon. *Nation as a Local Metaphor: Würtemberg, Imperial Germany, and National Memory, 1871–1918.* Chapel Hill: University of North Carolina Press, 1997.

Confino, Michael. "The *Soslovie* (Estate) Paradigm: Reflections on Some Open Questions." *Cahiers du Monde Russe* 49, no. 4 (October–December 2008): 681–699.

Conklin, Alice L. *A Mission to Civilize: The Republican Idea of Empire in France and West Africa, 1895–1930.* Stanford, Calif.: Stanford University Press, 1997.

Cooper, Frederick. "Empire Multiplied: A Review Essay." *Comparative Studies in Society and History* 46, no. 2 (2004): 247–272.

Cracraft, James. "Empire versus Nation: Russian Political Theory under Peter I." *Harvard Ukrainian Studies* 10, no. 3/4 (December 1986): 524–540.

Crews, Robert D. "Empire and the Confessional State: Islam and Religious Politics in Nineteenth-Century Russia." *American Historical Review* 108, no. 1 (February 2003): 50–83.

———. *For Prophet and Tsar: Islam and Empire in Russia and Central Asia.* Cambridge, Mass.: Harvard University Press, 2006.

———. "The Russian Worlds of Islam." In *Islam and the European Empires.* Ed. David Motadel. Oxford: Oxford University Press, 2014.

Cunningham, James W. *A Vanquished Hope: The Movement for Church Renewal in Russia, 1905–1906.* New York: St. Vladimir's Seminary Press, 1981.

Darwin, John. *After Tamerlane: The Global History of Empire since 1405.* New York: Bloomsbury Press, 2008.

Davletbaev, Bulat S. *Bol'shaia Oka: Istoriia sela.* Ufa: Ministerstva Pechati i Sredstv Massovoi Informatsii, 1992.

———. *Krest'ianskaia reforma 1861 goda v Bashkirii.* Moscow: Nauka, 1983.

Deak, Istvan. *Beyond Nationalism: A Social and Political History of the Habsburg Officer Corps, 1848–1919.* New York: Oxford University Press, 1990.

Demidova, N. F. "Upravlenie Bashkiriei i povinnosti naseleniia ufimskoi provintsii v pervoi treti XVIII v." *Istoricheskie zapiski* 68 (1961): 211–237.

DeWeese, Devin. *Islamization and Native Religion in the Golden Horde: Baba Tükles and Conversion to Islam in Historical and Epic Tradition.* University Park: Pennsylvania State University Press, 1994.

Di Cosmo, Nicola. "The Qing and Inner Asia: 1636–1800." In *The Cambridge History of Inner Asia: The Chinggisid Age*. Ed. Nicola Di Cosmo, Allen J. Frank, and Peter B. Golden. Cambridge: Cambridge University Press, 2009.

Dippie, Brian W. *The Vanishing American: White Attitudes and U.S. Indian Policy*. Middletown, Conn.: Wesleyan University Press, 1982.

Dixon, Simon. "The Church's Social Role in St. Petersburg, 1880–1914." In *Church, Nation and State in Russia and Ukraine*. Ed. Geoffrey A. Hosking. New York: St. Martin's Press, 1991.

Dolbilov, Mikhail. "Russification and the Bureaucratic Mind in the Russian Empire's Northwestern Region in the 1860s." *Kritika: Explorations in Russian and Eurasian History* 5, no. 2 (Spring 2004), 245–271.

———. *Russkii krai, chuzhaia vera: Etnokonfessional'naia politika imperii v Litve i Belorussii pri Aleksandre II*. Moscow: Novoe Literaturnoe Obozrenie, 2010.

Dolbilov, Mikhail, and Aleksei Miller, eds. *Zapadnye okrainy rossiiskoi imperii*. Series *Okrainy rossiiskoi imperii*. Moscow: Novoe Literaturnoe Obozrenie, 2006.

Donnelly, Alton S. *The Russian Conquest of Bashkiria, 1552–1740: A Case Study in Imperialism*. New Haven, Conn.: Yale University Press, 1968.

Dorofeev, Viktor. "Simvol goroda." In *Karavan-sarai*. Comp. Rim Z. Ianguzin and Gul'naz B. Danilova. 3rd ed. Ufa: Kitap, 1996.

Dowding, Keith, Peter John, Thanos Mergoupis, and Mark van Vugt. "Exit, Voice, and Loyalty: Analytical and Empirical Developments." *European Journal of Political Research* 37 (2000): 469–495.

Dowler, Wayne. "The Politics of Language in Non-Russian Elementary Schools in the Eastern Empire, 1865–1914." *Russian Review* 54, no. 4 (October 1995): 516–538.

Dudoignon, Stéphane. "Djadidisme, Mirasisme, Islamisme." *Cahiers du Monde Russe* 37, no. 1–2 (January–June 1996): 12–40.

Edelman, Robert. *Gentry Politics on the Eve of the Russian Revolution: The Nationalist Party 1907–1917*. New Brunswick, N.J.: Rutgers University Press, 1980.

Edgar, Adrienne Lynn. *Tribal Nation: The Making of Soviet Turkmenistan*. Princeton, N.J.: Princeton University Press, 2006.

Eklof, Ben. *Russian Peasant Schools: Officialdom, Village Culture, and Popular Pedagogy, 1861–1914*. Berkeley: University of California Press, 1986.

Elliot, J. H. *Empires of the Atlantic World: Britain and Spain in America, 1492–1830*. New Haven, Conn.: Yale University Press, 2006.

———. *Imperial Spain, 1463–1716*. London: Edward Arnold, 1963.

Elliott, Mark C. *The Manchu Way: The Eight Banners and Ethnic Identity in Late Imperial China*. Stanford, Calif.: Stanford University Press, 2001.

Emmons, Terence. *The Formation of Political Parties and the First National Elections in Russia*. Cambridge, Mass.: Harvard University Press, 1983.

———. "Russia's Banquet Campaign." *California Slavic Studies,* 10 (1977): 45–86.

———. "The Zemstvo in Historical Perspective." In *The Zemstvo in Russia: An Experiment in Local Self-Government*. Ed. Terence Emmons and Wayne S. Vucinich. Cambridge: Cambridge University Press, 1982.

Engelstein, Laura. *The Keys to Happiness: Sex and the Search for Modernity in Fin-de-Siècle Russia*. Ithaca, N.Y.: Cornell University Press, 1992.

———. *Moscow, 1905: Working-Class Organization and Political Conflict*. Stanford, Calif.: Stanford University Press, 1982.

Erofeeva, I. V. "Sluzhebnye i issledovatel'skie materialy rossiiskogo diplomata A. I. Tev-keleva po istorii i etnografii kazakhskoi stepi." In *Istoriia Kazakhstana v russkikh istochnikakh XVI–XX vekov*. Vol. 3. Comp. I. V. Erofeeva. Almaty: Daik-Press, 2005.

Etkind, Alexander. *Internal Colonization: Russia's Imperial Experience*. Cambridge: Polity Press, 2011.

Evans, R. J. W. *The Making of the Habsburg Monarchy*. Oxford: Oxford University Press, 1979.

Evtuhov, Catherine. *Portrait of a Russian Province: Economy, Society, and Civilization in Nineteenth-Century Nizhnii Novgorod*. Pittsburgh, Pa.: University of Pittsburgh Press, 2011.

Farkhshatov, Marsel' N. *Narodnoe obrazovanie v Bashkirii v poreformennyi period, 60–90e gody XIX v.* Moscow: Nauka, 1994.

———. *Samoderzhavie i traditsionnye shkoly Bashkir i Tatar v nachale XX veka (1900–1917 gg.)*. Ufa: Gilem, 2000.

———. "Ufa." In *Islam na territorii byvshei rossiiskoi imperii. Entsiklopedicheskii slovar'*. Vol. 4. Ed. S. M. Prozorov. Moscow: Izd. Firma Vostochnaia Literatura RAN, 2003.

Feldman, Noah. *The Fall and Rise of the Islamic State*. Princeton, N.J.: Princeton University Press, 2008.

Finkel, Caroline. *Osman's Dream: The Story of the Ottoman Empire, 1300–1923*. New York: Basic Books, 2005.

Firsov, N. *Inorodcheskoe naselenie prezhnego kazanskogo tsarstva v novoi Rossii do 1762 goda*. Kazan: Universitetskaia Tipografiia, 1869.

Fisher, Alan W. "Enlightened Despotism and Islam under Catherine II." *Slavic Review* 27, no. 4 (1967): 542–553.

Frank, Allen J. *Islamic Historiography and 'Bulghar' Identity among the Tatars and Bashkirs of Russia*. Leiden: Brill, 1998.

———. "Islamic Regional Identity in Imperial Russia: Tatar and Bashkir Historiography in the Eighteenth and Nineteenth Centuries." PhD dissertation, Indiana University, 1994.

———. "Islamic Shrine Catalogues and Communal Geography in the Volga-Ural Region: 1788–1917." *Journal of Islamic Studies* 7, no. 2 (1996): 265–286.

———. *Muslim Religious Institutions in Imperial Russia: The Islamic World of Novouzensk District and the Kazakh Inner Horder, 1780–1910*. Leiden: Brill, 2001.

———. "Russia and the Peoples of the Volga-Ural Region: 1600–1850." In *The Cambridge History of Inner Asia: The Chinggisid Age*. Ed. Nicola Di Cosmo, Allen J. Frank, and Peter B. Golden. Cambridge: Cambridge University Press, 2009.

———. "The Western Steppe: Volga-Ural Region, Siberia and the Crimea." In *The Cambridge History of Inner Asia: The Chinggisid Age*. Ed. Nicola Di Cosmo, Allen J. Frank, and Peter B. Golden. Cambridge: Cambridge University Press, 2009.

Freeze, Gregory. *The Parish Clergy in Nineteenth-Century Russia: Crisis, Reform, Counter-Reform*. Princeton, N.J.: Princeton University Press, 1983.

———. *The Russian Levites: Parish Clergy in the Eighteenth Century*. Cambridge, Mass.: Harvard University Press, 1977.

———. "The *Soslovie* (Estate) Paradigm and Russian Social History." *American Historical Review* 91, no. 1 (February 1986): 11–36.

———. "Subversive Piety: Religion and the Political Crisis in Late Imperial Russia." *Journal of Modern History* 68, no. 2 (June 1996): 308–350.

Gabdrafikov, Il'dar. "Etnokul'turnye rezul'taty migratsionnykh protsessov v severo-zapadnoi Bashkirii (konets XVI–nach. XX v.)." In *Etnologicheskie issledovaniia v Bashkortostane: Sbornik statei.* Ed. Il'dar Gabdrafikov. Ufa: UNTS RAN, 1994.

Gabdullin, I. R. *Ot sluzhilykh tatar k tatarskomu dvorianstvu.* Moscow: R. Sh. Kudashev, 2006.

Gainutdinov, M.V. "Razvitie obnovlencheskikh idei v tatarskoi obshchestvennoi mysli." In *Problema preemstvennosti v tatarskoi obshchestvennoi mysli.* Ed. R. M. Amirkhanov et al. Kazan: Institut Iazyka, Literatury, i Istorii im. G. Ibragimova, 1985.

Ganeev, R. G., V. V. Boltushkin, and R. G. Kuzeev, eds. *Istoriia Ufy: Kratkii ocherk.* Ufa: Bashkirskoe Knizhnoe Izdatel'stvo, 1981.

Gatrell, Peter. "Refugees in the Russian Empire, 1914–1917: Population Displacement and Social Identity." In *Critical Companion to the Russian Revolution, 1914–1921,* ed. Edward Acton, Vladimir Iu. Cherniaev, and William G. Rosenberg. Bloomington: Indiana University Press, 1997.

———. *A Whole Empire Walking: Refugees in Russia during World War I.* Bloomington: Indiana University Press, 1999.

Geraci, Robert P. *Window on the East: National and Imperial Identities in Late Tsarist Russia.* Ithaca, N.Y.: Cornell University Press, 2001.

Gerasimenko, Grigorii A. *Zemskoe samoupravlenie v Rossii.* Moscow: Nauka, 1990.

Gerasimov, I., S. Glebov, A. Kaplunovski, M. Mogilner, and A. Semyonov. "In Search of a New Imperial History," *Ab Imperio* 1 (2005): 33–56.

Gerasimov, Ilya, Sergey Glebov, Jan Kusber, Marina Mogilner, and Alexander Semyonov. "New Imperial History and the Challenges of Empire." In *Empire Speaks Out.* Ed. Ilya Gerasimov, Jan Kusber, and Alexander Semyonov. Leiden: Brill, 2009.

Gilyazov, Iskender. "Die Islampolitik von Staat und Kirchen im Wolga-Ural-Gebiet und die Batïr sah-Aufstand von 1755." In *Muslim Culture in Russia and Central Asia from the 18th to the Early 20th Centuries.* Ed. Michael Kemper, Anke von Kügelgen, and Dmitriy Yermakov. Berlin: Klaus Schwarz Verlag, 1996.

Glebov, Sergey. "Siberian Middle Ground: Languages of Rule and Accommodation on the Siberian Frontier." In *Empire Speaks Out.* Ed. Ilya Gerasimov, Jan Kusber, and Alexander Semyonov. Leiden: Brill, 2009.

Golden, Peter B. *An Introduction to the History of the Turkic Peoples: Ethnogenesis and State-Formation in Medieval and Early Modern Eurasia and the Middle East.* Wiesbaden: Otto Harrassowitz, 1992.

Gorenburg, Dmitry. "Identity Change in Bashkortostan: Tatars into Bashkirs and Back." *Ethnic and Racial Studies* 22, no. 3 (May 1999): 554–580.

Grell, Ole Peter, and Roy Porter. "Toleration in Enlightenment Europe." In *Toleration in Enlightenment Europe.* Ed. Ole Peter Grell and Roy Porter. Cambridge: Cambridge University Press, 2000.

Gurko, Vladimir I. *Features and Figures of the Past: Government and Opinion in the Reign of Nicholas II.* Ed. J. E. Wallace Sterling, Xenia Joukoff Eudin, and H. H. Fisher. Trans. Laura Matveev. Stanford, Calif.: Stanford University Press, 1970.

Gvozdikova, Inga M. *Bashkortostan nakanune i v gody krest'ianskoi voiny pod predvoditel'stvom E. I. Pugacheva.* Ufa: Kitap, 1999.

Haimson, Leopold, ed., in collaboration with Ziva Galili y Garcia and Richard Wortman. *The Making of Three Russian Revolutionaries: Voices of the Menshevik Past.* Cambridge: Cambridge University Press, 1987.

Halperin, Charles J. "Ivan IV and Chinggis Khan." *Jahrbücher für Geschichte Osteuropas* 51, no. 4 (2003): 481–497.

———. *Russia and the Golden Horde: The Mongol Impact on Medieval Russian History.* Bloomington: Indiana University Press, 1987.

Hanioğlu, M. Şükrü. *A Brief History of the Late Ottoman Empire.* Princeton, N.J.: Princeton University Press, 2008.

Harvey, L. P. *Islamic Spain, 1250–1500.* Chicago, Ill.: University of Chicago Press, 1990.

———. *Muslims in Spain, 1500–1614.* Chicago, Ill.: University of Chicago Press, 2005.

Heuschert, Dorothea. "Legal Pluralism in the Qing Empire: Manchu Legislation for the Mongols." *The International History Review* 20, no. 2 (June 1998): 310–324.

Hillis, Faith C. *Children of Rus': Right-Bank Ukraine and the Invention of a Russian Nation.* Ithaca, N.Y.: Cornell University Press, 2013.

Hirsch, Francine. *Empire of Nations: Ethnographic Knowledge and the Making of the Soviet Union.* Ithaca, N.Y.: Cornell University Press, 2005.

Hirschman, Albert O. *Exit, Voice, and Loyalty: Responses to Decline in Firms, Organizations, and States.* Cambridge, Mass.: Harvard University Press, 1970.

Hisao, Komatsu. "Muslim Intellectuals and Japan: A Pan-Islamist Mediator, Abdurreshid Ibrahimov." In *Intellectuals in the Modern Islamic World.* Ed. Stéphane A. Dudoignon et al. London: Routledge, 2006.

Hobsbawm, Eric. "Mass-Producing Traditions: Europe 1870–1914." In *The Invention of Tradition.* Ed. Eric Hobsbawm and Terence Ranger. Cambridge: Cambridge University Press, 1983.

Holquist, Peter. "'Information Is the Alpha and Omega of Our Work': Bolshevik Surveillance in Its Pan-European Context." *Journal of Modern History* 69, no. 3 (September 1997): 415–450.

———. "The Politics and Practice of the Russian Occupation of Armenia, 1915–February 1917." In *A Question of Genocide: Armenians and Turks at the End of the Ottoman Empire.* Ed. Ronald Grigor Suny, Fatma Müçek, and Norman M. Naimark. New York: Oxford University Press, 2011.

———. "Review of Brian J. Boeck, *Imperial Boundaries.*" *Journal of Interdisciplinary History* 41, no. 3 (Winter 2011). 461–463.

———. "To Count, to Extract, to Exterminate: Population Statistics and Population Politics in Late Imperial and Soviet Russia." In *A State of Nations: Empire and Nation-Making in the Age of Lenin and Stalin.* Ed. Ronald Grigor Suny and Terry Martin. New York: Oxford University Press, 2001.

Hosking, Geoffrey. *Russia: People and Empire, 1552–1917.* Cambridge, Mass.: Harvard University Press, 1997.

Humphreys, R. Stephen. *Islamic History: A Framework for Enquiry.* Princeton, N.J.: Princeton University Press, 1991.

Iakupov, R. I. "Teptiari: K istoriografii voprosa." In *Etnologicheskie issledovaniia v Bashkortostane: Sbornik statei.* Ed. Il'dar Gabdrafikov. Ufa: UNTS RAN, 1994.

Iamaeva, Larissa A., comp. *Musul'manskie deputaty gosudarstvennoi dumy Rossii, 1906–1917 gg.: Sbornik dokumentov i materialov.* Ufa: Kitap, 1998.

Ianguzin, Rim Z. *Khoziaistvo Bashkir dorevoliutsionnoi Rossii.* Ufa: Bashkirskoe Knizhnoe Izdatel'stvo, 1989.

Ianovskii, Abel' E. "Metricheskie knigi." *Entsiklopedicheskii slovar'.* Vol. 37. Ed. F. A. Brokgauz and I. A. Efron. Leipzig/St. Petersburg: Brokgauz and Efron, 1896.

Ibragimov, Galimdzhan. *Tatary v revoliutsii 1905 goda*. Trans. G. Mukhamedova. Kazan: Gosudarstvennoe Izdatel'stvo Tssr, 1926.

Ignat'ev, R. G. *Episkop Mikhail Byvshii orenburgskii i ufimskii po sluchaiu 40 let ot dnia konchiny ego*. Moscow: M. G. Volchaninov, 1898.

———. *Sud nad Brigadirom Aksakovym*. Ufa: Ufimskii Gubernskii Statisticheskii Komitet, 1875.

Il'iasova, A. Ia. "Osobennosti formirovaniia dvorianskogo sosloviia iz Bashkir." *Vestnik cheliabinskogo gosudarstvennogo universiteta* 38 (2009): 26–32.

Ishcherikov, Petr. *Ocherki iz istorii kolonizatsii Bashkortostana. Ot zavoevaniia Bashkortostana do epokhi raskhishcheniia bashkirskikh zemel'*. Ufa: Kitap, 2003[1933].

Ishkulov, Fazyl'ian A. *Sudebno-administrativnaia reforma v Bashkortostane*. Ufa: Kitap, 1994.

Iskhakov, Damir M. *Etnograficheskie gruppy tatar volgo-ural'skogo regiona*. Kazan: Akademiia Nauk Respubliki Tatarstan, 1993.

———. *Istoricheskaia demografiia tatarskogo naroda (XVIII–nachalo XX vv.)*. Kazan: Akademiia Nauk Respubliki Tatarstan, 1993.

Iskhakov, Salavat. *Pervaia russkaia revoliutsiia i musul'mane rossiiskoi imperii*. Moscow: Izd. Sotsial'no-Politicheskaia Mysl', 2007.

Islaev, F. G. *Islam i pravoslavie v povol'zhe XVIII stoletiia: Ot konfrontatsii k terpimosti*. Kazan: Kazan University, 2001.

Islam: Entsiklopedicheskii slovar'. Ed. L. V. Negria. Moscow: Nauka, 1991.

Istoricheskii ocherk narodnogo obrazovaniia v orenburgskom uchebnom okruge za pervoe 25-letie ego sushchestvovaniia (1875–1899 gg.). Orenburg: I. I. Evfimovskii-Mirovitskii, 1901.

Istoriia Bashkortostana s drevneishikh vremen do nashikh dnei, v dvukh tomakh. Vol. 1, *Istoriia Bashkortostana s drevneishikh vremen do kontsa XIX veka*. Ufa: Kitap, 2004.

Iunusova, Aislu B. *Islam v Bashkortostane*. Ufa: Ufimskii Poligrafkombinat, 1999.

Ivanova, Natalia A., and Valentina P. Zheltova. *Soslovnoe obshchestvo rossiiskoi imperii (XVIII–nachalo XX veka)*. Moscow: Novyi Khronograf, 2009.

Jahn, Hubertus. "For Tsar and Fatherland? Russian Popular Culture and the First World War." In *Cultures in Flux: Lower-Class Values, Practices, and Resistance in Late Imperial Russia*. Ed. Stephen P. Frank and Mark D. Steinberg. Princeton, N.J.: Princeton University Press, 1994.

———. *Patriotic Culture in Russia during World War I*. Ithaca, N.Y.: Cornell University Press, 1995.

Jasanoff, Maia. *Edge of Empire: Lives, Culture, and Conquest in the East, 1750–1850*. New York: Knopf, 2005.

Johanson, Lars, and Éva Ágnes Csato, eds. *The Turkic Languages*. London: Routledge, 1998.

Kalimullin, Baryi G. *Karavan-sarai v g. Orenburge*. Moscow: Izdatel'stvo Literatury po Stroitel'stvu, 1966.

Kamen, Henry. *Empire: How Spain Became a World Power, 1492–1763*. New York: Harper-Collins, 2003.

Kamenskii, Aleksandr. "Poddanstvo, loial'nost', patriotizm v imperskom diskurse Rossii XVIII v.: K postanovke problemy." *Ab Imperio* 4 (2006): 59–99.

Kanlidere, Ahmet. *Reform within Islam: The Tajdid and Jadid Movement among the Kazan Tatars (1809–1917), Conciliation and Conflict*. Istanbul: Eren, 1997.

Kappeler, Andreas. *The Russian Empire: A Multiethnic History.* Trans. Alfred Clayton. Harlow: Longman, 2001.

———. *Russlands erste Nationalitäten: Das Zarenreich und die Völker der Mittleren Wolga vom 16. bis 19. Jahrhundert.* Cologne: Böhlau, 1982.

———. "Tsentr i elity periferii v gabsburgskoi, rossiiskoi i osmanskoi imperiiakh (1700–1918)." *Ab Imperio* 2 (2007): 17–58.

Kasaba, Reşat. *A Moveable Empire: Ottoman Nomads, Migrants, and Refugees.* Seattle: University of Washington Press, 2009.

Kaspe, Sviatoslav. "Imperial Political Culture and Modernization in the Second Half of the Nineteenth Century." In *Russian Empire: Space, People, Power, 1700–1930.* Ed. Jane Burbank, Mark von Hagen, and Anatolyi Remnev. Bloomington: Indiana University Press, 2007.

———. *Imperiia i modernizatsiia: Obshchaia model' i rossiiskaia spetsifika.* Moscow: Rosspen, 2001.

Katz, Martin. *Mikhail N. Katkov: A Political Biography, 1818–1887.* The Hague: Mouton, 1966.

Keenan, Edward L. "Muscovy and Kazan: Some Introductory Remarks on the Patterns of Steppe Diplomacy." *Slavic Review* 26, no. 4 (December 1967): 548–558.

Kemper, Michael. "Entre Boukhara et la Moyenne-Volga: 'Abd an-Nasir al-Qursawi (1776–1812) en conflit avec les Oulemas traditionalists." *Cahiers du Monde Russe* 37, no. 1–2 (January–June 1996): 41–51.

———. *Sufii i uchenye v Tatarstane i Bashkortostane: Islamskii diskurs pod russkim gospodstvom.* Trans. Iskander Giliazov. Kazan: Idel-Press, 2008.

———. *Sufis und Gelehrte in Tatarien und Baschkirien, 1789–1889: Der islamische Diskurs unter russischer Herrschaft.* Berlin: K. Schwarz, 1998.

Khairutdinov, Ramil'. "Tatarskaia feodal'naia znat' i rossiiskoe dvorianstvo: Problem integratsii na rubezhe XVIII–XIX vv." In *Islam v tatarskom mire: Istoriia i sovremennost' (materialy mezhdunarodnogo simpoziuma, Kazan' 29 aprelia–1 maia 1996 g.).* Ed. Rafael' Khakimov. Kazan: Panoramy-Forum, 1997.

Khalid, Adeeb. "Backwardness and the Quest for Civilization: Early Soviet Central Asia in Comparative Perspective." *Slavic Review* 65, no. 2 (Summer 2006): 231–251.

———. *The Politics of Cultural Reform: Jadidism in Central Asia.* Berkeley: University of California Press, 1998.

Khamamoto, Mami. "Sviazuiushchaia rol' Tatarskikh kuptsov volgo-ural'skogo regiona v tsentral'noi evrazii: Zveno 'Shelkovogo puti novogo vremeni' (vtoraia polovina XVIII–XIX v.)." In *Volgo-Ural'skii region v imperskom prostranstve, XVIII–XX vv.* Ed. M. Khamamoto, N. Naganawa, and D. Usmanova. Moscow: Vostochnaia Literatura RAN, 2011.

Khanykov, Ia. V. "Raznye bumagi general-maiora Tevkeleva ob Orenburgskom krae i kirgiz-kaisatskikh ordakh: 1762 g." *Vremennik imperatorskogo moskovskogo obshchestva istorii i drevnostei Rossiiskikh* 13 (1852): 15–21.

Khodarkovsky, Michael. *Bitter Choices: Loyalty and Betrayal in the Russian Conquest of the North Caucasus.* Ithaca, N.Y.: Cornell University Press, 2011.

———. "'Ignoble Savages and Unfaithful Subjects': Constructing Non-Christian Identities in Early Modern Russia." In *Russia's Orient: Imperial Borderlands and Peoples, 1700–1917.* Ed. Daniel R. Brower and Edward J. Lazzerini. Bloomington: Indiana University Press, 1997.

———. "Non-Russian Subjects." In *The Cambridge History of Russia, Volume I: From Early Rus' to 1689*. Ed. Maureen Perrie. New York: Cambridge University Press, 2006.

———. "'Not by Word Alone': Missionary Policies and Religious Conversion in Early Modern Russia." *Comparative Studies in Society and History* 38, no. 2 (April 1996): 267–293.

———. *Russia's Steppe Frontier: The Making of a Colonial Empire, 1500–1800*. Bloomington: Indiana University Press, 2002.

———. *Where Two Worlds Met: The Russian State and the Kalmyk Nomads, 1600–1771*. Ithaca, N.Y.: Cornell University Press, 1992.

Khoury, Dina Rizk. "Administrative Practice between Religious Law (*Shari'a*) and State Law (*Kanun*) on the Eastern Frontiers of the Ottoman Empire." *Journal of Early Modern History* 5, no. 4 (2001): 305–330.

"Khutba." In *Islam: Entsiklopedicheskii slovar'*, ed. L. V. Negria. Moscow: Nauka, 1991.

Kiekbaev, M. D. *Bashkiry v gorodakh Bashkortostan: Istoriia i sovremennost'*. Ufa: NUR-Poligrafizdat, 1998.

Kiikov, A. *Iz bylogo urala. Materialy k istorii revoliutsionnogo dvizheniia na iuzhnom urale i v priural'i, 1905–1916*. Ufa: Izd. Bashkirskogo obl. Biuro Istparta RKP(b), 1923.

Kivelson, Valerie. *Cartographies of Tsardom: The Land and Its Meanings in Seventeenth-Century Russia*. Ithaca, N.Y.: Cornell University Press, 2006.

Klier, John Doyle. *Russia Gathers Her Jews: The Origins of the "Jewish Question" in Russia, 1772–1825*. DeKalb: Northern Illinois University Press, 1986.

Kliuchevskii, Vasilii O. *Istoriia soslovii v Rossii*. 3rd ed. Petrograd: Literaturno-Izdatel'skii Otdel Komissariata Narodnogo Prosveshcheniia, 1918.

Knight, Nathaniel. "Grigor'ev in Orenburg, 1851–1862: Russian Orientalism in Service of Empire?" *Slavic Review* 59, no. 1 (Spring 2000): 74–100.

Kosach, Grigorii. "A Russian City between Two Continents: The Tatars of Orenburg and State Power." In *Russia at a Crossroads: History, Memory, and Political Practice*. Ed. Nurit Schleifman. London: Frank Cass Publishers, 1998.

Kotsonis, Yanni. "'Face-to-Face': The State, the Individual, and the Citizen in Russian Taxation, 1863–1917." *Slavic Review* 63, no. 2 (Summer 2004): 221–246.

———. *Making Peasants Backward: Managing Populations in Russian Agricultural Cooperatives, 1861–1914*. New York: Macmillan, 1999.

———. "'No Place to Go': Taxation and State Transformation in Late Imperial and Early Soviet Russia." *Journal of Modern History* 76, no. 3 (September 2004): 531–577.

———. *States of Obligation: Taxes and Citizenship in the Russian Empire and Early Soviet Republic*. Toronto: University of Toronto Press, 2014.

Kratkii ocherk istorii orenburgskogo nepliuskogo kadetskogo korpusa. Orenburg: A. N. Gavrilova, 1913.

Kreindler, Isabelle T. "Educational Policies toward the Eastern Nationalities in Tsarist Russia: A Study of Il'minskii's System." PhD dissertation, Columbia University, 1969.

———. "A Neglected Source of Lenin's Nationality Policy." *Slavic Review* 36, no. 1 (March 1977): 86–100.

Kul'sharipov, M. M. "Otkrytie dukhovnogo upravleniia musul'man v Ufe." In *Sotsial'no-ekonomicheskoe razvitie i klassovaia bor'ba v iuzhnom urale i v Srednem Povol'zhe: Dorevoliutsionyi period*. Ed. Irek G. Akmanov. Ufa: Bashkirskii Universitet, 1988.

Kuzeev, Rail G. *Istoricheskaia etnografiia bashkirskogo naroda*. 2nd ed. Ufa: Kitap, 2009.

———. "O kharaktere prisoedineniia narodov volgo-uralskogo regiona k russkomu gosudarstvu i nekotorye voprosy ikh srednevekovoi istorii." In *Etnologicheskie issledovaniia v Bashkortostane: Sbornik statei.* Ed. Il'dar Gabrafikov. Ufa: UNTS RAN, 1994.

———. *Proiskhozhdenie bashkirskogo naroda. Etnicheskii sostav, istoriia rasseleniia.* Moscow: Nauka, 1974.

Kuznetsov, I. D., ed. *Natsional'nye dvizheniia v period pervoi revoliutsii v Rossii (sbornik dokumentov iz arkhiva byv. departamenta politsii).* Cheboksary: Chuvashkoe Gosudarstvennoe Izdatel'stvo, 1935.

Laitin, David, Roger Peterson, and John Slocum. "Language and the State: Russia and the Soviet Union in Comparative Perspective." In *Thinking Theoretically about Soviet Nationalities: History and Comparison in the Study of the USSR.* Ed. Alexander J. Motyl. New York: Columbia University Press, 1995.

Landau, Jacob. *The Politics of Pan-Islam: Ideology and Organization.* Oxford: Oxford University Press, 1994.

Lapteva, L. E. *Zemskie uchrezhdeniia v Rossii.* Moscow: Institut Gosudarstva i Prava RAN, 1993.

Larina, E. I. "Episkop Andrei i doktrina ministerstva vnutrennikh del rossiiskoi imperii v 'musul'manskom voprose.'" *Sbornik russkogo istoricheskogo obshchestva* 155, no. 7 (2003): 212–225.

Lazzerini, Edward J. "Beyond Renewal: The Jadid Response to Pressure for Change in the Modern Age." In *Muslims in Central Asia: Expressions of Identity and Change.* Ed. Jo-Ann Gross. Durham, N.C.: Duke University Press, 1992.

———. "Gadidism at the Turn of the Twentieth Century: A View from Within." *Cahiers du Monde Russe et Sovietique* 16, no. 2 (April–June 1975): 245–271.

Lebedev, V. "Bashkirskie vosstanie 1705–1711 gg." *Istoricheskie zapiski* 1 (1937): 81–102.

Leckey, Colum. *Patrons of Enlightenment: The Free Economic Society in Eighteenth-Century Russia.* Newark: University of Delaware Press, 2011.

LeDonne, John P. *Absolutism and the Ruling Class: The Formation of the Russian Political Order, 1700–1825.* Oxford: Oxford University Press, 1991.

———. "Building an Infrastructure of Empire in Russia's Eastern Theater, 1650s–1840s." *Cahiers du Monde Russe* 47, no. 3 (July–September 2007): 581–608.

———. *Ruling Russia: Politics and Administration in the Age of Absolutism, 1762–1796.* Princeton, N.J.: Princeton University Press, 1984.

———. "The Territorial Reform of the Russian Empire, 1775–1796: II. The Borderlands, 1777–1796." *Cahiers du Monde Russe et Sovietique* 24, no. 4 (1983): 411–420, 422–457.

Lentz, Thierry. "Imperial France in 1808 and Beyond." In *The Napoleonic Empire and the New European Political Culture.* Ed. Michael Broers, Peter Hicks, and Augustin Guimerá. Basingstoke: Palgrave Macmillan, 2012.

Leonard, Carol S. *Reform and Regicide: The Reign of Peter III in Russia.* Bloomington: Indiana University Press, 1993.

Leonov, Nikolai I. *Burzhuaznye reformy 60–70-x godov XIX v. v Bashkirii.* Ufa: Redaktsionno-Izdatel'skii Otdel Bashkirskogo Universiteta, 1993.

Le Torrivellec, Xavier. "Histoire des identités en Russie musulmane: La République du Bachkortostan (1969–2003)." PhD dissertation, École des Hautes Études en Sciences sociales, 2006.

Levitskii, V. "Pravye partii." In *Obshchestvennoe dvizhenie v Rossii v nachale XX-go veka.* Vol. III. No. 5. Ed. L. Martov, P. Maslov, and A. Potresov. St. Petersburg: Obshchestvennaia Pol'za, 1914.

Liashchenko, P. I. *Ocherki agrarnoi evoliutsii Rossii.* Vol. 2, *Krest'ianskoe delo i poreformennaia zemleustroitel'naia politika.* St. Petersburg: Ministerstvo Finansov, 1913.

Lieven, Dominic. *Empire: The Russian Empire and Its Rivals.* New Haven, Conn.: Yale University Press, 2000.

———. *Russia against Napoleon: The True Story of the Campaigns of* War and Peace. New York: Penguin, 2009.

Linton, Marisa. "Citizenship and Religious Toleration in France." In *Toleration in Enlightenment Europe.* Ed. Ole Peter Grell and Roy Porter. Cambridge: Cambridge University Press, 2000.

Litvak, Olga. *Conscription and the Search for Modern Russian Jewry.* Bloomington: Indiana University Press, 2006.

Liulevicius, Vejas. *War Land on the Eastern Front: Culture, National Identity, and German Occupation in World War I.* Cambridge: Cambridge University Press, 2000.

Lohr, Eric. *Nationalizing the Russian Empire: The Campaign against Enemy Aliens during World War I.* Cambridge, Mass.: Harvard University Press, 2003.

Longworth, Philip. "The Pugachev Revolt: The Last Great Cossack Peasant Rising." In *Rural Protest: Peasant Movements and Social Change.* Ed. Henry A. Landsberger. London: Macmillan, 1974.

Löwe, Heiz-Dietrich. *The Tsars and the Jews: Reform, Reaction and Anti-Semitism in Imperial Russia, 1772–1917.* Chur: Harwood Academic Publishers, 1993.

Lustick, Ian. *State-Building Failure in British Ireland and French Algeria.* Berkeley: Institute of International Studies, 1985.

Macey, David A. J. *Government and Peasant in Russia, 1861–1906: The Prehistory of the Stolypin Reforms.* DeKalb: Northern Illinois University Press, 1982.

Manchester, Laurie. *Holy Fathers, Secular Sons: Clergy, Intelligentsia, and the Modern Self in Revolutionary Russia.* DeKalb: Northern Illinois University Press, 2008.

Manning, Roberta Thompson. *The Crisis of the Old Order in Russia: Gentry and Government.* Princeton, N.J.: Princeton University Press, 1982.

Martin, Janet. "Multiethnicity in Muscovy: A Consideration of the Christian and Muslim Tatars in the 1550s–1580s." *Journal of Early Modern History* 5, no. 1 (2001): 1–23.

Martin, Terry. *The Affirmative Action Empire: Nations and Nationalism in the Soviet Union, 1923–1939.* Ithaca, N.Y.: Cornell University Press, 2001.

Martin, Virginia. *Law and Custom in the Steppe: The Kazakhs of the Middle Horde and Russian Colonialism in the Nineteenth Century.* Richmond, Surrey: Routledge-Curzon, 2001.

McDonald, David MacLaren. *United Government and Foreign Policy in Russia, 1900–1914.* Cambridge, Mass.: Harvard University Press, 1992.

McKenzie, Kermit E. "Zemstvo Organization and Role within the Administrative Structure." In *The Zemstvo in Russia: An Experiment in Local Self-Government.* Ed. Terence Emmons and Wayne S. Vucinich. Cambridge: Cambridge University Press, 1982.

Meehan-Waters, Brenda. *Autocracy and Aristocracy: The Russian Service Elite of 1730.* New Brunswick, N.J.: Rutgers University Press, 1982.

Metcalf, Thomas R. *Ideologies of the Raj.* Cambridge: Cambridge University Press, 1997.

Michels, Georg. "Rescuing the Orthodox: The Church Policies of Archbishop Afanasii of Kholmogory, 1682–1702." In *Of Religion and Empire: Missions, Conversion, and Tolerance in Tsarist Russia*. Ed. Robert P. Geraci and Michael Khodarkovsky. Ithaca, N.Y.: Cornell University Press, 2001.

Mikhailova, Saveia. *Kazanskii universitet v dukhovnoi kul'ture narodov vostoka Rossii*. Kazan: Kazan University Press, 1991.

Millward, James. "Eastern Central Asia (Xinjiang): 1300–1800." In *The Cambridge History of Inner Asia: The Chinggisid Age*. Ed. Nicola Di Cosmo, Allen J. Frank, and Peter B. Golden. Cambridge: Cambridge University Press, 2009.

Minkina, Ol'ga. *"Syny Rakhili": Evreiskie deputaty v rossiiskoi imperii, 1772–1825*. Moscow: Novoe Literaturnoe Obozrenie, 2011.

Mogilner, Marina. *Homo Imperii: A History of Physical Anthropology in Russia*. Lincoln: University of Nebraska Press, 2013.

Morrison, Alexander S. "Metropole, Colony, and Imperial Citizenship in the Russian Empire." *Kritika: Explorations in Russian and Eurasian History* 13, no. 2 (Spring 2012, New Series): 327–364.

———. "The Pleasures and Pitfalls of Colonial Comparisons." *Kritika: Explorations in Russian and Eurasian History* 13, no. 4 (Fall 2012): 919–936.

———. *Russian Rule in Samarkand, 1868–1910: A Comparison with British India*. Oxford: Oxford University Press, 2008.

Mukhamedova, R. G. *Tatary-mishari*. Moscow: Nauka, 1972.

Müller, Michael G. "Toleration in Eastern Europe: The Dissident Question in Eighteenth-Century Poland-Lithuania." In *Toleration in Enlightenment Europe*. Ed. Ole Peter Grell and Roy Porter. Cambridge: Cambridge University Press, 2000.

Naganawa, Norihiro. "Holidays in Kazan: The Public Sphere and the Politics of Religious Authority among Tatars in 1914." *Slavic Review* 71, no. 1 (Spring 2012): 25–48.

———. "Molding the Muslim Community through the Tsarist Administration: *Mahalla* under the Jurisdiction of the Orenburg Mohammedan Spiritual Assembly after 1905." *Acta Slavica Iaponica* 23 (2006): 101–23.

———. "Musul'manskoe soobshchestvo v usloviiakh mobilizatsii: Uchastie volgo-ural'skikh musul'man v voinakh poslednego desiatiletiia sushchestvovaniia Rossiiskoi imperii." In *Volgo-ural'skii region v imperskom prostranstve, XVIII–XX vv.* Ed. M. Khamamoto, N. Naganava, and D. Usmanova. Moscow: Vostochnaia Literatura RAN, 2011.

Nathans, Benjamin. *Beyond the Pale: The Jewish Encounter with Late Imperial Russia*. Berkeley: University of California Press, 2002.

Noack, Christian. *Muslimischer Nationalismus im russischen Reich: Nationsbildung und Nationalbewegung bei Tataren und Baschkiren: 1861–1917*. Stuttgart: Franz Steiner Verlag, 2000.

———. "Retrospectively Revolting: Kazan Tatar 'Conspiracies' during the 1905 Revolution." In *The Russian Revolution of 1905: Centenary Perspectives*. Ed. Jonathan D. Smele and Anthony Heywood. London: Routledge, 2005.

Nolde, Boris. *La formation de l'empire russe: Études, notes, et documents*. Vol. 1. Paris: Insitut d'Études Slaves, 1952.

O'Neill, Kelly. "Rethinking Elite Integration: The Crimean Murzas and the Evolution of Russian Nobility." *Cahiers du Monde Russe* 51, no. 2 (2010): 397–417.

Orlovsky, Daniel T. *The Limits of Reform: The Ministry of Internal Affairs in Imperial Russia, 1802–1881.* Cambridge, Mass.: Harvard University Press, 1981.

O'Rourke, Shane. *Warriors and Peasants: The Don Cossacks in Late Imperial Russia.* New York: St. Martin's Press, 2000.

Osterhammel, Jürgen. *The Transformation of the World: A Global History of the Nineteenth Century.* Princeton, N.J.: Princeton University Press, 2014.

Ostrowski, Donald. *Muscovy and the Mongols: Cross-Cultural Influences on the Steppe Frontier, 1304–1589.* Cambridge: Cambridge University Press, 1998.

Pagden, Anthony. *Lords of All the World: Ideologies of Empire in Spain, Britain and France c. 1500–1800.* New Haven, Conn.: Yale University Press, 1995.

Pallot, Judith, and Denis J. Shaw. *Landscape and Settlement in Romanov Russia, 1613–1917.* Oxford: Clarendon Press, 1990.

Pelenski, Jaroslaw. *Russia and Kazan: Conquest and Imperial Ideology (1438–1560s).* The Hague: Mouton, 1974.

Perdue, Peter C. "Boundaries, Maps, and Movement: Chinese, Russian, and Mongolian Empires in Early Modern Central Eurasia." *International History Review* 20, no. 2 (June 1998): 263–286.

———. *China Marches West: The Qing Conquest of Central Eurasia.* Cambridge, Mass.: Belknap Press of Harvard University Press, 2005.

Perrie, Maureen, ed. *The Cambridge History of Russia.* Vol. I, *From Early Rus' to 1689.* New York: Cambridge University Press, 2006.

Pipes, Richard. "The First Experiment in Soviet Nationality Policy: The Bashkir Republic, 1917–1920." *Russian Review* 9, no. 4 (October 1950): 303–331.

———. *The Formation of the Soviet Union: Communism and Nationalism, 1917–1923.* Rev. ed. New York: Atheneum, 1968[1954].

Pisarenko, E. E. "Kadet kniaz' V. A. Kugushev." *Voprosy istorii* 2 (February 1997): 150–156.

Pogorelskin, Alexis E. "*Vestnik Evropy* and the Polish Question in the Reign of Alexander II." *Slavic Review* 46, no. 1 (Spring 1987): 87–105.

Polunov, Aleksandr. *Pod vlast'iu ober-prokurora: Gosudarstvo i tserkov' v epokhu Aleksandra III.* Moscow: AIRO-XX, 1996.

Portal, Roger. *L'Oural au XVIII siècle: Etude d'histoire economique et sociale.* Paris: Institut d'Etudes Slaves, 1950.

Pravilova, Ekaterina. "The Property of Empire: Islamic Law and Russian Agrarian Policy in Transcaucasia and Turkestan." *Kritka: Explorations in Russian and Eurasian History* 12, no. 2 (Spring 2011): 353–386.

———. *A Public Empire: Property and the Quest for the Common Good in Imperial Russia.* Princeton, N.J.: Princeton University Press, 2014.

Prokof'eva, A. G., G. P. Matvievskaia, V. Iu. Prokof'eva, and I. K. Zubova, eds. *Neizvestnyi Vladimir Ivanovich Dal': Orenburgskii krai v ocherkakh i nauchnykh trudakh pisatelia.* Orenburg: Orenburgskoe Knizhnoe Izdatel'stvo, 2002.

Prucha, Francis Paul. *The Great Father: The United States Government and the American Indian.* Vol. 2. Lincoln: University of Nebraska Press, 1984.

Pushkin, Alexander. *The History of Pugachev.* Trans. Earl Sampson. London: Phoenix Press, 2001.

Quataert, Donald. *The Ottoman Empire, 1700–1922.* Cambridge: Cambridge University Press, 2000.

Raeff, Marc. "In the Imperial Manner." In *Political Ideas and Institutions in Imperial Russia*. Ed. Marc Raeff. Boulder, Colo.: Westview, 1994. First published as "The Style of Russia's Imperial Policy and Prince G. A. Potemkin," in *Statesmen and Statecraft of the Modern West*, ed. G.N. Grob. Barre, Mass: Barre Publishers, 1967.

———. *Michael Speransky: Statesman of Imperial Russia, 1772–1839*, 2nd rev. ed. The Hague: Martinus Nijhoff, 1969.

———. "Patterns of Imperial Russian Policy toward the Nationalities." In *Soviet Nationality Problems*. Ed. Edward Allworth. New York: Columbia University Press, 1971.

———. "Pugachev's Rebellion." In *Political Ideas and Institutions in Imperial Russia*. Boulder, Colo.: Westview, 1994. First published in *Preconditions of Revolution in Early Modern Europe*, ed. Robert Forster and Jack P. Greene. Baltimore, Md.: Johns Hopkins University Press, 1970.

———. *Understanding Imperial Russia: State and Society in the Old Regime*. Trans. Arthur Goldhammer. Foreword by John Keep. New York: Columbia University Press, 1984.

———. "Uniformity, Diversity, and the Imperial Administration in the Reign of Catherine II." In *Political Ideas and Institutions in Imperial Russia*. Ed. Marc Raeff. Boulder, Colo.: Westview, 1994. First published in *Osteuropa in Geschichte und Gegewart: Festschrift für Günter Stökl zum 60. Geburtstag*. Cologne: Böhlau, 1977.

———. *The Well-Ordered Police State: Social and Institutional Change through Law in the Germanies and Russia, 1600–1800*. New Haven, Conn.: Yale University Press, 1983.

Rakhimkulov, M. G., comp. *Bashkiriia v russkoi literature*. Vol. 1. Ufa: Bashkirskoe Knizhnoe Izdatel'stvo, 1989.

Rakhimov, R. M. *1905 v Bashkirii*. Moscow and Leningrad: Akademiia Nauk, 1941.

Rakhmatullin, Ural Kh. *Naselenie Bashkirii v XVII–XVIII vv. Voprosy formirovaniia nebashkirskogo naseleniia*. Moscow: Nauka, 1988.

Ransel, David L. "Implicit Questions in Michael Confino's Essay: Corporate State and Vertical Relationships." *Cahiers du Monde Russe* 51, no. 2 (2010): 195–210.

———. *A Merchant's Tale: The Life and Adventures of Ivan Alekseevich Tolchenov, Based on His Diary*. Bloomington: Indiana University Press, 2008.

Rawson, Don C. *Russian Rightists and the Revolution of 1905*. New York: Cambridge University Press, 1995.

Reichman, Henry. *Railway Men and Revolution: Russia, 1905*. Berkeley: University of California Press, 1987.

Riasanovsky, Nicholas V. *The Image of Peter the Great in Russian History and Thought*. Oxford: Oxford University Press, 1985.

———. *Nicholas I and Official Nationality in Russia, 1825–1855*. Berkeley: University of California Press, 1959.

Rieber, Alfred J. "The Comparative Ecology of Complex Frontiers." In *Imperial Rule*. Ed. Alexei Miller and Alfred Rieber. Budapest: Central European University Press, 2004.

Robbins, Richard, Jr. *The Tsar's Viceroys: Russian Provincial Governors in the Last Years of the Empire*. Ithaca, N.Y.: Cornell University Press, 1987.

Rodnov, Mikhail I. "Chislennost' tiurkskogo krest'ianstva ufimskoi gubernii v nachale XX v." *Etnograficheskoe obozrenie* 6 (1996): 121–131.

———. *Naselenie ufimskoi gubernii po perepisi 1920 goda: Etnicheskii sostav (Birskii, Zlatoustovskii, i drugie uezdy)*. Moscow: Institut Etnologii i Antropologii imi. N. N. Miklukho-Maklaia, 2014. http://static.iea.ras.ru/books/Rodnov.pdf, accessed July 22, 2014.

Rodnov, Mikhail I. et al. eds. *Istoriia Bashkortostana vo vtoroi polovine XIX–nachale XX veka*. Vol. 1. Ufa: UNTS RAN, 2006; Vol. 2. Ufa: Gilem, 2007.

Rogger, Hans. *Jewish Policies and Right-Wing Politics in Imperial Russia*. Berkeley: University of California Press, 1986.

Romaniello, Matthew P. "Absolutism and Empire: Governance on Russia's Early-Modern Frontier." PhD dissertation, Ohio State University, 2003.

———. *The Elusive Empire: Kazan and the Creation of Russia, 1552–1671*. Madison: University of Wisconsin Press, 2012.

———. "Mission Delayed: The Russian Orthodox Church after the Conquest of Kazan." *Church History* 76, no. 3 (September 2007): 511–540.

Rorlich, Azade Ayşe. *The Volga Tatars: A Profile in National Resilience*. Stanford, Calif.: Hoover Institution Press, 1986.

Rosenberg, William G. "The Problems of Empire in Imperial Russia." *Ab Imperio* 3 (2005): 453–465.

Roshwald, Ariel. *Ethnic Nationalism and the Fall of Empires: Central Europe, Russia, and the Middle East, 1914–1923*. London: Routledge, 2001.

Ross, Danielle M. "From the Minbar to the Barricades: The Tranformation of the Volga-Ural 'Ulama into a Revolutionary Intelligentsia." PhD dissertation, University of Wisconsin–Madison, 2011.

———. "In Dialogue with the Shadow of God: Imperial Mobilization, Islamic Revival, and the Evolution of an Administrative System for the Tatars, Bashkirs, and Mishars of Eighteenth Century Russia." MA thesis, University of Wisconsin–Madison, 2007.

Rudenko, Sergei I. *Bashkiry: Istoriko-etnograficheskie ocherki*. Moscow-Leningrad: Akademiia Nauk, 1955.

Ruedy, John. *Modern Algeria: The Origins and Development of a Nation*. 2nd ed. Bloomington: Indiana University Press, 2005.

Sahadeo, Jeff. *Russian Colonial Society in Tashkent, 1865–1923*. Bloomington: Indiana University Press, 2007.

Sanborn, Joshua. *Drafting the Russian Nation: Military Conscription, Total War, and Mass Politics, 1905–1925*. DeKalb: Northern Illinois University Press, 2003.

———. *Imperial Apocalypse: The Great War and the Destruction of the Russian Empire*. New York: Oxford University Press, 2014.

———. "The Mobilization of 1914 and the Question of the Russian Nation: A Reexamination." *Slavic Review* 59, no. 2 (Summer 2000): 267–289.

Schafer, Daniel E. "Building Nations and Building States: The Tatar-Bashkir Question in Revolutionary Russia, 1917–1920." PhD dissertation, University of Michigan, 1995.

———. "Local Politics and the Birth of the Republic of Bashkortostan, 1919–1920." In *A State of Nations: Empire and Nation-Making in the Age of Lenin and Stalin*. Ed. Ronald Grigor Suny and Terry Martin. Oxford: Oxford University Press, 2001.

Schrader, Abby M. *Languages of the Lash: Corporal Punishment and Identity in Imperial Russia*. DeKalb: Northern Illinois University Press, 2002.

Semenova, Natal'ia L. *Voennoe upravlenie orenburgskim kraem v kontse XVII–pervoi polovine XIX v.* Sterlitamak: Sterlitamakskii Gosudarstvennyi Pedagogicheskii Institut, 2001.

Semyonov, Alexander. "'The Real and Live Ethnographic Map of Russia': The Russian Empire in the Mirror of the State Duma." In *Empire Speaks Out: Languages of*

Rationalization and Self-Description in the Russian Empire. Ed. Ilya Gerasimov, Jan Kusber, and Alexander Semyonov. Leiden: Brill, 2009.

Seregny, Scott J. "Zemstvos, Peasants, and Citizenship: The Russian Adult Education Movement and World War I." *Slavic Review* 59, no. 2 (Summer 2000): 290–315.

Sessions, Jennifer E. *By Sword and Plow: France and the Conquest of Algeria.* Ithaca, N.Y.: Cornell University Press, 2011.

Shaiakhmetov, Fidail' F. *Mezhdu velikoi step'iu i osedlost'iu: Protsessy sedentarizatsii Bashkir i rasprostraneniia zemledelia v XVII–XIX vv.* Ufa: Bashkirskogo Gosudarstvennogo Universiteta, 2005.

Shakurov, R. Z., ed. *Bashkortostan: Kratkaia entsiklopediia.* Ufa: Bashkirskaia Entsiklopediia, 1996.

Shakurova, Faniia A. *Bashkirskaia volost' i obshchina v seredine XVIII–pervoi polovine XIX veka.* Ufa: BNT Ural'skogo Otdeleniia RAN, 1992.

Shepelev, L. E. *Tituly, mundiry, ordena v rossiiskoi imperii.* Leningrad: Nauka, 1991.

Shukshintsev, I. S. "Pervye vrachi iz Bashkir v orenburgskom krae." *Trudy Orenburgskoi Uchenoi Arkhivnoi Komissii* 11 (1903): 11–37.

———. "Volneniia v Bashkirii v 1835 godu." *Trudy Orenburgskoi Uchenoi Arkhivnoi Komissii* 11 (1903): 97–108.

Sinel, Allen. *The Classroom and the Chancellery: State Educational Reform in Russia under Count Dmitrii Tolstoi.* Cambridge, Mass.: Harvard University Press, 1973.

Skinner, Barbara. *The Western Front of the Eastern Church: Uniate and Orthodox Conflict in Eighteenth-Century Poland, Ukraine, Belarus, and Russia.* DeKalb: Northern Illinois University Press, 2009.

Slezkine, Yuri. *Arctic Mirrors: Russia and the Small Peoples of the North.* Ithaca, N.Y.: Cornell University Press, 1994.

———. *The Jewish Century.* Princeton, N.J.: Princeton University Press, 2004.

———. "The USSR as a Communal Apartment, or How a Socialist State Promoted Ethnic Particularism." *Slavic Review* 53, no. 2 (Summer 1994): 414–452.

Slocum, John. "The Boundaries of National Identity: Religion, Language, and Nationality Politics in Late Imperial Russia." PhD dissertation, University of Chicago, 1993.

———. "Who, and When, Were the *Inorodtsy*? The Evolution of the Category of 'Aliens' in Imperial Russia." *The Russian Review* 57, no. 2 (April 1998): 173–190.

Smirnov, A. P. et al. eds. *Ocherki po istorii Bashkirskoi ASSR.* Vol. I. Part I. Ufa: Bashkirskoe Knizhnoe Izdatel'stvo, 1956.

Smirnov, Iurii N. *Orenburgskaia ekspeditsiia (komissiia) i prisoedinenie zavolzh'ia k Rossii v 30–40e gg. XVIII veka.* Samara: Samarskii Universitet, 1997.

Smith, Alison K. *For the Common Good and Their Own Well-Being: The System of Social Estates in Imperial Russia.* Oxford: Oxford University Press, 2014.

Smolich, Igor K. *Istoriia russkoi tserkvi, 1700–1917.* 2 vols. Moscow: Izdatel'stvo Spaso-Preobrazhenskogo Valaamskogo Monastyriia, 1996.

Sneath, David. "Tribe, *Ethnos*, Nation: Rethinking Evolutionist Social Theory and Representations of Nomadic Inner Asia." *Ab Imperio* 4 (2009): 80–109.

Snyder, Timothy. *The Reconstruction of Nations: Poles, Jews, Ukrainians, Lithuanians, Belarusians, and Russians, 1569–1999.* New Haven, Conn.: Yale University Press, 2003.

Solov'ev, Sergei. *Istoriia Rossii s drevneishikh vremen.* Vol. 10. Moscow: Izdatel'stvo Sotsial'no-Ekonomicheskoi Literatury, 1963.

Sorensen, Thomas C. "The Thought and Policies of Konstantin Pobedonostsev." PhD dissertation, University of Washington, 1977.

Spannaus, Nathan. "The Decline of the Ākhūnd and the Transformation of Islamic Law under the Russian Empire." *Islamic Law and Society* 20, no. 3 (2013): 202–241.

Staliunas, Darius. "Did the Government Seek to Russify Lithuanians and Poles in the Northwest Territory after the Uprising of 1863–1864?" *Kritika: Explorations in Russian and Eurasian History* 5, no. 2 (Spring 2004): 273–289.

Stanislawski, Michael. *Tsar Nicholas I and the Jews: The Transformation of Jewish Society in Russia, 1825–1855.* Philadelphia, Pa.: Jewish Publication Society of America, 1983.

Steinwedel, Charles. "How Bashkiria Became Part of European Russia, 1762–1881." In *Russian Empire: Space, People, Power, 1700–1930.* Ed. Jane Burbank, Mark von Hagen, and Anatolyi Remnev. Bloomington: Indiana University Press, 2007.

———. "Making Social Groups, One Person at a Time: The Identification of Individuals by Estate, Religious Confession, and Ethnicity in Late Imperial Russia." In *Documenting Individual Identity: The Development of State Practices since the French Revolution.* Ed. Jane Caplan and John Torpey. Princeton, N.J.: Princeton University Press, 2001.

———. "To Make a Difference: The Category of Ethnicity in Late Imperial Russian Politics, 1861–1917." In *Russian Modernity: Politics, Knowledge, Practices.* Ed. Yanni Kotsonis and David Hoffman. Basingstoke: Macmillan, 2000.

Stepanov, Sergei A. *Chernaia sotnia v Rossii, 1905–1914.* Moscow: VZPI A/o Rosvuznauka, 1992.

Stoler, Ann Laura. "On Degrees of Imperial Sovereignty." *Public Culture* 18, no. 1 (2006): 125–146.

Stoler, Ann Laura, and Carole McGranahan. "Introduction: Refiguring Imperial Terrains." In *Imperial Formations.* Ed. Ann Laura Stoler, Carole McGranahan, and Peter C. Perdue. Santa Fe and Oxford: School for Advanced Research Press and James Currey, 2007.

Stoletnii iubilei ufimskoi dukhovnoi seminarii. Ufa: n. p., 1900.

Storozhev, V. "Votchina." In *Novyi entsiklopedicheskii slovar'.* Vol. 11. Leipzig and St. Petersburg: F. A. Brokgauz and I. A. Efron, 1906.

Strickland, John. *The Making of Holy Russia: The Orthodox Church and Russian Nationalism before the Revolution.* Jordanville, N.Y.: Holy Trinity Publications, 2013.

Sunderland, Willard. *Taming the Wild Field: Colonization and Empire on the Russian Steppe.* Ithaca, N.Y.: Cornell University Press, 2004.

Suny, Ronald Grigor. "The Empire Strikes Out: Imperial Russia, 'National' Identity, and Theories of Empire." In *A State of Nations: Empire and Nation-Making in the Age of Lenin and Stalin.* Ed. Ronald Grigor Suny and Terry Martin. Oxford: Oxford University Press, 2001.

———. *The Revenge of the Past: Nationalism, Revolution and the Collapse of the Soviet Union.* Stanford, Calif.: Stanford University Press, 1993.

Szeftel, Marc. "The Form of Government of the Russian Empire Prior to the Constitutional Reforms of 1905–1906." In *Essays in Russian and Soviet History.* Ed. John Shelton Curtiss. New York: Columbia University Press, 1965.

———. *The Russian Constitution of April 23, 1906: Political Institutions of the Duma Monarchy.* Brussels: Les Éditions de la Librairie Encyclopédique, 1976.

Tagirova, Leila F. *Kantonnye nachal'niki Bashkirii: Natsional'naia regional'naia elita pervoi poloviny XIX veka.* Ufa: UNTS RAN, 2012.

Tahir, Mahmud. "Abunasir Kursavi, 1776–1812." *Central Asian Survey* 8, no. 2 (1989): 155–158.

———. "Rizaeddin Fahreddin." *Central Asian Survey* 8, no. 1 (1989): 111–115.

Taimasov, Salavat U. "Rol' orenburgskoi ekspeditsii v prisoedinenii Bashkirii k Rossii (1730-e gg.)." *Voprosy istorii*, no. 2 (February 2008): 144–149.

Taylor, Charles. "Nationalism and Modernity." In *The State of the Nation: Ernest Gellner and the Theory of Nationalism*. Ed. John A. Hall. Cambridge: Cambridge University Press, 1998.

Thaden, Edward C. "Introduction." In *Russification in the Baltic Provinces and Finland, 1855–1914*. Princeton, N.J.: Princeton University Press, 1981.

Thornton, Russell. *American Indian Holocaust and Survival: A Population History since 1492*. Norman: University of Oklahoma Press, 1987.

Tillett, Lowell. *The Great Friendship: Soviet Historians on the Non-Russian Nationalities*. Chapel Hill: University of North Carolina Press, 1969.

Tilly, Charles. *Coercion, Capital and European States, AD 990–1992*. Rev. ed. Cambridge: Blackwell, 1992.

———. "How Empires End." In *After Empire: Multiethnic Societies and Nation Building. The Soviet Union and the Russian, Ottoman, and Habsburg Empires*. Ed. Karen Barkey and Mark von Hagen. Boulder, Colo.: Westview, 1997.

Todorov, Tzvetan. *On Human Diversity: Nationalism, Racism, and Exoticism in French Thought*. Trans. Catherine Porter. Cambridge, Mass.: Harvard University Press, 1993.

Tolz, Vera. *Russia's Own Orient: The Politics of Identity and Oriental Studies in the Late Imperial and Early Soviet Periods*. Oxford: Oxford University Press, 2011.

Toyokava, Koiti. *Orenburg i orenburgskoe kazachestvo vo vremiia vosstaniia Pugacheva, 1773–1774 gg*. Moscow: Arkheograficheskii Tsentr, RGADA, 1996.

Trepavlov, Vadim V. "'Dobrovol'noe vkhozhdenie v sostav Rossii': Torzhestvennye iubilei i istoricheskaia deistvitel'nost'." *Voprosy istorii* 11 (November 2007): 155–163.

———. "Kniazheskie rody nogaiskogo proiskhozhdeniia." *Materialy i issledovaniia po istorii i etnologii Bashkortostana* 2 (1997): 38–72.

———. "Nogai v Bashkirii, XV–XVII vv." *Materialy i issledovaniia po istorii i etnologii Bashkortostana* 2 (1997): 5–37.

Tsiunchuk, Rustem A. *Dumskaia model' parlamentarizma v rossiiskoi imperii: Etnokonfessional'noe i regional'noe izmereniia*. Kazan: Fen, 2004.

Tsviklinski, Sebast'ian. "Islamskaia model' modernizatsii? Zhizn' Gabdrashida Ibragimova v meniaiushchemsia mire (konets XIX–nachalo XX v.)." In *Volgo-Ural'skii region v imperskom prostranstve: XVIII–XX vv*. Ed. M. Khamamoto, N. Naganava, and D. Usmanova. Moscow: Vostochnaia Literatura, 2011.

Tuna, Mustafa O. "Imperial Russia's Muslims: Inroads of Modernity." PhD dissertation, Princeton University, 2009.

25 let pervoi revoliutsii. (Sbornik Istparta Bashobkoma VKP(b) posviashchennyi 25-letnemu iubileiu revoliutsii 1905 goda). Ufa: Tipografiia Imeni Dzerzhinskogo, 1930.

Usmanov, Abubakir N. *Prisoedinenie bashkirii k russkomu gosudarstvu*. Ufa: RIO Bashkirskoe Knizhnoe Izdatel'stvo, 1960.

Usmanov, Khamza F., ed. *Istoriia Bashkortostana s drevneishikh vremen do 60-x godov XIX v*. Ufa: Kitap, 1997.

——. *Razvitie kapitalizma v sel'skom khoziaistve Bashkirii v poreformennyi period, 60–90-e gody XIX v.* Moscow: Nauka, 1981.

——. *Stolypinskaia agrarnaia reforma v Bashkirii.* Ufa: Bashkirskoe Kniznoe Izdatel'stvo, 1958.

Usmanov, Mirkasim A. *Tatarskie istoricheskie istochniki XVII–XVIII vekov.* Kazan: Izdatel'stvo Kazanskogo Universiteta, 1972.

——. *Zavetnaia mechta Khusaina Faizkhanova.* Kazan: Tatarskoe Knizhnoe Izdatel'-stvo, 1980.

Usmanova, Diliara. *Musul'manskie predstaviteli v rossiiskom parlamente: 1906–1916.* Kazan: Fen Akademiia Nauk, Respublika Tatarstana, 2005.

Ustiugov, N. V. "Bashkirskoe vosstanie 1662–1664 gg." *Istoricheskie zapiski* no. 24 (1947): 30–110.

——. *Bashkirskoe vosstanie, 1737–1739 gg.* Moscow-Leningrad: Akademiia Nauk, 1950.

Uyama, Tomohiko. "A Particularist Empire: The Russian Policies of Christianization and Military Conscription in Central Asai." In *Empire, Islam, and Politics in Central Eurasia.* Ed. Tomohiko Uyama. Sapporo: Slavic Research Center, 2007.

Validov, Dzhamaliutdin. *Ocherk istorii obrazovannosti i literatury volzhskikh Tatar.* Vol. 1. Moscow: Gosudarstvennoe Izdatel'stvo, 1923.

Vásáry, István. "Clans of Tatar Descent in the Muscovite Elite of the Fourteenth to Sixteenth Centuries." In *The Place of Russia in Europe and Asia.* Ed. Gyula Szvák. Wayne, N.J.: Center for Hungarian Studies and Publications, 2010.

——. "The Golden Horde Term *daruġa* and Its Survival in Russia." In *Turks, Tatars, and Russians in the 13th–16th Centuries.* Aldershot: Ashgate Variorum, 2007.

Vasil'eva, O. V., V. V. Latypova, et al. *Doroga k khramu.* Ufa: Tsentral'nyi Gos. Istoricheskii Arkhiv Respubliki Bashkortostana, 1993.

Velychenko, Stephen. "Identity, Loyalty, and Service in Imperial Russia." *Russian Review* 54, no. 2 (April 1995): 188–208.

Vernadsky, George. *The Mongols in Russia.* New Haven, Conn.: Yale University Press, 1953.

Verner, Andrew M. *The Crisis of Russian Autocracy: Nicholas II and the 1905 Revolution.* Princeton, N.J.: Princeton University Press, 1990.

Veselovskii, Boris. *Istoriia zemstva za sorok let.* Vol. 4. St. Petersburg: O. N. Popov, 1911.

Vitevskii, V. N. *I. I. Nepliuev i orenburgskii krai v prezhnem ego sostave do 1758 g.* Vols. 1–5. Kazan: Kliuchnikov, 1889–1897.

Von Hagen, Mark L. "The Great War and the Mobilization of Ethnicity in the Russian Empire." In *Post-Soviet Political Order: Conflict and State Building.* Ed. Barnett R. Rubin and Jack Snyder. London: Routledge, 1998.

——. "Writing the History of Russia as Empire." In *Kazan, Moscow, St. Petersburg: Multiple Faces of the Russian Empire.* Ed. Catherine Evtuhov, Boris Gasparov, Alexander Osopovat, and Mark von Hagen. Moscow: OGI, 1997.

Vul'pius, Rikarda. "K semantike *imperii* v Rossii XVIII veka: Poniatiinoe pole *tsivilizatsii.*" In *Poniatiia o Rossii: K istoricheskoi semantike imperskogo perioda.* Vol. I. Ed. A. Miller, D. Sdvizhkov, and I. Shirle. Trans. V. S. Dubina. Moscow: Novoe Literaturnoe Obozrenie, 2012.

Waldron, Peter. *Governing Tsarist Russia.* Basingstoke: Palgrave Macmillan, 2007.

——. "Religious Toleration in Late Imperial Russia." In *Civil Rights in Imperial Russia.* Ed. Olga Crisp and Linda Edmondson. Oxford: Oxford University Press, 1989.

Wcislo, Francis W. *Reforming Rural Russia: State, Local Society, and National Politics, 1855–1914*. Princeton, N.J.: Princeton University Press, 1990.

Weber, Max. *Economy and Society: An Outline of Interpretive Sociology*. Vol. 1. Ed. Guenther Roth and Claus Wittich. Berkeley: University of California Press, 1978.

Weeks, Theodore. "Managing Empire: Tsarist Nationalities Policy." In *The Cambridge History of Russia, Volume II, 1689–1917*. Ed. Dominic Lieven. Cambridge: Cambridge University Press, 2006.

———. *Nation and State in Late Imperial Russia: Nationalism and Russification on the Western Frontier, 1863–1914*. DeKalb: Northern Illinois University Press, 1996.

Weil, Patrick. *How to Be French: Nationality in the Making since 1789*. Trans. Catherine Porter. Durham, N.C.: Duke University Press, 2008.

Werth, Paul W. "Arbiters of the Free Conscience: State, Religion, and the Problem of Confessional Transfer after 1905." In *Sacred Stories: Religion and Spirituality in Modern Russia*. Ed. Mark D. Steinberg and Heather J. Coleman. Bloomington: Indiana University Press, 2007.

———. *At the Margins of Orthodoxy: Mission, Governance, and Confessional Politics in Russia's Volga-Kama Region, 1827–1905*. Ithaca, N.Y.: Cornell University Press, 2002.

———. "Coercion and Conversion: Violence and the Mass Baptism of the Volga Peoples, 1740–55." *Kritika: Explorations in Russian and Eurasian History* 4, no. 3 (Summer 2003): 543–569.

———. "From 'Pagan' Muslims to 'Baptized' Communists: Religious Conversion and Ethnic Particularity in Russia's Eastern Provinces." *Comparative Studies in Society and History* 42, no. 3 (2000): 497–523.

———. "In the State's Embrace? Civil Acts in an Imperial Order." *Kritika: Explorations in Russian and Eurasian History* 7, no. 3 (Summer 2006): 433–458.

———. "Tsarist Categories, Orthodox Intervention, and Islamic Conversion in a Pagan Udmurt Village, 1870s–1890s." In *Muslim Culture in Russia and Central Asia from the 18th to the Early 20th Centuries*. Vol. 2, *Inter-Regional and Inter-Ethnic Relations*. Ed. Anke von Kugelgen, Michael Kemper, and Allen J. Frank. Berlin: Klaus Schwarz Verlag, 1998.

———. *The Tsar's Foreign Faiths: Toleration and the Fate of Religious Freedom in Imperial Russia*. Oxford: Oxford University Press, 2014.

White, James D. "The 1905 Revolution in Russia's Baltic Provinces." In *The Russian Revolution of 1905: Centenary Perspectives*. Ed. Jonathan D. Smele and Anthony Heywood. London: Routledge, 2005.

White, Richard. *The Middle Ground: Indians, Empires, and Republics in the Great Lakes Region, 1650–1815*. Cambridge: Cambridge University Press, 1991.

Wildman, Allan K. *The End of the Imperial Army*. Vol. 1. Princeton, N.J.: Princeton University Press, 1980.

Wirtschafter, Elise Kimerling. *Social Identity in Imperial Russia*. DeKalb: Northern Illinois University Press, 1997.

Wolfe, Patrick. "Land, Labor, and Difference: Elementary Structures of Race." *American Historical Review* 106, no. 3 (June 2001): 866–905.

Wortman, Richard S. *The Development of a Russian Legal Consciousness*. Chicago, Ill.: University of Chicago Press, 1976.

———. *Scenarios of Power: Myth and Ceremony in Russian Monarchy*. Vol. 1, *From Peter the Great to the Death of Nicholas I*. Princeton, Princeton University, Press, 1995.

———. *Scenarios of Power: Myth and Ceremony in Russian Monarchy*. Vol. 2, *Alexander II to the Abdication of Nicholas II*. Princeton, N.J.: Princeton University Press, 2000.

Yaroshevski, Dov B. "Attitudes towards the Nomads of the Russian Empire under Catherine the Great." In *Literature, Lives and Legality in Catherine's Russia*. Ed. A. G. Cross and G. S. Smith. Nottingham: Astra Press, 1994.

———. "Empire and Citizenship." In *Russia's Orient: Imperial Borderlands and Peoples, 1700–1917*. Ed. Daniel R. Brower and Edward J. Lazzerini. Bloomington: Indiana University Press, 1997.

———. "Imperial Strategy in the Kirghiz Steppe in the Eighteenth Century." *Jahrbücher für Geschichte Osteuropas* 39, no. 2 (1991): 221–224.

Zagidullin, Il'dus K. *Islamskie instituty v Rossiiskoi Imperii: Mecheti v evropeiskoi chasti Rossii i Sibiri*. Kazan: Tatarskoe Knizhnoe Izdatel'stvo, 2007.

———. "Osobennosti sobliudeniia religioznykh prav musul'man v rossiiskoi sukhoputnoi reguliarnoi armii v 1874–1914 g." *Journal of Power Institutions in Post-Soviet Societies* 10 (2009): 1–21.

Zaionchkovsky, Petr A. *The Russian Autocracy in Crisis, 1878–1882*. Ed. and trans. Gary M. Hamburg. Gulf Breeze, Fla.: Academic International Press, 1979.

Zakharova, Larissa. "Autocracy and the Reforms of 1861–1874 in Russia: Choosing Paths of Development." In *Russia's Great Reforms, 1855–1881*. Ed. Ben Eklof, John Bushnell, and Larissa Zakharova. Bloomington: Indiana University Press, 1994.

Zeldin, Theodore. *France, 1848–1945*. Vol. 2. Oxford: Oxford University Press, 1977.

Zelenogorskii, M. L. *Zhizn' i deiatel'nost' Arkhiepiskopa Andreia (Kniazia Ukhtomskogo)*. Moscow: Terra, 1991.

Zenkovsky, Serge. *Pan-Turkism and Islam in Russia*. Cambridge, Mass.: Harvard University Press, 1960.

Zlatoverkhovnikov, Ivan, comp. *Ufimskaia eparkhiia: Geograficheskii, etnograficheskii, administrativno-istoricheskii i statisticheskii ocherk*. Ufa: A. P. Zaikov, 1899.

INDEX

Page numbers in *italics* indicate a figure.
Entries for time periods in the index are as follows:

Abdiev, Akhmet'ian, 104
Abdülhamid II, Ottoman Sultan, 147, 180, 250
Abdülmecid I, Ottoman Sultan, 250
absolutism and empire (1730–1775), 42–77, 153–154, 278n132; August 20, 1739 law of, 55; Bashkir War of 1735–1740 and, 43, 47–54, 74–75, 242; census of 1740 of, 53, 54, 61; Cossack relationships with, 70–74; estate status distinctions in, 60; expansion of industry of, 59; February 11, 1736 decree of, 50–51, 54–55; forced conversions and repression of Muslims in, 40, 48, 57, 63, 81, 275nn80–81, 275n83, 277n121; governance strategies of, 43, 64–67, 75, 277n128, 278n129, 278n132; land redistributions by, 50–51, 54, 58–61, 69, 76, 89, 276n96; local administration of, 55–57, 60, 67–69, 75–76, 278n147, 279n149; migration and, 53–54; military service requirements of, 55, 66, 68–69, 90; Nepliuev and, 54–61; Orenburg project and, 42–47; Pugachev Rebellion against, 43, 65, 69–74, 79, 243, 279n157, 279n163; settled agriculture and trade goals of, 53–54, 60, 66–67, 69, 278n139; tarkhan status and, 67–69, 278n147; taxation policies of, 60–61, 276nn107–108; uprising of

1755 against, 61–63, 277n118; variations between east and west in, 75–77; Western models of, 42–44, 46–47. *See also* Orenburg project; Orenburg Province
Abulkhayir khan, 51–52
Adelman, Jeremy, 255n7
Afghani, Jamal ad-Din al-, 166
Agency of New Convert Affairs, 57
aimaks, 35, 284n53
Akchulpanov, Kucherbai, 289n134
Akhtiamov, Abussugaud, 167–168, 198, 214
Akhtiamov, Ibniamin, 205, 228–229, 322n117
Akhtiamov, Ibragim, 214–215
akhunds, 25–26, 51, 68, 74, 84, 164–165, 225
Akmanov, Irek G., 265n47, 268n107
Aksakov, Ivan, 236
Aksakov, P. D., 55, 59, 273n55, 274n72
Aksakov, Sergei T., 10, 82–83
Aleksandrovskii Military-Juridical Academy, 104
Alexander I, Tsar, 78, 80, 88–89, 110; administration of military colonies under, 101; centralized bureaucracy of, 80, 113–114, 291n176, 327n23; educational policies of, 102; Jewish cantons under, 112; land policies of, 89–91; Napoleonic war of, 78, 88, 90–91, 110; visit to Bashkiria by, 91, 110, 285n74
Alexander II, Tsar, 140; assassination of, 116, 141, 177, 180, 306n111; coronation of, 105; emancipation of serfs by, 120; Great Reforms under, 115–118, 147, 150, 250; Statute on Bashkirs of, 118–119, 124, 131, 294n43; twenty-fifth jubilee of, 115
Alexander III, Tsar, 141, 160, 163; coronation of, 115, 149–150, 300n2; police

CHARLES STEINWEDEL is Associate Professor of History at Northeastern Illinois University in Chicago.

www.ingramcontent.com/pod-product-compliance
Ingram Content Group UK Ltd.
Pitfield, Milton Keynes, MK11 3LW, UK
UKHW022154090225
454837UK00004B/162

9 780253 019264